ALL TRAILS LEAD TO SANTA FE

ALL TRAILS LEAD TO SANTA FE

An Anthology Commemorating the 400th Anniversary
of the
Founding of Santa Fe, New Mexico in 1610

The Official Commemorative Publication

SANTA FE

Note to Readers

Kindly report any errors in this book to:
Sunstone Press
Box 2321
Santa Fe, NM 87504-2321

© 2010 by Santa Fe 400th Anniversary, Inc.
All Rights Reserved.

No part of this book may be reproduced in any form or by any electronic or mechanical means including information storage and retrieval systems without permission in writing from the publisher, except by a reviewer who may quote brief passages in a review.

Sunstone books may be purchased for educational, business, or sales promotional use. For information please write: Special Markets Department, Sunstone Press, P.O. Box 2321, Santa Fe, New Mexico 87504-2321.

Book and Cover design ❧ Vicki Ahl
Body typeface ❧ Adobe Garamond Pro
Printed on acid free paper

Library of Congress Cataloging-in-Publication Data

All trails lead to Santa Fe : an anthology commemorating the 400th anniversary of the founding of Santa Fe, New Mexico in 1610.
　p. cm.
Includes bibliographical references and index.
ISBN 978-0-86534-760-1 (hardcover : alk. paper) --
ISBN 978-0-86534-761-8 (softcover : alk. paper)
1. Santa Fe (N.M.)--History.
F804.S257A45 2010
978.9'56--dc22

　　　　　　　　　　　　2010010143

WWW.SUNSTONEPRESS.COM
SUNSTONE PRESS / POST OFFICE BOX 2321 / SANTA FE, NM 87504-2321 /USA
(505) 988-4418 / ORDERS ONLY (800) 243-5644 / FAX (505) 988-1025

The Publication of This Book
is Generously Supported by
**REYNOLDS
INSURANCE**
the Oldest Independent Insurance Agency
in New Mexico.

Originally Founded in 1882
by
Paul Wunschmann

Impression of Santa Fe in 1882. From *Illustrated New Mexico, 1885* by W. G. Ritch.

CONTENTS

Foreword / Marc Simmons___13
Preface / Orlando Romero___17
Introduction / Joseph P. Sánchez___19
Listen / Valerie Martínez___35

1
Down at the Shell-bead Water / David H. Snow___37

2
A City Different Than We Thought, Land Grants in Early Santa Fe, 1598–1900 / Malcolm Ebright___65

3
The Viceroy's Order Founding the Villa of Santa Fe, A Reconsideration, 1605–1610 / James Ivey___97

4
Thirty-eight Adobe Houses, The Villa de Santa Fe in the Seventeenth Century, 1608–1610 / José Antonio Esquibel___109

5
The History of the Santa Fe Plaza, 1610–1720 / Stanley M. Hordes___129

6
A Window to the Past, The San Miguel and La Conquistadora Chapels and Their Builders, 1610–1776 / Cordelia Thomas Snow___147

7
Barrio de Analco, Its Roots in Mexico and Role in Early Colonial Santa Fe, 1610–1780 / William Wroth___163

8
In Her Own Voice, Doña Teresa Aguilera y Rocha and Intrigue in the Palace of the Governors, 1659–1662 / Gerald T. E. González and Frances Levine___179

9
On Establishing a Presidio at Santa Fe, 1678–1693 / Barbara De Marco___209

10
Vargas at the Gate, The Spanish Restoration of Santa Fe,
1692–1696 / John L. Kessell___219

11
The Pastures of the Royal Horse Herd of the Santa Fe Presidio,
1692–1740 / Linda Tigges___237

12
It Happened in Old Santa Fe, The Death of Governor Albino Pérez,
1835–1837 / Joseph P. Sánchez___267

13
"She Was Our Mother," New Mexico's Change of National Sovereignty and Juan
Bautista Vigil y Alarid, The Last Mexican Governor of New Mexico
Samuel E. Sisneros___279

14
They Came From the East, Importing Homicide, Violence and Misconceptions of
Soft Justice into Early Santa Fe, New Mexico, 1847–1853 / Michael J. Alarid___301

15
King Maker in the Back Room, Editor Max Frost and Hardball Politics in the Late-
Territorial Period, 1876–1909 / Robert K. Dean___317

16
Progressive Santa Fe, 1880–1912 / Robert L. Spude___339

17
The Cure at the End of the Trail, Seeking Health While Transforming a Town,
1880–1940 / Nancy Owen Lewis___361

18
Santa Fe in World War II, 1940–1947 / Judy Reed___383

19
Alcaldes and Mayors of Santa Fe, 1613–2008 / Albert J. Gallegos and
José Antonio Esquibel___403

Contributors___431
About the 400th Anniversary of Santa Fe___437
The 400th Anniversary of Santa Fe Book Committee___440
Publisher Acknowledgements___441
Notes___443
Index___525

Like the roads to Rome, all trails led to Santa Fe.
—Ruth Laughlin, *Caballeros*

Foreword
by
Marc Simmons

Origins of City Different Not So Simple
The Santa Fe New Mexican
October 2, 2009

When was Santa Fe founded? That is a question surely of interest to most New Mexicans, more so because the capital city launched a historical celebration to mark the 400th anniversary of that momentous event. Like much else in New Mexico, the actual founding date has become mired in controversy. That is because nearly all the official documents related to it have been lost.

An exception is the set of instructions issued on March 30, 1609 by Viceroy Luís de Velasco II and given to the newly appointed governor of New Mexico, Don Pedro de Peralta. Therein, Governor Peralta was ordered as his first duty to establish a new villa (town) and provincial capital for New Mexico, the "old capital" at colonizer Juan de Oñate's Villa de San Gabriel near San Juan Pueblo (Ohkay Owingeh) having been judged unsuitable.

A year or so earlier, the viceroy had learned that a plan already existed, no doubt hatched by Oñate, to create a second villa. Details about that remain quite vague, however. The story takes a twist now with a solider named Captain Juan Martínez de Montoya. Born in Spain's province Castile in 1561, he immigrated to Mexico City, where in 1599 he joined the first body of reinforcements being sent in support of Oñate's struggling colony on the Rio Grande. Upon Martínez's arrival here in December 1600, he ingratiated himself with Governor Oñate and over the next several years accompanied him on major expeditions.

He also served positions on San Gabriel's town council, or *cabildo*.

In August 1607, Juan de Oñate, in the face of repeated setbacks, submitted his resignation as governor. The following February 17, 1608, Viceroy Velasco sent him notice that his resignation had been accepted. At the same time, he announced that Captain Juan Martínez de Montoya should serve as the temporary governor until a permanent replacement could be dispatched to New Mexico.

The San Gabriel *cabildo* refused to accept Martínez for reasons it would not divulge. So it asked Juan de Oñate to resume the governorship, but he declined. The quirky *cabildo* then appointed Juan's teenage son Cristóbal to the office, a maneuver later rejected by the viceroy. Evidently, these curious steps reflected intense feuding among the Spaniards at San Gabriel, and that appears to have contributed to the early beginnings of Santa Fe.

As Thomas Chávez and other historians have reported, some kind of loose, unnamed settlement seems to have existed on or near the future site of Santa Fe by 1607, if not a year or two earlier.

Researcher José Antonio Esquibel has uncovered a handful of names identified as residents of the area "prior to the formal designation of the Villa de Santa Fe as a legally recognized municipality."

Our best guess is that these Spaniards moved down from overcrowded San Gabriel seeking fertile farmland, or left there owing to conflicts with Oñate and his clique.

Captain Martínez, on August 10, 1608, updated his service record and got it certified, no doubt intending to use it in seeking another job outside New Mexico, since he'd been denied the governorship. In that document, he claimed among his accomplishments that he settled "the plaza of Santa Fe." Note that besides "a municipal square," the word plaza can also mean a small village or a fortified place. It is significant, too, that the captain in his phrasing did not use the word villa.

There is no indication when or under what circumstances Martínez carried out this work. Nor do we know whether he acted on his own initiative or on orders of Juan de Oñate. Missing, in addition, is an explanation of why the name Santa Fe was chosen, its appearance in the 1608 service record being the earliest use of it, so far discovered.

Perhaps the naming was in honor of the historic town of Santa Fe in southern Spain that had served as the military headquarters of King Ferdinand and Queen Isabella when their armies defeated the last Moorish kingdom of Granada in 1492.

In his 1609 instruction to Peralta, Viceroy Velasco did not refer to Santa Fe by name. He merely indicated that the new governor should found and populate a villa, building on the slight efforts already made.

So, who should receive credit as the founding father of Santa Fe, and can we legitimately assign a date marking the city's birth? The three candidates for the honor of founder are Oñate, Martínez and Peralta. In all probability, successively each one played a role.

In my opinion, though, since Governor Pedro de Peralta, following orders, formally organized the Villa of Santa Fe as a royally chartered town in the first half of 1610, he deserves the accolades as founding father.

An early impression of Santa Fe. *From Report of Lieut. J. W. Abert of His Examination of New Mexico in the Years 1846–1847.*

Preface
by
Orlando Romero

Santa Fe, as a tourist destination and an international art market with its attraction of devotees to opera, flamenco, good food and romanticized cultures, is also a city of deep historical drama.

Like its seemingly "adobe style-only" architecture, all one has to do is turn the corner and discover a miniature Alhambra, a Romanesque Cathedral, or a French-inspired chapel next to one of the oldest adobe chapels in the United States to realize its long historical diversity. This fusion of architectural styles is a mirror of its people, cultures and history.

From its early origins, Native American presence in the area through the archaeological record is undeniable and has proved to be a force to be reckoned with as well as reconciled. It was, however, the desire of European arrivals, Spaniards, already mixed in Spain and Mexico, to create a new life, a new environment, different architecture, different government, culture and spiritual life that set the foundations for the creation of *La Villa de Santa Fe*. Indeed, Santa Fe remained Spanish from its earliest Spanish presence of 1607 until 1821.

But history is not just the time between dates but the human drama that creates the "City Different." The Mexican Period of 1821–1848, American occupation and the following Territorial Period into Statehood are no less defining and, in fact, are as traumatic for some citizens as the first European contact.

This tapestry was all held together by the common belief that Santa Fe was different and after centuries of coexistence a city with its cultures, tolerance and beauty was worth preserving. Indeed, the existence and awareness of this oldest of North American capitals was to attract the famous as well as infamous: poets, writers, painters, philosophers, scientists and the sickly whose prayers were answered in the thin dry air of the city situated at the base of the Sangre de Cristos at 7,000 foot elevation.

We hope readers will enjoy *All Trails Lead to Santa Fe* and in its pages discover facts not revealed before, or, in the sense of true adventure, enlighten and encourage the reader to continue the search for the evolution of *La Villa de Santa Fe*.

A commemorative publication like this would have never materialized without the support of the Santa Fe 400th Commemorative Committee, Mayor David Coss, City Councilors, and especially the Book Committee members—Adrian Bustamante, Cordelia Thomas Snow, Sandra Jaramillo, Joseph P. Sánchez and Gerald T. E. González—who had to read countless manuscripts before selecting the 19 presented here. And, of course, many thanks to the scholars who contributed to this anthology and to Sunstone Press for its suggestions and publication of this book.

—Orlando Romero
Chair, Call for Papers Committee

General view of Santa Fe. From *Harper's Weekly*, September, 1870.

Introduction
by
Joseph P. Sánchez

In 2010, the commemoration of the 400th year anniversary of the founding of Santa Fe offered the opportunity for scholars and citizens to collaborate in writing an anthology about the ancient city under the title, *All Trails Lead to Santa Fe*. This anthology complements other similar volumes that have been prepared about Santa Fe and covers a range of topics that may otherwise have gone unnoticed. The chapters contained herein portray events in Santa Fe's rich history, and each can be taken metaphorically or as a similitude of a pathway that leads toward a better understanding of Santa Fe's past. Some trails were physically on the ground; others were in the form of an historical event or reflected in the life-journeys taken by pre-historical and historical protagonists. Indeed, one of the chapters covers the prehistory of the area surrounding present Santa Fe, while the others are divided into different historical periods ending with modern-day Santa Fe and its municipal leaders as of 2010. Thus, this anthology contributes to a better understanding of all possible trails that lead to Santa Fe.

Santa Fe's history covers a period of more than four centuries. Predating Plymouth, Massachusetts, by ten years, Santa Fe was the northernmost seat of government of Spanish America in the seventeenth century and most of the eighteenth century until California was established in 1769 with its capital at Monterey. The settlement of New Mexico began in 1598, predating Jamestown by nearly a decade. In many ways, the histories of New Mexico and Santa Fe are inseparable. Since 1598 three different sovereigns, Spain (1598–1821), Mexico (1821–1848), and the United States (after 1848) have governed New Mexico from Santa Fe.

Among the Spanish colonial period capitals in the Greater Southwest of the United States, Santa Fe is particularly unique because it was the only city that remained as a capital after the Anglo-American occupation of the southwest. In Texas, for example, San Antonio was founded in 1716 but became the capital in 1772, which then moved to Austin in the nineteenth century. Similarly, in Arizona, the capital at Tucson, founded in 1776, was moved first to Prescott, then to Phoenix. Finally, the capital at Monterey, founded after 1769, in California was moved to Sacramento. These Spanish period capitals were centers of power with substantial voting Hispanic populations. The nineteenth century relocation of capitals away from Hispanic centers by newly established Anglo-Americans aimed at breaking up their political power. The location of the capital at Santa Fe has remained unchanged since its founding.

That New Mexico's capital at Santa Fe was not relocated in the nineteenth century likely resulted from two significant facts. First, the Hispanic population in New Mexico had settled along the Río Grande for several hundred miles. That meant any location for a new capital could never have been far enough away from a given Hispanic population center. Second, Hispanic politicians, as they had traditionally done under Spain and Mexico, quickly assumed a role in the governance of New Mexico Territory making relocation a moot point. Their training ground had been the Santa Fe *cabildo* (town council with elected and appointed members), or a Spanish land grant governing unit, or the *asamblea territorial* or territorial assembly under Mexico. Thus, New Mexicans held on to political control, while their cousins in Texas, Arizona, and California became strangers in their own lands. The struggle to recover their lost political control would take nearly 150 years.

Spawned in the Greco-Roman traditions of governance,[1] the *cabildo*, established in New Mexico by Juan de Oñate in 1598–99, worked hand-in-hand with the provincial governor until the end of the Spanish Period in 1821. After independence from Spain, the budding Mexican nation-state established a republican form of government in 1824. Under Mexico, the *cabildo* de Santa Fe, also known as the *ayuntamiento* de Santa Fe, became the *asamblea territorial*. Over two decades later, the United States acquired New Mexico following the War with Mexico in 1846–48. In the initial years of U.S. rule, Hispanic members of the defunct Mexican *asamblea*, along with Anglo-American representatives, formed the New Mexico Territorial Legislature. Sixty-two years later, in 1912, when New Mexico became a state of the Union, the Territorial Legislature became the New Mexico State Legislature. Throughout its history, the location of New Mexico's legislative body in Santa Fe never moved more than a few blocks. The history from *cabildo* to New Mexico State Legislature is a continuing legacy that has emanated from the Spanish Colonial and Mexican periods to the present. Thus, Santa Fe not only claims to be the oldest continuing occupied city in the United States, it is, with its predecessor capitals at San Juan de los Caballeros and San Gabriel, the longest termed site of the traditional basic unit of governance, the *cabildo*, in the United States.

Nestled in a small valley at the southern end of the Sangre de Cristo Mountain Range, Santa Fe has throughout the centuries hosted an historical pageantry of settlers, merchants, miners, governors, clergymen, traders, soldiers and others. As a result, the many layers of Santa Fe's cultural mixes often overlay each other and form an indistinguishable blurry moment in its fiestas and open markets. Yet in the every day hustle and bustle, the varied faces of Santa Fe mesh with Indian, Hispanic, Black, and Anglo manifestations seen in newscasts, political arenas, public, and work places. Still, visitors to Santa Fe often see a romanticized historical setting that caters to tourism in the unique setting of the Plaza de Santa Fe. This volume unravels the mysterious, mythical, legendary, and romantic Santa Fe that is buried deep in its rich history.

There is much more to Santa Fe than meets the eye. For over two hundred years, Santa Fe was the terminus of the *Camino Real de Tierra Adentro* (Royal Road of the Interior) that connected it to Mexico City. In 2000, the United States Congress designated 400 miles of the trail El Camino Real de Tierra Adentro National Historic Trail within the confines of the United States, recognizing it as part of our national story. The rest of the 1500-mile trail lies in Mexico. Indeed, the *Camino Real* is a binational historic trail.

But the *Camino Real* has an earlier history as an indigenous footpath since time immemorial. The primitive footpaths were formed by Native American traders and hunters, Nahua-speakers, Athapascans, and pueblos alike. The pathways became a broader trail when Spanish settlers introduced horses along it and modified the route for their uses. Later, when settlers brought *carretas* over the trail, it was once again changed to run their solid or spoke-wheeled carts along a flatter route of the trail. Eventually, with the invention of the automobile, the route was once again moved to accommodate paved roads along a flatter and less winding route. The *Camino Real* corridor today runs parallel to the historic route used by sixteenth-century Spanish settlers. The corridor includes a railroad line that follows portions of it, the modern day interstate I-25 from Las Cruces to Santa Fe, and flight patterns from El Paso to Albuquerque that follow the corridor overhead.

The ancient route from Santa Barbara in Chihuahua to El Paso is known as *La Ruta de Oñate* because he and his settlers blazed a straight-line north from Santa Barbara to the Río Grande at El Paso, which they named, and then north to San Juan. Earlier explorers had departed Santa Barbara eastward to the confluence of the Río Conchos and the Río Grande, then followed the river north to New Mexico. In time, another historic trail joined the Camino Real: the Santa Fe Trail from

Missouri. That trail became known as the Santa Fe-Chihuahua Trail as it wended southward from Santa Fe to Ciudad Chihuahua for trade. The trails not only crossed topographically, they crossed genealogically. The ancestors of old New Mexican families traveled the Camino Real with Oñate; later certain Anglo-Americans, who entered Santa Fe via the Santa Fe-Chihuahua Trail, married into Hispanic families. Like ancient roads that led to Rome, it can be said, metaphorically as Ruth Laughlin wrote in *Caballeros*, that "all trails led to Santa Fe."

Many questions abound about Santa Fe's history. Chief among them is when was Santa Fe founded and who was its founder? The answer to the dual question has intrigued many and varied writers and researchers for decades. For example, in summer of 1883, the planners of the commemorative celebration of Santa Fe, without a clue regarding the name of its founder, arbitrarily and erroneously agreed that the year of Santa Fe's founding was 1550 and set about to commemorate its 333rd anniversary.[2] Over the years, historians have evolved a large body of literature that traces the answer to the question, not in terms of *when* exactly Santa Fe came to be, but *how* it came to be. Purists argue a fine point when they state that Santa Fe was officially founded in 1610 by Governor Pedro de Peralta, who came from New Spain with instructions issued to him in 1609 by Viceroy Luis de Velasco II. The instructions empowered Peralta to establish a villa that would be the capital of the province of New Mexico. Others argue that the story evolved much earlier when, in 1598, Governor Juan de Oñate established New Mexico as a province of New Spain with its capital at San Juan de los Caballeros. Oñate's actions led to the establishment of an outpost called *San Francisco de Santa Fé, Real Campo de Españoles* (San Francisco de Santa Fe: Royal Spanish Outpost) south of San Gabriel.

In 1889, Hubert Howe Bancroft published his *History of Arizona and New Mexico*[3] largely based on documentation from collections found in historical archives in Mexico and the "Santa Fe archives." Uncertainty marked the text of his book to wit: "We have seen that San Juan was Oñate's capital from 1598, and that preparations were made for building a city of San Francisco in that vicinity. Naturally ... not during Oñate's rule, I think—it was deemed best to build the new villa on another site. I have been able to find no record of the date; but the first definite mention is in 1617, on January 3rd of which year the *cabildo* of Santa Fé petitioned the king to aid the 'nueva población.'"[4] He succinctly concluded: "Yet within this period, or rather between 1605 and 1616, was founded the villa of Santa Fé, or San Francisco de Santa Fé."[5]

A few years later, in 1896, Francisco de Thoma published his *Historia de Nuevo México* in which he expounded that "the exact founding of Santa Fe is unknown."[6] Although his statement rang true, Thoma explained that he had scant documentation that would verify the date. As Bancroft had concluded, he too knew

Santa Fe was founded during the administration of Governor Peralta. The dearth of documentation in his *Historia* did not impede him from writing a history of New Mexico, but he did commit, as had Bancroft, some historical distortions. Three decades passed before a more serious attempt was made to write a more precise history of Santa Fe.

In 1925, Ralph Emerson Twitchell published *Old Santa Fe: The Story of New Mexico's Ancient Capital*[7] that covered a period from 1598 to the twentieth century. His first chapter was entitled "Rèsumé of Events Preceding the Founding of the Villa Real de Santa Fé de San Francisco, A.D. 1598–1609. Don Juan de Oñate, Adelantado, Colonizer and Explorer. The Founders—Don Pedro de Peralta, Governor and Captain-General."[8] Unfortunately, Twitchell was no closer to establishing a definitive date for the founding of Santa Fe than were his predecessors. In his introduction, he concluded that "Although nearly all the early authorities, and ... later writers as well, credit Oñate with being the founder of Santa Fe, there are some writers and authorities who declare that the city was actually built by his successor ... Don Pedro de Peralta."[9]

Twitchell's work, however, was built on a more solid foundation of documentation and research than his predecessors. He deserves the distinction of having pioneered the first real history of Santa Fe, albeit at times sounding more anecdotal than factual. He also established themes substantiated with credible facts and a basic chronology that would be filled by future researchers.

For the most part, historians of the twentieth century, particularly those who wrote about the history of the state for the period 1610 to 1850, tended to approach the history of Santa Fe as the history of New Mexico. Still, in part, a sub-theme or an aside to the history of New Mexico, the historiographical undercurrents carried with them the question of the dating of the founding of Santa Fe. In 1927, Benjamin M. Read's "The Founder of Santa Fe," published in *El Palacio,* wrote that it was Juan de Oñate who established Santa Fe as the preeminent capital of New Mexico. A year later, Lansing Bloom retorted in his publication of the "Instructions for Don Pedro de Peralta, Governor and Captain General of New Mexico, in the Place of Don Juan de Oñate" (*El Palacio,* 1928) that the true founder was indeed Pedro de Peralta. Bloom's editor unabashedly wrote: "The dispute among historians whether Oñate or Peralta founded Santa Fe is settled by the instructions given Peralta upon his appointment as Governor and Captain General to succeed Oñate."[10] In 1929, Bloom insisted that the official founder of Santa Fe was Peralta and published his article "When Was Santa Fe Founded?" in the *New Mexico Historical Review.*

France V. Scholes carefully established, for the record, that other documentation existed that could clarify the origins of Santa Fe prior to 1610. In his article "Juan Martínez de Montoya, Settler and Conquistador of New Mexico," published in the 1944 issue of the *New Mexico Historical Review*, he alluded to some newly found documents that show Martínez de Montoya to be the founder of Santa Fe. Of his conclusions based on recently found documents, Scholes wrote:

> But the most interesting data recorded for the year 1607–1608 are brief references to a place called Santa Fé and statements indicating that some sort of post or settlement was being established there. In December, 1608, when messengers brought new reports to the viceroy, the latter was informed of plans to establish a new villa and provisional capital; and in his instructions to Pedro de Peralta, the new royal governor appointed in 1609, [Viceroy] Velasco stipulated that Peralta's first duty should be 'la fundación y población de la villa que se pretende.'[11]

Scholes' statements, however, proved inconclusive as he failed to cite the "newly found" documents from Maggs Bros. Ltd. Instead, he cited other known documents from the Spanish and Mexican archives, as well as the instructions given to Peralta that had been published in the the *New Mexico Historical Review*. The record regarding Martínez de Montoya is elusive because, aside from his brief sojourn in the province, he is not mentioned again in New Mexico's history, for he left the settlement in 1608 nevermore to return.

Aside from Scholes' efforts, no new documents shed light on the founding date of Santa Fe. Between 1929 and 1989, historians tended to 1609 or 1610 as the official founding dates for Santa Fe. While the issue of the founding date of Santa Fe seemed to be mellowing out in favor of 1610, the 1605 date was given new life toward the end of the twentieth century. The question, "when was Santa Fe founded," however, would not easily go away.

In 1989, Marc Simmons published *Yesterday in Santa Fe: Episodes of a Turbulent History*. Regarding the founding date of Santa Fe, Simmons carefully wrote that, "it has generally been assumed that the construction of the villa which became Santa Fe did not get underway until the spring of 1610."[12] A year later, Robert McGeagh, in *Juan de Oñate's Colony in the Wilderness*, noted that the viceroy had approved Peralta's relocation of the capital from San Gabriel because it was situated too close to the Tewa pueblos and therefore unsuited for defense purposes. Of Oñate's establishment of Santa Fe, he wrote: "It is possible that Oñate may have anticipated this decision during his tenure in office and founded a small settlement at a location at the southern end of a spur of the Rockies (later named the Sangre de Cristo Mountains)."[13]

By 1991 Simmons had reassessed Oñate's role in the founding of Santa Fe.

Having reviewed the notion that Santa Fe was founded earlier than 1610, he pulled away from his earlier conclusion. In *The Last Conquistador*, he wrote, "By now it also appears fairly certain that Oñate deserves partial and perhaps even primary honors for the founding of Santa Fe, which exists even today as one of the oldest cities in America and the first surviving municipality erected in the west."[14] Simmons explained that:

> It was about ... 1608, that the city of Santa Fe seems to have had its beginnings. Stray references point to some of the San Gabriel settlers moving twenty miles south, perhaps even as early as 1607, and establishing themselves in a narrow valley and at a place that was called, from the start, Santa Fe (Holy Faith).... What appears certain is that Don Juan, still de facto in charge, had approved this move. In dispatches sent to Mexico City ... in December 1608, the viceroy was informed of plans ... to establish a new villa and provincial capital.... The viceroy suggested later that it was the colonists and friars who were behind the transfer of the capital, but Oñate would have to acquiesce, at the very least.[15]

Simmons' explanation made it clear that no matter how the question regarding Santa Fe's founding is answered without Oñate's executive direction there would have been no Santa Fe as it is historically known today. Oñate's successor was Pedro de Peralta who, in 1609, was given instructions to establish Santa Fe as the official capital.

In 1992, David J. Weber reiterated McGeagh's wordings. Acknowledging that Santa Fe was founded circa 1610,[16] Weber straddled the historiographical fence by writing:

> Through most of the century, New Mexico had only one formal municipality, the Villa Real de Santa Fe, founded in 1610 under viceregal orders by ... Pedro de Peralta, who moved the capital from San Gabriel to a more defensible site in an unpopulated valley selected earlier by Oñate.[17]

Yet, Weber contradictorily wrote, "San Gabriel would remain the sole Spanish settlement in New Mexico until Oñate began to move some of his colonists south to Santa Fe, a more defensible and less crowded location, perhaps as early as 1608."[18]

In 1989, Thomas Chávez pursued the search for documents mentioned by Scholes in 1944. Of his success in locating the documents, Beverly Becker, publisher of *El Palacio,* wrote a commentary in the middle 1990s entitled "Santa Fe: Est. ~~1610~~ 1607."[19] In it, she told of the efforts by Thomas Chávez to acquire documents identified by Scholes regarding the services of Juan Martínez de Montoya. If the documents were to hold true, then it would follow that the date of establishment of Santa Fe would be dramatically pushed back to 1607.[20]

As the story goes, Scholes learned that the documents were held by Maggs Bros. Ltd. in London. In 1936, Scholes "stumbled upon mention of the documents … in a catalog from Maggs Bros." Becker speculated that Scholes did not go to London to see them; apparently he requested copies or a detailed description of their contents from the holder of the documents. Scholes, however, claimed he had read them when he wrote:

> Answers to these questions are found in documents, which I had the opportunity to examine several years ago. These papers contain … a document executed at San Gabriel on October 6, 1606, in which Juan de Oñate certified Martínez services in New Mexico up to that time, and a supplementary statement of services presented by Martínez before Cristóbal de Oñate on August 9, 1608.[21]

In 1944, Scholes wrote his conclusions from whatever sources Maggs Bros. Ltd. had sent him.

In 1989, Chávez wrote to Maggs Bros. Ltd. and inquired if the documents were still in their possession. If not, he asked whether the owners of the documents could be located so that he could communicate with them. After several attempts by Chávez and others to locate and request the documents, he finally received a portfolio, which contained the information he had sought.[22] The question remained whether the documents could, at least, clarify that a settlement or an outpost had been started at a place called "Santa Fe" and possibly its location. A new dawn had arisen over the debate.

In 2002, John L. Kessell weighed in on the issue. In his book, *Spain in the Southwest: A Narrative History of Colonial New Mexico, Arizona, Texas, and California*, he concluded that Oñate, Peralta, and Martínez de Montoya knew the place and founding date of the place called "Santa Fe." Of that moment in time, he wrote:

> Juan de Oñate and his replacement [Peralta] must have conferred, however stiffly. Don Juan, from the beginning, had intended to found a Spanish villa, or chartered municipality, and call it San Francisco, but circumstances had not favored the project…. Yet by 1607 or 1608, some of the proprietor's people, led by rejected interim governor Juan Martínez de Montoya, had begun a second settlement downriver on a more centrally located site unoccupied by Pueblo Indians. It lay along a pleasant southwestward-flowing tributary of the Rio Grande with fields nearby, abundant grazing

land, and wood for fuel and building. They were calling the place Santa Fe.[23]

Kessell pointed the way toward a more established documentation of sources that had been overlooked, although well known but not trusted, regarding the movement of Oñate's settlers toward a place that would be called Santa Fe.

The dual question regarding the founding date and the founder of Santa Fe has evolved into a multidisciplinary effort. Archaeologists and historical architects have contributed studies that date what has been found either underground or in the historic fabric of aboveground structures. It could be that genealogists, who look at the micro-aspects of history, may hold the key. The recent genealogical work by José Antonio Esquibel, whose chapter on early Santa Fe is published herein, offers documentation that Santa Fe was the site settled as San Francisco de Santa Fe, Real Campo de Españoles, during the tail end of the Oñate period. Still, it could be argued that "settled" is different from "established" or "officially established." In "Founders of the Villa de Santa Fe" in *Pariente*, Esquibel indicates that prior to 1610 births and baptisms had occurred in a settlement or outpost downriver of San Gabriel. The proposition begs the question: was Santa Fe the same place as San Francisco de Santa Fe, Real Campo de Españoles?

To some historians, the dates 1605 or 1608, do not ring true. To them, it appears that the date originated in a mistake made in the transcription of the numbers in the date, or a foggy recollection written years later by a chronicler, or the result of a faulty oral tradition. After all, Peralta and Oñate were mentioned as the founders in the historical documentation of the seventeenth and eighteenth centuries. Were such mentions made in error or based on traditional knowledge? Even so, the presence of documents regarding the role of Martínez de Montoya in the founding of Santa Fe can no longer be discounted.

The present volume, published specifically for the 400th Anniversary of Santa Fe's Founding, contains a number of chapters by well-known writers that spotlight certain themes in Santa Fe's history. The authors have dedicated their careers to archaeology, history, and genealogy and have published on a wide range of subjects dealing with New Mexico and the Greater Southwest.

Doubtless, this book complements other venerable studies mentioned above, including David Grant Noble's edited work, *Santa Fe: History of an Ancient City*, originally published in 1989. Noble's anthology, written by several authors, was republished in 2008 to coincide with the 400th Anniversary of Santa Fe's founding. Read together, they combine to cover a larger history of Santa Fe and add to a better understanding of the ancient city.

David H. Snow, "Down at the Shell-bead Water," explores, meditates, and ruminates about the Native-American past in Santa Fe. Of his perspectives, Snow wistfully writes, "The place called Santa Fe echoes but faintly in the recorded myths and legend of her Pueblo neighbors. There was at Santa Fe, however, a particular place the Tewa people called 'Quaking leaf water,' but it isn't there anymore…. It was a sacred place, and perhaps that memory remains, for within recent times elders from one Tewa pueblo came surreptitiously to place prayer feathers at its edge." Snow suggests an earlier Tewa name for Santa Fe, Ogapoge or Kapoge, "white bead-water place." If the Tewa and other Indian People, such as the Navajo, were not among those who settled the vicinity of Santa Fe, they were, at least, the ones who went there for spiritual reasons. Native American pathways from many directions led to Ogapoge, long before there was a Santa Fe.

In "A City Different Than We Thought, Land Grants in Early Santa Fe, 1598–1900," Malcolm Ebright discusses the realm of myth and history in telling the story of Santa Fe. Ebright deals with the Santa Fe Grant and other nearby land grants as they relate to the history of Santa Fe. He explains that pre-Pueblo Revolt Santa Fe was, from its earliest times, an occupied area comprised of a series of isolated settlements extending from its southernmost outpost at La Ciénega to the walls of Santa Fe. In between the two points were Cieneguilla, El Pino, Agua Fria, and the Barrio de Analco. All of these places constituted grants of land surrounded by common lands. In making his case, Ebright breaks a new pathway about how modern researchers should think about the founding of Santa Fe. Was it a historical act that can be captured in one moment in 1610? Or was the founding of Santa Fe part of an historical process that was formed by many other actions, inclusive of that "official moment," that resulted in a place called Santa Fe?

James Ivey in "The Viceroy's Order Founding the Villa of Santa Fe, A Reconsideration, 1605–1610," argues that the Juan Martinez de Montoya papers have put to rest the thesis that Pedro de Peralta was the founder of Santa Fe. He states that Martínez de Montoya is the "de facto founder" and Pedro de Peralta is the "official founder" of Santa Fe. Ivey bases his conclusion on the historiography of the founding of Santa Fe and recently acquired documents by the Palace of the Governors from Maggs Bros. Ltd. in London. He indicates that the documents point the way to further research, for there is always more documentation that could be found to explain the origins of Santa Fe.

José Antonio Esquibel, "Thirty-eight Adobe Houses, The Villa de Santa Fe in the Seventeenth Century, 1608–1610," adds to the historiography regarding the date of the founding of Santa Fe and its founder. Esquibel painstakingly sifted through the newly acquired documents from Maggs Bros. Ltd. and known documents from Spanish and Mexican archives and makes some astute observations. As a genealogist, Esquibel has explored extant documents and retraced birth dates of individuals who claimed to have been born before 1608 at a place called "Santa Fe." The historiographical trail to Santa Fe has taken on new life in Esquibel and Ivey's chapters.

In "The History of the Santa Fe Plaza, 1610–1720," Stanley M. Hordes examines the phenomenon of town founding in the Spanish Colonial period and its relationship to the establishment of Santa Fe. In particular, Hordes focuses on the construction of the *Plaza de Santa Fe* as it evolved before the Pueblo Revolt, during the pueblo occupation of Santa Fe, 1680–1692, and after the *reconquista* by Diego de Vargas.

In recounting the changes made to the *plaza* during the early eighteenth century, Hordes is able to reconstruct, at least theoretically, an image of the town square. The structures he describes include the *casas reales*, the residences and the *plaza's* historical configuration that can be overlaid on a modern map to show the approximation of its dimensions along certain present-day streets in the historic district. Colonial roads fed into the *plaza*. One of them was the Camino Real de Tierra Adentro, another was the Camino de Galisteo. Other roads emanated from settlements at San Juan, Santa Cruz de la Cañada, and Taos.

In "A Window To The Past, The San Miguel and La Conquistadora Chapels and Their Builders, 1610–1776," Cordelia Thomas Snow presents a fascinating history of San Miguel and La Conquistadora chapels and the people who built them, as well as those who later restored them. She explains that at the time of its founding, Santa Fe had two major neighborhoods. One was the Spanish Barrio de San Francisco on the north side of the Río Santa Fe, and the other was the Mexican Indian Barrio de Analco on the south side of the river. As a result, two churches emerged to serve the respective barrios. The author tells the story of both churches and adds biographical information about the artisans and architects who built them. Snow's excellent chapter adds another dimension to the story of early Santa Fe. Metaphorically, Snow extends our understanding of the historical pathways leading to Santa Fe.

The question regarding the early settlers of Santa Fe takes on a more complex view when one considers the possibility that Tlaxcalans or Nahua-speaking Mexican Indians had already settled the area prior to Hispanic settlers moving down from San Gabriel. William Wroth's "Barrio de Analco, Its Roots in Mexico and Role in Early Colonial Santa Fe, 1610–1780" examines one of Santa Fe's first settlements by Nahua-speaking Indians from Mexico who were traditionally loyal to the Spanish settlers. Wroth draws on analogies with other cities in Mexico with similar sites to explain the social underpinnings between Spanish Santa Fe and the indigenous Barrio de Analco. Indigenous pathways to Santa Fe took on a different look when Tlaxcalans and other Nahua-speakers settled on the south side of the river.

Gerald T. E. González and Frances Levine, "In Her Own Voice, Doña Teresa Aguilera y Rocha and Intrigue in the Palace of the Governors, 1659–1662," reconstruct a historical moment, the administration of Governor Bernardo López de Mendizábal and its multi-faceted history. While his term of office in New Mexico was fraught with serious philosophical and political differences between him and the clergymen who ran the missions, he also dealt with other events and activities that centered on the Palace of the Governors and the Plaza de Santa Fe. González and Levine focus on recreating the life and times of the period with particular insights about the governor's wife, Doña Teresa Aguilera y Rocha. González and Levine paint a poignant picture of life in the Palace of the Governor. Doña Teresa is representative of a frontier governor's wife who suffered through the intrigues and conspiracies against her husband. Eventually, she was caught in the same web. The authors also capture her descriptive comments about the Palace of the Governors in order to discern how it must have appeared during her residency. González and Levine take the reader to a time in Santa Fe and reveal the harried life of a governor and his wife at the terminus of the Camino Real de Tierra Adentro that led them back in ignominy whence they came.

In "On Establishing a Presidio at Santa Fe, 1678–1693," Barbara De Marco gives a view of the struggle by Fray Francisco de Ayeta to establish a much-needed presidio at Santa Fe. She traces Ayeta's 1678 proposal to establish a presidio or, at least, a garrison, to defend Santa Fe and its environs. When the Pueblo Revolt struck in 1680, Ayeta proposed that a presidio be established in El Paso. Ayeta hoped that once New Mexico was restored, a presidio would be constructed in Santa Fe. After Diego de Vargas retook New Mexico and re-established Santa Fe, the Presidio de Santa Fe was established.

John L. Kessell, "Vargas at the Gate, The Spanish Restoration of Santa Fe, 1692–1696," introduces new perspectives about the life and times of Diego de Vargas and the reconquest of New Mexico. No one tells it better than Kessell, general editor of the Diego de Vargas Project. Over many years, he and a team of researchers, successfully gathered and analyzed a large collection of documents of the period. Kessell weaves a step by step journey from El Paso, where refugees from the Pueblo Revolt set up a New Mexican government in exile, to the re-establishment of Spanish governance in Santa Fe and, consequently, New Mexico. Significantly, Vargas reopened the 400-mile segment of the Camino Real de Tierra Adentro that led from El Paso to Santa Fe.

"The Pastures of the Royal Horse Herd of the Santa Fe Presidio, 1692–1740" by Linda Tigges is a study about the location of pastures for animals, horses and mules, belonging to the Presidio de Santa Fe. Tigges introduces new documentation about one of Santa Fe's little known stories. Important to military operations and defense, Santa Fe's horse herd required special care. Following the reconquest by Diego de Vargas, land was set aside for pasturage of the presidial horses. By mid-eighteenth century, the horse herd was enlarged to accommodate the frequent campaigns against raiding warriors. Tigges identifies the location of the "*comedores*" or pasturage areas at Caja del Río, Santa Cruz, La Majada de Domínguez, Las Bocas, Los Cerrillos, San Marcos, and Maragua. Tigges' chapter presents another pathway leading to a better understanding of Santa Fe's history.

Joseph P. Sánchez, "It happened in Old Santa Fe, The Death of Governor Albino Pérez, 1835–1837," covers Mexican Period politics and culture. The Rebellion of 1837 resulted in the assassination of Pérez and proved to be a traumatic event in Santa Fe's history. The Mexican Period in Santa Fe's history is little known and less understood by the popular mind. Still, Sánchez' chapter recalls the event that sent shock waves southward on the Camino Real to Mexico City. The rebellion in New Mexico occurred a year after the Texas Revolt of 1836. As revolts rocked Mexico's northern frontier from Texas to California and other areas, Mexico's reaction to the New Mexico rebellion was not as severe as it had been in Texas and Zacatecas, where troops were sent to quell the disturbances. Instead, Manuel Armijo from Albuquerque, who had served a previous term as governor, was appointed as governor. Mexican officials assumed a *laissez faire* position toward New Mexico for the rest of the period. In time, a monument marked the place at a point on Agua Fria Street where Pérez fell.

In "'She Was Our Mother,' New Mexico's Change of National Sovereignty and Juan Bautista Vigil y Alarid, the Last Mexican Governor of New Mexico," Samuel E. Sisneros presents a chapter that serves to transition the Mexican Period story to the early Anglo-American occupation of New Mexico. Sisneros weaves an analysis of the life and times of Juan Bautista Vigil y Alarid, whose life spanned the late Spanish Colonial Period, Mexican Rule, and the early occupation of Santa Fe by the United States. The reader, therein, is introduced to a little known history of a man and his times. In doing so, Sisneros charts new directions in examining the history of Santa Fe. Juan Bautista Vigil y Alarid was the official tasked with meeting the occupation forces of the Army of the West led by Stephen Watts Kearny. The biographical sketch of this proud New Mexican breaks new ground and sheds new light about the descendants of the settlers of Santa Fe.

On the early Territorial Period in New Mexico, Michael J. Alarid, "They came From the East, Importing Homicide, Violence and Misconceptions of Soft Justice into Early Santa Fe, New Mexico, 1847–1853," covers a little known aspect of the early Anglo-American occupation of New Mexico. Anglo-American migration to Santa Fe increased criminal activity in the area. Between 1847 and 1853, Anglo settlers committed twelve of nineteen homicides in the city. The number, Alarid concludes, was high considering that the Anglo-Americans there represented 18% of the population. Alarid examines Santa Fe's society and explains how the Territorial courts worked to thwart newly committed crimes in the area.

In "King Maker in the Back Room, Editor Max Frost and Hardball Politics in the Late-Territorial Period, 1876–1909," Robert K. Dean presents an engrossing biographical sketch about Max Frost, a Civil War veteran and a member of the Signal Corps who established telegraph lines in New Mexico, Arizona, and Texas. Dean writes that Frost left his mark on the territorial period through his activities, some unethical and illegal, others magnanimous. For example, Frost assisted the Santa Fe Ring to steal land from Hispanics and others. On the other hand, he pushed for statehood and promoted commerce and development in New Mexico. He was also instrumental in the construction of the Scottish Rite Temple. Too, Frost "took control of the west's oldest newspaper, the *New Mexican,* and used its pages to rally the party faithful or to deliver the first blast against an opponent." As a consequence, Frost had his admirers and his detractors. Dean's chapter points to another pathway to Santa Fe's history.

In "Progressive Santa Fe, 1880–1912," Robert L. Spude examines the Progressive Movement that introduced new controls on vice, improved public health and made changes for the "common good," of the people of Santa Fe. Spude's chapter sheds light on the movement, which was multi-cultural in nature and presents new documentation and surprising themes to this little known facet of Santa Fe's past. The lasting legacy of the progressive movement in Santa Fe was its municipal Plan of 1912. Of it, Spude writes, "the plan would have been familiar to the previous city leaders, its plantings and beautification, where Riverside Drive became The Alameda. The philosophy was the same, to build a clean, healthy beautiful Santa Fe and was accomplishable.… [T]he Progressive citizens of the generation before had built a strong foundation on which to build the City Different." The pathway established by the Progressive Movement emanated from the east coast and changed Santa Fe's future in many ways.

The story about the thousands of people who came to New Mexico, and particularly Santa Fe, between 1889 and 1940, is told in Nancy Owen Lewis, "The Cure at the End of the Trail, Seeking Health While Transforming a Town, 1880–1940." The salubrious climate lured many people suffering from tuberculosis to Santa Fe. Among the many artists who came to Santa Fe during that period, Will Shuster is the most remembered, for the burning of Zozobra, the large puppet, was created by him as a joke but joined the many everlasting icons associated with the Fiesta de Santa Fe. Too, St. Vincent Sanatorium attracted health seekers to Santa Fe. Lewis introduces new sources regarding this history and adds yet another dimension to Santa Fe's enduring legacy.

In "Santa Fe in World War II, 1940–1947," Judy Reed contributes new insights toward understanding Santa Fe and the people that helped make it what it is. Reed's insights and strong research effort contribute a fascinating view of Santa Fe, one that would surely have been forgotten. Aside from the New Mexico National Guard 200th Coast Artillery (CA) Antiaircraft (AA) Regiment, which suffered high casualties in WWII, Reed writes that "Santa Fe's war years are imprinted with two other historical influences that also should not be forgotten—the Japanese Internment Camp and Bruns Army Hospital. Nothing remains of the internment camp except some photographs, documents, and memories. Bruns was transformed into what is now the College of Santa Fe. The threads of these three entities, the 200th CA (AA), Santa Fe Japanese Internment Camp, and Bruns General Hospital, do not intertwine so much on a practical level but each had a profound effect on the personal lives of the people of Santa Fe." Reed points out events associated with World War II that were spawned in the greater world and found their way to Santa Fe. Reed reminds us of a largely forgotten part of the city's history.

"*Alcaldes* and Mayors of Santa Fe, 1613–2008" by Albert J. Gallegos and José Antonio Esquibel, presents data that validates the claim that New Mexico has been continuously governed since its founding. Aside from the Pueblo Revolt years, when the settlers established their government in exile at El Paso, the authors establish that continuity by citing Peralta's instructions that established Santa Fe with a municipal government. The instructions provided for the election and appointment of municipal councilmen, who, in turn selected two *alcaldes ordinarios* with authority to hear civil and criminal cases in the jurisdiction of the villa within a radius of 15 miles. The authors compiled a list of the mayors of Santa Fe from the earliest records of Spanish Colonial rule to the Mexican Period and modern times. At the end of their chapter, they append a long list of names of those who have served Santa Fe's governance during the past 400 years.

Santa Fe's legacy continues to grow as it moves forward to its next birthday. It is our hope that this volume contributes toward an understanding of Santa Fe's past and present. Certainly, Santa Fe will always ignite the imaginations of people around the world who seek traditions, legends, and history. Santa Fe is like that.

View of the City of Santa Fe from Old Fort Marcy.
From *Frank Leslie's Illustrated Newspaper, July 21, 1883.*

Listen

by
Valerie Martínez
Santa Fe Poet Laureate 2008–2010

The city is murmuring—from the Sangres and southward,
along the trails become dirt roads become pavement;

into gullies and streams, into acequias, into Santa Fe River;
through calles and avenidas and caminos; up driveways

and through windows, out back doors and up into trees,
through our hair and through our sleeves. We want to say

it is the song of four hundred years, our song, but the words
are a tumult, cacophonous, many-tongued, hieroglyphic.

Stop, they seem to say. *Turn around. Turn ahead.*

Each second the present passes through us—we step forward,
it steps back and behind, becomes the history we revel in,

regret, defend—each second, each step, each person, thousands.
A song of the past comes together, falls apart, reconfigures

and we linger over the notes, diligent, so diligent perhaps
we forget it is the forward step, four hundred, four thousand,

that shapes the story of this place—its survival, our happiness,
the legacy we leave to the child who asks, *What is history?*

And we say: *Listen. Turn around. Turn ahead. It is everything
you imagine and create. It is the song you make.* And the child

walks carefully into blue air, into the light silver with sun,
into the city's steady murmuring: *what will come, what will come?*

Fort Marcy on the hill behind the Parroquia.
From *Report of Lieut. J. W. Abert of His Examination of New Mexico in the Years 1846–1847.*

1

Down at the Shell-bead Water
by
David H. Snow

W. H. Davis (1938: 39), writing of his experiences in New Mexico during the early years of Territorial government, claimed that Santa Fe occupied "very nearly the same site as the ancient capital of the Pueblo Indian kingdom ... and when the Spaniards first came to the country they found this point the center of their strength." More so than many other communities in North America, perhaps, interactions with Native Americans have played, and continue to play, a considerable role in defining the City Different's mystique: pseudo "Pueblo" architecture, Native American vendors under the Palace portal, and the annual Indian Market, continue to reflect the intimate relations between Santa Fe and her Pueblo neighbors. Nevertheless, the "ancient," or even the historic, footprints of Native Americans through the city's history are seldom remarked and are scarcely visible today. Here, I focus on a handful of the very fragmentary documentary accounts that reflect the bits and pieces of Santa Fe's Native American past.

Although Davis was correct in believing that Santa Fe was something of a focal point in an earlier Pueblo world, where Santa Fe is situated was a vacant place when a small settlement was established here sometime in 1605 or 1606. The nearby pueblo in "*la ciénega de Carabajal*"—today's La Ciénega, formerly occupied by Keres speaking people—was the only inhabited village of Pueblo people on Santa Fe's river prior to the establishment of the city as a formal *villa* in 1609. Sufficiently distant, perhaps, from La Ciénega, the early "plaza" established here by Juan Martinez de Montoya, and the subsequent villa, evidently were deemed "*sin perjuicio de los indios*"—'without prejudice to the Indians', as the 1593 Royal Ordinances advised. Scarcely mentioned subsequently, La Ciénega's "chief," along with others from Keresan San Marcos Pueblo, and the Tano Tewa villages of the Galisteo Basin, forewarned the Spanish authorities of the impending August revolt of 1680. When the Spaniards returned to stay in 1693, La Ciénega pueblo was deserted forever by its people.

Much of Santa Fe's Colonial, Mexican and Territorial Period histories, ably discussed by several generations of students and scholars, have focused on the foibles and fortunes of avaricious governors and their henchmen, on the sanctimonious and self-serving squabbles of church and state, the advent of the tumultuous "time of the gringo," and so on. But aside from the August 1680 sack and subsequent occupation of the villa by rebellious Pueblo people—a momentous, albeit, singular event in her "great traditions"—the presence and impacts of other Native Americans in Santa Fe's history are scarcely told. They are, in Eric Wolf's words, truly a "people without history," swept aside by the larger events that have created the legends and character of this "different city."

In what follows I have simply teased out some of the loose threads from readily accessible documents and printed materials, and from other accounts that speak to Native American involvement in this precarious settlement at the outermost edge of New Spain's far northern frontier. These are merely some of the tag-ends of the multifaceted 'small traditions'—the wefts—inextricably woven into Santa Fe's ongoing historic tapestry. My sources are referred to in the text and, where appropriate, the page(s) on which the information or citations can be found. The place called Santa Fe echoes but faintly in the recorded myths and legends of her Pueblo neighbors. There was at Santa Fe, however, a particular place the Tewa people called "Quaking leaf water," but it isn't there anymore. Still, there must be some of the people who know the name, or at least those who will understand to what is alluded by that curious name, as it recalls those esoteric beings who live in the creation stories and everyday life of the Pueblo people today. It was a sacred place, and perhaps that memory remains, for within recent times elders from one Tewa pueblo came surreptitiously to place prayer feathers at its edge. But I promised I'd reveal no more about that place, and note here only that it was but one among many such places sprinkled about the Pueblo world; places from whence the *Oxuhwa*, the cloud-people, the Kachinas, are summoned in solemn ceremony and ritual to bring rain, and to where they return until called upon again. But they no longer appear at the 'Quaking leaf water'—a place destroyed now and subverted by the shrines, the myths, and by the holy waters of another people.

J. P. Harrington's (1916) study of Tewa place names led him to suggest that this upper portion of Santa Fe Creek, in late prehistoric times, most likely was occupied by southern Tewa people—those called by the early Spaniards, "Tanos." Santa Fe is a place on the boundary between the Keres and Tewa pueblo worlds, and is called by the former the 'northeast corner', or simply, 'east country'. In the 16th century, at least, the Tano communities lay to the southeast of Santa Fe, in the Galisteo Basin, where the people occupied a group of villages that the Spaniards renamed Galisteo, San Cristóbal, and San Lázaro. Perhaps other southern Tewa people lived at places, now in ruins, that we know today as Pueblo Shé, Colorado, and Blanco, along the southern edge of that Basin.

Santa Fe Lake, Source of the Rio de Santa Fe. From *Old Santa Fe, The Story of New Mexico's Ancient Capital*, by Ralph Emerson Twitchell. 1925. Reprinted by Sunstone Press, Santa Fe, New Mexico 2007.

Up the canyon, the source of Santa Fe River also has a Tewa name—*katepokwi*—'leaf dwelling-place lake' and, together with its mountain, they define the eastern limit of the Tewa world. The Water People at Taos Pueblo—Tanoan speakers like the Tewas—say they came as fish up the mountain streams, thence down Santa Fe creek—*hulpâná*, 'shell river'—and up the Rio Grande to Ranchos de Taos. Perhaps "fishtail mountain," as Nambé people call it, near Lake Peak, recalls that migration of the Water People? Santa Fe also is called by Tewa speakers, 'down at the white (or olivella, or cowrie) shell bead water' *Ogapoge* (or simply, *Kuapoge*, 'bead-water place', at San Juan Pueblo).

Up the creek a short distance east of town was a place known as *pik'ondiwe*, 'the place where red clay is obtained' for use as body paint and for slip clay by Tewa potters. It is said also that Jicarilla Apaches came for this paint as late as the end of the 19th century, sometimes selling it to the Tewas. There is also a sort of yellow clay deposit a mile and a half or so up the canyon, where both Tewa and Jicarilla potters obtained clay. Apaches—"highwaymen," as one Spanish official called them—formerly came here for other reasons as well.

Southern Athapasksan-speaking people (Navajos and Apaches) relate to Santa Fe for other reasons. From the place called by the Diné—the Navajo—'White valley among the waters', or 'White shore', which is "near Santa Fe," they say, "very near the spot where Santa Fe stands," the place they call *tá'paha łialkai*—came the *tábaahá*, 'Among the Waters' clan of the Diné, producers of fine weapons and buckskin clothing. (Matthews 1994: 142) Santa Fe River the Diné call *yooto*—'bead-water', whence came also the *yoo'ó dine'*, the Bead People. (Van Valkenburgh 1999: 94; Young and Morgan 1951: 445) The Diné's familiarity with this "*Kuapoge*," or 'bead-water' place, was related by Hasteen Klah for Mary Cabot Wheelwright (1938: 6):

> Then the Gods took the older sister who married the Bear on a journey beginning at Taos.... The first person they met was the old woman who lives in the pointed mountain in the Rio Grande.... Then they went on south to Santa Fe Mountain (Yoh toh) and there were many ceremonies for them by the Turquoise Clan, and near La Bajada Hill they met the Bluebird people.

The Hopis of Second Mesa have a Bluebird clan—as the Tewas of San Ildefonso Pueblo once boasted a Bluebird kin group (and other Tewa kin groups included 'White shell', and 'Shell bead'). The Mountain Bluebird at Hopi has connotations of war, and Hopi migration stories say that the Bluebird clan came last as "guardians," bringing up the rear.

It is tempting to think that the Bluebird people were ancestors of those Tewas who, fleeing the wrath of the Spaniards following the 1696 Rebellion, sought refuge there on Second Mesa. We know that Tano Tewas from San Cristóbal and San Lázaro pueblos, as well as other Tewas from the Rio Grande Valley, took refuge among the Hopis during the last years of the 17th century; and there today on First Mesa is Hano, or Tewa Village. The Tewa's reputation as formidable warriors, so legend relates, led the Hopis to grant them a place to live at First Mesa in return for protecting the mesa's villages from nomadic raiders. (Parsons 1994: 175-77) As warriors of renown the refugee Tano Tewas were assigned to provide a guard village for the Hopi people near First Mesa. Perhaps the Bluebird people once served a like function as a condition of their acceptance by the Second Mesa community.

View of Hano (Tewa) Village, First Mesa, Hopi. From "A Study of Pueblo Architecture in Tusayan and Cibola," by Victor Mindeleff. Reprinted by the Smithsonian Institution Press, Plate 17, Classics of Smithsonian Anthropology. 1989.

White Shell Pueblo of Keresan Cochiti legend, a name that surely recalls the Tewa's *Ogapoge*, was destroyed, they say, by Tewas who lived near Pojoaque, and alludes, again, to the Pueblo people's association of shells imported from far off with war. The Water People's kiva at Taos is associated with the Kachinas—and with war. The Shipaulovi Hopi Snake dancer proclaims, "...I am the shell. I am a warrior;" and Ma'sewi, deity of war among the Keres people, wears a bracelet of olivella shells. (Parsons 1939) The Cochiti story also recounts their first meeting with the "whites," whom they defeated "after many days of battle."

> When the battle ended, the Whites sent their captain home ahead of them. The Indians met him at Santa Fe and they killed him there. [The anthropologist who recorded this story was told that "his grave is in Santa Fe now, near the main road."] His people spread out all over the mountains and tried to escape. Some were killed by the Indians. When they discovered so many whites killed on the mountains, the Cochiti Indians went up and brought their bodies down to the church to bury them. (Benedict 1982: 193)

History is a bit conflated here. Eye witness accounts say that it was Santo Domingo people who pursued the "captain" of the Spaniards—Governor Albino Pérez—and beheaded him, in 1837, near the junction of Hickox and Agua Fria Streets. Then, according to the story, a brief game of kick-ball with the former head of government ensued before the rebels returned home. Other governmental officials with Perez also suffered that day. Superintendent of Territorial Indian Affairs, John Greiner, recorded (May 7, 1852) that a "Santo Domingo chief took dinner today with us, told us of the killing of Abruya [Santiago Abreu] the judge near Santa Fe beaten to death he said. (Abel 1916: 205)

Among the inhabitants of Santo Domingo Pueblo are counted descendants of remnant Galisteo Pueblo Tanos who, apparently eschewing life on the Hopi Mesas, sought refuge at Tesuque Pueblo following the 1696 Rebellion. Residents in the converted *casas reales* during the interregnum, those few refugees were returned in 1705 to their former village near present Galisteo. Subsequently devastated by hostile Plains raiders, and ultimately driven from there in the 1790s, the survivors fled to Santo Domingo Pueblo. An irony of history, perhaps, is the likely participation of their descendants in the attack on an unpopular government at Santa Fe during the 1837 Rebellion. (Lecompte 1985)

Down the river is Agua Fria village, in colonial times called "*pueblo quemado*," as explained by the eminent visitor, Fray Atanasio Dominguez, in 1776. He noted that "*Quemado,*" [burned] a league west of the plaza,

> ...was an Indian pueblo in the old days, and because it was purposefully burned, it preserves to this day the name of the reason for its end. (Adams and Chavez 1954: 41)

'*Pueblo quemado*' was commonly used by Spanish colonists to characterize the ruins of ancient Pueblo villages in northern New Mexico, whose eroding middens of ash and charcoal from years of household cooking fires led the colonists to imagine—erroneously—that a disastrous conflagration, the result of 'nations' at war, had destroyed those ancient villages. Diego de Vargas' *Maestre de Campo,* Roque de Madrid, informed Vargas in 1693 that his parents and grandparents had lived on property they owned that he said stretched from the "*ojo fresco* [from which Agua Fria got its name] *hasta el pueblo quemado,*"—up to the burned pueblo—before the uprising in 1680. (Twitchell 1914: 476)

Pindi ruin (Tewa, *p'in dee*, 'turkey', named by archaeologists for the extensive turkey pens and remains found there), apparently was the "*pueblo quemado*" of Domínguez' note. Partially excavated in the early 1930s, one of the rooms there yielded the odds and ends from a bead-and-pendant-maker's workshop—fragments of olivellas, red shale and turquoise scrap—the residue from making *hishi* and other jewelry. Might not this ancient village have been home to Olivella Flower Boy, protagonist of many of Tewa tales?

Construction for the convention center in downtown Santa Fe consumed another 'burned pueblo', one known to the villa's colonial residents long before archaeologists discovered it. In 1693, Juan Lucero de Godoy requested a grant to his former lands lying about two *arquebus* shots distant from the villa (perhaps 400 to 600 yards). His property, he said (as translated by Twitchell 1914: 86), stretched south to the river "*desde el pueblo quemado*"—from the burned pueblo, "which is situated near another one, where the Captain Hno. Gonzales used to live." The original, cataloged by Twitchell as No. 54a in his Series II of the Spanish Archives of New Mexico, identifies Gonzales as *el Capn Juan Gonzales Lobon....*" On the east was land of Lucero's son, Antonio, whose southern boundary, in turn, was land of the same Captain Gonzales. It is, therefore, this 'other' *pueblo quemado*, at Gonzales' place, that was re-discovered by archeologists nearly 60 years ago:

> "The excavations for the new Santa Fe High School building have uncovered further evidence of a pre-Spanish occupation of this site.... Since the year 1610, when the Spaniards started building and farming, the location has been considerably torn up; however, the bull-dozers ... uncovered portions of ancient walls, refuse deposits,

> and burials of Santa Fe's first Indian citizens. Bits of broken pottery give clues to the period when Indians lived in this old village, indicating a date span from 1300 to 1500 A.D. Traces of old pueblos have been found from the vicinity of the Federal Building to the State Capitol, and La Fonda to Jefferson Street, Mr. Stubbs writes." (Anonymous 1951:81)

This ancient pueblo at Santa Fe—deserted long before the first *kwaek'u towa*, strange men dressed in metal, appeared at the edge of the Ancestral Tewa world—might well be the remains of that "ancient capital" of Mr. Davis' imagination.

The following appeared in the *Santa Fe New Mexican* for July 26, 1897: "DEVILISH DANCES. Indian Cruelty and Persecution Led by Them—They Should Be Stopped." (La Farge 1959:164-67). Occasional efforts by various Anglo officials and missionaries to ban Pueblo dances as barriers to their conversion to Christianity, or because such performances were considered mere idle diversions from efforts to make them over into 'productive' and enlightened citizens, were nothing new. Almost from the outset, pueblo ceremonies excited the Franciscan priests to a fever-like pitch. Former governor, Bernardo López de Mendizábal, accused in 1663 of various anti-clerical attitudes, also was strongly criticized by the Franciscans (and by the Inquisition!) for allowing Tesuque to dance *catzina* (Kachina) performances in Santa Fe's plaza.

The earliest use of that term that I have found is from Fray Juan de Torquemada, who identified "*Cacina*" as one of the three major pueblo "gods" in his voluminous *Monarquía Indiana* (1986: 681), published in Spain in 1615. In Tewa belief, Kachinas are among those deities who were present in the beginning, prior to the Emergence, but include the souls of the Made People—those who, in life, have achieved the uppermost positions in the Tewas' ritual hierarchy, and who are represented, like the familiar Hopi Kachinas, by masked figures. However, Kachina ritual no longer is public among the Rio Grande Tewa pueblos: "Long ago, when the *kwaek'u towa* (Mexicans) came ... the *oxuwahhe* [Kachina performance] was in the day time...." (Parsons 1994: 16-17) It was also related that the Spaniards cut off the masked head of a Kachina only to find beneath it a man. (Parsons 1994: 111) Eventually the Kachinas were forced underground by Spanish authorities, literally, into kivas, or at secret places outside the pueblo.

Testimony at Governor López de Mendizábal's trial provides an interesting link from the past to the ethnographic 'present'.

> ...the Indians were accustomed to perform a dance, which consisted of their coming to the plaza in very ugly masks, each one bringing

> in his hand some of the fruits which they eat, tied with a maguey cord, and depositing them one after another in a circle in the plaza. The Indians then put on masks representing aged persons and walk among the fruit, making ridiculous figures. Other Indians, either belonging to the place or strangers, come as freely as they wish. He who dares enter the circle to take the fruit, does so; he seizes what he wants, and flees. The Indians in the masks try to stop him and strike him with little paddles which they carry, whereupon those who are caught pay those who catch them, and so on until [the fruit is gone]. (Hackett 1937: 141-42)

Further, Governor Lopez had once occasioned a meeting of the Indians from the pueblos in the vicinity of Santa Fe, and "made them perform dances, even the *catzinas*, whereby the remainder of the kingdom was scandalized."

> Later, Lopez also ordered the Indians of his district to go to Santa Fe and dance the *catzinas*, and they donned their costumes and their devilish masks in the very *casas reales*, from which place they went out upon the plaza to dance ... [and] ... he gave them watermelons and other things customarily used and offered during these dances, and told them to go ahead and perform the *catzinas*. (Hackett 1937: 208)

In his defense before the Inquisition the governor argued that the *catcina* dance "contains nothing of superstition," and reminded the court that it had been danced before in the time of Governor Luis de Rosas, when it had been performed "even by Spaniards"(!). Both Lopez and interpreters of the various pueblo languages affirmed that the dancing "contained no distinguishable word," and that their songs meant nothing. It seemed, Lopez argued, that the dance was mere foolishness and "an entertainment which proved their fleetness of foot." Furthermore, he said that he wasn't aware that the dance was prohibited because it was "bad, nor for any other reason." Declaring, finally, that "were it not for the necessity of upholding his dignity as governor he would himself go out and perform those dances"—"and for a little," he said, "he would do it anyway." (Hackett 1937: 222) His colorful description of the performances, translated from the Inquisition trial documents, suggests a caricature for Spanish consumption, and not the rite found by the Franciscans to be so diabolical.

> "Ten or twelve Indians dressed themselves," Lopez related, in

the ordinary clothes which they commonly wear and put on masks painted with human figures of men; then half of them, with timbrels, such as are commonly used in New Spain, in their hands, went out to the plaza. The others carried thongs, or whips in their hands. They placed in the middle of the plaza four or six watermelons ... [and] those who were dancing continued to do so noisily, sounding the timbrels crazily, as they are accustomed to do, and saying, "Hu, hu, hu." In this fashion they circled around the plaza and the other Indians with the thongs went along, leaping, watching the watermelons, or prizes, from a distance, and allowing opportunity for other youths and boys, Indians or others, to slip in and snatch the watermelons. The one who did so they chased, and if they caught him they gave him many blows with the thongs, but if they did not catch him, he, being more fleet of foot, carried off the watermelon without receiving any lashes. When several had run away the dance stopped.... (Hackett 1937: 223)

Whipper Kachina (Tungwup Kachina), Hano (Tewa) Village. From, "A Pueblo Indian Journal, 1920–1921" by Elsie Clews Parsons. Memoirs of the American Anthropological Association No. 32, 1925, p. 54. Kraus Reprint Co., Millwood, New York. 1975.

Whipping with yucca 'thongs' by masked dancers—particularly, by the Whipper Kachinas—remains a significant aspect of various pueblo ritual ceremonies (Ortiz 1969; Hill 1982), and a performance quite similar to that described in 1663, was observed in 1891 by Fewkes at Tewa village on First Mesa at Hopi. The prizes, however, were stacks of *piki* bread (cornmeal wafers) instead of watermelons. Descriptions of the two performances, separated by very nearly 250 years, are remarkably similar:

> One after another, young men accepted the invitation to race by walking to a position in front of the line of kachinas, and at a signal raced across the plaza at top speed, pursued by a clown or a kachina. Only one pair raced at a time. If the kachina over-took his opponent he struck him once across the body or legs with a yucca blade which he held folded up in his right hand, tore the shirt from the body of his opponent, or cut off a lock of his hair. A prize was given to the lay runner by the kiva chief.... (Cited in Parsons 1974: 89-90)

Such continuity with past ritual remains an important aspect of today's Pueblo worlds.

"*Apaches salteadores*"—'highwaymen'—Juan Martinez de Montoya, the founder of Santa Fe's initial settlement, called them. They came seeking Spanish horses and cattle—and revenge. The assembled rebels in the fields of San Miguel, on the outskirts of the "suburb of Analco," on that fateful August morning in 1680, demanded of Governor Otermín that he turn over to them "all the Apache men and women whom the Spaniards had captured in war," as well as "all classes of Indians who were in [the Spaniard's] power," both those in the service of the Spaniards," and "those of the Mexican nation of that suburb of Analco." (Hackett and Shelby 1942:99) There is here a sense of solidarity—of "Indian-ness"—that, surprisingly perhaps, included even those of the "Mexican nation" serving the Spaniards.

Not even the rebellious Tanos who occupied the villa were safe during the Spaniards' absence, for Vargas was informed that the rebels feared those "Apaches de Navajo" who harassed them, "even beside the river." (Kessel and Hendricks 1992: 463):

> ...the Apaches spied on them, ambushing and killing them. They did the same thing when their women and children went out for firewood and water. Last week they had killed a boy and stolen some horses that were loose in the milpas.

Not long after, in 1697, Antonio Sisneros, suffered the recent loss of a mule and brought suit against Lorenzo de Madrid, citing Madrid's use of the animal "for the purpose of carrying an Indian servant to gather *tierra blanca*" (or *caliche*, for white-wash). The suit was settled in favor of Sisneros, since the mule had been lost when the Indian boy was killed by Apaches on the other side of the river. Hernando Martin, witness for Sisneros, declared that he had gone up river beyond the *cienega* to weed his corn field where he heard "an alarm toward the base of the hill by the road to Pecos" (today's Atalaya Hill where the old reservoir was). There, they "found dead said Indian who went for said dirt...." (Twitchell 1914: 64a)

For a time, the roads in and out of the villa were hazardous to travelers because of hostile Apaches, and governor Don Félix Martínez, was moved, as a result, to issue a *bando* (order) in 1716 requiring repair of those roads in order to make them safer:

> Whereas His Majesty (may God keep him), well-disposed as per His Royal Ordnances, that all Governors, Corregidors, Alcaldes Mayores, and other justices, each in his district, insure the cleanliness and order of the roads so that they may be traveled in safety, inasmuch as it is my concern as Governor of this kingdom, and that the roads from Pecos to this Villa, and that from this Villa to the Pueblo of Tesuque, and that to Taos and Picuris are very mountainous and broken, where with complete confidence the common Apache enemy and natives can ambush and commit murder and robbery against His Majesty's vassals, in order to avoid such harm, I order the Adjutant and Alcalde Mayor of Pecos Pueblo, Salvador Montoya, to require the Indians there to clear the roads to the [Arroyo?] hondo [and] to said Pueblo, cutting the trees down to the ground and removing them to the edge of the hills, so that as they dry out they are to be burned, and that the remainder be cleared off; and the same shall be done by Capitan Juan García de la Riva from the heights of this Villa to Tesuque Pueblo, cutting the trunks that might be in the road, and the Alcalde Mayor of Taos and Picuris shall execute the same, taking for this from their jurisdictions whatever Indians they deem necessary with hatchets... the 16th day of the month of April of 1716. (Twitchell 1914: 260; my translation)

Earlier still, in 1705, concern over the "constant thefts, damages, and murders" perpetrated by the "diverse nations of Indian enemies" who were continually at war with the citizens on this frontier, Governor Cuervo y Valdes issued a *bando* ordering all citizens,

> ..."of whatever quality and rank they might be," to have house-lots, gardens and corrals on the Royal Plaza and on the four public streets; that they build them by virtue of this order within the time limits granted and allowed by the laws of the kingdom, according to [conditions] in hostile countries, with the understanding that he who does not so build and construct [as ordered], those sites and lots will be declared unused and royal domain and will be given and commended as grants to persons who might build and construct thereon.... (Twitchell 1914: 1198; my translation)

Rumor has it—and this one has been around for a very long time—that San Miguel, the "oldest church" that looms across the alley from the "oldest house," was established by and/or for Tlaxcalan Indians who accompanied the colonists to Santa Fe. There is a certain mystique, seemingly, in the idea that Tlaxcalan Indians settled here early on (and I read once the assertion—but can no longer locate where I saw it—that Tlaxcalan deserters from Coronado's army actually founded Santa Fe a short time after 1542!). I remain unconvinced, in the absence so far of incontrovertible evidence in support of claims for Tlaxcalans settled at Santa Fe.

Allied with Cortez against the Mexicas ("Aztecs") of Tenochtitlan (Mexico City), the Tlaxcalan people subsequently were considered "loyal vassals" to His Majesty, for which they received special consideration not generally accorded other native groups in Mexico. Writing from Mexico City, in 1696, for example, the Bishop of that City, Juan de Ortega Montañes, suggested to Diego de Vargas—following his successful suppression of the 1696 Pueblo Rebellion—that the "peaceful [Pueblo] Indians and the governors of their pueblos who have remained obedient to his majesty," be accorded the "privileges of the Tlaxcalan Indians and favored as loyal vassals of his majesty...." (Kessell, Hendricks, and Dodge 1998: 947-48) Therein is the foundation of Santa Fe's Tlaxcalan myth, made up of whole cloth and woven willy-nilly into Santa Fe's historic tapestry.

The legend on the famous 1767 map of the villa by the engineer, Joseph de Urrútia, reads: "*Pueblo ò Barrio de Analco que debe su origen à los Tla[x]caltecas que acompañaron à los primeros Españoles que entraron à la Conquista deste Reino*" ['Pueblo or ward of Analco which owes its origin to the Tlaxcaltecas who accompanied the first Spaniards who entered into the conquest of this kingdom.'] Nevertheless, the legend does not tell us just which conquest, or when, exactly, those presumed Tlaxcalans came: either with Oñate in 1598, or with Vargas in 1693—certainly not with Coronado.

San Miguel Church as it appeared in the 1870s. From *New Mexico in the Nineteenth Century: A Pictorial History.* Andrew K. Gregg. University of New Mexico Press, p. 102.

Subsequently repeated by later 18th century writers, this claim appears in the writings of several Franciscan friars in December of 1693 (Simmons 1964), none of whom, it should be noted, were ever in Santa Fe. The accounts referenced by Simmons state that San Miguel was the parish church for the "Tlaxcalans who lived in the *barrio de Analco.*" Twitchell (in Harrington 1916: 463, note 1) cited an account from the "*Relación Anónima de la Reconquista,*" ostensibly taken from the campaign journals and letters of Diego de Vargas, to the same effect. Here, however, in his own words is what General de Vargas actually wrote in his journal:

> I ... went to inspect the church or hermitage that served as the parish church for the *Indians from Mexico City* who lived in this villa. Its title was the advocation of their patron saint, the Archangel Saint Michael. (Kessell, Hendricks, and Dodge 1995: 477, my emphasis)

Just "Mexican" Indians. What, apparently, is the earliest reference to the Native American population of the Barrio de Analco, in 1640, stated simply that they were "Indians of Mexico." (Cited by Chavez 1953: 143, from the Archivo General de Indias, Sevilla, Patronato, legajo 244, ramo 7, doc. 22, p. 182.)

As New Spain advanced her northern frontier in the latter half of the 16th century, settlements in the newly-conquered regions often included families of converted natives ("vassals"), including Tlaxcalans. Such natives performed churchly and other duties in the Spanish settlements, assisting the curate and *alcaldes mayores* at various functions. Equally important, as early converts to Christianity, they were deemed appropriate exemplars in missionary efforts to convert local "*infieles*"—as the unconverted Indians were termed. The *barrio* of San Estevan de Nueva Tlaxcala, at Saltillo, set aside for Tlaxcalan settlers is, perhaps, the most famous example. Similarly, at San Luis Potosí ("Tlaxcalilla"), Chalchihuites and Nombre de Díos in Durango, where *barrios* were established across the river ("*analco*") for various Native American "vassals." At the latter place, the *barrio de analco* was established originally for Tarascans and Mexican Indians. (The latter were Nahuatl-speaking Mexica, or Aztecs; Saravia 1993.)

Martín Lopez, who mustered with Oñate's colonists, gave his residence as Tlaxcala, but he was "Spanish," unaccompanied by a family, and left New Mexico when the majority of the colony deserted in 1601. (Snow 1998) Twitchell (1914: 36) said that the Britos—a well-known Santa Fe family—were Tlascalan Indians," but failed to provide the evidence for that assertion. There were no Tlaxcalans identified among the Indians with Oñate's colonists, although Marc Simmons (1964) suggested that one of Oñate's Franciscans was accompanied by a "Tlascalan assistant"—presumably, a lay brother—and he speculated that there might have been other such Tlaxcalan lay personnel with the expeditions' missionaries. While Catholic lay brothers were not necessarily bound by a vow of chastity, neither a congregation nor a *barrio* might such assistants have comprised or created.

Engineer Urrútia, like those before and after him, simply projected into Santa Fe an earlier practice of planting Tlaxcalans in several of New Spain's frontier settlements. In fact, her Mexican Indians came as individual household servants with Spanish families. Nothing more.

Elsewhere I attempted to determine the number and identities of Indians who came north with Oñate's colonists (Snow 1998). Forty-four "*indios*" are identified in the documents (there were most certainly others, however), 24 of them women, but the surnames of only seven are provided—all of them servants with various of the colonists. The majority of those hailed from the small community of Tepeaca in Puebla's *tierra caliente*, but several were evidently Tarasacan natives from Morelia, and at least two "*chichimec*" individuals accompanied the expedition's members as servants ("*chichimec*" was the term applied to all indigenous non-agricultural groups north of the Valley of Mexico). I was able to identify only six *español* families with Indian servants who remained at San Gabriel following the mass desertion in 1601—presumably their personal and household servants did also.

Returned to New Mexico with Oñate was Doña Inés, a young girl from one of the Tano pueblos, taken (willingly or not) to Mexico by Castaño de Sosa in 1591. Confident that he possessed in her person a second "Malinche" to assist him with the various Pueblo languages and customs, Oñate lamented later that she no longer recalled her native language (Hammond and Rey 1953: 321). No effort seems to have been made to return her to her people, and I suspect that she reappeared briefly as "*la doña ynés,*"—"*india ladina criada*"—who, along with a woman named Villafuerte, were "*indias*" in name only; for, as Fray Benavides wrote to the Holy Office in 1626, they were "*mas ladinas que las españolas.*" (Scholes 1935: 217n29)

Beatríz de los Ángeles, who also came with Oñate's colonists, and whom Friar Benavides also described as "*mui ladina y españolada,*" was a Tarascan, as was Juan with her, both of them in the personal service of Cristobal Brito. Juan, perhaps, was the same (or the father of?) Juan de Leon Brito, owner of a grant to lands in the 17th century *Barrio de Analco*. Beatriz was accused, before the Inquisitor (the same Fray Benavides) of witchcraft aimed at several of the colony's citizens, among them, her husband, Francisco Balón. His death was attributed to his wife's darker skills. (Scholes 1935:221) Balón (or his son) was a smithy who unsuccessfully courted Ynés, an *india ladina* servant—perhaps that same unwitting "Malinche" of Oñate's hope?

Fray Alonso de Benavides writing of his experiences in New Mexico in his

1630 Memorial, claimed that Santa Fe had "about seven hundred persons in service; so that, counting Spaniards"—250, he said—"mestizos and Indians, the total is about a thousand"—a ratio of nearly 3 servants per person (but it is not clear if Benavides also counted the *mestizos* as servants). Fray Gerónimo Zárate Salmerón, a contemporary of Benavides, writing in 1626, said there were only some 200 Indians under church administration at Santa Fe "capable of receiving the sacraments"—that is, Christian Indians (Scholes 1929: 46-47; Forrestal and Lynch [1954: 24; note 53] are mistaken in asserting that San Miguel was a "mission" for the Indians, since the villa's Native Americans were converts to Christianity and no longer required the indoctrination and ministrations of a missionary). In any event, no such numbers are evident in the accounts of Oñate's personnel and we must wonder just where they all came from, and when, as well as who, among the some 260 separate language groups in Mexico, were represented.

In the church that Benavides said he began construction on—shortly after his arrival in January of 1626—he noted that the friars had begun to teach "the Spaniards and Indians to read, write, play musical instruments, sing, and to practice all the arts of civilized society." (Forrestal and Lynch 1954: 24) Evidently he referred to those Native Americans "in service" to the Spaniards—those "capable of receiving the sacraments." How many of them, if any, were native Pueblo people who characteristically eschewed life among the Spaniards is unknown.

Among the presumed duties of the Mexican inhabitants of the *barrio*, is indicated by a *bando* issued by Governor Martinez, nearly a century later, in May of 1716, ordering that "the Indians come to put up *ramadas* on Corpus Cristi Day:"

> I order the Alcaldes Mayores of the pueblos that those mentioned in this order come, and they are the following: from Tesuque, ten Indians; from Nambe, eight; from San Ildefonso, twelve; from Santa Clara, eight; from San Juan, fourteen; from Pojoaque, six from Picuris, twelve; from Taos, one; from Cochiti, twenty; from Santo Domingo; ten; from San Felipe, twenty; from Santa Ana, twelve; from Zia, twenty; from Jemez, sixteen; from Laguna, ten; from Acoma, sixteen; from Isleta; eight; [and] *that by this order those pueblos [people] that pertain to Mexico,* together, bring the flowers that each pueblo might gather for the two days referred to, and that they name the dancers they want in order that they dance in the procession before the Blessed Sacrament, striving to dress themselves as decently as they can.... (Twitchell 1914: 251; my emphasis)

Requiring local Pueblo people to assist at Corpus Cristi celebrations was still a practice as late as 1808, when Governor Maynez ordered the *alcaldes* of Laguna, Jemez, and Zuni to send Indians to Santa Fe for constructing *ramadas* for Corpus Cristi; as well, he added, for "personal services" (Twitchell 1914: 2133), no doubt for mundane churchly activities required by the friars since Fray Benavides' time, when he eagerly extolled their participation at Easter and other ceremonies.

Some of those that 'pertained to Mexico', were likely residents of the *Barrio de Analco* prior to the 1680 Revolt, and were identified in the census taken by Vargas at El Paso in January of 1693, under the heading, "List of Indians *born in Mexico City* who have lived in the villa of Santa Fe in the company of the original Spanish settlers from there." (Kessell and Hendricks 1992: 56-58; my italics) Forty-five were adults, and 35 were children not yet 15 years of age (15 girls and 20 boys), the majority of them born in exile at El Paso. With few exceptions, their history, too, has been muted. Like the Spaniards who fled the villa in 1680, they were refugees, and on their return they and their descendants were rapidly absorbed into the villa's population of *españoles*—as were those hispanicized Mexican Indians who accompanied Oñate's colonists in 1598.

The only Native Americans mentioned with Vargas' expeditions to recover New Mexico for New Spain, he referred to simply as his "Indian allies" (100 of them), recruited from the missions at El Paso. Presumably they were Piro and Tiwa pueblo converts who had retreated to those missions some years prior to 1680, or local Manso Indian converts from El Paso. What role(s) they played in Vargas' successful assault on the villa, and their subsequent fate, are untold; but among those hispanicized Native American allies were two who, before the final assault on the Tano pueblo, managed to mingle with the rebels in order, perhaps, to be with family and relatives. Manuel Gomez and Lorenzo Simito left the rebel stronghold to inform Vargas of the rebel's preparations for the coming battle for the villa. According to Vargas' account:

> Lorenzo asked them why they are preparing [leather shields and arrows]; they replied to him that it was because they were going to hunt deer. The Indians told him that if he was a Spaniard why was he asking them why they were preparing their weapons? He replied that he was not a Spaniard, that he was an Indian, but he had grown up with the Spaniards. To this, they replied to him that if he was an Indian, why did he go about dressed like the Spaniards. (Kessel, Hendricks, and Dodge 1995: 519)

Gomez gave the rebels a similar response. Like the majority of those unheralded

Native Americans who debuted briefly in Santa Fe's historical pageant, Gomez and Simito disappear from the annals of history.

By the second decade of the century, as Governor Martinez' *bando* suggests, those Mexican-born Native Americans were referred to simply as "Mexicans." In his last will and testament in 1727, for example, Salvador Montoya provided for a piece of land on the south side of the river, that extended west from the vicinity of today's Camino de Monte Sol. On the west, he said, it was bounded by "lands of the Mexicans." (Twitchell 1914: 512) Still, not all of those Mexican Indians were relegated to life in the *barrio*, for Magdalena de Ogama was one of those Mexicans Indians in the El Paso census who returned with Vargas. She was the cook for her Mexican compatriots restoring San Miguel church (Kubler 1939) in 1710. As a *vecino* (like the Britos) in 1703 she owned land in the villa, and later sold property on the west side of the villa's plaza in 1711. (Twitchell 1914: 489, 1071) Health clubs, complete with steam rooms are nothing new in Santa Fe. Catalina Vernal had declined, she said in testimony in 1626, to join her sister-in-law at the *temascal,"* saying that she preferred to bathe in a washtub! (Scholes 1935: 237) *Temascal*, from Nahuatl (the language spoken by the Aztecs), '*tema*', to bathe, and '*calli*', house, was nothing more than a sudatorium—a room into which very hot stones were placed in the center and water poured to create cleansing steam—the traditional sweat-lodge of Native America. We can't be sure the villa's was a uni-sex facility, but another account in mid-17th century referred to the "room" where Governor Juan Manso "was in the baths taking a sweat...." (Hackett 1937: 155) Where those colonial sweat-lodges might have been located in the villa, how many might there have been, and what, precisely they might have looked like, perhaps one day will be revealed by archaeologists.

Aside from the prehistoric kiva discovered beneath the new convention center, a selling point of our local architectural 'style' referred to (surely with tongue in cheek?) as a 'kiva fire-place', also has historical precedence in our town. Called '*estufa*' by the early Spaniards here, they believed pueblo kivas to have functioned much like the familiar Mexican *temascal*—an error soon corrected, and efforts continued well into the 18th century to have such places of idolatrous worship stamped out. Several such features, apparently constructed above ground during the Tano occupation of the villa, were found—two of them on land belonging to Antonia de Moraga when she returned with Vargas' colonists. Testimony in her case referred to the one in which she took up temporary residence, as an "*estufa*" or "*torreon*" (tower), that had been built by the Indians who had occupied the villa. (Twitchell 1914:491) Is it possible that the early colonists also built structures much like pueblo kivas, and called them "*temascales*?"

New Mexican Spanish Torreon, Manzano, New Mexico. From, *The Cities That Died of Fear*, by Paul A. F. Walter. Photograph by Jesse Nusbaum. Reprinted 1931 by El Palacio Press.

A more famous kiva was the one that had been converted by the rebels in what seems to have been one of the torreones connected with the casas reales, and incorporated into their pueblo house-block. Offered by the Tano leader as a place of worship for Vargas' people during the winter of 1693, thereby providing access down through their pueblo "without having to go outside," Vargas ordered a doorway cut from an adjacent room, the walls whitewashed, an adobe altar built, and other doors opened into adjoining rooms for a sacristy and a dwelling for the priest. (Kessell, Hendricks, and Dodge 1995: 483) Upon completion, the father guardian was called to inspect the former kiva. All for naught, as he informed Vargas that

> ...the very reverend father custos had told him and ordered that the divine offices of the holy sacrifice of the mass not be celebrated in the kiva, because it had been a place the Indians had used for their prohibited juntas. Finally, he found other reasons why he should prohibit the kiva from serving as a place to say mass. (ibid, p. 485)

What other reasons the reverend father custos entertained are not recorded; but one assumes that no amount of exorcism, blessings, or holy water might have swayed his opinion.

The so-called "oldest house" isn't. The Palace of Governors, that "old molar," in Oliver La Farge's words, after all, was home to a long succession of governors, their families, and their entourage, servants, and hangers-on. The "oldest house," however, was the subject of a minor controversy that engaged some of the City Different's more distinguished visitors and celebrated historians. The issue was just who built and lived in it.

Pencil sketch of the Palace of the Governors by Governor Lew Wallace, 1889. From *New Mexico in the Nineteenth Century: A Pictorial History.* Andrew K. Gregg. University of New Mexico Press, p. 90.

Believed by some to be the remnant of the former "pueblo" of the Mexican Indians in the *barrio de analco*, W. W. H. Davis (1938: 39), informed his readers that "parts of two of the old buildings are standing on the west side of the river, on the road leading to San Miguel. The Indians resided here many years after the Spaniards made a settlement, but in course of time the pueblos fell...." Twitchell recalled that the structure had two stories when he first saw it, "but was later cut down to one story, as the top walls were crumbling away." He continued, arguing that:

The "Mexican Indians" did not build two story houses, nor did they

> build houses having opening in the top instead of the sides. *The "oldest house" had its entrance in the roof and the doors and windows now appearing are all of very late construction.* (Cited in Harrington 1916:463. My emphasis)

In New Mexican Spanish, the word '*coi*' is said to derive from the Tewa language, and refers to the lower rooms of the multistory Pueblo 'apartment' buildings (Cobos 1983: 32). I have been unable to identify the word either from Tewa or from indigenous Mexican language sources, but it was a conspicuous feature of pueblo architecture, visible today as the means of entrance, still, to some pueblo kivas.

Twitchell believed that the "oldest house," instead, was constructed by Pueblo Indians because of the entrance through the roof into the rooms below; but what he did not know is that Spanish settlers in the Rio Grande adopted that rooftop entrance for their own use, and the reader is referred to the brief account of a question of murder at Santa Cruz in 1713: did the husband beat his wife to death in their "*coy*," or did she fall into it from the ladder with a water jar on her head? (cited in Adams and Chavez 1956: 50)

Roof vigas from the "oldest house" were dated by the Laboratory of Tree-ring Research at Tucson, who determined that they were cut fresh between 1740 and 1767, or slightly later, suggesting either repairs to an existing structure, or one newly built in the 1760s. A further clue, at least to what the place might have looked like was described by Adolph Bandelier in 1890. He wrote that the wife of Esquipula Pacheco had told him,

> ...that the whole front where the old house now stands, including the corner of Pedro Martinez and Ramon Encinas, and as far as the house of Dona Rita Padilla, was formerly a two-story building as late as 40 years ago. It was then partly torn down, so that *the old house of today is only the last one of a small pueblo....* (Lange, Riley, and Lange, 1984: 101. My emphasis)

Doña Maria Rita Padilla and her husband, Francisco Garcia (for whom Garcia Street was named), occupied their residence near what once was called "five points" at the intersection of Arroyo Tenorio, Manhattan, and Garcia Streets—perhaps the easterly limits of the lands of the "Mexicans" referred to in Salvador Montoya's last will and testament?

The Oldest House. From Ralph Emerson Twitchell, "The Palace of the Governors, The City of Santa Fe, Its Museums and Monuments." Historical Society of New Mexico No. 29 1924, p. 47.

The Oldest House. From *Harper's Weekly*, September 13, 1879

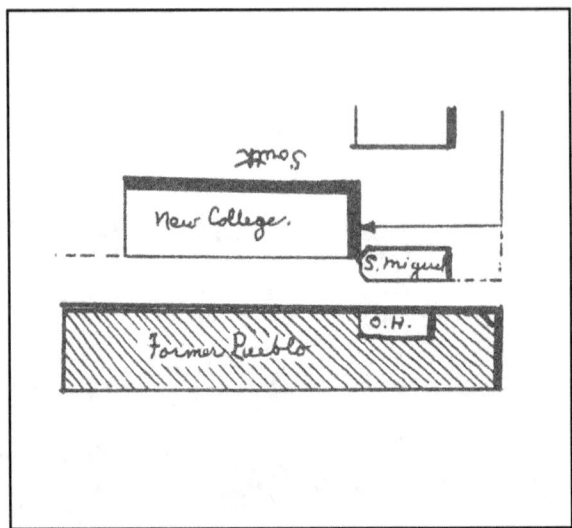

Sketch of the plan of the Oldest House by Adolph F. Bandelier, March 31, 1890. From *The Southwestern Journals of Adolph F. Bandelier, 1889–1892*. Edited and Annotated by Charles H. Lange, Carroll L. Riley, and Elizabeth M. Lange, p. 101. The University of New Mexico Press and the School of American Research Press. Albuquerque and Santa Fe. 1984; New Edition, Sunstone Press, Santa Fe, 2012.

Curiously, it was the son of that same hapless Governor Pérez—born, he said in the "oldest house"—who related an account of a party of Ute Indians who paid a visit to another governor in the *casas reales,* about 1844. (Mauzy 1960) In essence, Don Demétrio Pérez said, a large party of Utes entered the plaza requesting their annuity gifts which had always been furnished since colonial times to the less tractable native groups that surrounded and frequently harassed the New Mexican settlements—outright bribes in hopes of keeping them friendly and allied. Or at bay. Highly displeased, apparently, with their allotment that year, the Ute party threatened the governor with return the next day, following which they repaired to a vacant property for the night on the Rio Chiquito (Water Street). All night, Don Demétrio said, "their outcries & war songs kept the people of town terrorized fearing an attack by the Indians." Return they did, attacking the governor in his office with "knives and tomahawks," although he managed to hold them at bay with a chair, until his wife shouted the alarm, alerting the Palace guards who

> …gave the war cry to the Indians, who were ready to attack the Old Palace & kill indiscriminately all people they would meet in the Plaza & in the streets, but the troops were ready to check the

attack … & opened fire upon them & a struggle commenced here the Indians were routed loosing about 70 of their warriors & the remainder of them fled hurriedly taking their route down the San Francisco street…. (Mauzy 1960: 93)

Not unlike a similar incident faced by former governor Juan Treviño, in 1675, when 70 or more very angry Pueblo warriors—enough to fill two rooms of the *casas reales* (!)—threatened him with dire consequences should he fail to release 43 "sorcerers" (religious leaders) he had imprisoned for idolatry (Hackett and Shelby 1942:301)—among them, one named Popé, whose leading role in the subsequent 1680 Revolt only recently has been accorded the honor of his statue in the nation's capital (Kessell 2008). Popé and his fellow "sorcerers" were released immediately!

In any event, said Don Demétrio, the bodies of the Ute warriors were thrown into graves along the "south side of the arroyo running down [from the] Rio de Tesuque mountains"—almost certainly today's Arroyo de las Máscaras where, as far as anybody knows, they remain.

On December 30, 1693, General de Vargas ordered the execution of seventy rebel Tanos captured in the villa (Kessell, Hendricks, and Dodge 1995: 533), among them, the Tano governor, his assistant, Jose, and Antonio Bolsas, a Spanish-speaking spokesman for the rebels in the villa. Although not so identified, Jose and Antonio likely held the positions of War Chief and *cacique* in Tewa society, offices held by principal members of the religious hierarchy—the "Made People" of the Tewa world, as Alfonso Ortiz (1969) explained. As with the Utes, the bodies of the 70 rebels executed in 1693 have never been recovered. Still, the newspaper reported in 1884, the recovery of "many skeletons in the Palace patio," possibly the remains of the 1693 rebels (Shishkin 1972: 42)—but their spirits, I suspect, remain imprisoned beneath the former Quaking leaf-water place.

Among the finds under the new convention center was a kiva, the artifacts from which Tesuque claimed ownership for themselves (or, perhaps, on behalf of the greater Tewa community?). The objects were turned over to Tesuque Pueblo under an agreement between the City and the local Museum. If, as Harrington argued, Santa Fe was formerly Tewa country, as he was informed by his Cochiti informants, Tesuque's claims, perhaps, have considerable merit. Bandelier suggested, however, that any Tewa claim to Santa Fe merely reflected its brief occupation by Tano Tewas from Galisteo Pueblo during the Revolt. Be that as it may, we must remember that those who occupied the villa between 1680 and 1693 were not rebels from San Marcos, or their Keresan kin, but rather, were Tewa people.

Tesuque Pueblo. From Ralph Emerson Twitchell, "The Palace of the Governors, The City of Santa Fe, Its Museums and Monuments." Historical Society of New Mexico No. 29, 1924, p. 38.

Might not Doña Inés, Oñate's unwitting Malinche, uprooted from her Tano Tewa heritage and planted in an alien culture, be Santa Fe's very own "*Llorona*," grieving, perhaps, for the spirits of those of her kind similarly transplanted and forgotten in hub-bub of the City Different's "recent" history?

References Cited:

Abel, Annie Heloise. 1916. "The Journal of John Greiner," Old Santa Fe, Vol. III, No. 11, pp. 190-243.

Adams, Eleanor B. and Fray Angelico Chavez. 1975. *The Missions of New Mexico, 1776: A Description by Fray Francisco Atanasio Dominguez with Other Contemporary Documents.* University of New Mexico Press, Albuquerque.

Anonymous. 1951. "Construction Excavations in Santa Fe Uncover Archaeological Evidences." El Palacio 58(3):81.

Benedict, Ruth. 1982. *Tales of the Cochiti Indians.* University of New Mexico Press, Albuquerque.

Chavez, Fray Angelico. 1953. "How Old is San Miguel?" El Palacio 60(4):154-160.

Cobos, Ruben. 1983. *A Dictionary of New Mexico and Southern Colorado Spanish.* The University of New Mexico Press, Albuquerque.

Davis, W.W.H. 1938. *El Gringo, or New Mexico & Her People.* The Rydal Press, Santa Fe. New Edition, Sunstone Press, Santa Fe, 2010.

Forrestal, P.P., and C.J. Lynch, O.F.M. (translators and annotators). 1954. Benavides' Memorial of 1630. Academy of Franciscan History. Washington.

Hackett, C.W. (edited and annotated by). 1937. Historical Documents relating to New Mexico, Nueva Vizcaya, and Approaches Thereto, to 1773. (Vol. III). The Carnegie Institution of Washington. Washington, DC

Hackett, C.W., and C.C. Shelby (translators and annotators). 1942. *Revolt of the Pueblo Indians.* The University of New Mexico Press, Albuquerque.

Hammond, George P., and Agapito Rey. 1953. *Don Juan de Oñate, Colonizer of New Mexico, 1595–1628*. The University of New Mexico Press.

Harrington, J. P. 1916. The Ethnogeography of the Tewa Indians. 29th Annual Report of the Bureau of American Ethnology, 1907–1908. Government Printing Office, Washington.

Hill, W. W. 1982. An Ethnography of Santa Clara Pueblo (Edited and Annotated by Charles H. Lange). University of New Mexico Press, Albuquerque.

Kessell, John L., et al, editors and translators. 1992. *By Force of Arms*. The Journals of Don Diego de Vargas, 1691–1693. The University of New Mexico Press, Albuquerque.

1995. *To The Royal Crown Restored: The Journals of Don Diego de Vargas, New Mexico, 1692–1694*. The University of New Mexico Press, Albuquerque.

1998. *Blood on the Boulders: The Journals of Don Diego de Vargas, New Mexico, 1694–1697*. University of New Mexico Press, Albuquerque.

2008. *Pueblos, Spaniards, and the Kingdom of New Mexico*. University of Oklahoma Press, Norman.

Kubler, George. 1939. *The Rebuilding of San Miguel at Santa Fe in 1710*. The Taylor Museum, Colorado Springs.

La Farge, Oliver. 1959. *Santa Fe, The Autobiography of a Southwestern Town*. University of Oklahoma Press. Norman.

Lange, C.H., Riley, C.L., and Lange, E.M. (edited and annotated by). 1984. *The Southwestern Journals of Adolph F. Bandelier, 1889–1892*. The University of New Mexico Press, Albuquerque, and the School of American Research Press, Santa Fe. New Edition, Sunstone Press, Santa Fe, 2011.

Lecompte, Janet. 1985. *Rebellion in Rio Arriba, 1837*. University of New Mexico Press, Albuquerque.

Matthews, Washington. 1994. *Navajo Legends: Collected and Translated by Washington Matthews*. (reprint) University of Utah Press, Salt Lake City.

Mauzy, Wayne L. (editor). 1960. Recollections of Demetrio Perez: The Old Palace in Mexican Days," El Palacio 67(3):87-94.

Ortiz, Alfonso. 1969. *The Tewa World*. The University of Chicago Press, Chicago.

Parsons, E. C. 1939. *Pueblo Indian Religion*. University of Chicago Press, Chicago.

1974. A Pueblo Indian Journal, 1920–1921. Memoirs of the American Anthropological Association, Number 32. Menasha, Wisconsin (Kraus Reprint Co., Millwood, New York).

1994. *Tewa Tales* (reprinted, with a foreword by Barbara A. Babcock). Univeristy of Arizona Press, Tucson.

Saravia, Atanasio G. 1993. Obras IV. Apuntes Para La Historia de La Nueva Vizcaya. Universidad Nacional Autónoma de Mexico. Mexico, D.F.

Scholes, Franz C. 1929. "Documents for the History of the New Mexican Missions in the Seventeenth Century." New Mexico Historical Review IV:45-58.

1935. "The First Decade of the Inquisition in New Mexico." New Mexico Historical Review X(3) pp. 195-241.

Shishkin, J. K. 1972. *The Palace of the Governors*. Museum of New Mexico Press, Santa Fe.

Simmons, Marc. 1964. "Tlascalans in the Spanish Borderlands." New Mexico Historical Review 39:101-110.

Snow, David H. (compiler). 1998. New Mexico's First Colonists: The 1597–1600 Enlistments for New Mexico under Juan de Oñate, Adelantado & Gobernador. Hispanic Genealogical Research Center of New Mexico, Albuquerque.

Torquemada, Fray Juan de. 1986. Monarquía Indiana. Tomo I (Sexta Edición). Editorial Porrua, S.A. Mexico

Twitchell, Ralph Emerson. 1914. *Spanish Archives of New Mexico* (Volumes I and II). The Torch Press. Cedar Rapids. New Editions, Sunstone Press, Santa Fe, 2009.

Van Valkenburgh, Richard F. 1999. *Navajo Country, Dine Bikeyah: A Geographic Dictionary of Navajo Lands in the 1930s. Time Traveler's Maps*. Mancos, Colorado.

Wheelwright, Mary. 1938. *Navajo Creation Myth: The Story of the Emergence by Hasteen Klah*. Museum of Navajo Ceremonial Art, Santa Fe.

Young, Robert, and William Morgan. 1951. *A Vocabulary of Colloquial Navajo*. United States Indian Service, Phoenix Indian School, Phoenix.

A City Different Than We Thought
Land Grants in Early Santa Fe, 1598–1900
by
Malcolm Ebright

Santa Fe—established as the capitol of New Mexico 400 years ago in 1610—is still a mystery to many archeologists and historians. Because the archives of New Mexico were burned at the time of the 1680 Pueblo Revolt, the records generated by the Spanish authorities within New Mexico are no longer available for study, except for a few copies found in the archives in Mexico City, Seville, and smaller archives. These records would have provided a great deal of information about early Santa Fe, but would necessarily have given us only the perspective through the eyes of the Spanish conqueror. Myths and fiction have grown up around early Santa Fe and early New Mexico, myths that have been punctured only to be replaced by new myths. Basic historical questions are still debated by scholars: why did Governor Pedro de Peralta pick the present location as the site for the Villa of Santa Fe when later governors tried to move the villa,[1] when was the Villa of Santa Fe founded, and was there an existing settlement of Mexican Indians at the site of the Barrio of Analco prior to the founding of the Villa of Santa Fe?[2]

To begin to answer some of these thorny questions it is necessary to strip away several false ideas about early Santa Fe that have been imposed by nineteenth century lawyers, civic boosters, and historians. The following case studies deal respectively with the mythical Santa Fe League, and with the Cristóbal Nieto grant which was greatly stretched and expanded in size. Both claims were asserted before the Court of Private Land Claims (CPLC) in the 1880s and 1890s in an effort to establish title to land based on an imaginative history of early Santa Fe that was created to suit the needs of those late nineteenth century claimants trying to stake a claim to what had become valuable property in Territorial Period Santa Fe. After these fictions are exposed, it will be possible to draw a more realistic picture of early Santa Fe that truly represents the story of this place.[3]

The year 1610 was also a year of important literary happenings all over the world, which provide a sense of the European mindset at this moment in history. In England, William Shakespeare was working on his last major work, *The Tempest*, seen by some as an examination of the great encounter between the European powers and the natives of the new world represented by Caliban.[4] Ironically, Shakespeare's inspiration for *The Tempest* came partly from accounts of a 1609 shipwreck near Bermuda of one of a fleet of ships headed for Jamestown a year after its founding in 1607.[5] The shipwreck in a great storm, the wonders of strange lands, and the great gulf of understanding between Europeans and natives, were common elements in the play and in historical events in the Americas and in New Mexico. In Spain, the country whose conquistadors conquered the province of New Mexico, Miguel Cervantes was working on the second part of *Don Quixote*, published in 1615, (part one was published in 1605). It is appropriate that this great work encompassing the world of knights errant, heroic adventures, and the question of fiction's relationship to reality, was found in some early New Mexican libraries and was carried by some New Mexico governors in their baggage. It is a work we might consult today as we try to separate myth, fiction, and reality in the landscape of early Santa Fe.[6]

The Santa Fe Grant

Like many things connected with early Santa Fe, the notion that the king of Spain made a formal municipal grant to the Villa of Santa Fe is a myth. Like the "oldest house" in Santa Fe, which is not that old and more a tourist attraction than a historical building, the Santa Fe Grant never existed.[7] There never was a grant to the Villa of Santa Fe, though the Surveyor General and Court of Private Land Claims records include three long case files, litigated with numerous lawyers, all designated as "the Santa Fe grant."[8] The idea of a municipal grant to the Villa of Santa Fe first saw the light of day in 1874 and again in 1892 when petitions were filed with the Surveyor General of New Mexico and the Court of Private Land Claims, respectively, for confirmation of four square leagues of land (about 17,200 acres) to the municipality of Santa Fe, in spite of the fact that the area was already covered with almost fifty smaller grants (a list of those grants is attached as an appendix). Some of these small grants were confirmed prior to the Santa Fe grant case, some were joined as parties to that litigation, and some were what J. J. Bowden calls "ghost grants."[9] To piece together this complicated story of myths and reality it is best to start at the time when Spaniards first arrived in New Mexico.

After the sixteenth century explorations of Coronado, Espejo, Chamuscado-Rodríguez, and Castaño de Sosa revealed the existence of a large native population in New Mexico and the possibility of mineral wealth,[10] Juan de Oñate (1598–1608) established the first permanent settlement in New Mexico in 1598 at Ohkay Owingeh Pueblo (San Juan Pueblo) on the east bank of the Río Grande. A few months later the capitol was moved across the river to San Gabriel del Yunge Owingeh, which remained the capitol of New Mexico until Santa Fe was established in 1610 by Juan de Oñate's successor Governor Pedro de Peralta.[11] Early explorers such as Gaspar Castaño de Sosa[12] and Oñate were aware of the location that became Santa Fe, and as early as 1607 a military camp (*real*) had been established at the site that became Santa Fe.[13] In the spring of 1605 when Oñate crossed the Santa Fe River on his way to the Great Plains, he noted that the locale had many of the requirements for a new capitol: adequate water supply, fertile soil, abundance of timber, and a strategic position for dealing with hostile nomadic Indians.[14]

In 1609 Pedro de Peralta (1609–1614) was appointed governor of New Mexico and was ordered to establish a new capitol to be designated as a villa.[15] Peralta arrived in New Mexico late that year and by early 1610 Peralta had moved the capitol of New Mexico from San Gabriel to the site of present-day Santa Fe, on the ruins of the prehistoric pueblo of Kuapoge (bead-water place).[16] By May of 1610, if not before, the move to Santa Fe had probably been completed, the two main acequias dug, and the fields of the villa planted.[17] Viceroy Luís de Velasco had given precise instructions as to how the villa should be laid out, but it is unlikely that this was accomplished as called for by the viceroy. As was true of the other later villas of Santa Cruz de la Cañada (1695), and Albuquerque (1706), Santa Fe was primarily an agricultural settlement with ranches scattered along the Santa Fe River, rather than a compact urban municipality as myth would have it.[18]

The core of the villa was built north of the Santa Fe River around 1610, with later additions forming "a large government-military compound containing arsenals, offices, a jail, a chapel, and the governor's residence." The outer walls of these structures served as defensive walls of a compound which enclosed two interior plazas. The fortified villa had four watchtowers (*torreones*), two on the south wall, two on the north side, and only one gate. Outside of this enclosure were the homes and fields of the settlers. In 1610, or soon thereafter, a temporary church was constructed, but it collapsed after a few years.[19] A settlement of Mexican Indians, (mostly Tlaxcalans), who acted as servants to the Spaniards, presidial soldiers, and military auxiliaries on Spanish expeditions, formed the Barrio of Analco probably established between 1604 and 1608 and centered around the chapel of San Miguel south of the Santa Fe River.[20]

Although Santa Fe was designated as a villa when it was founded, no formal charter specifying the villa's ownership of the land within its boundaries had been discovered at the time of the litigation of the Santa Fe grant in the 1880s and 1890s.[21] This was crucial to the later claim by the municipality of Santa Fe that it owned four square leagues of land, measured from the center of the plaza, in a corporate capacity to be held in trust for the inhabitants of Santa Fe. Prior to the 1680 Pueblo Revolt it is difficult to know exactly how the Villa of Santa Fe acted in regard to the property it encompassed because of the scarcity of documents. When the Pueblo Indians and their Apache allies occupied Santa Fe after expelling all the Spaniards from the province and burned the archives, it is likely that many important documents concerning early Santa Fe went up in smoke. Thus historians are mostly left with archives outside of New Mexico to piece together the pre-Revolt history of the Villa of Santa Fe.[22]

In 1693, when Diego de Vargas was in El Paso gathering the soldiers and colonists needed for the reconquest of New Mexico, he told prospective members of his expedition that he would "give them the lands, homesites, and haciendas they had left at the time of the uprising."[23] However, since there was insufficient land to meet this promise, Vargas followed a resettlement plan that differed radically from the pre-Revolt settlement pattern. The Vargas plan involved an area of common pasture southwest of Santa Fe and another area of common woodlands north and east of the villa. Individual tracts were granted, both to pre-Revolt families and to new settlers of corn-planting land of one to two *fanegas* each (9-18 acres), together with pasture land. The resulting tracts were probably substantially smaller than what returning colonists claimed they owned before the Revolt. The only public land in Santa Fe at this time was the land where the governor's palace, the Santa Fe plaza, the churches, and other public buildings were situated. The lands of early Santa Fe are discussed further in the conclusion of this chapter.

A lawsuit between the *cabildo* or town council of Santa Fe and Diego Arias de Quiros in 1715 involved a kind of municipal property called *propios*. These were lands owned by the municipality as private property, which were rented by the municipal council with the rent applied toward public works for the benefit of all citizens. *Propios* were often confused with common property as was the case with the Ciénega property being litigated between Arias de Quiros and the *cabildo* of Santa Fe. The Ciénega of Santa Fe was a tract of spring-fed marshy land east of the plaza and the governor's palace that was initially used by Santa Fe residents to graze their animals in common.

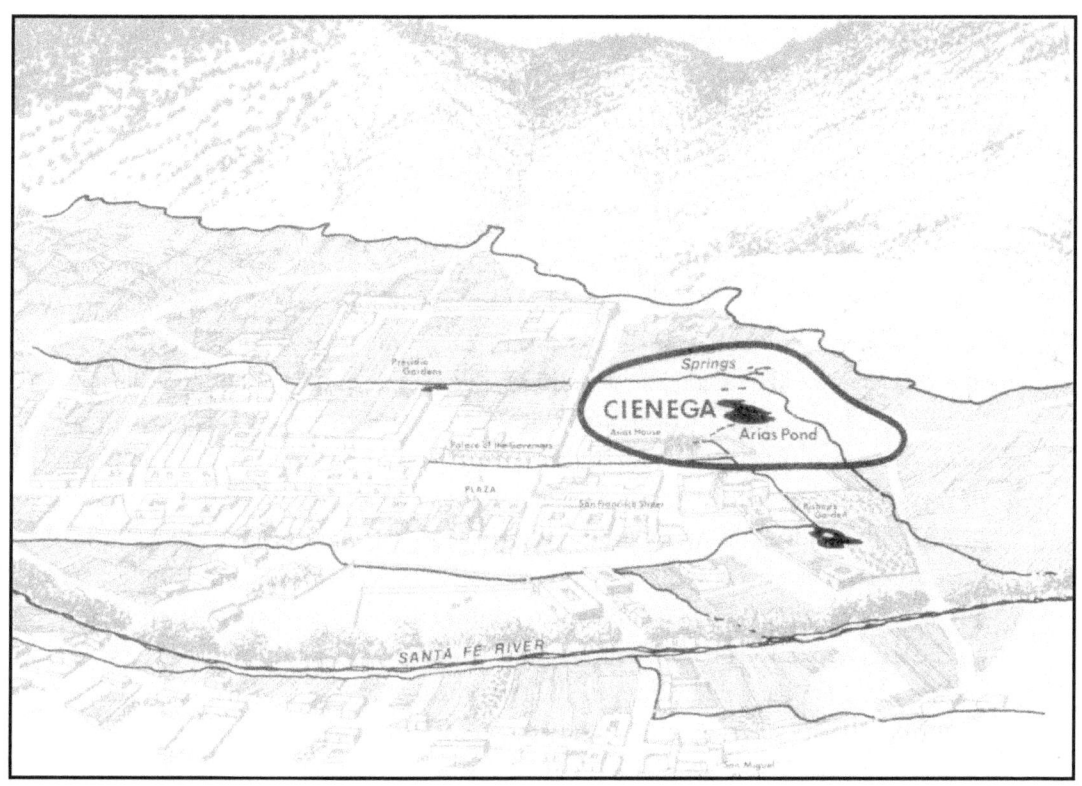

The Ciénega of Santa Fe drawn by Carrie Arnold (Malcolm Ebright, *Land Grants and Lawsuits in Northern New Mexico*, 93.)

Arias de Quiros owned land surrounding the Ciénega, and prior to 1715 he built a pond (*tanque*) on the Ciénega to collect water from one of the springs that kept the area wet and green. In July of 1715 the Santa Fe Cabildo (municipal council) ordered Arias to remove his pond, claiming that the Ciénega was municipal property and the pond was causing the area to dry up. Arias de Quiros responded by appealing directly to Governor Flores Mogollon (1712–1715) claiming that the Ciénega was unappropriated royal lands (*realengas*) not owned by the Villa of Santa Fe. The governor ordered the *cabildo* to produce any documents it might have showing that the Ciénega had been granted to the Villa, and after admitting it had no such document, the *cabildo* asked Governor Flores Mogollon to make a grant of the Ciénega to the Villa of Santa Fe. Flores Mogollon responded favorably to this request, giving the Villa the first written document granting it the Ciénega as its municipal property. This document would work against the later claim by the municipality of Santa Fe that it was entitled to four square leagues, either by express grant or by virtue of Spanish law.[24]

The first claim of a municipal four square league grant to the Villa of Santa Fe was made in 1874 by land developer and speculator Gaspar Ortiz y Alarid as Probate Judge for Santa Fe County.[25] Ortiz petitioned Surveyor General James K. Proudfit for a four square league tract of land to be measured from the stone monument in the center of the plaza, based on the possible existence of a written grant from the King of Spain and on Book 4, Title 5, Law 6 of the *Recopilación de Leyes de los Reyes de las Indias*, the book of Spanish laws affecting the Americas. Ortiz y Alarid claimed that this law provided a grant by operation of law to a community of at least thirty families as long as the settlement was at least five leagues from any other settlement and did not prejudice the interests of any Indian Pueblo or private party. If confirmed the grant would be held in trust for the inhabitants of Santa Fe until the city became incorporated and could then become the rightful custodian of the patent.[26] With unaccustomed alacrity and little or no investigation of possible conflicting grants, Surveyor General Proudfit recommended confirmation of the claim based primarily on the law cited in the petition supposedly providing four square leagues of land to a community of at least thirty families meeting the other requirements of the statute. Unfortunately Proudfit's staff did not thoroughly research the Spanish law cited as *Recopilación*, Book 4, Title 5, Law 6 as we shall see.[27] In September 1877 Deputy Surveyors Griffin and McMullin surveyed the Santa Fe grant and found it to contain 17,261 acres.[28] The Santa Fe Grant was submitted to Congress but no action was taken on the Santa Fe grant claim, which was still pending when the Court of Private Land Claims was established on December 2, 1891.[29]

The shaky foundation upon which the claim for a Santa Fe grant of approximately 17,000 acres was built was not evident until its examination by the Court of Private Land Claims. Ironically Gaspar Ortiz y Alarid, the petitioner on behalf of Santa Fe County, had constructed two massive land grant frauds himself just prior to his 1874 petition for the Santa Fe grant. In 1871 he succeeded in getting Surveyor General T. Rush Spencer to approve the fraudulent Roque Lovato grant which he stretched from a plot of about fifteen acres to a tract of six square miles or about 3840 acres. Then in 1873, Don Gaspar as he was called, claimed the clumsily forged Sierra Mosca grant. He was able to sell the Roque Lovato grant, whose ownership was based on a forged deed, before the forgery was detected by Will Tipton, handwriting expert for the Court of Private Land Claims. Like attorney James Purdy, discussed in the next section, Don Gaspar Ortiz y Alarid's reputation did not suffer because of his involvement with land grant boundary stretching, fraud, and forgery. In fact, his name is permanently affixed to the current landscape of Santa Fe: both Ortiz Street and Don Gaspar Avenue are named after him.[30]

A City Different Than We Thought, Land Grants in Early Santa Fe, 1598–1900

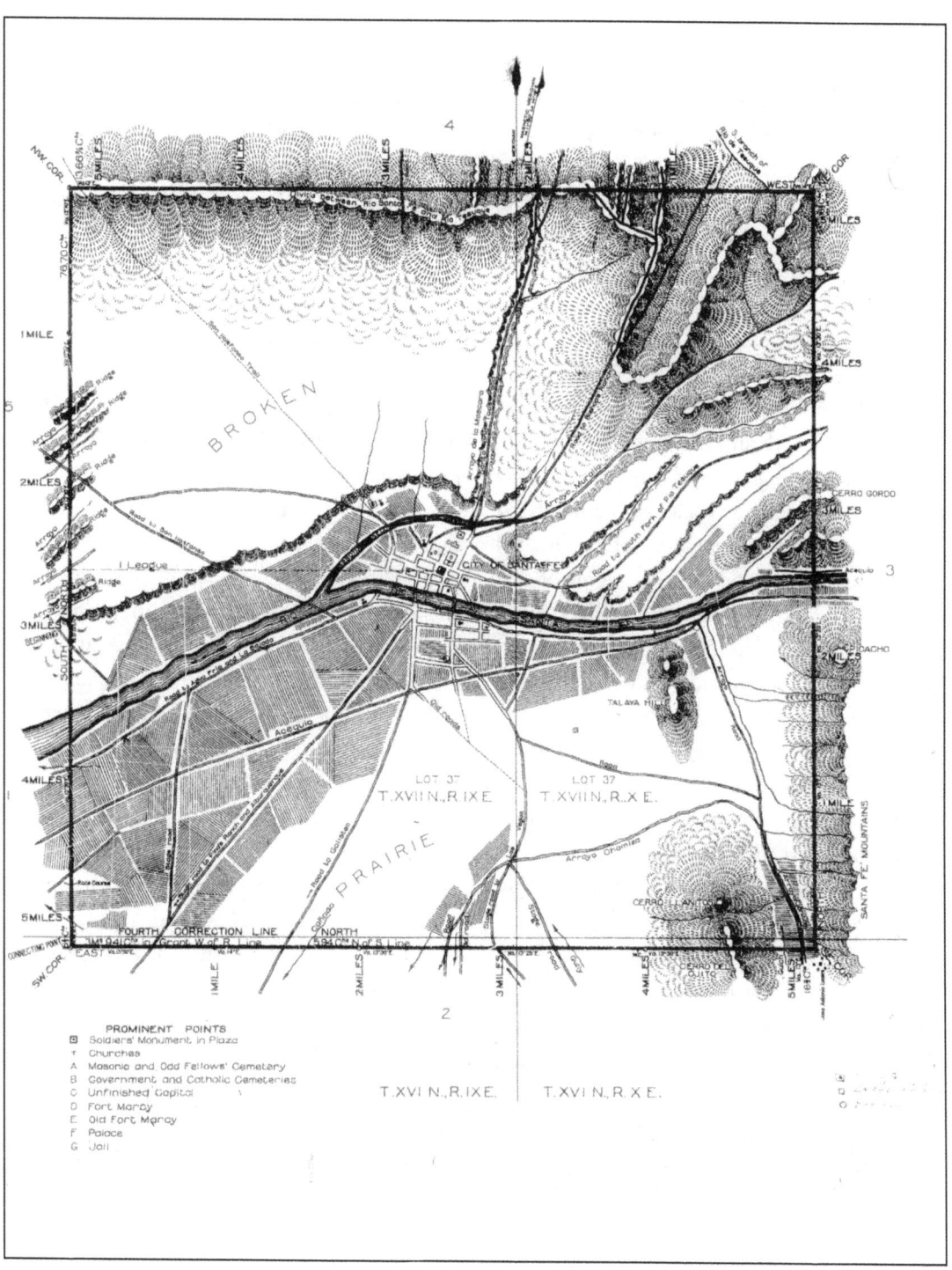

Plat of the Santa Fe grant. Bureau of Land Management, Santa Fe

Because of its importance the Santa Fe grant claim was one of the first submitted to the Land Claims Court. On July 14, 1892 the Board of County Commissioners of Santa Fe County filed its claim as successor to the ancient Villa of Santa Fe for confirmation of a four square league tract of land. The petition alleged that the King of Spain had made such a grant to the Villa, but the document could not be produced because of the destruction of the Spanish archives during the Pueblo Revolt of 1680. The complaint also alleged that the municipality was entitled to four square leagues by operation of *Recopilación,* Book 4, Chapter 5, Law 6 since the Villa of Santa Fe contained at least thirty families when it was reestablished in 1693 after the Pueblo Revolt, and met all the other requirements of the law.[31] However, the U.S. government, represented by U.S. Attorney Matthew Reynolds and his staff of experts such as Will Tipton and Henry Flipper, again failed to research and challenge the Spanish law cited by the city either at this point in the proceedings or later. Instead the government challenged the petition on the ground that the plaintiff had no authority to prosecute the claim on behalf of the Villa of Santa Fe.[32] The Court of Private Land Claims agreed and dismissed the petition without prejudice to the rights of the City of Santa Fe.[33]

About this time the City of Santa Fe was incorporated and in its new corporate capacity it filed another petition similar to the earlier July 1892 petition filed by the Board of County Commissioners. Again the city claimed a four square league grant both by means of a written grant from the King of Spain and by operation of *Recopilación,* Book 4, Chapter 5, Law 6. The population of Santa Fe had grown from about 6,000 to 7,000 since the 1892 petition was filed, but in most other respects the facts alleged in the two petitions were the same.[34] Again the U.S. objected to the petition partly on the ground that it failed to disclose the adverse claims by numerous claimants whose ancestors had received small land grants in Santa Fe.[35]

Finally, after three tries, the City of Santa Fe filed an amended petition naming the adverse claimants, and basing its claim solely on the provisions of the *Recopilación,* Book 4, Chapter 5, Law 6 which it claimed provided for a four square league grant of land to the villa by operation of law. No longer did the City of Santa Fe claim the existence of a written grant from the king, claiming instead that if such a grant had existed it was destroyed when the archives were burned during the Pueblo Revolt.[36] The amended petition was a bit more flowery than the earlier ones and was signed by no fewer than six lawyers. Instead of referring simply to the Villa of Santa Fe, the lawyers who drafted the amended petition said the predecessor to the City of Santa Fe was called: La Villa Real de San Francisco de Santa Fe, or San Francisco de Assis de la Santa Fe, or La Villa Real de Santa Fe. Most documents, however, including Governor Flores Mogollon's grant of the Ciénega to the villa, refer to Santa Fe simply as the Villa of Santa Fe. With its amended petition, the city had raised the issues that would decide the outcome of the City of Santa Fe Grant: was the Villa of Santa Fe and its successor municipality entitled to a four square league grant of land by operation of law?[37]

The United States joined those issues in its answer denying the grant by operation of law theory and alleging that the Villa of Santa Fe had never claimed ownership of any land within the four square leagues except for the Ciénega which had been granted to the villa in 1715 by Governor Flores Mogollon.[38] The adverse claims that were supposed to have been litigated during the main litigation between the City of Santa Fe and the U.S. were almost all represented by attorney James Purdy who joined the other five lawyers arguing the case.[39] With all the legal talent involved in this case, including the ever-present Thomas B. Catron, one would have expected a more vigorous legal discussion about Spanish law relating to municipalities. Instead it was Justice Murray of the Court of Private Land Claims who would provide the most incisive analysis of *Recopilación*, Book 4, Chapter 5, Law 6 and the grant by operation of law theory.[40]

The claim for the Santa Fe Grant finally came to trial starting April 21, 1894. The parties introduced transcriptions and translations of numerous Spanish documents into evidence, many of which came from the Territorial Library. Included among these documents were 1790 censuses for New Mexico and Santa Fe, Diego de Vargas's entry into Santa Fe on December 16, 1693 at the time of the Reconquest, and many miscellaneous documents included simply because they mentioned the Villa of Santa Fe. The plaintiff was attempting to show the existence of the Villa of Santa Fe, a historical fact of which no one had any doubt. Also introduced was a translation of *Recopilación*, Book 4, Chapter 5, Law 6 that was the basis for the municipality of Santa Fe's claim.[41]

Less than a week after the commencement of the trial, the case was submitted to the Court of Private Land Claims and decided by a majority opinion rendered by Chief Justice Joseph R. Reed and Associate Justice Thomas C. Fuller. The justices held for the city agreeing with its contention that the municipality of Santa Fe was entitled to four square leagues by operation of law.[42] The majority opinion recognized that Santa Fe's claim was analogous to claims of San Francisco, California and Brownsville, Texas, both of which had been upheld by the U.S. Supreme Court.[43] But this apparent victory for the City of Santa Fe was not the end of the story. Justice W. W. Murray wrote an incisive dissent, which examined *Recopilación*, Book 4, Chapter 5, Law 6 carefully for the first time in the litigation. First he pointed out that the law was mistranslated and he provided another translation. But more importantly he noted that the law applied solely to *empresario* grants, which existed only in Texas, not in New Mexico.[44] An *empresario* grant was made to a contractor who in return for bringing settlers onto a grant would receive one-fourth of the grant himself. Thus, *Recopilación,* Book 4, Chapter 5, Law 6 did not provide for four square leagues to a municipality, as the majority opinion had held. Rather it provided for an *empresario* grant of four square leagues to be allocated three-fourths to the inhabitants and one-fourth to the contractor after setting aside sufficient lands for a town site and for common lands, as long as the *empresario* met the terms of his agreement. The primary condition of the grant was that the *empresario* provide thirty families[45] who would each build a house and have a specified number of livestock.[46] If the *empresario* failed to meet the terms of his agreement, the four square leagues would revert to the crown and he would be fined 1,000 ounces of gold. This was not even close to providing for four square leagues of land to a villa or other municipality.[47]

Encouraged by the analysis in Justice Murray's dissent, the U.S. government appealed the Land Claims Court's decision to the U.S. Supreme Court which eventually reversed the decision of the Court of Private Land Claims. The Supreme Court's forty-three-page opinion written by Justice White, went beyond Murray's dissent on two major points. It cited additional historical evidence (mostly mythical and incorrect), about the early history of Santa Fe, and it discussed the Brownsville, Texas and San Francisco cases, claiming an analogy with the Santa Fe claim.[48]

Arguing the Supreme Court case for the plaintiff were Thomas B. Catron and William H. Pope. Catron was probably the lead attorney and though he was disliked by many Santa Feans for his aggressive acquisition and sale of large land grants and had narrowly escaped an assassination attempt a few years earlier,[49] he probably knew more about the history of the Villa of Santa Fe than anyone in the august chambers of the U.S. Supreme Court on that January day in 1896 when the case was argued. It is thus unaccountable that Justice Edward D. White could write in his opinion that Santa Fe was settled "in the midst of the native Indians ... as early as 1543 ... by deserters from the Spanish military force under Coronado who refused to accompany their commander on his return to Mexico."[50] This inaccurate statement indicates how far removed (both physically and in understanding), Justice White was from New Mexico, the southwest, and the laws of Spain. Ironically, however, there was a germ of truth in Justice White's statement in that there may well have been a settlement of Mexican Indians in the Analco area before Santa Fe was settled by Spaniards. Justice White's selection of citations for his opinion also reveals a snobbishness—even prejudice—against the laws he was charged with interpreting and indeed upon which the decision would turn. He cited Gustavus Schmidt's characterization of the *Recopilación* as "derived from the orders, decrees and regulations of different sovereigns and often temporary in their character [which] are often dignified with the title of laws," revealing a deep-seated prejudice against Spanish law that was all too common among lawyers and judges in the late-nineteenth century.[51]

Appointed to the Supreme Court in February of 1894, Edward D. White was a U.S. senator who had developed into a corpulent, thick-maned legislator whose position on virtually every public policy issue was "what is good for Louisiana sugar is good for America."[52] In *U.S. v. Santa Fe* Justice White held that *Recopilación*, Book 4, Chapter 5, Law 6 could not be construed as providing a four square league grant to the Villa of Santa Fe, and that the laws involved in the Brownsville and especially the San Francisco case applied only to settlements established after 1789. The 1789 Plan of Pitic (meant to apply to settlements established after that date), may have expanded the provisions of the *Recopilación* to provide for a four square league entitlement even when there was no grant, but simply an agreement to found a municipality. Even if the history of the founding of Santa Fe could provide a basis for such an agreement, the villa's founding in 1610 meant that the 1789 provisions of the Plan of Pitic would not apply. Thus the claim of the City of Santa Fe was rejected by the U.S. Supreme Court, reversing the decision of the Court of Private Land Claims.[53]

Since the Land Claims Court had rejected all the small private land grants submitted in the case, (see "Santa Fe Land Grants" at the end of this chapter), and since James Purdy (the lawyer for most of those claims), had not appealed that decision, the inhabitants of Santa Fe in 1900 were left in the rather absurd position of living in a no-man's-land: no one knew for sure who owned the land upon which Santa Fe was established almost 300 years earlier. Luckily the San Francisco case established a precedent for seeking relief from Congress, to which the city now turned for help.[54] On April 9, 1900 the U.S. Congress passed an act releasing and quitclaiming to the City of Santa Fe all the lands within the four square leagues for which the municipality had fought so hard. Thus, with the stroke of a pen the Santa Fe league was created where none had existed before. The city then issued deeds to occupants of land within the Santa Fe league holding under valid deeds, which served as quitclaims from the U.S. to the property described. The city retained "all parks, streets, alleys, vacant unoccupied lands or other public places," and the U.S. reserved its federal title to land and buildings located within the league such as the Federal Court House and Fort Marcy.[55]

Thus ended the saga of the Santa Fe league. It had never existed under Spain or Mexico but was, in effect, granted to the inhabitants of Santa Fe by the Congress of the United States in 1900. Though the decades of litigation of the Santa Fe grant might seem like a waste of time and legal talent, it was probably necessary to build the record of the historical existence of Santa Fe before Congress could act. It is unfortunate that the numerous documents introduced into evidence were not organized and indexed in some fashion, for this might have contradicted the mistaken notion enshrined in the Supreme Court opinion by Justice White that Santa Fe was founded as early as 1543 by Mexican Indians who deserted from the Coronado Expedition.[56]

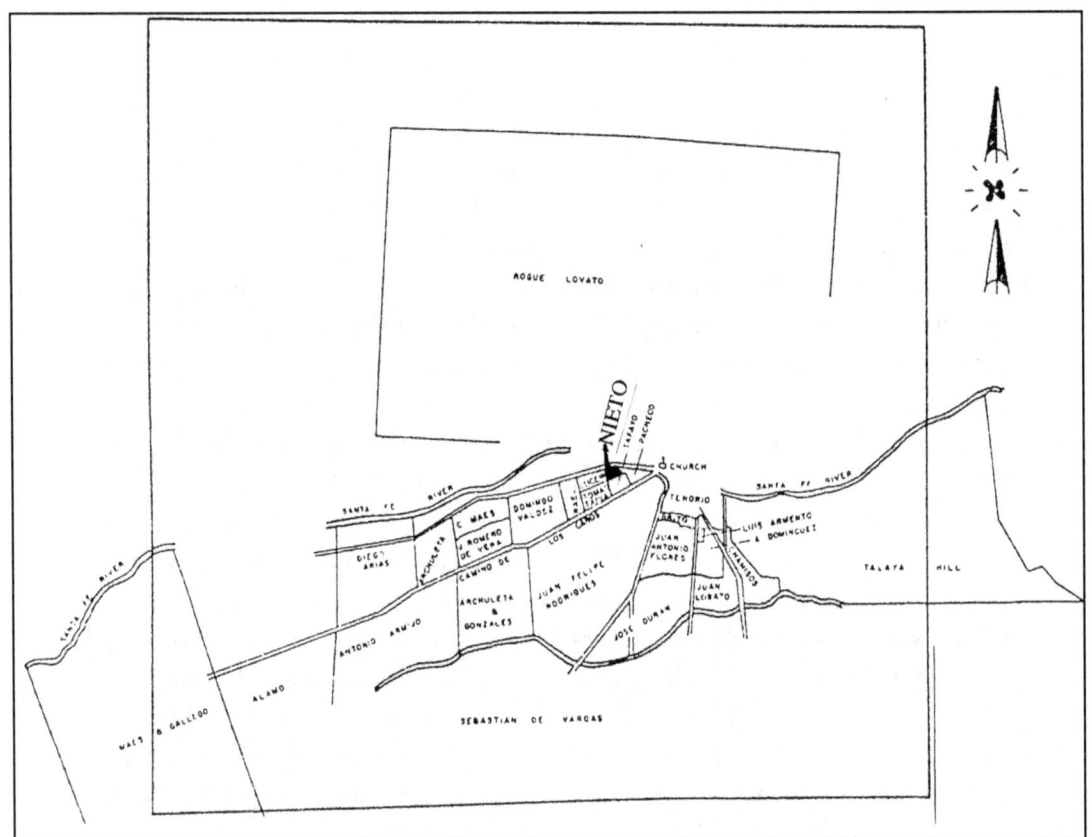

The Santa Fe League with smaller Santa Fe grants (Bowden, "Private Land Claims," 2: 270.)

Serious study of those documents, without the motive of acquiring land, might have shed light on questions about the early history of Santa Fe that we are still struggling with. It is supremely ironic that the most important document, the one which might have convinced the Supreme Court and all the judges of the Court of Private Land Claims of some official authorization for the founding of the Villa of Santa Fe, had not been discovered in 1894. It was found in the 1920s when historian Lansing B. Bloom discovered the instructions for the founding of Santa Fe in the

Archives of the Indies in Seville, Spain. This 1609 order directed Governor Pedro de Peralta to endeavor "before anything else, the foundation and settlement of the villa they claim and [he] shall order the same to be made there so people may begin to live there with some cleanliness. Until the above mentioned Villa shall have been founded and inhabited nothing else shall be attended to."[57] After Governor Peralta had chosen a site for the villa, he was to mark out an area in its center for *propios* (like the Ciénega), streets, and public buildings. Whether all that was done in 1610 is not clear, but this document establishes how important it was to Viceroy Luis de Velasco that the Villa of Santa Fe be established. The introduction into evidence of the Instructions of Viceroy Velasco could have changed the outcome of the litigation about the Santa Fe grant, though it was not the grant from the king that the plaintiffs had been searching for.[58]

One reason that such important historical evidence had not been discovered is that the disciplines of history, anthropology, and archeology were still in their infancy at that time. Many of the early historians of New Mexico, such as Ralph Emerson Twitchell and L. Bradford Prince, were lawyers who became interested in the field as they learned about New Mexico in their legal cases.[59] Adolph Bandelier was at the height of his career just about the time the Santa Fe case was tried. Other eminent archeologists, anthropologists, and historians were just beginning their careers in the first decades of the twentieth century, studying pueblo ruins and searching for documents (like the instructions for the founding of Santa Fe), in the archives of Spain and Mexico. The important work of scholars such as Lansing B. Bloom and of the next generation of scholars such as Herbert E. Bolton, France V. Scholes, George P. Hammond, Charles W. Hackett, Edgar L. Hewett, Frederick W. Hodge, Alfred V. Kidder, and Paul A. F. Walter would provide answers to many questions about the early history of New Mexico.

The Cristóbal Nieto Grant

Another mythical Santa Fe land grant was the Cristóbal Nieto grant whose fascinating history in the seventeenth and eighteenth centuries bore little relationship to the claim submitted to the Court of Private Land Claims in the late nineteenth century by lawyer James Purdy. Purdy's attempt to construct a bogus history whereby he stretched the boundaries of a fifteen-acre grant into 1200 acre one, changed the name from the Nieto to the Pino grant, and jiggered the genealogy to tie the claimant to the grantee, were reminiscent of the shenanigans of Gaspar Ortiz y Alarid, the first petitioner for the Santa Fe grant. Hidden behind the fake story was a fascinating real tale of abduction, captivity, and mixed blood children of Nieto's wife Petrona Pacheco that contained the makings of an episode of *Don*

Quixote or of Shakespeare's *The Tempest*. The most exciting parts of the story of the Cristóbal Nieto grant occurred before the grant was made and at the time of the adjudication of the so-called Pino grant in the late 1800s.

What happened before the Cristóbal Nieto Grant was made concerned Nieto's wife Petrona Pacheco more than Cristóbal Nieto. When Cristóbal Nieto's father, Alcalde José Nieto, heard the news of the Pueblo Indian uprising at Galisteo on August 10, 1680, he rounded up his family at his nearby *estancia* and tried to escape. Tragically, José Nieto, his wife Lucía, and his daughters María and Juana, were killed by Galisteo Indians, but fortunately for him, Cristóbal Nieto was away from home, either in Sonora or El Paso, and survived. Unknown to him however, Nieto's wife, Petrona Pacheco Nieto, and two of their children were taken captive by Pueblo Indians during the confusion. By May 10, 1700, when Cristóbal Nieto returned to Santa Fe and received a revalidation of a small land grant on the south side of the Santa Fe River, his wife Petrona had been through a saga of loss and captivity at Ohkay Owingeh Pueblo (San Juan Pueblo), that has the makings of a good Hollywood movie.[60]

At the time of the Reconquest of New Mexico in 1692, Petrona Pacheco Nieto was "rescued" from Ohkay Owingeh Pueblo (San Juan Pueblo), by Roque Madrid, at which point Petrona had given birth to three more daughters (these numbers vary), in captivity. Little is known about the conditions under which Petrona Pacheco Nieto was held captive by the Pueblo Indians, but apparently she was treated well and became part of an Ohkay Owingeh Pueblo (San Juan Pueblo), family. It was not uncommon for captive Spaniards to be adopted into Pueblo families and clans, to marry and have children, and sometimes be so well treated that they preferred to stay among their captors. This was the case throughout early America,[61] and was described by John Demos in his book about the 1704 capture of the John Williams family by Mohawk Indians in Deerfield, Massachusetts.[62] Of the five Williams children captured, all were released but Eunice Williams, who did not want to return because she had married a Mohawk man and been adopted by the tribe. Closer to New Mexico is the case of Juana (*la Galvana*) Hurtado living on a rancho near Zia Pueblo, who was also abducted at the outbreak of the Pueblo Revolt in 1680. Juana Hurtado lived with the Navajos for the next twelve years where she bore two children and may have been adopted into a Navajo clan. In 1692 Juana, *la Galvana*, was ransomed by her half-brother and returned to Spanish society. "Instead of being stigmatized by her experience, Juana used her connections with Spanish, Pueblo, and Navajo society to make trading contacts that allowed her to acquire a substantial amount of property."[63]

Unlike Juana Hurtado, who was only seven at the time she was captured, Petrona Pacheco Nieto was married with three children when she was abducted.

Like Juana, however—whose mother was a Zia Indian—Petrona's grandfather was a mestizo with some connection to Ohkay Owingeh Pueblo (San Juan Pueblo). In 1628 Geronimo Pacheco, a soldier at the Santa Fe presidio, was accused of "having taken part in certain pagan games at San Juan Pueblo. He denied the charges." Petrona's grandfather's connection to Ohkay Owingeh Pueblo (San Juan) may help explain her abduction.[64]

When Diego de Vargas entered Ohkay Owingeh Pueblo (San Juan Pueblo) on October 2, 1692, three Spanish captives were released to him, including Petrona Pacheco Nieto. In total seventy-six people of all ages surrendered and were baptized. Nieto's relatives recognized Petrona, who was released with "three sons and daughters, all of whom she had at this time."[65] Accounts varied sharply as to the number of children Petrona had with her when she was released from captivity. It was common knowledge among the New Mexico settlers at El Paso that "three or four *mestizas*" were being held captive by the Pueblos and rescuing them was one of the first priorities of the Reconquest of New Mexico.[66] Petrona was then taken to El Paso with a larger group of captives who had been held during the Revolt in various Pueblos. One of four Spaniards on the list of freed captives, Petrona Nieto is first on the list, "with five daughters and two sons" (again numbers are different in every account), escorted by Captain Roque Madrid.[67]

Next we flash back to August 25, 1680 when Cristóbal and his brother Francisco Nieto were part of the relief party mustered out at El Paso. Neither of the brothers had any idea that Cristóbal's wife had been captured at the time of the Revolt and was apparently alive at Ohkay Owingeh Pueblo (San Juan Pueblo). Cristóbal was described as "slender, medium stature, scant beard, aquiline face with the scar of a wound on the right eyelid," while Francisco was listed as a bachelor, twenty-six years old.[68] Cristóbal Nieto was listed as a twenty-nine year old widower, since he was unaware that his wife had survived the revolt when he enlisted on this relief mission. The circumstances of Cristóbal's reunion with the wife he thought was dead, and the children Petrona had borne in captivity, must have been quite emotional.[69] It is not clear which of Petrona Nieto's six surviving children were born in captivity, but the most likely are Josefa Pacheco who married Jacinto Perea, Sebastiana, and another Petrona.[70]

In 1697 Cristóbal Nieto and his wife Petrona were living in Santa Fe with their son Simón, and four daughters Sebastiana, María, Lucía, and Josefa (the young Petrona Pacheco does not appear until 1712). In that year, as part of a general distribution of livestock and supplies by the Spanish government, they received 10.5 *varas* of wool, 8.75 of baize, and 22 *mantas,* and animals consisting of 25 sheep, 3 cows and a bull. Cristóbal and Petrona (who is listed as Petronila in the livestock distribution), must have been farming land in Santa Fe at the time of the livestock distribution and in August of 1697 they apparently received a grant of the land from Governor Pedro Rodríguez Cubero (1697–1703).[71] Somehow the title papers to the 1697 land grant were destroyed before possession of the land could be delivered, so in 1700 Cristóbal Nieto asked Governor Cubero (this time serving his second term), to revalidate the earlier grant. Apparently there was no investigation by local *alcalde* Antonio de Aguilera as to whether the grant would prejudice Nieto's neighbors, and Alcalde Aguilera placed Nieto in possession of a tract of land south of the Santa Fe River bounded by the Camino Real, Domingo de la Barreda, and a small acequia.[72] From later records it appears that the grant covered a small tract of land south of the Santa Fe River in the Analco barrio near present-day Our Lady of Guadalupe Church.[73]

By early 1712 Cristóbal Nieto had died, but the composition of his family was clarified by a distribution of tools to Santa Fe settlers later in 1712. According to the list, five members of the Nieto family were living in separate households, as heads of families on the Cristóbal Nieto grant. In household 143 was Simón Nieto, who was buying and selling land in the area before and after the tool distribution. In household 144 was the widow Petrona Pacheco, who was living alone. Next to her was Jacinto Perea married to Josefa Pacheco, a daughter of Petrona by a Pueblo Indian man. Next to her in household 146 was Lucía Nieto, who was married to Salvador Olguín, a soldier at the Santa Fe Presidio who was absent at the time of the tool distribution. Finally, next to Lucía in household 147 was Petrona Nieto, the younger, another daughter of Petrona Pacheco by a Pueblo Indian man.[74] At least two of those listed in the distribution of tools were probably children of Petrona by a Pueblo Indian man, apparently from Ohkay Owingeh Pueblo (San Juan Pueblo). The Nietos listed in the 1712 tool distribution with Native American blood were probably the younger Petrona and Josefa Pacheco.[75]

Simón Nieto, the legitimate son of Cristóbal Nieto, was more interested in selling land he acquired through his marriage to Francisca Maese[76] than he was in consolidating his holdings and adding to the Cristóbal Nieto grant.[77] Simón's nephew, Francisco Nieto, the son of Simón's sister Lucía and the soldier Salvador Olguín, was just the opposite. By 1750 when a census was taken for the Villa of Santa Fe, Francisco was the only Nieto head of household left in Santa Fe. Francisco Nieto was living with his wife Isabel Gutiérrez, his aunt María [Magdalena] Nieto daughter of Cristóbal, his mother Lucía Nieto, and his aunt Petrona Pacheco, daughter of a Pueblo Indian man. Francisco's grandmother, Petrona Nieto, the elder, the former captive, died in 1750, so the reference to Petrona Pacheco in the 1712 tool distribution must have been to Francisco's aunt, his mother Lucia's half-sister, born in captivity.[78]

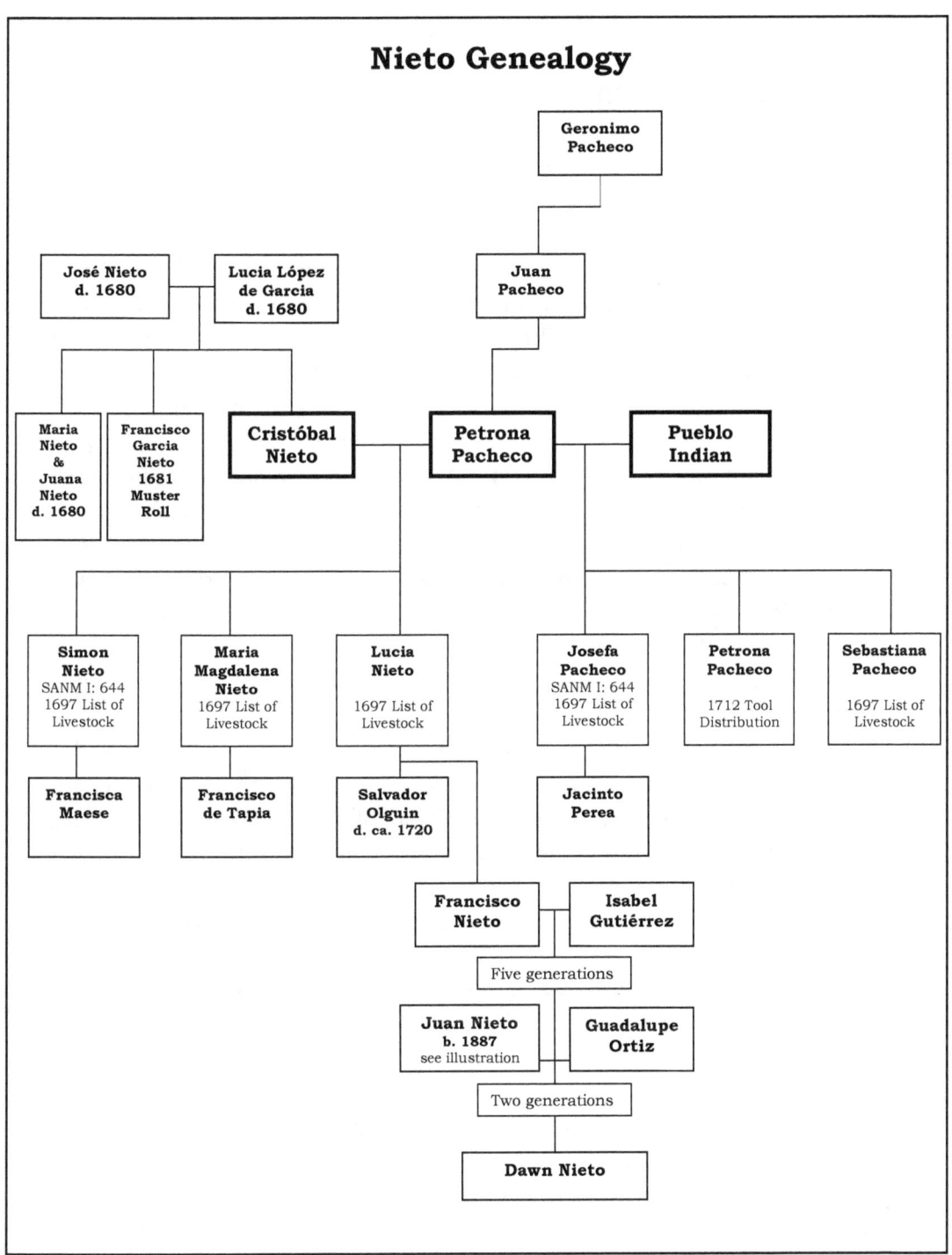

Genealogy of Cristóbal Nieto.

In 1765, Francisco Nieto, who was serving as a soldier in the Santa Fe Presidio, partitioned land south of Agua Fria that he had purchased from Andrés Montoya of Cieneguilla. This is the first document that connects a Nieto with the place called El Pino several miles from the Cristóbal Nieto grant. The land was described as being "in the locality of El Pueblo Quemado (Agua Fria), towards El Pino, Río Abajo," and bounded on the north by the hills, on the south by the Camino Real, on the east by an arroyo which divides the lands of Pueblo Quemado, and on the west, some tall oak trees marking the boundary of the lands of Lazaro Garcia at El Pino. Francisco Nieto had purchased the land from Montoya partly with funds provided by Jacinto Perea, husband to his aunt Josefa Pacheco who was one of the children fathered by a Pueblo Indian man during the time her mother, Petrona Nieto, was a captive at Ohkay Owingeh Pueblo (San Juan Pueblo). When Jacinto Perea married Josefa Pacheco she was described in the *diligencia matrimonial* (prenuptial investigation) as "a daughter of the church" or of unknown parentage.[79] Jacinto Perea was also a soldier at the Santa Fe Presidio, where he must have met Francisco Nieto. Jacinto was one of the few survivors of the 1720 surprise attack on the Villasur Expedition by Plains Indians [Pawnees] who killed thirty-two Spaniards and twelve Pueblo Indians.[80] In the partition with Francisco Nieto the property south of Agua Fria was divided in half, giving Jacinto Perea 4463 Castilian *varas* from east to west. Jacinto Perea had somehow accumulated sufficient funds to purchase this and other property in Santa Fe.[81]

After this point the documentation on the Nieto family in Santa Fe and at the Rancho at El Pino is sparse. In 1788 the ranch at El Pino was the subject of a partition suit by Rita Padilla, the daughter-in-law of Juan Garcia, who died owning an interest in "a Rancho of cultivable lands at the place of El Pino." This land was not part of the 1765 partition between Jacinto Perea and Francisco Nieto, nor was it part of the Cristóbal Nieto grant. Nevertheless, when the Cristóbal Nieto Grant was submitted for confirmation to the Court of Private Land Claims as the El Pino grant in 1893, this document was filed with the court. It seems to have been used by attorney James Purdy to expand the boundaries of the Nieto grant to 1200 acres, much more than the probable fifteen-acre size of the original Cristóbal Nieto grant.[82]

Piecing together all the evidence from the descriptions of the land covered by these and other deeds, the following picture emerges, incidentally shedding some light on the early history of Santa Fe. The *encomenderos* for La Ciénega and San Marcos Pueblos were Cristóbal and Francisco de Anaya Almazan, names that show up in the Francisco de Anaya Almazan grant west of the so called El Pino Grant.[83] Records of owners of *encomiendas (encomenderos)* refer to spheres of influence exercised around the pre-Revolt pueblos by Spaniards who later received land grants on or near the pueblo. The location of the Francisco de Anaya Almazan grant a little southwest of the El Pino tract towards Cieneguilla, suggests that the El Pino tract was a separate tract quite a distance from, and much larger than the Cristóbal Nieto grant in the Analco barrio.

In fact, there was no connection between the two tracts, except that Francisco Nieto and Jacinto Perea were members of the Nieto/Pacheco family. Francisco Nieto was a grandson (not a son, as claimed in the CPLC petition) of Cristóbal Nieto through his daughter Lucía, while Jacinto Perea was married to Josefa Pacheco, the daughter of Petrona Pacheco. The first use of the name El Pino is in the 1765 transaction whereby Francisco Nieto and Jacinto Perea partitioned the large tract of land the two had purchased near El Pino, partly with Jacinto Perea's money. By the 1890s largely through the efforts of attorney James Purdy, this had become the new Cristóbal Nieto/ El Pino grant.[84]

On February 11, 1893 a Juan Nieto, claiming to be a direct descendant of Cristóbal Nieto, filed a claim with the Court of Private Land Claims for confirmation of the Cristóbal Nieto grant. The land claimed was said to be known as El Pino or the El Pino Ranch and was described as containing 1200 acres. This was not the Cristóbal Nieto grant made by Governor Rodríguez Cubero in 1700. The boundaries of the claimed tract contained a combination of boundaries from the Cristóbal Nieto grant and the 1765 Francisco Nieto/Jacinto Perea purchase and partition. The boundaries claimed were the Santa Fe River on the north and the Camino de los Carros on the south, the land of Domingo de la Barreda (armorer of the Santa Fe Presidio), on the west, and the house of Domingo de la Barreda on the east. Since the location of the land of Domingo de la Barreda was not known, the description could cover land almost anywhere south along the Santa Fe River. Attorney James Purdy, who prosecuted most of the claims for land within the Santa Fe area, combined boundaries from the Cristóbal Nieto grant with boundaries from the much larger 1765 El Pino purchase/partition to make it seem like this was one large grant made to Cristóbal Nieto.[85]

Given this fictitious legal description, the land claimed by Juan Nieto could not be located on the ground. But no one realized this at the time because the land claims case never came to trial. The land shown on J. J. Bowden's map of Santa Fe grants as the Pino (Cristóbal Nieto) grant is the 1765 Nieto/Perea purchase, not the Cristóbal Nieto grant.[86]

Lawyer James Purdy had combined the legal descriptions of the two tracts (the Cristóbal Nieto grant in the Analco region of the Villa of Santa Fe, and the much larger El Pino Ranch purchase south of Agua Fria), to make a non-existent tract of land. Juan Nieto, the plaintiff before the Court of Private Land Claims, could tie himself to Cristóbal Nieto and his grant, but since that grant was relatively small, lawyer Purdy tried to tie Juan Nieto to other members of the Nieto family who owned other land in the Santa Fe area.

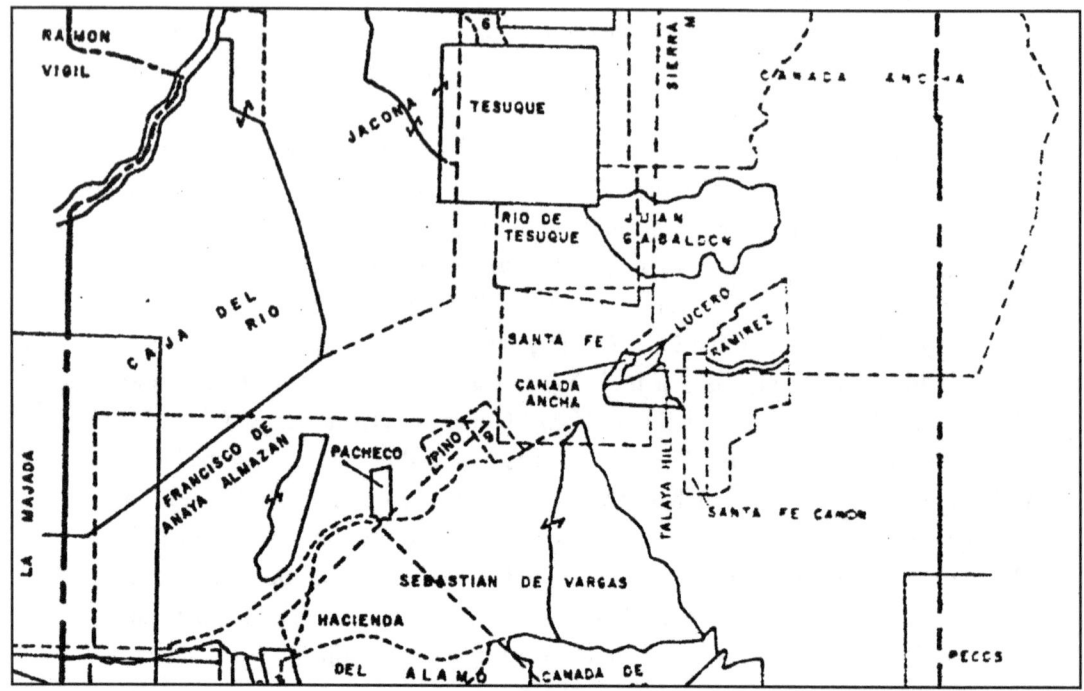

Partial map of Santa Fe grants (Bowden, "Private Land Claims," 2: 269.)

Lawyer Purdy did not worry about competing claims since he represented most of the small Santa Fe grants before the Court of Private Land Claims; Purdy simply drew the map of Santa Fe land grants to suit his purpose. Other grants like the Sebastián de Vargas grant, south of the El Pino tract, were also expanded without regard to the original boundaries.[87] When adjoining land grants were represented by the same lawyer there was a potential conflict of interest, because of the possibility that the common boundary might be in dispute.[88]

In addition to the creative construction of a new legal description to increase the size of the Cristóbal Nieto grant, Purdy submitted a genealogy for Juan Nieto that was also mostly false. While it seemed to connect Juan Nieto directly to Cristóbal Nieto, there were several other Nieto family lines that might also have had a claim to the Cristóbal Nieto grant that were unaccounted for.[89] The Nieto genealogy submitted to the Court of Private Land Claims showed the plaintiff Juan Nieto to be a direct descendant of Cristóbal Nieto through his only son Francisco Nieto. As we have seen, Cristóbal Nieto had three children who survived the Pueblo Revolt and Petrona Pacheco's captivity at Ohkay Owingeh Pueblo (San Juan Pueblo): Simón, María, and Lucía, but no Francisco. All three show up in the Santa Fe censuses and other records, and it is their heirs who were the descendants of Cristóbal Nieto. Lucía Nieto and Salvador Olguín had a son named Francisco, who used the name Nieto though his father was Olguín, and was probably the one involved in the 1765 El Pino partition with Jacinto Perea. It was convenient to link Juan Nieto, the petitioner, with Francisco Nieto since attorney Purdy needed to connect the 1765 El Pino tract with the Cristóbal Nieto grant. But there was no connection, since the El Pino tract was not a land grant but a land purchase and was located south of Agua Fria toward la Ciénega and Cieneguilla several miles from the Cristóbal Nieto grant. The only reason that could have justified inclusion of the El Pino tract in the Cristóbal Nieto claim would be if it had been acquired by the Nieto family as an addition to the Nieto grant and was adjacent to that grant. This was clearly not the case.

Even if the El Pino tract had been adjacent to the Cristóbal Nieto grant, it was not only the descendants of Francisco Nieto who would be entitled to the grant. Also entitled were the heirs of Cristóbal Nieto's other children through Petrona Pacheco (Simón and María Magdalena), and one of Petrona Pacheco's children through the Pueblo Indian: Josefa Pacheco. Josefa was married to Jacinto Perea, who put up at least half and possibly more of the purchase price for the El Pino tract. In another supreme irony, even if the Nieto grant and the El Pino tract had been connected, Juan Nieto, the claimant before the CPLC, would have had to share the land, not only with the descendants of Simón Nieto and María Magdalena Nieto, but also with the descendants of Josefa Pacheco who was the daughter of a Pueblo Indian man and not of Cristóbal Nieto.

The Court of Private Land Claims (CPLC) did not have the opportunity to unravel this mystery because there was never a trial. When the case came up for trial on June 11, 1898, Attorney Purdy announced that the plaintiff no longer wished to prosecute the suit and the court rejected the claim. Attorney Purdy had been successful in obtaining a few confirmations of Santa Fe grants, such as the large Sebastián de Vargas grant (also based on sketchy evidence), and he could see that it was unlikely that the Land Claims Court would confirm the Cristóbal Nieto grant.[90] As we have seen, the City of Santa Fe had been successful in 1894 in establishing its right to the so-called Santa Fe league, which partially conflicted with the Nieto/El Pino grant. Even though the opinion of the CPLC confirming the Santa Fe league was overturned by the U.S. Supreme Court in 1897, leaving the ownership of all the land in Santa Fe in limbo for a few years, the U.S. Congress quitclaimed to the City of Santa Fe all the lands within the four square leagues on April 9, 1900.[91]

Taking a motley assortment of deeds covering small tracts of land in seventeenth and eighteenth century Santa Fe, nineteenth century lawyers stitched them together and stretched them mightily to create a different Santa Fe, a mythical landscape peopled by a made-up genealogy connecting a nineteenth century claimant to a seventeenth or eighteenth century Santa Fe land grant. Drawing by Glen Strock.

Early Santa Fe: a different city

After the house of cards that was the Cristóbal Nieto grant collapsed, and the bubble that was the Santa Fe league burst, what are we left with? For one thing we have learned a great deal about the Nieto family and their place in the early history of Santa Fe which helps replace the myths of Santa Fe with a more nuanced history. Working with living members of the Nieto family like Dawn Nieto, who has investigated her place in the Nieto family story and who comes from the Cristóbal

Nieto side of the family tree through her grandfather Juan Nieto, we begin to see that many of the first generation Nietos were actually Pachecos, with ties to Ohkay Owingeh Pueblo (San Juan Pueblo), and possibly other pueblos.

Juan Nieto, grandfather of Dawn Nieto, with unidentified little girl. (Photo courtesy Dawn Nieto.)

Like Juana Galvan mentioned earlier, who used her captivity by Navajos during the Pueblo Revolt to her advantage, it seems likely that Josefa Pacheco was able to use her mestizo status, along with her mestizo husband Jacinto Perea, to their mutual advantage. This could be an example of James Brooks' theory about the special status of women captives during the Pueblo Revolt and their children: "children born in captivity seemed to be implicitly accepted as attached dependents, [and there was] an undercurrent of affinity between former captors [Pueblo Indians] and redeemed women and children."[92]

In other words, children like Josefa Pacheco, born in captivity, married to the mestizo Jacinto Perea, retained "an undercurrent of affinity" with her former captors that may have benefited the couple economically. This can be inferred from the fact that Jacinto Perea was a landowner at El Pino and was the one who put up a portion of the purchase price of the 1765 El Pino tract. As mestizos living in the Barrio of Analco, Jacinto Perea and Josefa Pacheco were able to negotiate between two worlds: the world of the Spanish *vecino* and landowner and the world of the Pueblo Indian.[93] The story of the Nieto/Pacheco family helps us piece together a more complete picture of early Santa Fe and the settlement south of the Santa Fe River known as Analco, where Mexican Indians, soldiers in the Santa Fe Presidio, and Genízaro servants of the Spanish elite lived. This is a hidden history not found in most land grant records.

As the myths and fiction about early Santa Fe are being discussed and debunked in this and other books and articles, new myths are springing up that are just as hard to lay to rest. One such myth: that the Villa of Santa Fe was founded, not in 1610 but in 1607 or 1608, or 1609, is not only damaging to the true and complete history of early Santa Fe, but it tends to emphasize the Spanish viewpoint almost exclusively with little regard for the Native American presence in and around Santa Fe. A disproportionate amount of scholarship and energy is thus focused on the Spanish presence and the possible earlier founding of Santa Fe by the Spaniards, viewing events solely through Spanish documents.

This new myth is based primarily on one document: a certificate of services of Juan Martinez de Montoya first discussed by France V. Scholes in 1944.[94] As a result of a 1944 article by Scholes, the Museum of New Mexico Foundation tracked down the document Scholes had studied, purchased it, and deposited it in the Fray Angelico Chavez History Library in Santa Fe in 1994. Also in 1994, an unannotated anonymous article in *El Palacio* suggested that Santa Fe was founded as early as 1607,[95] and another unannotated article in an on-line journal stated categorically that Santa Fe was founded in 1608 by Juan Martinez de Montoya.[96] Recently, some eminent scholars have lent credibility to this earlier founding of Santa Fe.[97]

Before rushing to judgment regarding a 1607 or 1608 founding of Santa Fe, it would be well to examine the Martinez y Montoya document more closely, as José Antonio Esquibel has done in his chapter for this volume, "Thirty-eight Adobe Houses, The Villa of Santa Fe in the Seventeenth Century, 1608–1699." Esquibel takes the phrase "*el haber hecho Plaza en Santa Fe*," upon which all the scholarly debate is based, and provides a translation, "he made a [military] post [or camp] at Santa Fe" rather than "he established the Plaza of Santa Fe." Based on an understanding of the totality of the situation at Santa Fe in the first decade of the 1600s, Esquibel's translation and other evidence shows that Santa Fe existed as a settlement and military post by 1604 or before, but the founding of the Villa did not take place until 1610.[98] If Santa Fe was a military post by 1604 or earlier, it is likely that the Analco settlement was in existence south of the Santa Fe River at that time, since many of the soldiers and most of the Indian auxiliaries were Mexican Indians. The Analco settlement was made up of people like the ancestors of Cristóbal Nieto and Juan de Leon Brito, both of whom received grants confirming their pre-revolt holdings in the Analco area.

The settlement pattern around Santa Fe can be inferred from the early land grants made by Governor de Vargas in the 1690s. As mentioned earlier, Governor Vargas had promised the members of his Reconquest expedition that he would give them the lands they had owned prior to the Pueblo Revolt.[99] Despite the efforts of Diego de Vargas to achieve a balanced land use pattern with most landowners having sufficient land to plant from 1 to 2 *fanegas* of seed corn (about 9 to 18 acres), there was a concentration of prime farming lands in the hands of a few elite in early Santa Fe, similar to the pre-Revolt land distribution pattern. Making this possible was the existence of various forms of common lands in the villa, which provided resources to all members of the community, or to those who acted in a public capacity like the governor and resident priests. These common lands in and around Santa Fe included the swampy Ciénega, lands attached to the *convento* (the residence of the priests), lands set aside for the governor's exclusive use, common lands farmed by the Analco Indians (*tierras de San Miguel* or *tierras de los Mexicanos*), and common grazing lands for the presidio horseherd.[100]

Even more important for the average citizen of early Santa Fe were the common woodlands located primarily to the north and east of Santa Fe, known as *el monte*. There was a public road east of the road to Tesuque that led to this area, and it was important to the people of Santa Fe that this road be kept open. It appears that a settlement or outpost (*puesto*) called Río Arriba was developing upriver and outside the jurisdiction of the Villa of Santa Fe by the 1690s. Whatever farmlands there were in the vicinity of the *puesto* de Río Arriba (located at Upper Canyon Road), were probably unirrigated and dependent on rainfall (*de temporal*), while most of the other land in this area was common woodlands available to the residents of Santa Fe for firewood, vigas, and other building materials.[101]

Just as the landscape and land ownership pattern of early Santa Fe may have been different than what is pictured in the mind's eye and in early maps, so were the early settlers a different lot than might be imagined. The language of the U.S. Supreme Court in *U.S. v Santa Fe* conjures a picture of early settlement "in the midst of Native Indians." Others paint a picture of a deserted place picked by the Spanish authorities because no Indians lived there. The truth is probably somewhere in the middle. While no Pueblo Indians were settled there, a group of Mexican Indians and mestizos may have lived in the Analco barrio even before Martinez y Montoya's arrival around 1607.[102] The Analco settlement, which may have started as early as 1604,[103] grew in size as it was situated on the best lands south of the

Santa Fe River, called *tierras de San Miguel* or *tierras de los Mexicanos*.[104] Analco's inhabitants who were mostly servants to Spanish families, presidial soldiers, and Indian auxiliaries:[105] people like Domingo de la Barreda, the presidial armorer whose land bordered the Cristóbal Nieto grant in 1697, and Petrona Pacheco's grandfather Geronimo Pacheco, a mestizo, probably the reason Petrona Pacheco was referred to as a mestiza. Geronimo was charged by the Inquisition with taking part in some type of ceremony at the Ohkeh Owingeh Pueblo (San Juan Pueblo) in 1628.[106] Although Geronimo Pacheco was a mestizo with ties to the pueblos, his daughters and granddaughters were married to elites such as Roque Madrid and Diego Arias de Quiros, both distinguished elites who each played a part in the events narrated earlier in this chapter. Arias de Quiros had battled the municipal villa of Santa Fe over the Ciénega in 1715 and Roque Madrid escorted Petrona Pacheco to El Paso in 1692, along with the other former captives of the pueblos. Since Petrona and Roque Madrid were related, this explains why he recognized her at Ohkeh Owingeh Pueblo (San Juan Pueblo), and why he was the one to escort her to El Paso.[107]

An understanding of the pre-villa (1610) settlement of Mexican Indians in Analco helps to answer the questions posed at the beginning of this chapter: why did Governor Pedro de Peralta pick the present location as the site for the villa when later governors tried to move it,[108] when was the Villa of Santa Fe founded, was there an existing settlement at the site of the Barrio of Analco of Mexican Indians?[109] Governor Peralta picked the location of the Villa of Santa Fe and its plaza at the current location because the more preferable site south of the river in the Analco barrio was already occupied. While the site north of the river had plenty of water from springs around the ciénega, there was too much water making much of the area a swamp. The earlier pueblo people picked the hills north of town in what became Fort Marcy to build their villages, the ruins of which would still have been visible to Juan de Oñate, Juan Martinez de Montoya and Pedro Peralta. But the area south of the Santa Fe River irrigated then and now by the Acequia Madre and called Analco was considered the most desirable area.[110]

Early Santa Fe was not a place where Spaniards settled in a vacant area, imposing their grid pattern villa on the empty landscape. Instead, the picture of early Santa Fe and its settlers appears as a series of isolated settlements, from south to north: La Ciénega, Cieneguilla, El Pino, Agua Fria, Analco, the fortified and walled Villa of Santa Fe, and the *puesto* of Río Arriba, all surrounded by common lands. This is what the land grant documents and property deeds tell us about early Santa Fe, a different picture than the map drawn by lawyer James Purdy or the mythical Santa Fe league.

Ancient Santa Fe with its early Mexican Indian presence in the Analco area pre-dating the founding of the villa, was a city different than we thought. Santa Fe continues to be different, in between myth and reality.[111] We would like to believe that Santa Fe began in an orderly rational way as Spain attempted in all her great cities: an ample plaza surrounded by a Governors' Palace, the principal church, municipal buildings, and the houses of the most important citizens. In fact, Santa Fe was scattered and fragmented rather than centralized and unified.[112] Even a century and three-quarters later Father Francisco Atanasio Dominguez described Santa Fe as "like a rough stone set in fine metal." He liked the setting but not the villa. Even Dominguez realized the tension between fantasy and reality inherent in the villa of Santa Fe: "as soon as its physical description is seen the reason will recognize the fantasy of the imagination and rightly replace it with the true facts."[113]

The facts were always at odds with the myths and fantasies of the imagination regarding Santa Fe. Over 100 years after Father Dominguez's description of Santa Fe, Governor Lew Wallace wrote about Santa Fe, the Governors' Palace, and his unfinished book in a classic statement about myth and reality co-existing at the same time and place in the governors palace: "the walls were grimy, the undressed boards of the floor rested flat upon the ground; ... nevertheless, in that cavernous chamber I wrote the eighth and last book of *Ben-Hur*.... It is curious this jumping from the serious things of life [being governor] to the purely romantic." Shakespeare and Cervantes, writing their classic works 270 years earlier at exactly the same time as the founding of Santa Fe, also appreciated the tension between the serious and the romantic, between myth and reality. Governor Lew Wallace, whose name is memorialized in a state office building only a few blocks from "the oldest house" and the San Miguel church, all in the Analco area, wrote the most famous words about how New Mexico, like the City Different, is different than anywhere else: "every calculation based on experience elsewhere fails in New Mexico."[114]

On the following two pages: 1766 map of Santa Fe drawn by Joseph de Urrútia.

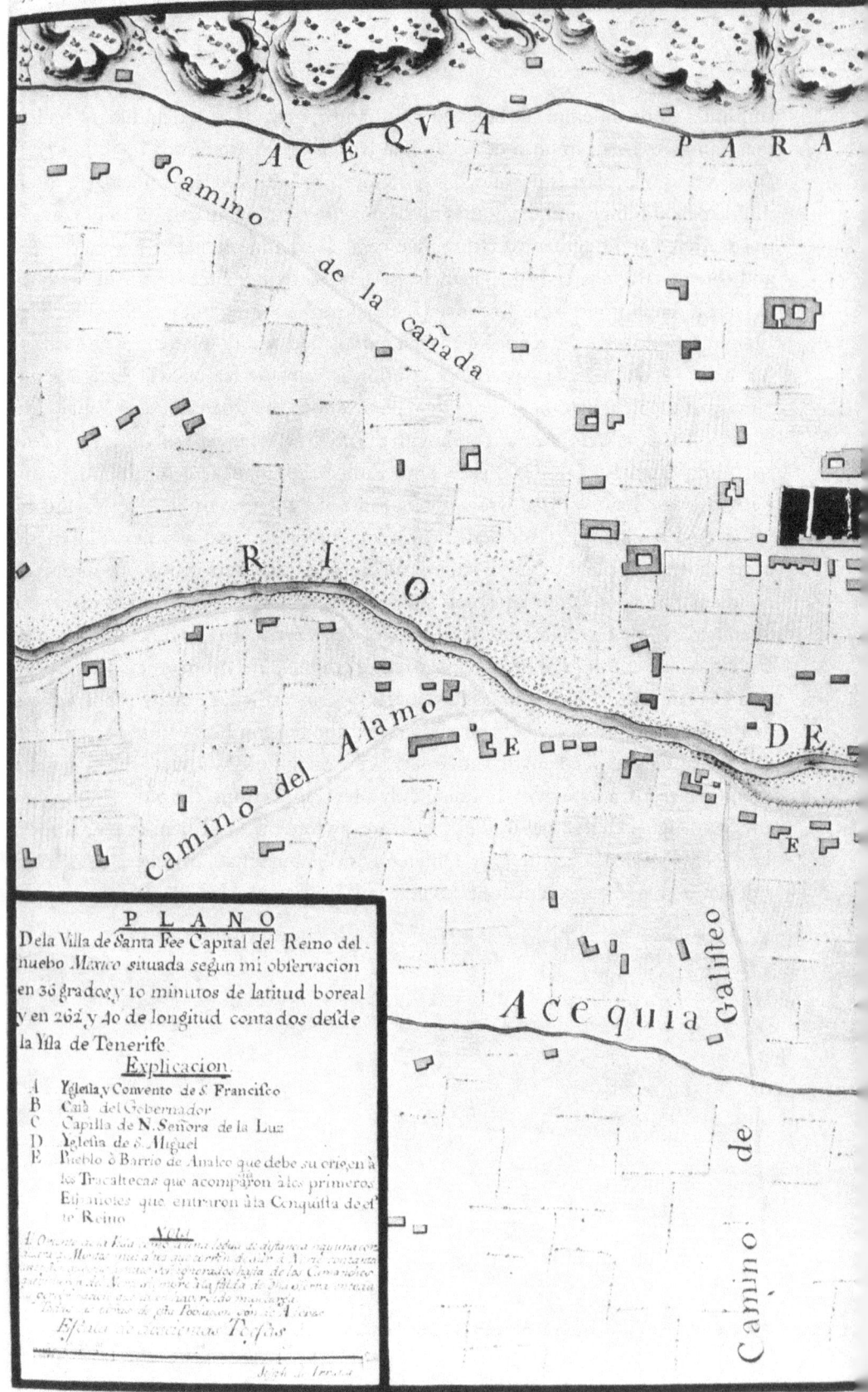

Lew Wallace from *Harper's Weekly*, March 6, 1886

Santa Fe Land Grants - Alphabetical

Date	Name of Grant
1769	Alamo – Chavez and Nieto
1693	Anaya Almazan, Francisco de
1742	Archuleta and Gonzales
1742	Archuleta, Juan Antonio
1742	Archuleta, Juan José
1742	Arias de Quiros, Diego
1733	Armenta, Luis
1769	Armijo, Antonio
1742	Brito, Juan de Leon
1785	Cañada de los Alamos
1742	Chamiso Arroyo - Marquez and Padilla
1742	Dominguez, Antonio
1743	Duran, José
1743	Flores, Juan Antonio
1742	Gonzales, Salvador - Cañada Ancha
1695	Griego, Maria
1714 (prior)	Hacienda del Alamo
1699	Jorge, Isabel
1728	Leyba, José de
1742	Lovato, Juan Cayetano
1785	Lovato, Roque
1693	Lucero de Godoy, Juan
1732	Lucero, José Antonio
1701	Lujan, Ana
1693	Madrid, Roque de
1790	Maes and Gallegos
1742	Maese, Catarina
1695	Maese, Luis
1695	Martín, Domingo
1697	Nieto, Cristóbal - El Pino Grant
1742	Pacheco, Felipe
1769	Pacheco, Joseph
1742	Padilla
1744	Rael de Aguilar, Alfonso
1742 (prior)	Rodriguez, Juan Felipe
1746	Romo de Vera, José
1698	Roybal, Ignacio
1742	Tafoya, Felipe
1731	Talaya Hill
1742	Tapia, Tomás
1732 (prior)	Tenorio, Manuel
1740	Trujillo, Andres
1742	Valdez, Domingo
1710 (prior)	Vargas, Sebastian de

3

The Viceroy's Order Founding the Villa of Santa Fe
A Reconsideration, 1605–1610
by
James Ivey

It has been almost a century since a small but sharp debate arose among the prominent historians of New Mexico concerning the date of the founding of the settlement of Santa Fe. At that time governor Pedro de Peralta's establishment of the Villa of Santa Fe in early 1610 was still unknown. In fact, not even the actual dates of the end of Juan de Oñate's rule and the beginning of Peralta's term as governor of New Mexico were known. This debate was apparently ended in 1922–1923 with the discovery in the Archivo General de Indias, in Seville, Spain, of the viceroy's order to governor Pedro de Peralta in 1609 to establish the Villa of Santa Fe in New Mexico upon his arrival. Subsequent documentary findings, however, have reopened the debate. They have shown that Santa Fe was privately founded before 1608, and changed our interpretation of the Peralta founding order.

In 1889, in the first in-depth historical study of the province of New Mexico, Hubert Howe Bancroft wrote that Santa Fe was established sometime between 1605 and 1617, and probably after the rule of Oñate. Bancroft cited evidence indicating that Oñate's rule ended about 1607 or 1608, and that Peralta was his probable successor.[1] In 1890, Adolph Bandelier argued for 1605, citing the statement by fray Alonso de Posadas, "*La villa de Santa-Fé ... descubrióla el año de 1605 el Adelantado D. Juan de* Oñate."[2] By 1893, however, Bandelier had concluded that the available documentation indicated a founding date after 1607.[3]

Ralph Emerson Twitchell, in his *Leading Facts of New Mexican History*, published in 1911, accepted Bandelier's earlier position.

Twitchell argued that Santa Fe was founded between 1605 and 1616, "in all probability in the first named year." Supporting his preference for this date, Twitchell included Bandelier's quotation from fray Posadas, including the ellipsis after "Santa Fe."[4] Two years later, however, in 1913, Lansing Bloom strongly disagreed with Twitchell, favoring the date of 1609 or later for the establishment of the town: "The colonial history of New Mexico had its beginning contemporary with the colonial period of the United States. The settlement of Santa Fe in 1609 yielded priority only to Jamestown, Virginia, in the Thirteen Colonies."[5] Bloom added that the "date of the founding of Santa Fe is not known exactly, but it is very improbable that it was earlier than the date given." He noted that Oñate was likely not the founder, and indicated that "the next governor," not yet shown conclusively to have been Peralta, was more probably the man who established Santa Fe.[6]

Twitchell, who was the editor of the magazine in which Bloom published these statements, took exception to Bloom's position. "There is no authority for Mr. Bloom's conclusion as to the date of the founding of Santa Fe," he stated. Twitchell again quoted the Posadas statement mentioned above (although this time he left out the ellipsis, which would suggest to the reader that there was no missing text in the quotation), adding "This would seem to settle the year, at least, in which the capitol of New Mexico was founded."[7]

Bloom fired back immediately, and his response was published in the next issue of the magazine. Bloom pointed out that the quotation from Posadas left out critical words, and that the full statement leaves no room for doubt that it was the discovery of the Gulf of California that Posadas was describing as having happened in 1605, not the "discovery" of Santa Fe. Bloom quoted the translation by Benjamin Read: "The villa of Santa Fe, center of New Mexico, is at 37 degrees in a straight line south, having the sea on the west, at a distance of 200 leagues. It was discovered in the year 1605 by the Adelantado Juan de Oñate...."[8] The phrase "it was discovered" in the second sentence, Bloom pointed out (*descubrióla* in the original Spanish), referred to "the sea," not to Santa Fe.

Twitchell grudgingly responded that "Mr. Bloom may possibly be justified in his conclusions," but added that "[a] strong circumstance against him is found in the fact that all of the earlier historians [unnamed] mention the Adelantado Juan de Oñate as the founder of Santa Fe, although no exact dates are given." Since Oñate left New Mexico well before 1609, said Twitchell, therefore the town had to have been founded before 1609.[9] However, by 1925 Twitchell had accepted Bloom's argument that the date of the establishment of Santa Fe was sometime after 1609.[10]

Beginning in January, 1926, *New Mexico Historical Review* published George Hammond's "Don Juan de Oñate and the Founding of New Mexico." This serial article, continuing into 1927, was subtitled "A New Investigation Into the

Early History of New Mexico in the Light of a Mass of New Materials Recently Obtained from the Archivo General de Indias, Seville, Spain."[11] The materials referred to had been gathered by Hammond himself in 1922–1923 during a year of research in Seville, and this long article was the published version of his doctoral thesis. Hammond found the instructions for the establishment of Santa Fe given by the viceroy don Luis de Velasco to Pedro de Peralta when he was made governor of New Mexico, and briefly summarized these instructions in the article.[12] Hammond indicated that Peralta undoubtedly established the Villa of Santa Fe promptly after his arrival in New Mexico at the end of 1609 or early 1610, but added, "That is as much as we are able to say with the documentary evidence available." In a footnote at this point he continued, "The writer among others has diligently searched the Spanish archives for some information to clinch the matter, but without success." What Hammond, "among others," was looking for was an official declaration of the actual founding of the Villa on some specific date, presumably in early 1610.

Although Hammond himself did not make the full text of the instructions to Peralta available in publication, Lansing Bloom relocated the document during his work in Seville in 1928. He transcribed the text of the instructions and sent a translation back to New Mexico, where it was published in *El Palacio* in June, 1928.[13] The editor, Paul A. F. Walter, added a note: "The dispute among historians whether Oñate or Peralta founded Santa Fe is settled by the instructions given Peralta upon his appointment as Governor and Captain General to succeed Oñate. The translation is by Lansing Bloom ... at present in Spain."[14]

A complete copy of Bloom's Spanish transcription of the instructions, and a new translation by Ireneo L. Chavez, were published side by side in April, 1929, in the *New Mexico Historical Review*.[15] Immediately after it in the April issue was an interpretive article by Bloom, "When Was Santa Fe Founded?," where he reviewed the available information in light of the Peralta instructions and the other new documentation available.[16]

He wrote, "[t]he answer to our question [posed by the title of the article] still must be that we do not know exactly, but we can now add the definite statement that the founding occurred during the term of the third governor of New Mexico, Don Pedro de Peralta ... and that the event took place in the spring of 1610 or shortly thereafter." Bloom discussed the known documents concerning Peralta's appointment and his trip to New Mexico, that indicated he had gotten only to Zacatecas as of early November, 1609. Considering the size and makeup of the baggage train, Bloom indicated that it would have been virtually impossible for Peralta to have reached San Gabriel before the end of February, 1610, although he admitted the possibility that Peralta and a few others of the mounted personnel in the wagon train could have pushed ahead and arrived by about the end of January.

Taking all the evidence into account, Bloom considered the establishment of Santa Fe to have happened about "the last of April, or early in May," 1610. No actual founding document had been located, and such a document continues to elude us today, eighty years later.

There the matter rested. But within fifteen years there were indications that things were not quite so cut and dried. In 1945, for example, in fray Alonso de Benavides's *Revised Memorial of 1634*, Benavides himself described the founding of Santa Fe: "This city was founded by the adelantado, Don Juan de Oñate" before his resignation in August, 1607.[17] In their notes for Benavides's text, Frederick Hodge, George Hammond, and Agapito Rey casually dismissed his statement: "The founder of Santa Fe was not Governor Juan de Oñate, as Benavides supposed, but Don Pedro de Peralta ... and the time of the establishment was the spring of 1610, not 1605, as had long been supposed."[18] Benavides had spent almost four years in Santa Fe in 1625–1629, only twenty years after its founding. His opinion was undoubtedly based on the statements of people who were present at the time of the original establishment. It had to be taken seriously in any discussion of when Santa Fe was founded.

In fact, Hodge, Hammond, and Rey were in error, and Oñate was indeed the one who approved the founding of the private settlement of Santa Fe, as Benavides claimed. Clear evidence that this was the case had been published a year earlier, in 1944. In the October, 1944 issue of the *New Mexico Historical Review*, printed about the same time that the galleys of the *Revised Memorial of 1634* were being prepared, France V. Scholes published a short note concerning a curious set of documents he had seen for sale in London "several years ago," probably in the late 1930s before travel to Europe was curtailed by World War II. These documents, he said, had the general title "D[on] Juan Saez Maurigade, vecino de esta Corte, sobre que se incluya en la descendencia directa del Capitan D[on] Juan Martínez de Montoya, descubridor, conquistador y poblador que fue en las Americas y Governador del Nuevo Mexico."[19] Scholes summarized the seventeenth-century documentation of the activities of Martínez de Montoya in New Mexico, and he included the startling statement that "the most interesting data recorded for the year 1607–1608 are brief references to a place called Santa Fé and statements indicating that some sort of post or settlement was being established there."[20] These documents concerning the career of Martínez de Montoya in New Mexico threw open the whole question of the date of establishment of Santa Fe once again.

Although most scholars who worked on the colonial history of New Mexico knew of this note by Scholes and the doubts it raised about the apparently settled question of the date of establishment of Santa Fe, little came of it because the documents themselves were unavailable.[21] Finally, in 1994, Tom Chavez, director of the Governors' Palace, in a sort of what-can-it-hurt gesture, contacted Maggs Brothers of London, the dealers that owned the Martínez de Montoya documents when Scholes saw them sometime before 1944, and asked them what had happened to the documents. To his surprise, the Martínez de Montoya papers had survived the bombing of London and were still in the hands of the dealers. Chavez made arrangements to acquire the papers for the Governors' Palace collection. As a result, the Martínez de Montoya documents are now available to scholars, and the question of what they have to say about the date of establishment of Santa Fe can now be answered.[22]

Juan Martínez de Montoya and the Founding of Santa Fe

Juan de Oñate, the founder of the province of New Mexico, was an *adelantado*, a private developer licensed by the king to place a colony on frontier lands. Juan Martínez de Montoya was not a member of Oñate's original expedition, but arrived with the relief expedition of 1600.[23]

In August, 1608, Juan Martínez de Montoya received certification from acting governor Cristobal de Oñate of his deeds and accomplishments, covering the time since he was granted an encomienda on October 6, 1606, for his services up to that date. Among these accomplishments, Oñate acknowledged Martínez as "*haber hecho Plasa en Santa Fe*," having established a *plaza* at Santa Fe, and as having "*poble en Santa Fe*," settled at Santa Fe.[24] This statement in August, 1608, indicates that the town had officially been granted at some earlier date. It was usual for the land to be put in use first, and if it proved to be acceptable, then an official grant would be requested from the governor. The town may have been unofficially established in 1605, and an official grant requested perhaps a year or two later.

The area where the plaza was established was a good central location in the province, and the natural resources and the lay of the land were appropriate for a town. There were good potential fields and the other necessary lands, a good water supply, and no nearby Pueblo settlement. The odd thing about the town site is Santa Fe's location on the north side of the river. Here was the swampy ground of the cienegas along the north and east sides of the present plaza, and the old oxbow along the south, just north of the historical river-bed. The Rio Chiquito, or "Little River" flowed here, perhaps both a smaller second channel of the Santa Fe and a small tributary. As a result, water was actually a little too abundant on the north side of the river. Carroll Riley has suggested that the south side of the river was already in use, the site of the settlement of Analco for Mexican Indians including Tlascalans, all of whom had special privileges for protected settlements on the frontiers.[25]

The town of Santa Fe apparently began as a governor's community grant, where the land was given by Oñate to Martínez de Montoya and his co-founders for their development under the usual regulations about appropriate use. Martínez de Montoya would have been accompanied to the site by an agent of the governor; here he would have carried out the standard ritual of possession, pulling weeds and throwing clods of dirt to the four winds, and so on. The "deed," actually a license for the use of the land without fear of interference by adjacent landholders or the government, would have been recorded in the governor's archives, but not outside the province (as apparently was the case for most of the other land grants made in New Mexico before the Pueblo Revolt—these documents were apparently all destroyed during the Pueblo Revolt, and so far none have been found to have been recorded at the viceregal level in Mexico City).

The settlement would have been laid out in a manner decided upon by the settlers themselves, but would have had some general similarity in plan to a typical Spanish town. How closely the founders adhered to the Laws of the Indies would have been determined by their expectations for the settlement. The survey would *not* have been under the direct regulation of the Laws of the Indies, as it would have been if the town was laid out as a result of the Viceregal grant making it a Villa; it was instead a private establishment and the plan was entirely the result of the decisions of the founders. Nonetheless, the later appearance of the town, and the scant facts about it in the few available documents, suggest that Martínez de Montoya designed a plan that met the requirements of the Laws of the Indies.

Martínez de Montoya left New Mexico for good in August, 1608. Formal permission to establish a new capitol was requested by someone in the province of New Mexico in mid-1608. The request was sent to the viceroy on the same wagon train of August, 1608, in which Martínez de Montoya traveled—this suggests that Martínez de Montoya himself carried the petition.

The reports carried in this convoy prompted the viceroy to appoint Pedro de Peralta as the new governor to replace acting governor Cristobal de Oñate, Juan de Oñate's son, and to order the establishment of a villa and new capitol "as petitioned," and to suppress the old capitol at San Gabriel.[26] The decision was part of a major legal change for the colony, removing the endeavor from the hands of the adelantado and placing it directly under the crown. The Oñates had been interested in making a return on their investment in their colony of New Mexico, and therefore were strongly in favor of conquest, mines and tribute: the military and economic exploitation of their section of the frontier. The viceroy's decision made the province a royal settlement with its emphasis on farming, ranching, and missionary work.[27]

When Peralta arrived, he carried out the wishes of the viceroy and made Martínez de Montoya's little *plaza* into the Villa de Santa Fe, capitol of the province of New Mexico. Oñate's settlement at San Gabriel immediately became an unimportant visita.

Peralta's viceregal grant of 1609 did nothing more than make the Paraje de Santa Fe into the Villa de Santa Fe, and officially granted it four leagues of land. The Martinez de Montoya papers make it clear that the settlement of Santa Fe was already in existence at the time Peralta was ordered to make it a villa and the capitol of the province of New Mexico. This changes the context within which the orders must be interpreted, and our conclusions about what they say.

The Orders to Peralta to Establish Santa Fe

The "Instructions to Peralta by Vice-Roy," the order authorizing the establishment of the Villa of Santa Fe, have been regarded with hopeful confusion since Hammond found them early in the twentieth century.[28] Because the order was considered to be the founding document for the settlement, it has been thought that, with the appropriate insight and comparison of the order with the Laws of the Indies,[29] surviving deed records and other historical documents,[30] and the Joseph de Urrútia map of Santa Fe prepared in 1767,[31] the order could be made to reveal details of the plan of Santa Fe as it was originally laid out.

It is apparent, however, that the document was not intended to found a town, lay it out according to the information in the "Instructions," and declare it the Villa of Santa Fe and capitol of New Mexico. Its intent, instead, was to grant the already-existing settlement of Santa Fe both the status of "Villa" and the full extent of the lands to which such a villa was legally entitled. The viceregal officials who drew it up simply included the standard boiler-plate information about the characteristics expected of a standard villa.

We are fortunate to have a similar document, the orders for the founding of the Villa de San Fernando (now San Antonio) in the Province of Texas in 1731, with the difference that the San Fernando document *was* intended to be the directive for the survey of a new town.[32] The governor of Texas and the new Canary Island settlers, however, chose to use the already-existing presidial town plan to form most of San Fernando's layout, adding only a small second, civilian plaza next to the presidial plaza, and most of the detail of the viceroy's order was not used.[33]

Note, for example, that the Santa Fe order contains no indication of *where* the new villa was to be placed. The corresponding order for the establishment of San Fernando specified the site and discussed its attributes; the discussion among the viceregal authorities as to the best location for San Fernando is also on record. That the details about the site of Santa Fe were not specified implies that nothing about the site was known to the Viceroy as of mid-1609 when the "Instructions" were written. The "Instructions" should, therefore, not be expected to have any *specific* information about the site or actual layout of Santa Fe.

From the viewpoint of legally providing for the full standard *fundo legal* of a villa, however, the order is more informative. Previously misconstrued internal evidence demonstrates that the order gives to the already-existing settlement of Santa Fe the generic attributes of a standard Villa as listed in the Laws of the Indies of 1573. First, consider the following clauses in the "Instructions":

Que los d[ic]hos alcaldes ordinarios y Regidores de la tal Villa pueden por treinta años señalar a cada vecino dos solares para Casa y Jardin y dos suertes para guerta y otras dos para Viña y olibar y quatro cavallerias de tierra y para el rriego de ellas el agua nescessaria aviendola obligandoles a hazer vecindad diez años continuos sin hazer avsencia con pena que si la hicieren quatro meses continuos sin licencia del Cavildo y Regimiento lo pierda todo y se rreparta su vecindad a otro.

That the said ordinary *alcaldes* and *regidores* of such a Villa may, for thirty years, assign to each resident two *solares* for house and garden and two *suertes* for irrigated fields and another two for vinyard and olive grove and four *caballerias* of land and the necessary water for the irrigation of these; obligating them to have to do ten continuous years without being absent to achieve the *vecindad*, with the penalty that if they are absent four continuous months without license of the *Cabildo* and *regimiento* they lose all and their *vecindad* is apportioned to another.

Señalara para propios de la d[ic]ha Villa seis Vecindades y una quadra de las Calles para hazer Cassas Reales y otras obras pp[ubli]ca.

For *propios* of the said Villa he will assigned six *vecindades* and a square of the streets for the construction of the *casas reales* and other public buildings.[34]

It is apparent from the statements in the first quotation that in the context of Peralta's order, a *vecindad* was not an area or district of the town, as it has previously been translated, but a "citizen's-right," the land to which an individual settler was entitled.[35] The quotation in fact defines this vecindad as consisting of two solares, four suertes, and four caballerias of land. On the northern frontier, solares are generally house lots in town, suertes are usually fields in the farmlands of the town, and caballerias are pasturing or grazing lots outside of the town lots. The statement about necessary water would probably have applied principally to the irrigated fields of the suertes, and secondarily to the solares and jardines (kitchen gardens), for household and garden water. The caballerias, being intended for general pasturage, would not have been considered to require irrigation.

The second clause indicates that the town would receive "a square of the streets" (the main plaza of the town) and six vecindades as its *propios*. Propios are lands to be rented by the town for income, and could be used for future expansion of the settlement. Propios are stated in the Ordinances of 1573 to be one-sixth of the total land of a town (Ordnance 90); therefore, this clause implies that thirty-six vecindades were established, of which six were apportioned to the propios of the Villa.[36] The rest was distributed among the original settlers, one to each family. If there were fewer than thirty families, the town kept the remaining vecindades as additional community property to be given to future settlers. The Ordinances say that a town cannot be smaller than that appropriate for thirty *vecinos*; it did not matter if the actual number of settlers was less than thirty—the town would be laid out for thirty regardless. San Fernando, for example, was founded by sixteen families, but the allotment of land was for the standard thirty.

The Villa Grant

With thirty-six vecindades, the town would have had a total of 72 *solares* divided by streets and arranged around a plaza, 144 *suertes*, and 144 *caballerias*, of which 12 *solares*, 24 *suertes*, and 24 *caballerias* would have belonged to the town as common lands. According to Barnes, Naylor and Polzer,[37] the following were standard measurements:

> Solar: 50 v. x 50 v.
> Suerte: 276 v. x 552 v.
> Caballeria: 552 v. x 1,104 v.

Rather than depressing ourselves with the usual endless recitations about how many possible sizes these units may have had, let us assume that they had these generic sizes, since this was a generic set of instructions. Seventy-two solares would form the center of town around the main plaza. Solares could vary considerably in size; the basic San Fernando solar, for example, was eighty varas on a size, but even in this case some solares varied from this base size. For our purposes here, the generic fifty vara size will be used. Each solar would have the allowance for a street around it, each street at least 11 varas (30 feet) wide. Extending the size of a solar by half a street width in each direction gives each the dimensions of 61 varas. Seventy-two of these is 267,912 square varas. Taking the plaza as the average size, 600 by 400 *pies*,[38] or 200 by 133.33 varas, plus half the width of a street all the way around, gives 211 by 144.33 varas, or 26,666 square varas for the plaza, for a total of about 294,578 square varas for the core area of town. One hundred and forty-four standard suertes amounts to an area of 21,938,688 square varas. The amount of 144 caballerias is a fairly large piece of land, equal to 87,754,752 square varas.

Adding the area of the plaza, solares, and streets at the center of town to the area of the suertes and the area of the caballerias gives an area of 109,961,352 square varas, using the standard sizes given above. One square league is 5,000 varas on a side, or 25,000,000 square varas, so the area included in the Instructions equals 4.4 square leagues, or a square 2.1 leagues on a side; this would be the equivalent of measuring 1.05 leagues (one league plus 250 varas) in each of the four cardinal directions from the front of the church, the usual center point of the town. This is close enough to precisely four square leagues, using the generic measurements of the individual units given above, to indicate that the actual size of one or another of the units was slightly different from that assumed here, and the Instructions intended to give the town precisely four square leagues.

What does all this tell us? Essentially, that the "Instructions to Peralta" were official permission to establish a town according to the Laws of the Indies, with four square leagues of territory in its *fundo legal*. However, this was only the idealized town plan presented by Peralta's orders, which had no particular relationship to the town plan actually laid out by Martinez de Montoya and his fellow settlers about 1605. The authorization to establish the Villa de San Fernando de Bexar (the present San Antonio, Texas) in 1731, for example, had a similar result. This set of instructions even went so far as to state not only the sizes of the streets, lots, and plaza but also described in detail the method to be used to lay out these units. In actuality, however, the governor accepted the already-existing plan of the presidial town and added a small plaza, even though these did not match the measurements in the instructions.[39]

The determination that the "Instructions" indeed granted a four-square-league tract to Santa Fe clears up a vexing historical Santa Fe question. In 1874, Gaspar Ortiz y Alarid, probate judge for Santa Fe County, petitioned the surveyor general James K. Proudfit for the confirmation of a grant of four square leagues to the city of Santa Fe, based on the assumption that the Villa had been granted such a tract originally "under the Spanish laws, usages, and customs." The surveyor general accepted Ortiz y Alarid's argument and surveyed a four-square-league tract centered on Santa Fe, but the land claim itself was never officially accepted, and in 1892 the Board of County Commissioners of Santa Fe County submitted the claim to the Court of Private Land Claims, established in 1891, with the United States acting as defendant. The court confirmed the grant of land to the city of Santa Fe in 1894, with two of the judges voting in favor of the grant and the third filing a dissenting opinion.[40]

The United States government appealed the decision to the Supreme Court, which in 1897 overturned the decision of the Court of Private Land Claims, and ruled that title to all property in the city of Santa belonged to the United States public domain.[41] The citizens of Santa Fe petitioned Congress, which had disposition of the public domain, for a final decision that would place ownership of their land in their own hands. In 1900, Congress passed an act which gave ownership of all the land within the original 1874 survey of four square leagues to the city of Santa Fe, with the provision that everyone who had held title to land in the city would receive "proper deeds of quitclaim" for their holdings. As a result, previous deeds are not considered to have been legal land ownership documents, and all property ownership in the city of Santa Fe is considered to begin in the first years of the twentieth century.[42]

The principal objection by the United States throughout the long legal fight was that there was no reason to think that Spanish law granted a four-square-league tract to every Spanish villa, nor was there any evidence that Spain had done so in the case of Santa Fe. It is clear, however, that the "Instructions" did indeed include such a grant to Santa Fe, and that the residents of Santa Fe had been correct all along in their contention that the town had a legitimate claim to four square leagues of land as its villa grant. The decision by the Supreme Court was in error. Had the "Instructions" been available in the 1880s and 1890s, presumably the Supreme Court would have ruled in favor of the decision of the Court of Private Land Claims, and the record of ownership of lots in the town would have legally extended as far back as the records are available, in some cases to the 1690s.

The 1994 acquisition of the Juan Martinez de Montoya papers and their subsequent availability to scholars has ultimately resulted in the rejection of Lansing Bloom's argument in 1913–1929 that Santa Fe was founded in 1609–1610 under Peralta, in favor of an earlier date around 1605–1607 under Oñate, as Adolph Bandelier and Ralph Emerison Twitchell had originally argued in 1890 and 1911, respectively. With the reacceptance of this original position, the "Instructions to Don Pedro de Peralta" acquire a different relationship to the settlement of Santa Fe than first thought. As demonstrated here, rather than being the order to create a new town named Santa Fe, the Instructions were, instead, simply the documents officially designating the already-existing settlement of Santa Fe to be a villa, and the allotment of a four-square-league grant of land to that villa.

4

Thirty-eight Adobe Houses
The Villa de Santa Fe in the Seventeenth Century, 1608–1610

by
José Antonio Esquibel

Personality of Place

There is an eminent presence of history in the City of Santa Fe. The visual impressions of the city characterize the most tangible evidence of this ambient history. Other aspects are less obvious and have even faded from current memory with the passing of time. Still, this presence embodies an association of traits that make up the personality of Santa Fe. It is a personality fostered over the course of four centuries by the experiences and cultural expressions of the many residents who made, and currently make, their homes in Santa Fe, creating a unique sense of place that is more than merely a geographic locale. Santa Fe as a place was, and continues to be, transformed by experiences of human intellect, emotions, and memories related to every day activities of home life, work, religious activities, civic duties, economic transactions, and political endeavors. The physical and mental energy of many generations of residents has engendered a unique cultural and historical geography embedded in landscape and inherited by those who live in the City of Santa Fe and felt by many who visit.

In the commemoration of four hundred years of history, the City of Santa Fe asks to be rediscovered. The *cuartocentenario* provides an opportunity to take another look at Santa Fe, to look closer and deeper into a variety of aspects of its personality that are more often taken for granted in the flurry of modern daily activity, to listen to new stories uncovered or re-told, and perhaps even to touch its textures and taste its flavors in new ways. This is an opportunity to be reflective of four hundred years of distinctive history of a place within the United States of America, which in its own particular history is two hundred and thirty-four years old in the year 2010.

Of Santa Fe's four centuries as a municipality, the first hundred years remain the least understood. When was Santa Fe founded? Who were the first residents of Santa Fe? What was life like for those who made their homes in Santa Fe during the seventeenth century? These are only a few of many seemingly unanswerable questions of Santa Fe's early history due to a lack of surviving records. Although historical accounts regarding Santa Fe's earliest decades are few and incomplete, this should not dissuade our curiosity.

Two sources for seeking partial answers are archival and archeological research. It becomes incumbent upon modern scholars to re-find the origins and early history of Santa Fe in fragments of information preserved in surviving historical documents or remains of buried material culture. Bringing new findings to light serves as a means for attempting to restore the memory of events and people of Santa Fe's past. There are a couple of intriguing questions to consider in the effort to rescue the memory of seventeenth-century Santa Fe. What is it that defines a place? And, what gives particular meaning to a place that is experienced as something unique by individuals?

It is an inherent aspect of human nature and experience to endow significance to places, engendering a sense of place that becomes imbued with emotions from the experiences of daily life. Intellectual energy, emotional energy, and memories related to daily activities of home life, work, religious activities, civic life, and economic and political affairs creates familiarity that becomes a bond between persons and place. Like other settlements, seventeenth-century Santa Fe was a place where people lived, loved, married, generated laughter, engaged in conflict, experienced sorrow, expressed religious beliefs and traditions, and gossiped, among numerous other human activities. Underlying the unique characteristics of Santa Fe are remnants of the blending of Spanish, Pueblo Indian, Mexican Indian, and Apache cultural influences during the seventeenth-century, a particular time in history when tribal warfare presented constant dangers and Native American and European societies met, clashed and merged.

Our understanding of Santa Fe is enhanced by becoming more familiar with its early history. Our sense of Santa Fe may even change as we gain glimpses of previous events and residents who made Santa Fe their home during the 1600s. To begin this endeavor, it is worthwhile to consider what is known about the origins of this four hundred year old municipality.

On the Origins of the Villa de Santa Fe

One of the limitations for uncovering the history of seventeenth-century Santa Fe is the lack of surviving documentation. The Spaniards of the Hapsburg Empire established and maintained extremely efficient systems of documentation and communication to keep royal government informed. Distinguished by adept coordination and management, the efficient system of Spanish government consisted of extremely effective laws, protocols and systems of communication that were administered over vast distances of territory from Spain to the Netherlands, Italy, India, Japan, the Philippine Islands, and throughout the vast territories of the north and south American regions. A remarkable network of roads and waterways connected all parts of the Spanish Empire so that even the most remote provinces were linked to vital centers of commerce and royal government. Although New Mexico's Spanish colony was established on the periphery of the empire, it was nonetheless well connected to the existing imperial mechanisms of secular and church governance and commerce.

When the Villa de Santa Fe was established as a formal municipality, it served as the seat of Spanish government and official documents were stored in an archive room located in the *casas reales*, the royal government building of seventeenth-century New Mexico, which today is known as the Palace of the Governors.[1] This archive most likely housed the early records of the Villa de Santa Fe, including the formal dedication of the villa and a list of the first residents. Unfortunately, these records did not survive the passage of time and were most likely destroyed during the Pueblo Indian uprising of August 1680 when many building and homes in the Villa de Santa Fe were set on fire and destroyed.

Only by extracting and collecting fragments of information found within numerous pages of official Spanish documents that were sent to officials in places like Mexico City and Spain can a few clues about the origins of Santa Fe be uncovered. The challenging aspect of these archival documents is the fact that the contents often relate to social and political conflicts and as such the records do not offer a well-rounded picture of other types of interactions among and between Spanish citizens and their relationship with Pueblo Indians, which in some cases were of an amiable nature that formed bonds of mutual respect, friendship, and even formed kinship groups.

The current fragments of information reveal several noteworthy circumstances pre-figuring the founding of the Villa de Santa Fe that are important to its origins:

- the toleration by the Pueblo Indians of the presence of Spaniards in the region and the formation of a mutually beneficial alliances;

- the establishment of a military garrison apparently at the future site of the Villa de Santa Fe during the era of Governor Don Juan de Oñate (1598–1608);
- the decline in prominence of the Villa de San Gabriel between 1604 and 1609;
- the extreme discouragement of the soldier-settlers following the unsuccessful expedition of Oñate to find the coast of the South Sea (1604–1605), which resulted in the request by the soldier-settlers to abandon New Mexico;
- the steadfast advocacy of the Franciscan friars for support by the royal crown to retain New Mexico as a province in order to preserve the Christian faith of those recently baptized and to introduce Christianity to other native people;
- and the royal order of 1608 to preserve New Mexico for the purpose of evangelization.

On the first point, various Pueblo Indian leaders actively negotiated a political and military alliance with the Spaniards in the early 1600s, seeking advantages and benefits for their people as well as strengthening the political and economic status of their respective communities within the region. Yet, consciously and with purposeful intent Pueblo tribal communities retained much of their cultural constitution and selectively adopted and adapted those aspects of Spanish European culture they viewed as beneficial. Without an alliance with Pueblo Indians, the Spanish colony established by Oñate would not have taken root in New Mexico, especially as the number of settlers dwindled over the course of 1601 to 1608. In fact, the Pueblo Indians of Ohkay Owingeh (San Juan Pueblo), allowed the Spaniards to make their homes at the nearby abandoned pueblo of Yunque, where the Spaniards established the Villa de San Gabriel in 1599.[2]

Following the lack of discoveries of silver and gold, it became clear that New Mexico as an extension of the Spanish realms was not a viable economic enterprise for Oñate, his followers, or the crown. As a result, the Spanish crown and Roman Catholic Church focused attention on the multiple communities of Pueblo Indians, including conversion of the Pueblo people to Christianity and protection of Pueblo communities against attacks by nomadic tribes. New Mexico would be known as *tierra de guerra*, land of war, throughout the seventeenth-century because of constant intimidations and hostilities inflicted on the Pueblo people and Spanish settlers by various tribes, in particular the Apache and Navajo. In regard to military protection, there is evidence that Santa Fe may have been the site of a garrison prior to becoming an official town.

In August 1608, Captain Juan Martínez de Montoya, who held the post of lieutenant governor under Oñate and served as governor for a brief period of about six months in 1608, sought an official certification of his services before as he made preparations to travel from New Mexico to Mexico City.[3] In this certification, reference was made to three specific geographical places, apparently all in New Mexico: 1) Santa Fe; 2) the *real de minas de San Buenaventura*; and 3) the Villa de San Gabriel. Curiously, this is the only surviving document dated before 1610 to specifically mention a place named Santa Fe in New Mexico, and the reference is made twice in this one document. In the first instance, the following string of military phrases were used, "*...el haber hecho Plasa en Santa Fe, y en el Real de San Buenaventura, Real de Minas, y sido en ayuda a descubrirlas, y he poblado en dicho Real.*"[4] The phrase "*el haber hecho Plaza en Santa Fe*" has been previously translated as "he established the Plaza of Santa Fe," thus attributing the founding of Santa Fe to Martínez de Montoya. Upon further study of the phrase, which is found in other historical sources, the term '*plaza*' appears instead to refer to a military post or camp.[5] An alternate translation is "he made post at Santa Fe," suggesting that he was stationed at a military camp that carried the name Santa Fe. Martínez de Montoya indicated that after serving at the military camp at Santa Fe and the royal mining camp of San Buenaventura, "*ansimismo poble en la Villa de S.ⁿ Gabriel, y hise Casa siendo en ella Alcalde Ordinario este año de mill seiscientos e ocho,*" "he also settled at the Villa de San Gabriel and constructed a house, becoming *alcalde ordinario* in this year of 1608."[6]

The second reference to Santa Fe in the certification of services of Martínez de Montoya recounts that he participated "*en guarda de la Yglesia e Real quando la Guerra de los Xumanas y poble en Santa Fe,*" "in protection of the church and royal mining camp during the time of the War of the Jumanos and he settled in Santa Fe."[7] This statement is revealing in that the "*real*" (camp) was most likely that of San Buenaventura, since the pueblo of Los Jumanos was also known as San Buenaventura de los Jumanos. It was in this area that Oñate and his soldiers organized salt mining operations, "*real de minas.*" Following the war of Los Jumanos in the early half of 1599, Martínez de Montoya then apparently settled at Santa Fe before eventually building a house at the Villa de San Gabriel where he served as *alcalde ordinario* in 1608.[8] If the military camp of Santa Fe was the site of a presidio or garrison, it may very well have been the same site as the future Villa de Santa Fe, strategically located in a direct route from the Villa de San Gabriel to the region of Los Jumanos, which was situated to the east of the modern-day Manzano Mountains in the lower Estancia Basin.

The implications from this brief study of the account of the services of Juan

Martínez de Montoya is that a military camp christened Santa Fe may have been established as early as 1599, but certainly prior to 1608. It is an assumption that it was located in the area associated with the Villa de Santa Fe, along the Santa Fe River. There are three other fragments of historical information that lend support to this assumption. Writing in the 1630s, Fray Alonso Benavides commented, "This city was founded by the *adelantado*, Don Juan de Oñate, when he entered with seven hundred married Spaniards, but the majority returned to Mexico."[9] What is significant about this statement is the very specific indication that the initial origin of Santa Fe occurred prior to the mass desertion of soldier-settlers in October 1601.[10] We can only presume that Benavides acquired his information first hand from conversation with individuals who came to New Mexico in 1598 during his tenure in New Mexico between 1626 and 1629. However, it is important to note there is no indication from known historical documents that Santa Fe was an official 'villa' during Oñate's tenure of governor.

The remaining two fragments of historical evidence pertain to information given by two men who declared they were each natives of Santa Fe with ages to indicate they were born between 1604 and 1607, prior to the formal designation of Santa Fe as a villa in 1610. Juan Griego consistently identified his birthplace as Santa Fe and just as consistently provided ages that place his birth as 1604–1605.[11] Hernán Martín Serrano, the younger, consistently indicated he was born 1606-1607, and on one occasion gave Santa Fe as his place of birth.[12] Unfortunately, there are no existing records of birth or baptisms to verify the dates of birth of these men. It is known from the historical record that the father's of both of these individuals served as soldiers in New Mexico during the early 1600s. As such, it is reasonable to consider that these soldiers settled at the military camp of Santa Fe.

Of the several hundred soldiers that came to New Mexico between 1598–1601, only about fifty Spanish soldiers, many with families, remained by 1608.[13] Along with a small number of Franciscan friars, this was the full constitution of Spanish citizens among tens of thousands of Pueblo Indians and Apache, Navajo and Ute Indians. Each of the Spanish soldiers who remained expended a great amount of their own finances, so much so that royal treasury funds were needed to supplement their welfare and to sustain their families.

The preservation of the soldier-settlers between 1606 and 1608 only continued to drain royal financial resources. In the words of Don Luis de Velasco, Viceroy of New Spain, sustaining New Mexico resulted in "excessive expense" for little return other than "the lacking and misery of the land and the great distance."[14] On August 24, 1607, the residents of the Villa de San Gabriel recorded their petition to the viceroy for desperately needed provisions and financial support from the royal *hacienda*, without which they planned to abandon New Mexico on the last day of June 1608 because, in their opinion and experience, "it seems impossible to keep this settlement."[15]

During this time, several Franciscan friars, notably Fray Francisco de Escobar, Fray Isidro de Ordóñez, and Fray Lázaro Jiménez, convincingly appealed to both royal and ecclesiastical officials in Mexico City for retaining a presence in New Mexico because so many Indians openly received the sacrament of Baptism and, in their opinion, were amenable to the Catholic faith. By February 1608, Felipe III, king of Spain, unequivocally decreed that New Mexico be sustained for the preservation and protection of *"nuestra sancta fee catholica,"* "Our Holy Catholic Faith."[16] The naming of the Villa de Santa Fe may very well stem from this phrase in relation to the stated purpose of retaining Spanish presence in New Mexico specifically for preserving the Holy Faith. The very name of the Villa de Santa Fe served as a continual reminder of that intention.

With the decision of the king to retain New Mexico, Viceroy Velasco, in consultation with the council of royal magistrate of the *Audiencia de Nueva España*, began to address the necessary measures for preservation of the province. In addition to dealing with the accusations against Don Juan de Oñate for the deaths of several soldiers and the mishandling of various situations under his command, and dealing with securing funds for the provisions to support the soldier-settlers and Franciscan friars, Velasco and his aids sought a qualified individual to appoint as governor. Velasco initially appointed Captain Juan Martínez de Montoya, whose short tenure as governor lasted from late February 1608 until his request to leave New Mexico in August 1608, leaving Don Cristóbal de Oñate acting as governor in the interim. The second appointment was given to Don Pedro de Peralta in early 1609.[17] On March 30, 1609, Peralta received specific instructions for founding a villa from Don Luis de Velasco in the form of a decree.[18] These instructions, preserved in a single document in the national archives of Mexico, represent the written origins of the lengthy civic lineage of Santa Fe, which has been uninterrupted for four hundred years. Velasco outlined orders for Peralta beginning with the need to establish a proper settlement for the *vecinos* (taxpaying citizens). He then referred to the election of four municipal councilmen, the *regidores*, who would elect two *alcaldes ordinarios* from among their number, with the authority to hear civil and criminal cases within the jurisdiction of the villa, extending about fifteen miles from the center of the town in all directions.

According to Velasco, and in accordance with Spanish custom, the *regidores* would elect those who would succeed them in the following year. In addition, the *regidores* had the authority to elect a notary and with the governor's approval an *alguacil mayor* (high sheriff). The decree outlined that the villa would consist of six *vecinidades* (districts) with a public square where the *casas reales* (royal government building) would be located along with other public buildings. The expectation of the viceroy was for Don Pedro de Peralta to establish and settle the new villa "with the greatest brevity," meaning as quickly as possible in order for the soldier-settlers to "begin to have and to live with some law and orderliness."[19]

One month later, in April 1609, Fray Francisco de Velasco submitted a brief memorial to Viceroy Velasco expressing reasons for not abandoning New Mexico in order to continue the work of bringing the native people to the Catholic faith. Fray Francisco made a revealing comment when he recommended, "It would be well also if your majesty ordered the confirmation of the town established at San Gabriel, and that it be organized with the status of a villa."[20] This statement is significant on two accounts. The first is the indication that although the primary Spanish settlement was referred to as the Villa de San Gabriel, it apparently did not hold the formal status as a legally recognized municipality. Secondly, Fray Francisco clearly expressed his personal preference for the primacy of San Gabriel as the recommended official villa.

The statement of Fray Francisco inferred that as of April 9, 1609, there was no Spanish settlement in New Mexico that held the legally confirmed status of a villa. Because of the lack of this status there was no sense of permanency among the soldier-settlers and Fray Francisco said as much when he also recommended that the crown order the establishment of a *custodia,* referring to local religious governance, "which would have the effect of settling the people permanently."[21] Although not expressed in the surviving historical records, there may have been a group of soldiers and families who preferred the location of the military camp of Santa Fe for receiving the designation of an official villa. This group most likely lobbied Governor Peralta upon his arrival in New Mexico in late 1609 and in response to his official orders to establish a villa "with the greatest brevity" he apparently bestowed the legal status upon the military camp of Santa Fe in 1610.

Because the first Spanish settlement of the Villa de San Gabriel was established out of necessity, and primarily as a military settlement, it could not be legally sustained as a Spanish municipality due to its close proximity to the Pueblo of of Ohkay Owingeh (San Juan). A number of families that came to New Mexico with Oñate remained as residents of the Tewa region near the Oque Owingue while others relocated to the new Villa de Santa Fe. Evidence accounts for eight soldiers, some with families, as original settlers of the Villa de Santa Fe in addition to one friar and Governor Peralta. There may have been a few additional first settlers whose

First page of instructions from Viceroy Don Luis de Velasco to Governor Don Pedro de Peralta on founding a villa with boundaries stretching five leagues in all directions and allotting two plots of land for each citizen, one plot for a house and one for a garden, plus additional land for orchards and farming. Archivo General de la Indias, Mexico 27, N63c, f.1r.

names remain unknown due to a loss of records. The small number of first settlers is consistent with that of other Spanish frontier towns. The names of the known first settlers of the Villa de Santa Fe are listed here for posterity:

Maese de Campo (Field Commander) Pedro Durán de Chaves, born circa 1556 Valverde de Llerena, Extremadura, Spain, and his wife, Doña Isabel de Bohórquez, born circa 1586, Mexico City.[22]

Sargento Mayor Francisco Gómez, born circa 1586, Lisbon, Portugal, who married Doña Ana Robledo, native of San Gabriel del Yunque, New Mexico.[23]

Juan Griego, born circa 1566, native of Negropote or Candia, Greece, and his wife Pascuala Bernal, parents of Santa Fe native Juan Griego, born circa 1604–1605.[24]

Juan López Holguín, born 1559, Funete Ovejuna, Andalucía, Spain, and his wife Doña Catalina de Villanueva, born circa 1576.[25]

Capitán Francisco Madrid, born circa 1593, who first married a daughter of *Capitán* Alonso Barba Martín and then María de la Vega Márquez.[26]

Capitán Hernán Martín Serrano, born circa 1558, Zacatecas, Nueva Galicia; the mother of his son and namesake was Doña Inés, a Tano Indian woman who was acculturated into Spanish society and was a long-time resident of Santa Fe.[27]

Capitán Juan Rodríguez Bellido, born circa 1556, Gibraleón, Andalucía, Spain.[28]

Capitán Alonso Varela, born circa 1566, Santiago de Compostela, Galicia, Spain, and his wife Catalina Pérez de Bustillo, very likely a native of Mexico City.[29]

Padre Fray Cristóbal de Quirós.[30]

Don Pedro de Peralta, Governor of New Mexico.

There are no known records to explain the reason for selecting the site of Santa Fe as a military camp and eventually as a villa. It may have been on the advice of Pueblo Indian allies that the site was accepted by the Spaniards as a strategic military position, particularly if the area was already a crossroad of Indian routes. The site was more central to both the northern and southern Pueblo Indian communities and in an area with ample access to water, wood, tillable land, and terrain suitable for protection.

There were fifty plots of land designated within the boundaries of the Villa de Santa Fe.[31] The governor assigned plots to himself and to those who settled in the villa. To persuade more soldier-settlers to come to the Villa de Santa Fe, Peralta apparently refused to allocate land and to assign Indian tributes (*encomiendas*) unless they became residents of the villa.[32] By 1612, some of the soldier-settlers living outside of the Villa de Santa Fe, most likely residing at the Villa de San Gabriel, expressed their dissatisfaction with the governor's measures and requested permission to leave New Mexico, which Peralta denied. Their request also went to royal officials and in August 1612 Fray Isidro Ordóñez arrived in New Mexico with what was purported to be a royal provision granting permission for the disheartened settlers to leave. The governor argued that because of the small number of Spanish residents, the loss of any number would place those who remained in severe danger.[33] Still, he was forced to comply by either allowing settlers to leave or allocating lands and assigning Indian tributes to those not living in the villa.[34] There is no clear indication that any settlers left New Mexico.

Cabeza de Estas Provincias—Capital of These Provinces

Between 1608 and 1620 the number of soldier-settlers in New Mexico changed very little, going from fifty soldiers-settlers in 1608 to an accounting of forty-eight soldier-settlers in 1617, most with families and probably consisting of around two hundred individuals.[35] It was only through alliances with Pueblo Indian leaders that such a small number of Spanish citizens managed to establish a new geo-political structure in New Mexico. Military protection lay at the heart of these alliances in which various Pueblo groups became a united military force in confederation with the Spaniards. Despite advanced European military technology, the Spaniards were far outnumbered and depended on allies to maintain their political authority and relied on cooperative relations for creating a sustainable economic infrastructure based on agriculture and raising livestock. In the early years of the history of the Villa de Santa Fe, Pueblo Indians leaders such as Cañasola, captain of the Pueblo of Pecos, Anda, captain of the Pueblo of San

Cristóbal, and Don Lorenzo, captain of the Pueblo of Pojoaque, were regarded as "friends of the Spaniards" and assisted in engaging more reluctant Pueblo groups as allies.[36]

Spanish and Pueblo Indian aesthetics combined in the Villa de Santa Fe to create a specific sense of place, a place that fostered bonds of human interactions among people of diverse cultural backgrounds. The decree of March 30, 1609, issued by Viceroy Velasco made the provision that the *regidores* (town councilmen) would allocate plots of land for houses and gardens with nearby fields for planting vegetables, vineyards, and with irrigation. Those who received such allotments were bound for ten years to remain as residents of the villa. The intent of the viceroy's instructions was to shape the locale in such a way as to anchor individuals to the villa and establish an attachment of the residents with that place.

Central to the new villa was the main plaza, referred to variously in seventeenth-century historical records as the *plaza principal*, the *plaza real*, the *plaza mayor*, and the *plaza pública*, and located on higher ground to the north of the river.[37] Indications are that the seventeenth-century plaza was twice a long as it is today, reaching all the way to the current location of the Basilica of Saint Francis and Cathedral Park. A passing reference made in 1662 mentions the presence of cottonwood trees on the plaza, and thus it was not merely an open space.[38] The plaza served as a gathering place for a variety of social, political, religious and economic activities.

Several essential structures were constructed along the sides of the plaza, representing government and religious authority and a visible connection to Spanish law, Catholic traditions, and European history. These structures were the *casas reales* (royal government building), the *casas de cabildo* (municipal government building), the Franciscan *convento* (living quarters), and the parish church. Of these four structures, only the *casas reales*, also known as the *casas reales de palacio* and better known today as the Palace of the Governors, survived the passage of time into the 21st century and still occupies the same space.[39] The Franciscan friars dedicated the *convento* to the *Limpia Concepción de Nuestra Señora*, the Immaculate Conception of Our Lady, and the adjacent parish church was presumably also dedicated to the same Marian devotion.[40] Thus, the original patron saint of Santa Fe was *Santa María*, also referred to in one seventeenth-century record as "*Nuestra Señora de la Villa*."[41] The church and *convento* were most likely located next to each other on the eastern side of the plaza in the area of the modern Basilica of Saint Francis. The town hall was also located along the plaza, but the precise site has yet to be determined by historical or archeological research.

The bottom half of this document begins to specify instructions for fortifying the Villa de Santa Fe after a request to move the villa was denied. The document, dated 1621, refers to repairs needed for the church and the *casas reales*, the modern-day Palace of the Governors. Archivo General de la Indias, Mexico 27, N45a, B2, f.5r.

The small number of Spanish residents of New Mexico in 1610, about fifty men, some with families, posed a particular challenge for constructing the main buildings of the new villa. Through necessity the Spaniards relied on Pueblo Indian ingenuity and skill in constructing abode structures. Given that the Pueblo Indians were a superior military force in New Mexico by sheer numbers, it is not likely that they were enlisted involuntarily to assist in the construction efforts. Pueblo Indian leaders and Spanish leaders may very well have worked out a mutual arrangement, or perhaps the Pueblo Indians leaders extended their assistance of their people with the expectation of specific political and economic favors from Spanish leaders. Through this relationship, in what ever manner it was formed, elements of European building design were incorporated with Pueblo structural design to produce a unique blending of architectural styles that is still admired and emulated today.

Unfortunately, the young villa and its first settlers did not have sufficient resources to feed and house the Pueblo Indian workers because of "the great poverty of the land" in the words of Fray Isidro Ordóñez.[42] During August 1612, Ordóñez, acting in his role as leader of the Franciscan friars in New Mexico, criticized Governor Peralta for having Pueblo Indians travel great distances to work in the villa without ample food along the journey nor in the villa.[43] It appears that Ordóñez and his friars intended to counter the request for Pueblo Indians to come in the Villa de Santa Fe as laborers, which drew the ire of not only the governor but some of the settlers.

The limitation placed on use of Pueblo Indian laborers may have been one of the underlying causes for discontent with the location of the Villa de Santa Fe. By 1620, a request was sent to royal officials to relocate the new villa to an area of better defense, although the preferred location was not specified in the response to the request. A royal decree dated January 5, 1621, and issued by Don Diego Fernandez de Córdoba y Cardona, Viceroy of New Spain, denied the request for relocating the villa. Instead the viceroy made provisions for sending materials to aid the *vecinos* in fortifying the defenses of the villa and making repairs of the *casas reales* and the church.[44] There was also instruction to build four towers and square the boundaries of the villa for better defense. Whether this fortification actually occurred is not known for certain. However, the Villa de Santa Fe remained at its location, and the main structures of the villa became prominent places for numerous interactions throughout the seventeenth century despite periods of disrepair and reconstruction.

Fray Alonso de Benavides, who resided in New Mexico between 1626 and 1629, noted that the Villa de Santa Fe consisted of "up to two hundred and fifty" Spanish residents and as many as 750 other residents, mainly Pueblo Indians and some *Indios Méxicanos*, referring to Indians from the Valley of Mexico in the area of Mexico City.[45] Three known *Indios Méxicanos* residing in the Villa de Santa during this time were Francisco 'Pancho' Balón, a blacksmith, and Domingo Sombrero and his wife Francisca, each living in the villa in the 1620s and early 1630s.[46] Unfortunately, the records are so sparse for this era that names of other such Mexican Indian residents remain unknown.

In 1638 the number of settler families living in the Villa de Santa Fe was stated as being fifty. In all of New Mexico the settler population was estimated to be about 200 individuals, consisting of Spaniards and *mestizos*.[47] In the following year of 1639, two figures of the general population of the Villa de Santa Fe were recorded, one indicating there were only thirty families living in the Villa de Santa Fe and the other accounting for fifty *vecino* households. In all it was estimated that there were about two hundred settlers who were described as a small number of people "in the presence of the enemy, with arms in hand, fighting continuously with the hostile heathen in defense of this new church and sustaining and guarding this kingdom for his Majesty."[48]

A census of the citizens of the Villa de Santa Fe and the outlaying settled areas of New Mexico was conducted in December 1644 by order of Governor Don Francisco de Argüello Carvajal.[49] To date, this census has not been located in any archive in Mexico or Spain. However, there is a contemporary list of settlements and the numbers of Indians living in forty-three Pueblo communities, as well as the number of Indians living in the Villa de Santa Fe. The first entry relates to the Villa de Santa Fe:

> The Villa de Santa Fe, the head of the said *Custodia*, where the governor and the Spaniards are assisted, [which] has a very good church in which is kept the Blessed Sacrament. Everything pertaining to divine worship is very complete and well arranged. It has a reasonable *convento* and 200 Indians under its administration capable of receiving sacraments.[50]

In regard to the geo-political landscape of New Mexico, each group of Pueblo Indians was a distinct community with its own customs, traditional constitution, language, and collective consciousness. Royal officials and Franciscan friars endeavored to bring these diverse tribes into permanent union as a single "kingdom" with common law and polity. For purposes of fiscal, judicial, and military administration, seventeenth-century New Mexico was divided into various jurisdictions commonly referred to as "*provincias*," provinces. By the mid-1600s seven jurisdictions formed the political geography of New Mexico with the Villa de Santa Fe serving as the center for royal government administration, the "*cabeza destas provincias*," "capital of these provinces," where the governor resided.[51]

Glimpses of People and Places

Elections for members of the municipal government, the *cabildo* (town council) of the Villa de Santa Fe, were held annually in early January of each year. Of the two *alcaldes ordinarios*, one was known as the *alcalde ordinario del primer voto* (first vote) and the other as the *alcalde ordinario del segundo voto* (second vote). These were the highest ranking town council positions. The other positions of the town council included two *regidores* (councilmen), the *alguacil mayor* (high sheriff), and the *escribano* (scribe/clerk). Men in these positions also took on the duties of *procurador general* and royal standard bearer. The town council met in the *sala del cabildo*, also known as the *sala de ayuntamiento*, the hall of the town council within the *casas de cabildo*, with main doors opening onto the plaza.[52]

Several families dominated the positions of the *cabildo de Santa Fe*. In particular, the Romero clan occupied as much as a fifth of the positions between the 1636 and 1680. Family names associated with this clan included Gómez Robledo, Guadalajara, Lucero de Godoy, and Salas. The Anaya Almazán and the Madrid families held various positions on the *cabildo* over several generations during the seventeenth century. A list of *cabildo* members and their positions from the year 1643 provides a brief example: Captain Mateo Romero, *alcalde ordinario*; Captain Francisco de Madrid, *alcalde ordinario*; Gaspar Pérez (a member of the Romero clan), *regidor* and *alguacil mayor*; Alvaro García Holgado, *regidor* and *procurador general*; Francisco de Anaya Almazán, *regidor*; Francisco Márquez, *regidor*; and Francisco [López] de Aragón, *escribano*.[53] These positions required literacy and an acumen for politics in addressing matters of justice, civic affairs, and military protection.

When an edict or decree was issued by the *cabildo* of the Villa de Santa Fe, it was given to one of the *pregoneros*, town criers, who posted copies of the documents on the doors of the *cabildo*, the doors of the *casas reales*, and the doors of the church. During the course of these posting, the *pregonero* proceeded to areas around the *plaza mayor*, shouting for people to gather, and he would read the decree in a loud voice for the public to hear. The *pregoneros* were generally Indians fluent and literate in the Castilian language. Only a few names of *pregoneros* are known, such as: Jusephe, *pregonero público* in 1641–1643; Antonio, an *Indio ladino* and a *pregonero* in 1643; Alonso Ramírez, *mulato* (part African and Indian), a *pregonero* in 1661; Juan Utaca, *Indio ladino*, a *pregonero* in 1662; and, Joseph, *Indio ladino*, a *pregonero público* in 1662.[54]

In October 1661, Governor Don Bernardo López de Mendizábal described Santa Fe as the only villa in New Mexico. He noted that the villa "consisted of only thirty-eight houses of adobe, inclusive of nine [houses] of widows."[55] Two of these houses belonged to *Sargento Mayor* Francisco Gómez Robledo, the eldest son of

Captain Francisco Gómez and doña Ana Robledo who inherited his father's large estate comprising of three estancias, one in the area of Taos Pueblo, one near San Juan Pueblo, and one at Las Barrancas south of the Pueblo of Isleta.[56] The house in which he lived he had bought for his sister. It consisted of "a living room (*sala*), three rooms, and a patio with its garden [or orchard] in the back."[57] The second house was that in which his mother lived, located "*de arriba*" ("just up") from the first house.[58]

Nicolás Durán, the younger, and his Apache wife, María, lived on the Durán family's Rancho Ribado, located along the banks of the Santa Fe River.[59] It appears María was raised in the household of Hernán Martín Serrano, who was himself part Spanish and part Tano Indian.[60] Martín Serrano operated an *obraje* in the villa, a textile manufacturing shop.[61] In all likelihood wool was the primary material woven into textile products such as stockings, pants and shirts by Indian employees. These items were either sold to local residents or sent by wagons for trade in towns of New Spain.

A number of goods produced in the Villa de Santa Fe and other parts of New Mexico found their way to homes and warehouses in the villa. In the early 1660s some of these products and their producers who resided in Santa Fe included: Antonio de la Serna, a shoemaker; Francisco Quasin, a leather jacket maker; Juan, a blacksmith who also made knives, latches, shackles and keys; and Juan Roche and José Lucas, wood gatherers.[62]

Some of residents of the Villa de Santa Fe stored goods in their own warehouses for commercial enterprise. Most of these people owned *estancias* and some were allowed to collect tribute from Pueblo Indians in the form of woven blankets and grain. Doña Ana Robledo, a widow living in Santa Fe owned a *bodega* (warehouse) in the villa where she stored a variety of goods, some for export to San José del Parral and Mexico City.[63] The governors also bought and sold items to local citizens and engaged in long-distance commerce through their own stores in the Villa de Santa Fe. Some of the merchandise sold in the store of Governor López de Mendizábal in 1661 included *chocolate* used for making a favorite drink of the time, packs of playing cards, bridles and spurs, taffeta cloth, ribbon, silver lace, and lace from Flanders.[64] These items catered to both men and women of the villa.

A *zapetería y coletaría* (shoe and leather jacket shop) also doubled as a *taverna pública* (public tavern).[65] It's not certain who owned this curious business, but in addition to selling shoes, leather jackets and pads, it also drew customers who came to drink sweetened *chocolate* and play cards while engaging in a variety of conversations. Trade merchandise was also stored at the *casas reales de palacio*, as was done in the late 1650s by the merchant Juan de Mestas, a native of Asturias, Spain. Mestas kept a supply of tablets of *chocolate*, loaves of sugar, men's and women's shoes, and yards of red *colonia* cloth in a room at the *casas reales*.[66] These items offer a sense of the type of merchandise that residents of the villa were most likely to purchase.

The *casas reales de palacio* served as the center of royal government in New Mexico and also as a center of commerce and military affairs. The parapets were a visible feature of the building as well as the tower, which fell to the ground by 1659. Public and church edicts often covered the main doors. The interior of the *casas reales* consisted of at least eighteen rooms around the mid-seventeenth century, each ranging in size according to function as indicated by the distinct terms that are found in the available historical records, such as *sala de recibimeinto* (receiving hall), *aposento donde estaba la mesa* (dining hall), *pieza de estrada* (drawing room), *aposento* (apartment chambers), *cuarto* (room), *pieza* (small room), *cuarto de cocina* (kitchen chamber), *capilla* (chapel), *alacena* (archive closet), *almacén* (storeroom), *carcel* (jail cell), harness room, and of course the governor's office.[67] In addition to the corridor within the building, a large corridor ran along the courtyard to the orchard or garden (*huerta*).

When Governor Don Bernardo López de Mendizábal took office in the Villa de Santa Fe in 1659 he found the *casas reales de palacio* in disrepair. He initiated major restoration work and construction of new rooms between July 1659 and October 1661. The man entrusted to conduct and lead this work was Juan Chamiso, an *Indio Méxicano* residing in the Villa de Santa Fe who was a master mason. Chamiso, working with several Tewa Indians, constructed a new chamber with several rooms and did restoration work on the interior and exterior corridors as well as the parapets and the fallen tower.[68]

Juan Chamiso, like other Indian residents of the Villa de Santa Fe, very likely lived in the *barrio de San Miguel*. This neighborhood was associated with the *hermita de San Miguel*, a small church for Indian parishioners of the villa that at one time was also part of the *hospital de San Miguel*, an infirmary operated by the Franciscan friars to help care for the sick.[69] Back in April 1640 when Fray Bartolomé Romero and a companion entered the Villa de Santa Fe they went straight to "the hospital of our Order under the title of San Miguel" where the Indians, mostly Mexican Indians, came out of the doors of the church of San Miguel to greet them on their safe arrival.[70]

It has been previously thought that Tlaxcalan Indians settled in the *barrio de San Miguel*. Seventeenth-century records relating to New Mexico do not indicate the presence of Tlaxcalans. Instead, an undetermined number of Mexican Indians from the Valley of Mexico made the lengthy journey to settle in New Mexico, mainly in the Villa de Santa Fe where most of the men worked as skilled tradesmen. In fact, Juan Chamiso, the master mason, still resided in the Villa de Santa Fe at the time of the Pueblo Indian uprising of August 1680. He managed to escape with a household of twenty members, including his wife, children, grandchildren and servants.⁷¹ Clearly, Chamiso's skills served him well between 1659 and 1680.

Religious ceremonies and traditions of the Catholic Church also shaped the daily lives of the residents of the Villa de Santa Fe in the seventeenth century. At mid-century, a procession of Franciscan friars and devout parishioners made its way around the plaza every Monday, Wednesday and Friday in line behind a large elevated crucifix of Jesus Christ.⁷² Numerous feast days of the liturgical calendar honored the memory of saints and deceased relatives and brought people together in solemnity, shared prayer, common devotion, and in some cases celebration. "*Las fiestas de Nuestra Señora de la Villa*" may have been the single most anticipated and widely celebrated event of the year, as mentioned in 1667.⁷³

Given that the patron saint of the *convento*, and presumably the church, was the *Limpia Concepción de Nuestra Señora*, the feast day on the liturgical calendar traditionally fell on December 8th of each year and was apparently celebrated over the course of several days in the villa. The "*cofradía de Nuestra Señora*" (confraternity of Our Lady), mentioned as early as 1641, may have been associated with this same devotion and with the image of *Nuestra Señora* brought to New Mexico by Fray Alonso de Benavides in the 1620s that is today known as *La Conquistadora, Nuestra Señora de la Paz*, whose chapel is within the modern-day Basilica of Saint Francis.⁷⁴

For many residents of the Villa de Santa Fe, faith and prayer brought solace and some measure of acceptance and tolerance of the hardships of frontier life in a land of war. Among these hardships were severe climate conditions. During the seventeenth century, the average annual temperature for the Villa de Santa Fe measured about 50 degrees Fahrenheit. In the summer months, high temperatures averaged 68 degrees and in the winter months the highs averaged 32 degrees.⁷⁵ The growing seasons consisted of about four to five months a year, and five years of drought conditions in the late 1630s affected the cultivation of various grains, principally corn and wheat, in addition to beans and squash.⁷⁶ Between the years of 1667 and 1672 extreme drought caused crop failures resulting in conditions of famine.⁷⁷

The increasing scarcity of food resources due to drought and the ensuing deaths from famine placed a strain on the social and economic relations between Pueblo Indians and Spanish residents. This social stress is one of the least studied factors underlying the erosion of the socio-political order of the previous seven decades resulting in the Pueblo Indian uprisings of the late 1660s and again in August 1680 in which the Villa de Santa Fe was sacked by Pueblo Indian warriors, forcing the residents to abandon their homes and flee for safety. The revolt splintered those Pueblo Indian and Spanish families that crossed cultural boundaries through intermarriage.

Thirteen years would pass before the broken bonds were reestablished.

During that time, the *cabildo* of the Villa de Santa Fe persevered in exile at El Paso del Río del Norte with the hope of someday returning to the physical location of their municipality. The citizens retained the continuity of Santa Fe's civic government despite exile. Tano and Tewa Indians occupied the villa until late December 1693 when Governor Don Diego de Vargas Zapata y Luján and some of the previous residents of the villa regained the town with the aid of Pueblo Indian allies.[78] Further negotiations with Pueblo Indians leaders such as Luis Tupatú, Domingo of Tesuque, Juan de Ye, Cristóbal de Yope, and Bartolomé de Ojeda led to securing the restoration of Spanish geo-political authority in New Mexico and once again the Villa de Santa Fe stood as the physical capital of a distant frontier realm of the Spanish Empire.

The advent of the eighteenth century saw peaceful and cooperative relations between Pueblo Indians and Spanish *vecinos* that created an enduring stability. Emigration of new settlers from communities such as Zacatecas, Fresnillo, Mexico City, and Puebla between 1693 and 1695 introduced additional families of diverse ethnic and regional origins as residents of the Villa de Santa Fe. During this period of re-forming the frontier society of the villa, the blending of new cultural influences engendered characteristics that redefined Santa Fe as a place.

Life experiences and culture are integral to sense of place. The fragments of historical information presented above are intended to augment the interpretation of the cultural history and historical geography of seventeenth-century Santa Fe, a period of time in Santa Fe's history that is least understood, but which is essential for understanding and appreciating the underlying unique characteristic of the personality of modern-day Santa Fe. In this respect, the influence of the physical setting and landscape in shaping experiences are vital considerations. Within the physical setting of the Villa de Santa Fe, each successive generation has further cultivated and modified a sense of place that has culminated in the identity of the modern City of Santa Fe as the "City Different."

5

The History of the Santa Fe Plaza
1610–1720
by
Stanley M. Hordes

In considering the historical development of the plaza of Santa Fe, it is difficult to refrain from imposing the present image of the square—manicured lawns, wrought iron benches, obelisk, gazebo, flocks of tourists, cameras clicking away—on the past. The romanticized image of the plaza and the Pueblo Revival facades on the buildings that surround it often get in the way of understanding the long transition that the plaza has undergone since the founding of Santa Fe in the first decade of the seventeenth century. I have undertaken what I call a first step in the examination of this long and complex historical evolution of the plaza and its relation to Santa Fe and its people over time, and to reconstruct the uses to which the plaza was put in its formative stages of development. Perhaps Santa Fe city planners will be able to utilize this, as well as future studies, in order to ascertain the true "historic" use of the plaza over the course of the past four centuries.

No attempt is made here to recount or analyze the general history of New Mexico, or even the history of Santa Fe, but rather how the events in that history have shaped the development of the plaza and it surrounding structures from 1610 to 1720. Undoubtedly research through yet undiscovered records will unearth information that will shed new light on Santa Fe's early years, and will alter my tentative conclusions.

In preparation, I first undertook a survey of the secondary literature, and followed with an analysis of the primary documentation. In considering the early years of Santa Fe's history, scholars have been frustrated by the absence of archival material relating to the period from 1610 to 1680. Since the Pueblo Revolt of 1680 resulted in the destruction of virtually all locally-generated documents produced during this period, historians have had to undertake a sketchy reconstruction of the pre-Revolt period based on correspondence from New Mexico received in Mexico and Spain, Inquisition records, and missionary accounts. The published efforts of these historians thus comprise the major source for my history of the plaza from 1610 to 1680. For the post-Revolt period, two major collections form the basis for the analysis presented here, the Spanish Archives of New Mexico (SANM), Series I, containing records relating to land and water issues, and Series II, consisting of administrative, military and judicial records, both housed at the New Mexico State Records Center in Santa Fe. Records from SANM I proved to be of inestimable assistance in reconstructing patterns of land ownership around the plaza, while the documents contained in SANM II helped to provide a human context for the study, putting meat on the bones of the skeletal land records.

My work here represents an updated and revised version of a section by the same title that appeared in an unpublished report prepared by the City of Santa Fe Planning Department edited by Linda Tigges in 1990.

The Founding of Santa Fe

From a physical perspective, perhaps the most obvious factor distinguishing the Spanish colonial enterprise in the Americas from that of the English and the French was the element of town planning. As the colonization of the Spanish Indies represented a government-sponsored endeavor to a much greater degree than the establishment of the English colonies of the east coast or the French settlements of the Mississippi River Valley, it is not surprising that Spanish colonial towns reflected a greater degree of planning and standardization than that of their northern European contemporaries. Formal standards for the establishment of towns, developed over centuries in Spain, and codified in numerous legal codes and regulations, served as theoretical basis for the laying out of Santa Fe, as well as for thousands of other communities in the New World over the course of the fifteenth through nineteenth centuries. While these standards were often changed to fit the exigencies of the local populace, as they were in Santa Fe, a brief examination of these standards will nevertheless be helpful in achieving a greater understanding of the establishment and development of the plaza of New Mexico's capital.

In 1573 King Phillip II of Spain issued the Reales Ordenanzas, a compilation of royal laws governing the Spanish possessions in the New World. For the most part, the Ordenanzas represented a codification of laws that had developed over the previous several centuries, adapted to fit the new physical and social environment in the Indies. The Ordenanzas mandated that towns be established on an elevated site, adjacent to good farming land, with adequate supplies of water, fuel and timber. "The plan of the place," the code continues, "with its squares, streets and building lots is to be outlined by means of measuring by cord and ruler, beginning with the main square from which streets are to run to the gates and principal roads, and leaving sufficient open space so that, even if the town grows, it can always spread in a symmetrical manner."

The hallmark of any Spanish colonial town was the plaza, the physical, as well as the social, cultural, and economic center of the settlement. The Ordenanzas specified that in each town, the plaza should be at least one and a half times as long as it was wide, in order to facilitate the celebration of fiestas. At a minimum, the plaza was to measure two hundred feet wide by three hundred feet long, and at a maximum, eight hundred by three hundred feet, with a recommended medium size of six hundred by four hundred feet. Eight streets were to run into the plaza, one each from the middle of each side, and two from each corner. Around the plaza, government buildings and shops were to be constructed, with private dwellings relegated to the streets leading to the plaza. The church was to be located some distance from the plaza, placed on an elevated site.[1]

Such was the theoretical formula that Pedro de Peralta carried with him when he began planning the Villa de Santa Fe in 1609 from his base at the former capital of New Mexico at San Gabriel. San Gabriel, located at the confluence of the Río Chama and Río Grande, near present day Española, had served as the capital of the new colony of New Mexico since 1600, when Juan de Oñate, founder of the first permanent colony and first governor of New Mexico, moved his headquarters across the Río Grande from the Indian Pueblo of San Juan de los Caballeros (also known as Ohkay Owingeh). Under the guidance of Oñate, the fledgling Spanish colony had not flourished. Failure to find sources of legendary mineral wealth, combined with only mixed success in winning the Indians over to Christianity, led to low morale among the colonists, and a lack of confidence in Oñate by the officials back in Mexico City, the administrative capital of the Viceroyalty of New Spain. The decision was almost made to abandon the colony, when reports of new missionary successes convinced the viceroy to give the effort another chance.

Early in 1609, Peralta was named governor of New Mexico, with instructions to re-establish the colony on sounder footing. Among Peralta's instructions from the viceroy was to relocate the capital. San Gabriel was considered too far north, too far from the center of Pueblo Indian population in the middle Rio Grande Valley. After scouting the region, Governor Peralta decided on Santa Fe, a small site settled at least two years earlier.[2] Santa Fe was close to a source of water, the Santa Fe River, with plentiful supplies of fuel and timber available in the nearby Sangre de Cristo Mountains. Moreover, the site was more easily defensible than San Gabriel, and, given the absence of Native American population in the area, the Spanish would not be competing for the same space and scarce natural resources as the Indians.[3]

By the spring of 1610, Governor Peralta had laid out the plan for the new Villa de Santa Fe. According to the instructions issued by the viceroy, he was to designate six *vecindades* (districts) and a square block for the *casas reales* (government buildings) and other public structures. The *casas reales*, according to the viceroy's wishes, should be designed to comprise arsenals, offices of royal officials, a jail, the offices and residence of the governor, and a chapel. Each of the residents was to be assigned two lots for a *casa y huertas* (house and gardens), two adjoining fields for vegetable gardens, and two others for vineyards and olive groves, four *caballerias* (ca. 421 acres) of additional land, together with water necessary for irrigation.

To the south of the plaza, across the river was the Barrio de Analco (Analco is the Nahuatl (Aztec) word for "on the other side"), which comprised the residences of the Mexican Indians who had accompanied Oñate on the original expedition to New Mexico. Serving the Barrio de Analco was the Chapel of San Miguel, on the site of the present San Miguel Church. To the south of this area were the *milpas* de San Miguel, irrigated by the Acequia Madre, cut from the Santa Fe River. On the eastern end of the plaza, a temporary church was built of *jacal* (mud mortar and posts), while the Franciscan prelate, Fray Alonso de Peinado, supervised the construction of a more durable structure. This church did not last but a few years, and Santa Feans found themselves worshiping in a building which doubled as a granary. By 1627 a permanent church finally had been raised, directed by Fray Alonso de Benavides. Commonly known as *la parroquia* (parish church), this structure was to last until the Pueblo Revolt of 1680. Although the exact shape and dimensions of *la parroquia* are not known, it is assumed that it was similar in design to its successor, built after the reconquest of Santa Fe from the Pueblos, or to the church constructed in the early seventeenth century at the Pueblo of Ácoma. It is known that this church did include a Capilla de Nuestra Señora (Chapel of Our Lady).[4]

The Santa Fe Plaza, 1610–1680

Despite the theoretical mandates of the Reales Ordenanzas of 1583 prescribing how a "standard" Spanish colonial town should be laid out, and despite the precise instructions given to Governor Peralta in 1609 regarding the requisite platting of Santa Fe, one can only speculate as to whether these specifications were ever actually implemented. As the Pueblo Revolt of 1680 resulted in the destruction of virtually every locally generated scrap of paper documenting everyday life in New Mexico, any physical description of the plaza between 1610 and 1680 has to be pieced together from only fragmentary evidence based on correspondence sent to

Mexico and Spain, post-reconquest recollections, and scanty archaeological evidence.

Most of the speculation has focused on the size of the plaza itself. Archaeologist Bruce T. Ellis suggested that the plaza originally was four times its present size, extending from Lincoln Avenue to the Cathedral, and from Palace Avenue to just a few feet north of Water Street, where the Río Chiquito once flowed. Ellis based his hypothesis on the assumption that Peralta would not have designed a plaza on the minimum size decreed—a mere 274 by 183 feet—and in fact seems to have opted for the maximum, at least in length." To further support this idea, Ellis cited documents relating to the construction of the church and *convento* in 1697, and several land transfers around the turn of the eighteenth century. The Ellis hypothesis was shared both by archaeologists David H. Snow and Cordelia Thomas Snow, based largely on the 1573 Reales Ordenanzas and the 1609 instructions to Peralta.[5]

That the plaza originally extended farther to the east than its present dimensions is beyond dispute. The idea that the elongated plaza pictured in the Urrútia Map of 1768 was in place a century and a half earlier is supported by land transfer documents of the immediate post-reconquest period, as well as by the opinions of most historians who have investigated the matter.[6] Whether Governor Peralta created a plaza that extended southward to the Río Chiquito, however, is less certain. A series of land transfer records in the plaza area from 1696 to 1707 suggests strongly that colonists maintained their houses and gardens on lots between the plaza and the Río Chiquito, at least in the later years of the pre-Revolt period.

In 1699, Governor Diego de Vargas granted a *merced* (land grant) to Ysabel Jorge de Bela, "on the southern side of the plaza, running to the [Santa Fe] river, which serves as the [southern] boundary...." By 1707, Jorge decided to divide her land into two parcels, north and south, with the Río Chiquito as the dividing point. The northern portion, comprising "a small house and lands for a garden," was bounded by the plaza on the north "... [and] the Río Chiquito on the south," thus clearly indicating that the plaza did not extend as far as the Río Chiquito after Vargas's reconquest of Santa Fe. But in her petition to the governor for the property in 1696, Jorge indicated that the property had belonged to her grandfather, Antonio Baca, prior to the Revolt. It is known that Baca was living in Santa Fe as early as 1628, serving as capitan in the army, living with his wife, Yumar Pérez de Bustillo, and three daughters. Unfortunately for Baca, he found himself on the losing side of a dispute between civil officials and Franciscan friars, and he was beheaded for conspiring to murder Governor Luis de Rosas in 1643. It is presumed that Baca's widow and children continued to occupy the property from 1643 until the Pueblo Revolt of 1680. If Baca and his family maintained their household on the lot regranted to Ysabel Jorge de Bela in 1699, then the assumption that the plaza extended southward to present day Water Street is thrown into question.[7]

The fact that Governor Peralta did not follow the Reales Ordenanzas of 1573, or even the more precise instructions issued him by the viceroy, should not be considered as surprising or exceptional. Far from being unusual, it was common, even expected, for viceregal officials in remote frontier areas to interpret their instructions loosely, in order to adapt them to fit unique local circumstances.[8] In fact, other Spanish colonial centers deviated from the model presented by the Ordenanzas, including San Agustín in Florida, and San Antonio, Texas, whose elongated plaza appeared to be almost identical to that of Santa Fe.[9]

The Plaza During the Pueblo Revolt of 1680

Severe jurisdictional problems between religious and civil officials, which had been brewing for most of the seventeenth century, combined with burdensome demands for tribute and labor placed on the Pueblo Indians by the Spanish, to lay the groundwork for a period of unrest among the Pueblos by the late 1670s. Unusual drought conditions and a resulting famine brought the conflict between Pueblo and Spanish to a head, resulting in the Pueblo Revolt of August 1680. Although the Revolt had widespread support among almost all the Puebloan groups in New Mexico, the spark for the outbreak emanated from the north with the principal leadership provided by Popé, from the Pueblo of San Juan (Ohkay Owingeh).

In Santa Fe, Governor Antonio de Otermín first received word of a widespread revolt on August 9. The following day, Otermín ordered all residents of the *villa* and its environs to assemble in the *casas reales* for protection, and in order to mount a more effective defense. On the thirteenth, all survivors from the outlying areas were instructed to abandon their homes and join those already assembled, swelling the number within the town to approximately one thousand. By this time, conditions were considered so desperate that it was deemed prudent for the priest to collect the sacred objects from the church and bring them to the *casas reales*. By the fifteenth, Santa Fe found itself under siege. Otermín summoned the leader of the attacking forces from the *milpas* de San Miguel, and met him on the plaza, unsuccessfully attempting to negotiate an end to the hostilities. Over the course of the next few days, the Indians set fire to the church and many of the houses surrounding the *casas reales*. The final blow to the chances of the Spanish withstanding the siege came when the attackers closed off the *acequia*, thus cutting off the precious supply of water to the colonists.

Realizing that he had no choice other than to launch a counter-attack, Otermín took the invaders by surprise on the morning of the twentieth, killing three hundred, and routing or capturing the rest. Despite this temporary victory, Otermín realized that his situation was untenable. Without food or housing, and aware that the Pueblos would soon regroup to resume the offensive, the decision was made to abandon Santa Fe and retreat southward. It would be another thirteen years before Spanish would reclaim the *villa* and repopulate the plaza.[10]

Cordelia Thomas Snow contended that on the basis of the documentation deriving from the period of the siege of Santa Fe by the Pueblos, it would have been impossible for one thousand refugees and several thousand head of cattle to have been housed within the confines of what is traditionally considered as the *casas reales*, limited to the buildings on the north side of the plaza. The area actually under siege, Snow contended, comprised not only the complex that presently consists of the Palace of the Governors, but the entire plaza and all the buildings that surround it. Extending the argument, Snow claimed that all the buildings around the plaza in the pre-Revolt period were part of the *casas reales* complex, leaving the clear implication that private residences were relegated to the area outside the plaza area.[11]

This hypothesis, intriguing as it is, depends on certain questionable assumptions: (1) that the plaza extended as far south as the Río Chiquito; (2) that no residences could be documented on the plaza during the pre-Revolt period; (3) that the Camino Real entered the plaza from the south in the area of present-day Shelby Street; and (4) that the military chapel would have been located at the south or west side of the plaza. The first two assumptions have already been challenged by the documentation of the pre-Revolt occupation of lands along that plaza by Antonio Baca and his descendants (see above). With regard to the placement of the Camino Real, it is far more likely that the highway from Mexico City followed the Santa Fe River from La Cienega and Agua Fría, and entered Santa Fe from the west, along what later came to be known as the Calle Real, and still later, Calle de San Francisco. Lastly, rather than be placed at the south or west side of the plaza, it would have been more likely for the tower to be located at the south or west side of the *presidio*, not at the present site of La Fonda, but at the corner of the Palace of the Governors. Thus, without more compelling evidence to the contrary, it is most likely that the casas reales occupied the position more or less on the site of the present Palace of the Governors, on the north side of the plaza.[12]

The Plaza During the Pueblo Occupation of Santa Fe, 1680–1692

As was the case with the period from 1610 to 1680, very little is known about the physical development of Santa Fe and its plaza during the twelve-year span between the Pueblo Revolt of 1680 and the initial reconquest of Santa Fe by Diego de Vargas in 1692. Accounts emanating from the reconquest and reoccupation efforts by Vargas's troops provide a brief glimpse of the plaza area as it was adapted by the Pueblos for their use. These accounts indicate that there were four large living quarters surrounding the plaza, varying in height from one to four stories.[13]

The Indians had "remodeled" the *palacio real/casas reales* complex to suit their needs. It must be remembered that in the seventeenth century this complex probably extended from the plaza northward to Federal Place, and could accommodate the some fifteen hundred Pueblo residents who were found living there in 1692. The complex included two patios, a large one on the west side, and the other on the east, behind the chapel, the Hermita de Nuestra Señora, and was surrounded by a high wall, which also served as the outside wall for the buildings. Four towers were built at the corners of the fortress, with only one entrance leading into the interior. The Indians had divided the plaza into two sections, with one kiva in each. Water was supplied by an *acequia* whose source was apparently in the *cienega*, or marshes, located to the east, and ran by the *casas reales*. This was the same *acequia* that the Pueblos had cut off from the Spanish in 1680 during the siege of Santa Fe.[14]

The Plaza During the Reconquest of Santa Fe, 1692–1693

After several unsuccessful attempts by the Spanish to recapture New Mexico from their base in El Paso through the 1680s, Diego de Vargas was named governor of New Mexico in 1691, charged with the task of defeating the Pueblos. The following year Vargas led a detachment of fifty troops, matched by fifty Indian allies and two Franciscan friars, northward in the hopes of retaking Santa Fe. They arrived at the walls of the *villa* on September 13, 1692. Several tense hours of negotiation ensued. Threats were exchanged, and the Spanish cut off access to the acequia that supplied water to the stronghold that had formerly served as the *casas reales/real palacio* complex. Finally the leaders of the Pueblos descended from the fortress to meet with Vargas in the plaza to discuss peace terms. The governor received them with overt gestures of kindness, signaling his conciliatory intentions to the other Indians. From his position in the plaza, he instructed the Pueblos to hang crosses around their necks and to erect a large cross in the middle of the patio in the complex.[15]

Later that day, Vargas and his troops set up their encampment "at the foot of the mountain, an arquebus shot from the plaza," probably at the base of Fort Marcy hill. Vargas then designated the *plaza de armas*, for the purpose of "holding audience to listen to and receive the rebel nations of the surrounding pueblos and provinces of this district and kingdom in peace." The next day the governor, dressed in his most splendid attire, boldly entered the fortress on horseback. He dismounted and kissed the cross that the Indians had erected. From the patio in the former *casas reales* complex, Governor Vargas raised the royal standard three times, and formally proclaimed possession of Santa Fe for the King Carlos II of Spain. Thus ended the bloodless phase of the conquest of the capital of New Mexico.[16]

The succeeding four years would witness a return to the hostility and violence that characterized relations between Spaniard and Pueblo a dozen years earlier. With the return of Vargas and a small colonizing expedition in the early winter of 1693, the plaza and *casas reales* complex-turned-Pueblo fortress once more served as the focal point of the conflict. The expedition left El Paso in October, arriving much too late to sow crops, but just in time to be greeted by snow and bitter cold. While a handful of Spanish were able to establish their residence within the fortress, most of the seventy families of colonists camped on the outskirts of town, ill prepared to face the onslaught of winter, with inadequate shelter and not much food. By mid-December, twenty-two Spanish had died, and the survivors were clamoring for entrance into the fortress. The Pueblos, however, had no intention of vacating peacefully. Hardening their position, they expelled the few Spanish residents and prepared for the inevitable attack.

On the 29th, Vargas' troops, supported by allies from Pecos Pueblo, began their assault on the Pueblo stronghold. After two days of pitched battle, the *casas reales* were taken, the Spanish troops first capturing one patio, and the next day the other. The Pueblos lost eighty-one warriors, killed in battle, executed, or having taken their own lives. The Spanish suffered only one fatal casualty. The complex conquered by Vargas's troops was so extensive that it took fifty soldiers almost an entire day to inspect and prepare an inventory of all the roomblocks. It was hardly "bloodless," but by New Years Day 1694, Santa Fe was finally captured, and the Spanish could now set about the task of rebuilding the capital.[17]

Reconstruction of the Plaza, 1693–1698

Although the rebellion among the Pueblos was far from over—major outbreaks against Spanish authority continued through 1696—Santa Fe was finally, and permanently, at peace. Colonists began putting the pieces back together, continuing where they and others had left off thirteen years earlier. Life was far from easy. New contingents of colonists arrived from farther south, some continuing on to found the new Villa de Santa Cruz de la Cañada, located immediately to the east of present-day Española, and others settling in the capital. By 1695 Santa Fe's Spanish population had reached over twelve hundred, comprising native New Mexicans returning to their old homes after their period of exile in El Paso, as well as new settlers from Mexico City and the mining areas of Zacatecas and Sombrerete.[18]

The effort of resettlement and reconstruction was hampered greatly by a lack of sufficient provisions for the colony. During the winter of 1695–1696, Santa Fe suffered famine and severe epidemics, in which several hundred settlers perished. For want of food, people were reduced to eating horses, dogs, and toasted hides. To make matters worse, rumors were rampant that the northern Pueblos had rebelled, and would again threaten the capital. Two years later it was alleged that Governor Vargas had been responsible for all these troubles, in that he had hoarded 2,400 *fanegas* (ca. 3,750 bushels) of corn that were supposed to have been distributed to the colonists, a charge of which he was ultimately found innocent.[19]

Given the overcrowded conditions in the *villa*, the lack of adequate housing, and the state of war that still existed between Pueblos and Spanish, Santa Fe had more of an appearance of a military base than a residential community. During the rebuilding effort, many of the newly-arrived settlers were assigned temporary quarters in the old Pueblo residences along the plaza, pending application and processing of royal grants for land to be distributed by the governor.[20] While land records pertaining to Santa Fe during the period are far from complete or comprehensive, it is clear that as early as 1695, colonists were being granted lands surrounding the plaza. While for some, these grants represented new assignments, for others they were confirming lands occupied by them or their families before the Revolt.

The last half of the 1690s witnessed the initial resettlement of the plaza area. On the western portion of the north side of the elongated plaza stood the *casas reales*, alternately known as the *real palacio, castilla presidial* and *real presidio*. Directly to the east of the *casas reales*, across the road that led to the *cienegilla de Tesuque* (presently Washington Avenue), were the house and fields of Diego Árias de Quirós. Árias, in addition to possessing title to 1.2 acres of agricultural land stretching to the north and east of the plaza, bears the distinction of being the most sued individual in Santa Fe in the years following the reconquest. Árias claimed title to the land based on a grant issued by Governor Vargas in 1697, but faced lawsuits by María and Juana Griego in 1703, Diego Trujillo and Antonia Bas Gonzales the same year, and by Bas Gonzales alone in 1704. Despite the fact that all of the plaintiffs presented seemingly credible evidence in support of their claims, the authorities ruled in Árias's behalf in each case. Undoubtedly, his cause was helped by his position as *alferez* (ensign) in Vargas's campaigns against the rebellious Pueblos in the period from 1692 to 1696.[21]

On the east side of the plaza stood the Franciscan *convento*, constructed in 1697, under the sponsorship of Governor Pedro Rodríguez Cubero, who had taken over from Vargas earlier that year. Before construction began, it was necessary to remove several residents who had already constructed their homes facing the plaza. The *convento* measured approximately 121 square feet, and was placed roughly just to the west of the ruins of the pre-Revolt *parroquia*. Vargas had vowed to reconstruct the parish church back in 1693, but was unable to do so during his administration. In years immediately following the reconquest, the faithful worshiped in the chapel that was located in the southeast corner of the *casas reales*. The church would not be built until 1717, immediately to the north of, and adjoining the *convento*, approximately on the site of the present Cathedral.[22]

The south side of the plaza began to be populated in the early years as well. As cited earlier, Ysabel Jorge de Bela, granddaughter of pre-Revolt settler Capitan Antonio Baca, petitioned Vargas for her ancestral lot between the plaza and the Río Chiquito in 1696. Next to her lot were the house and gardens of Juana Domínguez, who had been rescued from Indian captivity in 1692 with her five children. She was possibly the daughter of prominent pre-Revolt colonist Tomé or Antonio Domínguez de Mendoza.[23] Also found living on the plaza were: Capitan Diego de Medina and his wife, María Zapata Telles Jirón, and children Ramón and Josepha; Francisco Rodríguez Cubero, who came to New Mexico as a soldier in the retinue of Governor Rodríguez Cubero in 1698, and his wife, Gerónima Baca; and Sebastián Rodríguez, the black drummer and *pregonero* (town crier) in the administration of Governor Vargas, who lived on the plaza with his first wife, Isabel Olguín, and second wife, Juana de la Cruz, or Apodaca, and children Melchor and Esteban.[24]

Another resident of the plaza in the immediate post-reconquest years managed to achieve more notoriety than most of his neighbors. Agustin Sáez was a second generation New Mexican, driven out by the Revolt and enticed to join Vargas's reconquest effort in 1693. He was one of the people that was forced to flee the *casas reales* complex just before Vargas's troops stormed it in late December of 1693. After the successful retaking of the fortress, Sáez, his wife, Antonia Márquez, and daughter took up residence in a two-story structure within the complex. The family lived on the upper floor, above a warehouse belonging to Governor Vargas, fronting on the *plazuela de adentro*, one of the interior patios described above. In 1701 Sáez was convicted of adultery with Luisa Varela. During the trial, it was brought out that in 1694 he had stolen a considerable amount of soap and chiles from the warehouse that Vargas had established for the supply of his soldiers, apparently climbing down through a trap door at night to access the supplies. He was also accused of having stolen coconuts decorated with silver, and a quantity of *caxetas de dulce* (sweet caramel candies) from Vargas's residence. According to testimony, Sáez climbed through a small window on the north side of Vargas's house, which also was a two-story structure. For his adulterous behavior, Sáez was sentenced to live with his wife as a good and faithful husband, and fined forty pesos.[25]

Stability and Growth in the Plaza Area, 1698–1720

Through the first two decades of the eighteenth century, Santa Fe continued to grow along with the rest of Spanish New Mexico. In order to ensure greater stability for the colony, Governor Vargas and his successors issued land grants to entice new settlers to the region, and founded new towns to provide for a more effective defense against Indian attacks. Bernalillo was founded in 1695, as was Santa Cruz de la Cañada, and Albuquerque in 1706. Santa Fe participated in this growth as well. With the end of the troubles with the Pueblos, and the capital once more on a sound economic footing, the *villa* could resume a normal life.

Normality, however, did not infer total security from attack from what the Spanish labeled the *indios bárbaros*, the Apaches, Navajos and other hostile nomadic Indians of the plains. In 1705 Governor Francisco Cuervo y Valdes issued an order for all settlers of Santa Fe to build their "gardens, corrals and houses" around the plaza for greater security and mutual defense. The governor was concerned that colonists living down along the Santa Fe River near their farmlands would be vulnerable targets for Indian attacks, and through his proclamation he sought to establish a more effective stronghold. Those who did not comply were subject to having their grant annulled, and their property confiscated.[26] But to be sure, the plaza area could not have housed the over one thousand residents of the *villa* comfortably. Moreover, being an independent sort of people, most of the settlers felt it in their best interest to maintain the dispersed nature of their farmsteads, the governor's edict notwithstanding. A review of the land transactions located a distance from the plaza area in the early years of the eighteenth century, combined with a glance of the 1768 Urrútia map, demonstrates clearly the preference of Santa Feans to live away from the center of town, closer to their fields, herds, and flocks.

Over the course of the period from 1695 to 1720, the plaza slowly took on definition, with more residences constructed along the south and west sides. In order to gain a more accurate picture of the plaza, it must be pointed out that houses generally tended to be rather small, consisting of one living room, perhaps a bedroom, and a kitchen, surrounded by a small plot of land for use as a garden.[27] There were, of course exceptions to this rule, for example the comparatively palatial home of Capitan Nicolás Ortiz Niño Ladrón de Guevara, located on the south side of the plaza across from the church. Ortiz's residence comprised an entrance hall, parlor, bedroom, kitchen, and two additional rooms.[28] So too did the street pattern around the plaza become better defined, a pattern that has changed very little from the early eighteenth century down to the present. The major street in Santa Fe was the Calle Real, sometimes referred to as Calle Real de San Francisco, later as the Calle Principal, and today as San Francisco Street. Leading from the church, past the south end of the plaza to the west, the Calle Real became the Camino Real, linking Santa Fe with the communities of Río Abajo, El Paso, Chihuahua, and ultimately Mexico City.[29] To dispel any impression that the Calle Real had comprised a broad boulevard, it should be pointed out that in 1715 it was remarked that Félix Martínez had allowed his fields to encroach on the street to the west of the plaza, leaving a trail through which only a horse could pass. Moreover, Martínez had dug a pit to make his adobes right square in the middle of the right of way.³⁰

Bisecting the southern end of the plaza, and descending to the Santa Fe River, was the Camino Real a Pecos, now Shelby Street. Leading from the middle of the plaza to the north, the site of present-day Washington Avenue, was the Camino a la Cienegilla de Tesuque. Complaints similar to the one cited above with regard to the Calle Real were also noted about this road, which in 1715 was blocked by the fields of Diego de Veitia and Juana Apodaca. Leading north from the northwest corner of the plaza was the Camino a Tesuque, where Lincoln Avenue runs today.³¹

No evidence appears in the documentary record of Palace Avenue extending eastward or westward from the *casas reales*. It seems, rather, that the *acequia madre* ran in the area of present-day Palace Avenue from the *cienega* located in the area around what is today the Coronado Building and La Villa Rivera, westward through the *casas reales* complex, and thence slightly southwestward. This *acequia* apparently was the same that the Pueblos had cut off from the Spanish ensconced in the *casas reales* in 1680, and that Vargas's troops cut off from the Pueblos in 1693.³²

While new residential construction proceeded apace around the plaza, improvements to the *casas reales* complex appear to have lagged far behind. In 1697 Governor Vargas was not only replaced, but arrested by his successor, Pedro Rodríguez Cubero, for malfeasance in office. By 1703, Vargas had proven his innocence and regained the governorship. Upon his return, Vargas noted, perhaps with self-serving motives, that Rodríguez Cubero had let the defensive infrastructure of Santa Fe deteriorate to an unacceptable level.³³ Vargas died the following year without having the opportunity to implement the improvements that he sought. By 1708 the *palacio real* apparently had deteriorated to such an extent that Governor Marqués de Peñuela formulated plans to demolish the complex. It is uncertain how far these plans were able to proceed, but in July of that year, the viceroy expressed serious doubts of the wisdom of the move and demanded a report justifying the governor's action.³⁴

If the Marqués accomplished any improvement in the condition of the *casas reales*, it certainly did not show a few years later, when Governor Félix Martínez ordered that a report be prepared as to the status of the complex when it was handed over to him by his predecessor, Juan Ygnacio Flores Mogollón in 1715. To say that the palacio had seen better days would have been an understatement. The inspectors reported that the structure would have completely collapsed if it had not been for the nine buttresses supporting it. The only serviceable space consisted of one large room with high ceilings and a room that served as a chapel for the soldiers, which faced the plaza, no doubt the *capilla* on the southeast corner of the complex.

Governor Martínez' report contains more interesting details regarding the makeup of the *palacio*. The main entrance was on the south side, on the plaza. The passageway led to one of the patios, and to a coach house, which consisted of a two-story structure. Adjacent to the coach house was a chopping block and a dovecote. At the front corners stood two dilapidated adobe *torreones*, one of which served as an arsenal, filled with stores of gunpowder. Because of its obvious importance, Martínez ordered that the old door to the latter *torreon* be replaced with a more secure one. In one of the patios was a dry well, about four *varas* (ca. twelve feet) wide and forty *varas* (ca. 120 feet) deep. The complex included five broken benches, six chairs, two tables, two bedsteads, and one bruised and battered copper kettle. On the east side of the *palacio* was located a corral, surrounded by crumbling walls.[35]

Further architectural details regarding the *palacio* can be gleaned from a 1720 criminal trial against one Ysidro Sánchez for having stolen large quantities of clothes from the royal storehouse within the *casas reales*. According to Sánchez's confession, he was walking along the plaza one summer evening when he noticed the open balcony of the *palacio*, and "he was deceived by the Devil with the evil idea of climbing up the balcony." Using one of the posts as a ladder, Sánchez entered the storehouse through an open window and helped himself to as many clothes as he could carry. He stored his cache behind some vigas on the plaza, in hopes of reclaiming his booty at a later time. The next morning, however, some children kicked or threw a ball among the vigas, discovered the bundle, and reported the find to the authorities.[36]

Sánchez, together with dozens of other accused criminals, were housed at the *cuerpo de guardia* (guardhouse), within the *casas reales*, after their arrest. In at least two cases where women were arrested, they were placed either in the *casas de cabildo* or *casas del ayunatmiento* (building of the town council), or in the house of a soldier, since it was acknowledged that no jail for women existed in the *villa*.[37] The location of the *casas del cabildo* remains a mystery. The only reference that surfaces from the contemporary documentation is contained in the proclamation of September 16, 1712 by town council declaring September 14 as the day to formally commemorate and celebrate as a fiesta the reconquest of New Mexico by Diego de Vargas. The day that the proclamation was issued, the council had to meet in the house of Lieutenant Governor Juan Páez Hurtado, since the *casas del ayuntamiento* were damaged from the incessant rains that had occurred for the previous three days.[38]

The plaza area was the scene of several interesting events surrounding nasty disputes among neighbors in Santa Fe during these years. One particularly colorful case involved the murder of a soldier, Miguel de Herrera by Diego de Velasco, a one-legged master carpenter. One winter day, some of Herrera's cattle found their way onto Velasco's property. When the carpenter implored Herrera to kindly remove his animals, Herrera became enraged, calling him a "*cabrón cornudo, consentidón de su mujer*"—a rather descriptive epithet suggesting that Velasco's wife was engaging in sexual misconduct with his knowledge—and threatening that he was going to knock his horns off with a club. A fight ensued, in which Herrera was knocked down and killed. The carpenter made his way as fast as his one good leg could carry him to the Franciscan *convento* on the plaza, where he sought and received sanctuary from persecution. There he stayed for over a year, resisting persistent efforts by the alcalde to arrest him. Velasco ultimately surrendered himself to the authorities, and stood trial for murder. Although he was convicted, his sentence was relatively light, due in part to the nature of the provocation, but more to the fact that he was the only master carpenter in all New Mexico, and his services could not be spared. He was sentenced to say twenty-five masses for the soul of the deceased, and to perform several acts of community service utilizing his skills, including making a millstone and helping with the construction of the parish church.[39]

Another neighborly dispute that turned violent did not involve any residents of the plaza, but is illustrative perhaps of how some citizens coped with the problem of keeping neighbors off their property. Disturbed over the constant trampling of his yard by his next-door neighbor, Joseph Domínguez asked his fifteen-year-old son Manuel to plant some *nopales espinosos* (cactus) as a fence designed to keep trespassers out of his yard. Out came neighbor Catalina de Villalpando, about to track through Domínguez' property. Advised by young Domínguez that his yard was not a road, and asked to stop using it as such, Villalpando angrily started uprooting the cactus Domínguez had just finished planting. He shoved her, and she responded by throwing a barrage of rocks at him causing no small injury, an action for which she was arrested and tried.[40]

For all information pertaining to life around the plaza, very little data emerge shedding light on the use of the plaza itself during the period in question. Undoubtedly the plaza was utilized for mustering of troops and for the celebrations of fiestas, and possibly for growing of crops and corralling of livestock. The lone document detailing an occurrence that took place on the plaza involved an incident where Ana María Romero had the audacity to insult a prominent couple by calling the wife a *puta* (whore) in the presence of her husband. For this indiscretion, Romero was sentenced to exile for two years to Albuquerque. But before she left she was ordered to be paraded around the plaza and public streets on a horse, with a gag in her mouth, naked from the waist up—in January![41]

Santa Fe's first century was not an easy or tranquil one. Plagued by civil conflict between governors and friars, disrupted by the bloody Pueblo Revolt, suffering through bitter cold and food shortages during, and immediately after the

Reconquest, and enduring the growing pains of reestablishing a new town constantly under the threat of Indian attacks, the townspeople developed a certain toughness that would allow them to persevere in the face of adversity in the years to come.

As has been demonstrated, Santa Fe's growth and development did not exactly proceed according to plan. Despite the stipulations of the Reales Ordenanzas of 1573, and the instructions issued by the viceroy to Governor Pedro de Peralta in 1609, the new *villa* grew according to its own unique needs and agenda. The size and shape of the plaza appears to have diverged significantly from the standard pattern, taking on a narrower, rectangular configuration rather that the larger, more symmetrical model. The Pueblo Revolt exposed significant flaws in the design of the defensive infrastructure of the colony, problems that viceregal administrators attempted to remedy after the reconquest of Santa Fe in 1692–1693. Yet even after the painful lesson of the Revolt, the colonists still appeared to be reluctant to change their ways. Twenty years after wresting control of the *casas reales/real palacio* from the Pueblos, the defensive complex was still in shambles. Disregarding the orders of the viceroy, Santa Feans still displayed a dispersed settlement pattern, preferring to live a distance away from the plaza area, where they could be close to their fields and livestock.

Yet despite these problems, if Santa Fe did not thrive in the seventeenth and early eighteenth century, it did survive. While the density and character of the structures around the plaza have changed over the four centuries since the reestablishment of the *villa*, the essential pattern has remained surprisingly intact. Structures gradually filled in the eastern side of the plaza, but the Palace of the Governors, albeit greatly reduced in size from the original *casas reales* complex, still graces the north side, and *la parroquia*, with the Saint Francis Cathedral encapsulating it, still dominates the area on the east. Most significantly, the street pattern remains largely unchanged, with San Francisco Street representing a true *calle principal* or *calle real*, taking travelers to the highway to Albuquerque; Shelby Street still heading to Pecos; and both Lincoln and Washington Avenues still leading to Tesuque and points north.

Continuity is represented in other ways as well. While no one is using San Francisco Street as an adobe pit today, the issue of how wide city streets should be is still a controversial issue, much as it was in the early 1700s. Neighbors still sometimes resort to violence to settle their differences, occasionally resulting in the tragic loss of life. But, while prominent civic leaders still endure the insults of their fellow citizens, no one in recent memory has been forced to parade half naked around the plaza.

The documentary record is sketchy with regard to the actual public use of Santa Fe's plaza. It is assumed that it was utilized for the mustering and parading of troops, and for public fiestas. The plaza was the site of final negotiations for the capitulation of the *casas reales* by the Pueblos to Governor Diego de Vargas in December of 1693, as well as for the annual fiesta to commemorate Vargas's recapture of the town. It was from the plaza that the Devil seized Ysidro Sánchez that summer night in 1720 and compelled him to scale the balcony of the *palacio real* and raid the royal storehouses, and where his cache was discovered by children playing ball. The plaza also served as the place designated for the public humiliation of Ana María Romero after she had insulted a prominent Santa Fe couple.

It is hoped that in the continuation of this study through the eighteenth and early nineteenth centuries, additional primary documents will emerge that will offer a more complete and comprehensive picture of the historical use of the plaza and its surrounding structures. By examining and analyzing this documentation, and placing it in the larger context of the history of Santa Fe and New Mexico, planners and citizens will have a deeper understanding of the city's rich and diverse past, and they will be better able to make informed decisions about its future.

The author would like to acknowledge the contributions of several individuals who aided greatly in the preparation of this chapter. Karen Peterson assisted in the early stages of the research into land occupation patterns. Philip Davis and Dr. Meredith Dodge also served as research assistants, seeking out information from indices and primary documentation relating to social patterns in the seventeenth and eighteenth centuries. Special thanks are offered to Cordelia Thomas Snow, whose insightful and provocative hypotheses developed from her archaeological work proved extremely helpful in the formulation of the many of the conclusions contained in this report. The author would also like to acknowledge the efforts of the archival staff at the New Mexico State Records Center and Archives. Finally thanks are offered to Linda Tigges, former Deputy Planning Director for the City of Santa Fe for recognizing the importance of historical perspective in the planning process.

Central Plaza, Santa Fe. Illustration from *Illustrated New Mexico*, 1885 by W. G. Ritch.

6

A Window to the Past
The San Miguel and La Conquistadora Chapels and Their Builders, 1610–1776
by
Cordelia Thomas Snow

In 2008, Patrick Taylor, Senior Program Manager at Cornerstones Community Partnerships, Santa Fe, undertook a preliminary architectural assessment of San Miguel Chapel in Santa Fe to determine the overall condition of the building and the extent of structural damage to the chapel from runoff drains that undercut the southwest corner of the building. Upon completion of a visual assessment of the interior of the chapel, Mr. Taylor called to report that even though carved designs on the wood bond beams were slightly different, the designs on the carved corbels at San Miguel appeared to be identical to those in La Conquistadora Chapel in the Basilica of Saint Francis in downtown Santa Fe. Taylor also noted that the designs on some of the woodwork in the Santa Fe chapels appeared to be similar to that at Nuestra Señora de Guadalupe in present Ciudad Juárez, Mexico, formerly El Paso del Norte, even though N. S. de Guadalupe is more than forty years older than either San Miguel or La Conquistadora Chapels.

Unfortunately, funds were not currently available to do a detailed study of the woodwork in San Miguel or La Conquistadora chapels, or to compare the woodwork in those chapels to that at Our Lady of Guadalupe in Juárez; however, lack of funding does not preclude a preliminary study of the individuals responsible for restoration and/or construction of the buildings in the early 18th century.

When the Villa de Santa Fe was formally founded in 1610 under the direction of Governor Pedro de Peralta, the villa was divided into two barrios or neighborhoods. One was the Barrio de San Francisco on the north side of the Santa Fe River, and the other was Barrio de Analco on the south side of the River. Because the Ordinances of 1573, later known as the Laws of the Indies, forbade Spaniards and Indians from living together, the parroquia, or parish church, dedicated to Saint Francis served the Spaniards who lived north of the river, while San Miguel served the Mexican and local Indian slaves and servants of the Spaniards who lived in the Barrio de Analco south of the river. Both the parroquia and San Miguel were burned during the Pueblo Revolt of 1680, however, at some point during the absence of the Spaniards, the parish church in Santa Fe was razed and the area of the church used for planting corn. Comparatively speaking San Miguel suffered relatively little damage, eventually needing only repairs to the walls and a new roof to be serviceable.

Many years ago, George Kubler published an account of the 1710 restoration of San Miguel Chapel that had been found by A. von Wuthanau in the Ritch Collection at the Huntington Library.[1] This extraordinary document, a detailed account of the individuals involved in the many aspects of the restoration from fundraising to donation of adobe bricks, provides an unusual window to the past, especially when combined with other contemporary documents.

Without going into a detailed history of either the parroquia or Ermita[2] de San Miguel, the earliest reference to the parish church in the newly formed Villa de Santa Fe occurred July 7, 1613. On that date, Pedro de Peralta, Governor of the Province of New Mexico since 1609, found himself excommunicated and his chair—a symbol of the governor's civic authority—thrown from its place of honor in the parish church into the street by Fray Isidro Ordóñez.[3] Unrepentant, Peralta "ordered the chair ... *placed inside the door near the baptismal font, and there amongst the Indians he sat down*, the others, captains, alcaldes and cabildo being seated near the high altar."[4] Consequently, Peralta took his seat in the rear of the church, probably under the choir loft, near the main doors.[5] The fact that Peralta sat among the Native Americans suggests the Mexican and local Indian population living in the Barrio de Analco in 1613 did not yet have a church of their own and that San Miguel was not constructed until later.

Based on modern studies of Spanish Colonial mission churches by architectural historians Gloria Giffords and James Ivey, the earliest parish church in Santa Fe was, more than likely, a simple structure with a single nave and a rectangular or trapezoidal apse.[6] In short, as with other churches built before 1620 in New Mexico, the first parroquia in the Villa may have been longer and perhaps slightly wider than San Miguel is today, but it probably differed little in outward appearance from the present chapel. Whether that earliest parroquia had a transverse clerestory window, as found in many seventeenth century churches of the period in New Mexico, is unknown.

View of the back of San Miguel Chapel as it may have appeared after restoration in 1710. Illustration by Fritz Broeske from *The Santa Fean*, Early Summer, 1941.

The next reference to the parroquia appears in the 1620 during Juan de Eulate's term of office when the governor and cabildo, or town council, of Santa Fe requested permission to move the villa to a better location and build a new church.[7] According to the document, the viceroy denied the cabildo's requests, "inasmuch as there is already there a [parish] church and convent of Saint Francis, which seems sufficient for the number of residents."[8] Even though the viceroy denied the cabildo's request, he sent a quantity of tools, nails and other materials to repair buildings already constructed in the villa.[9] Ironically, the viceroy's comments notwithstanding, by 1626 the parroquia had a transept, that is, it was cruciform in plan, indicating the parish church had been either remodeled extensively or rebuilt entirely since first described in 1613.[10]

In 1623, Fray Alonso de Benavides became the Custodian or head of the Franciscans in New Mexico although he did not arrive in the province until late in 1625.[11] A reception celebrating Benavides arrival in Santa Fe was held in January 24, 1626 when he was greeted by the governor, alcaldes, cabildo and residents of the villa.[12] The following day high mass was celebrated in the parish church:

> At the time of high mass, the said governor, alcaldes, cabildo and all the other people and the harquebusiers came to the cell of the

said father commissary to accompany him to the church. This they did, the banner of our holy Catholic faith being carried before them in the hands of the said sargento mayor, accompanied by the captains ... in this order they entered the church up to the place of the father commissary, which was on the side of the gospel [on the left as one approached the altar] at the main altar. He had a kneeling chair with a cushion and opposite him, on the other side, a platform covered with a carpet where I, the present notary, sat and also the alguacil mayor and sargento mayor who carried the banner. The said governor [Felipe de Sotelo Osorio] *took his seat at the transept of the church* and high mass began....[13]

According to Kubler, who cited Scholes, the earliest reference to the Ermita de San Miguel is 1628 when Fray Alonso Benavides built it.[14] However, the fact of the matter is Benavides never said in either his *Memorial of 1630* or the *Revised Memorial of 1634* which church he built in Santa Fe, the parroquia or San Miguel, or for whom he built the church, the Spaniards or the Indian slaves and servants of the Spanish. Instead, Benavides said in his *Memorial of 1630* he built a church as, "the one they had was a poor hut,"[15] and because, according to his *Revised Memorial of 1634*, "their first one had collapsed."[16]

Although historians still debate which church Benavides built, it appears San Miguel must be the church built while Benavides resided in Santa Fe. There are several reasons why this must be so: there was only one church mentioned in the documents between 1613 and 1620, the parish church of Saint Francis; the church in which Benavides celebrated high mass January 25, 1626 had a transept which archaeological evidence has shown San Miguel never had; and, finally, Benavides says that he had local women and children help him construct the new church.[17] As Giffords points out,

"...based on what we know about pre-Conquest and post-colonial New Mexico, as well as on certain references by friars and soldiers, [native] women there most likely prepared adobe bricks, carried these to the walls of churches being built, and possibly even put the bricks into place; moreover, they engaged in the mud plastering or replastering of walls made from such bricks."[18]

By the 1660s, the Villa de Santa Fe had at least two churches, the parroquia and the Ermita de San Miguel, and may have had a third church, a military chapel in the casas reales, the governmental complex around the main plaza. At this same time, another church, Nuestra Señora de Guadalupe, was under construction in El Paso del Norte.[19] The mission church, built for the local Manso population, may have resembled the rebuilt parroquia in Santa Fe, in that N. S. Guadalupe had transepts.

> The wood work in the church, in addition to being very strong and unusual, is excellently finished. The church has a beautiful arch. The nave is ninety-nine feel long and thirty-three feet wide; the transept measures twenty-eight feet by forty-five feet; and the chancel is twenty feet long and twenty-one feet wide on the side of the transept. The altar steps are very beautiful..... [there follows a description of the church furnishings, some of which are still in place].[20]

The last of the New Mexico missions to be built, Our Lady of Guadalupe in Juárez is still in use. The carved vigas in the ceiling and other examples of wood-work are a monument to the master *carpinteros* of the 17th century and create a tapestry in wood that must have influenced carpenters and other woodworkers from the day the church was dedicated.

In Santa Fe, aside from the fact that San Miguel was partially destroyed during Governor Luis Rosas term of office, and later, after rebuilding was used as an infirmary, there is little mention of the Analco church in the years leading up to 1680.[21] Unfortunately, there is equally little reference to the parroquia in the fifty years before the Pueblo Revolt. Eyewitness accounts in August 1680 tell us that although both the parroquia and San Miguel burned, the latter fared much better than the old parroquia both during the Revolt and in the years between the Reconquest and restoration of the church.

When Don Diego de Vargas entered Santa Fe in 1692, he made a specific promise to "build the church and holy temple, placing in it the patron saint of that kingdom and the villa, Our Lady of the Conquest," a Marian figure which had been brought to Santa Fe in 1626 by Fray Alonso de Benavides.[22] However, when Vargas returned to Santa Fe in December 1693, he found the former parish church completely razed. At the same time, Vargas found the Ermita de San Miguel in the Barrio de Analco "that served as the parish church for the Indians from Mexico City who lived in the villa [prior to August 1680]," needed only a roof to make it suitable for services and so that "Our Lady of the Conquest might have a decent place."[23] Because it was winter, it was not possible to gather the necessary materials to cut and fashion the vigas and corbels to repair the roof, so Vargas commandeered the house of a former settler, "about a musket shot from the villa," and turned that into a church.[24] Apparently then, San Miguel remained without a roof and the interior exposed to the elements for nearly twenty years before it would be restored.

Meanwhile, in addition to the settlers who returned to New Mexico with

Vargas in December of 1693, additional settlers arrived in the spring of 1694. Recruited for the most part in Mexico City by Fray Francisco Farfán and Cristóbal de Velasco, these families included artisans, some of whom had already achieved the status of *maestro*, or master, whose trades and training would have a lasting effect on the colony.[25] Besides stonecutters, masons and carpenters, other trades included weavers, tailors, farriers, blacksmiths, and painters.[26] Initially, all the settlers who came to New Mexico in 1694 moved into the pueblo constructed around the former casas reales by the ousted Tano and Tewa residents of the villa. Eventually though many of the Farfán and Velasco recruits moved to Santa Cruz de la Cañada after it was founded in 1695, others remained in Santa Fe. Additional recruits led by Juan Páez Hurtado, who served as Lt. Governor for Vargas, came to Santa Fe in 1695.[27]

The west façade of San Miguel Chapel as it appeared in the mid-19th century. When described by Fray Atanasio Domínguez in 1776, this façade was very simple with a single door. Instead of a graduated steeple, there was a single small arch with a bell above the door. Illustration by Cleve Hallenbeck from *The Land of the Conquistadores* by Cleve Hallenbeck.

In 1709, Governor José Chacon Medina Salazar y Villaseñor, the Marquis de la Peñuela, appointed Agustín Flores de Vergara, the mayordomo of the Cofradia de San Miguel, to act, more or less, as the general contractor for the restoration of that church. Accordingly, Flores, who was an aide and standard-bearer for the governor, appointed two men, Pedro López and Bernardino de Sena, to carry the image of San Miguel "to collect alms in all the kingdom" to pay for the restoration.[28] Which of the several Pedro López's living in the colony at this time was selected to collect alms for the restoration is unknown; however, a great deal of information is known about Bernardino Sena, the other person appointed to raise funds for the restoration of the chapel. Sena was an orphan, only nine years old when he came to Santa Fe in 1693 with his foster-parents José del Valle and Ana de Ribera as part of the Velasco Farfán recruitment effort.[29] Twenty-five years old at the time of the restoration of San Miguel, Sena, a blacksmith by trade, already owned land in the Barrio de Analco.[30] Before his death in 1765 Sena amassed considerably more property including additional fields and an orchard in the Barrio de Analco, a ranch at Cuyamunque, and a two-story house in Santa Fe with nine rooms on the ground floor and seven rooms on the second-story.[31] Perhaps even more interesting, Sena was a syndic for the Franciscans and served repeatedly as mayordomo for the Cofradia of La Conquistadora who requested in his last will and testament that he be buried in San Miguel.[32]

Once fundraising had been organized, Vergara appointed other individuals to specific tasks. Among them, Pedro López Gallardo, a master builder, was employed as *oficial de la obra*, or clerk, and Juan Manuel Chiriños Martínez de Cervantes, a notary, became the project supervisor.[33] Although little is known of López Gallardo aside from his trade, Juan Manuel Chiriños stated he was twenty-seven years old when he left Mexico City to come to Santa Fe in 1693 with the Farfán-Velasco recruits; he later settled in Santa Cruz.[34] Andrés González, a native of Huejotzingo near Puebla was named *maestro de la obra* or "master workman," that is, he was probably a master mason, while Diego Velasco, a native of Guadiana [Durango] was identified as the carpintero, or carpenter for the restoration.[35]

Both Andrés González and Diego Velasco were well known residents of the villa. Andrés González was a soldier in his early 40s from Parral when he came to New Mexico with Vargas in 1692.[36] González would be involved in the inspection of the Palace of the Governors in 1716, and may have helped construct the new parroquia and La Conquistadora Chapel between 1714 and 1717.[37] Diego Velasco [Velázquez] was also known as the Lame Carpenter.[38] Velasco and his wife, María de Tapia [Herrera] inherited property granted to his mother-in-law by former governor Cubero.[39] The property was located in the Barrio de Analco and was sold in 1712 to Juan de los Rios.[40] In the same year, 1712, Velasco was found guilty of murdering

Miguel de Herrera. Velasco was sentenced to assist in construction of the new parroquia and to build barges to cross the Rio Grande at the Pueblo of San Felipe and El Paso del Norte.[41]

Other individual donors included: General Juan Páez Hurtado, Diego de Arias [de Quiros] and Tomás Girón [Jirón de Tejeda], all of whom donated goods toward the reconstruction of the church. Páez Hurtado had been responsible for bringing additional settlers to New Mexico in 1695. He served as Lt. Governor throughout both Vargas terms of office and acting governor on a number of occasions after Vargas's death. Páez Hurtado was majordomo of the Cofradia for La Conquistadora and a member of the Cofradia of San Miguel. In 1712, he loaned his house to members of the cabildo and others to plan an annual fiesta in honor of Vargas and La Conquistadora.[42] Diego Arias de Quiros came to Santa Fe with Vargas in 1692. He received property bounded on the west by the Palace of the Governors and was a member of the Cofradia of La Conquistadora.[43] Arias may be best known for developing a spring and creating a tanque in the cienega in 1715–1716 that caused a furor in villa before he was directed to close the pond.[44] Finally, Tomas Girón de Tejeda and his large family arrived in New Mexico with the Velasco-Farfán group. Tomas and his son, Nicolás were both listed on the muster rolls as *pintors*, or painters from Mexico City.[45]

Magdalena Ogano, or Ogama, the cook for the laborers was the only woman mentioned in the labor force for the restoration of San Miguel. She arrived with the settlers who accompanied Vargas in 1693 where she appears in the list of Mexican Indians who lived in Santa Fe prior to the Revolt.[46] In 1711, Sra. Ogama sold property she owned on the west side of the plaza in Santa Fe to Salvador Montoya. That property was bounded on the north by "the acequia madre which runs to the edge of this land and castle; on the south by the house of General Juan Páez Hurtado; on the east, said plaza; and on the west some bushes of roses of Castile."[47] As the north boundary of the Ogama-Montoya property was the "acequia madre which runs to the edge of this land and castle," it is possible that it was the ditch that once ran east west along present Palace Avenue. If so, it may be, the property was located about where the main office of the First National Bank now stands. Since Páez's house marked the south boundary for the Ogama-Montoya property, the general's house must have been located in the middle of the block, assuming the width of the plaza has not changed since 1711. In short, because the roof of the Casa de Cabildo leaked on September 16, 1712 when Páez Hurtado and others met to discuss the new fiesta in honor of Vargas and La Conquistadora, the meeting was held at the Páez house on the west side of the plaza.[48] Where the cabildo usually met is unknown.

Day laborers on the restoration of San Miguel included Joseph de Anaya,

Salvador Manuel, Nicolás Ramírez, Juan Rodelo, Felipe Rodríquez, Pedro de Rojas, Domingo Romero, Juan de Spinoza, and Pedro Vigil. Most of the day laborers cannot be identified; however, according to Chávez, Nicolás Ramírez was a native of Zacatecas known to have lived in Santa Cruz in 1696, while Pedro de Rojas Liscano was a native of Sombrerete and a soldier.[49] Finally, Chávez believed Pedro Vigil to have been part of the Montes Vigil family.[50]

Diego Brito, Agustín de la Cruz, Juan de Leon, Diego el Mexicano, Pedro López, Vizente Armijo, and [Cristóbal] Gongora were among those listed individuals who had donated goods or materials for the restoration.[51] Cristóbal Gongora, was a soldier in the Santa Fe Presidio, a singer in the church choir, and served as secretary of the cabildo in 1715–1716.[52] Three of these men, Brito, de la Cruz and Juan de Leon, were identified in the 1693 muster rolls as Indians of Mexico City who had lived in Santa Fe prior to the Revolt. The others appear to have been in the same category, but beyond that, they cannot be identified.[53] Also mentioned were Indians from Pecos Pueblo who supplied "one hundred and fifty planks and eighty spalls."[54]

Kubler discussed the restoration of San Miguel in detail in his 1939 publication; however, evidence uncovered during archaeological excavation in 1955 suggests strongly the restoration may have been more extensive than Kubler believed.[55] Stanley Stubbs and Bruce Ellis who conducted limited archaeological excavations at San Miguel believe "the main mass of the present church dates from 1710," and beside rebuilding the walls virtually from the ground up included construction of two windows and a door on the north wall of the chapel in their assessment.[56] Kubler, on the other hand, believed the restoration involved rebuilding the upper walls of the church to a height of about twenty-five feet, construction of a wholly new ceiling of round beams and a roof, and finally, construction of a choir loft. The loft included the ornately carved support beam with Governor Peñuela's and Ensign Flores de Vergara's names inscribed on it. The inscription on the beam beneath the choir loft reads *El Señor Marques de la Peñuela hizo esta Fabrica el aiferes Rl Don Agn Flos Vergara su criado Año de 1710*.[57] It is possible that Diego Velasco, the so-called Lame Carpenter, the only master carpenter known to have been involved with the restoration of San Miguel carved the choir loft beam. Presumably, Velasco was also responsible for carving the ceiling beams and the pair of corbels under the beam at the sanctuary.

When Fray Francisco Atanasio Domínguez described San Miguel in 1776, he mentioned first he had not been able to determine the founding date of the chapel.[58] Since Domínguez did not mention either the windows or door on the north wall of the chapel, it might be all traces of those features had been plastered over in the sixty-six years since San Miguel had been restored. The high altar was described as having an altar table of adobe with an altar stone and an adobe pediment or ledge on which the figure of San Miguel stood.[59] Interestingly, Domínguez did not mention a wood altar screen or the choir loft beam that had been donated by the Marques de la Peñuela in 1710.[60]

The west façade of San Miguel Chapel is shown here after it was restored in the early 20th centry. Illustration by Fritz Broeske from *The Santa Fean*, Easter Number, 1941.

In 1697, several years after the Reconquest, Pedro Rodríquez Cubero provided land for construction of a new convento for the Franciscans who served the colony and who apparently used the makeshift church provided by Vargas. Although Kessell et al. state that construction of the new parroquia started in 1703 with the construction of a chapel dedicated to La Conquistadora, other documents indicate construction of a wholly new parroquia and Conquistadora Chapel did not begin until ca 1712.[61] Unfortunately, it is not known if La Conquistadora was taken to outlying areas of the province to raise funds for the construction of Her chapel and the new church, nor is the building sequence known for the two structures. It may be pure conjecture that the Conquistadora Chapel was completed before the parroquia was finished. In any case, given the fact that the construction of the parish church and chapel was a much larger undertaking than the restoration of San Miguel, it is not surprising construction was still under way in 1716.[62] References to the church indicate that both the parroquia and Chapel dedicated to La Conquistadora had been completed by October 1717.[63] Finally, it should be noted that the little historical information known about the construction of the two buildings has been augmented by limited archaeological evidence.[64]

According to Fray Angélico Chávez's study of La Conquistadora, between October and December 1717, Bernardo de Sena:

> ...paid sixty pesos to the carpenter[65] Juan de Medina for building the high altar of the [Conquistadora] chapel, as well as its sacristy. He also paid another sum to Andrés Montoya for hauling lumber for the sacristy, and still another to Salvador Archuleta for thirty-five vigas.[66]

Based on the foregoing, it appears that Bernardo Sena may have acted as the project supervisor for construction of the two buildings and Juan Lorenzo de Medina was responsible for building an adobe altar. The problem is that there were two Juan de Medinas in the colony at this time, "Juan el Chico" and "Juan el Largo" only one of whom was a mason or builder, not a carpenter.[67] One of the referenced Medinas was responsible for inspecting the tanque that Diego Arias constructed in the cienega adjacent to his property in 1716. It is not clear whether it was "El Chico" or "El Largo." Whichever of the Medinas was referenced was likely a mason, not a woodworker.[68]

In addition, Chávez believes Andres Montoya and Salvador de Archuleta donated sixteen and twenty beams respectively toward the restoration of San Miguel.[69] Finally, it is known that Diego Velasco, the carpintero who worked at San Miguel had been sentenced to work on the new parroquia and La Conquistadora

Chapel for killing Miguel Herrera.[70] Other than the preceding individuals, it can only be surmised that the builders and/or masons, Pedro López Gallardo and Andrés González also worked on La Conquistadora Chapel in addition to the parroquia.

As the Conquistadora Chapel was attached to the north or Gospel side of the parroquia, the form of the new parish church was cruciform in plan. The chapel though was a simple structure with a single-nave and a rectangular or trapezoidal apse, just as it is today; however, based on historical and archaeological evidence the nave has been truncated and is about twelve feet shorter than it was once.[71] When Fray Francisco Atanasio Domínguez saw the chapel in 1776, he described it as follows:

> It is of adobes with walls nearly a vara [ca. 33"] thick. Its door is an arched opening in the wall at the place mentioned ['on the Gospel side of the main church at the head of the transept'], and from there to the wall of the high altar it is 20 [ca 55 feet] varas long, 7 [ca 19 ¼ feet] wide and 9 [ca 24 3/4 feet] high. Its beams are on the same level and there is no clerestory like that in the church. There are twenty-four new round ones (like those in the transept of the church), and they rest on the old corbels. The sanctuary is marked off by two small stairs, and from the upper one it is 4 [ca 11 feet] varas long through the center and as wide as the nave of the chapel. Its choir loft is above the entrance on twelve flying corbels, with a little balustrade, or railing. It is 3 [ca 8 ¼ feet] varas deep and as wide as the chapel. The floor is newly laid with wood. There are two windows with wooden gratings on the Epistle side spaced at proportionate distances, and they face east. Its furnishings, or adornment, are as follows:
>
> High Altar: There is no altar piece, but a large niche resting on a shelf serves the purpose along with two brackets on either side of the niche to hold two small niches (these and the large one are like shrines). All is painted mother-of-pearl with yellow fillets as if in tempera. In the large niche is an image in the round of Our Lady of the Rosary (or, as others say, of *La Conquistadora*) a vara tall.[72]

In short, the Conquistadora Chapel, as originally constructed, must have resembled very closely, the restored Chapel of San Miguel, even to the adobe altar without an altar screen. This, of course, stands to reason since the same artisans worked on both structures.

The San Miguel and La Conquistadora Chapels and Their Builders, 1610–1776

The parroquia, or parish church of St. Francis in Santa Fe with the Conquistadora Chapel on the left as they may have appeared after complete of construction between 1714 and 1717. Illustration by Cleve Hallenbeck from *The Land of the Conquistadores* by Cleve Hallenbeck.

Based on the foregoing, at least three of the individuals who worked on the restoration of San Miguel, Pedro López Gallardo, Andrés González and Diego Velasco, were either builders or masons (*albañiles*), master masons (*alarifes*), or in the case of Velasco, *a carpintero*, or carpenter. Although not mentioned as having taken part in the restoration of San Miguel, but known to have worked on construction of La Conquistadora Chapel, Juan Lorenzo de Medina was apparently also a master mason.[73] Each of the individuals mentioned was old enough at the time of his arrival in New Mexico that each must have attained the status of maestro, or master of his trade before coming to the province. In other words, each of these men had served as apprentices and journeymen before becoming a master and each was expected to own the tools of his trade.[74] Whether any or all of the masters involved in the restoration of San Miguel or construction of the parroquia and La Conquistadora Chapel trained apprentices is unknown. However, there can be no doubt that the work of each master influenced successive generations and gave rise to the "web of influence" among late 18th and 19th century carpenters, sculptors, painters and others not only in Santa Fe, but throughout New Mexico.[75] Today's visitors are fortunate to be able to see and admire the work accomplished by these four men, masters of their trades, and others during the restoration of San Miguel and construction of La Conquistadora Chapel three hundred years ago!

References Cited:

Adams, Eleanor B. and Fray Angelico Chavez. 1975. *The Missions of New Mexico, 1776: A Description by Fray Francisco Atanasio Dominguez with Other Contemporary Documents.* University of New Mexico Press, Albuquerque.

Ayers, Emma Burbank (Mrs. Edward E.), translator. 1916. *The Memorial of Fray Alonso de Benavides, 1630.* Annotated by Frederick Webb Hodge and Charles Fletcher Lummis, privately printed, Chicago. Reprinted in 1965 by Horn and Wallace, Publishers, Albuquerque.

Bloom, Lansing B. 1928. "A Glimpse of New Mexico in 1620," *New Mexico Historical Review* III (4):357-380).

Chávez, Fray Angélico. 1948. *Our Lady of the Conquest.* The Historical Society of New Mexico, Santa Fe; 2009. New Edition, Sunstone Press, Santa Fe.

—— 1949. "Santa Fe Church and Convent Sites in the Seventeenth and Eighteenth Centuries," *New Mexico Historical Review* XXIV(2):85-93.

—— 1992. *Origins of New Mexico Families: A Genealogy of the Spanish Colonial Period.* Revised edition, Museum of New Mexico Press, Santa Fe.

Chávez, Thomas E. 1985. "Santa Fe's Own: A History of Fiesta," *El Palacio* 91(1):6-17.

Ellis, Bruce. 1985. *Bishop Lamy's Santa Fe Cathedral.* Historical Society of New Mexico and University of New Mexico Press.

Esquibel, José Antonio and Charles M. Carrillo. 2004. *A Tapestry of Kinship: The Web of Influence among Escultores and Carpinteros in the Parish of Santa Fe, 1790–1860.* LPD Press, Albuquerque.

Esquibel, José Antonio and John B. Colligan. 1999. *The Spanish Recolonization of New Mexico: An Account of the Families Recruited at Mexico City in 1693.* Hispanic Genealogical Research Center of New Mexico, Albuquerque.

Giffords, Gloria Fraser. 2007. *Sanctuaries of Earth, Stone, and Light: The Churches of Northern New Spain, 1530–1821.* The University of Arizona Press, Tucson.

Hodge, Frederick Webb, George P. Hammond and Agapito Rey (editors and annotators). 1945. *Fray Alonso de Benavides' Revised Memorial of 1634.* Coronado Cuarto Centennial Publications, 1540–1940, Vol. IV, the University of New Mexico Press, Albuquerque.

Ivey, James E. 1988. *In the Midst of a Loneliness: The Architectural History of the Salinas Missions.* Professional Papers No. 15, Southwest Cultural Resources Center, Southwest Regional Office, National Park Service, Santa Fe.

—— 1998. "The Architectural Background of the New Mexico Missions," *Seeds of Struggle, Harvest of Faith: The Papers of the Archdiocese of Santa Fe Catholic Cuarto Centennial Conference on the History of the Catholic Church in New Mexico* edited by Thomas J. Steele, S. J., Paul Rhetts, and Barbe Awalt, LPD Press, Albuquerque.

Kessell, John L., et al., editors and translators. 1992. *By Force of Arms: The Journals of Don Diego de Vargas, 1691–1693.* University of New Mexico Press, Albuquerque.

—— 1995. *To the Royal Crown Restored: The Journals of don Diego de Vargas, New Mexico, 1692–1694.* University of New Mexico Press, Albuquerque.

—— 1998. *Blood on the Boulders: The Journals of don Diego de Vargas, New Mexico, 1694–1697,* Books 1 and 2. University of New Mexico Press, Albuquerque.

—— 2000. *That Disturbances Cease: The Journals of don Diego de Vargas, New Mexico 1697–1700.* University of New Mexico Press, Albuquerque.

Kubler, George. 1939. *The Rebuilding of San Miguel at Santa Fe in 1710.* Contributions of the Taylor Museum, Colorado Springs, Colorado.

Margo, Adair Wakefield. 1982. *Nuestra Señora de Guadalupe del Paso del Norte, its Foundation, Construction and Decoration 1668–1982.* Thesis, New Mexico State University, Las Cruces.

Scholes, France V. 1929. "Documents for the History of the New Mexico Missions in the Seventeenth Century, *New Mexico Historical Review,* IV (1):4-58; IV (2):195-201.

——— 1936. "Church and State in New Mexico 1610–1650," *New Mexico Historical Review* XI (4): 297-349.

Strout, Clevy Lloyd. 1978. "The Resettlement of Santa Fe, 1695, The Newly Found Muster Roll," *New Mexico Historical Review* 53 (3):261-270.

Stubbs, Stanley A. and Bruce T. Ellis. 1955. *Archaeological Investigations at the Chapel of San Miguel and the Site of La Castrense, Santa Fe, New Mexico.* Monographs of the School of American Research, No. 20, Laboratory of Anthropology, Museum of New Mexico, Santa Fe.

von, Wuthenau, A. 1935. "The Spanish Military Chapels in Santa Fe and the Reredos of Our Lady of Light," *New Mexico Historical Review* X (3):175-194.

7

Barrio de Analco
Its Roots in Mexico and Role in Early Colonial Santa Fe, 1610–1780
by
William Wroth

Barrio de Analco was founded on the south side of the Santa Fe River some time after the founding of the city in the early seventeenth century. By 1628 if not earlier, the barrio, which was also called Barrio de San Miguel, was established as a community for the Mexican Indian laborers and artisans and their families who accompanied the Spaniards in settling New Mexico. At this time, the early 1600s, Santa Fe consisted of the settlement around the plaza and the *casas reales,* and the settlement around the San Miguel chapel which was called an *ermita* or outlying chapel in the early documents. The center of Santa Fe was the plaza, also the administrative center of Nuevo México at the time, and the outlying San Miguel district was a barrio for the Indians. In this paper I will look at the antecedents for the establishing of Indian barrios in colonial New Spain in order to place colonial Santa Fe in a larger historical and cultural context and will also review the evidence for the history and ethnic make-up of the Barrio de Analco.

In the settling of the northern frontier of Mexico it was a common practice for the Spaniards to utilize Indian auxiliaries both as protection against hostile tribes and as support for the needs of the soldiers, settlers and friars in establishing new communities. A variety of social and contractual arrangements prevailed between the Spaniards and the Indians accompanying them, ranging from the limited entitlement accorded the Tlaxcalans (who had been instrumental in aiding the first conquistadors in defeating the Aztecs) to situations of full servitude. While the exact arrangements prevailing in Santa Fe are not known, the general situation mirrored that of other parts of New Spain's frontier in which a hegemonic relationship existed between the Spaniards and the subject Mexican Indians.

This relationship is quite clearly and succinctly stated by Fray Alonso de Benavides who was the Franciscan *custos* (custodian) for New Mexico from 1626 to 1629. In his *Memorial of 1630*, Benavides was the first to detail the demographic statistics for Santa Fe: "There reside the governors and the Spaniards *[Españoles]*, who number about two hundred and fifty, although for lack of weapons only fifty can be armed. Though they are few and poorly equipped, God has ... instilled into the Indians such a fear of them and of their harquebuses that at mere mention of a Spaniard's coming to their pueblos they run away. In order to keep them in constant fear they deal very severely with them whenever an occasion arises.... They have about seven hundred persons in service; so that counting Spaniards, Mestizos and Indians, the total is about a thousand." The 700 persons in service to the 250 Spaniards must have included a significant number of Mexican Indians who came with the Oñate expedition and with later wagon trains supplying the colony.[1]

The center of political power was the Santa Fe plaza, on the north side of the Santa Fe River where the governor and the *cabildo* (town council) ruled in the governmental offices (casas reales) and where the soldiers and citizens had their homes.[2] The hegemonic position of the Spaniards was enshrined in the city's official name found in seventeenth-century documents: "la villa de Santa Fee Rl [Real] de los españoles." Quite separate from the Españoles of Santa Fe, the majority of the Indians in their service lived on the south side of the river in the Barrio de Analco (a small number of domestic servants actually lived in the homes of the Spaniards around the plaza). The Indian residents of the Barrio de Analco were not directly represented in the government, but rather had Españoles representing them as members of the cabildo and officials (*mayordomos*) of the San Miguel church.

"Analco" is a Nahuatl word meaning 'the other side of the river,' as many New Mexico historians and writers have pointed out. "Barrio de Analco" is an apt place name to describe the separation of peoples by ethnicity which took place in colonial New Spain. In Nahua culture prior to the Spanish conquest of Mexico, urban centers and surrounding lands were divided into self-contained constituent entities known in Nahuatl as *tlaxilacalli* or *calpolli* (plural, *tlaxilacaltin, calpoltin*) which reflected the organic unity, as well as the diversity, of the Nahua social order. Taken together, four, six, or even eight tlaxilacaltin (the more commonly used term) formed the *altepetl*, the regional territory which constituted a sovereign state in central Mexico. Each tlaxilacalli had its own name, reflecting geographical features or the ethnic origin of the residents, and its own internal form of governance.[3]

View north from San Miguel College, Santa Fe, ca. 1880s. Homes and fields of Barrio de Analco in foreground, Santa Fe River and Loretto Chapel in middle ground, and Santa Fe Plaza in background. Photograph by William Henry Brown.

San Miguel Church, Barrio de Analco, Santa Fe, early 1880s. Photograph by William Henry Brown.

After the conquest the altepetl became synonymous, at least in the eyes of the Spaniards, with the municipality, a territory with an administrative urban center and outlying neighborhoods. In the colonial period, even in documents written in Nahuatl, the terms tlaxilacalli and calpolli were gradually replaced by the Spanish term *barrio*. The word *barrio*, reflecting Spanish social structure, has a connotation clearly different from that of the Nahuatl terms. It derives from the Arabic word *barri*, which means "outside." The barrio was originally, in medieval Spain, a settlement outside of the castle, citadel, or fortified (or defended) civic and spiritual center, perhaps reflecting the feudal social structure in which serfs lived outside the castle or city gates and worked as agricultural laborers and artisans. Thus unlike the tlaxilacalli, the barrio was not thought of as an integral part of the city. There were, however, traditional structured relationships based on social class distinctions between the residents of the barrio and the civic leaders. One could say a different type of organic relationship based on hierarchy prevailed in the traditional Spanish colonial city.

In the separation between the barrio and the civic center, the class and ethnic distinctions of colonial Mexico were embodied in urban space, providing a physical separation as well as a social and economic separation. The place name "Barrio de Analco" adds another powerful element to this social separation by placing the indigenous population literally on the other side of the river. In Santa Fe and elsewhere in Mexico the river provided both a physical and defensible barrier between the Spanish classes and the Indians who served them. It was also a symbolic barrier: rivers from early times have been boundary markers between different territories and different worlds. Thus to consign the Indian population to the Barrio de Analco was to place them both "outside" (barrio) and on the other side of the river (analco) from the civic center, the center of power and authority in colonial Mexico. In Santa Fe the choice of the north side of the river for the villa and the south side for the Indian barrio was also based upon water resources and the fertility of the land. The north side had many springs which were used to create ponds and provide abundant (for the arid climate) water resources for growing crops and feeding and watering livestock. The south side was much drier, requiring irrigation from the *acequia* for the cultivation of crops. Today's *acequia madre* still runs and is in use along the south side of the river. On the north side ponds were maintained and in use until the late nineteenth century, and a vestige of these abundant water sources is still to be seen today in the quite lush (but no longer wet) Bishop's Garden next to the Cathedral of San Francisco.[4]

Santa Fe was not the only place in colonial Mexico to have a Barrio de Analco. It is a common name for indigenous settlements that neighbor Spanish towns and villas, and those established in the sixteenth century no doubt served as prototypes for seventeenth-century Santa Fe. Among the Spanish cities with a neighboring Barrio de Analco are: Villa Alta in Oaxaca, Guadalajara, and Durango.[5]

In Oaxaca, the remote frontier town of Villa Alta, established in 1529, shared similarities with Santa Fe. It was laid out in the typical Spanish colonial grid pattern, with the government buildings, church and homes of the leading citizens placed around the central plaza. Outside the town, the Barrio of Analco, also called Papalotipac, was established by Nahuatl-speaking servants (*indios naborías*, free Indians), both Nahuas from the valley of Mexico (*Mexicas*) and Tlaxcalans. Most likely established when Villa Alta was founded, it gained official status in the mid-1550s, after complaints were voiced to the Viceroy by the "free" Indians that they were being treated like slaves by the Spaniards. Soon rules were established for the treatment of the residents of Analco, and they were allowed to have their own Nahuatl-speaking officials: *alcaldes*, a *regidor* (councilman representing them in the cabildo) and a mayordomo. Treatment of the Analco residents may have improved somewhat, but they were used by the Spaniards to help defend against attacks by hostile Mixes and Zapotecs. They were also forced to work as messengers, servants and laborers, often without pay. In the late 1500s a Zapotec barrio was also established in Villa Alta, and later, as in many places in colonial Mexico, the ethnic mix became more complex with the settlement of Chinantecs, Mixes and other groups.[6]

In 1541 a group of Mexicas from central Mexico accompanied the Viceroy Antonio de Mendoza in the campaign to subdue the indigenous tribes of Nueva Galicia. For their efforts they were allowed to establish their own barrio of San Juan Bautista de Mexicaltzingo when the city of Guadalajara was founded in 1542. Four years later Franciscan friars brought 500 Coca and Tecuexe Indians from the town of Tetlán to found the Barrio de Analco on the east side of the Rio San Juan de Dios, across the river from the plaza of Guadalajara. Due to the unhealthy marsh land on which Analco was situated, the friars soon moved their *convento* out of Analco across the river to the city proper. They, however, continued to minister to the people of Analco and they built a small ermita in Analco, dedicated to San Sebastián Mártir.[7] It is instructive to compare the treatment of the Mexica allies and the Cocas and Tecuexes. The latter had been participants in the Mixton War of 1540–1541, a desperate attempt by the indigenous groups of the region to repel the Spanish. As a result they were given marshy lands on "the other side of the river," while the Mexicas were given better lands closer to the center of Guadalajara. By the mid-seventeenth century more Indian barrios had been established in Guadalajara, and in 1667 Analco, Mexicaltzingo, and the Barrio of San Miguel de Mezquitán were all annexed and incorporated into the city of Guadalajara.

Of course Analco was not the only name given to Indian barrios in colonial Mexico, and larger urban centers often had several nearby Indian barrios providing both services to the city and a market for products. In sixteenth-century Mexico City the *ciudad de españoles (traza)* was founded in the heart of the former Aztec capital Tenochtitlan, surrounded by the four pre-existing central Indian barrios, thus keeping intact the geographic placement and social form of the pre-Conquest tlaxilacaltin. In later years this orderly form became more complex, as the Spaniards began to take up lands outside the central traza of Mexico City.[8] In the northern city of Zacatecas by the mid-sixteenth century there were at least four Indian barrios corresponding to the ethnic and linguistic origins of the residents. Tlaxcalan migrants lived in the barrio of Tlacuitlapan, northwest of the city center. Tlacuitlapan means in Nahuatl "in the back of things," a connotation similar to that of "Analco." Mexica migrants lived in nearby Mexicalpa (Mexicapan). There were two barrios of Tarascans from Michoacán to the west of the city proper, San José and Tonala Chepinque, and to the south Texcocans formed the barrio of El Niño Jesus.[9]

In 1556 Fray Diego de la Cadena, with the help of Lucas, an Indian lay brother from Michoacán who served as translator, established an Indian community at the future site of the villa de Guadiana, later named Durango, in Nueva Vizcaya. In 1562 the conquistador Francisco de Ibarra, searching for the mythical land of riches known as Copalá, brought Spanish settlers and soldiers north, and the next year he founded the Spanish villa of Guadiana. The Indian community next to it acquired the name of Barrio de San Juan Bautista de Analco. The first residents of this barrio were local Tepehuanes whom Fray Diego and Lucas had converted. Ibarra and later Spaniards brought Tlaxcalans and probably Mexicas with them to help establish Spanish domination of Nueva Vizcaya. By the mid-eighteenth century there were 610 Tlaxcaltecas living in the Barrio de San Juan Bautista de Analco.[10]

It is possible that the Barrio de Analco in Durango (which still exists today) was the immediate source for the naming of Santa Fe's Analco, since Durango was one of the closest cities to New Mexico. Although the name Barrio de Analco has not been traced in early seventeenth-century documents concerning Santa Fe, it is likely that the name was applied to the barrio before mid-century, since, as noted above, by 1629 there were already some 700 Indians, mostly of Mexican origin, living in Santa Fe. The church of San Miguel is first mentioned in documents in 1628. It may have been built some years earlier. It figures again in the documentary record in 1640 when Governor Luis de Rosas, in order to spite the Franciscan friars with whom he was fighting, ordered that the church be demolished. It was rebuilt some time between that date and 1680 when it is mentioned in accounts of the Pueblo Revolt.

Little information is available concerning the specific origins of the Indian residents of the Barrio de Analco in the early seventeenth century. Clearly, following the practice of all other expeditions to the north, the Spaniards accompanying Juan de Oñate in 1598 must have brought many Indian servants and laborers with them; however only a few are mentioned in the accounts of the expedition. The exhaustive inventory conducted before the expedition set out includes only scattered mentions of servants, few of whom, not surprisingly given their low status, appear in later New Mexico documents.[11] Among the participants in the expedition was Juan del Caso Barahona of Mexico City, probably a Mestizo,[12] who was fluent in Nahuatl and served as the translator during the expedition and later after settling in New Mexico. In 1599 at the Pueblo of Ohkay Owingeh (renamed by Oñate "San Juan Bautista") Caso Barahona was called upon to translate during the interrogation of a Mexican Indian named Jusepe (also known as Jusepillo), who had been a servant of Antonio Gutiérrez de Humaña on the ill-fated Leyva Bonilla and Gutiérrez Humaña expedition of 1593–1594. He gave his name as Jusepe Gutiérrez (having taken his master's last name) and said he was a native of the community of Culhuacán (a former Aztec altepetl) in the valley of Mexico. Jusepe stated that "approximately six years ago, a Spaniard named Antonio Gutiérrez de Umaña spoke to him at his own pueblo [Culhuacán] and took him away under an agreement whereby he was to serve him in some entradas that he was going to make."[13] Here Jusepe describes the typical "agreement" between Spaniards setting out on an expedition to the north and the Indians who accompanied them as servants. Doubtless many of the members of the Oñate expedition had similar arrangements with their Nahuatl-speaking servants, and there were enough of them to require the assistance of the translator Juan del Caso Barahona.

Oñate was replaced as Governor in 1609 by Pedro de Peralta who most likely included more Mexican Indians in his entourage when he traveled from Mexico City to New Mexico. After the founding of Santa Fe, throughout the 1600s more Mexican Indians traveled north as servants and laborers with the supply trains from central Mexico, which came up to the colony every few years bringing not only goods, but also more settlers and more missionaries. For instance, in 1631 the supply train which brought more Franciscan friars to New Mexico consisted of 32 wagons, more than 500 mules, a herd of livestock, and a military escort. In addition, it included a good number of servants and laborers who were needed to take care of all the daily issues involved in such an arduous long journey: "Under the procurator-general [friar in charge of the caravan] there served mayordomos who looked after the wagons, managed details of organization, and had charge of the drivers, lesser servants, and Indians who were employed for the journey. A small military escort accompanied each caravan." In the detailed inventory of the goods carried north on this journey the only mention of Indians accompanying it is for clothing purchased for two servants of the friars in charge: "Two suits of clothing, with shoes and shirts, for the two Indians who accompany the two friars in charge of the dispatch."[14]

In an appendix to his *Revised Memorial of 1634*, Benavides provides more evidence of Indians accompanying the supply trains. The caravan organized in 1624 included 17 Indians who were paid for their services: "This sum was paid in person and in cash on September 2 of the said year to seventeen Indians, seven of them married, the others single. This group went to the provinces of New Mexico with the sixteen wagons of his Majesty, in charge of Juan del Real, its mayordomo, bringing the belongings of the said Franciscan friars who were being sent there by order of the royal audiencia for the conversion and instruction of the natives of those provinces, and of the soldiers who went along as escort. They were paid at the rate of 130 pesos to each married Indian, 110 to the unmarried, and in return were to take care of the wagons during the round trip from Mexico and the stay in New Mexico." Benavides goes on to name each of the seventeen Indians, many without last names, for instance, Juan Francisco, Thomas Gerónimo, and

Cristobal Juan. He gives their marital status and places of origin, most of them from Mexica communities in central Mexico: San Juan del Mezquital, Tacuba, Tezcoco, Xocotitlan, Barrio of San Sebastián, as well as four from Zacatecas and two from New Mexico.[15] It is likely that some of these Indians did not make the round trip but stayed in New Mexico. There were doubtless many other Mexican Indians who made their way north to New Mexico in the 1600s with supply trains or by other means such as illegal trading expeditions.

By the second quarter of the seventeenth century Mexican Indians begin to figure more prominently in the documentary record in Santa Fe. Their occupations are occasionally given, ranging from domestic servants and cooks in the homes of the Españoles and in the *convento*, to artisans who practiced crafts essential for the maintenance of life in the remote villa. Among those mentioned by name as *Indios Mexicanos* are Francisco "Pancho" Balón, a blacksmith who was also identified in 1628 as being *de nación Mexicano*, and Agustín Brito, mentioned in two documents of 1663. In one of them he is called "Agustín, llamado Brito, el Yndio mexicano." Agustín was probably the progenitor of the Brito family whose connections with Barrio de Analco continued for nearly 100 years. An Agustín Brito and family (including a 14-year-old daughter) are among the Mexican Indians from Santa Fe listed in Diego de Vargas's census of 1693. Other Britos figure in early eighteenth-century documents, among them Diego Brito who held property in Barrio de Analco and assisted with the rebuilding of the chapel of San Miguel (see below). In a 1661 document Matías Morán was described by his Indian wife Francisca Tadeo as a cart driver, carrying dispatches to Parral in Nueva Vizcaya (now state of Durango), and he also served as a carpenter who made *carretas* and *carros*. He was likely a Mexican Indian; two families named Morán are in the Vargas 1693 census of Mexican Indians from Santa Fe. Juan Chamiso, identified as an *Indio Mexicano*, appears in a document of 1661 as master mason (*albañil maestro*), responsible for restoration work and new construction at the casas reales in Santa Fe. In August 1680 he fled Santa Fe with the Spaniards retreating to El Paso. His name appears again in the October 1680 muster roll made by Governor Antonio de Otermín in San Lorenzo where he is listed as having a household of 20, including servants.[16]

The Barrio de Analco and its residents figured prominently in the Pueblo Revolt of 1680. In August 1680 the rebellious Indians of the southern and eastern Pueblos (Tanos, Pecos and Queres) approached Santa Fe from the south, thus reaching the barrio before the plaza. Placement of the Mexican Indian community on the southern side of the river in the early 1600s now served one of its original purposes: a buffer protecting the plaza of Santa Fe from attacks from that direction. The advance of the hostile Indians is described in Governor Antonio de Otermín's first-hand report about the rebellion: "on the morning of the next day the army of the enemy was seen on the plain of the cornfields [*las milpas*] of San Miguel and in the houses of the Mexicans, which they sacked so shamelessly and in which they lodged in order to lay siege to the Villa, along with the rest of the people whom they were awaiting."[17] In a slightly later version of the events, a letter written by Otermín from Socorro to Fray Francisco Ayeta September 8, 1680, he specifically mentions the Barrio de Analco, the earliest mention we have found: "On Tuesday, the 13th of the said month, at about nine o'clock in the morning, there came in sight of us in the barrio of Analco, in the cultivated field of the *ermita* of San Miguel, and on the other side of the river from the Villa, all the Indians of the Tanos and Pecos nations and the Queres of San Marcos, armed and giving war whoops."[18]

Otermín attempted to parley with one of the leaders, a Tano named "Juan," "who had lived all his life in the villa among the Spaniards." Otermín's efforts were in vain because Juan came back from speaking with his cohorts, "saying that his people asked that all classes of Indians who were in our power be given up to them, both those in the service of the Spaniards and those of the Mexican nation of that barrio of Analco." Otermín states that the Pueblo rebels "were robbing and sacking what was in the said *ermita* and the houses of the Mexicans," and he ordered, again in vain, that they "immediately desisted from sacking the houses." The rebels then attempted an attack on the Santa Fe plaza but were repulsed by Otermín's soldiers, and then "they took shelter and fortified themselves in the said ermita and houses of the Mexicans, from which they defended themselves a part of the day with the firearms that they had and with arrows."[19]

It is of note that the rebels distinguished between the Mexican Indians of the Barrio de Analco and "those in the service of the Spaniards," suggesting that a difference in status prevailed. Many of those in the service of the Spaniards were captives from different tribes or were Pueblo people who for one reason or another no longer lived in their original villages. Also of note is Otermín's use of the phrase "las milpas de San Miguel." *Milpa* is a Nahuatl word meaning "cornfield" (literally *mil-li* "field" and *pa* "toward"). It is commonly used throughout Mesoamerica to designate the small cultivated fields surrounding Indian communities. Otermín's use of it suggests another important difference between the Indian barrio and the Spanish villa—a difference in the agriculture practiced by the Indians of Analco and that of the Spaniards across the river whose fields, where the European crops such as wheat and barley were grown, would be called *campos de los sementeros*, or *sementeras*, or *siembras*, as well as *pastos* and larger *estancias* for the grazing of livestock. Later in the same document Otermín himself makes this distinction. He writes that the Indians took possession "of the cultivated fields and houses of the villa" (del campo de los sementeros y casas de la Villa), these being the fields and homes of the Spaniards across the river from Analco.[20]

What was the fate of the Mexican Indians when their barrio was invaded by the rebels? Many immediately took shelter in the villa, and then they accompanied the Spaniards on their retreat to El Paso. Some, however, stayed in New Mexico, perhaps because by 1680 they had kinship ties with some of the Pueblos, or they were captured during the siege of Santa Fe.[21] Other Pueblo servants of the settlers later joined the retreating party, claiming they had to escape from the rebels. Before evacuating the villa during the siege approximately 1000 people, including many Mexican Indians from Barrio de Analco, were holed up in the plaza. The *alcalde ordinario* of Santa Fe, Francisco Xavier, testified that he gave clothing and "beasts" for transport to the 1000 souls about to retreat from Santa Fe: "I have distributed a large quantity of clothing to the Spanish soldiers, to all their families and servants, to the Mexican natives, and to all classes of people numbering more than one thousand souls who are in these casas reales in the siege which has continued for nine days by the rebellious enemy. Of shirts, clothing, coats, shoes, and provisions I have distributed a quantity apparently worth more than eight thousand pesos; and I have also given them beasts so that they may be able to march out of this villa."[22] Here again is the distinction, made this time by a Spaniard, between the servants of the Españoles and the "Mexican natives."

In El Paso at the end of September of 1680 Governor Otermín was already preparing for his abortive attempt at a re-conquest of New Mexico, and he did a detailed muster of the settlers and their families who had escaped in August. Most of the settlers included, along with their families, several (un-named) servants. A separate section at the end of his muster roll is devoted to the Indians and other non-Spanish refugees. Nine households of Mexican Indians are listed by the name of the head of the household, with a total of 75 individuals in all. Also listed, and totaling 59 family members, are four Mestizo households, one Mulatto household, and one Pueblo (T*eguas nación*).[23]

In 1680, after possibly as long as 75 years in Santa Fe, the Mexican Indians of the Barrio de Analco still formed a separate group, always distinguished from the Spaniards and from those in the domestic service of the Spaniards. Even more remarkable is that in January 1693 when Diego de Vargas made a census in the El Paso area of the refugees from New Mexico, there was still a coherent group of Mexican Indians from Santa Fe living in the community of San Lorenzo. After taking the census of the Spanish refugees in San Lorenzo, he was asked by them to include their Indian neighbors: "that those Indians born in Mexico City, who were living together with them in this real and pueblo of San Lorenzo and have accompanied and followed them since the uprising of the apostate Indians of the villa and principal town of Santa Fe and the kingdom of New Mexico … living and persevering with the hope of returning when this kingdom is recovered … be allowed to live and settle, accompanying them wherever they may settle...." This is followed by "List of Indians born in Mexico City who had lived in the villa of Santa Fe in the company of the original Spanish settlers from there...." Vargas then made a census of nineteen Indian households totaling 83 individual members and listing almost all their names.[24] A number of them or their descendants appear in eighteenth-century Santa Fe documents after the re-conquest. For instance, Magdalena de Ogano [also spelled Ogama] appears as a widow in the San Lorenzo census, living with her daughters Juana and María and two orphan girls, Pascuala and Gertrudis. She appears in Santa Fe involved in land transactions, 1703–1711, and in 1710 she served as cook for the crew rebuilding the San Miguel chapel in Barrio de Analco. She was replaced during the process by Juana Crisostome, possibly her daughter.[25]

In the 1693 census, the Mexican Indians are again distinguished not only from the Españoles, but also from the domestic servants of the latter, who are listed within the Spanish households. At least some of the Mexicans joined the settlers in the long and cold march north from El Paso to Santa Fe. Something of the role they played—indicating why the Spaniards wanted them along—was seen as soon as the caravan left El Paso and attempted to cross the Rio Grande. Vargas noted on October 5th that the ford across the river was in poor condition but he "overcame that difficulty by having the Indian allies who were nearby help with the wagon road. With their assistance it was repaired as well as possible." The rest of the day and the next day was spent in getting the carts and wagons across the river. The "Indian allies" included Pueblo Indians who had remained loyal to the Spaniards, but no doubt some of the Mexican Indians also played a role in this work and in the care of livestock and other manual labor during the long trip north.

After arriving in Santa Fe one of the tasks which Vargas attempted unsuccessfully to accomplish was to rebuild the San Miguel chapel in the Barrio de Analco to serve as a temporary church until a better one could be constructed. In his report of December 18, 1693 he notes that he went "to inspect the church or hermitage [ermita] that served as the parish church for the Indians from Mexico City who lived in this villa. Its title was the advocation of their patron saint, the Archangel Saint Michael."[26] Here Vargas affirms that San Miguel was, in the earlier seventeenth century, the church of the Mexican Indians and that Saint Michael was their patron saint. The restoration of this church, which had been burned and badly treated but not destroyed in the Revolt, did not actually take place until 1710. A number of individuals involved in the rebuilding of San Miguel, in addition to Magdalena Ogama discussed above, were residents of the Barrio de Analco. For instance, Diego Brito, member of a pre-Revolt Mexican Indian family, collected 500 adobes as alms, and "Diego el Mexicano" collected 100. The effort was directed by an Español, an aide to Governor Peñuela, Don Agustín Flores de Vergara, who also held the position of "mayordomo of the brotherhood of the Glorious Archangel Saint Michael in the Barrio called Analco" (mayordomo de la hermandad del Glorioso arcangel San Miguel en el Barrio que llaman de Analco).[27]

San Miguel Street (today De Vargas Street), Barrio de Analco, Santa Fe, looking east toward San Miguel Church, early 1880s. Photograph by William Henry Jackson.

Flores de Vergara's leadership of the confraternity of San Miguel raises the question of what role the Mexican Indians in the seventeenth and early eighteenth century played in the governance of the Barrio de Analco. It is likely that the Mexican Indians had some kind of unofficial form of government within the barrio. Traditionally in Mexico both pre-Conquest tlaxilacaltin and the barrios which succeeded them were governed internally by the residents, including both civil and ecclesiastical affairs, such as confraternities. In some cases the barrio even had a regidor (councilman) who had a seat on the city's cabildo (city council). Flores de Vergara's role as mayordomo, as well as the obvious power of the friar in charge of the chapel, suggests that the leadership positions were probably held by Españoles. No document has been found which suggests any form of internal governance in Analco until the year 1780 when a group of *Genízaros* living in the Barrio de Analco petitioned the Comandante General in Sonora to prevent the presidio from being moved to Analco and displacing them.[28]

A disputed question is whether or not the Barrio de Analco in Santa Fe was settled by Tlaxcalan Indians in the seventeenth century. The pre-Conquest Tlaxcalans, although Nahuatl-speaking, were enemies of the Aztecs and had been allies of the Spaniards in the conquest of Mexico in the early sixteenth century. Tlaxcalans continued to serve as auxiliaries to the Spaniards as they moved north; they helped in the subduing and Hispanizing of the "wild" Indian groups (*Indios bárbaros*), an assortment of northern tribes called *Chichimeca* in Nahuatl. Groups of Tlaxcalans migrated to these frontier areas and formed communities of varying sizes in many locations in Nueva Vizcaya and Nueva Galicia. For instance, in today's Coahuila and Nuevo León there were at least sixteen Tlaxcalan settlements, most of them established in the sixteenth and seventeenth centuries. As a result of their loyalty, the Tlaxcalan settlers were granted special privileges not accorded to other Indian groups, such as protection of their lands, freedom from paying tribute, and the right to ride horses and carry arms. In most cases they had their own internal government in their barrios and pueblos and a formal written *mandato* with the Spanish government concerning their rights and duties. In Santa Fe, as noted above, no evidence of a formal government exists for early colonial Analco, nor is there any evidence of an agreement or contract for its settlers with the Spanish government.[29]

There are a few documentary references to Tlaxcalans living in Analco, mostly in later eighteenth century. It may be that because the role of the Tlaxcalans in settling the frontier (for instance, the famed pueblo of San Esteban de Nueva Tlaxcala in Saltillo, established in 1591) was so well known that some writers assumed they also had settled the Barrio de Analco in Santa Fe. However, no mention of Tlaxcalans in New Mexico has been found in seventeenth-century documents. The terms most frequently used are *Indio Mexicano* or *de nación Mexicano*. *Mexicano* refers specifically to the Mexicas, the original Nahuatl-speaking residents of the valley of Mexico. The term *nación* refers to a tribe or an ethnic group speaking the same language and sharing the same traditions. Thus the chroniclers were referring specifically to Mexicas, not to a generalized concept of "Mexican" Indians in New Spain or to the "nation of Mexico" which of course did not exist until 1821. Also the frequent references by Vargas to the Analco residents as "Indians from (or born in)

Mexico City" further affirms their identity as Mexicas. The valley of Mexico (the site of Mexico City) was the center of population for the Mexicas, whereas their enemies the Tlaxcalans hailed from further south. Their kingdom, never conquered by the Mexicas, was in today's state of Tlaxcala.

It is of course possible that some Tlaxcalans made their way to Santa Fe, but it is highly unlikely that the Barrio de Analco was settled by a formal group of Tlaxcalan migrants. The Mexican Indians in the Barrio de Analco appear not have had the rights and autonomy that the Tlaxcalan settlers had in northern Mexico. Instead, they were a service class assisting the Spaniards in various realms such as farm labor, herding, hunting, and artisanal vocations, which placed them above the level of domestic servants and slaves, but below the level of full autonomy which, on paper at least, existed for the Tlaxcalans in their settlements.

San Miguel Street (today De Vargas Street), Barrio de Analco, Santa Fe, looking east toward San Miguel Church, soon after its restoration in 1887. (From sketch by John T. McCutcheon in Max Frost, *New Mexico: Its Resources, Climate, Geography, Geology, History, Statistics, Present Conditions and Future Prospects*. Santa Fe: Bureau of Immigration, 1894, p. 170, courtesy of the Laboratory of Anthropology Library, Museum of New Mexico.)

The ranks of the Indian population in seventeenth-century Santa Fe were swelled by the inclusion of some captured and enslaved Indians from the nomadic tribes of the region. The Spanish authorities in Santa Fe made a practice, from at least the time of Governor Juan de Eulate (1618–1625) of making slaves of captured nomadic Indians, such as the Apaches, many of whom they sold to mining and other communities further south.[30] Captured and detribalized Indians, known as Genízaros, gradually made up a significant class of people in colonial New Mexico, and by the eighteenth century many of them and their descendants were living in Santa Fe in the Barrio de Analco which gradually became known as a Genízaro community. By mid-century the population was so large that several outlying Genízaro communities such as Belén (1741) and Abiquiú (1754) were established.[31] By this time the Mexican Indians no longer formed a separate entity within Santa Fe. Following a pattern found throughout late colonial Mexico, they were absorbed into the larger poly-ethnic world that Santa Fe had become in the late eighteenth and nineteenth centuries.[32]

In Her Own Voice
Doña Teresa Aguilera y Roche and Intrigue in the Palace of the Governors, 1659–1662
by
Gerald T. E. González, JD and Frances Levine, PhD

Among the many events lived in New Mexico's Palace of the Governors in Santa Fé, the administration of Governor Bernardo López de Mendizábal captures a time when intrigue and danger swirled through the building and the town. The dramatic events of his term in office, from 1659 when he arrived in Santa Fe, to the summer of 1662 when he and his wife, Doña Teresa de Aguilera y Roche, were arrested by the Holy Office of the Inquisition, punctuate this period of Santa Fe's history. But for the efforts of the incoming Governor, Don Diego de Peñalosa Briceño y Berdugo, to prevent the Inquisition officials from embargoing all of Don Bernardo's goods when they arrested him, Don Bernardo might have been arrested at the Palace, along with his wife. Instead, he was arrested several hours before she was—at a separate location in Santa Fé to which he had been moved by Peñalosa—as is told in the records of his *residencia* and in the contemporaneous Inquisition trial records.[1]

All governors who served colonial administrations were subject to a *residencia*, an investigation of their conduct in office, which was conducted by the succeeding governor. The *residencias* also provided a means for an incoming governor to extort goods and money from a predecessor. Don Bernardo's administration was a contentious one, and from the time he left Mexico City to assume office in the Villa of Santa Fé, his style and actions heightened tensions between civil and ecclesiastical authorities. More to the point, the tensions between church and civil officials were a power and economic struggle that pitted the Franciscan friars and New Mexico governors against each other for control of the limited resources of the province of New Mexico. Some of the most important resources were the lands, persons and labors of Pueblo, Navajo and Apache people. The struggle for these resources played itself out through the tolerance—or lack of tolerance—each faction showed for the religious self-expression of Pueblo people. Each side characterized the other as morally corrupt. And there was adequate foundation for the mutual accusations.

Following the arrest of Don Bernardo late in the evening of August 26th, 1662 and that of his wife Doña Teresa by Inquisition agents on the morning of August 27th 1662, a litany of accusations were leveled against them—of his unbridled greed and sexual exploitation of women, of their blasphemy and hostility toward the church, and the suspicion that he and his wife were secret Jews. Because of the nature of the charges, the Inquisition record also includes fascinating details about social networks operating in New Mexico, and about the building that was identified during his trial for the first time as a "palace."

In 1660, Don Bernardo expanded the *casas reales* (the royal headquarters buildings, now known as the Palace), adding to the existing eighteen rooms. He requisitioned thirty Indian laborers: ten from Galisteo Pueblo, ten from San Cristóbal, and ten from San Lázaro. He also asked for women to do the plastering, a traditional task for Pueblo women. The Palace contained living rooms running along an orchard, a reception hall and archive for the governor's papers, a dining room and kitchen, quarters for several servants and members of the Governor's retinue, and rooms for bathing. The governor hired Juan Chamiso, a master builder and a native of the Valley of Mexico, to add a large central courtyard and surrounding portals, and to remodel a chapel, chamber, a *torreón* (defensive tower) and parapets.[2] Don Bernardo may have added to the Palace in part to create more space to store the tons of trade goods (chocolate, sugar, tobacco, fabrics and silver) he brought to New Mexico to trade for the *efectos del país*[3] (woven goods and knitted socks produced in the Río Grande and Hopi pueblos, piñon and salt collected in tribute from the Salinas area Pueblos, and tanned hides traded by Apaches and Pueblos that he then sent south to markets in Mexico. In 1660 alone he shipped 1,350 deerskins, 600 pairs of woolen stockings, 300 *fanegas* (roughly equivalent to bushels) of piñon, and untallied quantities of leather jackets, shirts, pants, salt and buffalo hides.[4]

While the Palace was undergoing these extensive repairs and expansions, affairs throughout New Mexico were in decline. By the 1660s the province was entering a growing drought cycle, Apache raids ravaged Spanish and Pueblo communities, and there was a resurgence of Pueblo religious practices that had been outlawed by the church.[5] Governor Don Bernardo further antagonized the church by permitting the reinstitution of Pueblo dances. Some historians have argued that the friars used their ultimate weapon, the Inquisition, to punish Governor López de Mendizábal for a variety of actions that they believed undermined their authority.[6] Among the Governor's actions that were within the letter of the law, but contrary to the interests of the missionaries, were his raising the daily wages of native peoples who worked on the mission farms, and his attempts to limit the work required by the missionaries which he believed left the Pueblo people unable to maintain their own farms. Don Bernardo argued that he took these measures in order to correct abuses by the friars.

The friars countered that the Governor was making unfair labor demands on Pueblo people to produce exports for his private business ventures. And when he permitted them to dance publicly, allowing them a liberty of conscious actions that the friars had long suppressed, this was heresy. There is no doubt that this, as much as the economic tensions between church and state, led to the indictment by the Holy Office. Other historians now judge Don Bernardo more favorably. Some historians have even proposed that Governor Mendizábal's policies might have forestalled the Pueblo Revolt by permitting Pueblos to take traditional means in response to the deteriorating climatic and health conditions in New Mexico.[7]

Franciscans and Governors also struggled for the loyalty of New Mexico's Hispanic colonists who, by the time of Mendizabál's tenure, had two and three generations of experience in this remote part of the Spanish empire. The colonists were an additional source of resources to be exploited, but their loyalty could also tip the balance of power between Franciscans and Governors. And the situation was even more complex as incoming and outgoing Governors cultivated their own adherents among the colonists. By the time Don Bernardo and his wife, Doña Teresa arrived in New Mexico, social structure had become clannish. There were family networks and alliances that, in addition to competing for moral high ground in the friction between Franciscans and Governors and Governors against Governors, also sought status through seeking official appointments and employment and securing their own claim on Pueblo-generated wealth through the *encomienda* system. The strands of all these interests came together in one place in New Mexico—the Palace. And they were critically aired during the *residencia* conducted by Peñalosa, Don Bernardo's successor, as well as during the Inquisition proceedings against Don Bernardo and Doña Teresa.

Don Bernardo's and Doña Teresa's troubles began even before they departed for New Mexico in Late December of 1658. Prior to their departure from Mexico City, Don Bernardo quarreled with Fray Juan Ramirez. Father Ramirez had been designated as the new Custodian of New Mexico's Franciscans as well as administrator of the Franciscan supply caravan itself that Don Bernardo and Doña Teresa would accompany for a large part of the journey to Santa Fe.[8]

During the journey, the differences between the two men intensified and the relationship deteriorated badly. At Parral, Don Bernardo, Doña Teresa, Father Ramírez and small group of the travelers left the main caravan and proceeded ahead to make better time. At Socorro, Don Bernardo excoriated the friar in charge for not welcoming him with appropriate ceremony. Don Bernardo took similar offense with his receptions at Sandia and Santo Domingo. At Santo Domingo, Fray Ramírez tarried behind, allowing Don Bernardo and Doña Teresa to arrive in Santa Fe where he was formally installed as Governor on July 11, 1659. Although it had been customary for the Governor and governing *Cabildo* to give the incoming Custodian a formal reception of his own, Don Bernardo declined to do so in this instance. This only added to the growing friction between the civil and religious elements of New Mexico's government.[9]

Don Bernardo's first major action, taken during the summer of his arrival, set the tone for his administration by alienating both clergy and a significant faction of the colonists: he increased the pay for Native American labor from one-half *real* a day to a full *real*. He ordered that Native Americans performing work for the Franciscans in the missions were to be paid as well. And he restricted the kinds of services Native Americans could perform to those related to what was necessary for the church or living quarters. Finally, he restricted the numbers of livestock the Franciscans could export to pay for church furnishings.[10]

Other missteps relative to the clergy and some of the colonists followed. He quickly began to build up a stock of goods to ship to Parral for sale. To facilitate this, he confiscated two hundred oxen from the settlers to pull nine wagons he required the Native Americans to build for him. He also pressed Native Americans into service to haul salt from the salt lakes east of the Manzano Mountains to sell in Parral. He also apparently organized an expedition to the plains to capture slaves from the nomadic tribes resulting in bringing back seventy captives—contrary to Spanish law. During his absence, Apache raiders struck the pueblos, carrying off captives and killing villagers. When the supply caravan returned to Mexico City in the fall of 1659, Fray Ramirez and a negative report on Don Bernardo's activities accompanied it. A second report followed by special messenger that November, in the wake of Don Bernardo's inspection of the various missions and pueblos. During that inspection he attacked the jurisdiction of the various prelates as well as attacking them personally, and he reversed policies with the effect of increasing the burden of the Franciscan missionaries while allowing the Native Americans to return to practices that had previously been forbidden and supporting them in claims and complaints they raised against the missionaries.[11]

Shortly after the supply caravan reached Mexico City in early 1660, the reports concerning Don Bernardo were heard by the Viceroy and his advisers. The

Inquisition also took testimony concerning New Mexico events in March and May.[12] By late 1660, the Viceroy had decided to replace Don Bernardo with a new Governor, Diego Dionisio de Peñalosa Briceño y Berdugo.[13]

Not accompanying the supply caravan on the return to Mexico City, despite the fact that he had been appointed as an official for the trip, was former Governor Juan Manso—Don Bernardo's immediate predecessor.[14] Don Bernardo waited to start the proceedings for Manso's *residencia* until after the caravan had left—using the *residencia* as an opportunity to extort wealth from Manso. When discussions concerning a bribe to speedily conclude the *residencia* broke down, Don Bernardo soon took possession of 100 *mantas* (coarsely-woven cotton or wool blankets), 27 oxen and 18 Apache captives that had belonged to Manso. As the *residencia* dragged into the spring, Don Bernardo also appropriated iron for making wagons, corn and wheat, and additional Apache captives from Manso. He also placed Manso under guard, alleging he had been told that Manso planned to escape. Inevitably, the *residencia* proceedings created one more faction among the colonists, many of whom had loyalty to Manso. Others became alienated from Don Bernardo as he removed some soldiers and citizen colonists from office, replacing them with others. In the end, some colonists not only helped Manso by carrying dispatches to the Viceroy on at least three occasions, but two helped him escape to Mexico City in September of 1660.[15]

In addition to his appointment and removal of various colonists from office, Don Bernardo also reassigned some of the *encomiendas* held by certain colonists. Under the *encomienda* system, the *encomenderos* were entitled to receive a certain amount of tribute from the households in an Indian pueblo in exchange for providing for the protection of the pueblo and supporting the Christianization of its inhabitants.[16] Because the *encomiendas* provided the colonists' families with sustenance as well as material wealth, they were highly prized.

Don Bernardo also pursued his business interests with considerable application. In Santa Fe at his store in the Palace, the seat of government, he sold and bartered goods to the colonists, including sugar, chocolate, clothing, imported textiles, and other goods. To satisfy the colonists' debts he sometimes confiscated portions of the *encomienda* receipts. During his tenure as Governor he also dispatched at least three wagon trains to Parral and Sonora loaded with goods for sale or exchange. At least thirty wagons were built for these purposes. In the end, he found himself at odds with the persons responsible for conveying the goods because, for various reasons, the return he expected never materialized.[17]

On February 1, 1661, following his arrival in Mexico City, Manso obtained a decree from the Viceroy that not only restored his property and that of the colonists who helped him escape, but also transferred jurisdiction over matters involving Manso from Don Bernardo to newly-appointed Governor Peñalosa. Peñalosa was directed to return the *residencia* records to Mexico City for review. Almost contemporaneously, Manso was appointed as *Alguacil* or bailiff of the Inquisition, and placed under Fray Alonso de Posada, who was replacing Fray Juan Ramírez as the Franciscan Custodian and Commissary of the Inquisition in New Mexico.[18]

Fray Posada left Mexico City in early February of 1661 and arrived in Santa Fe just before mid-May. Late in the same month he began to take evidence concerning the condition of the colony. Concluding that Native American ceremonies had gotten out of hand, on May 22nd, he issued an order forbidding the performance of kachina dances and requiring the burning of all dance paraphernalia.[19] Peñalosa arrived in mid-August of that summer. Shortly after his arrival, Peñalosa began taking evidence of Don Bernardo's activities as part of initiating Don Bernardo's *residencia*. It appears that initially there was significant cooperation between Peñalosa and Posada as each pursued the investigations under their respective charges.[20]

Posada dispatched the first batch of depositions he had taken from citizens and clergy to the Inquisition in Mexico City in December of 1661. These documents arrived eight months after the Inquisition had received other reports from Vice-Custodian Fray García de San Francisco, and almost a year after Fray Nicolás de Freitas had personally given a report to the Inquisition authorities on conditions in New Mexico.[21] Based on the earlier reports and four months before Posada's dispatches arrived, the Inquisition issued orders for the arrest of four of Don Bernardo's closest aides—Nicolás de Aguilar, Cristóbal de Anaya, Francisco Gómez Robledo, and Diego Romero—on charges of blasphemy and, in Gómez Robledo's case, of being a *judaizante*. The orders would be carried back to Santa Fe by Manso, along with his secret decree appointing him as *Alguacil Mayor* for the Inquisition's New Mexico activities. The Inquisitors—who already had accumulated accusations that, among other things, Don Bernardo and Doña Teresa were *judaizantes*—waited to take action regarding the two until Posada's reports were received. In March of 1662, following the arrival and review of Posada's reports, the Inquisition ordered the arrest of Don Bernardo and Doña Teresa.[22] Bernardo López de Mendizábal had succeeded in bringing about his own 'perfect storm' of disastrous consequences.

On May 2, 1662, Diego de Romero and Nicolás de Aguilar were arrested by the Inquisition at Isleta Pueblo as they arrived in the company of Governor Peñalosa from a patrol to Moqui—the Hopi country. Francisco Gómez Robledo was arrested in Santa Fe two days later, while Cristóbal de Anaya was arrested at Sandia on May 14. All four were then confined in specially prepared cells at Santo Domingo Pueblo.[23] On May 12, 1662, the Inquisitors in Mexico City ordered the arrest of Don Bernardo and Doña Teresa.[24]

As his *residencia* proceeded, more than seventy complaints against Don Bernardo were received by Governor Peñalosa. Many of these were from members of the clergy and the Indian pueblos, but over thirty were from individual colonists and soldiers. One was brought on behalf of the entire Hispanic colony by Captain Diego González Bernal, a member of the Santa Fe *Cabildo,* Santa Fe's *procurador general* or attorney general—and a former adherent of Don Bernardo's faction.[25] After receiving the usual allegation that Don Bernardo planned to flee, Peñalosa had him imprisoned. The *residencia* finally closed in mid-December of 1661 and the results were sent to Mexico City. Based on the evidence, the civil authorities reporting to the Viceroy absolved him of many of the charges, but found him guilty of others. He was sentenced to forfeit eligibility for any office for eight years, to pay 3,000 silver pesos to the Crown, and the claims made against him in the *residencia* were to be resolved. The sentence was delivered in Santa Fe by Diego González Lobón on August 19, 1662.[26]

When Diego González Lobón arrived from Mexico City, he also carried with him an order from the Inquisition calling for Posada to arrest Don Bernardo and Doña Teresa. After first meeting with Peñalosa, González Lobón left the same day for the Custodio offices at Santo Domingo to deliver the arrest order. Sometime on August 26, 1662, around 10 p.m., the Inquisition representatives arrested Don Bernardo. As we will see, Doña Teresa was arrested the following morning. At the time of his arrest by the Inquisition, Don Bernardo was being held under guard in the house of Pedro Lucero de Godoy where he had been moved from the Palace on orders from Governor Peñalosa. This was to allow Peñalosa to seize certain goods belonging to Don Bernardo immediately before his arrest—without having to surrender them to the Inquisition officials.[27]

The extensive Inquisition trial records for Don Bernardo actually begin before he even crossed the Río Grande into New Mexico, since they contain the complaints that Fray Ramírez sent to the Viceroy during the north bound journey he shared with the Governor in 1659, as these two men were becoming bitter enemies. These records also contain depositions given by servants, and by civil and church officials detailing the actions, reactions and sins of the Governor and his wife. But for our purposes the most engaging document of the Inquisition proceedings is the account of their life in New Mexico embodied in the defense statements prepared by Doña Teresa de Aguilera y Roche and given to the Inquisitors in 1663 and 1664.

Doña Teresa de Aguilera y Roche was the only woman from New Mexico ever tried before the Inquisition, though others were investigated for actions that were potentially blasphemous or construed as witchcraft. Doña Teresa was tried for 34 accusations related to alleged Jewish practices. In all, twelve New Mexican men were tried by the Inquisition for the alleged crime of heresy. Governor Don Bernardo,

Doña Teresa, and the four other men arrested near the same time, constitute half of the heresy cases originating in New Mexico.[28]

In Spain and Mexico, many women were brought before the Holy Office of the Inquisition, and in some cases their trial records are the only time when their voice was recorded. Few women in the seventeenth century, either in Spain or New Spain, were broadly educated. There is, in New Mexico, however, at least one case of a woman, Polonia Varela, who wrote out, signed and defended her request for annulment of a marriage forced on her by Governor Luis de Rosas in 1640. Widowed of Julián de Escarramán, and then forced to marry Juan Bautista de Zaragoza while they were both imprisoned by Governor Rosas, Polonia not only obtained her annulment, but subsequently married Juan González Bernal, son of Sebastian González, *encomendero* of Chilili Pueblo and brother of Diego González Bernal.[29]

In Spain and New Spain, women of stature did dictate wills, read and write letters to family,[30] give testimony in legal proceedings, and read a range of morally approved materials, but few could, as Doña Teresa did, read and write in several languages. The boldness of her testimony is surprising, and surely must have been unexpected in her own time when service, silence, and submission to authority were usual for women.[31]

Another famous Inquisition case involving a woman associated with New Mexico, though in a very different fashion, is the case of María Coronel y Arana or María de Jesus de Agreda.[32] Also known as the Blue Nun, her story was made famous—perhaps even manufactured—in New Mexico by Fray Benavides in 1631. In summary, Fray Benavides reported that the Blue Nun was known to have bi-located to the Pueblos of New Mexico through the intercession of the angels in the 1620s in order to preach the gospel. When called before the Inquisition to answer for her visions María Coronel was an adroit debater, always respectful and careful to tread lightly on the issue of whether her trances or her communion with the angels was the work of the Lord or of her overactive imagination. Or, perhaps it was her close relationship and correspondence with King Felipe IV that kept the Holy Office of the Inquisition enamored of her. In the end, she was not formally tried, but just reminded by the Inquisition that logical treatises on the nature of the mysteries were out of her realm. She herself dismissed the story of her bilocation to New Mexico, treating it as a youthful bout of religious zeal. Doña Teresa's ordeal with the Inquisition was a different matter, with many more appearances and a web of underlying intrigues.

Before describing Doña Teresa's ordeal with the Inquisition authorities, it would be useful to look at the Inquisition process itself.[33] Complaints or reports from *familiares*—employees of the Inquisition—or from ordinary citizens, could lead to an arrest or arrests on suspicion of heretical activity. An Inquisition proceeding generally began with a reading in church of the Edict of Faith, which urged anyone who might have anything to confess or information to provide concerning others' errors of faith to come forward voluntarily. Then the suspects would be arrested—usually sometime after midnight—and their goods and personal belongings immediately impounded and inventoried. The impounded goods would be used to pay for the expenses of housing and feeding the accused, as well as to pay for the administrative costs of the Inquisition process and its officials. The accused prisoners were generally allowed a bed, two sheets, a coverlet, and two complete changes of clothing, including undergarments.

The succeeding process was long and cumbersome, involving many interrogations, admonitions, reports, inspections and accusations. Once arrested, the accused were obliged to wait long periods between interviews with Inquisitors, forcing them to endure long periods of imprisonment between their arrest and the final outcome. Testimony from the accused, as well as voluntary and involuntary witnesses, would be recorded by a notary or scribe.

The accused ordinarily would have three audiences with the Inquisition officials following the accused's imprisonment. The first audience could take place weeks, months or as much as a year after the initial arrest and imprisonment. During the first audience, the accused was admonished not to conceal anything the prisoner might have said or done contrary to the Catholic faith. The accused was promised clemency if a full confession was made, but was not told what the charges were. Then the accused was required to give a complete account of the accused's life—a *discurso de la vida*—including describing close relatives going back two generations. The accused was then asked if she or he knew why they had been arrested. Finally, the accused was given the first of three formal admonitions to bare her or his conscience by confessing to any crimes the accused had committed.

Several months after the initial audience, the accused would be furnished with a formal accusation including an itemized list of the charges. However, the accused was not told who the witnesses were nor whose testimony was the basis for the charges. There was no opportunity to confront the witnesses. After consulting with a lawyer appointed by the Inquisition—and usually one selected from a list of three provided by the Inquisition—the accused would respond to the charges. Males accused of practicing Judaism would be required to submit to a physical inspection during this time. During this period, there would often be periodic, unannounced additional audiences and questioning, as well as two more formal audiences when the admonitions were again given to the accused.

The Inquisitors would then consider all of the information and render a sentence. Apart from acquittal, the sentences could range from exile and confiscation of the accused's estate to public penance or death. Execution, if it was called for, was carried out by civil, not religious authorities. Public penance required the convicted to appear in public and formally decked in penitential garments called *sanbenitos*, recant their errors. Executions by burning and public penance were carried out during a ceremony called the *auto de fé*. In addition to the public recantation, the lesser sentences of those who were to wear *sanbenitos* for life or for a designated period, also included other restrictions and penalties such as being forbidden to wear silk, gold, jewelry or silver, to ride on horseback, or to bear arms.

Doña Teresa's arrest by the Inquisition authorities occurred about 4 a.m. on the morning of August 27, 1662. Fray Posada carried out the arrest, which the notary accompanying him recorded in somewhat voyeuristic detail:

> On the twenty-seventh of the month of August of one thousand six hundred sixty-two, in the early morning about four, more or less, I the Father Custodian and Commissary, Alonso de Posada, in the company of the *Alguacil Mayor* of the Holy Office, Don Juan Manso, and assisted by Father Nicolás de Freitas, Captain Antonio de Salas and the Armorer Joseph Jurado, went to the house where Doña Teresa Aguilera y Roche lives and has lived, and having opened the door of the hallway that is there with a passkey, were found in said hallway, Doña Teresa de Aguilera y Roche, seated on her bed. She was half dressed and there, next to her were two beds. Doña Ana Robledo and Doña Catalina de Zamora were lying in one bed, and in the other, was Antonia González, all inhabitants of this Villa of Santa Fé who had gone to be companions to Doña Teresa. ... And said Alguacil having entered the hallway first, told Doña Teresa de Aguilera that she should surrender as a prisoner of the Holy Office by virtue of a special order which he had concerning her from Your Lordship. To this Doña Teresa, crying and showing her grief, responded by asking why, an important person like her, was being treated in this way. And saying that she was a Christian Catholic, and she did not know why she was being offended in this way. Turning her face twice toward an image of Our Lady, she asked for justice (with appeals) against whoever was the cause of outrages like those Our Lady had suffered. And that the Inquisitors would know who she was. And if they wanted to make her a martyr, to be done with it.
>
> And then they told Doña Robledo, Doña Catalina and Antonia González that they should get dressed and go to their homes. And they did this, taking their beds along with them. And with

kindness, Doña Teresa de Aguilera was ordered to finish dressing. And she put on a doublet of blue fabric, and beneath that a scarlet damask corset, a blouse of Rouen linen embellished with silk tufts. Then she put on a red petticoat with five tiers of silver tips, and an underskirt of *baieta* or the coarse cloth of this land, bracelets of coral, strings of beads, a thick braid of beads of blue and other colors and false pearls. All of her clothing, along with the shoes she had on, was soiled.

And having put on a red cape, he brought her as a prisoner and put her in custody in a cell of this *convento* which is immediately after the second door of the *convento*, and which had a closed window and a single skylight among the beams. After placing the sleeping bed with its two brown linen covered mattresses, two sheets of linen, pillows of linen, a cotton covering and a striped tablecloth in the cell, Doña Teresa de Aguilera said that the day before this day of her imprisonment, she had given to ... Peñalosa a black dress of moiré satin, an outer skirt, and doublet, a hooped petticoat and hoop for adornment of made of woven flowered cotton *manta*, a hooped skirt of blue finely-woven Holland linen silk, a scarlet cloak with blue point lace and embellished with silver.... [She continued on to describe many other items of clothing, jewelry and personal valuables conveyed to Peñalosa—all of which were later inventoried.]

And during this time said Governor took out of his house some homespun clothing that Dona Teresa had hidden, which were shirts of *manta*, breeches of the same material, buff embroidered jackets, and some chamois—although just a few. And for not being clear about how many they were, she does not say more. ... And she signed this along with the said Father Custodian and the *Alguacil Mayor*....[34]

Immediately following Doña Teresa's arrest, in accordance with Inquisition procedure, the arresting officers inventoried her goods, containing an impressive list of furnishings and ceramics brought from Mexico, as well as locally made textiles and ceramics. Her servants, Clara, a *mulatilla*, and a child Diego described as a seven or eight year old *mulatillo* were also listed on the inventory.[35]

Several days after their arrests, Don Bernardo and Doña Teresa were transferred to the Inquisition cells at Santo Domingo. It was from there that they and the New Mexicans left under guard on October 6, 1662, all destined for the Inquisition cells in Mexico City. They were received there on April 11, 1663.[36] Don Bernardo's first appearance before the Inquisitors was on April 28, 1663.

The main entrance to the headquarters of the Holy Office of the Inquisition in Mexico City. Fray Alonso de Posada would have entered through this doorway. Photograph courtesy of Gerald T. E. González.

On November 28, 1663, following the three admonitions during the spring and previous summer, Don Bernardo was presented with 257 articles of accusation. In addition to many detailing his defamation and mistreatment of the clergy, a number covered practices of his and Doña Teresa's that seemed Jewish in nature. Several also related to his failing to truthfully testify that his mother's grandfather, Juan Núñez de León, had been tried and found guilty of being a *judaizante* in 1603.[37]

The reception courtyard inside the main entrance to the Inquisition headquarters of the Inquisition complex, where Fray Alonso de Posada would have been received. Photograph courtesy of Gerald T. E. González.

Doña Teresa's initial appearance before the Inquisitors was four days after her husband first appeared before them. In giving her *discurso de la vida* and other information, she said: her parents, grandparents and relatives had been considered to be Catholic Christians without any racial taint; she was baptized in Italy at Alexandria de la Palla, and confirmed in Milán where she was taught in a convent; she had always attended mass on feast days, and confessed and took communion once a year as the Church required; she could recite all the appropriate payers in Latin and Spanish; and she could read well, but did not know how to write fluently. When asked if she knew why she had been arrested she replied that as a good Catholic Christian who would die to defend her faith, and while she knew the Inquisition did not arrest anyone without cause, she did not know why she had been arrested except because enemies of hers had given false testimony—whose specifics she did not know.[38]

Two tiers of prisoner cells in the prison section of the Inquisition complex in Mexico City. Prisoners were allowed occasional individual access to the internal courtyard while under guard. Individual cells had high ceilings, but were only large enough to accommodate a bed and minor items of furniture, like a small bench or table. Photograph courtesy of Gerald T. E. González.

An interior prisoner cell window in the prison section of the Inquisition complex in Mexico City. Photograph courtesy of Gerald T. E. González.

Doña Teresa had her second and third admonitions on May 9 and June 12 of that year. During the rest of that year, she appeared before the Inquisitors numerous times—mostly at her own request—in order to defend herself. On October 26, the forty-one articles containing the accusations against her were read to her. The accusations were based on the testimony of 26 persons. In addition to detailing the failure to attend to or fulfill various requirements to participate in church services, they also included allegations that she bathed and changed clothes and linens on Friday nights—possible signs of Jewish practices. On December 6, excerpts from the testimony against her were read to her without identifying the witnesses.[39]

Two of the witnesses whose testimony led to the charges levied against Doña Teresa and her husband, were Pedro de Artiaga and his wife, Josepha Sandoval who had accompanied Don Bernardo and Doña Teresa to Santa Fé from Mexico City in 1658.[40] They lived in the Palace, but at a distance from Doña Teresa's own quarters. On October 24, 1661, Pedro Artiaga had testified before Inquisition officials in Santa Fe that he knew:

> ...that Doña Teresa de Aguilera every Friday put on clean clothes with particular care, on her bed, as well as her person and on the table, and she washed her face; even in very bad weather, when it was snowing, she never failed to wash herself and change her clothes, as it was Friday; and she kept to herself when she did this; and she closed herself in her room ... for an hour each time; and his wife, Doña Josepha de Sandoval, had said that she would be cleaning her [private] parts, and that this witness suspected that she closed herself off for such fear when she left to clean her parts in the aforesaid room, when on other occasions she did not exhibit such fear when Doña Josepha would see her entire body in her bed....[41]

According to Josepha de Sandoval: "Every Friday, without fail, by order of [Don Bernardo] and [Doña Teresa], clean clothes would be put on the bed and the table, and although this could have been left to the next day, it wasn't permitted; and that the aforeseaid put on clean clothes on Saturday."[42]

Like a number of the servants, Antonia Ysabel gave her own version: "every Friday night Doña Teresa de Aguilera put clean linens on the bed, and she washed her face and feet, cut her fingernails, and put on a clean tablecloth."[43]

Following the 'publication of the charges,' Doña Teresa requested paper and pen to prepare a response. Her request was granted and on January 11, 1664. She filed with the Inquisition, a seven page hand-written reply to the charges. The close-lined seven pages of writing—each sheet written on both sides—constitute the remarkable document about to be described.

Page 195: The Inquisitorial attestation, signed by Doña Teresa near the bottom, stating that Doña Teresa de Aguilera's thirteen handwritten pages are being attached by being hand-sewn into the documents relating to her Inquisition proceedings. Archivo General de la Nación de México.

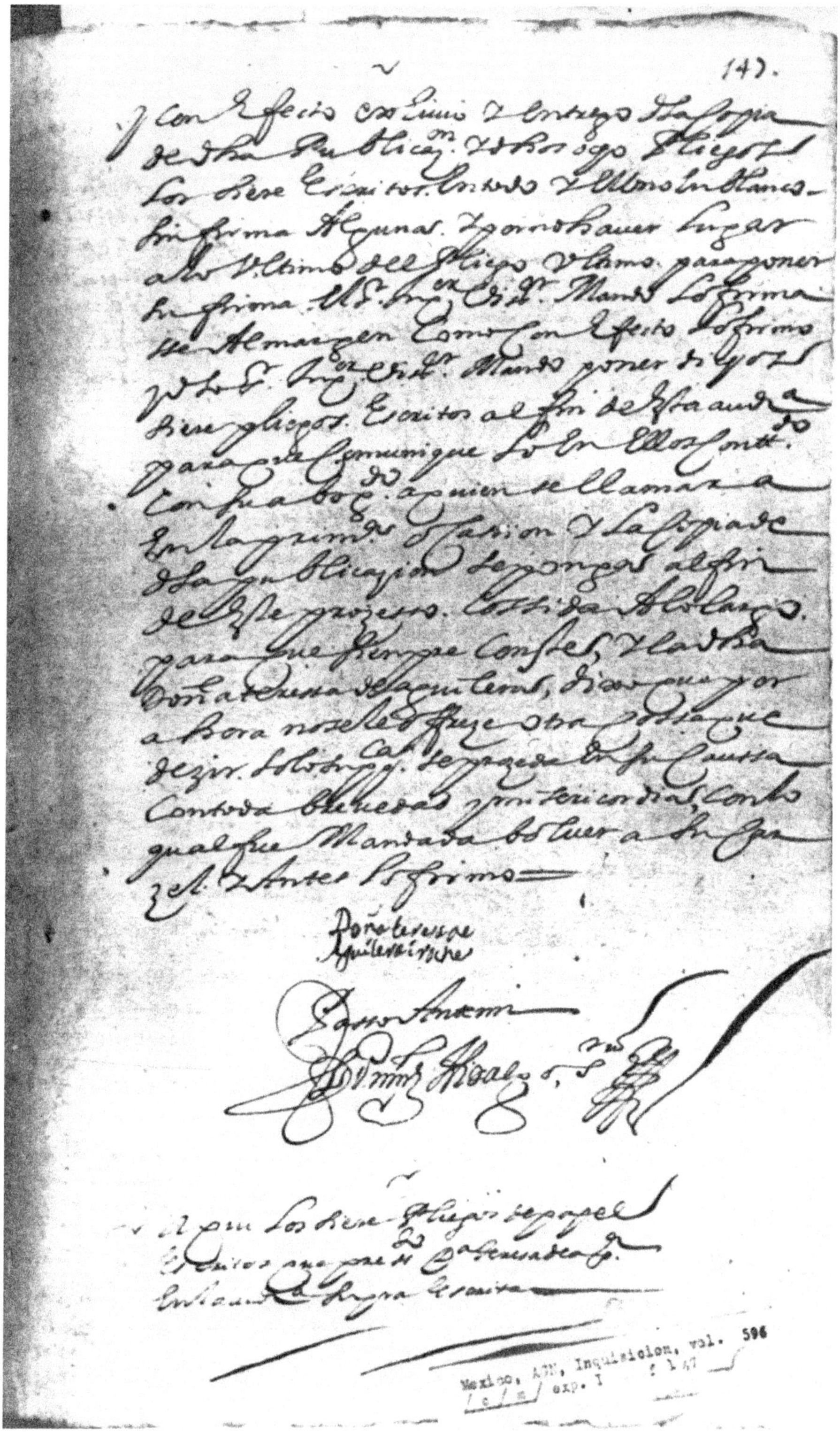

(4)

y con efecto escrivio y entrego la copia de dha publicaz.on y de los ocho pliegos los siete escritos enteros y el otro en blanco firma alguna y por no haver lugar a los ultimos del pliego ultimo para poner su firma. Su S.a el Sr Inq.or Vis.or Mando la firmase al margen como con efecto lo firmo y su S.a Inq.or Vis.or Mando poner de yo ts siete pliegos escritos al fin de esta aud.a para que comunique lo en ellos cont.do con su voto a quien se llamare en la prim.a ocasion y la copia de dha publicaz.on se ponga al fin de este proçeso. Y dicha Acus.on para que siempre conste. Y la dha Dona a dicha se que culpas, dixo que por ahora no se le ofrece otra cosa que dezir. Solo que se le de en su causa contoda brevedad y misericordia, con lo qual fue mandada bolver a su cassa y antes lo firmo =

Doña teressa
Aguilera y Roche

[signatures]

Y por los siete pliegos de papel
escritos que presentó ordenada de
enlo [illeg.] firma escrita

Mexico, AGN, Inquisicion, vol. 596
/ exp. 1   f 147

The first page of Doña Teresa's handwritten thirteen page defense. Archivo General de la Nación de México.

In her handwritten defense, Doña Teresa's view of New Mexico's frontier life was colored by her status as the wife of the governor. In it, surmising who might have been the unidentified witnesses, she named at least 72 Hispanic citizens, 6 Indian servants and named or referred to several African-American servants. She also named about a score of members of the clergy, whom she accused of sins and failings that ought to be considered in weighing their testimony. Some of her longest refutations were devoted to the persons deeply involved in her husband's *residencia* as well as the servants who worked and lived in the Palace. She opened her document by refuting the credibility of Don Juan Manso and some of his allies—as well as attacking other New Mexico colonists—all in order to undermine the validity of any testimony they might have given:

> Don Juan Manso would have surely given sworn testimony against me. He is an enemy because Don Bernardo was the judge for his *residencia* for which reason he had with him great differences about the *residencia*. And apart from that for different causes he had. He always complains of that and [Don Bernardo] was arrested to cause him injury because [Don Juan Manso] wanted to see that done. He was so disposed many times and finally he accomplished that from the offices of the *cabildo*. Don Juan Manso has always had and still has many complaints but Don Bernardo owes him nothing because of the Royal provisions which [Don Juan Manso] took. For which reasons [Don Diego de Peñalosa] took the provisions, saying they were a large amount of wealth, which should be returned to us. And thus Don Juan Manso was our enemy and resented a great deal that my husband quarreled with Ana Rodrigues[44] because of what happened in this [City of Mexico] with her nephew, Pedro de Valdes. And because they ejected him from the streets, for which causes and others, he had has always been and is, a mortal enemy, which my husband better understands.
>
> Pedro de Valdes[45] would have surely sworn. And [Don Bernardo] can explain it because I do not remember all that occurred. He is an enemy for same reasons as Don Juan Manso and because, like Juan Manso, [Don Bernardo] imprisoned him in the offices of the *cabildo*. And beyond that because he was a nuisance and I understand that [Don Bernardo] ordered him not to enter the house of Juan Griego[46] because of his scandalous conduct with Juan Griego's daughter. And after [Pedro de Valdes] returned with Don Diego [Peñalosa], who made [Valdes] his Lieutenant General, there were so many troubles and vexations that [he] inflicted on us that it is not possible to explain them nor even

mention them, except to say that Pedro de Valdes is and has been a mortal enemy.... And he demonstrated it by persecuting me in such a manner that he cut off my ability to communicate—as he did when he sent to have Juana Mohedano and Jusepa taken from the house. They had gone with me to church and he, having seen them, thereupon acted to order Antonio de Salas not to let us enter. And other times, knowing that [these two] were with me he sent others to oust them as was done on Palm Sunday. And there is no end to telling the story of the persecutions through which he demonstrated being an enemy and if it is necessary, this can be ascertained.[47]

As Doña Teresa continued her discourse, she next attacked the credibility of others in the web of Santa Fé residents who she also suspected of testifying against herself and her husband. In doing so, her words begin to paint the outlines of the clan-based nature of the colony's society emerging. Vividly depicted for posterity are relationships within and between families based on marriages, kinship, godparents and issue alliances. Provocatively, she also intimated that one of her potential accusers may have had a heretical—even crypto-Jewish—background:

> Juan Griego would surely have testified against us and he is, I am compelled to say, the son of another person of the same name who it is publicly known and said there [in New Mexico], died with a *capote* in his mouth and his face turned to the wall without wanting to make a confession or be a Christian, not even in that hour. Because of which reasons they say they buried him in the hills of Santa Ana or others—I'm not sure what truth this has.[48] And Juan Griego was an enemy since we went there because Don Bernardo removed him as an interpreter, a matter which he resented and all of his family resented very much and for this reason they became very aggrieved. And, also, Don Bernardo ejected his son-in-law from our house for being a thief and calling him a thief, and also because he asked Juan Griego for an accounting of the finances from the shipment that he took to Parral—and he still has not done that.[49]

After denigrating Juan Griego, Doña Teresa naturally next attacked the rest of the family—any number of whose members might have testified against herself and her husband:

> [Don Bernardo] also reprimanded [Juan Griego's] sister, a

Bernal, and her daughters for their bad life and he threatened her with whipping different times and finally he exiled her. It was a grave affront to him to send him on escort duty to Taos on one occasion that presented itself. He sent his son-in-law another time on another escort. And, in the same way, many other relatives of his—which is the general aggravation of all the inhabitants against the governors. Don Bernardo made a prisoner of various relatives [of Juan Griego's] for reasons that they gave him. He condemned him after seeing Juan Griego's sister sell one of her daughters to Don Juan Manso. And he found that out from the one who was given to Don Diego [de Peñalosa]. He reprimanded [Juan Griego's sister] for the comings and goings of Pedro de Valdes and the scandals of [Juan Griego's] daughters. And [Don Bernardo] was given to say that in order for a man there to have someone defend him, it only required that he get involved with a woman's family so that, as a consequence, all in her family would defend him—and [Don Bernardo] said this because he saw they all protected Manso.

[Don Bernardo] held Diego del Castillo, another son-in-law of Juan Griego's, prisoner and had him whipped, but not for me. And because of not just this, they are and have been my husband's enemies ... and besides that, mine as well, and they have shown this in all things without my having given them a single reason ... And I don't know if he is a complainant in the residencia.[50]

As she continued her disparagement of Catalina Bernal, Doña Teresa gives us glimpses of 'everyday life' in the Palace:

...since we went there she joined with Jusepa[51] because she would come to the house to make me some netting which she had some trouble in making and so she became very displeased as was her natural way ... And so as to make the most of the situation, she would come prepared with a small bag [hidden] beneath the underskirts or skirts that all of them wear so that when they would make ground chocolate, she would adjust her clothes and put the chocolate beans and the ground chocolate in [the bag]. And two of the persons who were grinding the chocolate, because they heard me complain about the large amount [of chocolate] that was missing ... revealed this so that I wouldn't blame them, except for their having seen what was going on. And so in this matter, I didn't forgive what was going on, and I reprimanded and embarrassed [Catalina Bernal] several times, which served only to make her want to get back at me more.

. . .

And this was not all that she did, because she muttered in front of me, believing that I would not understand Tegua. And because of circumstances I knew what she was saying, just not who she was talking about. Shocked that I understood what she was saying she said she would not say anything more in front of me. Later, on another occasion the other person told me what she had said.[52]

Some of the clans whose members Doña Teresa sought to undermine were those comprising the Domínguez and the Chávez families and their relations. In the case of the Dominguez-based clan, we easily see the tangled web of affiliations that characterized the colony. Tomé Domínguez, a member of the clerical faction among the colonists had been former Governor Manso's Lieutenant Governor and Captain General. When Don Bernardo arrived in Santa Fe, he replaced him with his brother, Juan Domínguez, another veteran soldier, administrative officer and local militia leader.[53] Juan's wife was Isabel Durán y Chávez, apparently the daughter of Pedro Durán y Chávez.[54] Tomé was appointed as Lieutenant Governor by Governor Peñalosa when he left for Mexico City in 1664.[55] Another brother in this family, Francisco Domínguez, carried notification to Don Bernardo's brother in Mexico City—and thereby to officials of the Viceroy—concerning Don Bernardo's imprisonment during his *residencia*.[56] In her holographic defense, Doña Teresa wrote concerning this family:

Tomé Domínguez surely testified against us as an enemy because he belonged to Manso's faction from the time we arrived and was his Lieutenant General—and because Don Bernardo removed him from office he was very resentful. And [Don Bernardo] sent him on military expeditions and also sent some of his relatives on escort duty, something they all complained about. And on one occasion, after having tolerated him considerably, when through his great presumptiveness [Tomé] annoyed him too much, he turned him around shoved him and had then him imprisoned in the Villa and his relations became greatly aggravated, saying that he had slapped him.

And [Don Bernardo] complained about [Tomé's] relatives, the [Pérez] Granillos because he had sent him on a dispatch to Sonora and for these reasons and many others including the petition or complaint of many of his relatives he is ... an enemy.

And apart from this during *residencia* and afterwards, he would come at night to the doorway to the street and call to his brother Juan Domínguez who was living in the [Palace] and they customarily spent a long time talking. And when his brother returned we usually asked him who had called him. And saying who, he would give us warnings and persuasions about why he should disassociate with my husband because the clerics threatened him, saying that if he did not, he would incur the greatest troubles that any man had experienced and many similar things. And he said this because he was very much in favor of the clergy, particularly Fray Salvador [de Guerra], secretary of the Custodio, who is the gravest enemy we have and who is his friend. In the end, despite these threats, they did nothing to him. And I do not know why, except they got him to complain against us so as to excuse the misdeeds they threatened him with having committed....[57]

Doña Teresa then tackled the Durán y Chávez relations who had acquired considerable wealth in the form of lands and livestock:[58]

The Chavez' ... are enemies because one is the son-in-law of Tomé [Domínguez] and the other is the father-in-law of Juan Domínguez. Because of all the reasons expressed by them ... they have many complaints of having been sent on escorts and military expeditions and because [Don Bernardo] upbraided them for being tricksters....

Doña Teresa, then returned to the Pérez Granillo family who she pointed out were cousins of Tomé Domínguez' wife, saying that in addition to the reasons just given for their being enemies another involved a shipment of goods Don Bernardo had sent to Sonora under the charge of Captain Francisco Pérez Granillo. According to Doña Teresa, fifteen days after leaving the Province of New Mexico, he was paid 7,000 pesos for the goods. And when Francisco returned a year and a few days later, he only brought back 2,904 pesos of silver, which Peñalosa then took possession of. And on top of this, Francisco then brought a complaint against Don Bernardo seeking the cost of freight for the mules that brought back the silver.[59]

Doña Teresa's detailing of the various clan groupings and how the people she named were allied against her and Don Bernardo pervaded her handwritten defense. However, she also paid attention to the persons who lived in and were associated with life in the Palace. Her attention to this group seemed motivated by her apparent understanding of what testimony these people gave or might have given and she took pains to discredit them. These individuals included Pedro de Artiaga, his wife,

Josepha Sandoval (or Jusepa as Doña Teresa called her), Diego de Melgarejo, her personal servants and slaves, and others who resided in the Palace for a time. Her testimony also traced some of the interactions between the Palace inhabitants and the members of Santa Fé society who lived outside the Palace:

> Pedro de Artiaga would surely have given testimony—and Diego Melgarejo as well. [And Pedro de Artiaga] is an enemy because while we were on the road to New Mexico, Don Bernardo reprimanded him for different reasons and he had him seized and shackled for days because he took advantage of his wife, even of her food. In Parral, because of his bad tendencies and because of tales told by [Miguel de] Noriega they left. Upon being returned they confessed this and resented having been returned and from there on they always had great hatred for us, as they demonstrated on all occasions.
>
> And upon arriving in the Villa [of Santa Fé], seeing them camped out, for the love of God we placed them in our house—only so that they would steal from us, something we caught them doing many times with the foodstuffs that were sent to the houses that were being fed, since they did not have adequate barns nor pantries for storing the food. Even the roasted sheep they would take over the walls at night using ropes, not being happy with the four sheep and two cows that were slaughtered each week. They would eat three because they were able to take them. And I was told at various times that they fed half of the Villa this way. And many times for these reasons we affronted them to no avail. Apart from this, I was informed that every night they would go sleep outside [of the palace with residents of the Villa].
>
> One evening when I felt ill, I sent the negress to bring a woman to treat me, and she returned hastily to say that she could see the people who were going outside [the palace]. Since my husband was undressed, he sent someone to find them—which they could not. Finally, after a half hour they found them and we assailed them. And because of the animals that were missing and could not be recovered on this occasion— and which every day they would take and eat making it necessary for us to look for them, which I could not stand—we reprimanded them, including [Jusepa], who was there at the time. And she would stand there calmly and abhor me. Apart from this, being told that at night they continued to escape—Jusepa along with them—to hold fiestas and dances in different houses, something that was documented, I had them relocated as was necessary in order not to be disturbed when they

returned since they left the door to the street open. And there being on another occasion a large whole in the wall, after finding the door closed up, the Apaches went out through it, even though they should have just gone to the patio.

And also on this occasion having gotten out of bed it was not possible to find where they were. And for these reasons and having little ability to correct the situation, we treated them badly and reprimanded them because it was necessary. And at that time Don Bernardo imprisoned them and told them that they had to repay the animals that were missing. And releasing them several days later, they promised to repay. And what they did was that they brought to the kitchen those who feasted with them, entertaining them there until we realized what was happening and we again reprimanded them saying they should not take anything. And on these occasions, because the negress had participated, I had her whipped because she was an accomplice and had given them tablecloths and other things for the feasts.[60]

Having a good idea that Josepha de Sandoval had given testimony to the Inquisition against herself and her husband, Doña Teresa, took the time in her written defense to take her to task. Interestingly, Doña Teresa indicates that despite the fact the Josepha lived within the Palace, she had not learned her surname—an indication that she maintained a certain distance from persons she did not see as being her social equal:

Jusepa, Pedro de Artiaga's wife, whose surname I do not know, surely testified against us. She is an enemy and leader, like her husband of all the ills that they did in my house and of the hostility they all had. And in this way because of all the matters which are expressed concerning her husband and Diego [de Melgarejo]. Furthermore, because she was a woman incompetent in her speech and without substantial wisdom and whose sole application is to whatever misdeed she could or might do. For that reason, it was a continual gyration I had with her from the first day. And there was no end to the occasions I had when I would not reprimand her.[61]

Doña Teresa then goes on to tell a tale concerning Josepha's indiscretions with a man not her husband in Parral, during the journey to Santa Fe. Because Don Bernardo reprimanded Josepha for this, it gave Josepha a reason to be his and Doña Teresa's enemy. Moreover, once in Santa Fé, Josepha, her husband and Diego de

Melgarejo would go "at night to different houses to dance, sing and be present and they would leave the door to the street open on these occasions and others so they would not have to call out when they returned. And having found this out was that they would not go out and, instead, they invited those they had fiestas with to come into the kitchen and there they had feasts and grand banquets causing incredible damage to my house."[62]

Doña Teresa also devoted a considerable effort in her defense to undermining the credibility of the various household servants. For example, regarding the negress who was one of the household slaves she wrote:

> The negress surely testified. She is an enemy because she is a slave as all slaves are respecting their masters. And also, we punished her many times for her scheming, great prattling, neglect and laxness—and not any less her fondness for trifles—and because since we were on the journey to New Mexico together, she allied herself with Jusepa and they became great friends. By happenstance we saw them together in a wagon, kissing and for that reason and their lack of consciousness, we reprimanded them greatly. Because of their great friendship, when we arrived in the Villa, she would help Jusepa with everything she did and would cover things up for her. And learning of some of these things, we whipped her. So both of them would get together and mutter against us, something that never stopped.[63]

This story was followed by a long description of how the negress had actually feigned a pregnancy—and was assisted in the deception by Josepha de Sandoval who kept up a close friendship with her—not only exchanging gossip in the kitchens, but also in the evenings when they would meet "for half an hour to an hour, talking with such great secrecy that a few times—having prepared beforehand to try and listen—I could not hear them, nor could some of the girls."[64]

Regarding Antonia Ysabel who had testified against her, she wrote:

> Antonia, an Indian who was a cook ... was a servant of Manso and when he fled she was brought as a prisoner. Don Bernardo struck her for complaining about [Manso's flight] as well as the imprisonment of the other enemies we had ... And when the cook we had fell ill we took her out of prison to replace the cook and like someone forced to do this she showed it always in her work ... And we ordered her not to leave the Palace without permission, something she resented so much it is unbelieveable. Finally she went to complain to Don Diego

[Peñalosa], asking for his permission to leave the Palace. He returned her and knowing all this, we told her we would pay her very well so she would stay. In turn she gave me a thousand complaints because I had had the key to her room when she was a prisoner, but had not cared for her at the time. I told her ... she had not told me then that she wanted to be a cook. When she did stay in my house, she was one of [Jusepa's] allies, sharing her hatred and ill will. And I reprimanded her because of this and because of things that went missing or were used up ... and her not wanting to do any work ... so she has been a mortal enemy as she demonstrated by fleeing from my home, having received one hundred pesos and transportation from [Juan] Manso.[65]

One thing that is clear from both the records of Don Bernardo's *residencia* and those of his and Doña Teresa's Inquisition trials, is that Don Bernardo was a philanderer. Doña Teresa obviously agonized over Don Bernardo's womanizing at the same time that she deftly used it as a way to counter testimony from the servants and others. In doing so, she also outlined the moral laxity that seemed to permeate the Palace as well as the Santa Fé colonists in general:

Petrona de Gamboa and her parents and siblings would surely have testified because they are enemies. She was brought to my residence as a prisoner, along with her parents, because her mother [María Pacheco] had killed a girl with a blow from a stick. And she was assigned to sleep in an apartment further in the [Palace] than mine where my girl helpers also slept. What she did was un-nail a board on the window there and then she would go out to sleep with whomever she wanted—although I did not realize this until later. And they told me that the negress accompanied her because they were good friends, something she would not have been able to do otherwise because they slept in the same place. In the early morning they would return through the same garden plot and window, so I reprimanded and mistreated her. I did the same with her mother because she denied the death she had caused with protestations and because of my compassion for the poor deceased girl, I could not stand it.

...

After the matter of her parents was concluded, Don Bernardo ordered that she go live with them. I later came to learn that both in the palace and outside, she had become entangled with [Don Bernardo] and when I was apprised of that I then learned that he would take

> her to an apartment in the residences [of the Palace] to see her. So, having requested the apartment's key to remove this bother, I sent word through Ana Carima, who was her aunt, not to come see me in my home because I would have her flayed or lashed since whenever Petrona de Gamboa would come to my home on the pretext of seeing me, she would see him either before or after. And having told my husband that if that was his desire—and having said other things as are necessary for a proper woman—he being blind to the sin's deception, resented what I said as all like him are wont to do....[66]

Doña Teresa then went on to describe how Petrona even tried unsuccessfully to get Don Bernardo to eject Doña Teresa from the Palace. In other instances, according to Doña Teresa, Don Bernardo had a liaison with Josepha de Sandoval in the Palace,[67] as well as with one of the daughters of Catalina Bernal.[68]

In addition to disparaging the members of principal families that made up the colonists' clans—the Apodaca, Durán, Gómez, González Bernal, González Lobón, Ledesma, Lucero de Godoy, Mondragón, Montoya, Romero, Salas, Telles Jirón, Trujillo, Vera, Zamora, and Xavier families among them—Doña Teresa also singled out a multitude of Franciscans for attack in her defense document. They included Fray Nicolás de Freitas, Fray Juan Ramírez, Vice-Custodio Fray García de San Francisco, and Fray Diego de Santander, among others. She gave various reasons why they were enemies of herself and her husband—including disputes over the disposition of various goods and her husband's treatment of the Native American pueblo inhabitants.

In the end, Doña Teresa's hand written document proved to be one of the lynch pins of her successful defense. At the same time, it succeeded in laying bare the rough details of Santa Fe and New Mexico's frontier, clan-based society—from the standpoint of someone who saw themselves at the apex of the social order.

Following the filing of her defense document, the attorney assisting Doña Teresa with her case filed a brief with the Inquisitors in March, pointing out that most of the testimony against her was not based on eyewitness observation. In preparing her defense and the documents that were filed by her attorney, it also did not hurt that one of the jailers, Juan de Cárdenas, had been a friend of her father's in Cartagena. As a result he had relayed secret inquisitorial information to Doña Teresa, her husband and the other four New Mexican prisoners—as well as gave her an idea of what was going on in the Inquisitors' proceedings.[69]

When the activities of Juan de Cárdenas came to light, Doña Teresa had to go through another round of hearings. Around this time, on September 16, 1664, her husband died and was buried in unconsecrated ground.[70] Her testimony during these hearings shows that Doña Teresa was most greatly concerned about the charges of engaging in Jewish practices. During the hearings she said that while it was true she had groomed herself, and put on clean clothes and changed bed linens on Fridays—which had become a matter of general public attention in Santa Fé—on one occasion when she was discussing all of this with her husband, she had a bitter disagreement with him because he had not warned her that the Jews bathed on Friday. So everything was his fault because she would not have chosen Friday if she had known this. By this time, the case had been diffused to the point that on December 19, 1664, the Inquisitors voted to suspend the case.[71]

While Doña Teresa refuted the charges of practicing Judaism, she never directly answered the charges relating to her religious failings, or her religious practices. At the same time, she painted a picture of life in the Palace and the Province of New Mexico so full of deceptions and conspiracy according to her that anyone—even the friars—were not credible witnesses. Was this why the Inquisitors suspended the case? Or was it that there was nothing substantive to support the charges? Or did she cleverly use the intrigues to diffuse the charges, and lead the Inquisitors away from a secret *crypto-Jewish* life lived in Santa Fé, on New Spain's remote northern frontier?

References Cited:

Archivo General de la Nación, Mexico City
Ramo de Concurso de Peñalosa
Ramo de Inquisición
Chávez, Fray Angelico. 1992. *Origins of New Mexico Families*. Revised Edition. Santa Fe: Museum of New Mexico Press
Clark, Colahan. 1999. María de Jesus de Agreda: The Sweetheart of the Holy Office in Mary E. Giles, (1999) *Women in the Inquisition: Spain and the New World* (pp. 155-170) Baltimore: Johns Hopkins University Press.
Coll More, María Magdalena. 1999–2000. "'Fio Me a de Librar Dios Nuestro Señor de Mis Falsos Acusadores': Doña Teresa de Aguilera y Roche al Tribunal de la Inquisición (1664, Mexico)," Romance Philology,Vol. 53, Special Issue, Part 2.
Dodge, Meredith D. and Rick Hendricks. 1993. *Two Hearts, One Soul. The Correspondence of the Condesa de Galve, 1688–1696*. Albuquerque: The University of New Mexico Press.
Esquibel, José Antonio. 2005. *Juan Chamiso, Albañil Maestro: Research and Summary Notes*. Prepared by José Antonio Esquibel, 2005 for the Palace of the Governors. Used by permission of the author.
Flint, Richard and Shirley Cushing Flint, (editors, translators, annotators). 2005. *Documents of the Coronado Expedition, 1539–1542*. Dallas: Southern Methodist University Press.
Giles, Mary E., editor. 1999. *Women in the Inquisition: Spain and the New World*. Baltimore: Johns Hopkins *Spanish Textile Tradition of New Mexico and Colorado*. Santa Fe: Museum of New Mexico Press.
Morrow, Baker H. (translator and editor). 1996. *A Harvest of Reluctant Souls; The Memorial of Fray Alonso de Benavides, 1630*. Niwot, Colorado: University of Colorado Press.
Riley, Carroll L. 2007. Bernardo López de Mendizábal; Could He Have Prevented the Pueblo Revolt? in *El Palacio112(3): 38-46.*
Riley, Carroll L. 1999. *The Kachina and the Cross: Indians and Spaniards in the Early Southwest*. Salt Lake City, Utah: University of Utah Press.

Scholes, France V. 1937. Troublous Times in New Mexico, 1659–1670. *New Mexico Historical Review*, Vol. XII, Nos. 2, 4.
—— 1938. Troublous Times in New Mexico, 1659–1670. *New Mexico Historical Review*, Vol. XIII, No. 1.
—— 1940. Troublous Times in New Mexico, 1659–1670. *New Mexico Historical Review*, Vol. XV, Nos. 3, 4.
—— 1941. Troublous Times in New Mexico, 1659–1670. *New Mexico Historical Review*, Vol. XVI, 1, 2, 3.
All in:
—— 1942. *Troublous Times in New Mexico*. Publications in History, Vol. XI. Albuquerque, New Mexico: University of New Mexico Press.

On Establishing a Presidio at Santa Fe, 1678–1693
by
Barbara De Marco

The presidio at Santa Fe came into being after Diego de Vargas reclaimed the territory of New Mexico for the Spanish Crown in the early 1690s.[1] In a series of documents, beginning in 1678, the Franciscan procurator general, Fray Francisco de Ayeta, made repeated pleas for the establishment of a presidio in Santa Fe. More persuasive than his written arguments were the events of the 1680 Pueblo Revolt, in light of which the council in Mexico could no longer argue against the pressing need for a military presence in northern New Mexico. In January 1681, with Father Ayeta present at court, the council in Mexico authorized the establishment of a presidio, with headquarters at El Paso until such time as the northern provinces could be reconquered.

A Royal Cedula, issued on 18 June 1678, sets the stage for Father Ayeta's protracted correspondence with the King, in which he discusses the welfare of the province and the need for a fifty-man presidio at Santa Fe. The Cedula authorized the reimbursement to Ayeta for unusual expenses incurred in the 1677 conveyance of supply wagons to New Mexico. In the course of that journey, as Ayeta was making his way north from Mexico City, he learned that a confederation of Indians had attacked the settlements at Salinas and Senecú. From the supplies intended for the Franciscan missions, he was able to provide aid to the more than three hundred families of "yndios christianos" in those settlements. Indian raids had been continuous since 1672, and it was in response to the earlier destruction of the settlements at Cuarac (Quarái), Jumanas, Abó, and Chililí that Ayeta was conducting an additional "socorro" of fifty men to the frontier in 1677. For various reasons, including the Indian attack at Salinas and Senecú, the trip took three months longer than the norm. A long paper trail, which accompanied Father Ayeta on his return from Santa Fe to Mexico City, set out the circumstances of the unforeseen expenses and provided a complete reckoning. Once the accounts were submitted to the Viceroy and approved by the fiscal in Mexico City, the entire series of documents was forwarded to Madrid.

The 18 June 1678 Cedula issued by the King was, in essence, a formal statement that Father Ayeta had satisfied all the terms of his contract, and a post facto granting of permission to reimburse Ayeta for the extra expenses incurred in the trip. Ayeta took the opportunity of the Cedula to formulate a petition to the King. The formal petition set out the rationale for a two-fold request: given the continued Apache raids and the most recent (1677) depredations of yet another two settlements (Salinas and Senecú), two measures were deemed essential: first, the provision of an additional fifty men (referred to as the "segundo socorro," inasmuch as it was a request for a second fifty-man supplementary force, like that which the King had authorized in 1677 in response to the attacks on Quarái, Jumanas, Abó, and Chililí), and second, the establishment of a fifty-man presidio at the Villa of Santa Fe for a period of at least ten years, modeled after the presidio at Sinaloa.

Father Ayeta's petition is of interest as much for the manner of its argumentation as for the argument itself. Ayeta justifies his pleas for additional manpower for the northern province by citing from a series of royal cedulas (nine in all, dating between 1602 and 1678, three of which he quotes in full). Copying out the entire text of the 18 June 1678 Cedula, Ayeta structures a three-fold argument by elaborating on the very words of the King ("y os encargo que en la primera ocasion que se ofrezca me deis quenta de lo que se ubiere obrado con ocasion de este socorro y del estado en que quedaren aquellas provincias y su pacificacion y sosiego"). He presents a brief report of the events of his nine-month journey from Mexico City to Santa Fe, including details of the cruel deaths of Franciscan friars at Senecú and Abó, as a considered reply to the King's request for a reckoning of the additional assistance he supplied in 1677 ("lo que se ubiere obrado con ocasion de este socorro"). To account for the present state of the provinces ("el estado en que quedaren aquellas provincias"), Ayeta writes that, having consigned the supplementary force of fifty men, since his return to Mexico in September 1678 he has heard of no new devastations to the northern settlements. Nonetheless, since the Apaches and their allies continue to conduct raids, he argues that it would be most appropriate for the King to agree to the two proposals set forth in his petition. To further support his argument, he cites from cedulas of 6 September 1670 and 21 October 1674, in which the King recommended an increase in the number of soldiers as a defense against continued Indian attacks in Nueva Vizcaya. Ayeta adds that a series of disasters that struck the province of New Mexico between 1670 and 1672 provides even more justification for the additional assistance: in 1670 a famine destroyed nearly half the population; in 1671 a plague further destroyed both people and livestock; in 1672 there was an Apache uprising in which the province was entirely sacked and plundered, and robbed of nearly all the livestock. Only by virtue of the assistance provided by the King was the province able to survive this wave of disasters.

Here Father Ayeta cites in full a Cedula dated 30 January 1635, which compares the halcyon days of the province to the harsh conditions that obtain in 1679. Ayeta provides the grim statistics of their actual situation: in an area extending north to south, from Taos to the banks of the Rio Grande, and east to west, from Oraibi to Salinas, the province contains 46 pueblos, 25 *conventos*, and 17,000 Indians, 6,000 of whom are armed with bows and arrows. In the entire settlement there are scarcely 170 settlers capable of bearing arms, and the Spanish populace is so spread out on the frontier and on *estancias* that, in case of sudden attack, the governor would be hard put to assemble even twenty armed men. By contrast, Ayeta asks the King (Carlos II) to consider the conditions of the northern province as they were described by fray Alonso de Benavides and reported by the King (Philip IV) in the 1635 Cedula.[2] At that time there were more than 100 religious to administer to 86,000 baptized Indians; each of the more than 100 pueblos had its own church, and Santa Fe was described as "una villa muy buena de españoles con otras estancias y haziendas pobladas de ellos." In the 1635 Cedula, the King instructed the Viceroy to give all possible aid to the provinces, to offer the Indians every care and protection, and to take care that the soldiers experienced no troubles of any kind. In light of those expressed sentiments, and in light of the far more difficult situation faced by the province in 1679, Ayeta argues that the approval of both his new requests—the "segundo socorro" of fifty additional men, and the fifty-man presidio at Santa Fe—are in perfect conformity with the royal desire for the welfare of the province.

The third point of Ayeta's argument addresses the King's request for information on the "pacificacion y sosiego" of the provinces. Ayeta argues that, even though the number of Apaches and their confederates is considerable, nonetheless, if His Majesty would (a) send fifty new recruits to the province, (b) establish the fifty-man presidio at Santa Fe, (c) retain Antonio de Otermín as governor, and (d) continue to support the missionaries, not only would there be more conversions in the province, but His Majesty would begin to reap the mineral wealth of the lands contiguous to New Mexico, and thereby receive some recompense for the amounts the Crown has spent on maintaining the province for so many years.

Father Ayeta submitted his carefully worded petition to the Viceroy, Archbishop Payo de Rivera, who on 10 May 1679 forwarded it to the fiscal in

Mexico City. The fiscal formulated his response in a letter of the same date, addressed to the King. The fiscal stated flat out that he was not convinced by Father Ayeta's arguments ("no persuaden bastantemente"). Referring to Ayeta's practice of citing earlier royal cedulas as justification for the present requests, the fiscal argued that, even though the King, in 1677, sent an additional fifty men to ward against Indian attacks in the northern province, the circumstances in the provinces in 1679 do not justify the request for yet another fifty men. If the King were to continue supplying aid in this way, the fiscal argues, all the money in the kingdom would not suffice.

Father Ayeta, having read the fiscal's response, adds yet one more letter, dated 28 May 1679, to the growing accumulation of documents. In this letter Ayeta stresses that he has served in the provinces of New Mexico as the chief ecclesiastical minister for six years, and he reiterates yet again (he states this request no less than six times in the course of his earlier petition) that if His Majesty would send another fifty men to the frontier and authorize the establishment of a fifty-man presidio at Santa Fe for a period of at least ten years, then not only would the missionaries be able to convert the Apaches and their allies, they would also be able to bring the Holy Gospel to the territories of "las Californias," in accordance with His Majesty's desires. This, in turn, would lead to the acquisition of new riches for the Crown. On 19 June 1679 the Archbishop forwarded the "escrito y representación" from Ayeta, making no specific recommendations of his own, merely asking His Majesty to consider the situation and the needs of the province, and the good effects that resulted from the assistance the King had already provided.

Several months later this assemblage of documentation reaches Spain. The fiscal in Madrid, in remarks dated 7 February 1680, notes that the Archbishop has forwarded Ayeta's petition to the council in Madrid without stating his own opinion on the matter. The fiscal insists that, in order for the council to make an appropriate decision, the Archbishop should inform them as soon as possible of the estimated cost that would be incurred in meeting Father Ayeta's request for the additional fifty-man supplement and for the establishment of a presidio at Santa Fe, as well as what harm might ensue if these measures were not put into effect. The fiscal also asks that the Archbishop advise the council of the best course of action to be followed, of the measures that he deems most appropriate, and as to whether the province of New Mexico can itself contribute to the expenses, and if so, in what amount.

These annotations, signed with the rubric of the fiscal, suggest that the council was poised to approve the additional aid that Father Ayeta had requested. However, the wording of the official response of the King, given in a Cedula dated 25 June 1680 (and addressed to the Marquis de la Laguna, fray Payo de Rivera's successor as Viceroy), reads somewhat differently. Beginning with the customary reiterations of earlier correspondence, the King refers to the Archbishop's letter of 19 June 1679, reprises his own 18 June 1678 Cedula, and acknowledges receipt of both Ayeta's letter of 28 May 1679 (with accompanying petition) and the fiscal's recommendations of 10 May 1679. The preliminaries established, he then instructs the Viceroy, in light of the continued Indian attacks, to apply whatever measures the Viceroy deems possible for the aid and defense of those provinces, and in whatever form he thinks necessary and appropriate. In other words, the Cedula does not simply and explicitly order the Viceroy in Mexico City to supply the additional men and establish the fifty-man presidio at Santa Fe, notwithstanding Father Ayeta's repeated entreaties. Even if it had, as events turned out, a cedula issued in Spain in June of 1680 would have reached the authorities in Mexico too late to be of any actual assistance to the province of New Mexico In fact, Father Ayeta did not see the 25 June 1680 Cedula until his return to Mexico City in early January 1681, that is, after the August 1680 Pueblo Revolt had already taken place.[3] At that juncture, and in light of Father Ayeta's reports on the aftermath of the Revolt, the council in Mexico City made haste to act. With the survivors of the Pueblo Revolt now settled in El Paso, however, there was clearly no immediate possibility of establishing a presidio at Santa Fe. On 10 January 1681, the Viceroy and members of the *junta general de hacienda* authorized expenditures for 150 "soldier-settlers" and a fifty-man presidio to be established at El Paso, along with provisions, arms, and supplies. On 17 January 1681, they further specified that the command of the presidio at El Paso would be entrusted to Governor Otermín, and that once the northern province was brought back into submission, the presidio would be moved to whatever place the Viceroy deemed best.

Several years passed before the presidio at Santa Fe could be established. In the winter of 1681, Governor Otermín staged an unsuccessful attempt to recover the territory lost in the Revolt. Not until the fall of 1693 was Diego de Vargas able to lead a recolonization effort from El Paso. In 1693, Father Ayeta received the news that, after a four-month campaign, Diego de Vargas had established "the symbolic reconquest of all New Mexico" (Kessell et al. 1989:59).[4] At this juncture, Father Ayeta sent a lengthy *memorial* to the King, in which he offered his retrospective on the 1680 Pueblo Revolt and his practical recommendations for the successful recolonization of the province. His remarks and recommendations to the King regarding the re-establishment of the Spanish presence in northern New Mexico were based on his years of experience in the provinces. For the events of the Revolt itself, he drew extensively on the documents he had received from Governor Otermín; from the end of August 1680 Ayeta himself was an eyewitness and a key participant in subsequent developments.

"The Adobe Palace," old Government House erected in 1650. From *Illustrated New Mexico, 1885* by W. G. Ritch.

The documentary history of the *memorial* merits some attention. The signed original is the last of four items, all dating to 1693, that are bound together in Archivo General de Indias, Guadalajara, legajo 139. An annotation to Ayeta's *memorial* reads: "Copy of [the *memorial*] that Viceroy Conde de Galbe refers to in his letter of 28 May 1693 ... concerning the restoration of New Mexico. To be placed together with the Viceroy's other letter of 20 May 1693 ...," that is, although Father Ayeta stated clearly that his intention was to describe to His Majesty how the provinces of New Mexico were lost in the events of 1680 and 1681, his *memorial* was filed with other papers from 1693 written in connection with Vargas' successful recovery of the northern provinces. It is perhaps by reason of this chronological filing that, notwithstanding the significance of the *memorial* as a retrospective on the Pueblo Revolt written by one of the key figures in New Mexico, the document was not included in either of the two major compilations of translated documents relating to the period: the *Historical Documents Relating to New Mexico ...* (Hackett 1937) or *Revolt of the Pueblo Indians of New Mexico* (Hackett 1942).[5]

Father Ayeta makes reference to a series of supporting documents that he is forwarding along with the *memorial*—an additional 500 folios in all (in modern terms, some 1000 printed pages). Although this supporting documentation is not bound with the *memorial* in AGI Guadalajara 139, Ayeta's descriptions of the contents, as well as the wording of the *memorial* itself, suggest that, were the missing attachments to be recovered, the supplementary documentation would correspond in great measure to the contents of Hackett's two-volume collection on the *Revolt of the Pueblo Indians of New Mexico and Otermín's Attempted Reconquest, 1680–1682*.

In a cover letter, Ayeta explains that he had been preparing the *memorial* even before he received news of Vargas's successful *entrada* into northern New Mexico.[6] His intention was to inform His Majesty of what occurred during the loss of the province of New Mexico in the years 1680 and 1681, so that the King might determine the most appropriate measures for the recovery of the provinces: "That this may be achieved, it may be most enlightening to know not only how the province was lost, but also what occurred when an attempt was made to recover it, since the petitioner, as eyewitness for the most part, is obliged by his conscience to relate what concerns him as chaplain and vassal of Your Majesty, as well as his concern over the quantity of blood that was shed by members of his Order in the conversion of that province."

The *memorial* itself is sub-divided into nine sections, describing in turn: the loss of New Mexico; details of the Revolt; representations made by Ayeta in Mexico City on behalf of the survivors; the 1681–1682 *entrada* into New Mexico; testimony taken down after the Revolt; Ayeta's impressions of the situation in New Mexico; opinions of the survivors as to whether to attempt the *entrada*; events that transpired in the return to El Paso after the unsuccessful *entrada*; and a final report from Ayeta, including his accounts of expenses in El Paso.

The closing passages of the *memorial*, relating most directly to the eventual establishment of a presidio at Santa Fe, are here excerpted at some length. Based on his experiences in the province, and especially as eyewitness to the *entrada*, Father Ayeta offers four specific suggestions for the successfully recovery of the province:

> First, the kingdom cannot be restored by those same settlers who lost it in the Revolt and the subsequent failed *entrada*. "They attempted the recovery of the kingdom only after they were constrained and compelled to do so [and] they performed harmful and damaging actions upon their return to the temporary settlement at El Paso," the evidence of which is contained in the accompanying autos.
>
> Second, any military campaign must not rely entirely on cavalry; rather, the main body should be comprised of infantry, with some cavalry for their defense. "To conquer, capture, and subjugate using only cavalry is an expense that yields nothing more than insolence

from the Indian and contempt for the Spanish nation, and what is more, it guarantees that once the Indian has taken to the hills, nothing can be done, and subjugation becomes impossible."

Third, in every presidio of the Indies at least one-third of the personnel should be infantry, and no soldier should enter into battle, or escort the wagons or mules, unless he is armed and wearing a cotton coverall (*sobretodo*) like those worn in Florida, or a leather jacket (*coleto*), which they call *cueras* in New Mexico.[7] Some do not even own weapons and are not required to purchase them out of their pay; all of them in general do not carry arms, using as their excuse that they are heavy and cumbersome. Thus their enemies are easily able to wound and kill the soldiers "because they are not carrying sufficient defensive force, not even against the weakest arrow. The evil consequences that result from killing a Spaniard are pernicious: they cut off his head and take his scalp and they dance all around it, then they send it out to all the other nations, so that they may celebrate their triumph, at which they all take heart, and any fear of the Spaniard is wiped out and the reputation of the Spanish nation is weakened."

Fourth, and of especial importance, is that the soldiers of the presidio should be virtuous men, at least twenty years old, so as to avoid certain problems which otherwise may occur.

Some closing words on the nature of the documentation itself are in order. The correspondence cited here is significant not only for what it reveals about actual persons and events in a crucial moment of American history, but also for what it reveals about the *modus operandi* of the courts in Madrid and Mexico City, and their extension into the far outreaches of the province of New Mexico and the Villa of Santa Fe. The evidence of elaborate, even belabored, exchanges of correspondence, in which an accumulation of previous documents are cited, copied, and recopied, or even, as in the 1693 *memorial*, the laborious and comprehensive compilation of reports to which there may be attached, literally, hundreds of folios of supporting documentation, inspires no little awe and, it must be admitted, not a little dismay. In their introduction to *The Presidio and Militia on the Northern Frontier of New Spain,* Thomas Naylor and Charles Polzer refer to "large portions of bureaucratic and dysfunctional rhetoric. In the typical Spanish document, paragraphs, even pages, can be consumed in repetitious formality" (page 12). The documents that form the background to this chapter reveal that, if anything, Naylor and Polzer understate the case. Nonetheless, to avoid repetitions in the presentation of texts by producing "a somewhat modernized version of the original, thus avoiding costly reproductions of questionable utility," though perhaps a justifiably pragmatic decision, obscures and even conceals valuable evidence offered by the documents themselves. The very presentation of the text on the page, the "conversations" that take place in the exchange of documents—including marginal notations, commentaries, and notes added by different hands, and even the original flourishes and rubrics are all valuable pieces of information. At times these annotations may be the only clues to dating the document with any precision; in any case, they offer crucial archeological evidence in the reconstruction of these paper kingdoms. With this in mind, it is to be hoped that the occasion of the 400th anniversary of the founding of Santa Fe will focus attention on the need to publish reliable Spanish editions of documents relating to the early history of the province of New Mexico and its capital, Santa Fe.

References Cited:

Cobos, Rubén. 2003. *A Dictionary of New Mexico and Southern Colorado Spanish*. Revised and expanded edition. Santa Fe: Museum of New Mexico Press.

De Marco, Barbara. 2000. "Voices from the Archives, II: Francisco de Ayeta's 1693 Retrospective on the 1680 Pueblo Revolt." *Romance Philology* Special Issue (Spring): 449-508.

De Marco, Barbara. 2005. "Fray Francisco de Ayeta and 1680 Pueblo Revolt in New Mexico: Preliminaries to a Biography." In *Francis in America: Essays on the Franciscan Family in North and South America* (proceedings of the International Franciscan Conference, Academy of American Franciscan History, Oakland, California, November 2000), editor. John F. Schwaller, 165-188. Berkeley, California: The Academy of American Franciscan History.

De Marco, Barbara, and Jerry R. Craddock, editors. 1999–2000. "Documenting the Colonial Experience, with Special Regard to Spanish in the American Southwest." *Romance Philology* 53. Special Issue in two parts (Fall 1999 and Spring 2000).

Espinosa, J. Manuel. 1988. *The Pueblo Indian Revolt of 1696 and the Franciscan Missions in New Mexico: Letters of the Missionaries and Related Documents*. Norman: University of Oklahoma Press.

Forrestal, Peter P., trans. 1954. *Benavides' Memorial of 1630*. With an historical introduction and notes by Cyprian J. Lynch, OFM. Washington, D C: The Academy of American Franciscan History.

Hackett, Charles Wilson, editor. 1937. *Historical Documents Relating to New Mexico, Nueva Vizcaya, and Approaches Thereto, to 1773*. Collected by Adolph F. A. Bandelier and Fanny R. Bandelier. Volume 3. Washington, DC: The Carnegie Institution of Washington.

Hackett, Charles W., editor, and Charmion C. Shelby, translator. 1942. *Revolt of the Pueblo Indians of New Mexico and Otermín's Attempted Reconquest 1680–1682*. Coronado Cuarto Centennial Publications, 1540–1940, 8-9. 2 volumes. Albuquerque: University of New Mexico Press.

Kessell, John L. 1987. *Kiva, Cross, and Crown: The Pecos Indians and New Mexico 1540–1840*. Albuquerque: University of New Mexico Press.

Kessell, John L. et al., eds. 1989. *Remote Beyond Compare: Letters of don Diego de Vargas to His Family from New Spain and New Mexico, 1675–1706*. Albuquerque: University of New Mexico Press.

Moorhead, Max L. 1975. *The Presidio: Bastion of the Spanish Borderlands*. Norman: University of Oklahoma Press. First paperback edition, with a foreword by David J. Weber, 1991.

Naylor, Thomas H., and Charles W. Polzer, S. J. 1986. *The Presidio and Militia on the Northern Frontier of New Spain. A Documentary History, 1570–1700*. Tucson: University of Arizona Press.

Nostrand, Richard L. 1992. *The Hispano Homeland*. Norman: University of Oklahoma Press.

Scholes, France V. 1930. "The Supply Service of the New Mexican Missions in the Seventeenth Century." *New Mexico Historical Review* 5:93-115; 186-210; 386-410.

Weber, David J. 1992. *The Spanish Frontier in North America*. New Haven & London: Yale University Press.

10

Vargas at the Gate
The Spanish Restoration of Santa Fe
1692–1696

by
John L. Kessell

Dismounted, the men crept forward in deep darkness—the snap of a dry branch, a muffled cough, the unintended clang of metal on metal. Anxiously, they groped on, peering ahead. The first tenuous light rising from behind the Sangre de Cristos cast hulking form to a strange fortress that now entombed the former palace of Spanish governors at Santa Fe. On Saturday, September 13, 1692, Diego de Vargas approached cautiously with his men-at-arms in close formation. On signal, all shouted in unison, "Praise be to the holy sacrament of the altar!" That brought crowds of Tano and Tewa Pueblo Indians to the flat roofs and terraces, the ramparts, as Vargas described the scene. The moment was critical. Four New Mexican Spaniards who knew the closely related Tano and Tewa tongues shouted up from the semidarkness that the Spaniards had returned in peace to pardon rebellious Pueblo Indians in the king's name. The occupants did not believe them. This must be some trick of Pecos or Apache enemies.

Urging calm, Vargas had bugle and war drum sounded. Now the Indians on the ramparts began a furious shouting that lasted an hour, screaming "many shameful things in their language," which dutiful interpreters translated for the governor. Still he refused to be drawn into battle. After sunrise, the angry dialogue continued. If he were indeed the new Spanish governor, he should come forward and take off his helmet so they could see him. This he did, removing even the kerchief from his head. He displayed his banner with the Blessed Virgin Mary on one side and the arms of Spain on the other. The vocal Pueblo tenants responded with a litany of earlier abuses committed by Spaniards. They demanded to know if Francisco Javier, Luis de Quintana, and Diego López Sambrano, their despised pre-Revolt tormentors, were among Vargas's company. He swore that they were not, and—dead or alive—that they would never return to New Mexico.

While the tense negotiations continued, Vargas had his small force of men-at-arms and Indian auxiliaries take up siege positions around the fortress and cut off its water supply. At the same time, outside the walls he greeted other Tewa delegations drawn from neighboring pueblos by the confrontation. He embraced them, literally. No one doubted this new governor's courage. Despite their urge to fight, Pueblo leaders inside the fortress noted that these Spaniards had not brought their women and children. Obviously they had not come to stay. Why not then let them perform their ritual acts and be gone?

Hence, on Sunday the fourteenth—a date still commemorated in Santa Fe's annual Fiestas amid mixed emotions—Diego de Vargas brushed aside his advisers' warnings and entered the fortress dressed in court finery without weapons. His bravado won the day. Gradually, Indian women and children crowded into the plaza to join their men. Before this assembly, the Spanish governor and three blue-robed Franciscan friars presided over the ceremonial repossession of Santa Fe and the absolution of hundreds of apostate Pueblo Indians, relying at every turn on the interpreters. Vargas permitted his honor guard to shout "Viva el Rey," throwing their hats in the air, but cautioned them not to fire their harquebuses in salute for fear that Indians outside the walls would assume that war had broken out.

The paramount Pueblo leader, don Luis el Picurí, alias Tupatu, put around his neck the rosary Governor Vargas had sent him as a safe-conduct. Don Luis appeared on horseback with his armed escort the next afternoon. He wore on his head like a diadem a plaited band set with a heart-shaped shell. The two leaders embraced in front of Vargas's campaign tent, talked of peace and war, and exchanged gifts. The following morning, Tupatu and other principal men knelt to accept absolution by the friars. After mass in the fortress on September 17, parents and guardians presented 122 infants and children born since 1680 for simple baptism. José, identified as captain of the fortress, and his wife Juana asked Governor Vargas to stand as godfather to their three girls. Half a dozen mothers brought babies to him "so that I might carry them in my arms, as I did, to receive the water of holy baptism." Whatever the ceremony of water meant to the infants' parents, Vargas came away with more Pueblo compadres. He rarely missed the diplomatic chance.

Throughout that fall and into the winter, pueblo by pueblo, from Pecos in the east—where restraint won him allies in future battles—to the Hopi pueblos in the west—where bluster failed to impress—Diego de Vargas staged similar scenes, then moved on. Before the end of December, he was back in El Paso, seat of the New Mexico colony in exile.

Diego de Vargas as a young man. Cuadra de San Isidro, Madrid, Spain. Courtesy of J. Manuel Espinosa.

Vargas's 1692 campaign journals and letters to Viceroy the marqués de Galve, which presented the reconquest of New Mexico as a fait accompli, inspired unrelieved praise and celebration in Mexico City, which Vargas made no effort to dispel.[1] Galve's court chronicler published a laudatory, thirty-six-page "news flash," or *mercurio volante*. The statistics resounded: numerous peoples and an entire kingdom restored to the Church and King Carlos II; 74 captives ransomed; 2,214 children baptized. Not a sword had been drawn, not an ounce of powder wasted, and most marvelous to relate, this peaceful victory of Spanish arms had cost the royal treasury not the thinnest copper coin. Grand propaganda indeed![2]

But Vargas masked the truth. A veteran administrator and military man, he knew the difference between a short-term truce and the renewed coexistence of Pueblos and Spaniards, between symbolic acts of repossession and actual reoccupation. Even at that, he gave too much credence to Pueblo leaders' compliance in 1692. Tupatu and other principal men had repeatedly lectured him that some Pueblos were good and others bad. Some had fallen in with Apaches and Navajos. Everywhere the Spanish governor went, Pueblo negotiators wanted Spaniards as allies to punish their own enemies. Governor Vargas, admonishing his interpreters, had tried to impress upon the Pueblo Indians with whom he parleyed that by renewing their obedience as vassals of the Spanish king, they would all be protected. Peace would return. That, many Pueblo adults recalled, had not been true in the grievous years before 1680.

Few Pueblo Indians, after experiencing Vargas's bold excursion through their towns in 1692, doubted that Spaniards would soon reappear in force with all their baggage. But because gathering, outfitting, and heading up a new wave of colonists took Vargas so long, Pueblo summer and winter councils had a full round of seasons during which to discuss their response. Divisions ran deep, nowhere more so than at Pecos, still one of the largest Pueblo communities. Younger men, especially warriors and plains traders of the winter people, saw benefit in the Spaniards' return. Their leader, Juan de Ye, spoke for the largest party. The venerable cacique Diego Umviro refused to listen: Spaniards were vermin.

No one had to remind Vargas that such factionalism favored resettlement, not only of Spaniards but also of temporarily displaced Pueblo Indians. Thanks to his most trusted Pueblo ally, Spanish-speaking don Bartolomé de Ojeda, the Spanish governor knew for certain of divisions among the Keresan people. Because Ojeda "was trustworthy and had his wife in the pueblo of El Paso," Vargas had hung a rosary around his neck late in September 1692, after Spanish "repossession" of Santa Fe, and sent him on a mission to treat with Keresan headman Antonio Malacate.[3]

A month later, don Bartolomé interpreted at a face-to-face meeting of Vargas and Malacate in the refugee pueblo where survivors from Zia, along with other Keres from Cochiti and Santo Domingo, had taken refuge on Mesa Colorada. As was his custom, the Spanish governor acted as godfather at the baptism of Malacate's son, appropriating another Indian namesake for the Spanish king. Vargas told Malacate through Ojeda to move his people back down to their pueblo in the valley. The Spanish governor would provide a saw so that they might cut timbers and reroof the damaged church. Once the meeting was over, Ojeda had warned Vargas that Malacate was not to be trusted.

Whatever faults don Diego de Vargas exhibited—arrogance and impatience prominent among them—the veteran Spanish administrator had learned to heed the counsel of trusted Indians. Without Bartolomé de Ojeda of Zia, Juan de Ye of Pecos, and others like them, the Pueblo-Spanish War—flaring in 1680, mostly smouldering between 1681 and 1691, and fanned anew by Vargas in the 1690s—might have dragged on into the new century. Its earlier resolution, however, resumed the measured, century-long dance of Pueblos and Spaniards in the Kingdom of New Mexico.

To Diego de Vargas late in 1693, it seemed like a fine idea, converting a Pueblo Indian kiva into a temporary Christian church. The Franciscan priest newly assigned to Santa Fe, fray José Díez, thought so too. The kiva resembled a squat tower protruding from one corner of the sprawling hive the Tewas and Tanos had superimposed on the former governor's palace. Along with outlying Spanish homes, they had torn down the previous Santa Fe church and planted corn in the ground where it had stood. While the gutted chapel of San Miguel might have been repaired, Indian leaders told Vargas that the snows lay too deep in the forests to cut new roof timbers. They invited him to use the kiva.

The Spanish governor went in person on December 20, 1693, to inspect the structure. "Having gone down the wooden ladder, I entered it and saw that it was round, and although its ceiling was low, it could serve for the winter." He accepted the Indians' offer and directed them to break a door through the wall at ground level for outside entry, make enough adobes for an altar, and whitewash the interior (an indication that kiva murals may have adorned the walls). The Indians objected to cutting an additional door into the interior of a resident's house to provide an adjoining two-room sacristy and priest's quarters with fireplace, but Vargas convinced them to do so. He loaned them crowbars, and two days later the space was ready.[4]

Only then did the Franciscan superior, Father custos Salvador Rodríguez de San Antonio, object. Since the Pueblo Indian occupants of Santa Fe had used this structure for "their prohibited juntas," the holy sacrifice of the Mass must not be performed within its walls. But the remodeling was complete, insisted Vargas. No matter, said the friar, there were other reasons as well why Christian worship could not take place in a Pueblo kiva, reasons the prelate did not expand upon. Recognizing the futility of further argument, the frustrated Spanish governor nevertheless reminded fray Salvador "that the main cathedrals of Spain had been Moorish mosques." Vargas also harbored an unspoken reason: if the Spanish reoccupation of Santa Fe came to war, the remodeled kiva offered a sure way into the fortress. With that in mind, the governor ordered Miguel Luján, a presidial soldier who understood Tewa and Tano, to move with his family into the unconsecrated kiva church and use it as a spy post.[5]

Restored Kiva, Pecos National Historical Park. Photograph by Fred E. Mang, Jr. Courtesy of Pecos National Historical Park.

The ragged migration north from El Paso of a thousand Spanish men, women, and children during the fall and winter of 1693—the second phase of Diego de Vargas's recolonization—had set new standards of misery. Experienced New Mexicans had told their impatient governor that early October was too late to head up the caravan. Given the overgrown and deeply eroded camino real, the inevitable breakdowns of wagons and carts, and the plodding pace of livestock on the hoof, they could not possibly reach Indian-occupied Santa Fe before winter set in.

Vargas had not listened. Now in mid-December, huddled in wagons, frozen tents, and makeshift lean-tos, "within view of the villa of Santa Fe, about two harquebus shots away" (several hundred yards), mothers struggled to comfort their babies in the fierce cold and blowing snow. At least twenty-two children died. Grieving fathers begged Governor Vargas to cease negotiations and force the Indian occupants to vacate Santa Fe and return to Galisteo or whatever pueblos they came from.

A majority of the adults in the Spanish camp were returning survivors of the Pueblo Revolt. They carried with them two venerated icons: don Juan de Oñate's original royal banner and the small image of the Blessed Virgin which fray Alonso de Benavides had transported to New Mexico in 1625, renamed La Conquistadora and temporarily housed in a wagon. Such symbols meant less to several dozen soldiers Vargas had recruited in and around Zacatecas earlier in the year, a few with families, who were new to the kingdom. Yet everybody in the snow-blanketed encampment was anxious. Members of the cabildo, Santa Fe's town council in exile, along with the ailing Franciscan superior, requested an open town meeting, and the governor agreed. Although he and his men-at-arms were sworn "to suffer all kinds of weather and misfortunes on campaign," Vargas recognized that such hardship was not incumbent on the friars or the colonists' families.

Therefore, on the two days following their sad Christmas of 1693, the colony's leaders crowded into Vargas's campaign tent to hear their earlier pleas read and to ratify them. The third individual to do so was sixty-year-old Sargento mayor Francisco de Anaya Almazán, whose protruding eyes gave him a look of perpetual amazement. He, as much as any Spaniard, personified the pre-Revolt, native New Mexicans who had come home to resume their interrupted lives. Anaya had buried his first wife in New Mexico as a young man. He had lived through the siege of Santa Fe in August 1680, losing his second wife and his children to the fury in the countryside. Married a third time in El Paso, he had come back and for the next twenty years would forge a link in the chain that bound pre-and postwar New Mexico. This day in December 1693, Anaya stood with the rest. The Indian occupants of Santa Fe, "shameless and sneering at the Spaniards," must evacuate their stronghold at once.[6]

Vargas had feared trouble, despite the Indians' token welcome and gift of tortillas. He doubted the sincerity of his compadre José, the Pueblo Indian captain whose three daughters had become his godchildren the previous year. He particularly distrusted the cunning, Spanish-speaking Antonio Bolsas, spokesman for the Pueblo occupants of Santa Fe, who "can easily sway the people of the villa to his will with persuasive words."[7] No Spaniard saw signs that the Indians were preparing to move out; in fact, others appeared to be moving in.

On December 27, after the town meeting had adjourned, distressing reports reached Governor Vargas. The Indians were arming. Before dawn on the 28th, the young son of Miguel Luján, housed in the remodeled kiva, carried messages through the snow to Vargas's tent. All night, the Indians had been working themselves up around bonfires inside the walls. Other multilingual informants had heard cries for war. Finally at first light, Spaniards observed that the Indian residents had taken up the ladders, barred the main gate, and manned the ramparts, shouting their defiance. Through a hail of arrows and stones hurled with slings, Miguel Luján and his family barely escaped, leaving their belongings behind in the kiva.

Vargas moved the camp forward, facing the main rampart, so that his men might more easily surround the fortress and prevent other Tewas and Tanos from entering. He and his secretary advanced from the siege line and shouted up to Antonio Bolsas that "they should come to their senses and come down; I would pardon them." But they kept screaming at him, until the Spanish governor gave up. Bolsas yelled that his people would talk and he would bring their decision out to the Spaniards. Vargas waited all day, but the Indian never came. That night, with the shouting and war chants reaching a crescendo, the Spaniards laid plans for a dawn attack, an *alborada*. Mounted patrols kept circling the stronghold all night.

On this occasion, Vargas's earlier diplomacy strengthened the Spaniards' hand in battle. Pueblo reinforcements counted on by the defenders did not arrive in sufficient numbers to break through the Spaniards' line or in time to affect the outcome. Moreover, the Spanish governor's restraint the year before at Pecos had brought him Pueblo allies willing for their own reasons to risk death or victory shoulder-to-shoulder with Spaniards. Refusing to sack abandoned Pecos Pueblo in 1692, Vargas had given its residents time to return and to welcome him. Now, on the eve of armed conflict, their governor, don Juan de Ye, and 140 Pecos fighting men put themselves under Vargas's command.[8]

The assault lasted just over twenty-four hours, from the moment Diego de Vargas shouted the charge "Santiago!" early on December 29 until the next morning when the defenders' women and children began streaming out of the war-torn complex. The Spaniards, seeing that their firearms had little effect from below, had built shielded ladders and clambered up them, taking one high position after another. As the besiegers sought to mine under the walls, Indians inside melted snow in iron kettles and poured boiling water down on them. Hacking and burning the heavy wooden gate and also breaking in through the remodeled kiva, the attackers gained the lower levels and overran the two interior plazas. Vargas ordered the royal standard and flag affixed to the highest rampart and a Christian cross placed over the main entrance.

A room-by-room search yielded fifty-four Tewa and Tano fighters. Vargas's compadre José, his right wrist broken, had hanged himself at dawn on the 30th, according to Antonio Bolsas. Governor Vargas condemned the male prisoners to death by firing squad, interpreter Bolsas among them. Not only had they risen against the Spanish king, but they had also smashed to pieces the patio cross and an image of the Blessed Virgin Mary, uttering countless blasphemies. Later, another sixteen men discovered hiding in the recesses of the fortress met the same fate. By Vargas's reckoning, "seventy were shot; nine died from the skirmishes; and two, without hope at the thought of defeat, hanged themselves."[9]

Unfortunately, no one sketched this odd building, rising in isolation from an open space the Indians had cleared by razing every adjoining Spanish structure. The building was unique in all the world, this pile laid up first by Spaniards, then occupied by Pueblos, and again by Spaniards who began at once punching holes in the lower walls so they could breathe and let in light. In the last days of 1693, they had retaken their capital. Reporting to the viceroy, the Santa Fe town council evoked a picture in words of the stronghold. "There are so many dwellings, which they have built on the top of the casas reales (which we here call the palace), that it took twenty soldiers and thirty Indian allies the whole blessed day until nightfall to search the fortress and the dwellings."[10]

The Pueblo-Spanish War, waged between 1680 and 1696, had entered its third and final stage, the Spaniards' hard-fought reentry into the Pueblo world. Although temporarily successful, Vargas's motley company of returnees had little cause to celebrate. Months removed from cousins in El Paso, holed up in the fouled casas reales, they doubted how they could possibly survive as snows swirled outside. But Governor Vargas, while acknowledging the urgent need for food, defense, and Pueblo Indian allies, appeared undaunted.

The four thousand fanegas (some ten thousand bushels) of corn, beans, and dried vegetables collected from the deepest corners of the building, no matter how carefully distributed among a thousand settlers and their four hundred captive Tano and Tewa women and children, would not last the winter. Arriving in mid-December, the Spaniards had planted no crops. They must exact provisions from Pueblos beyond the walls of Santa Fe, by negotiation or by force. Those natives who had escaped the siege had to be seen as enemies. Many Pueblo Indians who had nodded in token obedience in 1692 were now preparing to resist, laying up supplies, making arrows, and piling rocks at defensive sites atop steep-banked mesas. Rumors already circulated of Pueblo confederations forming to attack Santa Fe. Priding himself as a diplomat, Diego de Vargas believed he too could count on other Pueblo Indians as allies.

While en route north from El Paso, the Spanish governor had sent his Indian compadre Bartolomé de Ojeda among the Keresan people to enlist their allegiance. Now, on December 31, 1693, one day after the Spaniards had settled the matter of Santa Fe, Ojeda and a Keresan delegation arrived at the fortress. Their message was ominous. As Vargas fingered the four knots on the cord Ojeda handed him, the Indian recounted its significance: four days remained before a planned enemy convocation of Jemez, Navajos, and the faction of his own people from Cochiti and Santo Domingo swayed by old Antonio Malacate. Because the principal men of Zia, Santa Ana, and San Felipe had refused Malacate's invitation to march on Santa Fe, preferring instead to side with the Spaniards, they had become his enemies. Somehow Ojeda had persuaded his Pueblo kinsmen, brutalized by Spaniards five years earlier, to stand with him and ease the colonists' return.

Ojeda had a plan. If Malacate and two other agitators could be captured and brought to Santa Fe, their following would surely disperse. Characterizing Ojeda as "brave and cunning," Vargas concurred. "I promised him I would reward him, and he promised me he would effect the capture." Next, Juan de Ye, governor of the Pecos, came to Santa Fe on January 4 to warn through an interpreter of a large encampment of Tewas, Tanos, Picuris, Taos, and Apaches about two leagues (just over five miles) from Santa Fe. Ye thought they might assault Pecos and asked Vargas for help. Unable to go himself at this critical juncture, the Spanish governor dispatched Captain Roque Madrid, a native New Mexican conversant in Ye's Towa language, and thirty men-at-arms. They were back the next day. No attack had come, but Juan de Ye and his faction at Pecos had tested their pact with Vargas, "remaining assured of having the Spaniards so much on their side."[11]

Malacate proved elusive. The literate Ojeda wrote to Vargas, and the Spanish governor's secretary copied the letter into his campaign journal. Malacate and his Jemez comrades intended to make war on the pro-Spanish Keres before attacking Santa Fe. Ojeda had heard that Malacate was "worshiping the things of the devil every night in order to kill your lordship and the Spaniards." The Keres of Santa Ana, who were guarding some of the Spaniards' horses, begged "for the love of God to send them some soldiers." Addressing his reply to Bartolomé de Ojeda as "son and compadre" (also copied into the record), Vargas suggested that the Santa Anas withdraw temporarily to the more secure sites of Zia or San Felipe. He could not send soldiers until he had first reconnoitered the Tewa pueblos in force. Tested time and again, this pivotal alliance of Vargas and Ojeda—Spaniard and Pueblo—held strong throughout the restoration.[12]

Nor could Vargas put a price on the support of don Juan de Ye. While some Pecos traditionalists murmured against his leadership, Ye saw in the Spaniards' return a revitalization of his pueblo as a trade center. He led Pecos fighters in Vargas's initial, unsuccessful February and March assault on the embattled Tewas of San Ildefonso (or Black) Mesa, twenty-odd miles north of Santa Fe. He escorted Plains Apache leaders to Santa Fe to drink chocolate with the Spanish governor and talk of renewed trade fairs. Late in June 1694, Vargas called for a major military action to punish the Jemez confederation that had been harassing Zia, Santa Ana, and San Felipe. Ye and his scouts reported that the Rio Grande was running too high to cross safely even on rafts. Rather than disband the force, Governor Vargas added a pack train and led the cavalcade northward, intent on bargaining for food or simply removing stores from abandoned pueblos.

Four days out, the Spaniards made camp near Taos. Unwilling to parley with Vargas, the people of the pueblo streamed toward their refuge in a nearby mountain canyon. A band of Plains Apaches, friends of Juan de Ye, volunteered to arrange a meeting at the mouth of the canyon with Francisco Pacheco, Indian governor of Taos. Ye finally ventured too much, arguing passionately that the Taos return to their pueblo and accept the Spaniards' pardon. Pacheco feigned friendship. Since the sun was setting, he invited Ye to spend the night with him and talk more, and Ye agreed.

Sargento mayor Francisco de Anaya Almazán, sensing a trap, urged the Pecos governor not to go. Ye, insisting that he knew Pacheco well, dismounted from his mule, took off his spurs and the powder pouches from his belt, and handed over the harquebus that belonged to Vargas. He embraced the Spanish governor, Sargento mayor Anaya, and the others, "which the Taos Indians and their governor, Pacheco, closely watched." "God be with you," shouted Vargas. He would await them in his tent early next morning with chocolate. It was the last time any Spaniard saw don Juan de Ye. Later in Santa Fe, Governor Vargas tried to explain through interpreters to Ye's son Lorenzo. Presented with his father's cape and other effects, the Indian went away "satisfied, although sad."[13]

From communities in disarray, native residents of the Pueblo world closely watched Spanish colonists taking up homes again in the Kingdom and Provinces of New Mexico. Their reactions were not so different from those of their ancestors nearly a century before. A conspicuous few gave aid and comfort, more stood in angry opposition, and most kept to themselves their doubts about Spaniards as neighbors.

In 1694, three brooding citadels, one north and two west of Santa Fe, symbolized Pueblo resistance. Tewas and Tanos, who repulsed assaults in February and March, manned fortifications atop San Ildefonso Mesa; dissenting Keres of Cochiti and Santo Domingo, whose leader Malacate had been replaced by El Zepe, occupied the mesa of La Cieneguilla de Cochiti (Horn Mesa, Potrero Viejo); and defiant Jemez fighters defended their refuge on Guadalupe (or San Diego) Mesa. All fell in 1694, each stormed by combined forces of Spanish soldiers, militiamen, and Pueblo Indian auxiliaries. As they overran Guadalupe Mesa, the assailants captured 361 Jemez noncombatants. Vargas offered their return if surviving Jemez warriors would join his army to besiege San Ildefonso Mesa a second time. This they did, and the Spanish governor released the hostages. Tewa and Tano holdouts, observing Spaniards and other Pueblo Indians uprooting their crops in fields below, at last came down from the heights in September to be pardoned by Vargas. But they did not forget.[14]

Having forced the evacuation of the three mesa strongholds, Governor Vargas and his entourage toured the restored Pueblo communities, reinstalling native officials and assigning missionaries. They traveled first to Pecos, home of the vanished Juan de Ye. In September 1694, with familiar pomp, the Spanish governor addressed the assembly through two pre-Revolt colonists. He introduced fray Diego Zeinos. Pecos carpenters had already rebuilt living quarters for the friar and sawed beams to roof a temporary place of Christian worship between the standing north wall of the old convento and the mound where their former monumental church had stood.

Vargas asked the pueblo's principal men to confer and then present to him the individuals they wished to be their officers. The Spaniard bestowed on each a staff of office and administered the oath of loyalty. As Pecos governor, Diego Marcos headed a list of eighteen. Among the nine war captains, Vargas recognized Lorenzo de Ye, whom he dignified as "don." The newly legitimized Pecos leaders then requested that the Spanish governor appoint as their alcalde mayor old Francisco de Anaya Almazán, who had warned Juan de Ye of the danger at Taos. Vargas swore in Anaya. Last, asked who they wished to be the patron saint of their renewed mission, the Pecos replied that the pueblo's patroness should remain Our Lady of the Angels.[15] By the end of 1694, Governor Vargas had escorted Franciscans back to a dozen Pueblo communities and ordained their officers. In Santa Fe, meanwhile, the distressed colonists found fault.

Vargas had asked Viceroy Galve to authorize funding for a hundred presidial soldiers and five hundred colonist families, without which, he implied, the restoration of New Mexico would surely fail. Sixty such families, recruited in Puebla and the Valley of Mexico, had reached Santa Fe in June of 1694, straining available housing and food supplies. Worse, these subsidized newcomers, many of whom boasted a trade, considered themselves *españoles mexicanos* (Spaniards from Mexico) and superior to other New Mexicans. Vargas next sent his trusted, twenty-six-year-old protégé Juan Páez Hurtado to sign up additional colonists at government expense in New Spain's northern mining districts. Although charges of fraud and faking families of unrelated individuals (to collect the higher family rate) hung over this effort, by May 1695 another forty-four so-called family units had been added to New Mexico's rolls.[16]

Only partially pacified, the colony agonized during 1695. A widespread epidemic, unspecified in the documents, carried off Pueblos and Spaniards alike. As could be expected, more of the former died than the latter. Vargas himself took sick from recurring typhus; "at death's door," he dictated a hasty last will, then recovered.[17] Food shortages persisted. Drought-stricken crops attacked by worms were meager, and the beef and wagonloads of provisions driven north from Nueva Vizcaya were never enough. With so many pueblos reoccupied, that earlier source of confiscated foodstuffs had dried up.

To relieve crowding in Santa Fe—where Vargas must have set colonists to building defensive works—the Spanish governor decreed that the españoles mexicanos found a new villa, or chartered municipality, upriver at Santa Cruz de la Cañada, twenty-some miles north of Santa Fe and barely east of today's Española. This vicinity before 1680 had supported a considerable Hispanic farming and ranching population, Vargas's justification for again uprooting Tanos and Tewas. Taken together, such ill winds stirred a second, less general but no less passionate Pueblo revolt.[18]

Rumors of rebellion were rife during the winter of 1695–1696. The missionaries, alone in their pueblos, grew understandably nervous. They talked of withdrawing to Santa Fe, but in December decided against it. Governor Vargas got up from his sickbed to admonish the Tewa and Tano captains he had summoned to the capital. As a gesture of goodwill, he declared the freedom of forty-five of their women and children who had previously fled temporary servitude in Santa Fe. Christmas Eve, reportedly marked for the outbreak of an insurrection, passed without incident. Again, severe cold kept snow on the ground, making Vargas's emergency visits to various pueblos more burdensome.

Late in February, an officer awakened Vargas in the middle of Sunday night, delivering a warning from fray José Díez, the Franciscan who had agreed with him about the kiva church and who was serving now at nearby Tesuque. According to certain Tewas, even some of Vargas's Pecos allies were plotting against the Spaniards. The leader of the malcontents was said to be Juan de Ye's aggrieved son, don Lorenzo, who "intended to kill the father [missionary] first and come to do the same with the

Spaniards." Don Lorenzo would then retire with his faction to Piedra Blanca, an old pueblo belonging to the Pecos.[19]

The Franciscans begged Governor Vargas to station squads of soldiers in the missions, citing a growing "insolence" among their Pueblo congregations. Signs were everywhere. The Indians, swayed by itinerant agitators (*tlatoleros*), were carrying supplies to the mountains and digging horse traps. Father Díez anguished at Tesuque, "I do not know how, in conscience, I can say mass to apostates, which I know they already are in their knowledge of the uprising." For months, certain Indians had been meeting in Tesuque at the house of a "sorcerer," singing war songs and chanting, "Death to the Spaniards, what good are the Spaniards? We were better off before." Díez wanted a dozen soldiers—an overwrought request, given the colony's scarcely one hundred men-at-arms. He predicted that the blow would fall during the full moon in mid-March, "about eight days from now."[20]

Yet two more full moons waxed and waned. Then on Monday, June 4, 1696, during the week of the third full moon, amid seeming calm, Governor Vargas got the first garbled news of violence. As the people of Cochiti took to the hills, their missionary had barely escaped with his life. From Santa Ana, Bartolomé de Ojeda, senior Keresan war captain, reported that a gathering of Acomas was awaiting Hopis, Zunis, and Utes to launch an invasion.

A day or two later, Ojeda, writing to his old friend Father custos Francisco de Vargas at Santa Fe, allowed that the Acomas might have dispersed. Still, he was taking no chances, since if the enemy assaulted Santa Ana, "no one but Jesus Christ Himself will be able to protect it." The Indian asked Father Vargas (no relative of Governor Vargas) to inform Santa Ana's missionary, who had taken refuge in Santa Fe, that he had hidden the sacred vessels, vestments, and other items pertaining to Christian worship in a house that had been covered over with mud. Ojeda was not well. "I think I have caught typhus," he wrote to Father Vargas. "Nothing else, but may God Our Lord keep you for the many years I wish. Your lordship's servant and godson, Bartolomé de Ojeda."[21]

Alcalde mayor Roque Madrid at Santa Cruz de la Cañada heard that Tanos allied with Keres, Apaches, Hopis, and Pecos had risen. Immediately, Madrid ordered locals to catch their horses and assemble at the new villa. Governor Vargas, questioning the alleged participation of the Pecos, told Alcalde mayor Anaya to enlist a hundred Pecos warriors and, without betraying the least mistrust, escort them to Santa Fe. Two days later, led by their new governor, don Felipe Chistoe, they reported for duty, some on horseback, some afoot, eager to share in "the booty of clothing and maize."[22]

On campaign with Governor Vargas during June and July 1696, these Pecos men witnessed scenes reminiscent of 1680. Except for Tesuque, whose volatile governor decided at the last moment to side with the Spaniards, the other Tewas, along with Tanos, Tiwas of Taos and Picuris, and Jemez, had murdered outsiders and ransacked their missions. The scene at San Ildefonso sickened Vargas. Two Franciscans, huddled with members of a Spanish family inside the church as Indians set it afire, had suffocated of smoke inhalation. The bodies were decomposing. "I ordered the Pecos Indians and men-at-arms," wrote Vargas, "to cover them with adobes and a wall they tore down from the church itself; once they were buried, they could not be disturbed."[23]

One of the Franciscan victims at San Ildefonso had joined his brethren three months earlier in a debate about true martyrdom. He would gladly die, he professed, if his death would assure the salvation of some of his congregation. Believing, however, that his flock would rejoice, he questioned dying, "for two reasons: martyrdom is a crowning glory, and I do not deserve it; the other reason is that it would be rigorously an act of hatred of the faith."[24] In all, the summer outbreak of 1696 claimed the lives of five Franciscans and twenty-one Spanish colonists. A greater but unknown number of their Pueblo tormenters also died in subsequent fighting. As Vargas sought to suppress this latest insurrection, anger drove both Pueblos and Spaniards to acts of desperation and ultimately to exhaustion.

They clashed intermittently throughout the summer. Dictating such events in his campaign journal, Diego de Vargas rarely displayed emotion. When, however, his combined Pueblo and Spanish forces finally ran down and killed don Lucas Naranjo, whom he considered a prime mover of the 1696 revolt, Vargas let his hatred show. The Spanish governor had installed Naranjo as chief war captain at Santa Clara in 1694. Variously described as a mulatto or *lobo* (of Indian and African blood), Lucas may have been a son of the Naranjo suspected as the black representative of Poseyemu at the heart of the Pueblo Revolt in 1680.[25]

Heading a typically mixed column of presidial soldiers, volunteer Santa Fe militiamen, his Pecos allies, and a Franciscan chaplain, Vargas had set out from Santa Cruz de la Cañada before daybreak on July 23. The plan was to surprise Naranjo and his Tewa fighters hidden among the boulders in a rugged funnel canyon to the north. Felled trees lay across the entrance, forcing the attackers to dismount. When the exchange began, Naranjo evidently told his men to shoot at the chaplain, which infuriated Vargas. Had the friar not worn high leather boots, an arrow would have pierced his leg.

Advancing on the enemy's positions, Spaniards fired volley after volley. A shot from one of the militiamen "was lucky enough to hit Naranjo in the Adam's apple and come out at the nape of his neck." Another soldier shot the fallen enemy leader in the head and decapitated him. Tewas who were able fled, some leaving their blood on the boulders. This skirmish proved to be a turning point in suppressing the second Pueblo revolt. Not long afterward, the soldiers sent Naranjo's severed head to Vargas, who gloated: "I was very pleased to see that rebel apostate dog in that state: a pistol shot through the right temple had caused his brains to spill out, leaving the head hollow. What little remained was scooped out to take to his pueblo."[26]

As another bad winter set in, warfare trailed off. Despite recurring suspicions, it would never resume again in large scale between Pueblo Indians and Spaniards. Both peoples had suffered severe dislocations. Some families never returned to the homes they had left, while many others came back, reclaimed their property, and laid in food and firewood. The colonists of Santa Cruz de la Cañada, who petitioned to move downriver to sites they considered safer and more easily cultivated, were forced to stick it out. Their Tewa neighbors, who had withdrawn to uncomfortable but defensible locations in rough terrain during the troubles of 1696, straggled back, reoccupying most of their pueblos. Other Tewas joined an exodus of Tiwas from Picuris who ventured eastward to live with Plains Apaches. Vargas managed to bring some of them back in November 1696, while ten years later another Spanish column retrieved an additional sixty who had not adjusted to life on the plains.[27]

Given time and chance, Diego de Vargas believed he could reconquer the unrepentant Hopis, but he was denied both. A successor of somewhat more humble birth, don Pedro Rodríguez Cubero, presented his credentials to the town council at Santa Fe on July 2, 1697. Vargas, through agents in Mexico City, had maneuvered to block Rodríguez's appointment, even though don Diego had exceeded his own five-year term by more than sixteen months. The reconquerer of New Mexico desperately wanted a promotion to someplace else. Failing that, he supposed a grateful viceroy, no longer his patron Galve, would continue him in office. But the conde de Moctezuma y de Tula did not, and Rodríguez's papers were in order.

If only don Diego had accepted that fact. Instead, he set about convincing himself and anyone who would listen that he had been reappointed. Vargas's vanity, combined with the Spanish colonists' deep resentment toward him and his chosen circle of minions, explains why the former governor spent the next three years under house arrest in Santa Fe, for a time in leg irons. After conducting Vargas's uneventful, thirty-day judicial review, or *residencia*, Governor Rodríguez had presided as the cabildo of Santa Fe brought a litany of criminal charges against his famed predecessor. They ranged from misappropriation of government funds—the only charge that interested royal bureaucrats—to abuse of his authority, favoritism, and immorality. Vargas's ill-advised policies were blamed for every hardship suffered by New Mexico's returning colonists, including the loss of the twenty-two children who died in the snow outside the walls of Santa Fe in December 1693. Not until July of 1700, after the viceroy had summoned Diego de Vargas to Mexico City to present his accounts, did Rodríguez release him.

Meanwhile in Santa Fe, Governor Rodríguez had ordered a convento built for the Franciscans—at his own expense, he boasted. He also had workers tear into the defenses and alterations that the Indian occupants had constructed, renovating the casas reales and earning Vargas's curses for laying the capital open to attack. If only someone had sketched a plan of Santa Fe in 1700, what a find that would be for today's historical archaeologists.

Vargas's successor never liked New Mexico. When his five-year term expired on July 2, 1702, no one appeared to relieve Pedro Rodríguez Cubero. Suffering through another New Mexico winter, Rodríguez, whose health was failing, bolted from Santa Fe, not waiting for anyone. But by then, he knew who was to succeed him. Diego de Vargas, exonerated in Mexico City, had actually been reappointed.[28]

Vargas's reentry into Santa Fe in November 1703 stirred emotions all around. Rewarded with a noble title of Castile for his restoration of New Mexico, don Diego de Vargas, first marqués de la Nava de Barcinas, had sworn not to seek revenge. Nevertheless, prominent New Mexicans who had previously testified against him fell all over themselves in their efforts to ingratiate themselves anew. Pueblo leaders sent emissaries to welcome him. Few suspected that Vargas, just sixty years old, had only five months to live.

The following March, he decreed a campaign against Faraón Apaches who had been rustling scarce cattle and horses in the middle Rio Grande Valley. Through his district officers, Vargas summoned quotas of Pueblo Indian fighters to meet him and the soldiers at Bernalillo, just north of today's Albuquerque. A dozen pueblos had sent warriors expecting their share of the spoils. Don Felipe Chistoe's contingent from Pecos, numbering almost fifty men, was easily the most conspicuous. No mention was made of the steadfast don Bartolomé de Ojeda, who after 1702 faded from the historical record.

Four days into their operation, Vargas's campaign journal suddenly broke off. The governor, racked by stomach cramps and fever, could not go on. Pueblo Indians, probably carrying the Spaniard between them on a litter, conveyed him back to Bernalillo to the alcalde mayor's house. Juan Páez Hurtado galloped south with medication, but this time Vargas did not respond. On April 8, 1704, at about five in the evening, the once-and-future governor of New Mexico died, seemingly of dysentery.[29]

Although ten years older than Diego de Vargas, New Mexican Francisco de Anaya Almazán lived a decade longer, into his early eighties. Anaya owned a house on the reworked Santa Fe plaza and served as mayordomo of the religious confraternity of La Conquistadora. He must have attended Vargas's funeral. As the reconqueror lay dying in Bernalillo, he had dictated precise details for the honors he expected as a titled nobleman of Castile and captain general, including a pair of caparisoned riderless horses. He requested further that his body, borne to the Santa Fe church in his bed draped as a funeral bier, be buried in the main chapel "beneath the dais where the priest stands." He also provided that on that day fifty fanegas (about 125 bushels) of corn and the meat of twelve cattle be distributed in his name to the villa's poor.[30]

Years later, in 1712, Juan Páez Hurtado and other leading citizens petitioned a succeeding governor to proclaim Santa Fe's first fiesta commemorating Vargas's 1692 entry into Santa Fe two decades earlier. In 1714, a larger parish church was nearing completion. But because pertinent burial records have gone missing, we can only surmise that the people of Santa Fe, amid proper pomp, exhumed Vargas's remains from wherever that earlier structure stood and reburied them in the new church. Subsequent remodeling, construction of the present cathedral, and changes to the latter in the 1960s, have badly disturbed the site. Hence, even though Santa Fe's Fiestas in September annually resurrect don Diego de Vargas, Spanish recolonizer of the Kingdom and Provinces of New Mexico, no shrine marks his final resting place.[31]

Between the formal founding of Santa Fe in 1610—symbolic of the colony's transfer from proprietor Juan de Oñate to the royal crown—and the villa's restoration by Diego de Vargas in the 1690s, Pueblo Indians and Spaniards of the seventeenth century had worked out the basis of a dynamic coexistence. More by experience than by plan, more by peaceful exchange than by war, they had learned to live together yet apart. And they continue to do so today.

11

The Pastures of the Royal Horse Herd of the Santa Fe Presidio, 1692–1740
by
Linda Tigges

Beginning in the first part of the 18th century, it was apparent that the Santa Fe Presidio, separated as it was from the southern line of presidios located south of the Rio Grande, stood alone under the constant attacks coming from the surrounding hostile Indian tribes. It was also apparent that the natural resources needed to support the presidio in protecting the colony and to enable the colony to prosper, were limited. Extensive supplies from the central government in Mexico City and able governors with military ability were necessary for the colony to continue, and these were not always forthcoming.

In regard to protection of the colony, a strong and well supplied presidio with an effective military strategy was essential. Governors used the strategies of gift giving and trade with the hostile tribes when possible, but more often they used the strategy of mounted armed troops. Using mounted troops, rather than infantry, was necessitated by the size of the colony, the long distances traveled in campaigns, and more importantly, the increasingly effective use of cavalry tactics by many tribes as more horses became available to them.

Though the Indians had possessed horses for some time, the number of horses was greatly increased by the Pueblo Revolt, with large of numbers of Spanish mares and stallions left behind when the colonists abandoned the area for El Paso.[1] The warriors quickly adapted to the use of horses, with horse ownership becoming part of the culture and a sign of status. When the Spanish returned in the 1690s with their horse herds, raiding of settlements by mounted Indians and horses stealing followed.[2] By the 1720s and 1730s and throughout the

18th century, Santa Fe and New Mexico were considered by some to be under siege by the Faraónes[3] and other Apaches, Navajos, Utes, and the more recently arrived Comanches.[4]

Santa Fe had always been seen as a military as well as an administrative center for the colony both before and after the Reconquest, and the site was selected for its natural resources that would accommodate this, such as good water, timber, and pasturage.[5] After the Reconquest and as seen in the descriptions that follow, Vargas was careful to set aside land, not only for settlers, but also for the pasturage for the horses of the colony. As the eighteenth century wore on, however, the hostile Indians had more horses, became better armed, and were more adept at raiding. As a result, the size of the presidio horse herd was necessarily increased, even though it became increasingly difficult to provide sustenance for presidio horse herds while continuing to sustain the increasing number of sheep, cattle and horses herds of the settlers. The limited water and pasturage restricted both the protective value of the soldiers and the prosperity of the settlers.

The problem was the large numbers of horses needed for effective military operations, and the need for them to be strong enough to survive long distance expeditions. Presidio campaigns and expeditions could be extremely large affairs with as many as five to ten horses and a pack mule per soldier, with the militia and their animals, sometimes a cattle herd for food with some soldiers detailed to herd and guard them, and with the Indian allies, sometimes with their horses. The extra horses were needed because of the long distances, rough terrain and the heavy military equipment carried by the soldiers. It was also because in times of drought or when pastures were thin because of overgrazing, the animals were weak and tired easily.[6,7] In reviewing the data, detailed below, it was not uncommon for the presidio soldiers to take a *caballada,* or horse herd, of 400 to 500 horses and mules on a expedition, with the horses in the entire presidio herd numbering up to 1200 or more.

To feed all of the presidio animals, most of the grazing pastures for the horses and mules had to be located outside in the villa in places where water and feed could be found, but they had to be close enough to the villa so they could be protected from Indian raids. Grain and some forage were brought to the villa, and some hay was available from the *cienega* in Santa Fe and other areas, but most of the animals were driven to surrounding areas for grazing. Unfortunately, the grazing areas used by the presidio's horse and cattle herds were located in the same places as those used by the colonists for their horses, cattle and other animals, there being only so many watered areas and pastures available in the colony. This naturally led to a shortage for both the presidio and the colonist, which led to complaints from despairing officers or irate citizens about encroachments on assigned pastures. In turn this led to regulations and restrictions written by governors trying to sort things out.

The military background for this situation, data on the numbers of presidio horses and mules, the location of the designated outposts and pastures of the presidio, examples of the conflicts over pastures and forage, and efforts by a succession of governors to solve this problem and better protect the colony by expanding the entitlements of the presidio, are the subject of this chapter.

A description of the military campaigns and expeditions of Indian raids shows how threatened the colonists were and how preoccupied they were with defense. As a generalization, Frank Secoy in his study of the military patterns of the plains Indians, says that from the late 1600s to around 1720, certain tribes in New Mexico, particularly the Navajos and Apache, were using a post-horse, pre-gun or occasional-gun military technique. They had developed horse warfare, but most often used lances and arrows as weapons.[8] By 1720 if not before, as the French expanded their trading activities Indians were able to trade for guns, developing a post-horse, post-gun military technique. The Pawnee to the north and the Utes used this technique, though it was most effectively used by the Comanches.[9] Studies show that by the 1730s, the Comanches had taken over most of the river valleys of the southwestern plains. By the 1740s they had driven the Apaches south of the Canadian River, and by the 1750s, they had taken over the Texas plains.[10] Elizabeth John states that by the 1740s, "Comanche hostilities upon the eastern frontier of New Mexico so unsparing that it gradually depopulated the area."[11]

The adoption of armed cavalry warfare by the Indians necessitated the need for greater military preparedness by the Spanish. In the early eighteenth century, there were raids by mounted Navajo, Moqui, Utes, and Apache warriors. As the Apaches were driven south into Nueva Vizcaya, the raids on the New Mexican colony by the Comanches became more intensive. The Comanches had adopted the horse as part of their military tactics as well as part of their culture, with the result that the raiding of the horse herds of the Spanish presidios and ranchos became a regular occurrence. Because of this the Spanish in the northern frontier had to maintain supplies, horses and weapons and to develop effective military techniques at least as successful as those of their enemies.

To illustrate this situation, a selected list of the campaigns and military activities against hostile tribes in northern New Mexico from the first third of the eighteenth century includes:

> 1704 Vargas pursues Faraónes Apaches in the Bernalillo area. Dies of dysentery.[12]
> 1705 May. Cuervo y Valdés expedition against Navajo raiders.[13]

1705 June. Cuervo y Valdés leads a campaign against the Gila Apaches.[14]
1705 August. Roque Madrid leads a campaign against the Navajos.[15]
1705 September. Campaign against the Navajos.[16]
1715 Juan Páez Hurtado expedition against the Faraónes Apaches in eastern New Mexico.[17]
1716 Felix Martinez leads a campaign against the Moqui (Hopi) pueblos.[18]
1719 Valverde expedition against the Ute and Comanche.[19]
1719 Villasur expedition against the Comanche and Pawnee.[20]
1724 Bustamente expedition against the Faraónes Apache.[21]
1731 Cruzat y Gongóra campaign against the Faraónes Apaches.[22]
1734 Juan Páez Hurtado leads campaign against the Faraónes Apache.[23]
1741 Mendoza campaign against the Comanche.[24]

Though there are few recorded expeditions or campaigns for the later 1730s, the worsening situation with both the Faraónes and the Comanches is reflected in three government documents. The first is a March 30, 1737 *bando* from newly appointed Governor Olavidé y Micheleña ordering all able-bodied men, including the auxiliary Indians, to be prepared for campaigns. In the document, Olavidé states:

> "Because it benefits the Royal service of His Majesty (whom God may guard) that all the Spanish and Indians of this Kingdome (sic) are prompt and prepared for that which might be offered in the defense of this Kingdome due to the contingencies which could occur because we live surrounded by infidel nations, for which reason I order all the residents and natives of this Kingdom to be ready and prepared to join together in the Plaza De Armas [of Santa Fe] which I shall designate whenever the cases arises.... I order the Alcaldes Mayores ... to make it known in their respective jurisdictions and upon them knowing it, [that they] will leave [march] when the order is given, equipped with horses and offensive and defensive arms which they should have within the villa and the pueblos, along with sufficient people to provide for its safety and maintenance."[25]

The second set of documents is also from 1737. Alferez[26] Juan José Moreno, in requesting designation of specific presidio horse pastures, wrote to Governor Olavidé y Micheleña stating that there was no place for the horses to graze near the presidio, with the horses losing weight because of this. He stated that "the defense, garrison, and security of the Kingdom requires that the horses be fat [*gordo*, in good condition] and at hand for any invasion by Indians or hostility by enemies which occurs on a daily basis because the Kingdom is surrounded by them."[27]

The Governor supported Moreno's request, naming six sites, and ordered the settlers not to use them. He stated that he does this "…because the defense of it [the villa] consists of the robust, prompt and immediate [availability of soldiers] due to the incidents which occur on a daily basis in the wake of a revolt and invasion by the enemies.…"[28]

Olavidé did not order the presidio and the colonists to carry out any campaigns or expeditions, nor did his successor.[29] However, Olavidé was clearly aware of the threat to the colony and made some effort to address military preparedness.

Military officials throughout the eighteenth century asked questions, as they do now, about the most effective way to provide protection to the citizens and how to provide the protection most economically. Their questions were: How many soldiers were at the presidio and how were they and should they be used? How many horses did the presidio actually have and need? How many soldiers were needed to guard a grazing area, and how many should be left to guard the presidio and participate in escort service and other military operations? The results of their inquiries eventually led to the military regulations of 1729 and 1772 *Reglamentos*.[30] It also led to the keeping of muster rolls and inventories by the officers of numbers of soldiers, animals and equipment. Many of these remain and can be used to explain the needs of the Santa Fe presidio and to describe the efforts the governors and officers made to ensure adequate supplies of fodder and water to the horses.

The Vargas expeditions provide some initial information. For the initial 1692 expedition to the colony, 15 soldiers each were provided from three presidios near Parral and five from one, for a total of 50 soldiers. The muster roll included the number of horses and equipments showing that when Vargas began the reconquest, he proceeded to the north with 50 soldiers, 407 horses, and 36 mules for a total of 443 animals. The range of animals owned per soldier was 5 to 12, with the average being 9 per soldier. The muster roll did not include members of the citizen militia, allies or their animals.[31]

These numbers were small when compared with the number of animals that he brought to New Mexico in 1693. When Vargas returned to New Mexico in 1693, he brought with him 1,261 horses and 330 mules, of which 793 horses ran off or were lost or stolen. According to testimony from the colonists, the horses and mules could be counted in the *monte* or brush land surrounding the villa.[32] For the actual entrance into Santa Fe, Vargas used the 50 soldiers from what he called the flying squadron to make the entry with him.[33] He stated that each soldier of the flying squadron was to "take two horses and a saddle mule, if they have them."[34]

That is, the flying squadron for the *entrada* included 50 soldiers and a herd of 150 horses and mules. Vargas went on to say that there will also be "two squadrons of ten men readied with their military leader so that they may go to guard these horses and mules and the pack train. I am also ordering him [the leader of the squadron] to designate up to eighty pack mules with sacks and mantas and the muleteers who are assigned to the pack trains."[35] Given the number of animals on these expeditions, it was no wonder that Vargas almost immediately set aside pastures for the villa, as discussed below.

The second description of a military expedition is taken from the 1705 campaign of Roque Madrid against the Moqui (Hopi) northwest of Santa Fe. Though there was no record of the muster roll, Madrid's campaign journal states that the force included 65 presidial soldiers and citizens, and 100 Indian allies, and 700 horses. The number of horses must have been a concern to Madrid, because at one point he stated that, "God saw fit that day for it to rain a copious downpour that was sufficient to water all the horses, whose number surpassed 700 including those of the Indian allies."[36] Because Madrid only recorded the total number of horses, the number of horses per soldier cannot be calculated.

Better data is available for two later expeditions by Páez Hurtado and Martinez. In September 1715, Juan Páez Hurtado led 40 soldiers, 520 settlers and 150 Indian allies against the Faraónes Apaches. September was determined to "be an opportune time for it [the expedition], because there is much pasture and water for the horse herd."[37] Hurtado was to review the forces and equipment when they arrived at Picuris Pueblo rather than in Santa Fe, and after the review, "he will begin his march, making the journeys proportionately so that we may not lose the horse herd,"[38] whether because of lack of feed or by raids is unknown. The documents show that 40 soldiers arrived at the pueblo with 156 horses and 1 mule or 157 animals. This was an average of 4 animals per soldier, fewer than the 9 animals per soldiers of the earlier Vargas expedition. The citizens from Albuquerque, Santa Fe and Santa Cruz did somewhat better with a total of 21 men and 115 animals of which nearly one-third were mules. There was an average of 5.5 animals per soldier. There were also 149 Indians allies, but no mention of their horses or mules. The total number was 157 + 115 or 285 horses and mules.[39]

The 1715 expedition was followed the next year by that of Felix Martinez to the Moquis. This time the military review was held in Albuquerque, "on account of its fertile pastures and groves."[40] The review included 57 soldiers, not counting 11 soldiers leading the beef cattle. The 57 soldiers had 378 horses and 5 mules plus the 11 mounts for the cattle herding soldiers. The total number of animals was 383 for an average of 7 animals per soldier. The militia of Santa Fe, Santa Cruz de la Cañada, and Albuquerque numbered 41 men and 132 animals, which included 112 horses,

11 mules, 10 asses, and 1 burro. The average number of mounts for the military was 3, though some of these men only brought one horse or one mule. There were 155 Indian allies, but no mention of their horses.[41]

The data on the 1719 trek of Governor Valverde into the eastern plains is limited. A. B. Thomas says that Valverde took 50 soldiers to Taos for the muster, where they were joined by 45 settlers, 465 Pueblo Indian allies, and later, 196 Jicarilla Apaches. The Pueblos brought 680 horses, the Jicarillas brought 103 horses. Valverde provided 75 for the settlers. If, as Thomas estimated, each soldier had at least two animals, the grand total is 680 men and 850 horses and mules. Valverde describes the expedition as a useful reconnaissance, but there was no meaningful military action.[42]

For the ill-fated Villasur expedition the following year, it is known that 55 soldiers and citizens accompanied 60 Indian allies, but there is no known muster or inventory of the soldiers and animals.[43] One document records that l'Archiveque, one of the citizens, brought ten horses and six pack animals.[44]

Three years later, a muster of the Santa Fe presidial soldiers by retiring Governor Valverde for the newly appointed Governor Bustamante was held on June 18, 1723. The muster included 74 men, 418 horses and 8 mules for a total of 426 animals. The average number of animals per soldier was 6.[45]

The numbers from Bustamante's muster can be compared to a muster in the same year for the Janos Presidio in Nueva Vizcaya south of the Rio Grande. The muster showed that there were 50 soldiers with 514 horses and 50 mules, an average of 11 each. Each soldier had exactly ten horses and one mule except for the Teniente and Alferez who had 15 horses and 1 mule each, and the Sargento and Cave de Escuadra who had 12 horses and 1 mule each.[46] In his book on Anza, Donald Garate refers to the garrison at Janos as a crack unit, fully staffed where each soldier had the required arms, horses and mules.[47] The explanation for the larger number of horses at the Janos Presidio may be that Nueva Vizcaya was the location of ranchos and haciendas that raised and traded large numbers of horses. The horses did not have to be driven a far distance to the north with many of them dying or running off on the way. Examples of ranchos are San Mateo de la Zarca in the Durango area and that of Condé de San Pedro del Alamo, who, in the 1740s was considered one of the largest stockraisers in Nueva Vizcaya.[48]

Further information on the soldier/horse ratio is available in the 1720 *Reglamento* produced as a result of the inspection of the northern frontier by Pedro de Rivera in the late 1720s.[49] The regulations stated that the presidio of New Mexico was to have 80 men including officers[50] and that the captains should see that each soldier has six horses.[51] For purposes of comparison, the later 1772 *Reglamento* required that each soldier has "six serviceable horses, one colt and one mule; the captain shall not permit any animal to be kept that cannot endure the greatest hardships."[52]

In summary, the data show that for campaigns, the presidio in Santa Fe and the outlying royal pastures and outposts had to provide for at least 500 to 600 horses and mules, generally averaging five to seven animals per soldier. Another 300 to 600 should be added for the animals that were not taken on expeditions. In total, the royal pastures had to accommodate at least 800 to 1200 horses, not counting those of the settlers.

Though outside the period of this study, in the second half of the 18th century, as the military situation worsened, the number of horses in the presidio herd increased. In a 1794 report, Governor Fernando de Concha states that the size of the horse herd exceeded 2,000 animals.[53] Marc Simmons in *Spanish Government in New Mexico*, writing about the end of the 18th century, states that the *caballada* had upward of 1,000 horses and mules.[54]

Because the horse herds were prime targets for Indian raids, as well as theft by the colonists themselves, careful guarding of the horse herds was essential. Information on the horse herd guards is found in several sources. For example, in 1693, upon making his entrance into Santa Fe, Vargas assigned two squadrons of ten men each to guard the horses, mules, and the pack train.[55] This agrees with the later 1729 *Reglamento* stating that the number of soldiers on guard shall be no less than ten unless the company has less than 50 soldiers. The Reglamento also stated that the soldiers guarding the horses shall be rotated every fifteen days.[56]

Though later in the century, several items on the horse herd are of interest. For example, one of Governor Juan Bautista de Anza's muster rolls from 1779 to 1782 states that of the 100 Santa Fe Presidio soldiers, from 14 to 40 troops were assigned to the horse herds for an average of 24.[57] Concha, writing in 1794, said that the horse guard should be 30 men, whose command is given to one of three sergeants.[58] A muster by Santa Fe Governor Real Alencaster in 1808 showed that the presidio had 121 men of which 28 were assigned to guard the horse herds.[59]

An illustration of the horse guards on campaign, is found in the Segesser hide paintings. The painting shows eight mounted horse guard in close formation. Four of the guards are Spanish soldiers with flat broad brimmed hats, shields, guns and swords. There are four Indian guards with bows but no guns or swords. The Segesser hide paintings also include a mounted Spanish soldier.

Finally, information on the horse guards can be supplemented by that from Janos Presidio from the early 1720s where Juan Baptista Anza, Sr. (not to be confused with his son, Governor Anza mentioned previously) was alferez or lieutenant and the presiding officer. Documents in the *Archivo de Hildago de Parral* describe a roundup of horses from the caballada: "…the five soldiers who were presently on guard duty over the caballada were spread out, holding a long grass rope to keep the horse above that point. They had driven the herd in that morning before daylight and were waiting for the rest of the troops to arrive. When all was ready, five or six men at a time, again by order of rank and service, would enter the corral and stand in the middle of the caballada. As the band circled the handful of soldiers, each man would toss a rope round the neck of the horse he intended to ride as it trotted by him. He would then lead his mount for the day out of the corral and another soldier would take his place, until each was outfitted."[60]

Juan Bautista de Anza. From *The Land of the Conquistadores* by Cleve Hallenbeck.

The Spanish horse guards on campaign shown in the Segesser hide paintings. (From *The Segesser Hide Paintings* by Holtz Gottfried, 1991. Courtesy of Museum of New Mexico Press, Santa Fe, New Mexico.)

Mounted Spanish soldier shown in the Segesser hide paintings. (From *The Segesser Hide Paintings* by Holtz Gottfried, 1991. Courtesy of Museum of New Mexico Press, Santa Fe, New Mexicdo.)

Having documented the need for the large horse herds and something about how they were used and protected, the question becomes, where were the pastures for the horses located? Though mentioned in several documents, the only comprehensive list is found in a 1737 petition by Alferez Juan José Moreno to Governor Olavidé. In this petition, Moreno recommended a reservation of grazing pastures that had been used in the past, and names them. In this petition, Moreno urged that horse pastures be specifically assigned for use by the presidio and that the colonists be prohibited from using them. He said that "there is absolutely no place for the horses to graze, or if there are, they are at a distance, which means that the soldiers needed to protect the presidio are far away in time of need."

Moreno went on to state that while "there are grazing places (*parajes para comedores*) in close proximity to the Presidio *where they were grazed before* (author's emphasis) ... that they are sufficient to maintain them [the horses] the entire year without having to take them some thirty or forty leagues, [but] they are owned by someone, and their herds, cattle and sheep are given first priority to graze upon them instead of the horse herd which belongs to the King, which serves to safeguard not only the kingdom, but also the same herds." The places for grazing that Moreno names are: Caja de Rio, Santa Cruz, La Majada de Dominguez, Las Bocas, Los Cerrillos, San Marcos, and Maragua. In the petition, Moreno urged that the Governor proclaim that no settler can take their herds into any *comedores* or grazing area designated for the presidio horse herd.[61]

Governor Olavidé responded with a *bando,* or government order, doing just what Moreno had asked. He assigned the seven areas for the presidio horse herd, stating that they "are *ancient pasture lands for use by the royal horse herd*; (author's emphasis) they have tall grasses, an abundance of water and are secure from the enemies". He further stated, that "there being no fundamental right nor reason why some particular residents wish to have large numbers of herds of cattle and sheep and to pasture them at said places, as they are assigned for the said horse herds, and considering them as they should be considered as *ejidos* of His majesty, reserved for His Royal Presidio and garrison of this Kingdom." Olavidé added that the land shall be reserved for the presidio horse herd and if any vecinos have herds there, they shall remove the herds or incur a fifty peso fine.[62]

Locating these pastures on a map is not difficult, given that all but one or two, were land grants. The map included here is based on the land grants shown on United States Government Survey (USGS) maps and other sources and suggests their locations. Caja de Rio, Santa Cruz, La Majada, Los Cerrillos and San Marcos are easily identified as land grants located on the Rio Grande, the Santa Fe River, major drainages, or at springs. Though not a land grant, Las Bocas was described in the 1682–93 Vargas journals as being an outpost located near the confluence of the

Rio Grande and the Las Bocas River at the west end of the Santa Fe Canyon near the old pueblo of Cieneguilla.[63] Maragua was a land grant made in 1814 adjacent to the Galisteo Pueblo, though it can not be precisely located.[64]

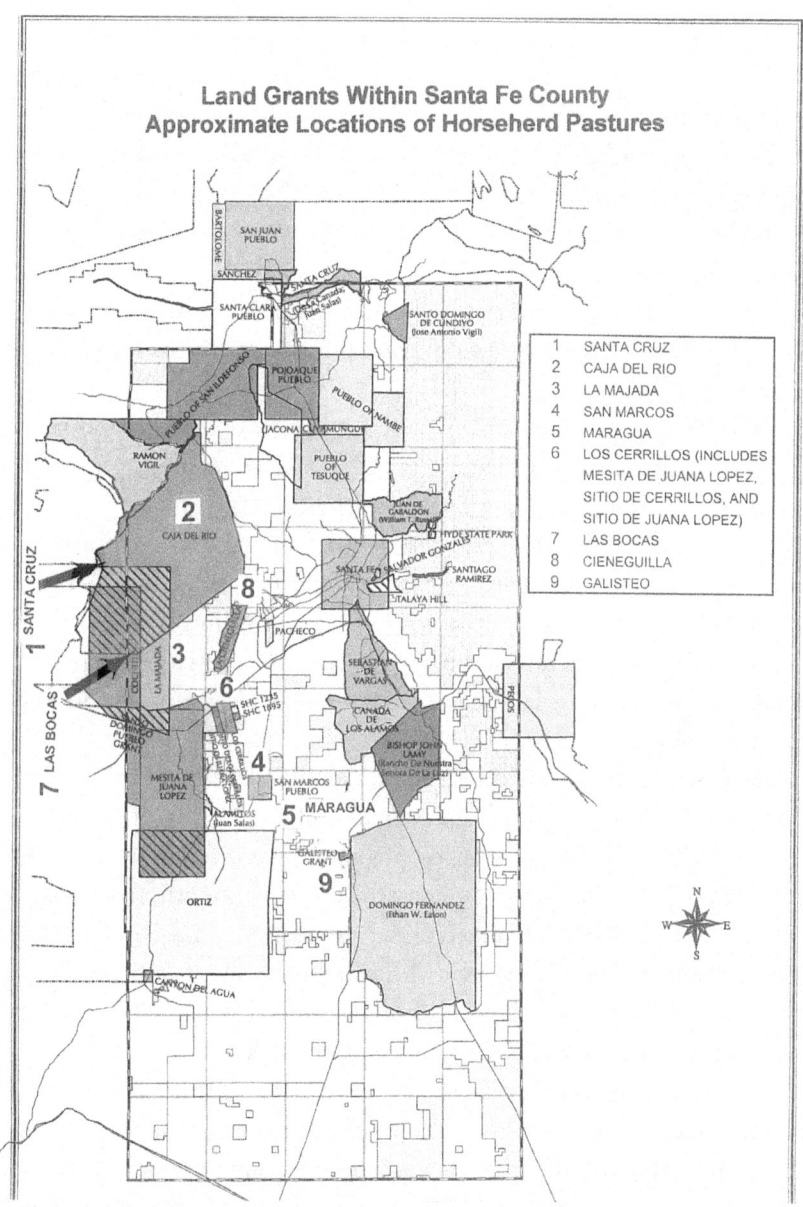

Map showing land grants within Santa Fe County showing approximate locations of Spanish Colonial horse herd pastures. Map prepared by Paul S. Casaus for the author, 2008, Santa Fe County Geographical Information System Office, Santa Fe, New Mexico

In looking at the list, one is faced with the question of when and how long these pastures had been designated as presidio grazing areas. Almost all of them were early land grants made to private individuals before 1737. If not, how did Moreno decide that they should be designated as such?

As shown above, both Moreno and Olavidé asserted that the designation of pastures for the presidio horse herd was from an earlier time. In Moreno's 1737 letter to the Governor, he said that pastures for the horses are near the presidio, "where they were grazed before". Olavidé went one further and calls them the *antiquos comederos* or ancient grazing lands. The land grant and other records provide evidence that some of the places designated by Olavidé had indeed been set aside for the grazing of the presidio horse herd before Olavidé wrote his bando. Other documents show that some pastures were included in pre-1737 land grants with a provision for common pastures for horses or just common pastures, but not with any reservation for the presidio. A few areas were designated as presidio pastures in land grants approved after 1737.

Caja de Rio. In the 1742 request for the Caja de Rio land grant made by Captain Nicolas Ortiz Niño Ladron de Guebara, he referred to the area in the grant as the "land called the Caja del Rio including the *potrero*," potrero being a pasture land for horses. That is, the land was used for horse grazing, but there was no mention of a reservation in the grant or pastures for the presidio. In making the grant, Governor Gaspar Domingo de Mendoza states that "according to the royal grant, the pasturage and watering places shall be in common, excepting the cultivable land."[65] The documents hint that the land had been used as grazing pastures, but there is no specific statement as such.

Santa Cruz. The site of Santa Cruz, (sometimes called Ojo de Santa Cruz, the Santa Cruz Cañada or the *virtientes* or drainage of spring of Santa Cruz[66]), is shown on a 1779 map of New Mexico prepared for Governor Anza by Miera de Pacheco. The Caja del Rio land grant lies to the north. The location is on the east side of the Rio Grande some distance north of the intersection of the Rio Grande with the Santa Fe River. The 1779 map shows it with a tiny symbol for *poblaciones dispenzas de los Espanoles*, (dispersed Spanish settlers) and the words, S. Cruz. A trail leads from the Cieneguilla area on the Santa Fe River to the place marked Santa Cruz.

An archaeological excavation carried out in the 1970s for the Cochiti Reservoir provides another map and additional information on the site.[67] According to the background report on the archaeological excavations, the area had been the site of a prehistoric pueblo, but in the 17th century was occupied by Spanish colonists. In 1731, following the Reconquest, there was a petition by Diego Gallegos for a "tract of land at the settlement of Santa Cruz which tract has been deserted by the year 80." The petition was denied because of the danger to the pastures of the cattle and horse herd of the Cochiti Pueblo.⁶⁸ Like the Caja de Rio grant, the document suggests that the area had been used for pasturage in the past, though not for the presidio horse herd.

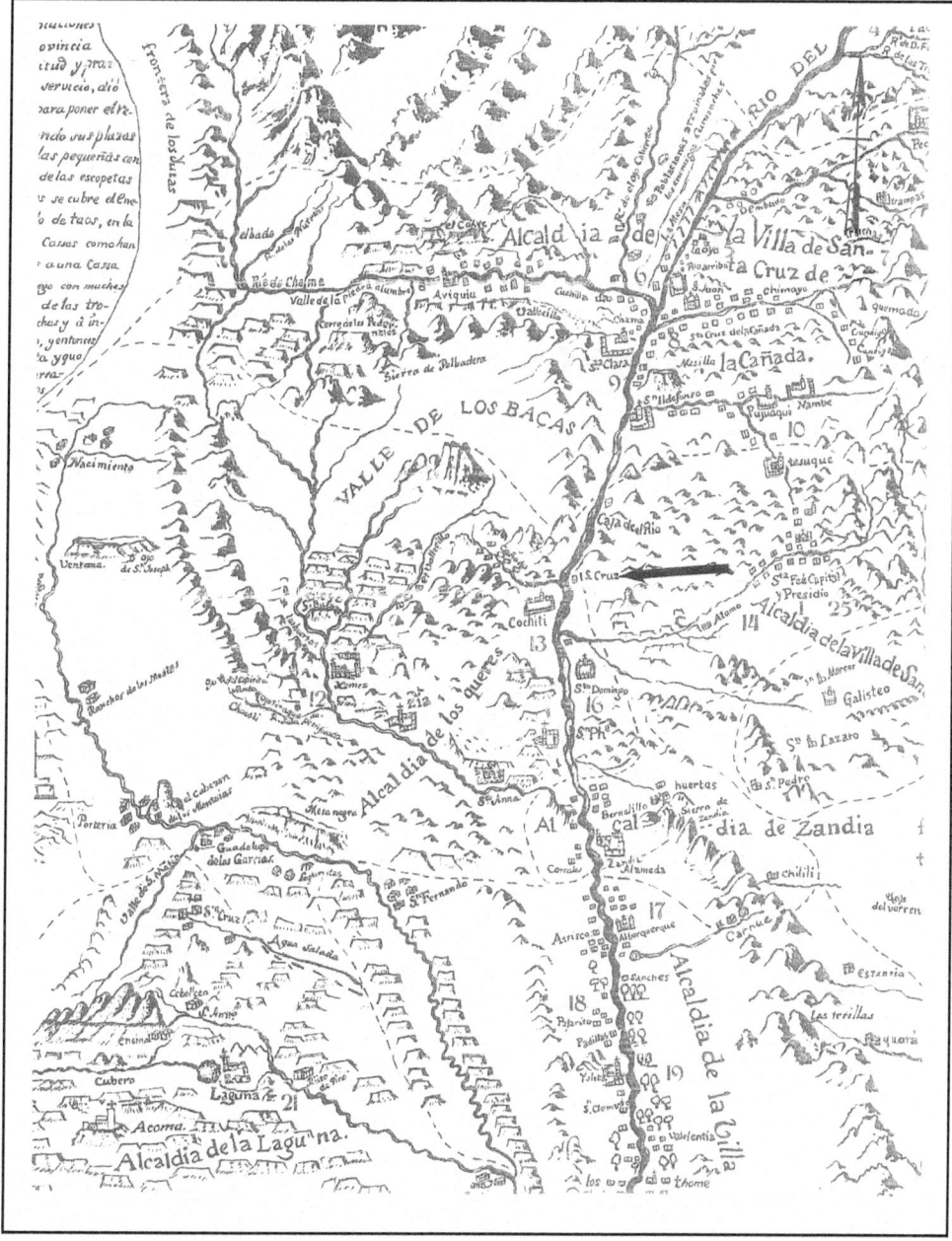

Portion of Miera de Pacheco Map of 1779. Courtesy of John L. Kessell. Located in the New Mexico State Archives, Santa Fe, New Mexico

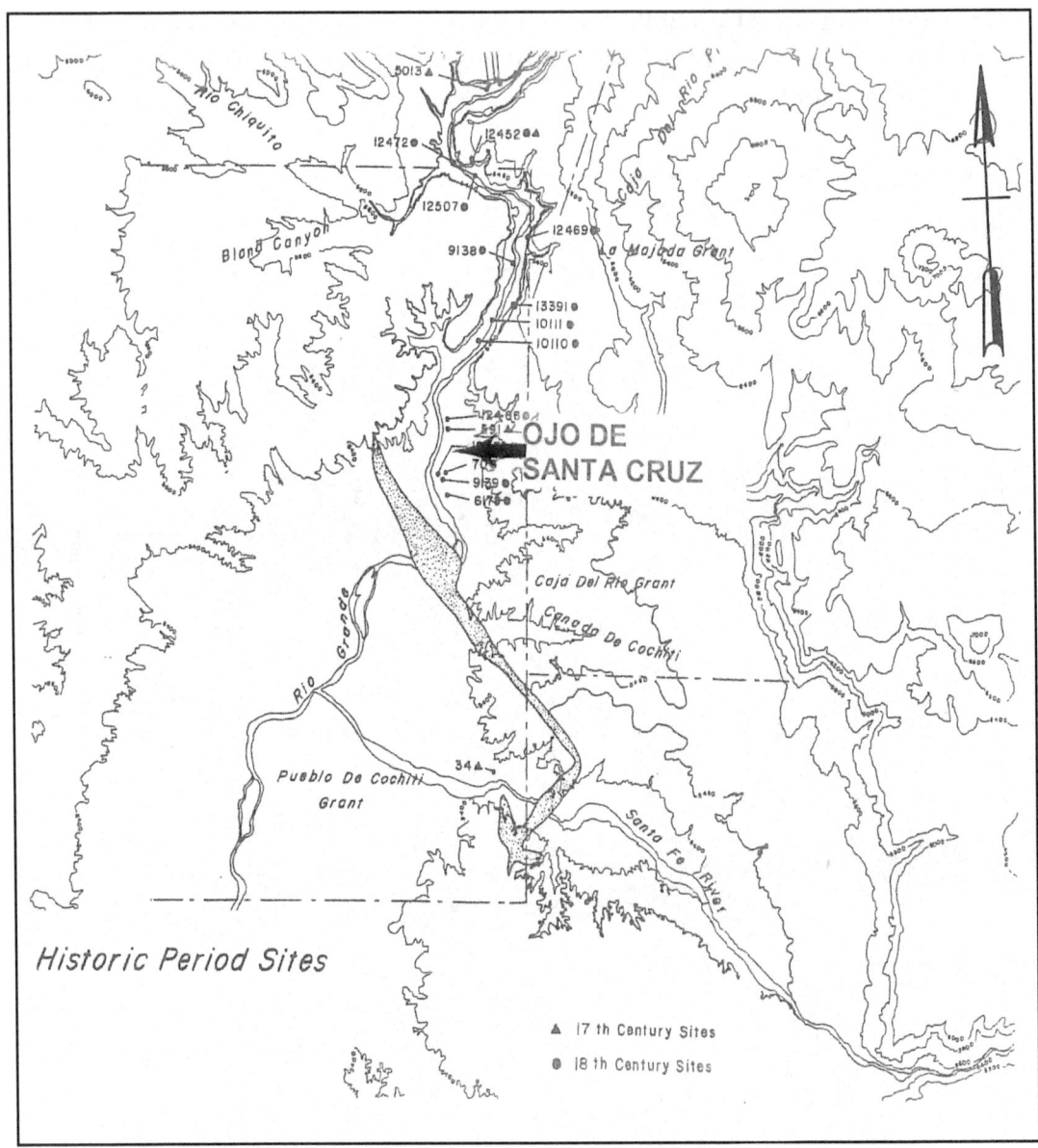

Map showing location of 17th and 18th century sites in the southern portion of Cochiti Reservoir from *Archeological Investigations in Cochiti Reservoir, New Mexico, Vol. 4, Adaptive Change in the Northern Rio Grande Valley*. Office of Contract Archeology, University of New Mexico, 1979, page 230, Albuquerque, New Mexico. Courtesy of Richard Chapman, University of New Mexico.

The Pastures of the Royal Horse Herd of the Santa Fe Presidio, 1692–1740   253

In 1744, Juan José Moreno, author of the petition to Governor Olavidé for horse herd pastures described above (see page 481 in Notes), also petitioned for a land grant for Santa Cruz. He asked for land for planting corn and for grazing, and stated that he would not disturb the presidio horse herd. The grant was approved by Governor Joaquin Codallos y Rabel with the condition that "the horses from the Royal Garrison, will graze on said lands in the proper time."[69] The reservation for the presidio horses may have dated from the 1737 bando of Olavidé.

Las Bocas. In 1692, Vargas, on his way to the *entrada* into Santa Fe, stated that after leaving Santo Domingo and crossing the Rio Grande, he called a halt at Las Bocas, a campsite on a plain surrounded by mountains.[70] The area has been identified as located in the Santa Fe Canyon where the Rio de las Bocas joins the Rio Grande, north of the Santo Domingo lands near La Cieneguilla, and that it is located where the Santa Fe River enters a narrow defile. The defile is called Las Bocas as shown in the map.[71, 72]

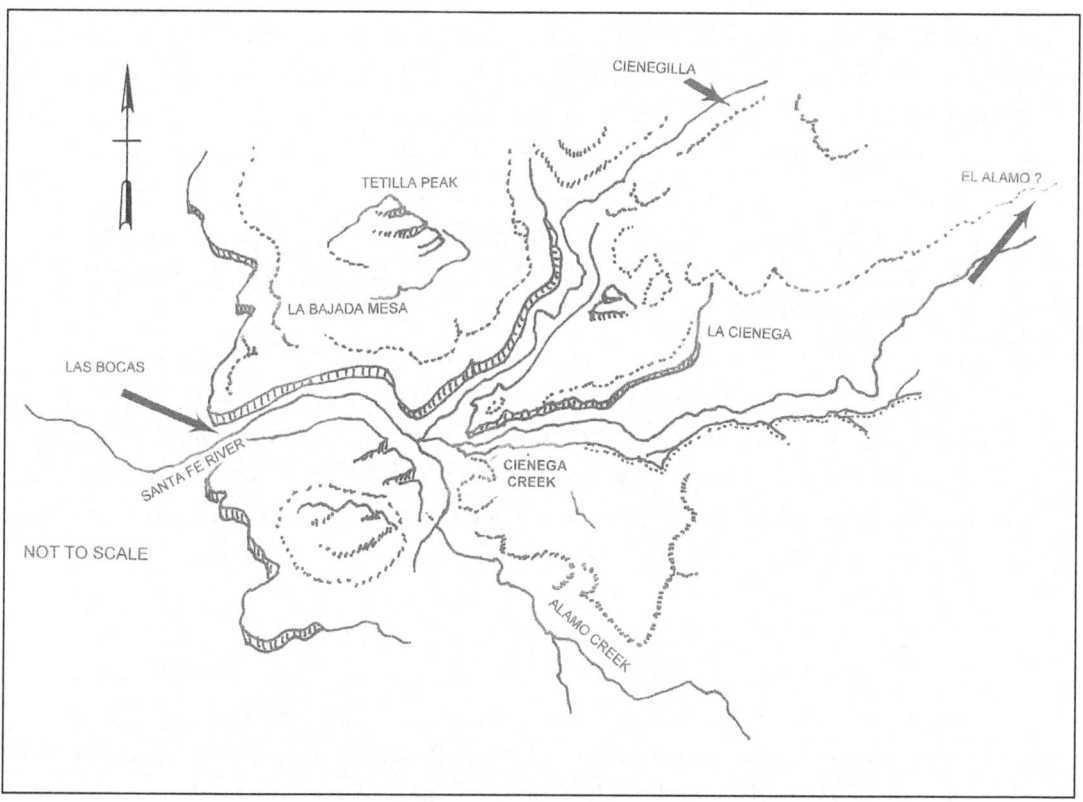

Approximate locations of Las Bocas, La Cienega, Cieneguilla, and El Alamo. Map prepared by the author.

In a 1693 letter to Viceroy Gálves, Vargas said that "It [Santa Fe] has plenty of firewood in the surrounding land and pastures. These can be set aside, leaving and reserving them from the entrance of Las Bocas, which begins along the road to Santo Domingo, seven leagues away."[73] This suggested that he saw the area at Las Bocas and also the land to the east of it, as pastures to be used by the colony, which would have included the horses of the soldiers.[74] Later in 1694, also in a letter to Gálves, Vargas referred to the "outpost" of Las Bocas at two small *cerros*, seven leagues outside the villa, suggesting that it had gained a certain military status.

In his campaign journal of 1696, Vargas said that while on campaign and returning to Santa Fe, he directed his officers to "cross [the Rio Grande] and spend the night around Las Bocas at the outpost of El Alamo, because I could see how exhausted the horses and mules were."[75] The statement suggests that Vargas saw Los Bocas as including the El Alamo area. An earlier statement he made in 1693 about El Alamo, showed that he intended the area to be reserved for the horses and mules of the colonists including the soldiers. He said, "The person who demonstrates his right to them [lands near the pueblo of La Cienega] will also be given the lands to the abandoned hacienda of El Alamo, with the limitation of not being able to make claims for the damage the horses may do.... That length and distance, with its ways in and out, is the site to be reserved, since it has been chosen as a commons, not only for the horses and mules of the settlers who will settle here, but also for those of the soldiers, the man-at-arms of the presidio, who are also to settle in that place."[76]

This area may have been considered one of the "ancient pastures." It also suggests that Vargas saw the colonists and presidio soldiers sharing the pastures on the entire west side of Santa Fe.

It is of interest that a much later report made in 1849 by Lieutenant Simpson on General Sumner's military reconnaissance of the Santa Fe area also described the area though without naming it. Simpson said "Debouching from the [Santa Fe] cañon, an extended plain—upon which I saw some fifty head of cattle grazing—stretches westward about six miles to the Rio Grande.... Not a tree is to be seen until you can look down upon the Rio Grande, and then the cottonwood is noticed sparsely skirting its banks."[77]

La Majada. Evidence that the La Majada grant was used or reserved for pasturage of the presidio's horses is difficult to find. According to grant documents compiled in the 1880s for the Surveyor General, the grant was originally made in 1695 by Vargas to one of his captains, Jacinto Peláez from the El Paso Presidio.[78] The grant was revalidated in 1698 by Governor Cubero before the death of Peláez in 1704. It was again revalidated by Vargas in 1710 for the daughter and heir of Peláez, Maria.[79]

The grant was bounded on the west by the Rio Grande, on the north by El Ojito and on the south by the lands of Santo Domingo Pueblo. On the east the boundary was Las Bocas, here called Las Bocas de Senetu. On the north were the spring of El Ojito and an unroofed house owned by Captain Francisco Lujan,[80] deceased, all of which was a league from the north boundary, and by another house in the Rio Grande bottom [land] which belonged to Captain Cristobal Fuentes.[81] The claimants to the grant stated that the original grant documents were lost. There is no mention of horse pastures in the later documents. There is no evidence that the lands could be considered an "ancient pasture."

Los Cerrillos. Though dated after 1737, the Los Cerrillos grant documents clearly referred to the pastures of the presidio horse herds. The 1750 grant papers included a request to Governor Velez Cachupin by the children of Alonso Rael de Aguilar for a revalidation of an earlier grant made to their father. They stated that

> "It being a grant for the place, Los Serrillos (sic), with its pastures, waters, timber, and watering places, as our deceased father had then settled, and a portion of the province revolted in the year ninety-six, our said father retired from the said Serrillos by order the Governor, where he had lived for years, and built houses, which fact is evidenced even to this day, by the remaining ruins, and it being true that he left us no other piece of land, except the said Serrillos and during the past years the place having been used as a pasture ground for the horse herds of this Royal Garrison, to which we all say, the horses are welcome to the pasturage as long as it may be required without any of us making objection unless pasturing in the cultivated grounds, as there is enough for all."[82]

Velez firmly responded that, "considering that so many governors, my predecessors, have refused to allow that section [Los Cerrillos] to be settled or occupied by any citizen, it being commons for the pasturage and subsistence of the large horse herd of this royal garrison, and being the place nearest the garrison, in the getting up at shortest notice of any necessary expedition in the royal service for the defense of the country, …that what these parties pray for cannot be entertained or permitted."[83] Velez's language is so similar to that used by the 1737 bando of Olavidé, it suggests he read it or was aware of it. Los Cerrillos would certainly qualify as an "ancient grazing land."

In an 1872 private land claims case for the heirs of Manuel Delgado for the Los Cerrillos Grant, it was stated that the property was the public grazing grounds and camp of the animals of the Mexican government.[84] Note that at this time, this is the only specific mention of a grazing ground for animals of the Mexican government.

San Marcos. In 1754, Governor Velez Cachupin did approve a grant to Antonio Urban Montaño for land in San Marcos which affected the presidio horse herd. In this case, the Governor stated that Montaño "shall not damage with his herds, the commons and the pasture of the horses of this royal garrison nor the pasturage of the herds kept for the supply and support of the soldiers of the royal garrison which are pastured and kept at those places. Should he do so, this grant shall be of no validity and cannot be of any force and effect, and he may be ejected there from."[85] In this case, it appeared that Velez was comfortable with sharing the pasture with a settler.

However, a much later document from 1809 shows that the Governors were not always consistent about this matter. A letter to acting Governor Manrique asked for permission for Don Francisco Ortiz and Captain Don Manuel Delgado to pasture their herds in the lands at San Marcos. The Governor responded negatively, stating that lands are "a common for pasturing the herd of horses of that company the greater part of the year" and that damages may result if it is assigned to others. Manrique also states that the pastures are reserved for the poor citizenry of the villa "pobre del vecinderos de dicho villa."[86] This suggests that at that time, the land was seen as reserved for the presidio and the poorer citizens, but not for private property owners.

There is some evidence that the area of San Marcos had been used for military purposes, if not for the pasturing of horses, at least since the time of the Reconquest. In his campaign journal for December 10 and 11, 1693, Vargas stated that he is ordering the families to depart from the Santo Domingo Pueblo, "regulating their travel so as to arrive early tomorrow morning at the arroyo and outpost with the most shelter, which they call San Marcos." The next day he said that he arrived "at the campsite and outpost they call San Marcos."[87] San Marcos may also qualify as an "ancient grazing land" or at least a former outpost.

Maragua. The final name on the list is Maragua, also called Santo Domingo de Maragua or rancho de Maragua.[88] It is described in the 1840 grant documents as a site located from "brow to brow" on both sides of the Galisteo Creek west of the settlers of Galisteo. The only hint of horse grazing pastures is that the grantees were forbidden from collecting damages because of the animals already there and from running off the loose animals from the common pastures (*no cobararan daño de animals sueltos no los correran por ser pastos communes*). The grantees were also required fence their fields and keep less than 100 ewes and cows on the land.[89] In 1897 when several old-timers who had worked on the property testified on past uses, none mentioned the use as horse pastures. Perhaps the use had been forgotten by that time. It is of interest that one of the persons testifying on the grant said that there were no houses on the site where he worked there as a boy in the 1820s digging acequias and breaking up the land, but there were ruins of some extinct pueblos.[90]

Further information on Maragua also shows that it was a common area, if not a horse pasture. In an 1830 petition to the Governor by Juan de Dios Peña and others for the La Gotera land grant located east of the Ortiz Mine grant and south of Galisteo, it is stated that the La Gotera property was located west of the *creston* (outcrop) of Maragua (also called Maragua Hill) and that the La Gotera grant was located "a little more or less below Maragua, which is public land" (*abajo de Maragua, terreno valdio*).[91] An accompanying document from Domingo Fernandez, alcalde of Santa Fe, places the petitioners in possession of La Gotera, stating that if the land is sold to the military, clergy or a religious community or society, "said tract shall revert back to the Mexican Nation and be known as public land, (*por bienes de realengas*), as Maragua continued to be."[92] This suggests that before the Mexican period, grants including La Gotera and Maragua, were given, Maragua was a larger area in what was seen as a common land. Though there is no documentation of it being an "ancient grazing pasture," it was likely that it was, given its location in the Galisteo Basin and proximity to San Marcos, which was clearly designated as a grazing pasture.

At this point, it should be noted that of the seven horse herd pastures named by Juan José Moreno, four were located along the Rio Grande, all in a row: Caja del Rio, Santa Cruz, Las Bocas, and La Majada. The other three, Los Cerrillos, San Marcos, and La Maragua, were located in the Galisteo Creek watershed. In other words, Moreno was urging that, excluding Pueblo land, the entire east side of the Rio Grande near Santa Fe and the nearer part of the Galisteo watershed, be reserved for the presidio horse herds. Excluded from the Galisteo area was the eastern part of what came to the known as the San Cristobal land grant and the pueblo of Galisteo. Though apparently the home of larger herds of wild horses in the 1920s, the San Cristobal area was probably excluded because it could not be defended from raiders from the east, or because La Maragua was within the San Cristobal area.[93] The Galisteo Pueblo area was almost certainly excluded from the list because is was still occupied by the Indians in 1737, as discussed below.

There are four remaining areas not listed by Moreno that are associated with the pastures of the royal horse herd, Galisteo, the Santa Fe cienega, Cieneguilla, and El Alamo. The discussion of the Santa Fe cienega differs somewhat from the others in that it includes information both on the horse herds and also on the entitlements for this kind of common land.

Galisteo. Though occupied as a pueblo until the late 1800s, Galisteo was seen as a bulwark against the raids of the Plains Indians, and from the mid 17th century on, presidio soldiers were assigned to the site. In 1750 Governor Vélez Cachupin directed that both the Pueblo of Pecos and Galisteo be garrisoned with 30 soldiers and that the walls of each pueblo be fortified.[94] An 1808 document shows that Governor Maynez assigned a corporal, three soldiers and members of the military to Galisteo.[95] In 1871 testimony before the Surveyor General on the Town of Galisteo Land Grant claim, Donaciano Vigil, a former official in both the Mexican and United States governments, stated that he had grown up in Galisteo, and that there was a house built there for a detachment of soldiers until 1814, the date when the Town of Galisteo Grant was made.[96] Presumably the soldiers' horses would have been pastured nearby. When the Town of Galisteo grant was made by Governor Maynez in 1814, a reservation was made giving "the people of Santa Fe and the vicinity the privilege of pasturing and herding their livestock on the land," but there was no specific reservation for the presidio herds.[97]

Santa Fe Cienega. The cienega was located within the Santa Fe villa and was described by Vargas as "a swamp and on low ground that makes the waters from the sierras and surrounding mesas collect."[98] Soils tests from the 1980s land development collected by this author in 1990, shows that the black, sticky swamp dirt of the cienega can be found in a triangular area with the greatest concentration east of Washington Avenue, north of Palace Avenue and south of Marcy Street.[99] The area has been drained and built over, though some structures, like the underground parking of garage of the Inn of the Anasazi, were built with sump pumps in the basement to collect ground water. A reminder is in the name of the one of the streets that passes through the area, Cienega Street.

Throughout the 18th century, the cienega was an important source of water and grass for the presidio and the community, so much so that the governor and citizens of the villa are on record as making efforts to protect it from encroachment. As discussed below, the records show that in the early 18th century, the land was considered an *ejido,* in this case, a kind of common area. Later it is referred to as "realengas" often translated as unappropriated land.[100] In the earlier years, the land seems to have been considered available for the horses of both the villa and the soldiers, though later, the presidio soldiers seemed to have claimed it as their own.

One of the relevant documents include a statement made in 1705 by Governor Francisco Cuervo y Valdés that at a certain time each year, no one should drive stock or horses on to the cienega so that they "shall not trample the grass that grows there so that anyone who needs it can mow it to feed their horses [*para dar de comer a sus Caballos].*" There was no mention of the grass being only for the presidio horse herd, though the Governor also stated that anyone violating this order was subject to a sentence of a month in jail for the first offense and for the second, two months of duty guarding the horse herd of the presidio garrison.[101]

A lawsuit in 1712 brought by Antonio de Moraga against Juan Sosa de Canela for lands in the "torreon of the cienega" described the cienega as an ejido (*q sirve de exideo de esta dha Villa*[102]). The term ejido was also used in a 1716 sale document from Antonio de Moraga to Diego Arias de Quiros for property adjacent to the cienega.[103] In neither case was mention made of the horse herd. Also in 1716, the Santa Fe cabildo made a presentation to Governor Flores Mogollon complaining that Arias de Quiros had made a pond in the cienega in unappropriated lands (*en tierras Realengas*). As part of the protest, the complainants stated they were defending the public because of the need to have "somewhere to cut a little grass with which to maintain all during the summer their horse herd (*mantener todo el Verano sus cavalgaduras*)."[104] The horse herd in question seemed to belong to the villa rather than to the presidio, or perhaps it referred to both.

In 1717 Lieutenant General Juan Páez Hurtado restated an annual order that the animals (cattle and hogs) in the villa be rounded up so that animals will not "trample or eat its [cienega's] grass in order that it may be mowed to feed to the horses of the presidial troops who escort those who go to the mountains to gather firewood and timber."[105] In 1748, Governor Codallos mandated that Santa Feans keep their animals away from the cienega which was for use of the military horse herd.[106]

These documents suggest that in 1705, it was not necessary to claim the cienega grasses exclusively for the presidio horse herd, though at a later date, in 1717 and again in 1748, it was. The site may not have been named in Moreno's list because it was already accepted as a source of water and fodder for the presidio's horses. Certainly the cienega would qualify as an ancient pasture, though it was not named by Moreno as such.

Cieneguilla. A second site, also called the Anaya Almazán grant, often discussed as a pasture for the royal horse herds is Cieneguilla, located, west of Santa Fe.[107] (See map shown previously.)

In the 1890s Cieneguilla grant approval, Surveyor General Henry Atkinson stated that, "It appears from the documents that in or about September 1693, Francisco de Anaya Almazán petitioned the Governor and Captain General [Vargas] for a grant to a *sitio* of land known as the Cieneguilla tract, distant about four leagues from the Villa of Santa Fe, and about one league from the Pueblo of Cienega. On September 2, 1693, Vargas declined to grant the sitio for the reason that it was included within the pasture lands of the Villa, though Vargas did grant to the petitioner, "one fanega of planting land, and also what may be necessary for raising the two hundred head of small stock or twenty head of large stock, besides the horses of his [military] service and oxen for his field or cart." In other words, Vargas was reserving at least some of the area west of the villa for common pasture lands, though it is not stated whether this was specifically reserved for the presidio horses. The document stated that the land was "bounded by El Alamo, the Cienega, the descent of the table land of Santo Domingo where Diego Gonzales was killed, and the other one where the roads to the Pueblo of Cochiti separate in front of the Pino [ranch]."[108]

El Alamo. As described above, a reference was also made by Vargas to the El Alamo site as including a common area for horses and mules. In 1693, Vargas stated that persons who demonstrated their right to them [it], would be given the abandoned hacienda of El Alamo, but that they could not make claims about the damage by horses. He further states that the site has been chosen as commons for horses and mules of the settlers but also for the soldiers.[109] Though the precise 17th and 18th century boundaries are unclear, the El Alamo hacienda as well as the Cieneguilla grant, described above, can be considered "ancient grazing pastures".

In summary, the information on the presidio grazing pastures named by Juan José Moreno showed that most of the sites were "ancient pastures" being reserved for horses by Vargas or other governors after the Reconquest, though in some cases, the pastures were not specifically reserved for the presidio horses. Specific reservations for the presidio horses were made for four areas, the Santa Fe cienega, Santa Cruz, Los Cerrillos, and San Marcos. Grants and other information for Caja de Rio, Las Bocas, Cieneguilla, and El Alamo referred to horses, but without a specific reservation for the presidio horses. There was no specific reservation for horse pastures belonging to the presidio or otherwise in the La Majada and Maragua grants.

All of the locations of the listed areas were less than thirty or forty leagues from the presidio. (For comparison purposes, a reference was made by Vargas to Isleta as being 30 leagues from Santa Fe.)[110] USGS maps and County water sensitive aerial photography shown that they are all currently, and probably were in the past, well watered. That is, they are in locations where there "are tall grasses for pasture and an abundance of water."

Given the needs of the presidio and the citizens and the limited amount of water and pastures, the situation in northern New Mexico led to encroachment of designated pastures and to complaints by both groups. These complaints necessitated regulations by the governors through a variety of bandos and other orders and to a determination of how common land could be used. As shown above, by 1737, the governor had determined that he had the right to reserve land for the presidio on property previously granted to colonists.

After the Reconquest, Vargas seemed to have avoided contention between settlers and soldiers over horse grazing pastures by reserving land for the horses and animals of the colony, including the presidio, not for the presidio horse herds alone. In the case of Cieneguilla, Vargas refused a large land grant to a soldier because the area was needed for the villa. He granted a small piece of land and insisted that the soldier pasture the presidio horses assigned to him on it. In the second case of El Alamo, Vargas stated that the land was to be shared by the grantees and by the horses of the colony.

In retrospect, one wonders why Vargas did not set aside land just for the presidio animals. It is possible that he did not anticipate how quickly the hostile tribes would adapt mounted military tactics. He may not have thought that the colony would be so beleaguered and so desperate for military protection and so dependent on effective cavalry operations that it had to be supported by a steady supply of horses and mules and the means to sustain them. Or he may have just run out of time.

A 1715 example of encroachment on an area reserved for the use of the community, and later for the presidio horses, was the disagreement over the Santa Fe cienega.[111] As stated above, the cienega was a source of water and particularly for fodder for the horse herd of the colony. Because the water in the cienega was being diverted into a pond by Diego Arias de Quiros for his own uses, a part of the cienega was drained. Complaints were made, and the Santa Fe cabildo ordered him stop. Arias de Quiros petitioned Governor Flores Mogollon who, most likely aware of the status of Arias as a soldier of the Reconquest and a Santa Fe alcalde, determined that Arias could use some of the water if he agreed to fill most of the pond and block two acequia connections. Arias ignored the requirement and after lengthy prevarication, the Governor insisted that Arias fill a part of the pond and block his connections to the acequia, a kind of compromise. The situation here was complicated, as it may often have been in Santa Fe, because Quiros was a soldier-settler. He was a colonist as well as a presidio soldier. If he went on military expeditions, it is likely that he rode the presidio horses. In this case at least, his attitude seems to have been that others could look after the presidio animals.

Probably the most significant example of a conflict between the presidio and the settlers is found in the 1737 petition, discussed extensively above, to Governor Olavidé de Micheleña from Juan José Moreno, *Alferez* and Sergeant of the Presidio Company. In the petition, Moreno asked the Governor to mandate that no settler can take their herds into any grazing area designated for the presidio horse herd and listing those areas.

Governor Olavidé responded with a *bando* restricting the seven sites for the purpose of grazing for the presidio horse herd and stating that "…there being no fundamental right nor reason why some particular residents wish to have large numbers of herds of cattle and sheep and to pasture them at said places, as they are assigned for the said horse herds, and considering them as they should be considered as *ejidos* of His majesty, reserved for His Royal Presidio and garrison of this Kingdom." As quoted in a section above, Olavidé went on to state that "the land shall be reserved for the presidio horse herd and a fine will be incurred by the settlers who used it."[112]

In this 1737 case, as well as with others, the problem had to do with how common areas with scarce resources, in this case the grazing areas, were to be used, with Olavidé unequivocally deciding that the needs of the settlers take second place to those of the presidio. Because defense was so important, the time for shared use of the pastures between the settlers and the presidio had long passed. The Governor gives a legal rationale for his decision, saying that the places assigned for the horse herds are "*ejidos de Su Magestad* reserved for His Royal Presidio and garrison of this kingdom ... the royal presidio shall have the fundamental right to its use by said horse herd." For good measure, he added, ominously, that "*there is no exempt place for its [royal presidio and garrison] maintenance*" (author's emphasis).[113] He was, in effect saying that any place, not just common land, but any land, including that granted to individuals, could be assigned by the governor for presidio and garrison purposes. In twenty-first century language, he was saying that regardless of entitlements, in times of a military crisis, property rights give way to military need.

In regard to the *ejidos Su Magestad,* Olavidés position seems to be that they were entitlements, but of a special kind. That is, they were the ejidos of His Majesty, and therefore to be used in the way that his representative, the Governor, chose. Moreno stated the case more clearly than the Governor in trying to pry the desperately needed pastures from the settlers. Moreno says, "The reason that the horses are not grazed at these said places is none other than because it is said that they are owned by someone and their herds, cattle and sheep, [and] are given the first priority to graze upon them instead of the horse herd which belongs to the king." Later he urged that the Governor promulgate a bando mandating that if these persons "insist that they are the owners of any of the places, we will recognize them [lands] as being vacant and without legitimate owners who can impede the use."[114] In saying this, Moreno was challenging the grant entitlements.

In Daniel Tyler's 1988 article, "Ejido Land in New Mexico," he pointed out that the word *ejido* was used in several ways, but it generally had to do with unplanted lands, unenclosed areas used for grazing or, sometimes, reserved land.[115] It had a more specific definition that "common" land. It could be part of a specific community or under total control of the sovereign.[116] In this case, Olvaidé and Moreno believed the pastures to be so valuable, that they belonged to the King, and were to be used for the benefit of the whole colony rather than for specific settlers.

In two examples from the 1750s, Governor Velez Cachupin seemed to agree, or partly agree, with Olavidés view. In the case of the Los Cerrillos grant discussed above, the Aguilera heirs requested ownership of a site that had been granted to their father and occupied before and after the Reconquest. They buttressed their claims by stating that they thought there was enough pasturage for both the colonists' animals and the royal horse herd, similar to the arrangement that Vargas had made west of the villa years earlier. Velez Cachupin disagreed, stating that the area was set aside for the presidio horse herd only. In San Marcos grant, Velez Cachupin, for whatever reason, is more compromising. He approved the grant request, but stated that the grantee, Urban Montaño, was not to damage the pastures of the horses and herds of the royal garrison.

This situation of scarce resources for the horses that were desperately needed for protection of the colony became, if anything, more severe in the later 18th century. Military personnel in the southwest continued to find the availability of water, fodder, and the consequent deterioration of the horses to be an on-going concern in the face of increasing hostilities.[117] The deterioration of the horses meant fewer useful horses for the soldiers and militia, severely limiting their ability to provide protection for the colony.

The governors of New Mexico continually commented on the situation. In a 1771 report from Governor Mendinueta to Viceroy Bucareli, the Governor stated that his 80 soldiers and the settlers were barely able to defend themselves. He adds, "Because, while it [New Mexico] abounds with men apt, scarcity of arms makes them useless; much more so the lack of horses, for war in this land cannot be made afoot."[118] In 1779, Governor Anza, found that while he was able to mount the soldiers, there were few mounts owned by the settler militia that could be used on a campaign. Anza said that, "Because of their [settlers] wretchedness, the best equipped presented themselves with two riding beasts, the most of them almost useless".[119] In 1780, Inspector General Teodoro Croix stated that in New Mexico, the practice of putting the horses out to pasture made the animals unfit for duty as the forage was insufficient to maintain their strength.[120] Viceroy Gálvez expressed his concern about the province in his *Instruccions* of 1786: "The enemy Indians upon our frontiers well know how to surprise and destroy our troops in the mountains and on the plains. They are not ignorant of the use and power of our arms; they manage their own with dexterity; and they are as good or better horsemen than the Spaniards."[121]

The problem continued through the nineteenth century. Frank McNitt quotes General Sumner, leader of 1849–1850 Navajo campaigns, as stating that, "It is impossible to make long marches [in New Mexico] with cavalry on grass alone, loaded down as they [the soldiers] are with arms, accoutrements and clothing, and to have the horses equal to the Indian horses in speed or bottom… [C]onsequently our Cavalry horses are a great embarrassment…. Indeed I would prefer that 4 Companies of horse should be withdrawn, even if they cannot be replaced by other troops." McNitt points out the difficulty of supplying forage, and states that in 1850–1851, "there was a steady insistence from the quartermasters at Fort Marcy upon the selection of new posts in regions offering an abundant supply of forage. The valley of the Mora and the western slopes of the Chuskas were mentioned repeatedly in reports to Washington. And so the sites of Fort Union and Fort Defiance were chosen".[122]

By the end of the first third of the eighteenth century, it began to be apparent that New Mexico did not have the resources to be a sustainable, economically viable community while at the same time continuously fighting the various hostile tribes, unless there was a higher level of support from Spain than they were ever given or likely to get. The situation continued to worsen throughout the 1700s and, in fact was still a problem in much of the nineteenth century.

Bibliography:

Baxter, John O. *Las Carneradas*. University of New Mexico Press, Albuquerque, 1987.
Bob, Bernard. *The Vice-Regency of Antonio María Bucareli in New Spain 1771–1779*. University of Texas Press, Austin, 1962.
Bloom, Lansing, editor. "A Campaign Against the Moqui Pueblo". *New Mexico Historic Review*, Vol. 6, #2, 1931, pages 158-201.
Blyth, Lance R. *Los Vaqueros Buenos. The Presidial Soldiers of Santa Fe, 1779–1805*. A Thesis for Degree of Master of Arts. Colorado State University, Fort Collins, Colorado, 1997.
Bowden, J. J. *Private Land Claims in the Southwest*. Graduate Thesis. Southern Methodist University, Dallas, Texas, 1962.
Brayer, Herbert O. *Pueblo Indian Land Grants of the "Rio Abajo", New Mexico*. The University of New Mexico Press, Albuquerque, 1939.
Brinkerhoff, Sidney, and Odie B. Faulk. *Lancers of the King*. Arizona Historical Foundation, Phoenix, 1965.
Calloway, Colin G. *One Vast Winter Count*. University of Nebraska Press, Lincoln, 2003.
Chavez, Fray Angelico. *Origins of New Mexico Families*. William Gannon, Santa Fe, 1975.
Christmas, Henrietta Martinez. *Military Records. Colonial New Mexico. Notas y Revistas*. Hispanic Genealogical Research Center, Albuquerque, 2004.
Concho, Fernando de la. "Advice on Governing New Mexico", *New Mexico Historical Review,* Vol. 24, 1949, pages 236-254.
Ebright, Malcolm. *Land Grants and Lawsuits in Northern New Mexico*. University of New Mexico Press, Albuquerque, 1994.
——"The Galisteo Grant," Paper for website of the New Mexico State Archives, 2008.
Fehrenbach, T.R. *Comanches*. Anchor Books, New York, 1974.
Gálvez, Bernardo de. *Instructions for Governing the Interior Provinces of New Spain, 1786*. Translated and edited by Donald Worcester. The Quivera Society, Berkeley, California, 1950.
Garate, Donald T. *Juan Bautista de Anza*. University of Nevada Press, Reno, 2003.
Hadley, Diana, Thomas H. Naylor, and Mardith K. Schuetz-Miller. *The Presidio and Militia on the Northern Frontier of New Spain. A Documentary History. The Central Corridor and the Texas Corridor, 1700–1765*. Vol. 2, Part 2. University of Arizona Press, Tucson, 1997.

Haggard, J. Villasana. *Handbook for Translators of Spanish Colonial Documents.* University of Texas, Austin, 1941.

Hämäläinen, Pekka. *The Comanche Empire.* Yale University Press, New Haven and London, 2008.

Hammond, George P. and Agapito Rey, editors. *The Rediscovery of New Mexico*, University of New Mexico Press, Albuquerque, 1995.

Hendricks, Rick and John P. Wilson. *The Navajos in 1705. Roque Madrid's Campaign Journal.* University of New Mexico Press, Albuquerque, 1996.

Hildinger, Erik. *Warriors of the Steppe.* Da Capo Press, Cambridge, Massachusetts, 2001.

Hotz, Gottfried. *The Segesser Hide Paintings.* Museum of New Mexico Press. Santa Fe, 1970.

Jackson, Hal. *Following the Royal Road. A Guide to the Historic Camino Real de Tierra Adentro.* University of New Mexico Press, Albuquerque, 2005.

John, Elizabeth A. H. *Storms Brewed in Other Men's Worlds.* University of Nebraska Press, Lincoln, 1975.

Kessell, John. *Kiva Cross and Crown.* University of New Mexico Press, Albuquerque. 1979.

—— *Spain in the Southwest.* University of Oklahoma Press, Norman, 2002.

Kessell, John and Rick Hendricks, editors. *By Force of Arms.* University of New Mexico Press, Albuquerque, 1992.

—— *Royal Crown Restored.* University of New Mexico Press, Albuquerque, 1993.

—— *Blood on the Boulders.* University of New Mexico Press, Albuquerque, 1997.

—— *That Disturbances Cease.* University of New Mexico Press, Albuquerque, 2000.

—— *A Settling of Accounts.* University of New Mexico Press, Albuquerque, 2003.

McNitt, Frank, editor. *Navaho Expedition. Journal of a Military reconnaissance from Santa Fe, New Mexico to the Navaho Country Made in 1849 by Lieutenant James H. Simpson.* University of Oklahoma Press, Norman, 2003.

Moorhead, Max L. *The Presidio, Bastion of the Spanish Borderlands.* University of Oklahoma Press, Norman, 1975.

—— "The Soldado de Cuera: Stalwart of the Spanish Borderlands". *Journal of the West.* Vol. 8, 1969, pages 38-55.

Naylor, Thomas H. and Charles W. Pozer. *Pedro Rivera and the Military Regulations of Northern New Spain, 1724–1729.* University of Arizona Press, Tucson, 1988.

New Mexico Land Grants Private Land Claims of the Surveyor General (PLC), Microfilm at the New Mexico State Archives.

New Mexico Land Grants Surveyor General (SG), Microfilm at the New Mexico State Archives.

Noyes, Stanley. *Los Comanches. The Horse People, 1751–1845.* University of New Mexico Press, Albuquerque, 1992.

Pinart Collection: Documents P-E 46-1 and P-E 46-2. Bancroft Library. University of California, Berkeley.

Rose, Martin, Jeffrey S. Dean, and William Robinson. *The Past Climate of Arroyo Hondo, New Mexico, Reconstructed from Tree Rings.* School of American Research, Santa Fe, New Mexico, 1981.

Secoy, Frank Raymond. *Changing Military Patterns of the Great Plains Indians.* University of Nebraska Press, Lincoln, 1953.

Snow, Cordelia Thomas. "The Evolution of a Frontier: An Historical Interpretation of Archeological Sites" in Jan V. Biello and Richard C. Chapman, *Archeological Investigations in Cochiti Reservoir, New Mexico, Vol. 4, Adaptive Change in the Northern Rio Grande Valley.* Office of Contract Archeology, University of New Mexico, Albuquerque, 1979.

Simmons, Marc. *Spanish Government in New Mexico.* University of New Mexico Press, Albuquerque, 1968.

Spanish Colonial Archives, Volumes I and II. Microfilm, New Mexico State Archives, Santa Fe.

Thomas, Alfred Barnaby. "Governor Mendinueta's Proposals for the Defense of New Mexico, 1772–1778". *New Mexico Historical Review,* Vol. 5, 1931, pages. 21-39.

—— *Forgotten Frontiers. A Study of the Spanish Indian Policy of Don Juan Bautista de Anza Governor of New Mexico. 1777–1787.* University of Oklahoma Press, Norman, 1932.

——— *After Coronado*. University of Oklahoma, Norman, 1935.
——— *Teodoro de Croix and the Northern Frontier of New Spain, 1776–1783*. University of Oklahoma, Norman, 1941.
Tigges, Linda. "Soils, Tests, the Cienega, and Spanish Colonial Occupation in Downtown Santa Fe", in *Santa Fe Historic Plaza Study I*. City of Santa Fe, 1990, pages 75-84.
Twitchell, Ralph Emerson. *The Spanish Archives of New Mexico. Volumes I and II*. The Torch Press, Cedar Rapids, Iowa, 1914.
Tyler, Daniel. "Ejido Lands in New Mexico" *in Spanish and Mexican Land Grants and the Law*. Malcolm Ebright, ed. Sunflower Press, Manhattan, Kansas, 1987.
Walker, Henry Pickering. *The Wagonmasters. High Plains Freighting from the Earliest Days of the Santa Fe Trail to 1880*. University of Oklahoma Press, 1966.

12

It Happened in Old Santa Fe, The Death of Governor Albino Pérez, 1835–1837
by
Joseph P. Sánchez

On Saturday, June 15, 1901, a group of New Mexicans met in Santa Fe to dedicate a monument to the memory of Albino Pérez.[1] Leading the parade were the First Cavalry and the New Mexico National Guard Band. The parade marched from the plaza to a point along Agua Fria Street and stopped near the spot where Governor Pérez fell sixty-four years before.[2] The rest of the marchers reached the place of dedication. First, the Daughters of the American Revolution, then some members of the Rough Riders, followed by the National Guard, firemen and a contingent of interested citizens.[3] As they gathered around, gusts of wind and dust attacked the on-lookers, while overhead clouds began to darken the late afternoon sky. The ceremony began and one of the participants unveiled a marble boulder polished on one side with the inscription:

On this spot, Governor Albino Pérez
was assassinated, August 9, 1837[4]

The paraders listened to speakers while wind and dust disturbed them and the rain clouds became evermore menacing. After a round of introductory remarks, Demetrio Pérez of Las Vegas made an apologetic and brief presentation punctuated with forgive the brevity of my remarks.[5] Demetrio Pérez, son of Albino Pérez,[6] expressed his appreciation for the honor extended to the memory of his father. As he ended his speech, a driving hailstorm scattered the crowd and cut short the ceremony.

Like the gathering storm of 1901, the opposition against Governor Albino Pérez increased until certain of the citizenry of Santa Fe and nearby villages vented their wrath against him. In 1837 Pérez, *jefe político* or governor of New Mexico, and his followers were killed in a rebellion allegedly led by Pueblo warriors. Although Pérez' death occurred during the revolt, the circumstances leading to his demise suggest a conspiracy on the part of Hispanic New Mexicans. They had been unhappy under Mexican rule that began with Mexican independence from Spain in 1821 and ended with the War of 1846 between Mexico and the United States.

Appointed to the military-governorship of New Mexico by Mexican Dictator Antonio López de Santa Anna in 1835,[7] Pérez' unquestioned loyalty to the central government in Mexico City, and his military experience made him a fine choice for the New Mexican mission.[8] Pérez' objective, to prepare the people of New Mexico for the change from an outlying frontier province to a territorial department[9] inspired opposition from New Mexican frontiersmen who interpreted the change to mean that they would surrender local power to a distant central government. Consequently, an explosive political issue regarding home rule worked to undermine his mission.

A native of Veracruz, Pérez was an outsider to Santa Fe's politics. Ultimately, New Mexicans openly opposed him and after his untimely death, New Mexico's native son, Manuel Armijo, became governor of the politically fragmented *territorio de Nuevo México*. Armijo ruled until the American invasion of 1846.

In 1835, Albino Pérez worked to prepare the Santa Fe legislative assembly for departmental status. While introducing necessary reform measures, Pérez inadvertently intruded on a local political situation. Consequently his administration became increasingly unpopular among New Mexicans, who opposed the departmental plan.

Early in his administration, Pérez undertook an inspection tour of Northern New Mexico so that he could better assess the situation there and promote the reformation of New Mexico's government. Hoping to sway them to accept the change in governmental form, Pérez addressed the people of Santa Fe in patriotic and flowery terms. He said,

> Compatriots: A series of extraordinary circumstances have come together to furnish me with the most pleasant references to speak to you for the first time. As of today, it is thirty-four days that I have the honor to govern you, and already I can count thousands of examples of your gentleness, your love for order, your submission to justice and a true complement of many civic and moral virtues which God has joined here so as to illuminate His Omnipotence in this majestic retreat.[10]

Pérez continued speaking of the "patience of a truly paternalistic government, proud of its Mexican origin and ... heroic ... because it is supported by the unanimous vote of the Nation." The speech was published and circulated throughout New Mexico where it was received with indifference.

The departmental plan mirrored the strongly centralized government under Antonio López de Santa Anna, president-dictator of Mexico. Quickly changing the form of government from a federal republic to a dictatorship, the national congress in Mexico City, early in 1835, abrogated the self-governing powers of the states. Each state or department, thereafter, was permitted a five-member council which reported directly to the congress. In November 1835 a provisional departmental council met in Santa Fe in conformity with Mexican directives. The convocation of a provisional council signaled Nuevo México's preparation for departmental status. Seven months later, the Mexican government recognized the first permanent council for New Mexico under the Constitution of 1836.[11] By that time New Mexico, with its departmental capital in Santa Fe, had been divided into several districts each one administered by a *prefecto*, with judicial and political powers.[12] The *prefectos* were appointed by the *jefes políticos* of each department throughout the Mexican Republic. Thus, the *prefectos* reported to Pérez, as the *jefe político*, who in turn communicated with the national congress and reported directly to the Dictator Santa Anna. Subsequently, once the departmental assembly was established and linked to the prefect system the chain of governmental command connected local control with the central government.

Yet controversy continued to shroud the department system in New Mexico, and the leadership provided by Albino Pérez became the focal point of attention among New Mexicans. The causes of discontent resulted from legislative action initiated by the *jefe político* as well as the consideration that Albino Pérez was not a native of the area he governed. Chief among the issues was direct taxes imposed on the inhabitants of New Mexico by the Pérez administration. Demands made by Pérez on the people for aid against marauding Indians became another point of complaint, for the people felt that the central government should provide military assistance. Lack of cooperation for the new form of government by New Mexican frontiersmen became evident to Pérez and his administration.

Pérez's activities, no matter how practical, became increasingly unpopular. On October 16, 1835, for example, Pérez announced legislation regulating trade with Indians and Anglo-American traders along the Santa Fe-Chihuahua Trail. Threatening a lucrative illegal Indian trade which the *jefe político* accurately tied to increased Comanche, Apache, Ute, and Navajo attacks by well-supplied raiders, the October law provided that:

1. *Estrangeros del norte* (Anglo-Americans) be prohibited from trading in New Mexico with all classes of Indians.
2. Both *estrangeros* and citizens of New Mexico not be permitted to trade arms and ammunition to *naciones barbaros* who surrounded the territory and raided into Chihuahua.
3. Trade with Indians be permitted only with a license issued by the departmental government.
4. No Mexican citizen, native or naturalized, be permitted to trap beaver without license from the departmental government.
5. No citizen be permitted to use his license to trap beaver for any *estrangero*.[13]

Pérez also required that monies be used to outfit troops for combat against raiders. But New Mexicans viewed the law as an example of Pérez' role as an agent of the centralist government bent on destroying home rule through stronger regulations.

Eight months later, in June 1836, Pérez announced another regulatory law. This time foreign merchants were the target. The law,[14] weighted with details, provided that taxes be levied on each wagon bringing foreign merchandise into Santa Fe, on each animal involved in freighting, and on each horse or mule brought into New Mexico for sale. The June law also provided for taxes per head for driving herds of cattle or sheep through the streets of Santa Fe. Cutting timber required a license; and, fees for attendance at theaters and dances were charged in accordance with the law.

Far reaching in scope, the June legislation made it mandatory that all foreigners as well as natives of New Mexico who resided outside of Santa Fe report themselves to the *alcalde* within three days after their arrival in that city, and that each person state his business and occupation under penalty of fine. The *prefectos* of the territory were instructed to keep a list of all inhabitants within their respective districts listing occupations of all persons. Unemployed individuals who could not prove that they subsisted without illegal means were to be punished. Justices failing to comply with the requirements of the law were to be censured, fined and removed from office. Notwithstanding the practicality of his actions, the earlier October law and the June enactments effected many facets of the New Mexican economy. Using little discretion, Albino Pérez signed the law into being.

Although the law placed the burden of taxes on foreign traders they, in turn, passed it on to their New Mexican customers by raising their prices on trade items. Josiah Gregg, American trader in Santa Fe, noted the attitude of the people when he stated that although it was "necessary for the support of the new organization to introduce a system of direct taxation ... the people ... would sooner have paid a doblón through a tariff than a real in this way."[15]

While his economic reforms caused much debate among foreigners and citizens Don Albino turned his attention to other problem areas. Knowing of the up-and-down history of education in New Mexico, Pérez proposed a remedy. The *jefe político* did not have far to go for examples of illiteracy. The 1836 report of the *ayuntamiento* de Santa Fe, for example, indicated that two of the seven deputies of that departmental *junta* could neither read nor write.[16] Pérez called the state of education in the department deplorable. He cited that children in the streets as well as juveniles who were given to "evil dispositions, abandoned to laziness, and practicing vices" ought to be in school. Moreover, he described the prevailing thievery, immorality, desertion and poverty as "the most humiliating shame of the city."[17] On July 16, 1836, Pérez proposed a change. His prescription called for the establishment of two schools dedicated to primary instruction in Santa Fe. Threatening parents and guardians with fines, Pérez announced that all children ages five to twelve were to attend school. The fines ranged from to one to five pesos, double for the second offence and triple for the third. Anyone, who could not pay the fines, was subject to arrest for a minimum of three days. The time of detention increased with each arrest.[18]

Pérez detailed how his compulsory education system would work. Several Commissioners of Public Instruction, stationed in every block of Santa Fe, made lists of inhabitants and kept track of school age children and their attendance in school. Aside from making monthly attendance reports, the commissioners, or *comisarios*, selected students for their academic or vocational programs. As prescribed by the law, the *comisarios* explained to each parent as many as three times the stipulation of the law regarding education and the financial responsibility of each family to support the school by paying fees agreed upon by the school master.

Performing their duties under penalty of law, the *comisarios* followed additional instructions to seek "idle and suspicious" individuals and give them notice to find employment. The *comisarios* kept records of the population within their sectors and reported the whereabouts of people who moved out of their blocks. To assure that the *comisarios* performed their duties, the law stipulated penalties for commissioners who failed in their jobs.[19] The people of Santa Fe particularly resented Pérez's watch-dog intrusions into their lives.

If any doubt remained concerning Pérez' authority to suggest or decree taxation provisions within laws, it soon disappeared with the Decree of April 17, 1837.[20] Sent from Mexico City, the decree spelled out the role of *jefe políticos* in directing their departments toward improved fiscal efficiency. Granting investigatory, advisory and appointive powers to department governors, the decree, for example, allowed Pérez to supervise treasury officials in Santa Fe. He even reviewed the monthly and annual cash statements made by officers of the *Hacienda,* or Treasury. Overall, if he observed omissions and abuses, the law empowered him to report and suspend employees who did not perform their duties loyally. In the same way, control of customhouses throughout New Mexico came under his control. The Decree of 1837 had significantly enlarged Pérez' power.

As a result of Pérez' increased authority, the undercurrent of opposition began to move swiftly gathering the discontented and opportunistic elements of New Mexico's society. The optimism described in Pérez' inaugural speech began to disappear. Slowly his political enemies revealed themselves. One of the first to do so was Juan Estevan Pino, a wealthy associate judge. Realizing that Pérez had surrounded himself with a few local politicians whom he favored, Pino used his office to voice his opinion about them. He openly criticized Santiago Abreu,[21] a New Mexican and close associate of Pérez. Opposing the appointment of Francisco Sarracino, another Pérez favorite, to the office of *sub-comisario*, Pino forced his removal in 1836. Because charges against Sarracino involved embezzlement, Pérez inspected the account books kept by the accused and found them to be correct. Yet Pino's enmity ran deeper than the situation indicated, for he was not about to let Sarracino go so easily. Supporting Pino, Juan Bautista Vigil, postmaster, and Manuel Armijo, interim *sub-comisario*, formed the opposition. Inadvertently, Pérez had intruded on a local political feud that would negatively affect his relations with all involved. In Santa Fe, the Pino-Sarracino rivalry had reached a breaking point. In late October 1835, Sarracino, under orders from Pérez, investigated Juan Bautista Vigil. Charged with mismanagement of the mail service, Vigil stood accused by Miguel Sena, loyal follower of Pérez.[22] Upon recommendation by Sarracino, Vigil was removed from office. Appealing the decision before the departmental court, Vigil found able support in Manuel Armijo who wrote a counter-draft to Sena's complaint. Consequently, Vigil, restored to his position,[23] became an invaluable ally to Armijo, whose friendship with Judge Pino was personal as well as political.

In 1836, Sarracino was accused of embezzlement and removed from office. Meanwhile, the anti-Pérez faction maneuvered Manuel Armijo as his replacement. The following year Sarracino was brought to trial, despite Pérez' inspection of his books. Presiding over Sarracino's trial, Juan Estevan Pino expeditiously found him guilty of embezzlement. In complete disregard for the verdict, Pérez reinstated Sarracino to his position but acting *sub-comisario* Manuel Armijo refused to give up the office when Sarracino approached him. Understandably so, aside from the political struggle to reduce Pérez's power, Armijo had, in the interim, become accustomed to the position that paid 4000 pesos a year. Besides, controversy surrounded Pérez's action to restore Sarracino. Pino openly questioned Pérez' authority to change a decision issued by a court.[24]

Pérez's enemies gathered strength. The Sarracino episode had defined the factions, the laws on education and taxation had focused on the significance of outside interference, the Decree of 1837 demonstrated the power of the central government, and local feuding supplied the emotion required to make the situation explosive. Taking a strong stand against Pérez, Manuel Armijo denounced the power given to *jefe políticos*. Opposing factions objected to all obnoxious features of taxation and prophesized on the possible precedents the law had set such as a tax on poultry or that "husbands would be taxed for the privileges generally attaching to connubial bliss."[25] At the heart of unrest was opposition to the departmental plan.

In the backlands of northern New Mexico, trouble brewed for the Pérez faction. A seemingly innocent court case in out-of-the-way Santa Cruz de La Cañada began a chain of events that led to the political confrontation with the *jefe político*. Presiding over a trial involving relatives, Juan José Esquivel, acquitted them. Next, the case was reviewed by Ramon Abreu, a supporter of Pérez, who not only reversed the decision but had Esquivel arrested when he refused to comply with the reversal.[26] Public sympathy favored Esquivel, who sat in jail serving out his term. Moving swiftly a mob formed outside his cell, liberated him and escaped to a mountain stronghold. Observing the situation, Josiah Gregg, noted that it was "an occurrence that seemed as a watchword for a general insurrection.[27] Momentarily, Esquivel became the protagonist in the struggle against the *jefe político*, but in reality, the pretext for a rebellion.

On August 3, 1837 a revolutionary junta was formed. It was made up of twelve persons who called their district the Cantón de La Cañada. They drew up their position, which stated nothing about the Esquivel incident, as follows:

Long live God and the Nation and the faith of Jesus Christ. The principal points that we defend are as follows:

1. To be with God and the Nation and the faith of Jesus Christ.
2. To defend our country to the last drop of blood in order to attain victory.
3. Not to admit the Departmental Plan
4. Not to admit a single tax.
5. Not to admit the bad order of those who are trying to effect it.

God and the Nation. Santa Cruz de la Cañada. August 3, 1837. Encampment.[28]

The term "Encampment" boldly signaled that the rebellion had begun. The Hispanic rebels gathered at the encampment with their counterparts "the principal warriors of all the northern pueblos."[29]

Meanwhile as word reached Pérez of impending trouble, he hastened to gather a militia but could muster only "a hundred and fifty men including the warriors of the Pueblo of Santo Domingo."[30] With his small force, Pérez left Santa Fe on August 7, 1837 to suppress the rebellion. Having spent the night at the Indian Pueblo of Pojoaque, they continued the march to Santa Cruz. En route the rebels attacked them. Francisco Sarracino later recalled that their attack was "in a disorderly manner ... giving us a lively fire.... Colonel Pérez approached the cannon and said to me these words 'Friend Sarracino do not abandon the cannon.'"[31] Needless to say, the cannon was abandoned, the battle lost, most of Pérez' men either fled or were captured or defected to the rebels. Pérez was chased back to the outskirts of Santa Fe where on August 9 he was caught and brutally killed. Josiah Gregg described the atrocity: "His body was then stripped and shockingly mangled: his head was carried as a trophy to the camp of the insurgents; who made a football of it among themselves."[32] Gregg's report on the death of the governor was second hand; but he did claim to see the death of Jesus María Alarid:

> I saw them surround a house and drag from it the Secretary of State, Jesus María Alarid, generally known by the sobriquet of El Chico. He and some other principal characters who had taken refuge among the ranchos were soon afterwards stripped and scourged, and finally pierced through and through with lances.[33]

Santiago Abreu was similarly killed, yet even more brutally.[34]

The rebel forces now two thousand strong, almost all of them Pueblo warriors, marched on Santa Fe. Preparing for the worst, the inhabitants fortified themselves in their homes. The rebels entered the city and elected a governor, José Gonzales whom Gregg described as a "good honest hunter, but a very ignorant man."[35] Two days after their entry into Santa Fe, they left.

News of the rebellion reached the Hispanic villages on the *Río Abajo,* the lower Río Grande from Cochiti Pueblo to, at least, Socorro. Despite their dislike of Pérez and his administration, the people of the *Río Abajo* could not support the rebels and their illegitimate grasp for power. On September 8, 1837, representatives of most of the *Río Abajo* villages met at Tomé, south of Albuquerque. They called for the suppression of the rebellion which by then had centered on Santa Fe and surrounding villages north of there. Sensing that the tide of sentiment for rebellion had ended, Manuel Armijo joined them in denouncing the uprising.[36] At Tomé, Mariano Chávez, announced, "I know of no one better qualified to lead our army than Manuel Armijo."[37] After nominating Armijo, he asked the assembly to declare Armijo as the leader of the army.

As soon as he could muster a fighting army, Manuel Armijo attacked the rebels just north of the Santa Cruz Valley and routed them. By early 1838, Armijo, with reinforcements from Chihuahua, had captured and executed Gonzales, thus crushing the revolt. Next he reported to the central government that the situation was under control. He informed Mexican officials that there was no need to send troops northward. Armijo petitioned for the governorship and received it. Granted that concession, New Mexico was restored to its native sons.

With Pérez dead, New Mexicans could ignore most of the directives from Mexico City. Earlier, the government of Antonio López de Santa Anna had suffered political and military defeats in the Texas and California revolts of 1836. Instability in Mexico allowed New Mexico to revert to its customary pattern of isolation. But for the next decade New Mexicans fared poorly under subsequent Mexican administrations and an annexationist cause began to grow. As an alternative to Mexican rule, leading New Mexicans desired annexation to the United States. When Stephen Watts Kearny and his Army of the West marched into Santa Fe, during the War of 1846, members of the New Mexico upper class welcomed them. A new, troublous era had begun for the *hispanos* of New Mexico. But the memory of Albino Pérez seemed to haunt them.

Sometime after Governor Pérez's death, a ballad or corrido called a *decima glosada,* which contained 40 lines with a certain rhyme pattern, appeared in Northern New Mexico. The decima "*Año de mil ochocientos treinta y siete desgraciado,*" memorialized Pérez' tragic death. The balladeer sang of the event in point of fact. In the ballad, Pérez is portrayed as an innocent victim of circumstances, who died as a result of "Vengeance and hatred" on the part of the people he tried to govern. Angrily, yet wistfully the balladeer criticized his generation for the disgrace that reflected on New Mexico.

Año de mil ochocientos[38]	O year of eighteen hundred
Treinta y siete desgradiado	and thirty-seven—be damned!
Nuevo Mexico infeliz	O miserable New Mexico
¿Que es lo que nos ha pasado?	What has happened to us?
Ya murio el juez de distrito	Our district judge is dead
murio el prefeto y el jefe	So too our prefect and our chief
y asi, ninguno se queje	Let no man cry in grief
cuando pague su delito	For the guilt upon his head
estaba desvueladito	This innocent man was led
cuando pago, el inocente	To doom, sleepless and exhausted,
y que padezca la gente	Now let the storm be inflicted

este crecido tormento	On the people, let them dread;
siempre te tendre presente	You will always be remembered,
año de mil ochocientos	O year of eighteen hundred
Junta de departamento	Departmental Council convoked
constituida por la fuerza	Convened by force;
¿quien ha de tener a bien	Who can, as a matter of course, accept
la inicua desobedencia?	such a wicked revolt?
¿Quien sera aquel que no tema	Who will now not fear to speak
hablar por su territorio	For his land, having seen
viendo la venganza, el odio	the vengeance and hatred
de lo que nos ha pasado?	Which upon us did wreak?
No quisiera haberte visto,	I wish I had never seen you
treinta y siete ¡desgraciado!	Eighteen hundred thirty seven, be damned.
Desgraciado territorio,	Damned territory
¿que hicistes con la pacencia	What became of your patience
con la cuerdura, obedencia,	Your good judgment, the obedience
que era tu unico tesoro?	which was your only treasure?
Es lo que mas siento y lloro:	That which I lament and mourn
Verte hoy desacreditado	Your reputation soiled,
de la fuerza cautivado	By violence despoiled,
sin defensa ni salida;	Defenseless and forlorn;
llora, llora tu desdicha,	Cry, cry for your misfortune,
territorio desgraciado.	Damned territory
Conquistadora feliz,	Contented Conquistadora
tu has de traer el consuelo	You must bring your consolation
y que no permita el cielo	That heaven not permit
la discordia entre nosotros;	The discord among us
Madre mia, nuestro amparo,	Mother mine, our true salvation,
siembra tu la paz y union	You sow your peace and unity among us,
entre nos, tus moradores	
de este reino conquistado,	your dwellers in this conquered land
Yo estoy confuso y no se	I am confused and don't
que es lo que nos ha pasado.	know what has happened to us.

"Año de mil ochocientos trienta y siete desgraciado" thus represents a nineteenth century personal perspective on the death of the hapless *jefe político*.

But dissatisfaction with Mexican rule persisted in New Mexico and a small vocal annexationist party emerged. Similar to the experience in Texas, one of the consequences of the Rebellion of 1837 was the growth of an annexationist movement that provided for separation from Mexico and union with the United States. That development accounts for the easy occupation of New Mexico by the U.S. in 1846, for when Stephen Watts Kearny and his army entered Santa Fe, they were greeted by leaders of the movement who were tired of an unstable Mexican administration. In time, *hispanos* of nineteenth century New Mexico came to doubt the advantages of American occupation, and a new period of discontent began.

Standing in the Plaza de Santa Fe on September 18, 1846, Kearny addressed the people of New Mexico. His words, however, were no match to those of acting Governor Juan Bautista Vigil y Alarid. His words echoed with a certain *tristeza* throughout the Plaza. Looking intently at Kearny, Vigil y Alarid said,

> Do not find it strange if there has been no manifestation of joy and enthusiasm in seeing this city occupied by your military forces. To us the power of the Mexican Republic is dead. No matter what her condition, she was our mother. What child will not shed abundant tears at the tomb of his parents?... Today we belong to a great and powerful nation.... [We] know that we belong to the Republic that owes its origin to the immortal Washington, whom all civilized nations admire and respect.[39]

With those poignant words, New Mexico slipped into the hands of the United States.

Yet, it was the Revolt of 1837 that provided the dynamics for such a consequence. The years 1834–1838 were, indeed, critical to Mexican unity with its frontiers to the north. During that period California, Texas, Zacatecas, Sonora and New Mexico resisted control by a centralist government in Mexico City. For New Mexico, in particular, the result was greater political instability and uncertainty. The Revolt of 1837 had far reaching effects for *hispanos* of New Mexico, whom the balladeer chastised with the words *"Nuevo México infeliz. que es lo que nos ha pasado?* Oh Unhappy New Mexico, what has happened to us?"

"She Was Our Mother"
New Mexico's Change of National Sovereignty and Juan Bautista Vigil y Alarid The Last Mexican Governor of New Mexico

by
Samuel E. Sisneros

As the last Mexican Governor of the department of Nuevo Mexico, Juan Bautista Vigil y Alarid addressed the public at the plaza in Santa Fe on August 19, 1846. Paradoxically, his speech, which articulated emotional and patriotic sentiments towards the Nation of Mexico, was a response to Brigadier General Stephen Watts Kearny's better known and often quoted proclamation announcing the American military occupation of New Mexico.[1] In the name of the citizenry Vigil y Alarid accepted the seizure of New Mexico by the United States of America and pledged his and his fellow Nuevomexicanos' loyalty and allegiance.[2] At the onset his address, delivered in Spanish, demonstrated conflicting thoughts and sentiments towards the change of national sovereignty.

Vigil y Alarid was the official left with the task of dealing with the U.S. take-over. This was a result of Governor Manuel Armijo's inability to defend New Mexico and his abrupt flight from Santa Fe leaving Vigil y Alarid in charge. Vigil y Alarid began his address with praise for the United States and hope for the "wonderful future that awaits" New Mexico. After stating that the inhabitants of New Mexico "humbly and honorably" submitted their loyalty and allegiance, he exclaimed, "No one in this world can successfully resist the power of him who is stronger," indicating a sense of futility and reluctance. He passionately continued with the following statement:

Do not find it strange if there has been no manifestation of joy and enthusiasm in seeing this city occupied by your military forces. To us the power of the Mexican Republic is dead. No matter what her condition she was our mother. What child will not shed abundant tears at the tomb of his parents?

He continued with a justification of Mexico's "misfortunes" as the result of civil war. Calling Mexico "one of the grandest and greatest countries," he then, in the following sentence, patronized and esteemed the nation of the United States. With mounting contradictions, his speech again resonated with a sense of defeat when he suggested that it would have been worse if New Mexico were "invaded" by a European nation. He ended his address by swearing obedience and respect to the laws and authority of the "Northern Republic."[3]

Juan Bautista Vigil y Alarid's submissive yet ambivalent speech, as well as other public expressions he made during his political career, demonstrate how the people of New Mexico faced and dealt with the dilemma of whether to maintain sovereignty with Mexico or accept political and cultural dominance by a foreign government.[4] Examining Vigil y Alarid's political life and the forces that put him in this precarious position to determine New Mexico's future presents a comprehensive perspective of this pivotal point and the subsequent decade in New Mexico's history.

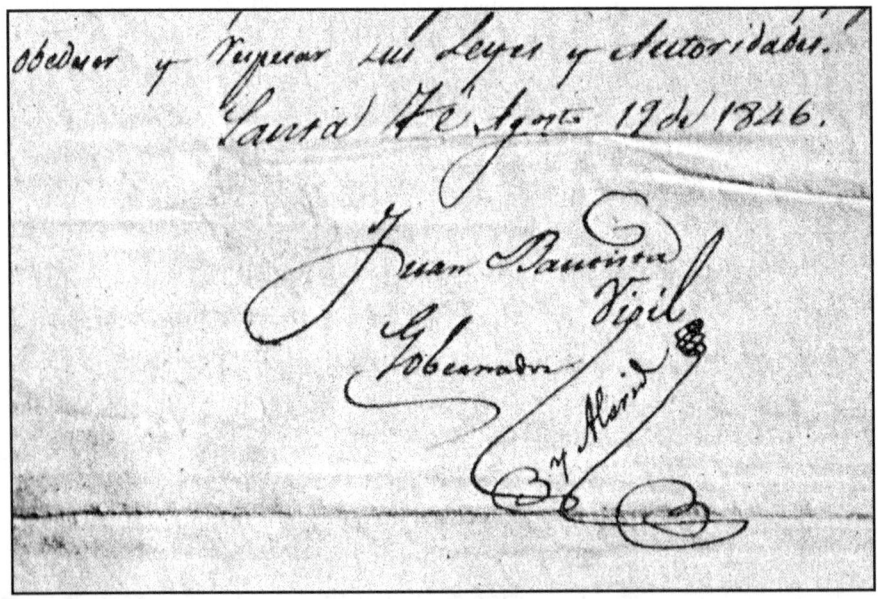

Signature and rubric of "Gobernador" Juan Bautista Vigil y Alarid from bottom of page of Acceptance of Allegiance speech, Ralph Emerson Twitchell, *The Military Occupation of the Territory of New Mexico from 1846 to 1851*, page 77.

The expressions of nationalistic loyalties towards Mexico, determined by how the people of New Mexico, both Indian and Mexican Hispanic, chose to react to the United States varied. Some showed complete acceptance and assimilation and participation in the United States' political system, while others responded with resistance, such as organized military confrontation, guerrilla warfare, open revolt, repatriation to Mexico and challenge of the United States' legal system. Others simply survived in isolated cultural enclaves. As with the people of Nuevo México, Vigil y Alarid's choices were often based on practical needs. In this dichotomy of resistance and acceptance, he expressed loyalty towards not only Centralist Mexico and Nuevo México, his "*Patria Chica*", but also to his principles of justice.[5]

This predicament faced by the people in New Mexico, which was the outcome of the aggressive takeover by the United States of nearly half of Mexico's northern territory, had its antecedents in two earlier conflicting episodes. One was the westward expansion of the United States along with its ideology of Manifest Destiny, and the other was Mexico's desire to populate Texas in an attempt to protect its interior provinces against enemy Indian and foreign attack. As a result, *Americanos* quickly populated Texas, who along with some *Tejanos*, rebelled against Mexico. After achieving independence from the Mexican Department of Coahuila, Anglo-Texans, backed by the United States, soon looked to expand into New Mexico. These two national entities would soon collide in the Mexican territories of Texas, New Mexico, and California and spread southward to Mexico City. In the end, this confrontation proved to be a tremendous benefit for the United States, and a great loss for the Republic of Mexico. This situation created a political and economic tug of war which, according to one's own vantage point, allegiances were questioned and formed.

A poignant example of the confrontation between native Nuevomexicanos and newcomers at the time of U.S. occupation is found in the memoirs of Lieutenant J.W. Abert, a member of the Corps of Topographical Engineers who came with Kearny. In his travel journal Abert wrote about his observations of Nuevomexicanos and their response to the U.S. invaders. He reflected his and his fellow Americans' bigotry towards Mexicans, often using the word "indolent" to describe Nuevomexicanos. To him they were more of a hindrance than an aid to what he called his "fact-finding" mission. He complained that throughout New Mexico, and in particular the Río Abajo area, the people answered his queries with the usual expression of "*quién sabe*" (who knows), or "*quizás*" (perhaps). Abert later admitted that the people in New Mexico were not necessarily unintelligent in their answers, conceding that their "laconic" and noncommittal replies to his queries contained much wit and finesse, but he still referred to the New Mexicans as degenerates and ignorant. He arrogantly said that they would make "Cervantes weep." A few Nuevomexicanos, perhaps realizing his attitudes towards them, took reparation by stealing the ropes off his mules.

Though Abert's mission was to survey New Mexico and other areas, it appears that his main interest was to find mines. In his relentless inquiry into the whereabouts of mines, Nuevomexicanos often sent him to far away places, and warned him that many "discontented" Mexicans lurked inside the mines and caverns attempting to "revolutionalize" the people. In the town of Manzano, on the other side of the mountain east of Belén, the town's people confronted Abert with their guns drawn demonstrating the existing tension that almost resulted in a violent confrontation.[6] These incidents reveal that there was apprehension and mistrust on both sides with regard to Albert's undertaking in conquered New Mexico.[7] Abert reveals his distrust of *Nuevomexicanos* and their resentment of him and the U.S. when describing these events:

> The people have a lingering inclination for the old government, and although none of their institutions have been changed, yet it will be some time before they will regard the entrance of Americans otherwise than as an intrusion.[8]

Vigil y Alarid surely witnessed similar tensions as he watched the change of three national sovereignties in New Mexico. He lived through the end of the imperialistic Spanish colonial era in the Americas and saw the birth of the new nation of México, which he came to call his "Mother." He witnessed and participated in the subsequent takeover by United States forces and the "death" of the nation, which he loyally served as a government official.[9]

The historiography regarding the role Vigil y Alarid played before, during and after the United States occupation and the patriotic sentiments of the Nuevomexicanos during this time, is limited. Early Anglo-American historians tended to perpetuate the "bloodless conquest" myth of New Mexico and viewed Vigil y Alarid as a friendly collaborator with the United States. They mentioned him only in the context of his short term as the last Mexican governor of New Mexico and his famous acceptance of allegiance speech. Nor did they present his political sentiments and those of other Nuevomexicanos of his generation. Mexican historians on the other hand treat this episode with disdain and describe Vigil y Alarid as a traitor and expansionist.[10]

A pioneer American historian on New Mexico history, Ralph Emerson Twitchell, in his 1912 multi-volume *Leading Facts of New Mexican History*, concluded that friendly feelings between New Mexican and Anglo traders and a weak allegiance to Mexico that was unable to resolve the "trouble with marauding Indians", created sentiments in New Mexico that favored a change in sovereignty. Furthermore, he stated that due to New Mexico's predominant mixed class (Spanish and Indian), New Mexicans were never loyal to Spain or Mexico. These assertions by Twitchell indicated the biases and attempts to justify the United States occupation shared by many early Anglo American writers.[11]

One of the earliest Hispanic New Mexican historians to write on the issue of New Mexican allegiances was George I. Sánchez. Writing along the lines of the previous Anglo American authors, he stated that the Mexican regime "had little effect upon the life of the New Mexicans." He presented an apathetic New Mexico towards change in any administration whether it be Spanish, Mexican or United States, and a fatalistic approach stating that "far removed from the currents of civilization, the New Mexican has been forced to live in a world of his own making." Sánchez states that the common people comprehended the United States occupation as nothing more than another governing power. Sánchez contends that the educated and elite, who were involved with commerce, were aware of the democratic conditions of the United States and were in favor of New Mexicans becoming citizens of the United States. He presented Vigil y Alarid's acceptance speech as evidence of this sentiment. Sánchez spoke of the New Mexicans' willingness to be part of the United States, suggesting, "the New Mexican quickly and wholeheartedly accepted his foster parents." He diminished the many attempts of resistance by stating the standard cliché of the bloodless occupation and contented that the Hispano and Pueblo Indian "rebels" who participated in the Taos Revolt[12] were a minority of "malcontents who did not have the sympathies of the native leaders or of the masses." Although Sánchez does not include notation of sources and often contradicts himself, he does exemplify the myths and historical memory that existed in the 1960's. Sánchez' work along with earlier writing perpetuated the belief that New Mexico was isolated and uniquely separate from Mexico.[13] These beliefs are still prevalent in New Mexico and responsible for much internalized racism, or at least, ethnocentrism, among Anglos and Native Hispanics towards recent immigrants from Mexico.[14]

David J. Weber in his book *Myth and the History of the Hispanic Southwest* wrote that the historiography of New Mexico during the Mexican administration has been "notably unbalanced, ethnocentric, and incomplete."[15] This call for a more balanced study has been taken up by a handful of historians who have looked into the issue of Mexican nationalism and patriotism in New Mexico. In his biography of Padre Antonio Martínez, a contemporary of Vigil y Alarid, Hispano historian Fray Angélico Chávez discusses the issue of patriotism and nationalism in New Mexico prior to and during the United States occupation.[16] Padre Martínez, a well-known parish priest, educator, prominent leader in New Mexico politics and "a peoples' priest," Chávez states, cherished his Mexican patriotism. His sermons often included

"Mexican impassioned narration," including a quote from a civic celebration honoring Mexican hero Don Miguel Hidalgo, in which Martínez alluded to a Mexico oppressed since the days of Cortéz. Chávez discusses Martínez' adherence to the Plan de Iguala of 1821, which resulted in independence and proposed that all classes of people were to be considered equal citizens. Padre Martínez, Chávez implies, was the main influence on the common folk in New Mexico whom he claimed "had no way of knowing about any such decree of racial equality unless they had been told about it and here is were Martínez comes in." Chávez states that Martínez, who openly vaunted Mexican patriotism, centered his writings on human rights and affirmed that "one can safely assume that his preaching and conversation throughout the north country often touched upon these matters, and with impassioned references to Padre Hidalgo and the Iguala laws of equality and freedom." He mentions that Vigil y Alarid, and Manuel Armijo were involved in a plot to embarrass Martínez by accusing him of complicity in the Rebellion of 1837 which was the only uprising of New Mexicans against the Central Mexican government. Spurred by discontentment with forced taxes and abuse from Mexico City, Governor Albino Pérez and sixteen of his officials were killed.[17]

A nephew of Fray Angelico Chávez, author Thomas E. Chávez, in his epilogue to the memoirs of the Spaniard, Manuel Alvarez, a naturalized American citizen and the United States consul to New Mexico, discusses trade restrictions under Spanish rule in New Mexico. He mentions that because of their location, New Mexicans found themselves between two expanding European traditions. Upon independence from Spain, New Mexico, now a northern frontier of the Republic of Mexico (1821–1846), saw relaxed trade laws and became a Mexican port of entry. Chávez notes that Alvarez mentioned in his memoirs that the Mexicans in New Mexico were negligent of the trade treaties and were corrupt, revealing "they have profited by the present circumstances, under the appearance of exalted patriotism, to find fault and create difficulties with the American merchants and particularly myself (Alvarez)." Alvarez highlighted his own conflicts at this time, which showed much tension between Nuevomexicanos and U.S. officials.[18]

Robert Tórrez, another Nuevomexicano historian, has come to the forefront in the discussion of Mexican nationalism in New Mexico. He argued that New Mexicans indeed were very patriotic towards Mexico. He sites several documents that demonstrate that state officials and the general public expressed patriotism through regular and elaborate celebrations of the *16 de Setiembre*, Mexico's independence from Spain. In addition, he presents documents that support New Mexicans' allegiance to the central Mexican government, including an insurrection in 1847 against the United States, where as many as three hundred Hispanos and Pueblo Indians, gave their lives in defense of their loyalties to Mexico. This was, as Tórrez states, "an ultimate expression of Mexican patriotism."[19] Tórrez explored this patriotism expressed as resistance to the United States in a subsequent work that offers a new and revisionist look at the New Mexican revolt and treason trials of 1847, following the United States occupation. As a result of the revolt in Northern New Mexico, many people were accused and tried for treason, which was in violation of the Treaty of Guadalupe Hidalgo. Provisions in the Treaty of Guadalupe Hidalgo stated that the citizens in the occupied territory were to retain their citizenship up to one year; therefore they could not be tried for treason against the United States if they were not United States citizens. Tórrez proposes that we re-evaluate this period in New Mexico history and consider revising the place in history of those involved who died resisting American invasion. They should, as Tórrez puts it, "be remembered, not as rebels and traitors, but as Mexican patriots who died defending their country."[20]

In order to add context to this historiography, it is important to focus in on the chronology of events in the political life of Juan Bautista Vigil y Alarid.[21] Born a citizen of New Spain around 1788 at Santa Fe, New Mexico, Juan Bautista Vigil y Alarid spent his childhood as a subject of the Spanish Crown. Information of his childhood up to the time of his marriage is sparse. An 1808 matrimonial record reveals that at Tomé, New Mexico, Vigil y Alarid married María Encarnación Rafaela Sánchez. His parents were listed as Domingo Vigil and María Francisca Alarid who were from military families and lived in the presidio of Santa Fe.[22]

Little is known of the activities of Vigil y Alarid from the time his marriage up to the Independence of Mexico. At this point in his life he most likely received news of Miguel Hidalgo's 1810 *"Grito de Dolores"* which resulted in Mexico's independence from Spain in 1821. This was the beginning of New Mexico's participation with the new nation of Mexico and when we first see the political actions of Vigil y Alarid. His service to Mexico in various political positions lasted throughout the twenty-five years New Mexico was under the Republic of Mexico. He served intermittently as Secretary starting under Governor Francisco Javier Chávez in 1822 through 1847 under Governor Manuel Armijo.[23]

Since the beginning of his political career, Vigil y Alarid found himself at odds with the central Mexican government and local officials. Yet he continued to serve in various political capacities. In May of 1824, just a few years into his political career as Secretary of State, Vigil y Alarid was named deputy to State Congress in Chihuahua.[24] As a representative of New Mexico, which at that time was called a *provincia* of the *"Estado interno del Norte"* in Chihuahua, Vigil y Alarid reported suspicion of the actions of the delegate to the *Cortes* in Mexico City, Jóse Rafael Alarid (relation not mentioned), who also signed Mexico's first Constitution (October 4,

1824). On July 6, 1824, delegate Jóse Rafael Alarid was granted his petition that New Mexico be separated from Chihuahua and no longer a province in the union of the *Estado interno del Norte*, which included Chihuahua and Durango.[25] As a result, New Mexico became a territory of the Mexican Federation and Chihuahua became its own separate State, transferring El Paso del Norte from its traditional jurisdiction in the province of New Mexico to the State of Chihuahua.[26] Vigil y Alarid, who was not alone in his objections, voiced his opinion that Nuevo Mexico should have remained part of the "confraternity" of the Northern Provinces. Perhaps it was his contention that New Mexico remains united in the far frontier rather than centralize being that was the most northern province and needed protection from native and foreign enemies. As a result of this change in jurisdiction, Vigil y Alarid returned from Chihuahua city to New Mexico.[27]

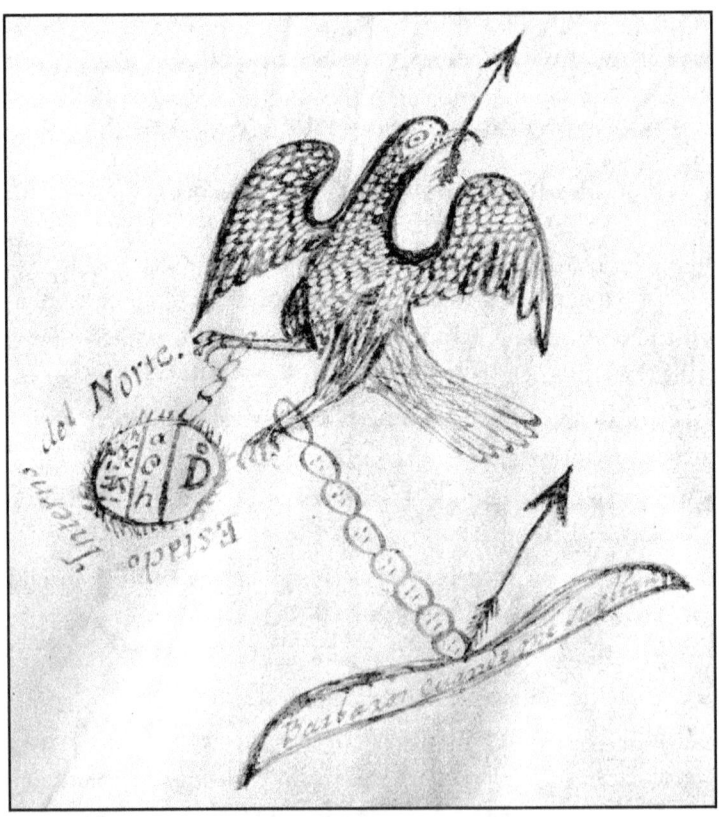

Bottom of cover page to the Journal of Provincial Deputation, 1824, Mexican Archives of New Mexico, Serial # 10151, NMSRCA. This representation of the fraternity of the three provinces (Nuevo Mexico-NM, Chihuahua-Cha, Durango-Do) or *Estado Interno del Norte* was most likely drawn by Vigil y Alarid when he was secretary.

Back in Santa Fe, Vigil y Alarid resumed his position as Secretary to Governor Bartolomé Baca and soon after became New Mexico's first Customs Agent. As a consequence of Mexico's relaxed trade restrictions, New Mexico became an important commercial throughway between the interior of Mexico and the United States via the Santa Fe-Chihuahua Trail. This trade created economic loyalties and partnerships between elite Nuevomexicanos and trappers, prospectors, squatters and adventurers who came down from Missouri and beyond. High quality and low prices created a dependency for United States products. In 1826, the Central Government in Mexico City created the position of customs collector to administer trade regulations and payments of duties. Vigil y Alarid was appointed to this position in New Mexico. This position was new to New Mexico and because of the distance from Mexico City, tariffs were difficult to enforce or regulate against abuse towards foreigners. This may have contributed to accusations against Vigil y Alarid and subsequent dismissal from his position after being accused of failure to arrest an illegal American.[28]

In 1845 Vigil y Alarid again became the secretary under Governor Manuel Armijo and soon after not only faced problems with incoming American merchants but also with the eventual invasion of American troops. Texas independence from Mexico brought many Anglo Americans to New Mexico. As a result Vigil y Alarid came into conflict with various Anglo individuals. One of them was Charles Bent, a sly businessman and land prospector who later became Governor of New Mexico.

In the case of Bent, historical documents reveal a series of unfavorable transactions between Bent and Vigil y Alarid while he was the Custom Agent. This comes into light through obscure letters written in February 1841 from Bent to the United States Consul Manuel Alvarez.[29] Bent's letters reveal that he and William Workman chastised a certain Juan B. Vigil for presenting, in writing, false accusations against them.[30] It is not clear what the accusations were, but Workman, who was suspected of attempting to introduce Texas control of New Mexico, was involved in a plot to assassinate Governor Manuel Armijo. Nevertheless the letter mentioned that Workman struck Vigil with a whip and beat him with his fist until Bent pulled him off stating that he "thought he had given him enough." Workman left for California, perhaps after this incident.[31] Bent, who did not have faith in Governor Armijo's judgment in this case, mentioned that he could have had Vigil arraigned for slander but this did not give him as much satisfaction as beating Vigil. He arrogantly stated "I had rather have the satisfaction of whipping a man that has wronged me than to have him punished ten times by the law." The letter ends with a mention of Vigil trying to protect some property from the hands of creditors Branch and Lee. As a result of either the beating of Vigil or the accusations that angered him, Bent was put under house arrest.

This incident happened in the middle of the Texas-Santa Fe Expedition which was an attempt by the Texas Republic to claim New Mexico. Perhaps Bent, Workman, Branch and Lee were the Texan agents sent by President Mirabeau Bonaparte Lamar to infiltrate New Mexico. Some of these agents were arrested for attempts to murder Governor Manuel Armijo, a long time political colleague of Vigil y Alarid. The agents soon after were followed by a party of over three hundred armed Texans instructed to seize all property in New Mexico and select a representative to the Texas Congress. These invaders met opposition headed by Armijo. They were captured, made prisoners, and taken on a tedious and brutal forced march to Mexico City.[32] This episode of resistance came up later during treaty ratifications where Luis de la Rosa, Mexican Minister of Foreign Affairs argued that the Republic of Mexico should not abandon New Mexico. Referring to the Texas-Santa Fe Expedition of 1841, he honored the Nuevomexicanos by claiming:

> These worthy and dignified Mexicans should not be sold like a herd of sheep, who being misfortunate and without any protection, put aside their inconveniences and rising against the invaders (United States) spilled their own blood so that they may continue to be part of the Mexican family.[33]

Regardless of Bent's troubles during Texas' interventions in New Mexico, he became civil Governor of New Mexico on September 1846 after the United States takeover. He served precariously until his murder on January 19, 1847. Insurgents of the Taos revolt assassinated Bent along with other officials such as Louis Lee, who was the creditor confronted earlier by Vigil. These insurgents were New Mexican Hispanos and Pueblo Indians who formed the revolutionary movement to rid New Mexico of Anglo-Americans and attacked them in their homes in Taos. This inspired other uprisings in at least five other northern New Mexico villages, which were quickly quelled by the well-armed U.S. cavalry.[34] Though Juan Bautista Vigil was not implicated in Bent's murder, it is evident that he did have a motive. Tension certainly existed between Anglos and Mexicans in New Mexico. The Texas-Santa Fe Expedition, the beating incident mentioned above, the Taos rebellion, Abert's observations, and other events give solid evidence that should put to rest the myth that the conquest of New Mexico was peaceful and bloodless. Additionally, these examples represent a manifestation of discontent and an expression of loyalty to Mexico or at least to the local Mexican community and culture.

Though similar confrontations occurred prior to the Treaty of Guadalupe Hidalgo, which in 1848 ended the United States war on Mexico, the Treaty offered another means in which New Mexicans were able to express their loyalty to Mexico. As stipulated by Article VIII of the treaty, the Republic of Mexico provided Mexicans (Hispanic and Indian) residing in the occupied territory, known today as the Southwestern United States, the opportunity to repatriate to Mexican soil in order to retain Mexican citizenship. They were left to make hard decisions as to their national identity. In 1850, more than four thousand Mexican citizens from northern New Mexico and from what is known today as the El Paso valley made the choice to repatriate. They emigrated to the south side of the Rio Grande, which was the new boundary of Mexico's diminished northern half of its national territory. In the State of Chihuahua, they established the towns of Mesilla (present day Doña Ana county in southern New Mexico), and San Ignacio and Guadalupe, which are located forty to fifty miles down river from Ciudad Juárez in Chihuahua, México.[35] Vigil y Alarid also crossed the receding border and made his new home in Guadalupe which is a little known, but significant, fact that historians had overlooked.[36]

Juan Bautista Vigil y Alarid, like his predecessor Manuel Armijo, moved southward to Chihuahua. He first moved to Aldama some time between 1847 and 1850. Perhaps during his days as Congressional Deputy in Chihuahua City he had made contacts that welcomed him at Aldama, just north of Chihuahua City.[37] Soon after he moved to Guadalupe and San Ignacio to be with his fellow New Mexican repatriates.[38] In Guadalupe, on Feb 10th, 1852, Vigil y Alarid was elected to the local Council as Secretary. Head of the Council was Padre Ramón Ortiz, also a Santa Fe native.[39] Shortly after the start of his new political career in Guadalupe problems began to develop with him and local authorities. The first case of Vigil y Alarid's difficulties in the colony of Guadalupe started in June 1852 when he refused to hand over the sum of fifty pesos owed to the *Suplente de la Jefetura Política de Cantón Bravos* (itinerant Chief Magistrate) Don Joaquín Alvarez. Vigil y Alarid believed Alvarez held his political position with out legal authority, because Alvarez was both employed as the *Aduana Fronteriza* (Director of Customs) in El Paso del Norte and also employed by the Federal government. He argued that there was no law that authorized a federal employee to take a state position and proceeded to explain how this is an insult to the supreme powers of the State. Vigil y Alarid justified his actions and even quoted articles from the Constitutional law, something that clearly demonstrates that Vigil y Alarid was educated and familiar with the law, which is something he utilized to his advantage and to the benefit of others.

His confrontation with Alvarez resulted in a criminal investigation and consequently, Vigil y Alarid placed a guard in front of his house. Military Captain, Miguel Castro expressed that Don Juan Vigil presented himself and submitted to him his military dispatches and credentials as a military Captain from the supreme governor. Castro continues by saying that Vigil was given these legal titles in virtue of his service to the nation against the invading forces of the United States. As commanded he protected Vigil because he (Vigil) maintained privileges and special protection *(gosa de fuero de guerra)*, due to his military service to the Mexican

Republic. Regardless of Vigil y Alarid's *fuero* or even the efforts of Castro, Vigil y Alarid was sentenced to thirty days in prison for lack of respect and insults towards the Magistrate.[40]

It is not known if Vigil y Alarid served the thirty days in jail but soon after he again confronted the authorities. Apparently, discontent grew between the ex-governor of New Mexico and Padre Ramón Ortiz, who was the emigration commissioner of the colonies and responsible for recruiting the repatriates. Ortiz, who was a parish priest at the mission of Nuestra Señora de Guadalupe, established himself as the most influential and affluent person in El Paso del Norte.[41] In 1853 Vigil was mentioned as the primary complainant in a Foreign Ministry investigation into Padre Ramón Ortiz's dealings as emigration commissioner. This investigation led to Padre Ortiz's exoneration and replacement by Guadalupe Miranda, another prominent politician from New Mexico. Ortiz was accused of mishandling funds during the settlement of the colonies and insults directed towards the people of Guadalupe and San Ignacio when they gathered to adhere to the *Plan de Guadalajara*, which was a national attempt to overthrow the Government of Presidente Arista. In the investigation of Padre Ortiz, Vigil y Alarid complained about the conduct of Padre Ortiz and, in addition, filed a complaint against infractions made by Chihuahuan authorities in regards to the repatriation efforts.[42]

The preceding complaint might account for a letter written on October 3, 1853 from the Chihuahuan state Government to the Ministry of Foreign Affairs, which was included in the investigation of Padre Ortiz. The letter did not take seriously the complaints made by Vigil y Alarid but attacked him instead. It mentioned that Vigil "all his life, in New Mexico, occupied himself by complaining against the authorities." The letter also stated that when the "*Americanos*" occupied New Mexico, Vigil was named Governor, and held this title as a "representative of the United States of America." It claims that after U.S. authorities took over his leadership, he lived in New Mexico and was "reputed" to be an American citizen, and than repatriated as a Mexican citizen, first to Cantón Aldama and then to Guadalupe. It is also noted that the citizens of Guadalupe lived peacefully until Vigil's arrival. In Guadalupe, the civil government accused Vigil y Alarid of inciting divisions between colonists from New Mexico and those from Isleta, Socorro and San Elizario, Texas. Vigil y Alarid, the report said, attempted to position himself as a leader and commenced to expel those that were not from New Mexico. Additionally it was reported that he also tried to collect contributions intended for the Justice of the Peace. For these reasons the military commanders sent troops from El Paso del Norte to Guadalupe. Again Vigil y Alarid claimed exemption because of his *fuero de guerra*. The letter noted that his claims of exemption were not valid because not only did he (military commander inferred) remain in New Mexico after the occupation but he also held public office as Governor under the United States. The letter expresses that the "disfavorable" proceedings be remedied soon because it is very likely that Vigil y Alarid would continue with his "old habits."[43]

Vigil y Alarid's pattern of confronting the authorities also came to a head just a couple of years after the problems with Padre Ortiz. In 1855, Vigil y Alarid again arose to the occasion in defense of his beliefs. An example of Vigil y Alarid's writing which best exemplifies his siding with those that are most affected by class, race and gender dominance and struggles with church officials is found in a letter he wrote to the Bishop of Durango during the latter's holy visitation to the El Paso del Norte area.[44] The letter, dated May 22, 1855, is a complaint about the mistreatment of an Indian woman by a parish priest. He began the letter by stating that it was written to his Excellency as a humanitarian act. He claims that the priest, whose name he said he "omits for the time being," was guilty of canonical impediments according to the sacred canons and ecclesiastical laws. The priest, Vigil y Alarid claims, hit and beat a defenseless Indian woman, causing her bruises and open wounds. Vigil noted that the priest bragged about owning a purchased Indian slave whose name he never mentioned. Vigil y Alarid appeared insulted by this, stating that it is expressly prohibited, under the fundamental civil laws of the Republic of Mexico, to partake in such "contraband." Furthermore, Vigil y Alarid said that the priest forcedly brought this woman from territory lost by the Republic of Mexico as a result of the Treaty of Guadalupe Hidalgo in 1848. This situation, Vigil y Alarid claimed, tested the patience of the authorities and became a public scandal in the town where the priest resided.[45]

Vigil y Alarid continued with a detailed and sympathetic account of how this woman had suffered so much that she was at the point of suicide. In an emotional if not poetic plea, Vigil y Alarid stated that this slave women "tired of so many cruel and insufferable impediments, and remote is a remedy to her fate, on this day she has cried an ocean of tears and on her knees with deep sighs of bitterness (*exsaltando suspiros amargos*) she has entreated me to have the compassion to bring all this to the attention of your excellency." Vigil y Alarid asked the Bishop to free her from her servitude and also from the imminent suicide that "the devil has put in her mind." According to Vigil y Alarid, suicide was a practice among the tribe that she was born into and though she was baptized as a Christian, he alluded to the possibility that she may revert to these tribal ideas of suicide. Vigil y Alarid ended his letter stating that he wrote it not for his sake but for the sake of his "client" and for humanity.[46]

This incident reveals much about Vigil y Alarid and also about the society in which he lived. It gives an indication that Vigil y Alarid was conscious of his social responsibilities to protect those who were oppressed. It also shows that slavery or a remnant of it still existed in the outer fringes of Northern Mexico. This demonstrates that Vigil y Alarid was compassionate and ready to challenge church authority. The letter reiterates that Vigil y Alarid was literate, skilled in the written language and knowledgeable in the laws of the land. The affair is an example of how one can belong to the dominant class and break from their rank to aid those that the same class has designated to keep subjugated. Perhaps Vigil y Alarid wrote this letter as a result of his convictions and appreciation for the revolutionary ideas as advocated by Padre Miguel Hidalgo, the same appreciation that first drove Juan Bautista Vigil y Alarid and others to repatriate to Mexico.

Meanwhile the colonists in Guadalupe and San Ignacio were not only caught up in Vigil y Alarid's undertakings but were also part of the national reform in Mexico. At the same time, they sought to separate from the Cantón Bravo District and form their own municipalities. Guadalupe's residents were the most reverent supporters in the Cantón Bravo District of the Reforma.[47] Led by Luciano Telles, an armed force of several hundred men from Guadalupe and San Ignacio set out to dispose of the present liberal authorities in El Paso del Norte, headquarters of the district. Guadalupe and San Ignacio resident's involvement in the Reforma and their petition to form a separate municipality in Chihuahua along with a temporary exile to the U.S. side of the border showed that not only were the repatriates united but they were also independent and connected to the Church Party.[48]

Vigil y Alarid's involvement with the Reforma is not known. His name does not appear in any petitions or official records dealing with the rebellion. This upheaval, his troubled political life and confrontations with church officials could have pushed him to move back to his "old" New Mexico society. Perhaps he moved back because he had bigger battles to fight in his native land. Regardless of his reason, he returned to Santa Fe and is listed in the 1860 U.S. Territorial Census as Juan B. Vigil y Alarid, age sixty seven, with the occupation of "Apotocary" which at this time was not necessarily a pharmacist but could also have been a folk healer or *curandero*. The census listed the value of his personal estate as $1500.00, which appears to be lucrative compared to his neighbor's estates.[49] Another contemporary source notes that Vigil y Alarid was not only a doctor but was also a poet and a painter.[50]

Attempting to reground himself and perhaps re-enter into in the higher echelon of New Mexican society, Vigil y Alarid became involved with the issue of land ownership in New Mexico. Caught up in a legal battle, which came to a head in 1859, Vigil y Alarid and two other individuals claimed to be legal owners of a land grant, which was confirmed on February 4, 1846 by Governor Manuel Armijo and the Departmental Assembly. As his own attorney Vigil y Alarid provided documents and gave testimony to prove that they were the original petitioners and legal grantees of a tract of land, which totaled two and a half million acres, known as Jornada del Muerto. The large tract of land spanned the counties of Doña Ana and Socorro. On

August 29, 1859 the U.S. Surveyor General rejected the grant which was deemed void and therefore "rightfully belonged to the public domain of the U.S." It was rejected primarily because the original Spanish documents were never presented and the grantees were not in compliance with the original land grant stipulations. For example, they were to dig two wells with tanks to "relieve and aid" travelers and their livestock. They were also obligated to cultivate the land and build a "modern factory" along with providing protection from Indian attacks.[51] Vigil y Alarid and his partners soon hired a law firm to make an appeal, which was upheld by the Territorial Supreme Court of New Mexico. The case continued in the courts until it was reversed in 1871 a few years after Vigil y Alarid's death.[52]

1860 U.S. Census Schedule, Santa Fe County, City of Santa Fe, page 24, Serial # 5667, NMSRCA. Detail shows dwelling #181 is that of Vigil y Alarid.

Dealing with the new foreign political system may have become too taxing for Vigil y Alarid. Perhaps bitter from his experiences with the Surveyor General, he engaged in an ultimate expression of resistance against United States dominance. In several New Mexico courts he took the witness stand in defense of land grants claims. As in the past, he demonstrated his advocacy through his words. On October 22, 1860, Vigil y Alarid wrote a rebuttal to Santiago Collins, Editor of *Gazeta Seminario de Santa Fe* in an attempt to fight off American land titles and defend the property rights of Nuevomexicanos.[53] He knew the law well and quoted various articles and cited from past cases. He was especially ardent in his reference to the Treaty of Guadalupe Hidalgo and accused the Surveyor General of violation of its articles. Then, as it is now, land ownership is essential in the New Mexican psyche.

Perhaps it can be concluded that to the Nuevomexicano, retaining one's family land is the greatest form of resistance. This possibly is due not only to the fact that New Mexicans are connected to the land by a cultural and ancestral indigenous past but also because of legal continuous titles granted to them by both the Spanish Crown and the Mexican Republic. The Mexican Republic fought not only to include provisions for the protection of the peoples' choice of national sovereignty, but also the protection of their culture, language, religion and property rights. The latter has become the basis of the last political stronghold in New Mexico's over one hundred and sixty years of resistance and acculturation to the United States occupation. Prevailing national and cultural identity issues and historical memory in New Mexico as expressed by land ownership and family/tribal history are still passionately discussed and debated among New Mexico Native Hispanic and Pueblo people.[54]

This dichotomy of national and cultural identity as manifested in the connection to the land and property rights came to surface by New Mexico's remapping into a new political and cultural space.[55] This new space caused shifts in national identity and preferences.[56] After making a complete circle in his journey to maintain a sense of national loyalty, connection to his Nuevomexicano patriots and his New Mexican landscape, Vigil y Alarid returned to his birthplace of Santa Fe. He perhaps realized that, for him, his "mother' the "nation" of Mexico was indeed dead and the mourning period was over. His need to be with his *patria chica* grew stronger than his nationalistic affinities. Since he no longer was a political official, the "official nationalism" no longer fit into his ideals and commitment to his Mexican national identity. His allegiance, along with those citizens who did not repatriate, was to his *Patria Chica*. The association to Mexico, because of change in political borders now only existed in their connection to the land that was granted to their Spanish, Pueblo and Mexican ancestors. As in his acceptance of allegiance speech, Vigil y Alarid perhaps still spoke for the citizenry of New Mexico when he expressed, possibly for the last time, their underlying needs and nationalistic sentiments when he quoted from a land case in his letter to the editor of *Gazeta Seminario de Santa Fe*:

> The people change their loyalties; their relations to their old sovereigns are broken; but their relations among themselves and their property remain permanent."
>
> U.S. vs. Rencheman[57]

A few years after he sent this letter to the *Gazeta Seminario de Santa Fe*, Juan Bautista Vigil y Alarid died on April 20th 1866 at the age of seventy-two and was buried in the Rosario Chapel in Santa Fe, New Mexico.[58]

Following are the Proclamations by Kearny and Vigil y Alarid from *The Military Occupation of the Territory of New Mexico from 1846 to 1851*, by Ralph Emerson Twitchell, p. 75:

General Stephen Watts Kearny's Proclamation:

> New Mexicans: We have come amongst you to take possession of New Mexico, which we do in the name of the government of the United States. We have come with peaceable intentions and kind feelings toward you all. We come as friends, to better your condition and make you a part of the Republic of the United States. We mean not to murder you or rob you of your property. Your families shall be free from molestation; your women secure from violence. My soldiers shall take nothing from you but what they pay for. In taking possession of New Mexico, we do not mean to take away from you your religion. Religion and government have no connection in our country. There, all religions are equal; one has no preference over the other; the Catholic and the Protestant are esteemed alike. Every man has a right to serve God according to his heart. When a man dies he must render to God an account of his acts here on earth, whether they be good or bad. In our government, all men are equal. We esteem the most peaceable man, the best man. I advise you to attend to your domestic pursuits, cultivate industry, be peaceable and obedient to the laws. Do not resort to violent means to correct abuses. I do hereby proclaim that, being in possession of Santa Fe I am therefore virtually in possession of all New Mexico. Armijo is no longer your governor. His power is departed;

but he will return and be as one of you. When he shall return you are not to molest him. You are no longer Mexican subjects; you are now become American citizens, subject only to the laws of the United States. A change of government has taken place in New Mexico and you no longer owe allegiance to the Mexican government. I do hereby proclaim my intention to establish in this Department a civil government, on a republican basis, similar to those of our own states. It is my intention, also, to continue in office those by whom you have been governed, except the governor, and such other persons as I shall appoint to office by virtue of the authority vested in me. I am your governor—henceforth look to me for protection."

Juan Bautista Vigil y Alarid's Acceptance of Allegiance speech (English translation):

General: The address which you have just delivered, in which you announce that you have taken possession of this great country in the name of the United States of America, gives us some idea of the wonderful future that awaits us. It is not for us to determine the boundaries of nations. The cabinets of Mexico and Washington will arrange these differences. It is for us to obey and respect the established authorities, no matter what may be our private opinions. The inhabitants of this Department humbly and honorably present their loyalty and allegiance to the government of North America. No one in this world can successfully resist the power of him who is stronger. Do not find it strange if there has been no manifestation of joy and enthusiasm in seeing this city occupied by your military forces. To us the power of the Mexican Republic is dead. No matter what her condition she was our mother. What child will not shed abundant tears at the tomb of his parents? I might indicate some of the causes for her misfortunes, but domestic troubles should not be made public. It is sufficient to say that civil war is the cursed source of that deadly poison which has spread over one of the grandest and greatest countries that has ever been created. Today we belong to a great and powerful nation. Its flag, with its stars and stripes, covers the horizon of New Mexico, and its brilliant light shall grow like good seed well cultivated. We are cognizant of your kindness, of your courtesy and that of your accommodating officers and of the strict discipline of your troops; we know that we belong to the Republic that owes its origin to the immortal Washington, whom all civilized nations admire and respect. How different would be our situation had we been invaded by European nations! We are aware of the unfortunate condition of the Poles. In the name, then, of the entire Department, I swear obedience to the Northern Republic and I tender my respect to its laws and authority.

Juan Bautista Vigil y Alarid (Rubric)
Governor
Santa Fé, August 19, 1846.

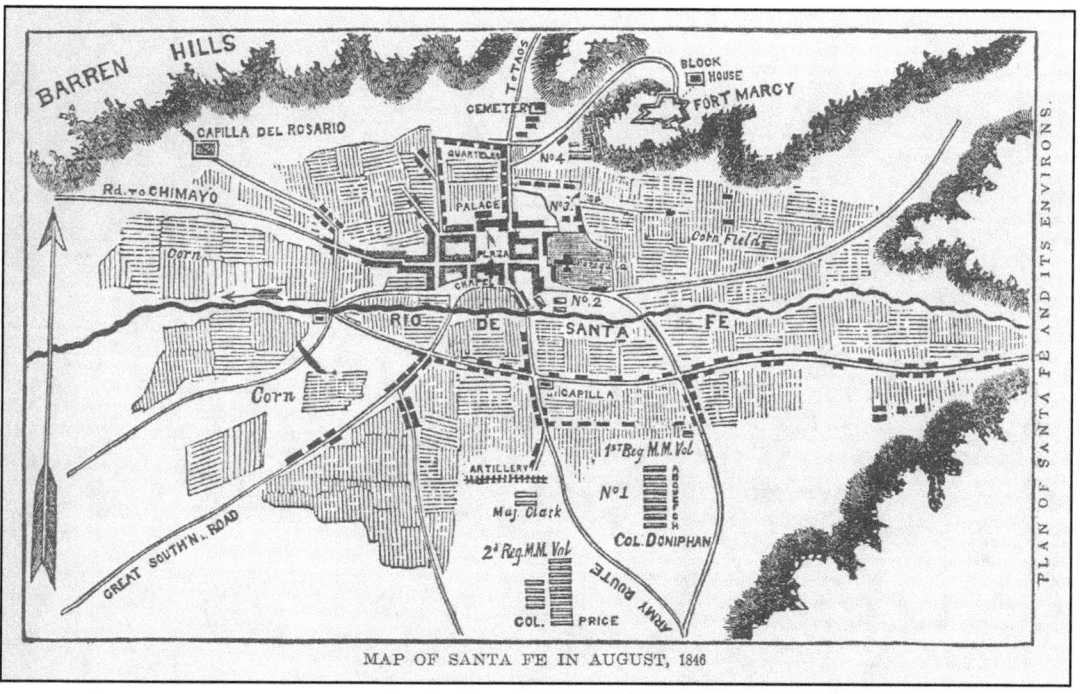

Map of Santa Fe in August, 1846. From *Doniphan's Expedition* by John T. Hughes, 1850.

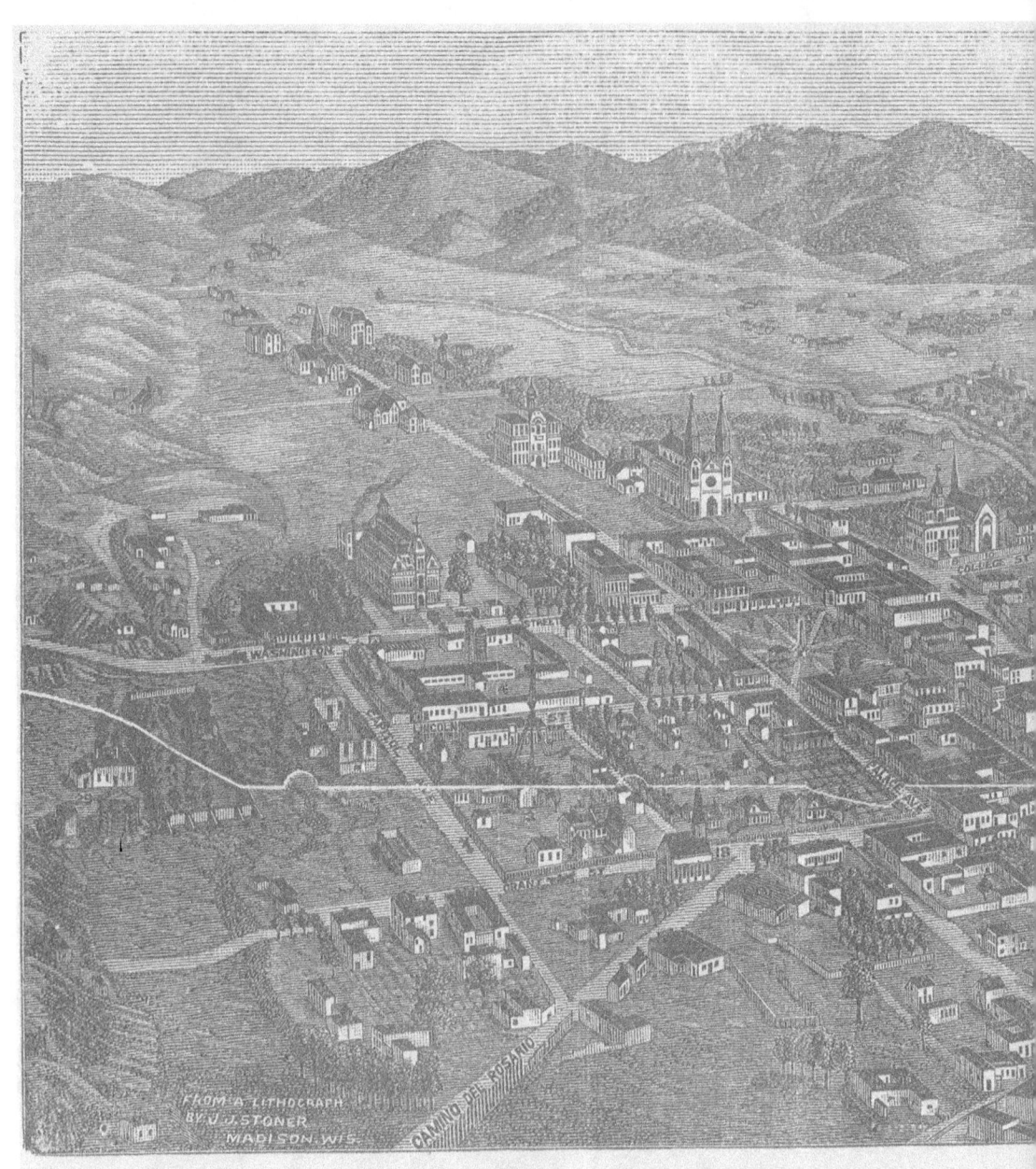

Impression of Santa Fe in 1882. From *Illustrated New Mexico, 1885* by W. G. Ritch.

San Miguel Cemetery.　　　　　　　　　　　　　　　El Atalaya.
Fe.)　Bishop's Garden.　Camping Ground U. S. Army, Aug. 18, 1846.　Santa Fe Trail.
oretto.　San Miguel Church and College.　Rio de Santa Fe.
ess.　　　　　　　　　　　　　　　　　　　　Territorial Penitentiary.
　　　　　　　　　　　　　　　　　　　　　　Congregational Church.
Northern R. R.　　　　　　　Guadalupe Church.　A. T. and S. F. R. R. Depot.
　Methodist Church.　　　　　　　　　U. S. Indian School. (Gov. Vigil Place.

, NEW MEXICO.
Presented by the Bureau of Immigration, New Mexico.

14

They Came From the East
Importing Homicide, Violence, and Misconceptions of Soft Justice into Early Santa Fe, New Mexico, 1847–1853

by

Michael J. Alarid

With the consolidation of New Mexico as an American Territory, routes once reserved for traders and explorers increasingly saw their share of prospectors, new businessmen, and American soldiers. Informed by residual propaganda from the U.S. Mexican War and disparaging accounts of a people marked by their depredations, these migrant groups brought negative preconceived notions that judged the New Mexican community as uncivilized. Operating under these presuppositions, American authorities labored to install a legal apparatus they hoped would both enforce excessive laws and administer harsh punishments to a community perceived to be uncivilized and in desperate need of authority.

Ironically, new Anglo settlers[1] were 1.6 times more likely to be indicted for criminal activity than were members of the Nuevo Mexicano community[2] and though they comprised only 18% of the population of Santa Fe, Anglo settlers were responsible for twelve of the nineteen homicides committed from 1847–53.[3] Statistically, it is undeniable that Anglo settlers were ten times more likely to commit homicides than members of the older New Mexican community, which more than doubled the overall homicide rate in New Mexico.[4] Incidents between Anglo settlers and Nuevo Mexicanos[5] were not common; instead, violence was more frequently committed by and against drifters and transients who had recently arrived from Texas and other parts of the United States. Anglo settlers were more likely to target fellow Anglos, and were both more likely to attack them and more efficient in killing their victims than their Hispanic counterparts. The Americans had arrived in Santa Fe, and an increase in violent crime came with them.

It is telling that through the entirety of the Mexican Period (1820–1846) in all of New Mexico, a detailed homicide study conducted by Jill Mocho revealed evidence of only 11 homicides during the full 26 year period.[6] That the records from the Mexican period are incomplete is undeniable, but accounting for lost records still reveals a pre-American New Mexico far less homicidal than the city of Santa Fe in just the first seven years under American suzerainty. Still, the older New Mexican community would continue to be maligned as a lawless society that failed to enforce justice and allowed absconding murderers to escape without punishment.

Of the cases actually heard by the Santa Fe District Court, there was likely a 50% conviction rate, which was in actuality very high for homicide litigation. What remained low was the number of individuals brought before the court system, as only 42% of those indicted are confirmed to have engaged in the judicial process.[7] Still, these numbers are somewhat misleading when taken cumulatively, largely because the majority of guilty verdicts were passed down against Nuevo Mexicano perpetrators by Nuevo Mexicano juries. Of the twelve homicides committed by recent Anglo settlers, only one guilty verdict was returned, a second likely returned, and a third pronounced by a rogue jury during a lynching. Additionally, there were at least two not guilty verdicts, at least one decision not to prosecute, two granted successful changes of venue, and at least four remaining either unsolved or undocumented.[8] Territorial law seemed both harsh and clear, with Article I, Section 1 of the Kearny Code, dictating that, "If any person shall be convicted of the crime of willful murder, such person shall suffer death."[9] However, a further reading of the legal code reveals in Article II, Section 1, "Every person who shall kill another in the necessary defense of his own life, or that of any other persons, or of his own house or property, or in the legal execution of any process, or in order to prevent great bodily harm to himself or another, shall be deemed guiltless."[10] That more perpetrators did not hang had nothing to do with the alleged leniency of the older New Mexican community, but instead was the byproduct of the rational interpretation of law by both American and New Mexican Alcaldes. For these Alcaldes, proof of malice dictated capital punishment and very few cases adjudicated before the bench satisfied this prerequisite.

This article focuses on eight of these homicide cases, including one double homicide, in Santa Fe, New Mexico. These cases have been chosen primarily because they are the most heavily documented among the existing nineteen. The cases examined herein are representative of greater homicide trends and include random acts of unprovoked violence by recent immigrants, homicides stemming from drunkenness, domestic homicides, and calculated execution style murders. They are organized into three categories: *transient homicides* committed by drifters and very recently arrived immigrants; *community homicides* comprised of violence within and against the old New Mexican community; and *homicides at fandangos*, social gatherings where both groups came together. Examining homicide in Santa Fe within these categories illuminates the degree to which recent Anglo immigrants, while bemoaning the high rates of violence and judicial leniency in Santa Fe, were in fact responsible for both sources of their own frustrations.

The Exchange Hotel, once known as the Inn at the End of the Trail or La Fonda, was purchased in 1847 by Anglo settlers. The building was not altered until it was purchased again in the 20th century by a corporation that demolished the original structure and built the Hotel La Fonda, which remains at the original site on the plaza. (Photographer unknown, Museum of New Mexico Negative No. 39368)[11]

Another view of the Exchange Hotel or La Fonda. From *Harper's Weekly*, April 21, 1866.

Yet another view of the Exchange Hotel. From *Illustrated New Mexico, 1885* by W. G. Ritch.

Transient Homicides

As night fell in the dusty Santa Fe streets that Saturday, 12 November 1853, the plaza was quiet, families had settled in for the evening, and the working citizens were nestled into various local drinking houses passing their time with booze, gambling, and wayward women. The spirits flowed, producing a casual merriment among the local townsfolk, and men everywhere risked their salaries in the popular games of the day, including Monte,[12] poker, and faro.[13] The quietude of this mountain city was interrupted by the sound of gunfire, which echoed from the Exchange Hotel across the plaza. Two more shots rang out, and the citizens in the backroom of the Exchange Hotel, who had been eagerly losing their money at Monte, wrestled the perpetrators to the dusty floor. "We're Texans, we can take this town," the prisoners repeated through their drunkenness.[14] On the same floor lay Judge Hugh N. Smith, mortally wounded by a projectile that passed through his lungs and lodged itself into his shoulder.

Violence of this sort was not normative in Santa Fe, but when confrontations such as this occurred they usually involved recently arrived Anglo setters and transients. For their part, Stephenson and Gillion Scallion were two Texans who had recently arrived and had been drinking most of the evening while loudly proclaiming their Texas heritage.[15] By 1853, the mutual enmity between Texans and New Mexicans was well known; the Texans had attempted to invade New Mexico in 1841 with dire consequences and New Mexicans were always suspicious of their presence.[16] All evening these two Texans had been drinking heavily, proclaiming their superiority as Texans, and finally their binge led them into the very popular Exchange Hotel.

The Texans entered, approached the bartender, and hearing of the backroom game of Monte demanded a $10 loan from the hotel.[17] When the bartender refused, the intoxicated pair shouted, "We're from Texas, we could take this whole town if we wanted to!"[18] Rebuffed, the Texans went to the backroom and upon hearing that one of the dealers was named Stephens, the Texan Stephenson voiced his bet that he could whip anyone in New Mexico Territory with that name. The argument escalated when a newly arrived New Mexico resident retorted, "If you came from Texas, as you keep saying, you will find that at Santa Fe there are men to whom no name or country can communicate terror."[19] Stephenson, who the eyewitness claims was more intoxicated, then escalated the event but before the fighting could ensue the quieter Scallion pulled his colt revolver and opened fire on the group while shouting, "I'm going to clear this room."[20] The first shot struck Stephenson, his fellow Texan, in the hand, the second was embedded in Judge Smith, and the third missed altogether.

Stephenson was taken to the Jailhouse, while Scallion was cornered by the local citizenry. Across the plaza word spread through the streets that Judge Smith had been gunned down by a Texan. While the physician was cutting the bullet from Judge Smith, who would not survive the night, those not already outside the Exchange Hotel were beckoned, and the gathering mob milled about the plaza wanton for vengeance. Surviving documentation indicates that Anglo settlers comprised the leadership of the angry mob, and from this collection there was immediately drawn a jury, and an eyewitness acting as judge to adjudicate the murder case at the Exchange Hotel.[21] Scallion was reportedly asked how he could fire upon unarmed men, and allegedly responded, "I don't care a damn, if you don't like what I have done, help yourselves."[22] Gillion Scallion was found guilty by the mob court and sentenced to death by hanging. Scallion was marched across the old plaza, that sight of so much brutality and public mirth, and illegally lynched by the angry mob of Santa Fe residents.[23]

This was neither the first nor last time an individual would be lynched in Santa Fe, though the rate of lynching in Santa Fe would never rival other areas of the New Mexico Territory. Historians like Stephen J. Leonard have asserted that lynch mobs were thought to save both time and resources, but legally this lynching should have been treated as another homicide case; this was an act of violence committed by an angry mob bent on retribution, though charges were never filed against the citizens who murdered Gillion Scallion by hanging him outside of the exchange hotel. As there were no gallows, Scallion was actually strangled to death, a process which would have been slow and extremely painful. Because of the quick drop that ideally snaps the neck, death at the gallows supposedly spares the victim from an extended period of pain, which might be construed as torture.[24] But in an age that had supposedly moved beyond violence against the body, the lynch mob in Santa Fe reveled in the justice that slow asphyxiation by strangulation seemingly afforded.[25]

Scallion was not the first Texan to suffer this fate; a previous lynching occurred 14 June, 1851 when another Texan had entered the Exchange Hotel, taken a glass of brandy, and commenced firing his pistol at random.[26] The Texan discharged his weapon four times, striking one person in the arm and an unknown lawyer in the abdomen, then was tackled and detained. When asked for his motive, the Texan replied, "A friend of his from Texas was killed in Santa Fe, and all the inhabitants of the place were cut-throats, robbers, and murderers."[27] The lynch mob arrived later that night, took the Texan, and hung him in the backyard of the Exchange Hotel.

It is significant that both individuals lynched in Santa Fe were Texans, that both acted violently as part of a larger dispute between Texans and New Mexicans, and that both were condemned outside the judicial process. On only two other occasions were individuals lynched in Santa Fe between 1847–1923, one in 1857 and another in 1880.[28] Statistically Santafesinos were neither prone to mob justice nor to ignoring the judicial process; but Anglo settlers were, just as they were prone to lynching Texans as part of a larger dispute over territorial integrity and interstate rivalry that manifested in acts of violence. The lynching of Texans was meant as a political message as much as it was meant to deal justice.

Neither illegal act of violence perpetrated by the uproarious community was condemned, either by the state or the local press. An eyewitness account of the lynching of Gillion Scallion published in the *Santa Fe Weekly Gazette* feigned lamentation of the mob justice, offering:

> Another reason that had its effect in producing the closing scene in this sad affair, is the fact that many murders have been committed in this Territory within the last two or three years, some of them of the most unprovoked character, and the guilty parties have invariably escaped without punishment; some from the insufficiency of the jails, and others from being acquitted by jurors when the proof was most positive against them, and others from being permitted to escape without even an arrest.[29]

Echoing the complaints of the *Gazette* editors, this eyewitness reinforces the misconception of a forgiving New Mexican justice system devoid of reckoning capacities. In truth the emotionally charged issue of homicide distorted the Anglo settlers' sense of reality, as they attributed low conviction rates for homicide to all forms of crime, and this mislead them into assuming that criminals were seldom found guilty by juries and judges alike. Despite an excessively high conviction rate of 62% from 1847–1853 in the Santa Fe District Courts, both the press and prominent public officials continued to advance the misconception that juries in New Mexico were prone to acquittal. In fact, the rate was even higher for members of the older New Mexican community, who were convicted 71% of the time they went to court as opposed to Anglo settlers who were convicted 51% of the time during that same period.

Fueling the misconception of lawlessness was the fact that of the nineteen homicide cases filed in Santa Fe, only thrice were the perpetrators found guilty in this early period by the judicial system. Of the three, only Andrew Jackson Simms was sentenced to capital punishment.[30] This low rate of murder conviction was disconcerting to many of the outspoken citizens in Santa Fe, the loudest of whom were recent Anglo immigrants inclined to judge the New Mexican people themselves as lawless and uncivilized. As late as 1857, Governor Abraham Rencher echoed the falsehoods promulgated by the Gazette in 1853, lamenting to Secretary of Treasury

Howell Cobb the need for a penitentiary, "The necessity of which is seen and felt every day as a consequence of the insecurity of most of the county prisons as well as from the great unwillingness on the part of our juries to find a verdict in favor of capital punishment."[31] Complaints of absconding prisoners, indeed transients who had committed murder, hint that there may be records missing from this seven year period; but if the records are complete or close to it, one must conclude that the local civic leaders overreacted to the mere four individuals that escaped trial. Considering how few actually escaped trial, it seems more reasonable to believe that what troubled civic leaders and Anglo settlers was not a broken system, but rather the hesitancy of local judicial representatives to issue capital punishment.

Of the eleven men legally hanged in Santa Fe County, only three were executed before 1895.[32] Recently arrived Missourians like Henry Wheeler, who in late October 1849 shot and murdered Captain Alexander Papin of The United States Army, did not necessarily commit their crimes in ways Alcaldes believed demanded capital punishment.[33] Wheeler, a merchant from Missouri, was in an affray with the recently arrived fellow Missourian named Papin over slanderous proclamations Wheeler had posted on bulletin boards and buildings about town.[34] Captain Papin angrily pulled one of the postings down from outside the store Makers, Austin, and Dalton and entered the building cursing Wheeler as a rascal. Papin was unaware that Wheeler had followed him into the store, and upon noticing his person confronted Wheeler, demanding to know if it was his signature inscribed on the document. Wheeler asserted that it was, and Papin raised a yardstick and struck Wheeler, who in turn drew his pistol and shot Captain Papin in his right temple.[35]

Though there is no record of the verdict, Henry Wheeler is listed as a prisoner in the Santa Fe County Jail in the 1850 Unites States Census, more than two months after perpetrating the murder.[36] Historian Robert J. Torrez highlights the case of Andrew Jackson Simms to buttress his point that justice in New Mexico Territory was swift, and sentences were usually carried out equally as fast.[37] It can be inferred that the verdict of imprisonment was passed down to Wheeler, which provides insight into how Anglo Alcaldes interpreted the Kearny Code as well as the rational decisions they passed down. Wheeler was certainly guilty of murder, but the circumstances attest that it was responsive and could be construed as self defense. The judge likely determined, however, that Wheeler's response was excessive and warranted some type of punishment. Like judges everywhere, Santa Fe County judges willingly asserted their discretion in sentencing at murder trials, just as they had done in petty larceny cases when assigning lashes. In this way, the Kearny Code proved to be more malleable under the gavels of New Mexican Alcaldes than both citizens and public officials preferred.

Community Homicides

Of the eight homicide victims that were members of the old community, one was accidentally killed, two were murdered by a mentally ill person, three were violently murdered by members of the community, and three were victims of violent assaults perpetrated by recently arrived Anglo settlers. Of the three Anglo settlers accused of homicide against members of the Nuevo Mexicano community, all were either granted outright acquittals or found not guilty. Interestingly, Anglo settlers blamed jury incompetence and bemoaned the inability of the New Mexican community to deal justice to supposedly culpable transgressors.[38] The irony is twofold: not only were Anglo settlers more homicidal, but the juries deliberating cases with Anglo settler defendants were exclusively comprised of other Anglo settlers.[39] That members of the older New Mexican community were active as jurors is certain, but when a homicide case involved Anglo settlers in any capacity the surviving jury lists indicate that Anglo jurors were exclusively selected.

The jury deliberating the exceptionally violent case of the farmer Pablo Rael was drawn from the Nuevo Mexicano community and provides a window into how the New Mexican community interpreted judicial responsibility. The twenty-four year old Rael committed one of the few double homicides on record in the Territory, taking an axe and striking first his wife Maria on left side of her head and then his sister Rufugia on the right side of the head.[40] After interviewing witnesses and the defendant, the jury determined that Rael was guilty of both murders; however, it was also determined that Rael was mentally ill and incapable of determining right from wrong. The judge seems to have agreed and with no options available to assist the mentally ill, Rael was released into the custody of his two brothers, Jose de la Paz and Bartolo Rael, where he remained through 1850.[41] In exercising personal discretion, the judge and jury no doubt incited animosity from the general Anglo settler public, adding to their grievance against the judicial system.

In truth, there are no records indicating that the older New Mexican community executed prisoners in the Mexican period, even when perpetrators were deemed guilty.[42] Community justice in New Mexico, as in many parts of Latin America, was based on the notion that redemption was possible; community members who participated in the implementation of the new legal apparatus remained informed by this credence. Some historians have insinuated that this was racially motivated and that while Nuevo Mexicano juries refrained from convicting and executing defendants who were members of the old community, they did not do so for Anglo settler defendants such as Andrew Jackson Simms.[43] This proves to be most untrue, for in reality juries peopled with Nuevo Mexicanos were unlikely to suggest capital punishment for anyone, regardless of their surname. The fragmentary case file of Andrew Jackson Simms proves this: Simms was convicted of murdering Johnson Jackson and sentenced to death, but the foreman of the jury is clearly listed as Horace Long, which is not a known Spanish surname.[44] Regardless of the defendant's ethnic origin, the tradition of not instituting capital punishment, and thereby not promoting violence by the state, was applied by Nuevo Mexicano juries whenever they were called upon to pass judgment.

Another indication of community based jury and judge discretion is the case of Manuel Sandoval, adjudicated by Alcalde Edward Hoffman in early 1850. The charges indicate that the seventeen year old Sandoval, "Being moved and seduced by the instigation of the devil on the first day of November," assaulted Rafael Gonsales by throwing a stone at him.[45] The rock struck Gonsales in the right temple, leaving a gash two inches long and two inches wide on the right side of his head. Gonsales remained bedridden, groaning in pain, until Christmas day when death finally overtook him. Judge Hoffman and the community based jury determined that Sandoval had not intended to murder Gonsales, and Sandoval was convicted of manslaughter and sentenced to six months in imprisonment and a one dollar fine.[46] Though Sandoval clearly was not premeditating murder when he cast that stone, a public determined to see hard punishment could hardly have recognized the sentence as satisfactory.

In contrast to the community juries, the verdict of not guilty was returned in the case James C. Brady by an exclusively Anglo jury. Brady was accused of murdering a Nuevo Mexicana community member named Maria Antonia Lenoia on the night of 25 January 1847.[47] The primary witness was Sheriff James Powers,[48] who swore under oath to Hugh N. Smith that Brady was guilty of going into Ms. Lenoia's place of residence and murdering her. The prosecution charged that the perpetrator loaded his pistol, held it to the head of the victim, and discharged the leaden bullet into her head. The bullet, the prosecution details, penetrated Maria Lenoia's head to the depth of six inches, instantly killing her.[49] The witness James Powers, as acting Deputy Sheriff in Santa Fe County, should have carried a great deal of credibility with the jury. But Brady possessed enough capital to hire criminal defense attorney Allen Clark, whose personal notes contend that Brady was not guilty because no one could describe either the details of the assault or the manner Brady held the pistol while executing the victim.[50] There seems to have been no eyewitness at the moment the gun was discharged and, though Sheriff Powers witnessed Brady entering and exiting the crime scene, the evidence was deemed circumstantial.[51] The Anglo jury determined that the defense's case was persuasive enough to return the verdict of not guilty and no one was punished for the execution style murder of Maria Antonia Lenoia. In spite of several witnesses attesting to various aspects of the murder, including the Deputy Sheriff, the lack of an eyewitness outweighed the case presented by the prosecution.[52] It is likely that racial bias played a role in this decision, given the history of racially disproportionate punishments.

Racial bias was also overt in the adjudication of the case of New Mexico v. Oliver P. Anderson, who was indicted for the murder of Nuevo Mexicano community member Joseph Garcia.[53] Anderson was accused of assaulting Garcia and of concluding his assault by shooting Garcia above his right eye, killing him instantly.[54] Anderson allegedly murdered Garcia 10 November 1850, but through a series of skillfully filed legal petitions, Anderson was able to acquire continuances on two separate occasions.[55] Anderson first petitioned to have the case dismissed on 4 September 1851, but this was denied by an irritated Judge Grafton Baker who thenceforth ordered the prisoner remanded until trial.[56]

The trial finally occurred 17 March 1852, six months after Anderson was originally jailed for suspected murder. This was an unusually long delay but was no fault of the judicial system, which statistically tried cases within six weeks of arrest. Anderson and his attorney calculated that Judge Grafton Baker, the man who had ordered several public lashings, was more prone to hard justice and this suspicion was confirmed by Baker's decision to imprison Anderson indefinitely after he petitioned for a dismissal. Anderson and his unnamed attorney considered it prudent to continuously file extensions until the Honorable Judge Horace Mower was adjudicating. Irregularly, Mower ordered that a special jury session be conducted with twenty-four Anglo settlers to determine the validity of the case against Oliver P. Anderson.[57] Nowhere in the criminal dockets, the court docket books, or district court records is there either precedent or another instance of a special jury being formed in this manner for deliberation. Through whatever avenue Anderson and his unnamed attorney were able to appeal, the irregular conduct of Judge Mower was both a questionable and suspicious modification of the judicial process. On 22 March 1852 the all Anglo jury returned the verdict of not guilty, and Anderson was released from custody and exonerated of all charges.[58] As was the case with the execution style murder of Maria Antonia Lenoia, the execution of Joseph Garcia went unpunished.

Homicides at Fandangos

That fandangos are remembered as violent and drunken debacles is tragic, but not surprising considering that entertainment was the most easily commodified resource the New Mexican community had to offer. As such, the lively fandangos that traditionally celebrated community and good will were transformed into entertainment packages that incorporated excessive drunkenness and gambling for purchase by the highest bidder. Early travelers to New Mexico wrote voluminous accounts of the fandangos they attended and while their opinions of the New Mexican people differ, there was a common thread reported when violence or bad behavior occurred at fandangos: the presence of both numerous Americans and whiskey.[59] Thus, fandangos must be divided into two types: those that were traditional and community based and those that were commodified for the purpose of eliciting liquid capital from both soldiers and settlers alike.[60] It should not be surprising that violence and ultimately an incident of murder had occurred at a non-traditional fandango; fortunately the details of this particular homicide offer insight into the process of investigation, social divisions among Anglo settlers, and the hesitation of the traditional Nuevo Mexicano community members to cooperate with the new judicial apparatus.

The not guilty verdict returned against Christian Mild for the murder of United States Army Private William H. Bolt is another example of how Anglo jurors, and not the Nuevo Mexicano community, failed to satisfy the Anglo settlers' own desire for more convictions. Certainly the investigators had gathered the case competently, as Sheriff E. L. Vaughn conducted a formal inquest and produced a written record of this procedure that meticulously provided witness testimonies, physical evidence, and the details of the assault for the jury to consider.[61] Sheriff Vaughn, accompanied by a twelve member grand jury, arrived at the home of Jesus Romero where the murder of William Bolt occurred the night before, on 13 September, 1847. Romero had been hosting a commodified fandango, for which he had provided music, dancing, and drinking.[62]

In fact, a group of German immigrants and German born soldiers had commissioned Jesus Romero to host this celebration.[63] Difficulties arose when a significant number of American soldiers arrived and were turned away for refusing to pay admission fees to the German hosts.[64] The Americans departed, but returned with greater numbers determined to either enter the fandango or break the celebration up.[65] All that is agreed upon by witnesses is that there was an affray, confusion ensued, and multiple gunshots were fired from inside the house.[66] Outside of the home of Jesus Romero, the body of William Bolt lay mortally wounded from a bullet that struck his heart.[67]

The inquest commenced with an inspection of the body, as the members of the grand jury examined the remains of William H. Bolt. Next, the six Nuevo Mexicanos who had been present at the fandango (likely the very individuals that hosted the celebration) were questioned consecutively, beginning with Jesus Romero. The host explained that he had arranged the fandango for the Germans, the Americans had returned and tried to force their way in, he heard gunshots, but saw nothing and could tell nothing.[69] Elvino Romero was of no help to the inquisitors, as he claimed to be elsewhere at the time of the murder.[70] Jose Patricio Romero explained that he heard the shots, but remembered nothing; Miguel Gonzales' reply was more in depth, but he also claimed to have seen nothing.[71] Francisco Martinez claimed to have been asleep during the affair and testified that he was awakened by the gunshots, though E.L. Vaughn notes, "Witness contradicts himself about guard waking him up."[72] Thomas Alverez concluded the Nuevo Mexicano testimonies by explaining that there was a conflict between Americans and Germans at the door, but that he knew nothing.[73] Criminal court records indicate that Nuevo Mexicanos regularly testified against parties irrespective of race, but very little evidence exists that they did so in homicide cases; in the least it can be concluded that if the Nuevo Mexicano hosts knew anything about this murder, they were not willing to share it with either the sheriff or the grand jury.

Only eight years removed from Mexican rule, this depiction mirrors fandangos in Santa Fe, which were filled with peoples of all classes and ethnic origins. As in the picture, Santa Fe fandangos featured ornately decorated rooms with crucifixes, pictures of saints, and damsels waltzing with men of all backgrounds. The depiction here is of a more humble fandango, very common in the countryside, but ornate fandangos with champagne and fine foods were held at wealthier homes and within the Palace of the Governors. The fandango remained an important part of Santa Fe culture after American settlers arrived, though they became increasingly violent when whiskey drinking Americans participated. Nuevo Mexicanos had used the fandango to transcend cultural and class barriers; wealthy Nuevo Mexicanas could be seen waltzing with poor farmers, Native Americans with Nuevo Mexicanas, and wealthy elites with poor vecinas. [C. Castro, J. Campillo, L. Auda and G. Rodriguez "Mexico y Sus Alrededores," (Alicante: Miguel de Cervantes Virtual Library, 2006), Casimiro Castro y J. Campillo, "Trajes Mexicanos: A Fandango," (1855), pp XXIX)][68]

The testimonies of the ten Anglos and Germans, mostly comprised of American soldiers, were both far more detailed and accusatory. Joseph Donahue and Stephen Huffington both claimed they witnessed the murder weapon being passed by Mild into the hands of a Nuevo Mexicana, who absconded with the evidence, which might explain the Nuevo Mexicanos unwillingness to talk.[74] William Price concurred, testifying that he witnessed Mild loading the weapon in the backroom of the house and identified Alejandra Ortiz as Mild's girlfriend, the woman who allegedly disappeared with the murder weapon.[75] George Morgan, who was one of the Americans outside the home, verified seeing the weapon in the possession of Mild and believes he shot Private Bolt, but confessed that he never actually witnessed it being discharged.[76] A.J. Mitchell added that he believed the shots fired by the prisoner were not aimed at any particular individuals, rather that Bolt was the unfortunate recipient of a stray projectile.[77]

The other five testimonies given by these soldiers and settlers had nothing significant to contribute toward the grand jury deliberations. Other particulars that emerged during the inquest included confirmation that Mild had been guarding the door, that the Americans were trying to push their way through the door, and someone restraining the Americans discharged his firearm, causing Bolt to exclaim that he was wounded.[78] Though there were many women dancing at the fandango, the only woman questioned by the grand jury was Alejandra Ortiz, whom Huffington, Price, and Donahue had accused of concealing the murder weapon. Just as the Nuevo Mexicano males, Ortiz was terse during her testimony, claiming that she had no clue who gave her the weapon and submitting, "I had it in my hand, but it was left on the bench and another person took it."[79] The grand jury asked Ortiz if the individual who transferred the weapon to her person was Mexican, but Ortiz claimed no knowledge. Ortiz testified that when she heard someone was shot both she and her sister, who also knew nothing of the affair, departed forthwith.

The refusal of Nuevo Mexicanos and Mexicanas to impart knowledge to inquisitors may also be representative of a larger difficulty within the early system. The omission of Nuevo Mexicanos from participation in the jury pool in homicide cases during the first two years of occupation likely made Nuevo Mexicanos less likely to cooperate. Additionally, Nuevo Mexicanos were accustomed to a statutory code-based legal system that did not utilize the jury as a form of examination. The process was foreign, potentially intimidating, and was likely not well received by Nuevo Mexicanos accustomed to their own practices. This unwillingness contributed to more disparaging remarks about the lawless New Mexico, a misconception that American Richard W. Weightman, the self proclaimed protector of the people, argued against before the United States House of Representatives. Petitioning for an autonomous New Mexico that should be governed by the Nuevo Mexicano people, Weightman explained to Congress that it was unnecessary to, "Prolong your apprehension that crime will go unwhipped of justice; you may safely lay them aside; the criminal courts will be held, murder will not go unpunished."[80] The surviving criminal court records support Mr. Weightman's contention, as Anglo juries deliberating homicides committed by Anglos returned verdicts of not guilty in three of four cases, while Nuevo Mexicano juries convicted perpetrators of all crimes at a significantly higher rate.[81]

The exclusion of Nuevo Mexicanos from these three cases and the subsequent resistance to the transitional judicial authorities is indicative of the initial mistrust that accompanied the merging of two different cultures. When Nuevo Mexicanos were more involved in the jury process they more actively participated as witnesses in the judicial system.[82] More accustomed to the American judicial apparatus, Anglo settlers were willing to actively participate in these cases by providing both their knowledge of events and their personal speculations regarding details they did not witness. The exclusion of Nuevo Mexicanos from the juries in the cases of Anderson, Brady, and Mild is representative of the selection process in homicide cases involving Anglo perpetrators. The unified refusal of Nuevo Mexicanos to communicate their knowledge in the Christian Mild case may be representative of the Nuevo Mexicano response to their estrangement from the new judicial apparatus. Still, the witnesses were consistent in accusing Christian Mild of firing the shot that killed Private Bolt, and the grand jury charged Mild as the perpetrator. The Anglo trial jury was presented a case that in the least proved Mild was guilty of manslaughter, but as in other cases the Anglo jury returned the verdict of not guilty.

Given the reluctance of Anglo settler juries to convict fellow Anglo settlers of murder, it can be concluded that the murder committed by Andrew Jackson Simms must have been judged excessive.[83] The indictment against Simms contains a key phrase, "That Simms did willfully and with malice and forethought make an assault."[84] Other cases contain this language, but the jury and judge concurred that Simms had premeditated the murder of Jackson Johnson, though the surviving documents offer no motive to his perceived malice. The indictment contends that Simms assaulted Johnson, then pulled out his pistol, placed it to the right temple, and fired a shot that instantly killed the victim.[85] The details conveyed by the surviving court documents mirror the execution style murders of Nuevo Mexicano community members Maria Antonia Lenoia and Joseph Garcia, the sole difference being that the victim Johnson was an Anglo settler. It is likely that because the victim was a fellow Anglo and not a Nuevo Mexicano, the Anglo jury convicted Simms. The judge's instructions to Sheriff C.H. Merritt familiarly dictated that Simms be "Hanged by the neck till he be Dead! Dead! Dead!" but did not dictate Simms be hanged immediately.[86] Uniquely, the sentence called for a six month period of incarceration, after which Simms was legally hanged.[87]

All indications are that the Anglo settler public desired more justice of the Andrew Jackson Simms type; that they blamed the older Nuevo Mexicano community for their own propensity for leniency; and that they operated under the mistaken notion that excessive punishment dissuades criminals. The failure of the Anglo settler press, public officials, and the local citizenry to distinguish between murder trials and criminal trials explains the mistaken observations of both Anglo settlers and subsequent historians. Statistically, criminals were not going unpunished in Santa Fe; instead, Anglo settlers who committed homicides were being exonerated seemingly regardless of what the evidence suggested. The emotionally charged issue of homicide distorted the Anglo settlers' perception, as they attributed low conviction rates and lenient punishments for homicides to all forms of crime, and this induced them to operate under the assumption that criminals were seldom found guilty by juries and judges alike. Anglo settler dissatisfaction manifested through expressions of public outrage, petitions to modify the laws, and ultimately vigilantism in their efforts to combat the violence that they themselves had brought on the road to Santa Fe.

15

King Maker in the Back Room
Editor Max Frost and Hardball Politics in the Late-Territorial Period, 1876–1909

by
Robert K. Dean

In January 1867, fifteen-year-old Max Frost walked into a Brooklyn recruiting station, lied about his age, and joined the U. S. Army.[1] Having come of age during the Civil War, Frost was not the first youngster to see himself as seasoned beyond his years by that bloody conflict. So when he faced the recruiter on his enlistment day just twenty-one months after Lee surrendered to Grant, Frost figured he deserved the independence owed the twenty-one-year-old man he claimed to be. He was his own man. He wanted to be a soldier. The postwar army of 1867 marched in two directions, south and west. Frost's first two assignments sent him south to serve in an army deployed to impose order during Reconstruction.[2] The second phase of his army career took him west, where soldiers acted in the cause of Manifest Destiny—America's self-proclaimed sense of superiority and self-validated claim to land stretching across the continent.

The army, assigned by the federal government to protect white settlers and put down Native Americans who pushed back, picked Frost for the Signal Corps and sent him to get the telegraph lines humming in New Mexico, Arizona, and parts of Texas. His office was in Santa Fe, but he was no office-bound clerk. Charged with building the line, he had to travel across the territory. Whenever Frost set foot in a new town along the route, the words of his boss, Lieutenant S.C. Vedder, ran through his brain. The army promised to put in place a staff of polite operators and a network of reliable equipment, a system that in Vedder's words was to be "a helper to the people without the distinction

317

of persons" and a supplier of news to fill the newspapers "on terms that will barely pay for compiling and transmitting it."³ Inspired by Vedder's pledge, Frost the Signal Corps sergeant got hooked on newspapering. He saw almost immediately the power of the newspapers to write the story and the power of the telegraph to flash it across the country.

To the U. S. government, the telegraph was nothing less than an essential tool in taming the west, and Frost saw the mission of the telegraph and the newspapers as one in the same. Through circumstance, he matched opportunity to ambition. The newspapers gobbled up the news he keyed into the system; the telegraph job gave him an advantage in getting newspaper work on the side. He signed on as a frontier correspondent for a number of eastern newspapers, accompanied a Santa Fe reporter on a trip around the New Mexico territory, and wrote his first freelance story for the *Santa Fe New Mexican* in 1876.

From those first tentative steps in New Mexico, Frost would end up leaving a large imprint on the late-territorial period. He helped the Santa Fe Ring steal land. He promoted commerce of all kinds and pushed statehood, the close cousin to development. He paved the way for construction of the Scottish Rite Temple. He took control of the west's oldest newspaper, the *New Mexican,* and used its pages of to rally the party faithful or to deliver the first blast against an opponent. Some praised him as a brilliant editor, and others condemned him as a political dictator.⁴ To his critics, he became "a lying scoundrel."⁵ To admirers, he stood for a generation as "the power behind the throne" in the territory.⁶

The answers to three questions help establish Frost's place in territorial history. First, what shaped his views on political power and the public good? Second, what was the nature of political and economic power in Santa Fe so that a young man, particularly one like Frost who accepted the dominance of the federal government, might tap into it? Third, what tools did he use and how well did he use them to enter the circle of power and exert influence once he did?

Max Frost, as much as anyone during his time, wrote the rules of hardball politics in New Mexico's corrupt late-territorial period. From his eastern roots, he brought with him, less than a generation beyond U. S. military occupation of New Mexico, a sense of American overconfidence wrapped around a preference for economic power, military order, and federal authority. Growing up in the midst of the Civil War, Frost learned early in his life how to talk a good game, and in New Mexico he mastered the ins and outs of the bureaucracy. Armed with an insight into how power really worked and an impatience to make things happen, Frost never hesitated to twist an arm to get what he and his pals wanted.

To that brash newcomer to the west, making money was the highest calling for people and the best use of the land. In that way, he represented well his self-assured, ambitious, land-hungry nation. Frost's military experience showed him the value of order, brotherhood, and can-do assertiveness. He gazed on all that open space in the west and concluded that only the sprawling federal government could get control of such an unwieldy place. Captivated by the beauty and majesty of New Mexico, he saw that wealth was inextricably linked to the land. Few people, a shortage of water, and natural resources too meager to fuel industrial expansion left land as a rare marketable commodity. A clever landowner could turn the land, its livestock, and crops into supplies for sale to government-run forts and Indian trading posts.

After the army, Frost made his home in Santa Fe, where elective office was not the path he chose to power and influence. He left his imprint in many other possible ways, operating mostly on the edge of public life. He formed lasting bonds with his Masonic brethren, served four years recording and certifying property claims in the federal land office, and mastered the machinery of the dominant Republican Party. All the while, he deepened his association with the *New Mexican*, becoming in time an editor, publisher, and owner who was willing to turn his newspaper into the mouthpiece for every one of his causes. First and foremost, he protected the interests of the shadowy Santa Fe Ring, and when it weakened he lent his influence to the contentious, thirty-year campaign for statehood.

A complete telling of history blends many stories and truths from diverse points of view. This is one story. Frost and his colleagues embodied Manifest Destiny, the doctrine that justified and propelled American expansionism. The consequences of that, reflected in Frost's words and deeds, were concrete: trails and railroads that stretched west; policies that encouraged men to take minerals and other natural resources from the earth; and a system for acquiring land to expand the public domain.[7] Largely missing in this short biography are truths from the people who lived with the fallout of American expansion, the Hispanos and Native Americans and their communities who before U. S. occupation had an identity and sense of place deeply rooted in the New Mexico soil. This limited biography, then, is a narrow piece of territorial history based primarily on the articles, documents, and reports published in Frost's time. That body of material represented mostly the one-dimensional experience of white settlers from the eastern United States and recorded in that context Frost's activities as a career-minded transplant who moved to Santa Fe midlife.

To date, no study has singled out Frost for a biography. But Porter Stratton, in *The Territorial Press of New Mexico 1834–1912*, found Frost a leading player and concluded that he helped usher in progress but used bad politics to get there.

Stratton hinted in 1969 that a historian at some future date ought to examine Frost as a research topic, for he embodied the paradox of territorial public life. Frost spoke up for development, statehood, and the rights and dignity of Spanish Americans, while he also joined up with the forces of greed, intimidation, and machine politics.[8] Frost also was prominent in Howard Lamar's *The Far Southwest*, the classic study about the interplay of politics and money in the American west. The federal budget paid for jobs, government, and forts. So the men who came to New Mexico to make money adapted to a colonial point of view, relying on the federal government to subsidize their political and business ambitions.[9] To Lamar, the significance of the newspapers and editors like Frost was this: A strong press that held the line at home and Washington friends who kept the dollars flowing were a packaged deal that satisfied the power brokers.[10] New Mexico historian Marion Dargan's study about the struggle for statehood called Frost a "masterful editor."[11] The study, serialized from 1939 to 1943 in the *New Mexico Historical Review*, portrayed Frost as a man fighting the odds. Press support of statehood was strong and consistent, but over a long period too few readers agreed with the pro-statehood message delivered by the newspapers.[12] From the historians' work and Frost's own writings, a portrait emerged of a man with a laser focus who was ready to engage his opponents and willing when necessary to get his hands dirty.

Frost's early life was a mystery. For reasons that were unclear, Frost changed his story several times about both when and where he was born. The earliest public records on him were his enlistment papers. Those papers—the first but not positively the most accurate record—said Frost was born in Vienna, Austria, in 1852.[13] He later claimed New Orleans as his hometown.[14] Along with his three brothers and three sisters, he was orphaned after his mother died at a young age and his father fell in battle during the Civil War.[15] While living in New York City, he joined the army less than two years after the war ended. He gave his age as twenty-one.[16] He really was fifteen. He finished his first tour of duty in New Orleans and after that served in Arkansas and Colorado before getting his big break with the Signal Corps.[17]

Americans' movement west was an eclectic mix ranging from pioneers who dragged plows across the plains to speculators and crooks who brought along their get-rich-quick schemes. Alongside them rode a modern Signal Corps still in its infancy. The Signal Corps took control of the telegraph system in 1867, and Congress made it responsible for a national weather service in 1870. The telegraph shortened the distance between commanders in the east and the far-away outposts on the vast plains, but to do the job Signal Corps soldiers needed specialized training, a need the army met when it established a new training center in Washington, DC.[18] Frost landed one of the training slots.[19] Not many soldiers won an assignment to the Signal Corps, and when they did, because the army needed its highly trained telegraph operators and because qualified replacements were in short supply, soldiers in the Signal Corps tended to stay in the army a long time.[20] The Signal Corps was to be on the leading edge of America's western expansion, and so was Frost. The corps assigned the young sergeant to Santa Fe in 1876. Over the next four-and-a-half years, he was in charge of construction and maintenance, traveling across the territory and making friends wherever he went.[21]

From Santa Fe, the telegraph line pointed south to El Paso and west to Phoenix, a swath of land Frost came to treasure. He wrote later in his life, "New Mexico stretches in abundance and beauty, waiting for those who are wise enough to investigate its resources."[22] His travels introduced him to people in all parts of the New Mexico territory. His job was to plant the poles, string the line, and make the wires talk. A press report favorable to Frost late in his life went so far as to say that people on the frontier gave Frost credit for the mysterious, magical gadget called the telegraph.[23] Signal Corps inspectors, too, thought highly of Frost's work. They recognized him for keeping the offices neat, the services efficient, and instruments in good shape.[24] Still, to people who embraced the federal government's mission, the technical and physical precision of the line was his masterpiece. "The telegraph lines [are] … a fine piece of work, symmetrical and durable," a reporter wrote after viewing the project. "The poles are all of uniform size and height and numbering precisely 25 to the mile all along the line, measured with a tape-line at the time they went up."[25] At twenty-four, Frost was succeeding exactly as his country wanted. The uniform gave him self-respect, the smooth operation of his line gave him a sense of accomplishment, and the young territory gave him hope. In the bigger picture, the young man filled with optimism thought that if settlers could fill the land, commerce and prosperity were sure to follow.

A turning point for Frost came in December 1876 and January 1877, when he teamed up with a *New Mexican* correspondent for a trip across the territory to observe and assess the state of affairs in New Mexico. Writer William Dawson sent back home twenty-three dispatches filled with vivid images of tidy fields that produced crops, mines that pumped out riches, and pastures that sustained sheep and cattle by the thousands. On one particularly memorable evening, the Santa Fe men shared a camp fire with famed cattleman John Chisum, who boasted that his business was booming. Dawson reported: "He informed me that his herd numbers some 40,000 head, with headquarters on the Pecos river in Lincoln County, but that it is increasing to such an extent that he is compelled to hunt up new ranges in isolated regions further west. At his ranche [sic] on the Pecos and with his hands elsewhere he employs 90 herders, whom he furnishes with horse, wagons, camp equipage and provisions."²⁶ For Frost and Dawson, the future was clear: Let ranchers and merchants like Chisum take hold, and "the advancing tide of civilization" would lift all New Mexicans.²⁷ Overall, news reports from the expedition had a heavy pro-development slant. Dawson's reports practically ignored Hispanos of the Rio Grande valley, choosing instead to appeal to whites in the east who might be tempted by opportunities in New Mexico and inspired by examples of successful "American energy and enterprise."²⁸

In the territorial period, fraternal, benevolent, and civic organizations became gathering places for Santa Feans for whom the Catholic Church was not a spiritual home. Until about 1850, the faith communities were organized almost exclusively around the Catholic parishes or Native religions. To serve a growing number of white immigrants, the Masons and the Odd Fellows organized in the early 1850s. The Masonic lodge, in particular, became "the American church" in the eyes of Spanish Catholics in Santa Fe.²⁹ As one of the white immigrants who settled permanently in the town, Frost threw himself into the work of the Masonic lodge.³⁰ It was an association that became one of the defining features of his life. He did not live to see the Scottish Rite Temple in downtown Santa Fe, but he led the effort to raise the seed money and buy the land for the temple.³¹ In a town that was heavily Hispanic, Spanish speaking, and Catholic, Frost was none of those, so he gravitated as well to social circles and fraternal organizations that sprang up steadily as the flow of immigrants from the east continued. For a time, he served as president of the Fairview Cemetery, the final resting place for many Jews and Protestants.³² The one-time military officer on the go became a busy man about town, a trim figure of five feet, five inches, with a handsome mustache, a dark complexion and hair to match, and piercing black eyes behind a pair of studious wire-rimmed spectacles. He took a leadership role in the Odd Fellows lodge and joined the library board, the historical society, archaeological association, the bar association.³³

The quiet of the lodge hall or society meeting room had a counterpoint, the rough-and-ready life in the territorial militia. Under three governors between 1778 and 1885, Frost served as adjutant general of New Mexico. In that capacity, he fought rustlers and participated in several Indian campaigns. Later he held the rank of colonel in the First Regiment of the New Mexico National Guard, and again he led a campaign to put down a Native uprising to the north.³⁴ During that campaign, the horse he rode threw him, causing injuries that would slow him the rest of his life. Frost, marked for life in more than one way by his military experience, clung self-consciously to the privilege of rank and never stopped calling himself colonel.

Max Frost in Santa Fe, 1882. Courtesy Palace of the Governors Photo Archives (NMHM/DCA), negative number 009876.

Max Frost as a colonel in the National Guard from 1882 to 1886. Courtesy Palace of the Governors Photo Archives (NMHM/DCA), negative number 007224.

A presidential appointment to the federal land office changed the course of Frost's career. The man who had spent most of his working days in the field became the man in the back office. He found the keys to making money and peddling influence buried in the stacks of maps, charts, and paper work. At first he was deputy surveyor, and then in 1881 President James Garfield appointed Frost register of the land office. The office kept an inventory of what land was claimed and unclaimed; arranged for and recorded the sale of open land; and reported the details for tax purposes.[35] In New Mexico, the job boiled down to sorting out the Spanish and Mexican land grants, government giveaways issued many years earlier as payback to families and communities that had been willing to settle the northern territory.

When New Mexico became a U. S. territory in 1848, the United States agreed to honor existing property rights but not to give blanket acceptance of the old land grants. In 1854, Congress created a bureaucracy to verify the grants, define property boundaries, and identify leftover public lands. Land was abundant and cheap. The Spanish and Mexican governments, not seeing the value of land in monetary terms, handed out parcels "in the most lavish and extravagant fashion."[36] The old documents were notoriously vague. The language of one, for example, specified only enough land "on which to plant a cornfield," while another designated vaguely a pasture for a "small stock and horse herd."[37] Even in the case of well defined boundaries, a clash of cultures created a fertile ground for fraud. Simply put, the grant holders and the speculators lived in different worlds with incompatible notions about property. While the Spanish and Mexican tradition emphasized community ownership and working the land as the basis of a valid claim, the U. S. economy favored private ownership, the profit motive, and the view that land was a commodity.[38] Conditions were right for a land grab.

Land stealing took several forms, but it all started with fraudulent surveys that exaggerated the size or manipulated the boundaries of the grants.[39] Some speculators preyed on land-grant descendants with low-ball offers that seemed like riches to the poor people of New Mexico. At other times, a lawyer would represent a community of grantees in exchange for a piece of the grant. Once the grant was certified and the lawyer's ownership established, the lawyer could then sell that portion of land. Another method of snatching land resulted in the fraudulent purchase of grants from communities or families. Many of those grants were made in the name of a single representative, but an unscrupulous lawyer with the help of the land office could buy the grant with a payoff to that one name on the grant. The rushed process of adjudicating the land claims included sloppy surveys, forgeries, made-up testimony, and maps that were a joke. In 1885, former Indiana congressman George W. Julian accepted the presidential appointment as surveyor general and the assignment to clean up the mess. Although he was a newcomer among the veterans in the adjudication process, he had national political standing. He dug through old records, and his blunt assessment of the damage done inside the land office thundered over the territory. "Millions of acres of the public domain were thus appropriated to the uses of private greed," Julian said.[40] At the heart of his analysis was the bold assertion that a ring of business and legal interests was behind the land fraud and corruption in the land office.

Santa Fe has debated for generations the very existence of a ring and wondered out loud about the varying depths of its misdeeds. The Santa Fe Ring was either a collection of opportunists brought together by coincidence or a tight regime that would stop at nothing, including murder, to keep its grip on New Mexico's affairs. Most likely, the ring was something in between, an enigmatic association of lawyers, bankers, and politicians who dominated territorial politics and business from the 1860s to the mid-1880s. People who saw firsthand what was going on felt no doubt: The ring was real, it was ruthless, and it stole New Mexico. "Notorious" was the verdict from frustrated land reformer Julian. He declared:

> They have hovered over the territory like a pestilence. To a fearful extent they have dominated governors, judges, district attorneys, legislatures, surveyors-general and their deputies, marshals, treasurers, county commissioners, and the controlling business interests of the people. They have confounded political distinctions and subordinated everything to the greed for land.[41]

Julian's blistering attack was neither the first nor the last on the matter. In 1884, *The New York Times* had presented the case against the ring, from stealing land to deploying a band of assassins, all designed to crush the independence of New Mexicans. "They are oppressed to such an extent that their property and often their personal safety are at the mercy of that compact, well-organized, unscrupulous, and cruel association of Federal officials and ex-officials known as the New-Mexican land ring," the *Times* said.[42] Intimidated by the ring's might, few victims went public with cases that would pit them against the full weight of the machine. Years later, however, Miguel Antonio Otero detailed how members of the ring conspired to steal his family's mine. Otero, a member of a prominent banking family in northern New Mexico, served as one of the last territorial governors. His memoirs included a vivid portrait of the ring in action. The land office changed the boundaries on the Otero land grant; the ring seized control of their mine; the courts refused to hear the Mexican government's land-grant expert who could have straightened out everything; armed guards locked down the mine; and lawmen under ring control threw some of the Oteros in jail.[43] Otero, still angry fifty years later, left no doubt where he stood on the ring's role. "The territory of New Mexico was dominated by one of the most corrupt, unscrupulous, and daring organizations ever connected with its history," he said. "Nothing was too rotten for the well-known Santa Fe Ring to undertake."[44]

The ring growled and bit back against its critics. The men who knew how to get things done were not about to let attacks from the likes of Julian go unchallenged. Besides his report to the president, Julian also made his findings public in an article in the *North American Review*. The article named names: Stephen W. Dorsey, a former U. S. senator from Arkansas; Stephen B. Elkins, a former U. S. attorney in New Mexico and future U. S. secretary of war; Thomas B. Catron, a one-time attorney general in the territory who would go on to represent the state of New Mexico in the U. S. senate; and Charles H. Gildersleeve, a lawyer and leader of the Democratic Party. Julian dismissed the lot of them as politicians "for revenue only."[45] Land owner Dorsey, standard bearer for the ring, delivered a powerful defense in his own *North American Review* article. Brushing off Julian as a political hack who knew nothing about New Mexico, Dorsey said that sorting out land claims was messy, but it had to be done quickly in order to calm the environment for buying and selling. Further, he emphasized, land-grant issues could only be understood in the context of the New Mexican terrain and climate. Small farms and ranches would not be viable in the arid region. "Wise in their own deceit," he said, some men saw what they wanted to see—a farming paradise. Others saw the reality—miles and miles of dry grazing land. "Practical men of affairs look at things as they find them," Dorsey concluded.[46]

By attacking the accuser instead of the accusation, Dorsey used a well worn tactic of the ring. Frost carried on, using Dorsey's same approach on the same issue. Results were what counted to defenders of the ring, and those included getting the land claims out of the way so development could proceed. "[T]he blight of unstable tenures of land which has so long characterized New Mexico is now removed," Frost said some years later. "When purchasing a piece of land now it need not be feared that a lawsuit is bought on account of counter claim of some concealed owner or claimant."[47]

The constant discussion about corruption in New Mexico was a vexing issue for Washington. Grover Cleveland won the presidency in 1884 as a reformer, and one of his promises was to clean up New Mexico. Based on Julian's investigation, the government charged Frost with taking money to register a fraudulent land claim. At trial, he avoided conviction because of one holdout juror. The case went to trial a second time, and Frost was convicted and sentenced to a year in prison. On appeal, the territorial Supreme Court ordered a new trial. Before the third trial, some of the evidence was lost or destroyed, and Frost was finally acquitted.[48] Not content only to take its chances in court, the government pursued him administratively as well. During his years in the land office, Frost studied for admission to bar, and, not surprisingly, he specialized in land claims.[49] After leaving the office, he sought permission to represent clients in land-office matters. The Department of the Interior barred him from handling federal or state land cases.[50]

The legal troubles only compounded the difficult times Frost was experiencing at home around the same time. He met and married Lyda Hood, the daughter of Kansas preacher Graehme W. Hood. Before long in 1889, Lyda was pregnant. Graehme Hood Frost was born in September, and the mother died soon afterward, perhaps related to childbirth. Lyda was just twenty-two. The young father was not able to care for the boy at all times, and Frost sent Graehme to be with his maternal grandparents in Kansas at least part of the time. Frost remained single for ten years and then married Maud Pain in Kansas City on Dec. 19, 1899.[51] Her father, Henry Pain, worked on the business side of the *Kansas City Times*. Maud was in her twenties, and Max was almost forty-eight.[52] She outlived her husband, remarried, and lived for years in Santa Fe. Maud's second husband was Miguel Antonio Otero, the same man who years before had been victimized by the Santa Fe Ring.[53]

Frost's trial and acquittal in the land-office scandal coincided with the end of the Santa Fe ring. As the wide-open days of wheeling and dealing in the territory drew to a close, Frost and his friends increasingly focused on statehood as the next leap forward for New Mexico. In their minds, statehood was the key to development. Not only would statehood validate New Mexico as a stable environment for business investment, but it also was the only way to earn its rightful share of federal tax dollars.[54] Frost, as any able attorney might, laid out the case point by point in his most familiar arena, the newspaper. He wrote:

> The United States has given to thinly populated states and territories other than New Mexico, sections 16 and 36 in every surveyed township, to each state university 90,000 acres of public land, and special donations of many thousand acres for state agricultural, normal and mining schools and institutions for the insane and helpless. The swamp lands in the Mississippi basin and on the coast as in Florida have been given by millions of acres, and these gifts have stimulated immigration, educated the people, encouraged enterprises, developed resources, and multiplied industries till they have become populous and enlightened and prosperous states.
>
> To New Mexico during forty years not one acre has been donated. On the contrary, by official decisions the people have been robbed of much land in their rightful possession.[55]

Frost was frustrated for most of the 1890s. Why did men of that era own newspapers? A newspaper can take the voice of one, amplify it, and turn it into a roar. But that was only half the answer. Men also owned newspapers to make money. The territorial capital of Santa Fe was a good place to be. As long as Republicans ruled Washington and the territorial government, that was good news for the party faithful and for a loyal hometown publisher. The government did a lot of paper work. Frost's publishing company was in position for lucrative government printing contracts, especially when his political allies were in charge of ordering reports, ballots, legal notices, brochures, and forms of all kinds. But the tables turned just as surely when Frost's friends were out of power. Cut out of the government-printing business, Frost's company suffered through the first Democratic administration of Grover Cleveland. The Democrats were out of office only four years when Cleveland returned for a second term starting in 1893. Frost was not sure his company could survive another Democratic administration.

Frost hatched a plan that was brilliant, audacious, and, above all, pragmatic. He leased the *New Mexican* to a group of Democrats and got out of the newspaper business.[56] The announcement in the *New Mexican*, which did not mention that Gov. W.T. Thornton himself would be president of the new corporation, offered no specifics about the transaction, just that the circumstances were beyond Frost's control.[57] There was much more behind the deal. The loss of the printing subsidy during the earlier Democratic administration told Frost that the *New Mexican* needed a monopoly position if it were to survive political ups and downs. Before the power shift in 1893, a weekly called the Santa Fe *Sun* was the printer favored by Democrats who passed out contracts. When the Democrats took over the *New Mexican*, they closed the weekly. The *New Mexican* became the monopoly Frost prized, a situation that would benefit him should the Republicans regain control and Frost reclaim the newspaper.[58] For all of its forty-four years until the lease to the Democrats, the newspaper had been Republican, but the time had come for the editor to put profit ahead of politics.

Frost walked away from the newspaper business, yet, at just forty-two, he was not ready to retire. Before long, he surfaced as secretary of the territorial department of tourism and commerce, known then as the Bureau of Immigration. He cranked out a book promoting the "Land of Sunshine" to the rest of the country, 340 pages of boosterism that demonstrated the writer's breadth on topics from rainfall to mineral deposits, from tax policy to crop prices.[59] He stayed at the bureau for twelve years, a tenure that overlapped with his eventual return to the *New Mexican*.[60] Meantime, he practiced law on the side. He performed three distinct jobs and worked out of two separate offices, but he wrote with one voice, as this routine item from an editorial column in 1903 showed: "[Santa Fe advertising] is bearing good fruit, as the large number of tourists and healthseekers in the city abundantly shows."[61] Frost's role as New Mexico's official promoter proved how comfortable the newsman could be blurring that line between words meant to inform and words intended to sell.

One election cycle later the clouds parted, the Republicans returned to the White House, and on Jan. 23, 1897, the Democrats who had the *New Mexican* for four years ran a headline saying simply, "Adios." The Democrats sold the newspaper. Max Frost, Republican, was back in charge. Two days later, the newspaper declared its return to the Republican ranks and, with a disarming understatement that only accentuated the editor's self-importance, noted: "Mr. Frost, who assumes control, is tolerably well known throughout the territory as a staunch Republican."[62] After more than twenty years of coming and going at the *New Mexican*, Frost was back in the editor's chair, and for good this time until the ravages of terminal illness eventually would force him to retire. The fight for statehood would be back on page one.

Four times in the first fifty years of territorial history, Washington came close to making New Mexico a state. It seemed that Washington kept playing a cruel joke by dangling then withdrawing the possibility of self rule.[63] Without a doubt, historian Stratton found, "the *New Mexican* was the most consistent and strongest advocate of statehood throughout the period."[64] Frost met every objection with a clear, strong rebuttal. A number of anti-statehood arguments that made the rounds in Washington came wrapped in ethnic and cultural prejudice. One of the doubters looked for "familiarity and sympathy with our institutions" and for "all the elements that go to make up good citizenship."[65] In New Mexico, the students did lessons in Spanish, the faithful worshipped the pope's church, and the small farmers remained poor. Those factors worried Washington. One of the fears most distressing to Frost focused on whether Spanish descendants truly pledged their allegiance to the United States. "The native people of New Mexico have repeatedly proved their loyalty to the American flag and their patriotism is unquestioned," Frost fired back.[66] Even at the height of American patriotism brought on by war in Cuba and the Philippines, he spoke up for the civil rights of Spanish Americans.

As the defense of the people demonstrated in that case, Frost was at his best when the topic steered him away from party and electoral politics. He rarely missed a chance to promote railroads and to say so in a way that presumed he spoke for all New Mexicans. "It must be remembered that this railroad age is one of surprises and that New Mexico stands ready to be pleasantly surprised any time by the coming of a new railroad," he wrote.[67] The editor looked for outlets for his humor. When two government officials lost their way in a car, he wrote that "they became confused as to roads and directions and yesterday spent five hours in the beautiful scenery of the Ortiz Mountains trying to find a road."[68] At the turn of the century, the obsession with national identity and white superiority crowded out progressive views on race. Frost showed the courage to take on the issue. He wrote:

> [I]f anybody is entitled to the appellation of American it certainly is the people who are descendants of men and women who lived in New Mexico when the ancestors of the later comers were probably living in the squalor of some European hamlet or Asiatic village. But aside from that, the word American is not at all distinctive, for the United States occupies but one-fifth of the area of the Americas, has but one-half of their population and its population is about as mongrel as that of any nation on the face of the earth.[69]

Frost could be petty, vindictive, and caustic when the target was an enemy of the Republican establishment. In politics, there was no middle ground for the editor. And Democrats did not get all the attention. Governor Herbert J. Hagerman was a reform-minded Republican appointed to take on the entrenched party leadership. Frost used his considerable talent for a surgical strike on a Hagerman appointee. "He really does not know enough about educational matters to go into a schoolhouse when it rains, but nevertheless and notwithstanding, he was appointed assistant superintendent of education, an appointment which is disgraceful and detrimental," Frost said.[70] The editor had the skill to use words. No one argued that point. But his colorful words also cut deeply, and that was a sore point with others. Long before, Frost showed he was after power, not popularity, but increasingly he grew unpopular even among former friends.

Throughout the first decade of the century, his health weakened, and he lost his teeth, his eyesight, and the use of his legs. He dictated editorials. A clerk read to him each edition of the *New Mexican* front to back so he could direct news judgments. He improvised to stay current with public affairs. For instance, his wife read to him in the evening from eastern newspapers, books, and magazines. He bragged to an interviewer, "I can do more work in ten minutes than most men can in an hour, as, being blind, I have nothing to distract my attention."[71] Although the public heard only that his spirits stayed high and his intellect remained sharp, Frost's physical breakdown likely darkened his outlook and widened his mean streak.

The *New Mexican*'s rigid nature and nasty tone in electoral politics hurt its effectiveness. Frost showed he could be insightful and sensitive in social and cultural affairs, but he approached politics willing to win at any cost. He learned when his company was out of favor for government contracts that readership alone could not keep the *New Mexican* profitable. His newspaper needed to cozy up to power. On the issue of statehood, the *New Mexican* and other papers that followed its lead tried to rally support in the territory and to overcome objections in the east. The efforts largely failed, however, simply because the newspapers had too few readers.[72] The population was growing but was still small. In 1850, the territory had 61,547 residents, and the number almost doubled to 119,565 by 1880 and grew to 195,310 by 1900. Based on the argument that New Mexico would receive disproportionately high representation in Congress, the population numbers justified for Washington the delay in bringing a small state into the union. Statehood proponents made the reverse argument, that statehood would encourage growth. The numbers eventually supported the argument. From 1900 to 1920, New Mexico's population grew eighty-five percent to 360,350.[73]

While New Mexico demanded action on statehood, Congress formed a subcommittee. The act of empanelling the committee itself helped little to propel the issue forward. But from that day in June 1902, statehood for New Mexico seemed just a matter to time. "New Mexico will not pull down its flag and surrender in its fight for statehood," Frost wrote.[74] The issue lurched forward with a congressional proposal in 1906 to bring Arizona and New Mexico into the union as a single state. The idea seemed crazy to people in the southwest. To Congress, it made perfect sense. The two territories made a neat square on the map; further, joint statehood restricted the representation of the area to two senators, and the densely populated eastern seaboard liked that.[75]

Frost was so eager for statehood that he clenched his jaw, changed his mind, and accepted joint statehood. He even said he could stomach giving up the name New Mexico to accept Arizona as the name of the would-be state. As the vote in both territories approached, the *New Mexican* was typically upbeat, saying: "All that it will take, is a united pull, a long pull and strong pull of the friends of statehood, and on the seventh of November the tidings will be shouted from Phoenix to Clayton, from Carlsbad to Yuma: 'Hail to the newest of the states, the great state of Arizona!' "[76] All the fuss produced nothing. New Mexicans voted for statehood, but Arizona voted it down. In heavily Hispanic and Catholic northern New Mexico, where political leaders and the church never favored statehood, the resolution failed. The counties of Santa Fe and Rio Arriba in Frost's backyard voted more than two to one against statehood.[77]

The vote proved that the results did not match the rhetoric of Frost and his Republican buddies. Throughout the fall, he and Holm O. Bursum, the boss of Socorro County, exchanged letters that documented their efforts to twist press coverage in order to manipulate the vote. Bursum urged, "Keep your Spanish weekly full of statehood stuff.... Try and get all the letters and interviews you can favoring statehood."[78] Voters in favor were not easy to find in the northern counties, Frost replied, continuing, "I doctor the interviews to make them as favorable as possible to joint statehood."⁷⁹ Bursum kept the pressure on and offered this plea: "If we can whoop her up with interviews throughout the Territory…, it will do a great deal towards discouraging and disheartening the Democrats"⁸⁰ The issue of statehood hinged on the most basic democratic right, the right of people to elect leaders and make laws. Frost and Bursum pleaded with Congress to be fair to New Mexicans, but behind the scenes the cynical bosses did not trust people with the facts. They talked a good game about self government, but they could not trust their own neighbors with free choice.

Congress united around statehood in late 1908 and placed it on the agenda for 1909. At almost the same time, the *New Mexican* announced that the owner was too ill to go on. Frost sold the newspaper and retired immediately.⁸¹ He spent most of his last nine months in a Kansas City sanitarium, suffering from dementia and the loss of body control, a condition called locomotor ataxia that doctors typically associated with latent syphilis.⁸² Offering another explanation, his obituary attributed his physical breakdown to permanent injuries sustained when a horse threw him during his National Guard days. Frost died October 13, 1909, in his home. He was fifty-seven. Poet and biblical scholar E. McQueen Gray, who for a short time served as president of the University of New Mexico, officiated at the funeral. As Gray drew the service to an end, Frost's Masonic friends filed out in solemn silence, each placing an evergreen twig on the coffin.⁸³

In the years leading up to his death, the imperious Frost found that, just as the onset of ill health changed his life, the end of machine politics changed his world. On Thanksgiving 1906, the editor was at the office because the newspaper had to get out, even on a holiday. His phone rang. Being blind, he fumbled for the handset but could not get a grip. Frustrated, he tried to summon help. "Boy. Boy," he shouted, widening his mouth with each louder cry. His false teeth fell out, and his jaws snapped together with such force that the jawbone fractured.⁸⁴ The ringing telephone was not really the issue. Someone was supposed to answer, all right, and put an end to the unnerving noise. But the underlying truth was that times had changed for boss Frost. He hollered for the news boy, and the news boy did not come. The boy, having put turkey before task, was home for dinner. There had been a time when, if Frost hollered, the news boy always came.

In Santa Fe, the one-time orphan and army wanderer had found a home. Frost arrived as a foot soldier for Manifest Destiny who felt duty bound to remake Native Americans and Hispanos culturally, religiously, and economically in his image of American superiority. He exhibited his Signal Corps self-confidence the rest of his life, along with the title of colonel. In middle age, Frost went to the land office out of a desire to clear the way for development and got sidetracked by the temptation to skim off the top. Land was money, and money was power. Greed applied to political power, too, and Frost's associates clung to that at any price. As a telegraph operator, Frost connected quite naturally with the *New Mexican*, and that connection became a career. The *New Mexican* kept him close to powerful Republicans, and he unapologetically made the newspaper a mouthpiece for the machine. As an editor, he was a brainy, skillful loud mouth when the political currents favored him, and he relied on government patronage when business was not so good.

In Frost's last years, as statehood for New Mexico drew near, Theodore Roosevelt and the progressives were on the march. They were ready to take on the old-style politics. If old-style politicians like Frost stood in their way, the reformers were ready to take them out. Reformers judged Frost's ways harshly. He was a man of many talents and good deeds, but he too often crossed the line. His desire for personal gain tainted his public service. He was opinionated and arrogant to the point that it was hard to distinguish where persuasion stopped and bullying began. His pragmatism was so expansive that it accommodated corruption.

References Cited:

Archives

Manuscripts Collection, Center for Southwestern Research, University Libraries, University of New Mexico, Albuquerque.
Missouri State Archives, Jefferson, Missouri. Missouri Marriage Records, 1805–2002. Microfilm Collection. Ancestry.com database online. Provo, Utah: The Generations Network, Inc., 2007 (accessed September 13, 2008)
National Archives and Records Administration, Washington, DC. U. S. Army. Register of Enlistments, 1798–1914. Records of the Adjutant General's Office, 1780's–1917. Record Group 94. Ancestry.com database online. Provo, Utah: The Generations Network, Inc., 2007 (accessed June 2, 2008).
National Archives and Records Administration, Washington, DC. U. S. Department of Commerce. Bureau of the Census. Decennial Census of the United States, 1880 and 1900. Ancestry.com database online. Provo, Utah: The Generations Network, Inc., 2004 (accessed September 20, 2008).
Rio Grande Republican, Las Cruces, New Mexico from December 19, 1908, to October 22, 1909.
Santa Fe New Mexican, Santa Fe, New Mexico from September 28, 1876, to October 14, 1909.

Government Reports

Copp, Henry Norris. *Public Land Laws Passed by Congress from April 1, 1882, to January 1, 1890, with the Important Decisions of the Secretary of the Interior, and Commissioner of the General Land Office, the Land Opinions of the Attorney General, and the Circular Instructions Issued from the General Land Office to the Surveyors General and Registers and Receivers During the Same Period*. Washington, DC: Office of the Librarian of Congress, 1890. U. S. Department of Commerce. U. S. Census Bureau. New Mexico's Resident Population, 1850–2000. www.census.gov (accessed September 14, 2008).
U. S. Department of the Interior. National Park Service. Fairview Cemetery, Santa Fe, New Mexico National Register of Historic Places Registration Form. Prepared by Corinne P. Sze, Fairview Cemetery Preservation Association, August 2004. U. S. War Department. *Annual Report of the Chief Signal-Officer, to the Secretary of War: For the Year*. Washington: Government Printing Office, 1878.

Primary Sources (Books and Articles)

Dorsey, Stephen W. "'Land Stealing in New Mexico.' A Rejoinder." *North American Review* 147 (October 1887): 396-410.
Frost, Max. *New Mexico: Its Resources, Climate, Geography.* Official Publication of the Bureau of Immigration. Santa Fe, New Mexico: New Mexican Printing Co., 1894.
Julian, George W. "Land Stealing in New Mexico." *North America Review* 145 (July 1887): 17-32.
"New-Mexico's Land Ring: Gigantic Swindles Accomplished in the Territory." *New York Times.* May 18, 1884.
Otero, Miguel Antonio. *My Life on the Frontier, Vol. 2: Facsimile of Original 1939 Edition.* Santa Fe, New Mexico: Sunstone Press, 2007.
"Passing of Frost: New Mexico's Blind Boss a Picturesque Figure." *Stevens Point Journal.* March 18, 1909.
"Shouting, Broke His Jaw: Queer Accident to Col. Max Frost, Blind Editor of Santa Fe." *New York Times*, December 1, 1906.

Secondary Sources (Books and Articles)

Agnew, Jeremy. *Life of a Soldier on the Western Frontier*. Missoula, Montana: Mountain Press Publishing, 2008.
Anderson, George B. *History of New Mexico: Its Resources and People.* Los Angeles: Pacific States Publishing, 1907.
Dargan, Marion. "New Mexico's Fight for Statehood 1895–1912." *New Mexico Historical Review* 14 (January 1939): 1-33; (April 1939): 121-142; 15 (April 1940): 133-187; 16 (January 1941): 70-103; (October 1941): 379-400; 18 (January 1943): 60-96; (April 1943): 148-175.
Gomez, Laura E. *Manifest Destinies: The Making of the Mexican American Race.* New York: New York University, 2007.
Lamar, Howard R. *The Far Southwest, 1846–1912: A Territorial History.* New Haven, Connecticut: Yale University Press, 1966.
Langston, LaMoine. "The History of Montezuma Lodge No. 1, Santa Fe." *A History of Masonry in New Mexico 1877–1977.* Roswell, New Mexico: Hall-Poorbaugh Press, 1977.

Leonard, John William. *Who's Who in Finance and Banking.* New York: Who's Who in Finance Inc., 1922.
Melzer, Richard. Foreword to 2007 Edition of *The Military Occupation of New Mexico: Facsimile of Original 1909 Edition* by Ralph Emerson Twitchell. Santa Fe: Sunstone Press, 2007.
Prince, L. Bradford. *New Mexico's Struggle for Statehood: Sixty Years of Effort to Obtain Self Government.* Santa Fe, New Mexico: The New Mexican Printing, 1910. New Edition, Sunstone Press, Santa Fe, 2010.
Raines, Rebecca Robbins. *Getting the Message Through: A Branch History of the U. S. Army Signal Corps.* Washington, DC: Center of Military History, 1996.
Stratton, Porter A. *The Territorial Press of New Mexico 1834–1912.* Albuquerque, New Mexico: University of New Mexico Press, 1969.
Torrez, Robert J. Introduction to *New Mexico in 1876–1877: A Newspaperman's View, the Travels and Reports of William D. Dawson*, edited by Robert J. Torrez, 1-12. Los Ranchos de Albuquerque, New Mexico: Rio Grande Books, 2007.
Twitchell, Ralph Emerson. *The Leading Facts of New Mexican History, Vol. I: Facsimile of Original 1911 Edition.* Santa Fe, New Mexico: Sunstone Press, 2007.
Whiting, Lilian. *The Land of Enchantment: From Pike's Peak to the Pacific.* New York: Little, Brown, and Company, 1910.

Military District of New Mexico in Santa Fe. The further of the three residences facing Grant Street was the quarters of Ex-President Grant and family, when they visited Santa Fe, in 1886. Illustration from *Illustrated New Mexico, 1885* by W. G. Ritch.

                                        Cañon of the Rio Santa Fe.
                        The Fort.
            Palace Hotel.   Old Spanish Government Palace.
                        Residence of Gen. L. P. Bradley, Com'dg Dist.
                                                    General Offices.

rs' Quarters.
ast.
esident Grant and family, when they visited Santa Fe, in 1880.

STRICT OF NEW MEXICO.
nta Fe.)

16

Progressive Santa Fe, 1880–1912
by
Robert L. Spude

Around the turn of the last century, Santa Feans spoke of "progress" as a means to end all ills. The idea of progress was more than economic development; it had come to symbolize not only a city-wide but a nation-wide movement for reform. Historians give the period roughly 1890 to 1917 the name the Progressive Era, and in Santa Fe it manifested itself in a period of "Americanization" of the former Spanish and Mexican capital, where "progressive" minded citizens strove to reform government, social and cultural values, and the very appearance of their city. New residents with Eastern and Midwestern values desired to reshape the community to fit their image of what they had had back home, but, maybe, better. Civic leaders, men and women, including a series of significant mayors, brought controls on vice, improvement of public health, and, in general, changes for the common good, described here as how they believed the common good should be.

None of the new residents spoke more of being progressive than the town newspaper editor, Maximilian Eugene Frost of the Santa Fe *New Mexican,* the territory's most influential newspaper. Historian Ralph Twitchell said: "Through the columns of that newspaper he was able to mold public opinion in a manner unsurpassed by any journalist in the west."[1] Frost, whose southern genteel manner hid a bundle of energy, a steel hand in a velvet glove, held the editorial quill pen all but three years from 1887 until his death twenty-two years later. He wanted new residents, new homes, new businesses, economic expansion "to ensure a progressive city," which meant an end to "adobe town," the moniker given by the capital city's critics. In a piece titled "Progressive Santa Fe" in 1891, after a hard won fight for city incorporation, he declared that of Santa Fe, "her long lethargy has been cast off, and day by day, she makes gigantic strides in the rank of progress." Through his newspaper or as secretary of the territorial Bureau of Immigration he not only recorded events of the era, he influenced them.[2]

The outspoken editor of the Santa Fe *New Mexican*, Max Frost, helped shape "Progressive Santa Fe" of the 1890s and early 1900s. Sketch from *Las Vegas Daily Optic,* Courtesy Palace of the Governors Photo Archives (NMHM/DCA), negative number 7222.

The 1890s was not the first period the territorial press used the term "progressive" to describe new developments as a positive good. It took over press rhetoric when the Atchison, Topeka and Santa Fe Railroad's subsidiary began building across New Mexico and approached the capital. The railroad set off a boom and bust cycle that gave Santa Fe its one moment of Wild West popular culture mythology that most would not have called "progressive." In 1880, the railroad held up the good citizens of Santa Fe for $150,000 worth of county bonds in order to build them an 18 mile spur track of outmoded rail and below-standard grade. But the town leaders were euphoric and began the first major construction projects, mostly water system, which failed, and gas lights, which were outdated the moment they went into operation, to accompany a handful of Victorian business buildings and hotel built around the plaza. The wild and wooly moment came in the early eighties. (Even Billy the Kid came to town to spend a short while in the jail.) A mining boomlet occurred in the Cerrillos Hills, where every public official bought into a share of the mining claims; the Chicago & Santa Fe smelter, built on the edge of town—a sure sign of progress—belched a few puffs of smoke then closed permanently. Wild Bill Hickock's pard, Buckskin Charley Utter, moved from Deadwood to Santa Fe and opened the Little Church saloon on south San Francisco Street. The bust was hard, and by 1884 the financial panic hit, closing mines, businesses and Charley Utter's saloon, which moved to Socorro. The town's only salvation was the eastern and French money put into Catholic religious schools, hospital and completion of the magnificent cathedral. Just as important was the success of Santa Fe's political delegation led by the irascible Thomas Catron, which secured funding for the construction of Santa Fe's territorial capitol building, finally, and a penitentiary. Quipped an editorial in the *Kansas City Star*: "A penitentiary is exactly what they want—a large county penitentiary, and then some few laws, an incorruptible judge or two, and a corps of honest officers [of the law]."[3]

Editor Frost, himself caught up in the speculative boom and bust of the 1880s, took the chair of the *New Mexican* to help influence the drafting of "some few laws." Santa Fe county had a tumultuous government, where ballot boxes were stolen during elections, and the county clerk went to jail rather than certify an elected official. Frost, as did many other residents, saw the need for incorporation and creation of a separate municipal government as also necessary to change the city's tarnished reputation. Such papers as the Saint Louis *Republican*, *Harpers Weekly* of New York, *Kansas City Star*, and Chicago *Inter Ocean* described Santa Fe in the late 1880s–1890s as, besides corrupt, "musty with antiquity," having "no air of thrift," impoverished, and, with racist intent, "the land of the Greaser."[4] The generation of progressive reformers had to overcome overwhelming negative press.

By 1891, when the incorporation issue came to a head, the local economy had rebounded. The Atchison, Topeka & Santa Fe Railroad (AT&SF), during 1887–1888, completed track into Chicago and connecting it with Los Angeles, making it the longest railroad in the nation, and for Santa Fe brought more investors looking over opportunities for investment in the capital city. Just as importantly, a connection from the capital to the narrow gauge Denver & Rio Grande Railroad, a competitor to the AT&SF, was completed in 1887. Following the D&RG were a group of Denver speculators ambitious to invest in Santa Fe. Denverite E. T. Webber built the first three-story business block on the plaza, platted and promoted the city residential neighborhood of Buena Vista, and helped tout the region's agricultural and mineral potential to fellow Coloradans. He joined Frost in the push for city improvement, especially through the creation of a responsible government.[5]

A committee of businessmen—the Committee of Forty—raised funds to draft incorporation papers, decide on a boundary, and take a census. Although the Santa Fe River valley had an estimated 8,000 residents, the committee selected a boundary that ensured a positive voter outcome, from Irvine Street on the west to the brewery up Canyon on the east, and roughly the bottom of the valley north and south. Inside the boundary were 3,880 residents, with 1,083 eligible to vote. The *New Mexican* pointed out the good and the bad: how "all modern progress depends on incorporation." Frost published a letter by "tax payer" (probably Frost, who often published leading letters under a pseudonym), that outlined what was wanted, and what benefits would arise: street improvements, sidewalks with curbs, gutters, and a good sewage system. The town needed a marshal and more garbage carts, lighted streets, new streets opened and better bridge repair. He wanted jobs for the poor. Lastly, he wanted someone to stop saloons and restaurants from dumping slop and emptying spittoons in the street. He complained, behind the saloons of lower San Francisco was a cesspool with "a stench unequaled in any city in the world." He suggested tourists should visit the spot in order to give them a strong whiff of "a genuine Santa Fe smell." Incorporation would put workers to work cleaning this up and stopping it from happening again.[6]

A small group, mostly Hispanics, questioned the plan for municipal government and suspected it just another "scheme of Americans to drive the Mexican-speaking [sic.] people out of town." Frost detailed benefits to all, especially for the Hispanics in his Spanish language edition, *Nuevo Mexicano*. In the end, on June 2, 1891, the town voted 8 to 1 for incorporation. The town celebrated, while Frost added: "The young Spanish American showed his true colors to-day. Set him down in favor of progress."[7]

The subsequent election of the town's first two mayors, Missourian William Thornton and Santa Fe native Manuel Valdez, was important in the setting of a positive beginning for the government. Thornton, a successful cattleman and mine speculator had been a lawyer. He ran unopposed on the "businessman's non-partisan" ticket and received every vote but one of the 569 votes for the unpaid position. He was essential, along with council member Ed Bartlett, the sitting territorial attorney general, in establishing the framework for the legal code, taxes and ordinances, and franchises—for a new water system, electric plant, telephone lines, and a street car, all built except the latter. He also hired the first town marshal and deputies, mostly Hispanic, garbage cart men, street sprinkler wagon, physician, and attorney. Considered able, Thornton a life-long Democrat would be appointed governor less than a year after leaving the mayor's chair in April 1892.[8]

The first contested election pitted grocer and land owner Manuel Valdez against long-time resident merchant Bernard Seligman. The Democrat Seligman called his opponent a "Mexican," which brought Frost out swinging. "The *New Mexican*," he wrote, "deplores this issue of race that is being raised in the city campaign." He defended Valdez, stating, the opposition calls him a "Mexican, … which in its ordinary sense there is a great deal of honor, chivalry and bravery attached to this term, but as used by these individuals it implies a disrespect." Frost and voters should respect Valdez as not only "a native of Santa Fe," but as "a true American citizen." Valdez became the first Hispanic mayor by 21 votes. Oddly he took the predominately American ward, while losing in the predominately Hispanic ward, not unusual in the contentious Santa Fe political arena. Hispanics would be active participants in the city government from its initiation and within a few years they had taken over what was thought an American trick to "drive them out of town," and had held the mayor's seat four times (Valdez, 1892–1893; Pedro Delgado, 1896–1897; R. L. Baca, 1899; Amado Chavez, 1901–1902) and were the majority (after 1898) in the city council. Mayor Valdez followed in Thornton's footsteps on major issues, while adding a spirit of volunteerism for the common good. As mayor he donated land for the extension of city streets across his west Santa Fe lands. Probably the most contentious issue facing the council, besides taxes, was the opening of roads through agricultural lands to create a city grid, especially to connect new developments or "city additions" with the core. Valdez led the way for expanding the city grid.[9]

The politics of Santa Fe's African American community is little known. Residing near the railroad yard and along Johnson Street adjacent the African American Methodist church and the home of African American pioneer Henry Johnson, their vote was split into two different wards making it difficult to gauge their impact. William Slaughter, a popular barber on the plaza and owner of the Alameda Bath House and Barber Shop, was a member of the Republican central committee as a delegate at large. Republicans strongly supported incorporation, and voted for Valdez. Supposedly, the party of Lincoln continued to hold the African American voters within its membership.[10]

Valdez worked with councilman Bartlett to develop an agreement with the newly formed Woman's Board of Trade and Library Association to do broadly defined "good works" for the city, including taking over management of the town plaza. This fit into the progressive philosophy of using "volunteerism" to accomplish good for the community. It also provided an outlet for women of some leisure—barred by custom, perhaps also by inclination, from having careers—needed outlets for their surplus time and unused talents. The Woman's Board of Trade and Library Association was incorporated in May 1893, but the women who organized it had for nearly a decade worked toward making Santa Fe "the prettiest city in the Southwest." First president Cora Bartlett, wife of councilman Bartlett, was the leading spirit with, wrote Frost, "some very energetic and true women who have the good of the city and its advancement in every way at heart." Ida Rivenburg, wife of the owner of the Santa Fe Nursery, became second president and first head of the city's parks committee. They took over the plaza management through hiring of a police guard to patrol and tidy the grounds; raised funds for stone curbing and walks; and initiated the replacement of the town well and spout—what Frost called the "fountain of death"—with the Lamy Memorial Fountain. New grasses, with their "keep off the grass signs," tree plantings, and repaired gazebo appeared through the 1890s, making the plaza "one of the beauty spots of the valley." They helped not just the plaza; they maintained library rooms, a gym, did relief work, had a committee on the prevention of cruelty to animals; and had a reception committee that took over formal receptions for visiting dignitaries. This was an organization of upper middle class elites—wives of bankers, lawyers, large property owners and businessmen—that not unlike their counterparts in other Progressive Era communities provided city services, especially city beautification, yet to be totally funded by governments.[11]

The Woman's Board of Trade gained in stature if not real power with its successes. Probably the greatest coup was acquisition of the abandoned lands of Fort Marcy for the city's school board. Located north of the plaza, Fort Marcy had been closed by the military once the protective arm of Secretary of War Stephen B. Elkins was removed. The military base lands were transferred to the Department of Interior, which was besieged by the women. Fortunately, Elkins was now a U. S. Senator and aided, along with many others, in the transfer of the property to the city. In 1903, after his May 5 visit to Santa Fe, President Theodore Roosevelt formally transferred the grounds. The board leased or sold lots for school needs while the women sought money from the Carnegie Library Fund and other groups. They built their show case office and library on the grounds. The women were also influential in other arenas. Although not a suffrage group their members pressed for suffrage and were instrumental in the passage of a territorial bill allowing women to serve on school boards. (Taos had the first female member.) They also pushed for universal suffrage and formed a lobbying group when New Mexico's first U. S. Senator, Thomas Catron, unwisely let it be known he opposed woman suffrage. Unfortunately, the women of Santa Fe would have to wait until passage of the 19th amendment to the Constitution in 1918 before they received universal voting rights.[12]

Among the many legal minds set to work to help the women's club was Ralph Waldo Emerson Twitchell. Known today for his history writings, Twitchell, as a young man, had become embroiled in Santa Fe politics. He served as district attorney and then mayor during one of its most violent periods. The more academically minded author/lawyer Twitchell was thus thrust unprepared into the realm of cleaning up vice and corruption.[13]

Arriving in Santa Fe in 1883, Twitchell represented, in his own words, the "new people, imbued with modern ideas and a full realization of the future," who came to New Mexico in the late 19th century. He had grown up in Missouri listening to the tales of Mexican War veterans, and, after graduating from the University of Michigan law school, was hired as a junior corporate lawyer for the Atchison, Topeka, and Santa Fe Railroad based in their Santa Fe headquarters. At age 33, he was convinced by Republican party leaders to run for mayor; he was elected, as he liked to claim, to be the youngest mayor of the oldest city. His former home town newspaper, the *Kansas City Star*, made much of the young mayor, praised his abilities and waxed poetic about his young adventurer image right out of a gay nineties novel by Richard Harding Davis. Twitchell later recalled, he served as mayor for only one year, but it was "365 days of grief."[14]

While in the position he pushed hard for the progressive ideals laid out in 1891—he had streets graded, new sidewalks built, new roads opened. He worked to have the main business street curbed and paved and have sewers built, against recalcitrant business owners. He found himself unpopular for new taxes, such as the one on bicycles. He tried to close saloons on Sunday, denied the permit for a bull fight, and temporarily closed the opera house because of a "naughty show." The Presbyterians complained to him for not removing a pig pen from near their church. And it was discovered the city had no record of its Spanish grant for the town's land, a major issue for the remainder of the decade finally resolved in the city's favor by Congress. He worked with the boosters at the Chamber of Commerce to publish his booklet on Santa Fe as a health resort, and wrote a long running bit of town promotion for the *New Mexican*. But he was burdened by petty feuds over his selection of city employees and consultants. In frustration, he sent a letter to Max Frost, who published his tirade. He whined, "will this city ever find room to discuss anything other than politics and public office?" He listed needed city improvements, but further complained: "Our supposed best citizens will congregate around the Arcade corner and discuss these propositions as though the whole world and its right to revolve depended upon some applicant for a $12 a week job." The only praise was to the women's work on the plaza as "advertisement of progress."[15]

Twitchell's problems included a volunteer fire department ready to quit unless they received new equipment—Frost called them little better than a mob. He resolved their complaints by gaining a public subscription for new equipment and commitment for a new fire hall. More troublesome was bar room violence, even his brother Beecher was beat up by a gang. However, the appointed police force he inherited had become violent and unruly, or derelict of duty—wrote Frost, "God help Santa Fe, for assuredly her people have deserted her." He set up a separate city committee to oversee the force, provide reforms and justify the firing of two city police officers.[16]

The "youngest mayor of the oldest city," Ralph E. Twitchell served one year, 1893–1894, but recalled it as "365 days of grief." Sketch from *New Mexican* September 9, 1891.

Unfortunately, tragedy followed this act. An impending series of political rallies necessitated the immediate appointment of temporary city police. Twitchell appointed city councilman Canuto Alarid policeman to aid Alarid's brother, the city marshal, keep peace during the rally. A mixture of alcohol and insults led to gun shots. The mayor witnessed a one-time Texas gunslinger now county deputy sheriff, out of his jurisdiction but not his party line, gun down Alarid. Twitchell sought peace through the courts and committees, even after out of office. Santa Fe had been the scene of several murders, including the year before of newly elected councilman Francisco Chavez, Santa Fe county's ex-sheriff. The committee initiated reforms to get "politics out of the police force." In concert with former Mayor Thornton, now governor, the city also raised rewards and pursued the murderers. But the reform of the police in town would still be a complaint of the last mayor under the territorial days, a problem for progressives. For Santa Fe, the shoot outs continued to hurt the town's image, one where the muckraking *San Francisco Examiner* and the *Kansas City Star* claimed "the pistol and the bowie knife are important factors in native politics." For the next election, Twitchell at least shut down the saloons to keep liquor from disrupting the polls.[17]

Vice was a major city concern during the Progressive Era. A number of laws and regulations ended, or at least more closely controlled, prostitution, gambling, and saloons. Santa Fe's reforms and history would follow the national pattern. The territorial legislature passed an act in 1889 making it illegal for women to enter saloons for drinking, singing, playing cards, playing musical instruments, dealing cards or running other games, which was slowly enforced. In Santa Fe, one of the first acts of Mayor Thornton was to ensure the police kept drunk women from the streets, per ordinance. The council also made prostitution illegal, though it was a law more to enhance revenue than eliminate the sin. For example, Frost reported the city marshal arresting a madam, who was fined five dollars and charged seven more for court fees, but was shortly back on the streets. In 1901, the legislature passed another law restricting red light district cribs from 700 feet from any school, church, fraternal lodge, seminary, opera house or public hall. The city council debated whether to further restrict the prostitutes by putting them in one fenced-in area. The ordinance failed to pass, but the prostitutes and their places of work were kept hidden, especially from the eyes of young girls who might wander by.[18]

Legalized gambling came under attack as well. Frost's newspaper, according to a historian of the New Mexico press, was "more than any other single paper became the spokesman for the reform movement in New Mexico ... particularly effective in helping to end legal gambling and in closing saloons on Sundays."[19] The first major impetus came from the outside, when the Congressman from Maine pushed for Federal legislation eliminating gambling from the territories. The Santa

Fe school board and others protested the possible tax revenue loss and the bill was defeated. But pressure for anti-gambling legislation continued. Ex-mayor Charles Speis now in the territorial legislature wrote an anti-gambling bill which finally passed in 1907. All gambling halls and devices were to be shut down by January 1, 1908, leaving Nevada the last vestige for gambling.[20]

Saloons had been affected early, when the council passed its first liquor license fee. Before it went into effect, Frost noted, "many of the *tendejones* about the suburbs are already closed. The owners of these little gin-mills will henceforth engage in other business." After restricting prostitution and ending gambling, Santa Fe progressives continued the attack and in 1909 Mayor José Sena and the city council voted 5 to 4 to rid the city of saloons. An uproar ensued including a lawsuit that nullified the city decision until the territory could pass a local option law. In the meantime, the council raised the saloon license fees. A final vote in 1915 barely failed to close the saloons, but the liquor dealers agreed to be more self-regulating and eager to pay the license fees. In 1917, with state-wide prohibition Santa Fe went officially "dry."[21]

Another major issue for New Mexico progressives was public health. The Progressive Era coincided with rapidly evolving and more successful medical practices. New Mexico had been swept by contagious diseases since founding of the colony, but the railroad and the easy movement of infected individuals brought a series of disastrous epidemics in the 1880s and 1890s. The worst problem was a series of small pox epidemics. In the words of resident Thomas Catron, "the Mexican has a horror of the small pox. Where skilled physicians are scarce it is his greatest enemy."[22]

One of the first acts of the new city government was to set up a board of health, appoint a city physician, and provide funding for medicine for the poor. Dr. John H. Sloan served as first city physician as well as three terms as mayor at a critical time during these epidemics. Sloan was born in Missouri but trained at the University of Cincinnati Medical School, specializing in lung diseases. In 1883 he moved to Santa Fe, then experiencing a growth spurt, and quickly developed an extensive private practice. As city physician he initiated a haphazard program for vaccinating school children and providing drugs for the poor. The medicine provider, a local drug store, when discovered gouging the city was ousted in favor of the Sisters of Charity's St. Vincent Hospital.[23]

During Sloan's administration the new, more reliable city water system began operation under the franchise with the Municipal Investments Company of Chicago, which provided better water service. He also continued pushing the construction of sewers. But as Frost editorialized, "warm weather and standing filth will make Water street a hot bed of contagion." Sloan ordered the clean-up of pools of stagnant water, which bred disease as well as the removal of a slaughterhouse and cow corrals from the city limits. Still an open pool on Johnson Street bred disease, making 40 residents sick in 1895. Mayor Hudson, who served between Sloan's terms as mayor, became ill from the water, had a severe "gastric disease" and died in office; his acting and then short-term replacement mayor R. L. Baca, also became ill.[24]

During New Mexico's small pox epidemic of 1898, the last and worst, Santa Fe was hit in 1898–1899. Mayor Sloan had a quarantine hospital built a mile out of town, something necessary because the illness needed to be isolated. He ordered all school children vaccinated, critical to the control of the disease, but still parents were reluctant to conform. Frost used the press to alleviate any concerns about complications—that modern science had made the small pox vaccination successful. We do not know the impacts of the efforts. Frost reported only three deaths, but noted many more outside the town in the county. Statistics are unavailable (a proposal by an early city council to record births and deaths unfortunately was tabled and not until the 1920s was a regular vital statistics system inaugurated by the state), but, for example, church records showed 151, mostly children had died in Tome Parish. The 1900 and 1910 census include information about the number of children born to each woman as well as the number of their children still living. Santa Fe women's responses revealed a shocking number of childhood deaths. One sixty year old woman had borne twenty-six children but only six were still alive. The 1910 census suggests that women who had children born after the 1898 epidemic—and after the city had initiated a public health system—had a higher survival rate. Clean water, vaccinations, and ridding the town of open cesspools were undoubtedly factors in the decline in childhood deaths in the city. The territory followed suit with a 1901 law requiring all children be vaccinated. This was followed by corporations, primarily railroads, which transported much of the disease, requiring that all employees show proof of vaccination prior to employment.[25]

The regulation and control of corporations, especially railroads, were Progressive Era goals. Railroads were the dominant industry of New Mexico during the Progressive Era, and during those years, the Atchison, Topeka & Santa Fe Railroad (AT&SF) controlled New Mexico's economic life. The AT&SF had blocked the Denver & Rio Grande from building into Santa Fe through a stock take over and short-term shot gun wedding. After the D&RG reached Santa Fe in 1887 through local businessmen's effort, the AT&SF used every means to successfully block any construction south. Through its "headquarters" office in Santa Fe, attorney Henry Waldo and his assistant Ralph Twitchell manipulated legislators and wrote legislation favorable to the firm. Corporate attorneys were ridiculed in Frost's *New Mexican*, except for Waldo. Although a life-long Democrat, he was a power behind the Republican party as well. The power of the AT&SF briefly broke down with the financial panic of 1893, which eventually led to the line's bankruptcy. The economic depression of 1893–1896 swept the country and with it the many small and large businesses of the West. During the mid-1890s, Santa Fe lost a bank, stores, hotel, and saloons. With a reorganization, the AT&SF transferred its Santa Fe offices to Las Vegas, and with it went its solicitors, Judge Waldo and Ex-Mayor Twitchell. The railroad's and the territory's prosperity would not return until the late 1890s.[26]

The Atchison, Topeka & Santa Fe Railroad's hegemony was also threatened during the third wave of transcontinental railroad building at the beginning of the twentieth century. In 1900, the Chicago, Rock Island & Pacific announced that it would build across the Southwest to southern California. At the same time, George Gould began making hints of extending his Denver & Rio Grande Western Railway possibly to the Gulf of Mexico via Santa Fe and southeast New Mexico. The Rock Island and Gould's ambitions sparked a group of New Mexicans into action. Willard S. Hopewell, with a number of Pennsylvanians led by politician William H. "Bull" Andrews, proposed building a rail link between the end of the Denver & Rio Grande at Santa Fe to a connection with the under construction Rock Island line in eastern New Mexico.[27]

Hopewell, a Sierra county rancher and mine owner, had served in the territorial legislature and was on a key committee to end the capital removal ambitions of residents of Albuquerque (although some would say the only way to get the capital out of Santa Fe was to get Max Frost out of the capital). He also was on the commission to build the new capitol, completed in 1899, but dedicated in 1900. Hopewell opened an office in Santa Fe and began speculating on lands in the town and in the Estancia Valley to the south. He proposed building the Santa Fe Central, with Bull Andrews relocated to New Mexico as president, and with Pittsburgh capital. Andrews became a political force in New Mexico and served as its Delegate to Congress, 1905–1912. Their railroad proposal met with support from the city, where the city fathers donated land for the yards near the AT&SF depot, after Hopewell agreed to build a "Union Depot" with the D&RG.[28]

The AT&SF stayed out of the agreement, showing its continued anathema for anything related to the competition—and much to the consternation of Union depot booster Max Frost. With the construction of the Santa Fe Central, the booster rhetoric in the *New Mexican* written by Frost was unequaled by anything he had written before. The Santa Fe Central was to link Santa Fe with the great Rock Island line, providing a better, alternative route than the AT&SF to El Paso to the south, and Kansas City and Chicago to the East. In hushed rumors, the press spread stories also of George Gould acquiring the Santa Fe Central as part of his empire building line to the Gulf, placing Santa Fe on the mainline of a significant railroad (Gould would abandon the proposal, instead extending his D&RGW not south from Santa Fe but west from Utah to California—to the disappointment of Santa Fe town boosters).[29]

> # THE
> # Santa Fe Central Railway Co.
> ## SUNSHINE ROUTE VIA. TORRANCE, N. M.
> ### GATEWAY
>
> Connects at Torrance, N. M., with the El Paso & North-Eastern and the Chicago, Rock Island & Pacific Ry. Systems. At Santa Fe with the Denver & Rio Grande Railway. Route Freight via. C. R. I. & P., via. Torrance New Mexico. Best, Safest and Shortest Route to all points, for Passengers and Freight.
>
> **W. H. ANDREWS,**
> Prest. & Gen'l Mgr.
>
> **S. B. GRIMSHAW,**
> Asst. to Pres. & G. M.
>
> **J. A. KNOX, T. F. & P. A.** F. DIBERT, Gen'l Immigration Agt.
>
> **SANTA FE, NEW MEXICO**

Advertisement for the Santa Fe Central Railroad, "the Sunshine Route," in the *New Mexico Business Directory, 1905–1906.* Denver: Gazetteer Publishing Co, 1905.

The completion of the Santa Fe Central in 1903 connecting Santa Fe to the Rock Island system coincided with a period of modest economic growth and prosperity for Santa Fe. The solid basics of sheep raising and wool shipments, coupled with agricultural produce were the economic lifeblood of the county. The operation of a few mines in the southern part of the county helped with the tax base. The costs of living had dropped with cheaper coal for heat and electric power brought by rail from nearby fields as an example (although outside journalists continued to revel in showing Santa Fe's burro alley and the burros laden with wood for residential fireplaces). The council funded more sewer lines and sidewalks, street lights and paving. Business leaders still touted the region's healthy climate and sunshine while the new building and loan association provided cheaper loans for the new business blocks going up around the plaza and nearby. Brick cottages and newer revival style residences—Dutch colonial, Bungalow—appeared, especially in the Buena Vista neighborhood and the north east side.[30]

Santa Fe had three different rail lines, more than any other New Mexico rail center. Here, the New Mexico Central, formerly the Santa Fe Central, runs a special out of Santa Fe's Union Depot, ca. 1910s. T. Harmon Parkhurst photographer. Courtesy Palace of the Governors Photo Archives (NMHM/DCA), negative number 169617.

Twitchell wrote, "the promoters of the enterprise [Santa Fe Central Railroad] encouraged and brought others to see and learn, whose influence on the community was immediately noticeable." During this period a group of young, new voices took over the city government and pushed for more extensive progressive changes. The young Turks included Ishmael Sparks, who had arrived from Denver as builder of the town's first telephone system in 1893, now managed its electric plant as well, and Adelbert R. Gibson, a Cleveland railroad builder whose tuberculosis caused his move to Santa Fe, who constructed the Sunmount Sanatorium. Both would serve as mayors. Sparks caused a split in the Republican party ranks and became mayor after the Old Guard's retreat. Sparks proposed a more beautiful river front, a new "Riverside Drive" along a more landscaped Santa Fe River (and properly defined river bed and property boundary lines). He also pushed for the Santa Fe Central Railroad concessions and for the union depot; being echoed by Frost in an editorial on the vision for the future: "Santa Fe should cease to rely on a reverence for the antique to attract visitors. Ancient possessions are all very well, so far as they go, but for every person attracted to a city because of relics a dozen might be induced to come by modern conveniences and evidence of progress."[31] The newspaper reported somewhat blandly of the destruction of historic adobe buildings and their replacement with newer stores and business blocks. Ex-Governor LeBaron Bradford Prince and other preservation minded residents fought the new group to save the old Palace of the Governors, which he had slowly taken over as the museum of the New Mexico Historical Society. Prince's outrage— at as well as edification of—the newcomers began by comparing the "Palace" to Faneuil Hall in Boston and Independence Hall in Philadelphia.[32]

Bungalows and cottages, the residential neighborhoods around the core of the old town began to acquire the look of a comfortable Midwestern townscape. The Buena Vista development seen here was promoted by Denver transplants during the 1890s. The new penitentiary is in the distance, along future St. Francis Drive. Aaron B. Craycraft photographer. Courtesy Palace of the Governors Photo Archives (NMHM/DCA), negative number 16537.

Besides his interest in history, Prince had an avid interest in natural history and was an experienced horticulturalist. This brought him into collaboration with the new city leaders. While territorial chief justice and later as governor, Prince also put his over-active energy to raising fruits and vegetables, planting orchards and flower beds around Santa Fe and in the nearby Santa Cruz River valley. The son, grandson, and great-grandson of horticulturalists in the east, one considered the founding father of horticulture in colonial New England, Prince organized and became first president of the New Mexico Horticulture Society. He gathered a following that started an annual horticulture fair in Santa Fe through the late 1890s and into the early 1900s. He brought in Grant Rivenburg, a German who began an extensive nursery just east of the cathedral between the German's Queen Anne home and the Santa Fe River—"no prettier spot in the Southwest," wrote Frost. Rivenburg also put in an ice plant and cannery. Prince influenced Hispanics as well as other Anglos. For example, Marcelino Garcia, from an old family of the area, developed a Jersey cow dairy adjacent Santa Fe and a fruit orchard 18 miles to the north.[33]

His horticultural pursuits would lead him to be one of the leaders in one of the western progressive's self-proclaimed greatest triumph, the irrigation movement. Prince was active in the National Irrigation Congress beginning with one of its first meetings in Albuquerque in 1895, and was a participant in the passage of the 1902 Federal reclamation or Newlands Act, which provided for Federally supported irrigation projects. He organized the Santa Fe Irrigation and Improvement Company consolidated lands and water rights, with hopes of converting more Santa Fe River valley lands to orchards and farms, through the new act. A major new dam higher up the river, lateral canals and branches were proposed. Irrigation was the new Western cure-all, and he and Frost touted it. Dubbed by one contemporary, "The Horace Greeley of the Southwest," Frost as secretary of the territorial Bureau of Immigration used its publications to promote irrigation as the way to bring more settlers west. However, Frost and Prince's vision brought them into immediate conflict with Hispanic water users in the Santa Fe River valley.[34]

Previously, some river water rights were consolidated by a Chicago-based company for the city water system, but clashes had already erupted with the older acequia owners. Prince had limited empathy for Hispanic economic systems—at a National Irrigation Congress speech he belittled the Spanish system while praising the Mormons as the true irrigation pioneers. However, in New Mexico an acequia is a cultural institution more than an irrigation ditch, which is a basic economic unit of agricultural production. Prince's plans for consolidating the water into a rational system of irrigation based on a bureaucratic water district model did not fit the long traditional use of the farmers of the Santa Fe valley. While Max Frost might praise the Hispanic farmers of the Mesilla Valley for giving up "wasteful acequias" and their water rights for the larger, Federal Rio Grande project (and today criticized for that act), the Santa Fe valley water users saw no advantage. And they were a powerful political force. All knew there were three local governments in Santa Fe: the county, the municipal, and the acequias and their *mayordomo*. Prince's company attempted to use the courts to condemn the land owned by Hispanics for his 2,192 acre reservoir, but lost. Hispanics' fear of Anglos taking their land was well founded. Prince's proposed Santa Fe Irrigation company failed to "rationalize" the water in the valley by the time the economic Panic of 1907 put an end to his over-ambitious company. Prince left the company but a new backer later constructed a dam on the Rio Hondo south of Santa Fe that failed to meet the promoter's expectations. The Progressive Era agenda of large irrigation projects were not feasible in the Santa Fe valley without damaging or ending the acequia system.[35]

The Panic of 1907 did further damage to Santa Fe's economy. The already financially strapped Santa Fe Central Railway began its slow fall into bankruptcy, only to limp along afterwards as the re-named New Mexico Central. Long before that, Hopewell had closed his office and moved to Albuquerque to become one of its leading boosters. He was followed by Gibson, who sold out his Sunmount sanitarium to the Mera brothers. Sparks went into real estate development. In the last years of the territorial period, Santa Fe's leadership shifted to the Old Guard, including lawyer-politician Tom Catron, Jose Sena of a prominent family dating back to Spanish colonial years, and Arthur Seligman, son of a pioneer merchant family. Although famed for their work in other spheres, Catron and Sena are best known in the Santa Fe community for their long term commitment to its school system.[36]

Santa Fe had in place religious schools and Indian school by 1890, but the early public school system lacked organization and support. The early attempts for an effective public school territorial law was opposed by Bishop Lamy and the Catholic church, which preferred religious schools that provided education of the whole person, including the spiritual, not just the "Godless" three Rs of the Yankee system. "Nothing," Lamy declared, "shall induce us to admit a system of schools which is positively condemned by the Holy Apostolic Roman Catholic Church." In 1891, after Lamy's death, the legislature passed a public schools system act with teeth; Governor Prince placed Santa Fe native Amado Chavez in charge as first superintendent of public instruction, who set up the secular system. Santa Fe's incorporation coincided with the new law and worked to introduce the new system, but was hampered by lack of funds (the local bank often giving interest free loans to the city in order to keep the schools open). The passage of a congressional act in 1896 giving New Mexico public land to be leased for school operations, helped but more importantly was the successful acquisition of the 17 acres of the former Fort

Marcy by the school board. The school board sold acreage to businesses that helped fund the system. Coincidently, Amado Chavez served as mayor when the land was guaranteed to the school board. Mayors Catron and Sena, though antagonistic toward each other on many issues agreed on helping the public schools and carried out the popular wishes of building new schools, the Catron School being one. They also pushed for the mandatory attendance of all 2500 of Santa Fe's school-age children. Sena, a former educator himself, also saw that the much coveted high school diploma was available to all, a Progressive Era goal. Sena High School was named after the mayor for his long-term school board work.[37]

By the end of the period, Santa Fe citizens faced a number of new challenges not the least of which was the appearance of the automobile, the first arriving in the territory in 1900. Mayor Sena moved the council to regulate the "devil wagons." The city Fathers passed an ordinance limiting the speedsters to 4 mph along congested San Francisco Street and 14 mph out Cerrillos Road. The legislature created the Good Roads Commission, fore-runner of the state highway commission, in 1909, too, which surveyed and the next year built the winding auto road down the La Bajada to Albuquerque, a boon for travel between the capital and the largest city. The Good Roads Commission also boosted a "New Santa Fe Trail" to Kansas City, part of a nation-wide Old Trails System (and eventually, in 1926, part of the new Route 66). In 1911, they marked the end of the old Santa Fe Trail with an etched stone at the southeast corner of the plaza. Within the city limits, garages and auto camps were built to serve the growing number of "tin lizzie" tourists.[38]

During Mayor Sena's term the city leaders also began the shift toward more actively promoting the town's history to the increasing number of tourists. In 1909, the community came together to support the creation of a Museum of New Mexico by the territorial legislature, and to house the new museum in the Palace of the Governors. In many ways, the birth of the Museum of New Mexico marks the beginning of the new era of Santa Fe development, still fitting into the philosophy of progressives, but one more receptive to capturing the flavor of the historic city. Twitchell, who would soon move back to the town, with Sena, became a leading proponent of this new movement. That year he authored a pamphlet for the town's three-hundredth anniversary, about the "New—Old Santa Fe," and then began publishing his long string of history books. This movement, the City Different and the creation of the Santa Fe Style—the use of Spanish mission and Pueblo Indian architectural elements and crafts—would redefine the city in the twentieth century. We don't know what Max Frost would have thought of Santa Fe Style for on October 13, 1909, "death gained a victory" against the editor. In his last years, the slowly going crippled and blind editor had news copy read to him by his wife. He meticulously edited the paper until near the end. He was buried by the Masons, being a 33d degree member and its historian. His memory is kept in that building as flamboyant and expressive as the editor, the town's Masonic Scottish Rites Temple.³⁹

Frost and his progressive contemporaries built the core of a city that they had envisioned. In 1910—the year statehood legislation passed and progressivism would move into high gear in the larger state arena—the Santa Fe born, thirty-nine year old mayor Arthur Seligman took hold of the city and would boast of building or paving more roads, building more concrete bridges, and providing more for the common good at schools, charities and public health (more vaccinations) than his two predecessors—a politician's boast that would help him eventually gain the governor's chair.⁴⁰ The aging Ex-Governor Prince, relegated to the idle ranks of the town's abundant appointive ex-politicians, was still in charge of part of the adobe Governors' Palace as a museum and reliquary for the ancients; author of a half dozen books he was not without his bias. The short, dignified man with the long graying beard and wrinkled face, with silk hat and cane, sometimes backed sometimes opposed by the old families, the Senas, the Delgados, the Ortizes, and his histories corrected in the Spanish language history by Hispano Benjamin M. Read.⁴¹

Progressive Santa Fe: three story brick business blocks (the 1891 Webber Building at right), cement curbs and sewers placed by the new city government, electric power and telephone lines of Mayor Sparks' company, and a shaded plaza thanks to the Women's Board of Trade. The automobile section of the De Vargas Pageant, July 4, 1911, is circling the plaza. Henry Dendahl photographer. Courtesy Palace of the Governors Photo Archives (NMHM/DCA), negative number 15262.

Throughout the 1910s the town retained something of simplicity and bucolic charm. Most of the valley inhabitants were Hispanic, *gente* of the soil—descendants of those who had moved in with the founding of the capital, and people of some means who came from the smaller villages. It was a city of homes. The *ricos*, among them the Princes and the Senas, by no means ostentatious dwelt for the most part on Palace Avenue. Here were the commodious *haciendas* or two story town houses being added to by the new merchant princes with their Victorian, Queen Anne and other "revival" architecture style homes, still standing on the east side. Most people walked to their work, in the field or in the offices and businesses about the plaza. It was a friendly city. The best of men would pause and refresh themselves at the old Lamy fountain on the plaza and to exchange pleasantries; and all through the Sunday afternoons the young men would stroll around the plaza while the young ladies promenaded in the opposite direction, each not speaking to the other. The plaza was the gathering place softened by the years, and by shade trees and grass.[42]

Weekends were crowded with hunting parties or fishing outings to the Pecos, quilting bees, fraternal lodge meetings, church, or baseball. Special days like the festival of Corpus Cristi or Memorial Day brought the crowds. The old gray headed men, the Civil War veterans, would be reduced in numbers with each Memorial Day's parade; their remains sometime in uniform being carried, usually from the Cathedral, down past the Soldiers Monument, the obelisk they built in the center of the plaza, and to the National Cemetery. Grand Army of the Republic local commander Antonio Ortiz, then Perfecto Armijo marched behind the caskets, then they too followed their comrades of Val Verde and Glorieta to the last call for duty.[43]

In the waning days of the territorial years, the AT&SF railroad began running its "Tourist Flyer," soon after renamed the "Navajo," the prelude to the grand era of passenger train travel.[44] The train stopped at the new Fred Harvey house, El Ortiz, at Lamy, which set the mythic "land of *poco tiempo*" ambience for the traveler. The run from there on the upgraded track to Santa Fe ended at the AT&SF's Spanish mission style depot, completed in 1909. The increased tourist traffic started Santa Fe on its new economic panacea, tourism. At work were the mayor and the town on a new municipal plan to make their town more appealing, the Plan of 1912, especially to the increasing number of visitors. But the plan would have been familiar to the previous city leaders, its plantings and beautification, where Riverside Drive became The Alameda. The philosophy was the same, to build a clean, healthy beautiful Santa Fe and was accomplishable. For the progressive citizens of the generation before had built a strong foundation on which to build the City Different.

Subsequent generations have criticized the work of Santa Fe's progressives. Not their efforts in public health, or in establishing city government, or education, for that has, for the most part, been forgotten, but their efforts to create a physical environment imitative of contemporary Midwestern capitals, an instant Topeka, or recreated Des Moines. The reminiscences of Ruth Laughlin, daughter of progressive lawyer/banker Napolean Bonaparte Laughlin, is an example: after the success of the City Different movement, she wrote that "the decision was not made without a struggle, however, for the herd instinct of building every American town alike was strong in those American pioneers who had come in with the railroads to make a new center out of an old Spanish capital."[45] The respect for the ambience and built environment of the "Spanish capital" was worthy of preservation and protection from some of the misguided desires of the railroad-riding newcomers, but the progressives deserve a more fair appraisal of community building, broadly defined, and their part in Santa Fe's history.

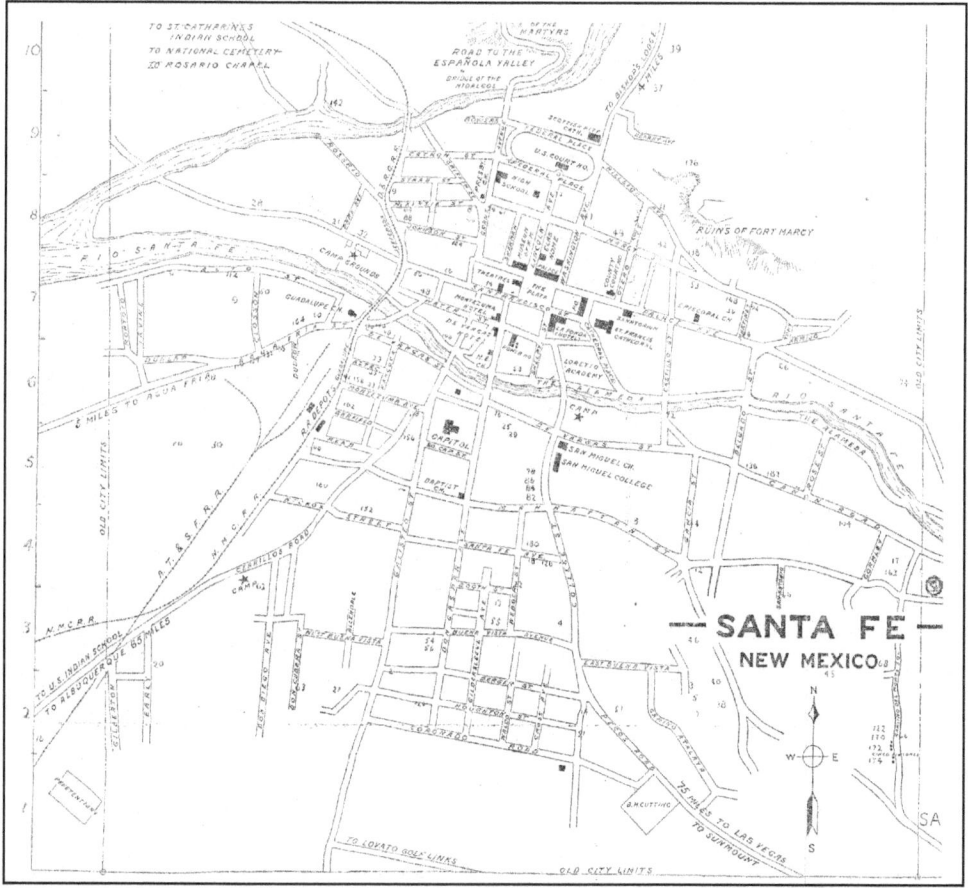

A map of the city the progressives built, ca. 1910s, shows the three railroads, the more uniform street grids of the new neighborhoods around the historic core, and prominent landmarks, such as the new capitol, penitentiary, power plant, road to Sunmount Sanitarium, and a golf course. Chamber of Commerce, Map of Santa Fe, n.d., author's collection.

17

The Cure at the End of the Trail
Seeking Health While Transforming a Town
1880–1940

by

Nancy Owen Lewis

Thousands of invalids journeyed to New Mexico from 1880–1940 seeking a cure for tuberculosis, the leading cause of death in America. Although the tubercle bacillus had been discovered in 1882, the development of streptomycin and other effective drugs would not occur until the 1940s. During the intervening decades, the medically approved regimen consisted of nutritious food, fresh air, and rest, preferably in a high, dry, and sunny place. New Mexico, with its high elevation, abundant sunshine, and arid climate was considered ideal. The New Mexico Bureau of Immigration, established in 1880, wasted no time in advertising the territory's healing climate as a way to promote New Mexico during its long struggle for statehood. Santa Fe began touting its own therapeutic properties and would soon become a major health destination.

Josiah Gregg, in fact, raved about the city's salubrious climate in his 1844 publication, *Commerce of the Prairies*.[1] A lawyer by training, he became a Santa Fe trader after his physician prescribed a trip to the high prairies as a cure for consumption. By the time he reached Santa Fe from Independence, "his relief was so satisfactory that he at once engaged regularly in the trade and continued the business for many years, enjoying comparatively excellent health."[2]

In the absence of x-rays or other tests, Gregg's doctor, like other nineteenth century physicians, would have based his diagnosis on severity of the symptoms. If the patient had a persistent cough, irritation in the throat, pains in the chest, and a racing pulse, the diagnosis would likely be consumption, especially if there was a fever or blood in the sputum. A chronic disease characterized by acute attacks alternating with periods of remission, it could take years for a patient to reach the final stage of extreme emaciation, uncontrollable diarrhea, and hemorrhaging resulting in death.

Until 1882, tuberculosis was not considered contagious. Those who developed it were thought to have an inherited predisposition that could be exacerbated by living in a cold, damp climate or having an "irritating" occupation such as the law, ministry, or teaching.[3] Professors, for example, might be advised to take up farming in a more salubrious climate, except that physicians couldn't agree on what that was. As a result, the American Climatological Association was founded in 1884 in order to educate physicians about the nature and variety of climates to be considered in determining where to send tuberculosis patients. Florida, Cuba, the Adirondacks, and the Southwest were frequently recommended, but before 1880, travel to New Mexico was difficult. In his 1875 treatise on climate, W. D. Bizzell,[4] states:

> New Mexico has in some sort of vague way, for a long time, been spoken of as promising much to phythisical invalids ... but I have been able to find very little that was definite in regard to it. No doubt its inaccessibility and the comparatively few invalids who could undertake so toilsome a journey, has deterred medical men from recommending it before this.

In 1880, this would change with the arrival of the Atchison, Topeka, and Santa Fe Railroad. But after the Santa Fe Trail passed into oblivion, the city of Santa Fe experienced a precipitous decline, for the territorial capital lay in a steep basin unsuitable for the main track. In 1890, Santa Fe, with a population of 6,185, was still the largest city in the territory, but within the next thirty years, its population would shrink by 23 percent, while New Mexico's would double.[5]

By 1900 both Albuquerque and Las Vegas surpassed it in size. When legislators talked about moving the territorial capital to Albuquerque, Santa Fe leaders responded quickly. The town, they agreed, needed to improve its image in order to attract more people. Paul A. F. Walter suggested that "removing manure heaps from the central plaza" might be a place to start.[6]

To bolster its economy, local leaders decided to promote Santa Fe as a health resort. At the same time, they agreed that people would be more likely to come if the city looked "more American." For as a Lordsburg newspaper noted in 1892, newcomers were attracted to the railroad towns of Las Vegas and Albuquerque, which they considered American cities. Santa Fe, on the other hand, was seen as remote and foreign, "an out of the way place [whose] population ... is largely Mexican." General William T. Sherman, in fact, told a largely Hispanic audience:

> You must get rid of your burros and goats. I hope ten years hence there will not be an adobe house in the Territory. Yankees don't like flat roofs, nor roofs of dirt.[7]

The *Santa Fe New Mexican* began criticizing merchants who failed to modernize their buildings. In a series of articles published between 1882–1892, the paper campaigned for the removal of portals, as they "make the streets look narrow and have not a business like appearance." When the archbishop's nephew, Juan B. Lamy, ordered his portal torn down, notes Chris Wilson,

> The paper congratulated him for being "sensible" and "patriotic." Those who followed his example would give their buildings more air and sunlight—a growing concern in a city beginning to tout itself as a tuberculosis health resort.[8]

But Santa Fe had a resource that other communities lacked—a hospital. In 1865, the Sisters of Charity converted a one-story adobe building, previously used as the Episcopal residence, into St. Vincent Hospital. In 1878 construction had begun on an imposing three-story building to be used as an industrial school for girls. But plans changed mid-stream, for Archbishop Jean Baptiste Lamy decided that a modern hospital, with bed space for tuberculosis patients, was a more pressing need. St. Vincent Sanatorium opened in 1883. Complete with steam heat and a mansard roof with a cupola on top, it was the tallest building in Santa Fe. In keeping with efforts to "Americanize" Santa Fe, the facility was built in the French Second Empire style popular in other U. S. cities. The sanatorium had a ward for "coughers from the East," but it treated other patients as well. An appropriation from the legislature helped cover the cost of services for indigent residents.

Meanwhile, the Territorial Bureau of Immigration continued to tout New Mexico's healthful climate. *New Mexico: The Tourists' Shrine*[9] boasted that:

> The lowest death rate from tubercular disease in America is in New Mexico. That the Territory has superior sanitary advantages, as represented in high altitudes, equable temperatures, dry atmosphere, generous sunshine, and mineral and hot springs is manifest.

Built in 1883, St. Vincent Sanatorium provided medical care for health seekers and other patients until 1896, when it was destroyed by fire. Courtesy Palace of the Governors Photo Archives (MNM/DCA), Negative Number 067744.

These claims, however, failed to impress Eastern politicians, who still viewed New Mexico as a cultural backwater not worthy of statehood. General William T. Sherman suggested starting a war with Mexico to make them take New Mexico back.[10]

Health seekers, however, arrived in increasing numbers. Individual cities promoted their own healing properties and adopted special slogans. Santa Fe, "The World's Only Sanitarium," competed for health seekers with Albuquerque, "The Heart of the Well Country," and "The Silver City with the Golden Climate." In 1890, Reverend Edward Willcocks Meany[11] described Santa Fe as "the queen of health resorts for the pulmonary sufferers." Santa Fe, he explained, has all "the requisites of a climate curative of consumption—altitude, dryness, equability of temperature, light and sunshine and a porous soil." Citing an eminent German authority, Meany noted that "great altitudes furnish a gymnasium where the respiratory organs are compelled to be exercised, and consequently become larger and more efficient." A similar claim was made in *Santa Fe: The Climatic Mecca*,[12] which also noted that Santa Fe, "has the most equable climate in the world, continuous sunshine, and not a single wind or sand storm during the year."

The perception of tuberculosis and its treatment, however, began to change in response to several new developments. In 1882 German scientist Robert Koch discovered *Mycobacterium tuberculosis*, the bacillus responsible for tuberculosis. The disease, long thought to be hereditary, was now considered contagious. Tuberculosis sanatoriums were established in Germany, but they didn't come into vogue in the United States until Edward L. Trudeau, a New York physician suffering from consumption, cured himself during a retreat in the Adirondack Mountains. In 1885, he established the Adirondack Cottage Sanatorium, which became a model for the rest of the country.

Although not exclusively for tuberculosis, St. Vincent Sanatorium continued to attract its share of health seekers, but its days were numbered. On June 14, 1896, it caught on fire and burned to the ground. Patients were relocated to one of the other church-run facilities, which by this time also included a hospital annex and orphanage. Authorities sifted through the ashes, unable to determine the cause of the fire, which erupted from the roof, reducing the facility to "shapeless ruins."[13] The *Santa Fe New Mexican* attributed a failure to save the building to deficient fire equipment, lack of water pressure, and poor organization." Although losses were estimated at upwards of $75,000, only $11,000 was covered by insurance, as the premiums on some of the policies had not been paid.

Consequently, when Sister Victoria Fulweiler, the current superior, appealed to the Motherhouse in Cincinnati for funding, the request was rejected; "the burden could not be assumed."[14] The following year, Sister Victoria was replaced by Sister Eulalia Whitty, who converted the burnt-out sanatorium grounds into a lawn tennis court and invited local youth to play.[15] Although St. Vincent Sanatorium was eventually rebuilt, more than a decade would pass before the necessary funds were obtained.

In the meantime, city leaders began exploring other options, including the possible use of Fort Marcy. Dating from 1846, Fort Marcy was one of a number of military forts built in New Mexico during the mid 1800s. No longer needed, they began to be viewed as possible sanatorium sites. In 1892 a bill was introduced into Congress "looking to the establishment of a national sanitarium at one of the abandoned military posts in either New Mexico or Colorado." The Spanish

American War finally provided the impetus, for by 1898 the U. S. Soldiers Home in Washington DC was inundated with consumptive veterans. It soon became apparent that facilities in a more salubrious climate were needed.

In 1899, the government established two facilities in New Mexico—the U. S. Marine Hospital Sanatorium at Fort Stanton near Lincoln and a U. S. Army General Hospital for tubercular soldiers at Fort Bayard near Silver City. These two institutions helped legitimate New Mexico's claims as a health resort, for in his 1908 Report to the Secretary of the Interior, Territorial Governor George Curry[16] wrote: "The splendid successes in the treatment of tuberculosis … furnish constant and convincing proof of the right of New Mexico to the title of 'the nation's sanatorium' and to the wonderful effect of the climate in checking the white plague."

For the next several years, Santa Fe residents would discuss the pros and cons of converting Fort Marcy into a sanatorium. The American Invalid Society, in fact, had submitted a proposal to Congress, which if approved, would make Santa Fe one of the leading centers in the country for the cure of consumptives. Although recognizing its economic potential, Santa Fe's Board of Trade expressed concern over the magnitude of the proposed facility.

> The prospect of a large colony of consumptives being planted here is not alluring, neither is it pleasant. The presence of a limited number of persons so afflicted is in no way dangerous to the health of the community, but there is grave danger in the assembly of a large number of consumptives in one locality. Consumption is the most insidious of all known diseases, and once let it become endemic in Santa Fe, the city will become a veritable pest house to be shunned by everybody.[17]

Although President William McKinley eventually issued an executive order to set aside Fort Marcy for a sanitarium, no facility was ever established. The issue was still being debated in 1902, but the proposal had changed. The latest scheme involved the establishment of a military sanatorium, the pros and cons of which were discussed in "Does Santa Fe Want the Sanitarium?" which appeared in the March 4, 1902 issue of the *Santa Fe New Mexican*. On June 13, 1902, the newspaper reported that the Department of the Interior was preparing to sell the property. Eighteen months later, the *New Mexican* announced that President Theodore Roosevelt had granted Fort Marcy to the city of Santa Fe for public use.[18]

Health seekers, however, continued to arrive. Some checked into the old St. Vincent Hospital, while others stayed in hotels or rooming houses. Many lived in tents.

> In and around the town, in fact, throughout the entire county, can be seen tents here and there occupied by health seekers or their families, and by owning their own tents and providing their own meals, health seekers can live at an expense of only $4 a week, without stinting themselves of the essentials for recovery.[19]

In fact, in their 1906 promotional brochure on Santa Fe County, Max Frost and Paul A.F. Walter[20] actually advised health seekers to "go into the forests and hills surrounding Santa Fe and camp out."

> The life of the tent dweller is the best treatment for incipient pulmonary tuberculosis. A year's out-of-door life in the dry, bracing air will arrest most cases of pulmonary tuberculosis, if the sufferer has the necessary strength and vitality to begin such a course of treatment and takes ordinary precautions against undue exposure and over-exertion.

With the defeat of the Fort Marcy proposal in spring 1902, Santa Fe still needed facilities to address the needs of health seekers. A few months later, two local businessmen stepped up to the plate. In August 1902, A.R. Gibson and F. H. Mitchell announced their plans to establish Sunmount Tent City for consumptives on land east of town. Modeled after a summer tent city at California's Coronado Beach, the developers planned to build a year-round suburb as part of a larger real estate venture. Lots would be sold, and tents would be available for rent, starting at $10 per month.

Santa Fe enthusiastically embraced the project, and for the next several years, its progress was given front page coverage in the *Santa Fe New Mexican*. On November 4, 1902, the paper reported that "many lots have already been sold to people of means, scattered over the country, among them bankers, merchants and professional men." Plans to establish a casino, pleasure pavilion, and park were announced. One month later, on December 18, the paper praised Sunmount for making "the Capital City of New Mexico famous as the Mecca for those suffering with bronchial and pulmonary troubles." It went on to state that prominent physicians throughout the east are sending their patients there. On February 17, 1904, the paper noted:

> It is a common remark that the buoyant looking stranger on the streets of Santa Fe is a lunger at Sunmount, while if a visitor asks about some haggard, careworn looking individual he is told, "Oh, that's only a native, there is nothing the matter with him."

Several articles commented on its financial success. The September 23, 1904 issue of the *Santa Fe New Mexican* described Sunmount as "one of the most flourishing enterprises in the vicinity of Santa Fe" and reported that "over fifty large sanitary tents now cover the ground." In 1906, Frost and Walter[21] noted that "Sunmount, the pioneer tent city in New Mexico, has been in operation sufficiently long to demonstrate its success and permanency."

In reality, it was on the verge of collapse, for by 1906 Sunmount Tent City was heavily mortgaged and deeply in debt. The administration building remained unfinished, and the communal recreation rooms had never been built. By late spring it went out of business. Santa Fe was back to square one. To compete as a health resort, it needed an up-to-date facility, for health seeker began bypassing Santa Fe for Albuquerque and Silver City, both of which offered sanatorium care in modern facilities.

Although Santa Fe still had no TB sanatorium, this was about to change. On June 1, 1906, the *Santa Fe New Mexican* announced that Sunmount Tent City had been "purchased by Dr. Mera who will make repairs." Frank Mera, with the help of brother H.P. Mera, also a physician, planned to establish a new sanatorium on the grounds of the failed tent city. Although the previous settlement was almost always full of TB patients, there had been no doctor and no control over the patients. Unlike the previous proprietors, Frank Mera was a trained physician. He had also been a health seeker, himself, and wanted to ensure that patients received the very best treatment, which meant avoiding the harsh regimen that he had endured.

In 1902, while a medical intern at Grace Hospital in Detroit, Mera was diagnosed with TB. Following his doctors orders, he headed West and ended up in Las Vegas, New Mexico, where the "cure" nearly killed him. In addition to daily sunbaths, he was required to drink four quarts of milk a day, eat four raw eggs after every meal, and engage in "limited" exercise. The latter included mountain climbing and working as a ranch hand during haying season.

Instead of getting stronger, he became weaker and lost weight. After two years, he left and checked into a tuberculosis sanatorium in Colorado Springs, where he recovered his health. During his recovery, he read everything he could find about tuberculosis and decided to start his own sanatorium. At the recommendation of a friend, he visited Santa Fe, where he found the climate extraordinary and a tent city available for purchase.[22]

The Mera brothers planned to open the new facility on September 1, 1906. However, before the first patients arrived, the main building needed to be renovated, new furnishings purchased, a billiard table ordered, and forty tents remodeled. Although recognizing the importance of fresh air in fighting tuberculosis, Frank Mera also believed that a patient needed more substantial lodging than that provided by the existing tents. Eventually they would be replaced by cottages, but in the meantime Mera planned to put the tents on a firm foundation and shingle each roof.[23]

For the first few years, they kept the original name, but in a brochure on *Sunmount: The Land of the Large and Charitable Air*,[24] Frank Mera announced that "Sunmount Tent City has been remodeled and after January 1, 1908 will be used as a sanatorium for the treatment of tuberculosis." The rates for Sunmount Sanatorium, as it was now called, included an entrance fee of $3.00 plus $12.50 per week, which covered all expenses, including medical attention and general nursing. By this time Frank Mera was on his own, for his brother had moved back East. Although H.P. Mera returned to Santa Fe in 1922, he was no longer actively involved in Sunmount. Instead he became a county health officer. Developing a passion for New Mexico prehistory, he later served as curator of archaeology for the Laboratory of Anthropology.

Sunmount Sanatorium, circa 1907. John Gaw Meem Photograph Collection, Image No. 23504, Courtesy of the New Mexico State Records Center and Archives.

Within the next few years, Frank Mera transformed Sunmount into a sanatorium with a national reputation. It attracted so many artists and writers that Mera began advertising it as "The Sanatorium Different." In reality, however, the treatment it provided was similar to that of other New Mexico facilities, including St. Vincent Sanatorium, which had been rebuilt in 1910. In short, the treatment regimen was based on four major principles—fresh air, rest, ample food, and an optimistic frame of mind.

Of these, fresh air was considered key, for to take full advantage of New Mexico's healing climate, physicians encouraged their patients to be outdoors as much as possible. As one reporter observed, "while 'climate is fate,' in many cases it is more assuredly so in the treatment of tuberculosis."[25] Patients were encouraged to sit in the sun, and in many sanatoriums mirrors were used to direct the sun's rays down the throat, a practice called heliotherapy. By the early 1900s, the more substantial cottage with sleeping porch had replaced the flimsier tent as the preferred housing. Sunmount's "Rules and Hints for Patients"[26] offered the following advice:

> In this climate there is no reason why the patient except on rare occasions cannot spend all of his time outdoors, with slight intervals in the house for meals etc. When it is stormy one may find sheltered parts of the porches in which to sit. At night the sides of the cottages are to be put down so that patients are practically outdoors all night as well as during the day.

A typical lunger cottage at Sunmount Sanatorium. Photograph by Jesse L. Nusbaum, Courtesy Palace of the Governors Photo Archives (MNM/DCA), Negative Number 061393.

In contrast to the nineteenth century regimen of strenuous activity, sanatoriums prescribed rest. Sunmount patients, for example, were required to get nine hours of sleep every night and to rest at least half an hour before and after each meal. L.G. Rice,[27] president of the New Mexico Board of Health, recommended that patients relax in "a comfortable chair, preferably of the Adirondack type, located where there is lots of fresh air, without exposure to drafts and storms." At Sunmount, patients were not allowed to exercise except on advice of the physician. Graduated exercise, however, soon became the norm, beginning with "a short walk of five minutes, which is gradually run up to full time."[28]

Physicians encouraged their patients to eat lots of nourishing food. Since pulmonary tuberculosis literally consumed its victims, who became weak and thin, gaining weight was considered an important indicator of progress. In fact, in his 1901 Report to the Secretary of the Interior, Territorial Governor Miguel Otero[29] provided a list of 100 patients at Fort Stanton and the amount of weight gained or lost during the previous week. Frank Mera, told his patients at Sunmount: "Your progress will depend to a large extent on the amount of food you can take. Be prompt to meals and eat even if you have no desire."[30] Sunmount, in fact, had its own jersey cows and chickens so that patients could have a regular supply of fresh milk, butter, and eggs.

Bedroom with sleeping porch at Sunmount Sanatorium. John Gaw Meem Photograph Collection, Image No. 23560, Courtesy of the New Mexico State Records Center and Archives.

Chasing the Cure at Sunmount Sanatorium. John Gaw Meem Photograph Collection, Image No. 23523, Courtesy of the New Mexico State Records Center and Archives

Some sanatoriums, however, plied their patients with too much food, for as Albuquerque physician LeRoy Peters observed:

> I have known patients who were drinking 26 glasses of milk and swallowing a dozen raw eggs per day, and in addition were making a brave attempt to eat three meals that would do credit to a harvest hand. Perhaps the oversupply of nourishment was sufficient to produce a state of inertia in bugdom, and the helpless tubercle bacillus was so over fed that it became inactive through corpulence. I do believe that better results can be obtained by a suitable diet than by the old method of gluttony.[31]

Another key element of treatment was a positive outlook, for as L.G. Rice[32] pointed out: "a cheerful and hopeful spirit has a great influence over the processes of the body." Given the seriousness of the disease and the strict regimentation of sanatorium life, keeping patients happy was no easy task. To fulfill this need, sanatoriums provided recreational opportunities, which were often described in lavishly illustrated promotional brochures. At Sunmount, for example:

> Horse-back riding and several day camping-out trips are very numerous and break the ordinary routine of this life. Here we find a group of pleasure disposed people indulging in a game of croquet, while in the Administration room, is gathered a quiet crowd engaged in playing pool, cards, chess and checkers, while others read books and periodicals, and several young people of musical inclinations are gathered about the piano singing and playing.[33]

Croquet was one of the many pastimes enjoyed by patients at Sunmount Sanatorium. John Gaw Meem Photograph Collection, Image No. 23505, Courtesy of the New Mexico State Records Center and Archives.

Sunmount also sponsored plays and Mariachi concerts and took patients on excursions to nearby Pueblos and old Spanish missions. It hosted archaeology lectures by Sylvanus Morley and poetry readings by Carl Sandberg and Vachel Lindsay. Like other sanatoriums, Sunmount offered classes in arts and crafts and provided outlets for the products. Some sanatoriums encouraged patients to produce newsletters as a part of occupational therapy. Billed as the "world's latest newspaper," the first issue of the Sunmount Cub hit the stands in August 1919.

Patients at Sunmount enjoy a game of billiards. John Gaw Meem Photograph Collection, Image No. 23671, Courtesy of the New Mexico State Records Center

In 1914, a group of lungers at the Methodist Deaconness Hospital in Albuquerque launched the *Killgloom Gazette*, which would be read by health seekers throughout New Mexico. Each issue was chocked full of jokes and poems such as the following, which appeared in the July 1914 issue.

> Little Bo Peep,
> Could not sleep,
> But coughed the whole night thru
> She scattered the bugs
> All over the rugs
> Now her sheep have T.B. too.

The *Gazette* also published serious articles, many written by physicians. By this time, a popular terminology and approach to recovery had developed, as reflected in the following advice offered in the August 1914 issue:

> The other day our attention was called to the attitude of a health seeker [who] made the remark that he didn't like to think of himself as a lunger. [That] attitude is certainly a detriment to a speedy and thorough cure. [The] sooner he realizes that he is a T.B. and begins to act like one, the better off he will be. The TB is not like other folks and never will be unless he thinks of himself as a TB and acts like one, which means to

watch his temp, his diet and to conserve every energy—*which is to chase*.

In 1912, a physician in Silver City began experimenting with a new procedure called artificial pnemothorax, the deliberate collapse of a lung to allow it to rest and heal. This entailed introducing an inert gas into the pleural cavity, a procedure which patients described as "very painful." It often required many applications before a lung was fully collapsed, and for two years, recalled LeRoy Peters, we worked without advantage of x-ray equipment.

> Lungs were over-compressed [and] diaphragms pushed downward with displacement of liver and other abdominal viscera, and many times the unhappy patient made worse than better.[34]

The procedure was refined and became part of the standard treatment regimen at other facilities, including Sunmount Sanatorium and St. Vincent Sanatorium in Santa Fe.

Sanatoriums soon began touting their success rates. On September 18, 1911, the *Santa Fe New Mexican* carried the following headline: "100 Per Cent Have Been Cured. Report of Sunmount Sanatorium Shows Value of Climatic Treatment. Tuberculosis in the First Stages Readily Yields to Dry Bracing Air." The article went on to state that:

> All or one hundred per cent of patients suffering with tuberculosis of the first stage and remaining here three months or more are reported discharged as cured. This statement speaks volumes for the benefits of this climate which is being recognized more and more in the medical world as presenting ideal conditions for the treatment of lung and throat troubles.

Sunmount, like most private sanatoriums, upped the odds by refusing to accept people who were "suffering with tuberculosis in the last stages." Like most private sanatoriums, it focused on patients in the incipient phase of the disease. Fifty years later, however, Frank Mera recalled "there were so many TB patients whom we couldn't save."[35]

Despite claims of spectacular cure rates, many health seekers never lived to see their first anniversary. One national study estimates that from the beginning of the sanatorium movement through the 1940s, nearly 25 per cent of patients died in the hospital, while 50 percent of those released succumbed within five years of discharge.[36]

Despite this grim reality, health seekers continued to arrive. New Mexico, in fact, continued to encourage tuberculars long after other states tried to restrict their immigration. In 1909, the state health officer for Texas proclaimed *Consumptives Unwelcome in Texas*.[37] In contrast, *The Land of Sunshine*, published in 1906 by the Bureau of Immigration, stated: "Health seekers are invited. New Mexico does not intend to shut the door upon them." In 1903, the Territorial Legislature offered tax breaks for sanatorium construction. Five years later, New Mexico ranked fifth in the nation for the number of tuberculosis beds. By the time New Mexico achieved statehood in 1912, nearly thirty sanatoriums had been established, and another thirty would be built in the decades that followed.

Health seekers with sufficient funds to pay the $50–$100 monthly fee usually checked into at a sanatorium for an average stay of nine months. Thousands, however, arrived with scarcely enough to pay for their train ticket. Instead, they "chased the cure on their feet," hoping the climate alone would be sufficient. In fact, so many health seekers arrived, that by 1910, New Mexico's death rate from tuberculosis, once touted as the lowest in the country, far exceeded the national average of 153.8 deaths per 100,000.[38] In Albuquerque alone, the rate was 1,133.1 per 100,000. Most of the victims were new arrivals.

Unfortunately, many health seekers lacked the means to support themselves. New Mexico, observed Dr. C. M. Mayes[39] in 1909, has become a dumping ground for indigent patients.

> They are sent to us or drift here in all stages of the disease, and only too often without income or friends, and for the most part unable to perform necessary manual labor for their support. They sit about our parks, on our curbs, in our places of amusement and recreation. In the saloon, breathing tobacco smoke and air otherwise contaminated. Friendless, homesick and only too often poorly clad, badly housed, and hungry, or at least without necessary food. A menace to the exposed, and a burden both to themselves and our citizenship. Could anything be sadder?

Physicians from other states, he warned, should "notify their patients that unless they have an income [and are prepared to] stand an expense of at least $14.00 per week indefinitely, they should remain at home...."

Santa Fe, like other communities, began to fear exposure, as an increasing number of health seekers arrived and set up tents within the city limits. Sanatoriums had strict rules concerning the disposal of sputum. Patients at Sunmount, for example, were "allowed to expectorate only in sputum cups. When these are full they are to be put in a place designated from where they are taken and burned." Failure to do so was grounds for dismissal. Those living elsewhere, however, were under no such restrictions. Alarmed, members of Santa Fe's Women's Board of Trade put up handbills around the city, urging citizens to refrain from expectorating on public streets. Spitting, however, had become such a problem that in 1907 the Territorial Legislature passed an ordinance prohibiting spitting in public places.

Tents had become a problem as well. On April 24, 1908, the *Santa New Mexican* announced:

> The City Council will pass an ordinance prohibiting the erection and occupation by consumptive persons of tents within the city limits hereafter. The step will be one in the right direction and will meet with the approval of the citizens generally as well as prove for the benefit of the city.

Some hotels refused to accept health seekers. Bishop's Lodge, for example, announced that "the Lodge positively does not entertain tubercular guests."[40]

But the movement had a positive side, for it brought hundreds of creative and productive citizens to Santa Fe. "They came to heal, but stayed to paint," and in the process helped transform a sleepy little town into a thriving art community and a major tourist destination. One of the first artists to arrive was Carlos Vierra, who came to Santa Fe in 1904 after experiencing lung trouble in California. He first resided in a little cabin on the Pecos River, but after contracting a severe cold, he checked into a sanatorium. Vierra recovered and was hired by Edgar Lee Hewett, founding director of the School of American Archaeology[41] and the Museum of New Mexico, to produce murals for an exhibition in San Diego as well as for the Fine Arts Museum in Santa Fe.

Tuberculosis had brought Hewett to Santa Fe as well. An educator from Illinois, Hewett was teaching in Colorado when his wife Cora contracted TB. Hoping that fresh air and sunshine would restore her health, he put her in a horse-drawn camp wagon and spent summers touring the west. When the Hewetts came to Santa Fe, they checked into St. Vincent Sanatorium, where guests of patients could stay for $3 a night. Cora succumbed to tuberculosis in 1904. Hewett, however, had developed a passion for Southwest archaeology, which led to a doctorate at the University of Geneva and the founding of the School and Museum in Santa Fe. He soon began hiring staff, which included another health seeker, Kenneth Chapman, an artist and illustrator from Chicago, who had gone to Las Vegas, New Mexico for a lung condition.

In 1909, the territorial legislature granted Hewett permission to house the School and Museum in the Palace of the Governors, on the condition that he renovate the building in keeping with "the Spanish architecture of the period." By 1909, popular Victorian styles had replaced much of the city's Spanish colonial architecture. Even the 300-year old Palace of the Governors had undergone a Victorian facelift, complete with an ornate railing on top and square posts holding up a classical-style porch. Efforts to modernize the city, however, had failed to attract more people. Its population continued to decline, and by 1910, it had shrunk to 5,072.

Impressed with the ongoing renovation of the Old Palace, city officials sought the School's help to reverse the city's thirty-year economic decline. On January 6, 1912, New Mexico finally achieved statehood. Two months later, Mayor Arthur Seligman created a planning board chaired by Harry. H. Dorman, president of the Chamber of Commerce. Hewett and staff member Sylvanus Morley became deeply involved and suggested that to encourage growth, the city needed stress its unique heritage. The board finally agreed and the Chamber of Commerce soon began touting Santa Fe as the "City Different."

Santa Feans applauded the restoration of the Palace of the Governors, completed in fall 1913, and wanted the city to return to the architecture of their forebears. The *Santa Fe New Mexican*, which twenty years earlier had insisted that the portals be demolished, now called for their return.[42] Other buildings followed suit, giving birth to Santa Fe style. Artist Carlos Vierra would soon become involved, but it would be another health seeker, John Gaw Meem, who would refine the style and take it to new heights.

John Gaw Meem, an engineer by training, contracted tuberculosis while working at a bank in Brazil. Sent to New York City for a second opinion, he later described the experience to colleague Douglas W. Schwartz, who relates it as follows:

> John Gaw Meem was told by his doctor in New York that he had three options—Saranac in New York, the mountains of North Carolina or Santa Fe, New Mexico. John had not heard of any of these places, so he thanked the doctor, whose office was on Times Square. By the time he got outside it was deep twilight. As he pondered what to do, he looked up into the sky and saw a sign flashing 'Santa Fe, Santa Fe.' Of course it was an advertisement for the Santa Fe Railroad. But that was how he made his decision of which of the three places he should go. So it was a chance observation of a neon sign on the top of a building in Times Square, New York, that changed the character of New Mexico architecture.

A friend later told Meem about a cousin who was "quite happy at Sunmount Sanatorium," so he bought a ticket and headed for New Mexico.[43]

He was 26 years old when he entered Sunmount in 1920. He left eighteen months later, renewed both physically and mentally, to pursue an apprenticeship with a leading architectural firm in Denver. His fascination with the Spanish-Pueblo style architecture developed during his stay at Sunmount, for as Nancy Meem Wirth explained:

> Frank Mera was a major influence in my father's life because unlike most sanatoriums where tuberculosis was thought of as a disease where you were confined, Dr. Mera thought that the patients should get out and do things. So he took trips throughout New Mexico, which is how my father got excited about the Franciscan missions. Because of Dr. Mera, he truly fell in love with New Mexico.

Tuberculosis also brought artists Sheldon Parsons, Arthur Musgrave, Datus Meyers, and Will Shuster to Santa Fe. The burning of Zozobra, a puppet originally created by Shuster as a joke, would change the face of fiesta forever. In fact, Williams and Fox[44] suggest that the inspiration for Zozobra may have come from the Joyflingers, a "loose group of jokesters" at Sunmount. Other artists came as well. Following his stay at a sanatorium in Albuquerque, Gerald Cassidy eventually settled in Santa Fe as did William Penhallow Henderson, who moved to the city after his wife Alice was diagnosed with tuberculosis. An artist as well as an architect, Henderson designed a number of major buildings, including the Wheelwright Museum and the Amelia White estate, now home to the School for Advanced Research.

Alice Corbin Henderson was one of many literary artists who "chased the cure" at Sunmount Sanatorium. Writer Yvor Winters met his wife, poet Janet Lewis, while both were patients there. Poet Witter Bynner decided to relocate to Santa Fe after visiting Alice Corbin Henderson at Sunmount. Bynner stayed for over six weeks, an experience he recalled with both apprehension and delight.

> Though it troubled me at first to stay in a building which was half hotel, half sanatorium for tuberculars, I was soon persuaded that I was safer at Sunmount than in a New York Trolley car.... Alice Corbin's room, perhaps purposely, was opposite the doctor's office. She was not only a bed patient but under strict watch as to care and diet.... Waitresses would bring coffee for groups in this or that private room.... Now and then we would enjoy in our coffee cups a fill or two of Taos

lightning, that firey corn whiskey which we keg-rolled in the backs of our cars.... Finally even the head doctor would be there and almost grunt that these trespasses upon rules were doing his patient good.[45]

Others came to Sunmount as well, including silversmith Frank Patania; Dorothy McKibben, gatekeeper for the Manhattan project; and Wayne Mauzy, who later served as director of both the School of American Research and the Museum of New Mexico. Mauzy, in fact, claimed that two venerable Santa Fe institutions, the Indian Arts Fund and the Old Santa Fe Association, originated from conversations at Sunmount.[46] Physician Robert O. Brown was treated at Sunmount and upon recovery became medical director of St. Vincent Sanatorium. Pioneering aviator, Katherine Stinson, met her husband, Miguel Otero, Jr., while both were patients at Sunmount. Miguel Otero recovered to enjoy a successful political career as state treasurer, attorney general, and district judge. Otero was a close friend of Bronson Cutting, a wealthy New Yorker, who had contracted tuberculosis while a student at Harvard. Shortly after graduation, Cutting became deathly ill and was brought to Santa Fe on a stretcher. He recovered to become publisher of the *Santa Fe New Mexican* and a powerful U. S. senator.

During the 1920s, an estimated one third of Santa Fe's artists and intellectuals originally came to the city because they suffered from tuberculosis or other respiratory ailment.[47] In fact, as Mera later recalled, "if it wasn't TB that brought you to New Mexico from the East, you were looked on with suspicion."[48] By 1920 Santa Fe's population had grown from 5,072 in 1910 to 7,236. Health seekers now comprised an estimated ten per cent of New Mexico's population.[49] But they weren't the only ones affected by tuberculosis. It had become a serious problem among locals as well.

In 1918, Governor Washington E. Lindsey, frustrated by the lack of health care for tubercular soldiers, commissioned Dr. J. W. Kerr of the U. S. Public Health Service to conduct a statewide health survey. Kerr had not yet completed his survey when the 1918 flu broke out. In the absence of a state health department, he coordinated relief efforts. When he finally finished his survey, the results were in marked contrast to a report issued twelve years earlier by the Territorial Bureau of Immigration, which claimed "that the native people of this section experience such wonderful immunity from tuberculosis." In contrast, Kerr's study revealed that:

> The Spanish American element suffers increasingly from tuberculosis, and the Indian is extremely prone both to tuberculosis and trachoma. Overcrowding and unhygienic habits adversely affect both

Mexicans and Indians, while economic factors affect many of the whites who came to the Southwest in search of health.... It is a matter of record that the death rate from tuberculosis among the Indians in New Mexico is over twice that of the average in the Registration Area and that disease is estimated to cause over 800 deaths (not migratory healthseekers) annually in our State.... New Mexico needs an adequately financed and efficiently organized state department of health and she needs it now.[50]

In 1919, the New Mexico Legislature finally established a Department of Health, which immediately began tackling the state's many health problems, including tuberculosis. The Albuquerque Indian Hospital was built in 1934. Two years later, the state established a tuberculosis sanatorium in Socorro, which provided free treatment for local residents.

St. Vincent Sanatorium was rebuilt in 1910. Dr. Robert O. Brown, a former patient at Sunmount, served as medical director. Photograph by Jesse L. Nusbaum, Courtesy Palace of the Governors Photo Archives (MNM/DCA), Negative Number 061373.

During the 1930s, however, the health seeker movement dwindled sharply as the nation plunged deeper into the depression. "People who formerly flocked to climatic resorts found their pocketbooks too flat to make the venture," explained LeRoy Peters.[51] "The private sanatorium, east as well as west, was deserted for the public institution." Many came to realize that it was the sanatorium regimen—with its emphasis on rest, diet, and fresh air—that was critical, not its location.

But the final end to the sanatorium movement came in 1944 with the discovery of streptomycin, followed by other drugs, which proved highly effective in treating tuberculosis. Sanatoriums had become medical anachronisms. One by one they shut their doors. Sunmount closed in 1938, and after a brief stint as a resort hotel, it became a Carmelite Monastery. In 1954 St. Vincent Sanatorium was remodeled for use as a convent and nursing school and renamed Marian Hall. The state later purchased the building and converted it into offices.

One by one the TB doctors died as well—Robert O. Brown in 1949 and Frank Mera in 1970. Although the health seekers have long since gone, their legacy lives on in the contributions they made to a sleepy little town and the vibrant community it became.

18

Santa Fe in World War II, 1940–1947
by
Judy Reed

New Mexicans suffered an unusually high casualty rate in World War II—a statistic resulting from federal activation of the New Mexico National Guard 200th Coast Artillery (CA) Antiaircraft (AA) Regiment. About nine hundred of the 1,800 men of the 200th died in battle or at the hands of their captors through torture, killing, and starvation as POWs.[1] This statistic held true for sixty-six[2] men from Santa Fe who sacrificed their lives in the Far East theater. The loss of so many New Mexicans as they tirelessly defended the Philippines touched nearly every city, pueblo, Indian reservation, and community.

Santa Fe's war years are imprinted with two other historical influences that also should not be forgotten—the Japanese Internment Camp and Bruns Army Hospital. Nothing remains of the internment camp except some photographs, documents, and memories. Bruns was transformed into what is now the College of Santa Fe. The threads of these three entities, the 200th CA (AA), Santa Fe Japanese Internment Camp, and Bruns General Hospital, do not intertwine so much on a practical level but each had a profound effect on the personal lives of the people of Santa Fe.

Several families tearfully and proudly welcomed home the 200th after the war; many more were never to see their loved ones again. One of the worst aspects for the families was the lack of information on the status of the members of the 200th. Were they dead, alive, suffering, in the Philippines, Manchuria, or Japan? Did they have a chance of getting home or was it all over except a funeral that could never be? The Japanese relocation program carried out by the War Department spiked the already cynical attitudes towards the Japanese. Bruns Hospital had an entirely different effect on Santa Fe. It boosted the economy and inspired hope in a town whose own troops seemed to have been written off as expendable by the difficult decisions made by those in power.

The precursor to the New Mexico National Guard was the Colonial Militia, formed in 1606 when New Mexico was a province of New Spain. As its designation morphed through the years to become the 200th Coast Artillery Regiment (Antiaircraft) of the New Mexico National Guard, the ground work for other world-shaping events was being laid on the opposite side of the world. In 1823 Satō Nobuhiro crafted "A Secret Strategy for Expansion."[3] The goals were clear—the entire world would be provinces and districts of Japan. The plan lingered with little impetus behind it for some time until the population density of Japan threatened full consumption of the country's natural resources. The desire to assume power over all Oriental countries as a strategy to access and control the much needed resources gave Nobuhiro's plan new life. The new twentieth century plan that sprouted from Nobuhiro's seed was the "Greater East-Asia Co-Prosperity Sphere." The first foreign land taken into the fold of Japanese expansion was Manchuria, China.

Alarmed at what seemed to be an overwhelming number of immigrants from the Far East, the U. S. Congress passed the Asian Exclusion Act in 1924, thus prohibiting Oriental immigration.[4] These immigrants were, for the most part, seeking opportunities to improve their personal lives rather than change the underpinnings of the country's democratic foundation. Humiliation Day, as the Exclusion Act was known in Japan, followed by a series of U. S. embargos on natural resources into Japan, hardened the Japanese leadership's perspective against the United States. The Japanese government bombarded its citizens with heavily weighted propaganda and revelations of recently enacted discriminatory U. S. laws against Orientals in the 1930s as an effort to foster anti-U. S. opinions.

At the same time, Japan's Prime Minister of War Hideki Tojo and other influential military men modified the *Bushido* code of the highly revered samurai to "whip the Japanese people into a war mentality".[5] Rape, murder, torture, and a repugnance for surrendering to an enemy were inserted into the code and put into action as the Japanese advanced through China. By 1939, Japan occupied all the cities of coastal China, north China, and the Yangtze Valley up to Hankow.[6] For all its foreign policy maneuvering, the U. S. was impotent as a world power while Japan and Germany callously pursued their dreams.

During the Great American Depression of the 1930s, it was difficult to obtain financing for U. S. military purposes. The New Mexico National Guard facility in Santa Fe occupied property along Washington Avenue in downtown Santa Fe. As the offer of a steady paycheck enticed more and more young men, the National Guard grew, quickly rendering the Washington Avenue facility inadequate.

Plans for a new complex on nine acres of land owned by the National Guard on College Street (now Old Pecos Trail) were finalized on April 22, 1938, and requests for construction bids advertised a year later.[7]

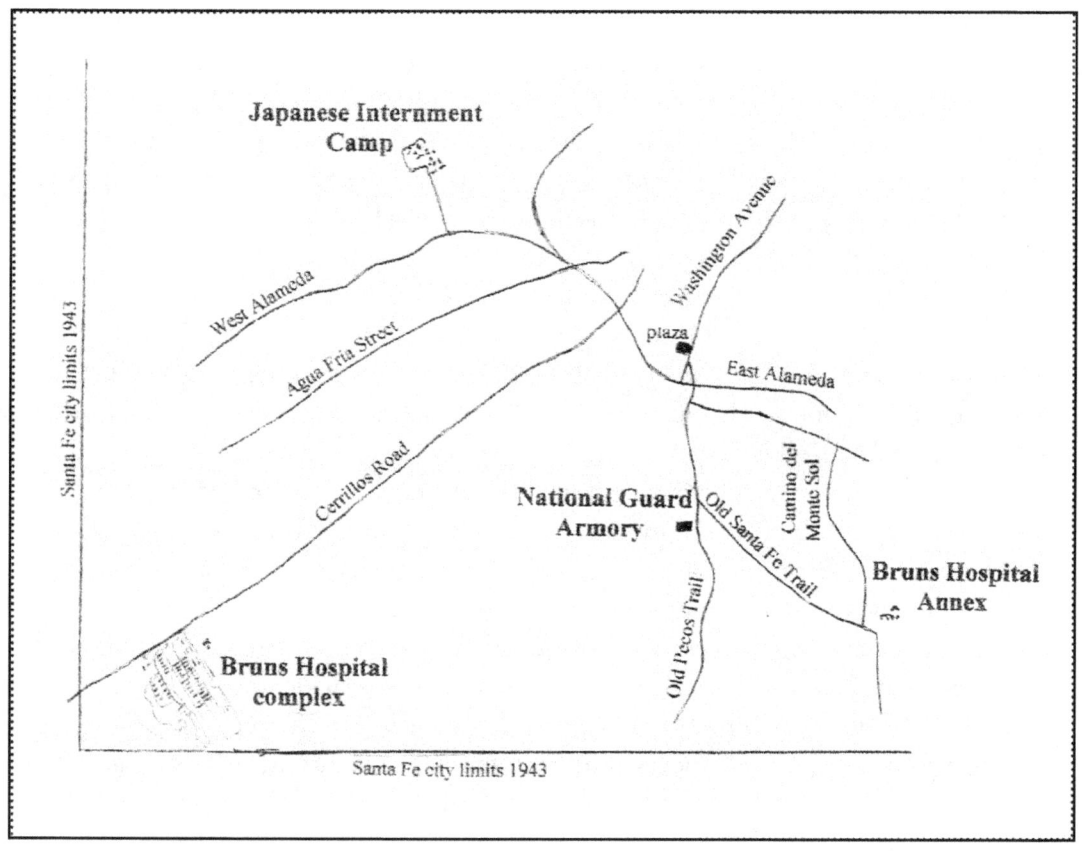

Historic World War II locations in Santa Fe, New Mexico, with some streets identified. Map courtesy of the author.

What has become the highly visible "Santa Fe Architecture" popularized by John Gaw Meem, was taking root. The new armory was slated to conform to this new style.[8] Construction commenced on the heels of closing the bidding process. It was an exciting time of possible rejuvenation from the long years of the depression and dust bowl. But for the Santa Fe boys who took their oath of induction at the new armory and perished in the Far East during WWII, it was the beginning of the end of their lives. Today the armory is fittingly the home of an exceptionally fine Military Museum.

The U. S. government was acutely aware of the woeful condition of its military defenses. In contrast, the brutal powers of Japan and Germany continued to grow. In the summer of 1940, the U. S. Army and National Guard initiated a series of training classes in the use of coastal artillery equipment at Fortress Monroe in Virginia. Within six months and continuing through the summer of 1941, Colonel Charles G. Sage along with more than twenty officers and a considerable number of enlisted men of the 200th successfully completed three months of intense antiaircraft training.[9] Colonel Sage, from Deming, New Mexico, was eventually promoted to general and was the commander of the 200th while in the Philippines. The soldiers were impressed with Sage—the tall, mustachioed, well respected man with the natural bearing of a general.[10] Colonel Sage was equally, if not more, impressed by the men of the 200th and genuinely shaken by their fate.

The 200th was inducted into Federal service on January 6, 1941, at one minute past midnight[11] for the purpose of providing one year of intense training as an antiaircraft unit.[12] Battery C of the 200th was formed entirely of Santa Feans. Men from Deming, Albuquerque, Gallup, Clovis, Carlsbad, Silver City, and Taos comprised the other batteries and headquarters staff. The pay scale had been increased over the year before; a private first class rank now earned $66 a month.[13]

While the community carried on with the normal course of living, such as raising children, working, visiting with friends, going to dances, and sitting in the comfortable smoker lounge chairs at the Lensic Theater to watch *Gone with the Wind,* the 200th was quarantined for ten days before moving out to their training grounds at Fort Bliss.[14] Quarantine was a standard preventive measure to stem the spread of any communicable diseases. Their around the clock home at the armory had no other social activities beyond enjoying the radio but these "men," most of whom were high school seniors or recent graduates, were content in having an income.

The 200th loaded their equipment onto trucks and themselves on the train on January 15, 1941, and made their way to Fort Bliss in El Paso, Texas, when the quarantine ended. The barracks were temporary structures but nonetheless solid with screened windows and enough room to be comfortable.[15] Soon after arriving, a circus tent was set up for socializing and movies. The men anticipated the showing of *Gone with the Wind* scheduled for one evening in March. A strong wind, however, blasted through on that day and blew away the tent along with their anticipation.

A heightened sense of impending danger seeped through the days of February and March. Governor Miles proclaimed February 12th–22nd as "National Defense Week."[16] The War Department called up 34,500 additional National Guardsman to be activated by June. The *USS Grant* deposited more than 500 U. S. troops in the

Philippines as Japan revealed to the world the concepts of the Greater East-Asia Co-Prosperity Sphere.[17] New recruits and draftees steadily flowed into the 200th once it was at Fort Bliss.

The 200th practiced weeks of dry runs on antiaircraft equipment at Fort Bliss before the time came for live firing. The target was a long cloth sleeve about the size of a bomber fuselage.[18] A large airplane towed the target at the end of a 500-yard cable. Brigadier General Spiller, commander of the country's antiaircraft training program, attended the live shoot. He thought little of the "boy scouts from New Mexico" and was unabashedly fond of the Washington, DC, antiaircraft unit simultaneously training at Fort Bliss.

During the live firing, the 200th shredded the target and the cable with four rounds. When the plane returned with a new target, the DC unit took their turn at demonstrating their marksmanship but with disastrous results. Their aim was so poor that the shells exploded closer to the airplane than the target. In an act of self preservation, the pilot ditched the cable with its target and left the area. At the end of the day, Batteries B, C and D of the 200th had the highest accuracy.

The achievements of the 200th quickly caught up with them. Their reputation as the "best anti-aircraft regiment, regular or otherwise, then available to the U. S. armed forces"[19] led to an early departure five months prior to completing their training. On September 16, 1941, their first battalion arrived in Manila, Philippine Islands, via the *USS President Pierce* by way of San Francisco.[20] The remainder and majority of the regiment put into the Manila dock aboard the *USS Coolidge* ten days later.[21] The Fort Stotsenberg-Clark Field installation located seventy-five miles north of Manila was their new home.

In the ten weeks before the Japanese attack on Pearl Harbor, Clark Field, and Fort Stotsenberg, the 200th set up camp, unpacked equipment, acclimated to their new surroundings, and did some target practice but without ammunition.[22] None was available. The lack of equipment, ammunition, men, and training were pervasive. Fort Stotsenberg, for instance, was protected by one-fifth the number of men required by its size and strategic location.

A Japanese envoy met with Ambassador Cordell Hull in Washington, DC regarding the ever straining relationship between Japan and the *U. S. News* articles following up the talks were disappointing. In the article describing the one hour and twenty-three minute meeting, Japanese Admiral Nomura replied to an inquiry with a brief "many things said."[23] What was left unsaid is probably the grandest omission of all—Japanese submarines were headed to Hawaii. Orders to attack Pearl Harbor were given on December 2nd. Japan had made a fateful decision. The 200th, now at a level of 1,809 men[24] along with the other troops in the Philippines and Hawaii, were soon to pay the price.

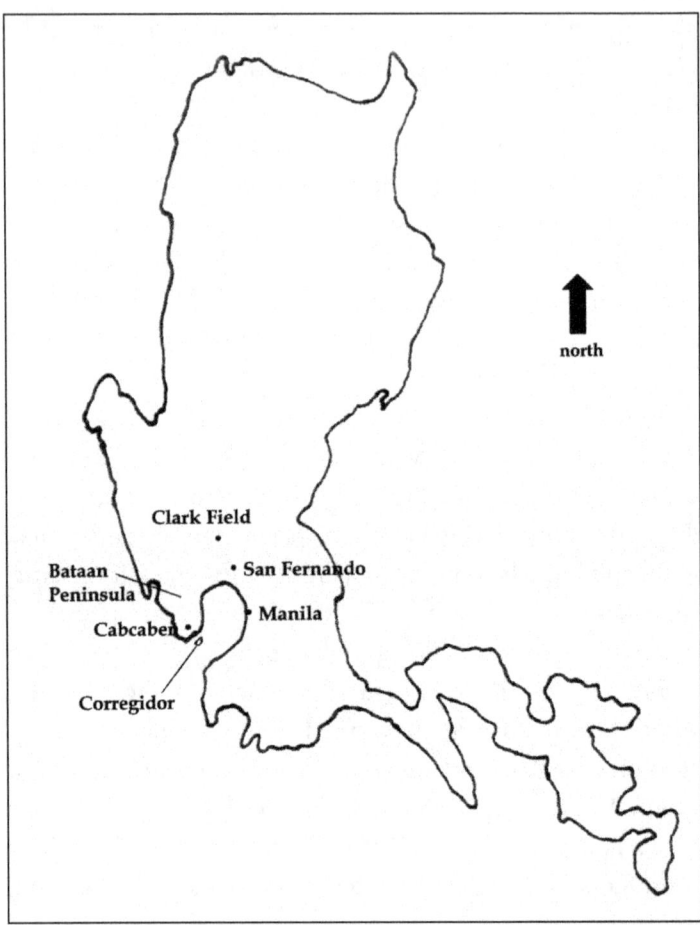

Luzon, the main island in the Philippines. Map courtesy of the author.

Pearl Harbor was attacked by the Japanese on December 7, 1941, sinking or damaging nineteen ships and killing 2,300. On the same day in the Far East (i.e., December 8th) Japanese airmen also bombed Guam, Philippines, Wake, Hong Kong, and British possessions. Interestingly, the decoy P-40 airplanes made from straw by Japanese contractors hired by the U.S. military before the attack were left as untouched targets on the tarmac of Clark Field—an unbelievable coincidence to some.[25] The number of Filipino troops outnumbered Americans six-to-one. The 1,809 men of the 200th was the largest American military unit in the Philippines and it was their job to protect Clark Field.[26] The larger, better trained, and battle hardened force, however, was the Japanese under General Homma.

A broadcast over a commercial radio station about the fate of Pearl Harbor reached the 200th at 3:00am on December 8th.[27] Many of the men of the 200th had never before heard of Pearl Harbor but they did not have time for a geography lesson. The first bombs dropped near the 200th was around 7:00 am when ninety-six twin engine Japanese bombers flew over Mount Pinatubo.[28] The regiment spent the remainder of the morning in position and on high alert. The bombing resumed on a much grander scale at 12:35pm, first by high altitude bombers followed by fast flying fighter planes.[29] When the thick clouds of smoke finally cleared, the 200th found that two men from their regiment from Chavez County in New Mexico lost their lives to one of the first bombs dropped on Clark Field by a direct hit on their truck. The movie theater, where *Gone with the Wind* was scheduled to be shown that night, was demolished.[30] At least one man, Sergeant Richard Daly of Santa Fe, was beginning to develop an aversion to ever wanting to see the movie!

Felipe Trejo was the only Santa Fean killed in combat in the Philippines.[2,28,31] Trejo was part of an antiaircraft crew with Frances VanBuskirk, Richard Daly, and others. Daly and Trejo were sitting on a mound of excavated dirt from a foxhole in front of their gun emplacement. Their crew mates were firing upon "Photo Joe," the Japanese reconnaissance plane, and his dive bomber escorts. The World War I vintage American shells were badly corroded. About half were complete duds and never exploded. On this unlucky day a defective shell exploded as it left the gun barrel. Shrapnel struck Trejo. He was evacuated to the closest hospital but died two days later in the first week of January 1942. Japanese bombing raids came regularly at noon every day from December 8th until Christmas Eve when the allied forces began their retreat into Bataan.[32]

Understandably, the people back home in New Mexico were paying more attention to the attacks in the Philippines than Pearl Harbor. Their loved ones were there. Others noticed the connection, too. New Mexico Governor Miles received a telegram from Shuji Fujii, editor of the *Doho*, a Japanese-American newspaper.[33] Fujii "vehemently" condemned Japan's attack on "our democratic Americans" and informed the governor that he had wired President Roosevelt urging an immediate declaration of war against Japan. The governor issued a proclamation declaring "a full emergency to exist and urge[d] that all citizens of this state cooperate to the fullest extent with municipal, county, state, and Federal governments, and in full harmony, strive in our common cause until our armed forces have time to exact just retribution from our treacherous, despicable, and infamous foe." [34] The citizens of Santa Fe reacted. A series of Civil Defense meetings garnering widespread attendance were held. The meetings were encouraged as a way to dispel war hysteria, discourage "witch hunting," prevent "mob spirit" from prevailing, and allay fears.[35]

Once the brass had time to reconnoiter the bombing blitz of the Philippines, they realized that a prime target, Manila, had no antiaircraft protection.[36] Men were peeled away from the 200th and sent to Manila to uncrate recently arrived antiaircraft equipment and set up defenses around the city. Eventually they were designated as the 515th Coast Artillery (AA) and they joined the machine gunners already in place in Manila. The 200th was assigned to protect northern Luzon while the 515th assumed protection of southern Luzon. The perseverance and success of the 200th and 515th boosted the morale of the allied infantry. It gave them some level of protection in a desperate situation.

News of the bitter fighting filtered into Santa Fe the day after bombardment of the 200th. Individuals and groups proudly demonstrated support of the men. Groups began buying up defense bonds, collecting scrap metal, and volunteering their time towards the war effort. A cross section of Santa Feans sent letter to Governor Miles offering assistance: The United Brothers of Carpenters and Joiners Santa Fe Local Union Number 1353; Star Lumber Company; Santa Fe Central Labor Union; Lions Club; Architects Kruger and Clark; Department of Public Welfare; etc.[37] With volunteers from such organizations the governor formed the State Council on National Defense.

Despite efforts to ward against mob spirit and witch hunting, pockets of the country reached a feverous pitch of anti-Japanese sentiments early on. Violence erupted on the west coast two weeks after Pearl Harbor was attacked.[38] Riots filled the streets of Berkley and San Francisco and several Japanese were killed. Citing the need to control the violence, Roosevelt decided to err on the side of caution "even if civil rights do take a beating for a time." He issued Executive Order 9066 on February 21, 1942. The order empowered the Secretary of War to prescribe certain areas in the U. S. and its territories as military zones where any person or groups of people could be excluded for the duration of the war in order to safeguard the country.[39] About 40,000 *Issei* (Japanese born immigrants to U. S. and non-citizens) and 70,000 *Nisei* (children born in U. S. of the *Issei*) were removed from their homes under EO 9066.[40] Among the tens of thousands removed, about 5,000 were interned throughout the entire war.[41] By the end of this embarrassing episode in our history, one person was found guilty of spying for Japan. At the time the U. S., including its territories and possessions, had a population of 150,621,231.[42] Among these, 113,874 were identified as non-citizens of Japanese descent. New Mexico's population was 531,818 with 186 Japanese (114 citizens; 72 non-citizens).

Full retreat into the Bataan peninsula was in motion by the end of 1941. Malaria and lack of food were constant. Medicine was nearly nonexistent. Most had their extra clothing burned in the initial bombings. The 200th and 515th were the last into Bataan as they provided the main defense to cover the hordes of retreating men. On January 1, 1942, the retreat was complete and the bridges blown up to slow the advancing Japanese, but they found Bataan more inhospitable than from where they had come. Bataan held the distinction as the worst malaria-plagued place in the world[43] and three quarters of the allied combat forces were suffering from the disease[44] with an estimated 1,000 new cases occurring daily.[45] Hospitals were no more than hammocks stretched between trees with mosquito nets hanging over them.[46] General Wainwright, who had been left in charge of the allied troops upon MacArthur's departure from the Philippines, notified his superiors that all food, including c-rations, would be exhausted by April 15th.[47] Orders came to cut the troops rations to one-fifth their normal allotment.[48] They killed all the cattle, mules, horses, carabao, monkeys, and anything else edible to supplement their diet.[49]

The exhausted and starving men of the 200th and 515th did better than could reasonably be expected. War Department Chief of Staff George C. Marshall bestowed honor and distinction on the 200th and 515th for their gallant defense against overwhelming numbers of hostile forces on two particular occasions against an enemy "enjoying unopposed superiority in the air, these regiments maintained a magnificent defense through outstanding technical ability and courage and devotion to duty...."[50]

In the U. S. it was thought that relief could reach the doomed troops if enough money could be donated to purchase and ship food. Governor Miles issued a memorandum to all his departments suggesting that "at least one-half of one day's salary" from each employee be donated to the Red Cross to benefit the armed forces and the suffering civilians in war zones.[51] A collection box was set up in the state capitol for donations but the supplies bought were years in reaching the starving, sick troops.

The first U. S. troops arrived in Britain on January 26, 1942. Perhaps this was the sign-off from Washington for the men in the Philippines. The U. S. commitments had shifted to Europe rather than reinforcing those desperate souls in the Far East. Secretary of War Henry Stimson's words to Governor Miles that "everything possible is being done to feed, supply, and protect our soldiers in the Philippines"[52] were not untrue but rang hollow. A choice was made at the expense of the defenders of Bataan and it left a bitter taste in the mouths of many.

When the defenders' lines broke, droves of disorganized Filipino troops dressed in their blue denim and some khaki-clad American soldiers came running to the rear but none from the 200th or 515th. Ultimately the battle was lost due to starvation, disease, and lack of ammunition in the face of an overwhelming number of Japanese troops, and the inability of the U. S. military to send reinforcements. Back home, the USO held a rally at La Fonda on the plaza in Santa Fe. Their goal was to raise $32,000,000 in three months for the benefit of the troops serving overseas.[53] Santa Feans contributed generously but the aid could not get through to the men of the 200th and 515th.

Two newly formed agencies, the War Relocation Authority and the Wartime Civil Control Administration, were assigned the responsibility of formulating and carrying out a program for the planned relocation of persons evacuated from "potential military areas."[54] The entire west coast was proclaimed as such in early March 1942. The rationale given for the program was two-fold: In the event the west coast would become a combat zone, persons of Japanese ancestry there would be "possible cause[s] of turmoil and confusion which could seriously jeopardize military operations" and "military considerations cannot permit the risk of putting an unassimilated or partly assimilated people to an unpredictable test during an invasion by an army of their own race." Henceforth, U. S. law now allowed for the forcible removal of Japanese from their homes and placement in relocation centers.

In addition to the several relocation centers, the Federal Bureau of Investigation identified Japanese in the U. S. who were likely to carry out acts against the security of the country. They were placed in the "Enemy Alien Program" administered by the Department of Justice and put into high security camps such as the Santa Fe Japanese Internment Camp.[55] These camps received very little publicity and they were established swiftly and quietly. The FBI seized 12,000 "enemy aliens" during the first year America was at war. Over half were Japanese, the others were German, and people from both groups were held in camps in New Mexico. In February 1942, James Matsu wrote from his dormitory room at the University of New Mexico in Albuquerque that "Last week thirty Japanese from Clovis were sent to Ft. Stanton to be interned."[56] Japanese in New Mexico were being taken into custody.

The New Mexico State Prison Board granted the Immigration and Naturalization Service use of the eighty-acre pre-war Santa Fe Civilian Conservation Corps (CCC) camp.[57] Expectations were that 1,400 Japanese enemy aliens would be held there. At its peak in 1945, it held 2,100 men removed from places across the U. S. and other parts of the world including Hawaii, Alaska, Peru, Bolivia, Dominican Republic, Haiti, and Panama.[58] Modifications of the forty-two buildings in the CCC complex began March 3rd, the day after permission was granted to the INS to use the camp.[59] The first 357 *Issei* arrived by train at the newly designated Santa Fe Japanese Internment Camp on March 23rd, along with another 209 arriving three days later.

Amidst the turmoil of identifying Japanese-free zones, establishing relocation centers, and identifying "enemy aliens," the notion was put forth to establish Japanese colonies on farmable land in the American west, similar to the Indian reservation system, for the purpose of containing the Japanese. New Mexico was touted as a place where 60,000 Japanese-American colonists could settle.[60] Talk about it was everywhere and opinions flared like wildfire. The topic was in the forefront of the newscasts, newspapers, social events, conversations between neighbors, and political speeches. With the exception of a handful of people, attitudes were firmly set against allowing Japanese colonization in New Mexico.[61] The uproar in New Mexico over colonization within the state seemed to have its desired effect. The government dropped the idea and proceeded with the smaller, contained relocation centers and enemy alien camps. The final plan was announced in late May 1942. In the meantime, Governor Miles remained unconvinced that a colonization strategy would be abandoned. He spoke out in opposition of the idea at every possible opportunity and promised the full use of his "emergency police powers if necessary to prevent the colonization of New Mexico districts by Japanese."[62]

Orders to surrender to the nearest Japanese contingent around noon on April 9, 1942, reached the 200th and 515th on April 8th.[63] The men were heartsick but not surprised. A total of 36,853 allied forces surrendered.[64] Of these the Japanese reported that 6,700 were American. Thousands of Filipino troops had been relieved of duty a few weeks before. It would not be until January 1943 that Japan would begin to release information on American POWs.[65] The 200th and 515th were to destroy their antiaircraft equipment and organize as infantry to protect the line south of Cabcaben airfield until the time came to surrender.[66] The 200th and 515th were the only organized units remaining and, therefore, the only ones to receive orders to defend anything. So under the dark sky of a moonless night they carried out their orders.

The Japanese were unprepared to handle the huge number of surrendering men. Corregidor, a rock fortress island off the southern tip of Bataan, did not surrender simultaneously. Japanese infantry and tanks were streaming through the glut of Americans and Filipinos turning themselves in. Most of the 200th and 515th were on the front lines and, therefore, closest to the rapidly approaching Japanese. This would be one of the few blessings to come their way over the next three and one half years. The advancing Japanese army needed to get through en mass to be within range for their attack on Corregidor.[67] A convoy of Japanese infantry was dropped off at Cabcaben shortly after surrender. The empty trucks were used once to haul some of the 200th and 515th to San Fernando where they were dropped off at the train station before reloading the trucks with incoming Japanese reinforcements. Thus, the POWs who were transported by truck missed the grueling fifty-four-mile death march from Cabcaben to San Fernando.[68]

Many members of the 200th and 515th, however, walked the death march to the railroad station in San Fernando. They were eyewitnesses to POWs having their heads bashed in with rifle butts for talking or roughly prodded along with bayoneted rifles and, every once in a while, randomly executed.[69] One sure death sentence was to be caught in possession of any Japanese item. Killing the marchers in as many sadistic ways as they could think up became a sort of sport. Beheadings, stabbings, dismemberings, and clubbings predominanted. The prisoners marched day and night with minimal stops for rest although the Japanese guards were replaced with fresh soldiers often. Water was withheld from them, turning the phrase "dying for a drink" into reality. Some desperate souls dared to try to get water from the roadside artesian wells and were slain in a perfunctory manner. Others simply died from the lack of it.

News of defeat in the Philippines quickly reached Santa Fe.[70] Families paid five cents to read the bad news in the *Santa Fe New Mexican*. The bold headline "BATAAN CRUMPLES" pierced their hearts. The glum news spanned four pages. "Doubt if Many Can Get Away." "Bulk of Defenders Army Lost." "Fighting New Mexican Regiment Somewhere on Luzon at Finish of Gallant Defense." Mayor Manuel Lujan, Sr., immediately called for a meeting to confer with all civic organizations regarding the role of the Santa Fe Council of National Defense.

The governor attempted to prop up the people's courage through a series of proclamations after the fall of Bataan. His first was as "A Day of Prayer in New Mexico"[71] asking for the "spiritual aid of the Almighty in the strenuous and difficult days ahead," as it was "entirely fitting that we beseech the blessing of God for those who may be in prison camps and for those who are still fighting the battle of survival. With God's help we will hasten the day when the defenders of the Philippines can return to their families and homes and carry on again their civilian lives in peace and security."

Conditions in the Japanese POW camps where Americans, Filipino, and other allied forces were held were dire and improved only slightly towards the end of the war. Some 2,100 Americans and 37,000 Filipinos died in the Philippines during their first few days of captivity between April 12th and 24th.[72] One out of every six American POWs, a total of 1,450, died from malaria in the first six weeks of being held prisoner.[73] The dead were piled in contorted heaps reaching three feet high in the morgue until a burial detail could haul them out. A constant parade of death flowed as the dead POWs were taken in stretchers to be buried.[74]

With the fate of the 200th unknown, a need to pay some sort of tribute to them grew. A committee of Santa Feans came up with a solution that involved moving the 200th's regimental marker from Fort Bliss to the State Capitol grounds.[75]

A solemn dedication ceremony followed.[76] The concrete marker was hand made by the men of the 200th as their regimental sign post at Fort Bliss. Its design is the official antiaircraft insignia incorporated with the Zia symbol of the state flag. Santa Fe philanthropist Amelia White referred to the monument as "preposterous" and "a hideous object."[77]

News of surrender fueled other problems. The issue of Japanese colonization in New Mexico was far from over after all. Piles of letters protesting colonization besieged Governor Miles' office. Among them were two in favor of the idea. One of the two writers, Mr. John Wight of Los Angeles, went as far as to inquire of the Secretary of State in Washington, DC, about the possibility of purchasing or leasing some 25,000 to 50,000 acres of privately owned irrigated land in New Mexico for the purpose of establishing a Japanese colony.[78] Governor Miles was quick to reiterate the attitude in New Mexico that "our people are bitterly opposed to Japanese colonization in any form" citing economic, social, and political reasons for the opposition as well as the fact that more than 2,000 New Mexico men were now prisoners of the Japanese."[79] Bitter opposition was somewhat of an understatement. One letter to the governor suggested that "planting Jap colonies over this country would be worse than filling our water supply with typhus germs."[80] The people's voices prevailed and nothing more was said.

Another 192 *Issei* from California[81] arrived and were quietly put into the Santa Fe camp as the stormy discourse on colonization re-emerged. Camp population fluctuated from month-to-month throughout its life. Internees were shuffled from one camp to another for various reasons and many were repatriated to Japan. Among Japanese-Americans who renounced their American citizenship, 1,098 were considered hard core patriots of Japan and incarcerated at Tule Lake in California. Their applications for repatriation were usually approved without delay and, in groups ranging from 70 to 650 people, they were moved from Tule Lake to the Santa Fe camp to await repatriation.[82] About forty percent ultimately refused to return to Japan.

The radical Tule Lake internees, who account for the majority of the total 2,100 internees in Santa Fe in 1945[83], sported shaved heads, rose each morning to face the rising sun, and prayed for the Emperor and Japanese military success. They beat up one *Nisei* who would not renounce his U. S. citizenship.[84]

The only incident of note in the history of the Santa Fe internment camp occurred in March 1945.[85] The Tule Lake group refused to turn in their sweatshirts bearing emblems of Japanese organizations supporting Japan's march to victory in the war. The following day a search was conducted by thirty Border Patrol inspectors from El Paso, Texas, to forcibly remove the contraband. Two days later a demonstration arose when three known trouble makers of the group were to be transferred out of camp. A crowd of between 250 and 300 internees congregated with the intent to interfere with the transfer. Guards threw several gas billeys and tear gas grenades into the crowd. The internees responded by hurling rocks at the guards and administration buildings. All guards were called in. They carried sub-machine guns, riot guns, and other weapons and secured the perimeter while sixteen officers with night sticks and gas billeys went into the compound to break up the riot and disburse the group. Eventually the guards acquired the upper hand. Several rioters were injured during the incident but all recovered.[86]

The pre-existing large wooden barracks covered in tar paper left standing from the CCC days housed most of the Japanese men.[87] The others were put into sixteen-by-sixteen-foot plywood huts, four men to a hut. They slept on mattresses suspended slightly off the floor by iron cots. Each of the CCC barracks had its own latrine inside. Spanish Embassy representatives regularly visited the camp in accordance with EO 9066 to facilitate Japanese requests, especially those for repatriation, hear grievances, and inspect the facility. The internees were allowed a limited self-government and selected a spokesman to convey messages between camp command and internees. Grievances were to be brought to the attention of inspectors by the spokesman. Each week each man was given three clean hand towels, two bath towels, two bed sheets, one pillow case, and two pounds of meat.[88]

Among the first complaints received was the lack of traditional baths although they had access to unlimited hot showers.[89] Bath tubs were installed immediately. Although applications for repatriation were quickly processed and hearings held, the internees were dissatisfied with the time it took to learn the verdict of their hearings. But all-in-all the Spanish Consul inspectors found the men well treated, of high morale, and living in a "spotless" facility from the first inspection through the last.

The detainees cooked their own meals, were allowed unlimited visitors, and practiced their own religions whether it be Christianity, Buddhism, or Shinto.[90] Facilities included a staffed hospital, several barracks, a softball diamond, croquet sets, a library with both English and Japanese material, horse shoe tossing area, radios, censored in and out mail service, a canteen, a bakery, a recreation hall, a kitchen for preparing Japanese cuisine, a hot house to grow vegetables, a twenty-acre garden, a laundry, and several other service buildings. Although the internees favored playing softball above all recreational activities, others such as watching movies, performing dramas, competing in judo and ping pong tournaments, orchestral performances, and conducting science classes had a dedicated following.[91]

Around the first of July 1942 a fire broke out at the Japanese internment camp and destroyed the internees' and officers' mess halls and several other buildings. Five weeks later all of the Japanese were evacuated.[92] After attending to some paperwork and cleaning out the camp, it was abandoned. The dormancy of the camp lasted most of the winter. In February 1943 it was expanded to accommodate 2,000 people[93] and six weeks later the second phase of use began with the relocation of 357 internees from the Lordsburg, New Mexico, camp.[94] This number was added to in a few days hence by moving 150 Japanese internees from Livingston.

By December 17, 1944, Japanese evacuees held in American concentration camps were indexed into three groups:[95] 109,000 were cleared to go anywhere in the U. S. come the following January; 4,963 malcontented men who had renounced their American citizenship were to be kept in relocation centers (mostly at Tule Lake); and 4,810 men, most of whom had asked for expatriation to Japan, were to simply be excluded from the West Coast. As the war in both theaters proceeded in favor of the allies throughout 1945, improvements continued to be made at the internment camp—a new recreation hall, a new electric sterilizer in the hospital, improved clothing supply house, a new Judo gymnasium, a new outdoor wrestling ring, new ping pong tables, new beer hall, new soccer field, new equipment for the shop, a new shoe stitcher, four new latrines and six wash basins, improvements to the golf course, an addition of 778 books to the library along with new shelving, new screen doors, and more than a dozen other upgrades.[96]

Initially medical situations beyond the capabilities of the Santa Fe Japanese Internment Camp were treated at St. Vincent Hospital in downtown Santa Fe. Just after the camp re-opened in March 1943, a tract of land tucked into the southwest corner of the city limits was petitioned for condemnation on behalf of Bruns Hospital through Federal District Court by the U. S. Government.[97] Bruns was soon functioning and replaced St. Vincent as a back up to the internment camp hospital.

The doors to Bruns opened on April 19, 1943, to admit its first patient and was formally dedicated on September 22nd.[98] The hospital was named for the late Colonel Earl Harvey Bruns of the Army Medical Corps and former chief of Fitzsimons Hospital in Denver. He was an internationally known authority on pulmonary disease and thoracic surgery. Colonel Bruns died of pulmonary tuberculosis, the very disease upon which he had built his reputation.[99]

Bruns admitted 1,352 patients in the first year of operation.[100] Army installations established to handle war casualties were, by policy, placed about 400 miles inland of the coast to reduce their vulnerability yet be close enough to transport patients from a port to a hospital within one day. Hospital sites were selected on the basis of climate, terrain, utilities, transport systems, communication systems, available labor, housing, and accessibility to larger training camps. Santa Fe was deemed perfect.

Brigadier General Larry B. McAfee was the longest tenured commander of the facility. At its peak Bruns employed almost 1,000 civilians, 500 military men and 100 military nurses, had the capacity for 2,500 beds, pumped $4.5 million a year into the economy, and covered 250 acres.[101] Between 500 and 1,000 surgical operations were accomplished each year.[102] The paid staff was augmented by the "Gray Ladies of Santa Fe"[103] who visited with the patients and furthered their physical therapy program by teaching them to knit, crochet, or paint. Sometimes they simply read to them.

Bruns was one of fifty-one general hospitals built during WWII for the Army but it was never intended to be a permanent facility.[104] The buildings were constructed either of wood and plasterboard like so many in Los Alamos during the Manhattan Project or metal Quonset huts. By 1944 the Bruns Hospital complex had grown to 196 buildings. Outdoor facilities included a handball court, volley ball court, badminton court, shuffleboard, clock golf, tennis court, horse shoes, football field, and softball field.[105]

Reclassifying and relocating allied POWs in the Philippines started around November 1942. The Japanese began shipping them to labor camps where they worked for civilian companies producing materials, equipment, transportation systems, and energy for Japan's military. The healthiest POWs were selected for the work. Conditions in their new locations in Japan or occupied China were a little better but the work was much harder.[106] Before embarking on their transport ships, they were usually given new clothing made of lightweight denim, received their first "bath" in over seven months, and were given their first meal since December 1941. They had been subsisting on a rice ball or two a day since their surrender.

The bath was not for the comfort of the POWs but to decontaminate them before coming into close contact with Japanese civilians. They were stripped of their clothing, hosed down outside sometimes in freezing temperatures upon arriving at the Japanese docks, treated with a chemical substance, told to dress, and marched off towards the train that took them to their new camps. Several men perished on the voyage, others froze to death when hosed down, and hundreds more died of the cold temperatures during their first winter.[107]

A few American POWs escaped their Japanese captors and made their way into friendly hands during the winter of 1943–1944. The news relayed to the military about the treatment and condition of allied POWs was grim but accounts of the Death March was withheld from the public until January 1944.[108] More atrocities were exposed a year later when POWs from the 200th were rescued in a daring raid on Cabanatuan Prison Camp and returned to Bruns Hospital in Santa Fe to tell their stories. Sadly, no men from Santa Fe were in the group. Those still alive were incarcerated across the Far East.

Public outrage combined with heavy military losses for the Japanese during allied offensives probably led to opening up some lines of communication with POWs in Japanese camps. POWs began receiving mail from home in the spring of 1944, about one year after they were allowed to send their first message home.[109] The tide of war turned and it was getting worse for the Japanese early in 1945 despite the advantage of about 4 million armed Japanese men against 1.5 million armed U. S. troops in the Pacific Theater. It was only a month later that the Super-Fortress B-29 bomber laid waste to military targets in Tokyo and an all out invasion of Japan, named Operation Downfall, was finalized.[110]

As expected, the mood at Bruns hospital was completely different than at the prisoner camps.[111] A radio system, the Bruns Broadcasting System, was piped into every ward. Patients attentively listened to accounts of D-Day in Europe. Patients well enough to walk spent most of their day at the Post Exchange (PX) or out and about town on a furlough pass. Changes in 1944 brought about the re-designation of Bruns as a specialized center for chest diseases, medicine, and POWs. Seven hundred fifty beds were allotted for tuberculosis patients and seventy-five German POWs were brought in from Roswell as maintenance workers for the hospital.

In the middle of February 1944, a convalescent reconditioning annex to Bruns opened five miles away from the main hospital.[112] It had recently been operating as the Santa Fe Inn set on seventeen acres at the south end of Camino del Monte Sol near Old Santa Fe Trail. Their success rate was impressive. All of the men who received treatment at the annex returned to duty. The big lounge at the inn was used in the winter for indoor athletics and calisthenics but the principal components of the rehabilitation facility was its physical therapy clinic, occupational therapy shop, and physical and educational programs. Therapy treatments were those familiar to us today: short-wave diathermy, infra-red and ultra-violet lamps, electrical stimulation, whirlpool baths, massage, and passive and active exercise by professional physical therapists.

Miss Mela Ortiz y Pino dropped in regularly to instruct about a dozen interested patients in learning to speak Spanish.[113] A post orchestra formed and played for local dances. The PX was a combination general store, restaurant, soda fountain, and drug store where one could get a hair cut, clothes laundered, checks cashed, and clothes tailored. The social atmosphere of the PX made it the most popular spot at Bruns. After hours the lounge at the annex served as somewhat of a night club with beer, crackers, other cold drinks, pool tables, phone booths, and a juke box. The Army mandated the expansion of all its hospitals between May and June 1945 to handle the incoming wounded expected at the close of the war.[114] This consequently prompted Bruns to solicit one hundred additional civilian employees.[115] The end of the war in Europe in July 1945 led to the repatriation of the 150 Italian POWs being treated for tuberculosis at Bruns.[116] The space freed up by their departure was critical in order to treat the wounded U. S. servicemen returning to the states.

The massive destruction of cities and the tremendous loss of life in Japan brought about the end of the war in the Pacific. A series of incendiary bombings of Tokyo, Yokohama, Nagoya, Osaka, and Kobe took 300,000 lives and left one million homeless. Rather than concede, the Japanese continued to prepare for an allied invasion of their homeland. The Americans estimated the human cost of Operation Downfall to be somewhere between another quarter of a million to one million lives on both sides.[117] As the clock ticked closer to its implementation, President Truman made the historic decision to use the newly developed atomic bomb. American airplanes opened their bomb bay doors first to drop leaflets warning Japanese citizens to evacuate cities and then, several days later on August 6, 1945, to let loose the first atomic bomb. It was detonated 1,900 feet above Hiroshima causing unbelievable damage. Still, no signs of surrender. Conventional bombing of Tokyo resumed and a second atomic bomb was released over Nagasaki. The next day, August 10th, Japan put forth a tentative surrender but the allied bombings continued until Japan ordered its military to lay down its arms. That day came on September 2, 1945, the same day the official Instrument of Surrender was signed on board the *USS Missouri*.

Once the emaciated allied troops were fed, clothed, and rescued from their POW camps, soldiers of the 200th began returning home. Five hundred of them were admitted and treated at Bruns.[118] Fifty-eight percent were replete with tropical parasites, the most common being ascaris and hook worm. A few stories were passed around by the modest ex-POWs.[119] Tony Montoya became known as the "Angel of the Hospital" because he continually nursed the sick while in the Philippines. Evans Garcia faced a firing squad rather than squeal on another POW who had stolen food to feed the sick. Thankfully, they did not shoot him.

The federal government lifted restrictions from Japanese-Americans in January 1945.[120] The doors of the Santa Fe Japanese Internment Camp closed in April 1946 after having detained 4,555 Japanese men throughout the war. The Japanese detention program officially ended on June 30, 1946, leaving a scar on this country's record of human rights. About the same time the Japanese were given back control of their lives, the 200th reverted to National Guard status.[121] On the anniversary of the bombing of Pearl Harbor and the Philippine Islands, certain members of the 200th Coast Artillery were presented medals under the "Act of Recognition of Service in Bataan" for bravery, loyalty, and devotion to duty.[122]

Bruns' days were numbered, too. Mayor Lujan, all city counselors, and the

Santa Fe Chamber of Commerce petitioned the federal government to disburse Bruns as one unit so it could remain in town instead of being sold off building-by-building.[123] By resolution, the city backed a successful plan to turn it into a college to be run by the Christian Brothers of New Mexico.[124] In March 1947 the War Department awarded an interim permit to the College of Christian Brothers for 22 acres and 51 barracks.[125]

Pressure on the U. S. government coordinated through the National Council for Japanese American Redress out of Chicago led to congressional legislation offering amends to Japanese-American victims incarcerated and deprived of their constitutional rights. In 1950 thirty-eight million dollars in reparations were distributed and another $1.2 billion followed in 1987 with an apology from the American government.[126] U. S. civilians held in Japanese prison camps and servicemen who labored for the Japanese have received no compensation. Seventy-three Bataan Death March veterans, their families, and friends were offered an in-person apology from Ambassador Ichiro Fujisaki on behalf of the Japanese government in a historic address on May 30, 2009, at the last convention of the American Defenders of Bataan and Corregidor held in San Antonio, Texas. Ambassador Fujisaki said in part "we extend a heartfelt apology for our country having caused damage and suffering to many people including prisoners of war, those who have undergone tragic experiences in the Bataan Peninsula, in Corregidor Island in the Philippines, and other places."[127]

19

Alcaldes and Mayors of Santa Fe
1613–2008
by
Albert J. Gallegos and José Antonio Esquibel

The origin of the municipality of the Villa de Santa Fe is documented in the decree of don Luis de Velasco II, viceroy of Nueva España, dated March 30, 1609, in which he committed to paper and for posterity the instructions to Governor don Pedro de Peralta for the establishment of a formal villa in New Mexico.[1] The decree specifically referred to the election of four municipal councilmen, the *regidores*, who would elect two *alcaldes ordinarios* from among their number with the authority to hear civil and criminal cases with the jurisdiction of the villa, extending about fifteen miles from the center of the town in all directions.

For purposes of fiscal, judicial, and military administration, seventeenth-century New Mexico was divided into various jurisdictions. By the mid-1600s there were seven administrative jurisdictions outside of the jurisdiction of the Villa de Santa Fe. From the northern region southward the jurisdictions were Los Tewas, Los Tanos, Cochití, the Isleta and Sandia, and Los Piros.[2] On the east side of the Manzano mountains of New Mexico was the jurisdiction of Las Salinas. To the far west was the jurisdiction referred to as *Las Provincias de Moqui* reaching into modern-day Arizona, and by the 1650s the outpost and region of El Paso del Río del Norte in the far south was clearly another administrative jurisdiction of New Mexico. These jurisdictions formed the political geography of New Mexico with the Villa de Santa Fe serving as the center for royal government administration.[3] An *alcalde mayor* was appointed by the governors to represent the crown and serve as ministers of justice and as military leaders in each of the jurisdictions. However, in the jurisdiction of the Villa de Santa Fe the chief magistrates were the two *alcaldes ordinaries*, both members of the *cabildo*, town council.

During the era that New Mexico was administered as part of the Spanish crown, elections for members of the *cabildo* of the Villa de Santa Fe were held annually in early January. Of the two *alcaldes ordinarios*, one was known as the *alcalde ordinario del primer voto* (first vote) and the other as the *alcalde ordinario del segundo voto* (second vote). One, or sometimes both, *alcaldes ordinaries* also held the title of *capitán de guerra*, literally war captain, referring to the role as captain of the local militia. The other positions of the town council included two *regidores* (councilmen), the *alguacil mayor* (sheriff), and the *escribano* (scribe/clerk). Men in these positions also took on the duties of *procurador general* and royal standard bearer. During the 1700s the two positions of *alcalde ordinario* became known as *alcalde mayor*, consisting of *alcalde mayor* of the first vote and *alcalde mayor* of the second vote. In 1821, the same positions were titled *alcaldes constitucionales*. With the advent of New Mexico's U. S. territorial era the term *alcalde mayor* was eventually substituted with that of mayor, as traditionally known in English-speaking municipalities.

In addition to being leaders of civic governance, the *alcaldes ordinaries*, and later the *alcaldes mayores*, served primarily as chief magistrates of their jurisdiction. The *alcalde ordinario/mayor* of the first vote presided over cases for residents of the first district and that of the second vote presided over cases for residents of the second district. The boundaries of these jurisdictions are difficult to ascertain due to a lack of maps or general descriptions of the district. These magistrates received and reviewed a variety of petitions from citizens, reviewed civic complaints, presided over proceedings related to a variety of types of civil and criminal lawsuits, property ownership, land disputes, and sales and donations of land. They also served as the certifying judge for last wills and testaments and oversaw proceedings related to settlements of estate.

The town council held meetings in the *sala del cabildo*, also known as the *sala de ayutamiento*, the hall of the municipal council, located in a building referred to as the *casa del cabildo/ayuntamiento*.[4] The precise location of this building during the 1600s is uncertain, but it is known that the doors of the building faced the *plaza mayor*, also known as the *plaza principal*, and was most likely located opposite of the *casas reales*, now known as the Palace of the Governors. During the 1700s, the *casa de cabildo* may have been situated on the south side of the plaza. In 1836, the *casa de ayuntamiento* was located on the east side of the plaza.[5]

During the seventeenth-century, when an edict or decree was issued by the *cabildo* of the Villa de Santa Fe it was given to one of the *pregoneros*, town criers, who would post the decree on the doors of the *cabildo*, the *casas reales* and the church. During the course of this posting, the *pregonero* would proceed to areas around the *plaza mayor*, shouting for people to gather, and would read the decree in a loud voice for the public to hear. Only a few names of *pregoneros* are known from the seventeenth century, such as:

- Antonio, Indio *ladino* (an Indian who was literate in spoken and written Spanish), *pregonero* in 1640;
- Alonso Ramírez, *mulato* (part African and Indian or African and Spaniard), *pregonero* in 1661;
- Juan Utaca, *Indio ladino, pregonero* in 1662; and
- Joséph, *Indio ladino, pregonero público* in 1662.[6]

In the early seventeenth century, the members of the *cabildo* were required as part of their duties to attend mass and special feast day celebrations as a group. An edict from the viceroy of New Spain dated November 1714 specified sixteen mandatory feast days to be attended by *cabildo* members. A list of these dates recorded on January 8, 1715, reminded the Santa Fe *cabildo* members of their obligation to attend these religious celebrations:[7]

1. January 1st, New Years Day
2. January 25th, Feast of the Conversion of San Pablo, titular saint of New Mexico
3. February 2nd, Feast of the Purification of Our Lady
4. *Viernes de Dolores* (Friday of Sorrows), honoring Nuestra Señora de los Dolores on the Friday before Palm Sunday
5. Palm Sunday
6. Holy Thursday
7. Easter Resurrection, second day
8. May 1st, Feast of San Felipe and Santiago, the birthday of King Felipe V
9. Feast of Corpus Christi with vespers
10. August 15th, Feast of the Assumption of Our Lady
11. September 14th, Feast of the Exaltation of the Cross promised by the Villa for protection from *los rayos* with vespers[8]
12. 1st Sunday of October, Feast of the Naval Battle[9]
13. October 4th Feast of Nuestro Padre San Francisco
14. December 8th, Feast of the Immaculate Conception of Our Lady
15. December 25th, Christmas, second day
16. 2nd day of the Feast of Espiritú Santo

As a matter of practice, the *cabildo* held meetings on specific days of the month and minutes were kept, although most of these records for the seventeenth and eighteenth centuries appear to have not survived the passage of time. An inventory of the *cabildo* archives was apparently conducted at the beginning of each year. At the end of each year, the members of the *cabildo* were required to provide a fiscal account for the previous year and a record of proceedings. Only a few of these types of records are preserved.[10] The majority of archival documents preserved in the Spanish Archives of New Mexico, Series I, dating from 1682–1821, relate to cases brought before the *alcaldes ordinaries* and *alcaldes mayores* of various communities of New Mexico, in particular the Villa de Santa Fe.

There is documentation that on at least two occasions in the history of the *cabildo* of the Villa de Santa Fe the *alcaldes* were appointed or commissioned by governors. In January 1715, due to the small number of councilmen, Governor Don Juan Ignacio Flores Mogollón commissioned General Juan Páez Hurtado and Captain Juan García de la Riva as *alcaldes ordinarios*. Don Francisco Guerrero, who first served as an *alcalde ordinario* in 1733 and again in 1742, received an appointment from Governor Don Francisco Antonio Marín del Valle (1754–1760) as *alcalde mayor* and served for as many as seventeen terms between 1733 and 1777, making him one of the longest serving *alcaldes* in the history of the town council of Santa Fe.

Other men who dedicated many years of services as *alcaldes* of Santa Fe include: Captain Don Diego Arias de Quirós, who is know to have served eighteen terms between 1697 and 1731; Don Antonio José Ortiz, who served as many as seventeen terms between 1777 and 1795; Captain Don Antonio Ulibarrí, who served at least fourteen terms between 1732 and 1754; and Don Francisco Bueno de Bohórquez y Corcuera, who held the post of *alcalde mayor* for as many as nine terms between 1714 and 1724. Each is deserving of particular recognition for their lengthy service, which stand as a testament to the high degree of trust and respect with which they were regarded by their peers and the citizens of Santa Fe. Perhaps modern city leaders will consider honoring their memory when considering names for city projects, buildings, or roads.

It is also worthwhile to note that as many as eighteen *alcaldes* of Santa Fe during the eighteenth and early nineteenth centuries were members of a large extended family clan. This clan dominated the politics of Santa Fe as influential leaders and established themselves as the socially prominent members of the community. The common ancestors of this large clan were Captain Antonio de Montoya, an *alcalde ordinario* between 1692 and 1713, Captain Juan Páez Hurtado, an *alcalde ordinario* between 1712 and 1737, and Miguel José de la Vega y Coca, an *alcalde ordinario* between 1724 and 1726. The complex network of relations of this clan is illustrated in the genealogy chart below and serves as an outline for future study of the political dominance of this extended family.

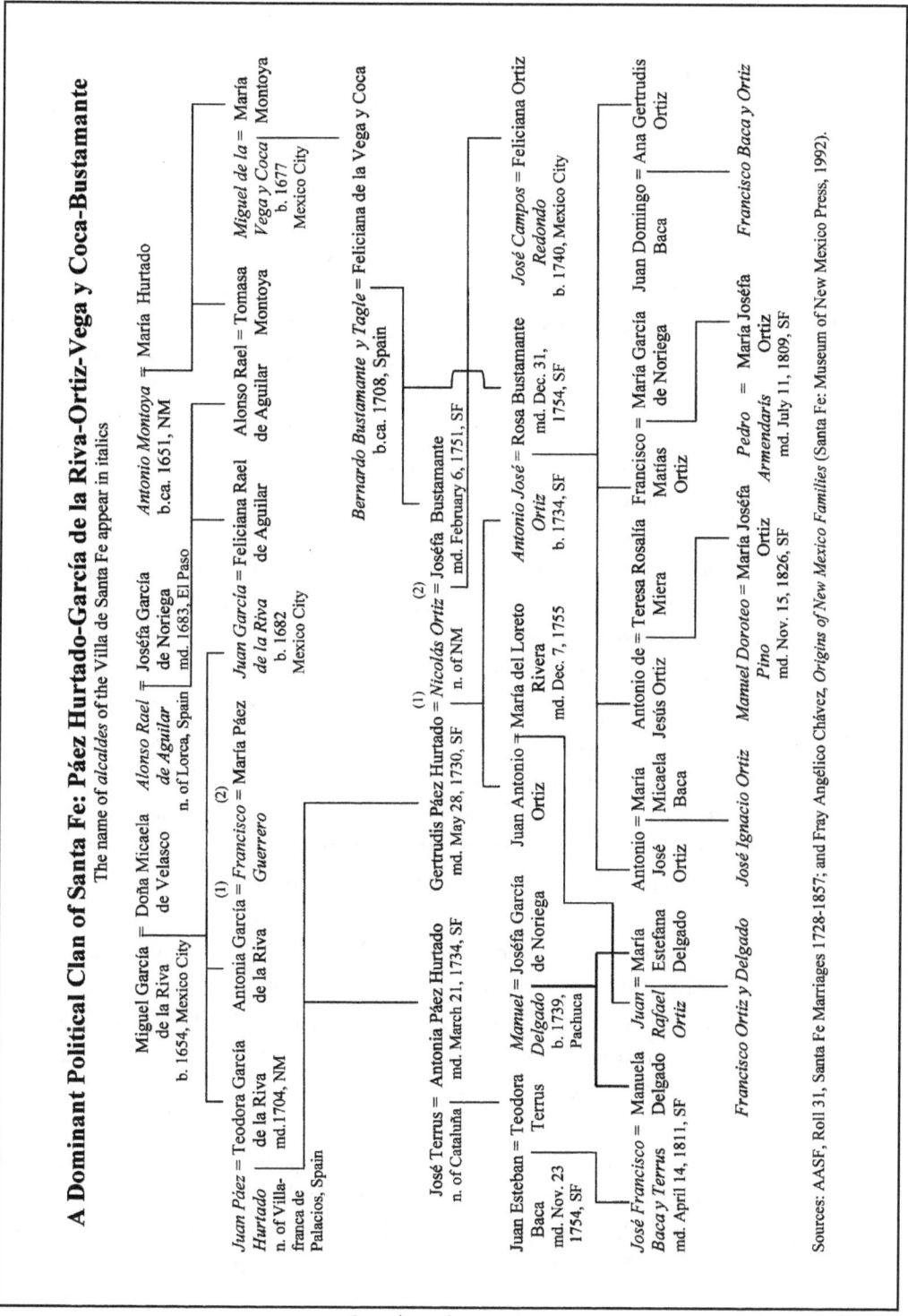

Genealogy chart.

The town council of Santa Fe has existed continuously since 1610 through eleven eras of distinct government administration over the course of four centuries. Santa Fe held the status of a villa from 1610 until 1819 when it became recognized administratively as a *ciudad* (city).[11] Under the government of the United States of America, Santa Fe became officially incorporated as a city on June 17, 1891, by popular vote of its citizens.[12] Because of a loss of records for the period of 1610 through 1693, the names of many of the *alcaldes ordinarios* for that period remain unknown. The records begin to improve in 1692 and there is almost a continuous account of the municipal leaders of Santa Fe to the modern day, with a gap in names for the period of 1858 through 1890. Although an effort was made to locate primary sources that identify the mayors for this gap, no records were uncovered. It appears that between 1858 and 1890 many of the official and legal mayoral duties were carried out by the elected commissioners and clerk of courts of the County of Santa Fe. No minutes of town council meetings for that period were located in a search of various archival collections.

A seen below, names for more than two *alcaldes* were uncovered for several years. There are a number of reasons to consider for this occurrence. In some cases, a particular *alcalde* was unable to perform his duties for a short period of time or unable to complete his term due to illness, absence from the town due to travel, or because of removal from office. As such, a *regidor*, councilman, was selected to serve as an acting or provisional *alcalde* or was elected to replace the *alcalde* for the remaining term. In January 1716, Captain Francisco Lorenzo Casados was elected as *alcalde ordinario* of the second vote while absent from the Villa de Santa Fe on travel. The *regidor* Salvador Montoya was selected to serve as *alcalde ordinario* until the return of Casados.[13] Travel became an impediment to electing *alcaldes* in Santa Fe. Many of the eligible men made their living in commerce and traveled out of New Mexico for as much as four to six months of the year, according to an account by Governor Fernando Chacón recorded in 1799.[14] Social, economic and political conflicts contributed to difficulties in completing full terms for some *alcaldes ordinarios*. The list of *alcaldes* for 1833, 1837, 1841, 1844 (see below) are examples of politically eventful years when several *alcaldes* did not complete full terms due to conflicts of interest and indictments for alleged misconduct or partiality.[15] As a result, others were selected to fill their positions.

In 1833, Don José Francisco Baca y Ortiz, 1st *Alcalde Constitucional*, was accused of abuse of power in a case in which he forcibly dispossessed a citizen of his property.[16] Baca y Ortiz was apparently replaced by Don Juan García, who came to hold the title of 1st *Alcalde Constitucional* for the remaining part of the year of 1833.[17] In 1837, *Alcalde* Don Juan García could not complete his term of office, finding himself "unable to exercise his duties as a magistrate on account of his infirmities."[18] Citizens of Santa Fe complained about "irregularities" in the January 1841 election results of the town council. It was determined that there existed "immediate relations that unites individuals" among the group of newly elected officials, most likely referring to very close familial ties.[19] Following an investigation, the entire town council was replaced through a second election process. Despite the replacement of councilmen, problems surfaced later in the year with the removal of Don Francisco Ortiz y Delgado, 1st *Alcalde Constitucional*, due to allegations of "arbitrary and scandalous irregularities" on his part.[20] Ortiz y Delgado was replaced and also in that same year the 2nd *Alcalde Constitucional* was either removed from office, resigned, or was unable to continue his term.

The list of *alcaldes* and mayors presented below is based on consultation of numerous primary documents and is an expansion of the compilation of *alcaldes* and mayors made by Linda Tigges as part of her Santa Fe Historic Plaza research. While conducting the historic Santa Fe plaza study, Tigges reviewed numerous primary documents. Her research collection of transcriptions and translations of many of these documents are invaluable sources and served to guide the additional research presented below. The expanded compilation not only adds the names of additional men who served as *alcaldes* of Santa Fe but also adds more documentation from primary sources. The following list represents an updated, comprehensive account of the main municipal leaders of Santa Fe from 1613 to the present.

Alcaldes and Modern Mayors of the Villa and City of Santa Fe

First Period of the Cabildo de la Villa de Santa Fe
Era of the Spanish Empire
Viceroyalty of Nueva España, 1610–1680

1613
Captain Don Juan de Escarramad, Alcalde Ordinario[21]
Juan Ruiz de Cáceres, Alcalde Ordinario[22]

1614
Captain Juan de Vitoria Carvajal, Alcalde Ordinario[23]

1615
Captain Asencio de Archuleta, Alcalde Ordinario[24]

1626
Captain Francisco Pérez Granillo, Alcalde Ordinario[25]

1628
Captain Bartolomé Romero II, Alcalde Ordinario[26]

1631
Captain Diego de Santa Cruz, Alcalde Ordinario[27]

1636
Captain Francisco Gómez, Alcalde Ordinario[28]

1639
Captain Don Roque Medón de Casaus, Alcalde Ordinario[29]
Captain Francisco de Madrid, Alcalde Ordinario[30]

1641
Antonio Baca, Alcalde Ordinario[31]

1643
Captain Matías Romero, Alcalde Ordinario[32]
Captain Francisco de Madrid, Alcalde Ordinario[33]

1644
Don Fernando Durán y Cháves I, Alcalde[34]

1650s
Francisco de Madrid II, Twice Alcalde Ordinario[35]

1660
Sargento Mayor Francisco Gómez Robledo, Alcalde Ordinario[36]
Captain Diego Romero, Alcalde Ordinario[37]

1661
Captain Bartolomé Romero II, Alcalde Ordinario of 1st vote[38]
Captain Pedro de Leyva, Alcalde Ordinario[39]

1662
Captain Francisco de Anaya Almazán, Alcalde Ordinario[40]
Sargento Mayor Diego López del Castillo, Alcalde Ordinario[41]

1663
Maese de Campo Juan Domínguez de Mendoza, Alcalde Ordinario[42]
Maese de Campo Tomé Domínguez de Mendoza, Alcalde Ordinario[43]

1664
Captain Juan Domínguez de Mendoza, Alcalde Ordinario[44]

1668
Captain Bartolomé Romero III, Alcalde Ordinario[45]
Maese de Campo Pedro Lucero de Godoy, Alcalde Ordinario[46]

1669
Captain Juan Domínguez de Mendoza, Alcalde Ordinario[47]

1680
Captain Francisco Xavier, Alcalde Ordinario of 1st vote[48]
Sargento Mayor Juan Lucero de Godoy, Alcalde Ordinario of 2nd vote[49]
Gregorio de Valdés, Alcalde Mayor[50]

Second Period of the Cabildo de la Villa de Santa Fe
Exile at El Paso del Río del Norte
Era of the Spanish Empire
Viceroyalty of Nueva España, 1681–1693

1681
Sargento Mayor Lorenzo de Madrid, Alcalde Ordinario[51]
Sargento Mayor Juan Lucero de Godoy, Alcalde Ordinario[52]

1682
Maese de Campo Francisco Xavier, Alcalde Ordinario[53]
Juan Lucero de Godoy, Alcalde Ordinario[54]

1683
Captain Francisco Ramírez de Salazar, Alcalde Ordinario[55]

1684
Sargento Mayor Lorenzo de Madrid, Alcalde Ordinario[56]
Captain Juan Severino de Zuballe, Alcalde Ordinario[56]

1685
Francisco Gómez Robledo, Alcalde Ordinario[58]

1689
Juan Lucero de Godoy, Alcalde Ordinario[59]

1690
José Telles Jirón, Alcalde[60]

1692
Sargento Mayor Francisco de Anaya Almazán, Alcalde Ordinario of 1st vote[61]
Captain Antonio Montoya, Alcalde Ordinario of 2nd vote[62]

1693
Alonso Rael de Aguilar, Alcalde Ordinario[63]
Sargento Mayor Lorenzo de Madrid, Alcalde Ordinario[64]

**Third Period of the Cabildo de la Villa de Santa Fe
Reestablished in Santa Fe
Era of the Spanish Empire
Viceroyalty of Nueva España, 1694–1776**

1694
Maese de Campo Lorenzo de Madrid, Alcalde Ordinario[65]
Francisco Romero de Pedraza, Alcalde[66]

1695
Francisco Romero de Pedraza, Alcalde Ordinario[67]
Maese de Campo Lorenzo de Madrid, Alcalde Ordinario[68]

1696
Maese de Campo Lorenzo Madrid, Alcalde Ordinario of 1st vote[69]
Antonio de Aguilera y Isasi, Alcalde Ordinario of 2nd vote[70]
Francisco Romero de Pedraza, Alcalde Ordinario[71]

1697
Captain Diego Montoya, Alcalde Ordinario[72]
Captain Don Diego Arias de Quirós, Alcalde Ordinario[73]

1698
Captain Don Diego Arias de Quirós, Alcalde Ordinario of 1st vote[74]
Antonio Lucero de Godoy, Alcalde Ordinario[75]
Antonio de Aguilera y Isasi, Alcalde Ordinario[76]

1699
Antonio Lucero de Godoy, Alcalde Ordinario[77]
Antonio de Aguilera y Isasi, Alcalde Ordinario of 2nd vote[78]

1700
Agustín Sáez, Alcalde Ordinario of 1st vote[79]
Antonio de Aguilera y Isasi, Assistant Alcalde Ordinario and then Alcalde Ordinario of 1st vote[80]
Captain Francisco Romero de Pedraza, Alcalde Ordinario[81]

1701
Francisco Romero, Alcalde Ordinario[82]
José Rodríguez, Alcalde Ordinario of 2nd vote[83]

1702
Antonio de Aguilera y Isasi, Alcalde[84]
Captain Antonio de Montoya I, Alcalde Ordinario of 2nd vote[85]
José Rodríguez, Alcalde Ordinario of 2nd vote[86]

1703
Captain Antonio Montoya I, Alcalde Ordinario[87]
Maese de Campo Lorenzo de Madrid, Alcalde Ordinario of 2nd vote[88]

1704
Maese de Campo Lorenzo de Madrid, Alcalde Ordinario of 1st vote[89]
Captain Don Diego Arias de Quirós, Alcalde Ordinario[90]
Captain Antonio de Montoya I, Acting Alcalde Ordinario of 2nd vote[91]

1705
General Juan de Ulibarrí, Alcalde Ordinario of 1st vote[92]
Captain Don Diego Arias de Quirós, Alcalde Ordinario of 2nd vote[93]

1706
Captain Don Alonso Rael de Aguilar, Alcalde Ordinario of 1st vote[94]
Captain Diego Arias de Quirós, Alcade Ordinario[95]

1707
Captain Don Alonso Rael de Aguilar, Alcalde Ordinario of 1st vote[96]
Captain Antonio de Montoya I, Alcalde Ordinario of 2nd vote[97]

1708
Juan García de la Riva, Alcalde Ordinario of 2nd vote[98]

1710
Captain Juan de Ulibarrí, Alcalde Ordinario[99]
Captain Diego Arias de Quirós, Alcalde Ordinario[100]

1711
Captain Diego Arias de Quirós, Alcalde Ordinario[101]
Sargento Mayor Juan de Ulibarrí, Alcalde Ordinario[102]
Captain Alonso Rael de Aguilar, Alcalde Ordinario[103]

1712
Captain Diego Arias de Quirós, Alcalde Ordinario[104]
Captain Don Alonso Rael de Aguilar, Alcalde Ordinario of 2nd vote [105]
General Don Juan Páez Hurtado, Alcalde Ordinario[106]

1713
General Don Juan Páez Hurtado, Alcalde Ordinario of 1st vote[107]
Antonio Montoya I, Alcalde Ordinario[108]
Captain Juan García de la Riva, Alcalde Ordinario[109]

1714
Captain Francisco Bueno de Bohórquez y Corcuera, Provisional Alcalde and then Alcalde Mayor & War Captain[110]
Captain Juan García de la Riva, Alcalde Mayor[111]
Juan de Ulibarrí, Alcalde Ordinario[112]
Captain Don Diego Arias de Quirós, Alcalde Mayor & War Captain[113]

1715
General Don Juan Páez Hurtado, Alcalde Ordinario of 1st vote[114]
Captain Juan García de la Riva, Alcalde Ordinario of 2nd vote[115]
Captain Don Alonso Rael de Aguilar, Alcalde Ordinario[116]
Captain Diego Arias de Quirós, Alcalde Ordinario & War Captain[117]

1716
Captain Juan García de la Riva, Alcalde Ordinario of 1st vote[118]
Captain Francisco Lorenzo de Casados, Alcalde Ordinario of 2nd vote[119]
Salvador Montoya, Acting Alcalde Ordinario of 2nd vote[120]
Captain Don Diego Arias de Quirós, Alcalde Ordinario & War Captain[121]

1717
Captain Francisco Bueno de Bohórquez y Corcuera, Alcalde Mayor[122]
Juan García de la Riva, Alcalde[123]
Salvador Montoya, Alcalde[124]

1718
Captain Francisco Bueno de Bohórquez y Corcuera, Alcalde Mayor & War Captain[125]

1719
Captain Francisco Bueno de Bohórquez y Corcuera, Alcalde Mayor & War Captain[126]

1720
Captain Francisco Bueno de Bohórquez y Corcuera, Alcalde Mayor & War Captain[127]
Miguel Tenorio de Alba, Alcalde Mayor[128]

1721
Captain Francisco Bueno de Bohórquez y Corcuera, Alcalde Mayor & War Captain[129]
Juan de Pineda, Alcalde Mayor[130]
Captain Don Diego Arias de Quirós, Alcalde[131]

1722
Captain Francisco Bueno de Bohórquez y Corcuera, Alcalde Mayor & War Captain[13]
Captain Don Diego Arias de Quirós, Alcalde Mayor & War Captain[133]

1723
Captain Francisco Bueno de Bohórquez y Corcuera, Alcalde Mayor & War Captain[134]

1724
Captain Francisco Bueno de Bohórquez y Corcuera, Alcalde Mayor[135]
Miguel José de la Vega y Coca, Alcalde Mayor[136]

1725
Captain Francisco José de Casados, Alcalde Mayor[137]
Miguel José de la Vega y Coca, Alcalde Mayor & War Captain[138]
Antonio Montoya, Alcalde Mayor & War Captain[139]

1726
Miguel José de la Vega y Coca, Alcalde Mayor[140]

1727
Captain Don Diego Arias de Quirós, Alcalde Mayor & Alcalde Ordinario[141]

1728
Captain Don Diego Arias de Quirós, Alcalde Mayor & War Captain[142]
Captain Antonio Montoya II, Alcalde Mayor & War Captain[143]

1729
Captain Antonio Montoya II, Alcalde Mayor[144]
Captain Don Diego Arias de Quirós, Alcalde Mayor & War Captain[141]

1730
Captain Don Diego Arias de Quirós, Alcalde Mayor & War Captain[146]

1731
Captain Don Diego Arias de Quirós, Alcalde Mayor[147]

1732
Captain Antonio de Ulibarrí, Alcalde Mayor & War Captain[148]

1733
Captain Antonio de Ulibarrí, Alcalde Mayor & War Captain[149]
Don Francisco Guerrero, Alcalde Mayor[150]
Captain Antonio Montoya II, Alcalde Mayor & War Captain[151]

1734
Captain Antonio de Ulibarrí, Alcalde Mayor[152]

1735
Captain Antonio de Ulibarrí, Alcalde Mayor[153]

1736
Captain Antonio Montoya II, Alcalde Mayor[154]
Captain Antonio de Ulibarrí, Alcalde Mayor[155]

1737
Captain Antonio de Ulibarrí, Alcalde Mayor[156]
Juan García, Alcalde Mayor[157]

1738
Captain Antonio Montoya II, Alcalde Mayor & War Captain[158]
Captain Juan Rodríguez, Alcalde Mayor[159]

1739
Captain Antonio Montoya II, Alcalde Mayor & War Captain[160]

1740
Lieutenant General Don Juan Páez Hurtado, Alcalde Mayor & War Captain[161]
Captain Antonio Montoya II, Alcalde Mayor & War Captain[162]

1741
Lieutenant General Don Juan Páez Hurtado, Alcalde Mayor[163]

1742
Captain Don Antonio de Ulibarrí, Alcalde Mayor & War Captain[164]
Don Francisco Guerrero, Alcalde[165]

1743
Captain Don Antonio de Ulibarrí, Alcalde Mayor & War Captain[166]

1744
Captain Don Antonio de Ulibarrí, Alcalde Mayor[167]

1745
Captain Don Antonio de Ulibarrí, Alcalde Mayor & War Captain[168]

1746
Captain Don Antonio de Ulibarrí, Alcalde Mayor & War Captain[169]

1749
Don José de Bustamante de Tagle, Alcalde Mayor[170]
Captain Don Antonio de Ulibarrí, Alcalde Mayor[171]

1750
Don José de Bustamante y Tagle, Alcalde Mayor[172]
Don Bernardo Bustamante y Tagle, Alcalde Mayor[173]

1751
Don José de Bustamante y Tagle, Alcalde Mayor & War Captain[174]
Captain Don Antonio de Ulibarrí, Alcalde Mayor[175]
Manuel Gallegos, Lieutenant Alcalde Mayor[176]

1752
Don José de Bustamante y Tagle, Alcalde Mayor & War Captain[177]
Manuel Gallegos, Lieutenant Alcalde Mayor[178]

1753
Don Nicolás Ortiz, Alcalde Mayor & War Captain[179]
Manuel Gallegos, Lieutenant Alcalde Mayor[180]

1754
Don Nicolás Ortiz, Alcalde Mayor & War Captain[181]
Don Antonio de Ulibarrí, Alcalde Mayor[182]

1755
Don Francisco Guerrero, Alcalde Mayor & War Captain[183]

1756
Don Francisco Guerrero, Alcalde Mayor & War Captain[184]

1757
Don Francisco Guerrero, Alcalde Mayor & War Captain[185]

1758
Don Francisco Guerrero, Alcalde Mayor & War Captain[186]

1759
Don Francisco Guerrero, Alcalde Mayor & War Captain[187]

1760
Don Francisco Guerrero, Alcalde Mayor & War Captain[188]
Felipe Tafoya, Alcalde Mayor[189]

1761
Don Francisco Guerrero, Alcalde Mayor & War Captain[190]
Manuel Gallegos, Alcalde Mayor & War Captain[191]

1762
Manuel Gallegos, Alcalde Mayor & War Captain[192]

1763
Manuel Gallegos, Alcalde Mayor & War Captain[193]
Don Carlos Fernández, Alcalde Mayor[194]

1764
Don Francisco Guerrero, Alcalde Mayor[195]

1765
Don Francisco Guerrero, Alcalde Mayor[196]
Tomás Antonio Sena, Alcalde Mayor[197]

1766
Don Francisco Guerrero, Alcalde Mayor & War Captain[198]
Don Felipe Tafoya, Alcalde Mayor & War Captain[199]

1767
Don Francisco Guerrero, Alcalde Mayor[200]
Don Manuel García Pareja, Alcalde Mayor & War Captain[201]
Vicente Sena, Alcalde Mayor[202]

1768
Don Francisco Guerrero, Alcalde Mayor[203]
Don Felipe Tafoya, Alcalde Mayor & War Captain[204]

1769
Don Felipe Tafoya, Alcalde Mayor & War Captain[205]
Don Manuel García Pareja, Alcalde Mayor & War Captain[206]

1770
Don Felipe Tafoya, Alcalde Mayor & War Captain[207]

1771
Don Manuel García Pareja, Alcalde Mayor & War Captain[208]
Don Felipe Tafoya, Alcalde Mayor[209]

1772
Don Manuel García Pareja, Alcalde Mayor[210]
Don Manuel Gallegos, Alcalde Mayor[211]

1773
Don Manuel García Pareja, Alcalde Mayor & War Captain[212]

1774
Don Manuel García Pareja, Alcalde Mayor & War Captain[213]
Don Francisco Guerrero, Alcalde Mayor[214]

1775
Don Manuel García Pareja, Alcalde Mayor & War Captain[215]

1776
Don Manuel García Pareja, Alcalde Mayor & War Captain[216]
Don Francisco Guerrero, Alcalde Mayor[217]

**Fourth Period of the Cabildo de la Villa de Santa Fe
Era of the Spanish Empire
Provincias Internas, 1776–1785**

1777
Don Antonio José Ortiz, Alcalde Mayor & War Captain[218]
Don Francisco Guerrero, Alcalde Mayor[219]

1778
Don Felipe Tafoya, Alcalde Mayor & War Captain[220]
Don Antonio José Ortiz, Alcalde Mayor & War Captain[221]
José Miguel de la Peña, Alcalde Mayor[222]

1779
Don Felipe Tafoya, Alcalde Mayor & War Captain[223]

1781
Don Antonio José Ortiz, Alcalde Mayor[224]

1782
Don Antonio José Ortiz, Alcalde Mayor[225]

1783
Don Antonio José Ortiz, Alcalde Mayor & War Captain, Alférez Real & Captain of Militia[226]

1784
Don Antonio José Ortiz, Alcalde Mayor & War Captain, Alférez Real & Captain of Militia[227]
Manuel García Pareja, Alcalde[228]

1785
Don Antonio José Ortiz, Alcalde Mayor & War Captain, Alférez Real & Captain of Militia[229]
José Miguel de la Peña, Alcalde[230]

Fifth Period of the Cabildo de la Villa de Santa Fe
Era of the Spanish Empire
Viceroyalty of Nueva España, 1786–1792

1786
Don Antonio José Ortiz, Alcalde Mayor & War Captain, Alférez Real & Captain of Militia[231]
Don José Campos Redondo, Alcalde[232]

1787
Don Antonio José Ortiz, Alcalde Mayor & War Captain, Alférez Real & Captain of Militia[233]
Manuel García Pareja, Alcalde Mayor[234]

1788–1792
Don Antonio José Ortiz, Alcalde Mayor & War Captain, Alférez Real & Captain of Militia[235]

Sixth Period of the Cabildo de la Villa de Santa Fe
Elevated to a Ciudad in 1819
Era of the Spanish Empire
Provincias Internas, 1793–1821

1793–1795
Don Antonio José Ortiz, Alcalde Mayor & War Captain, Alférez Real & Captain of Militia[236]

1799
José Miguel de la Peña, Alcalde Mayor[237]

1800
José Miguel de la Peña, Alcalde Mayor of 1st vote[238]
Francisco Montoya, Alcalde Mayor of 1st vote[239]

1802
José Miguel de la Peña, Alcalde Mayor[240]
Juan Rafael Ortiz, Alcalde of 2nd vote[241]

1803
Don José Antonio Beita, Alcalde[242]
Don Pedro Bautista Pino, Alcalde of 2nd vote[243]

1804
Manuel Delgado, Alcalde of 1st vote[244]
José Francisco Ortiz, Alcalde[245]
Francisco Montoya, Alcalde[246]

1805
Don Bartolomé Fernández, Alcalde of 1st vote[247]
Manuel Delgado, Alcalde of 1st vote[248]
Francisco Montoya, Alcalde of 1st vote[249]

1808
Don Juan Rafael Ortiz, Alcalde of 1st vote[250]

1810
Don José Campo Redondo, Alcalde Mayor of 1st vote[251]
Don Diego Montoya, Alcalde of 1st vote[252]

1811
José Miguel Tafoya, Alcalde Ordinario[253]

1812
José Miguel Tafoya, Alcalde of 1st vote[254]
José Miguel Trujillo, Alcalde[255]

1813
Don Juan Cristóbal Vigil, Alcalde Mayor of 2nd vote[256]

1814
Matías Ortiz, Alcalde of 1st vote[257]

1815
Matías Ortiz, Alcalde of 1st vote[258]
Juan Estévan Pino, Alcalde of 2nd vote[259]

1816
Matías Ortiz, Alcalde[260]

1817
José Francisco Baca, Alcalde of 2nd vote[261]

1819
José Francisco Ortiz, Alcalde[262]

1820
José Francisco Ortiz, Alcalde of 1st vote[263]

**Seventh Period of the Cabildo de la Ciudad de Santa Fe
Era of the Empire of Mexico: Constitucional Monarchy
Provision Government Junta, 1821–1823**

1821
Juan Rafael Ortiz, Alcalde Constitucional[264]

1822
Don Pedro de Armendáriz, Alcalde of 1st vote & Captain of Militia[265]
Don José Francisco Baca, Alcalde[266]

**Eighth Period of the Cabildo de la Ciudad de Santa Fe
Era of the Republic of Mexico
Departamento de la Nación Méjicana, 1824–1846**

1824
Santiago Abreu, Alcalde of 1st vote[267]
José Ignacio Ortiz, Alcalde of 2nd vote[268]

1826
Don José Francisco Baca, First Alcalde Constitucional[269]

1827
Don José María Martínez, Alcalde Constitucional[270]
Juan Vigil, Acting Alcalde Constitucional[271]
Vicente Baca, Acting Alcalde Constitucional[272]

1829
Juan Bautista Vigil y Alarid, Alcalde[273]

1830[274]
José Ignacio Ortiz, Alcalde Constitucional[275]
Domingo Fernández, Second Alcalde Constitucional [276]

1831
Pablo Montoya, First Alcalde Constitucional[277]
Domingo Fernández, Alcalde[278]
Francisco Archibeque, Acting Alcalde[279]
Vicente Martínez, Acting Alcalde[280]

1832
Juan García, First Alcalde Constitucional[281]
Francisco Rascón, Second Alcalde Constitucional[282]
Don Pablo Montoya, Second Alcalde Constitucional[283]

1833
Francisco Baca y Ortiz, First Alcalde Constitucional[284]
Juan García, First Alcalde Constitucional[285]
Manuel Antonio Sena, Second Alcalde Constitucional [286]

1834
Santiago Abreu, First Alcalde Constitucional [287]
Juan Gallegos, Alcalde Constitucional[288]

1835
Manuel Doroteo Pino, First Alcalde Constitucional [289]
José Maria Ribera, Alcalde[290]
Don Francisco Ortiz y Delgado, Second Alcalde Constitucional[291]
Don Francisco Trujillo, Alcalde[292]

1836
Agustín Durán, First Alcalde Constitucional[293]
Gregorio Sánchez, Alcalde[294]
Don Juan Rafael Ortiz, Provisional Alcalde[295]

1837
Luis Robidoux, Alcalde Constitucional[296]

Ramón Abreu, Alcalde Constitucional[297]
Francisco Ortiz y Delgado, Alcalde Constitucional[298]
Don Felipe Sena, Third Alcalde Constitucional[299]
Juan García, Third Alcalde Constitucional[300]
Don Francisco Baca y Ortiz, Alcalde Constitucional[301]

1838
Manuel Doroteo Pino, First Alcalde Constitucional [302]
Antonio Sena, First Alcalde Constitucional[303]
Don Felipe Sena, Second Alcalde Constitucional [304]

1839[305]
Gaspar Ortiz, Second Alcalde[306]

1840[307]
Domingo Fernández, Second Alcalde Constitucional[308]

1841
Francisco Ortiz y Delgado, First Alcalde Constitucional[309]
Don Justo Pino, First Alcalde Constitucional[310]
Don Albino Chacón, Second Alcalde Constitucional[311]
Don Simón Apodaca, Second Alcalde Constitucional[313]
Antonio Montoya, Alcalde[313]

1842
Don Pedro José Perea, Alcalde Constitucional[314]

1843
Antonio Sena, First Alcalde Constitucional[315]
Francisco Ortiz y Delgado, Second Alcalde Constitucional[316]
Santiago Armijo, Second Alcalde Constitucional [317]

1844
Francisco Sena, First Alcalde Constitucional[318]
José Francisco Baca y Terrus, Second Alcalde Constitucional[319]
Tomás Ortiz, Second Alcalde Constitucional Ex-offcio/Acting Alcalde and
    First Alcalde Constitucional [320]
Don Francisco Ortiz y Delgado, Alcalde Constitucional[321]
Santiago Flores, Acting Alcalde Constitucional[322]

1845
José Francisco Baca y Terrus, First Alcalde Constitucional[323]
Francisco Ortiz y Delgado, Second Alcalde Constitucional[324]

1846
José Miguel Romero, Alcalde[325]
Trinidad Barcelo, Second Alcalde Constitucional[326]

Ninth Period of the Cabildo de la Ciudad de Santa Fe
Military Occupation by the United States of America, 1846–1849

1848
Henry Maidew, Alcalde[327]

1849
Rufus Bench, Alcalde[328]
José Francisco Sena, Alcalde[329]

Tenth Period of the Town Council of the City of Santa Fe
United States of America
Territorial Era, 1850–1912

1850
Lorenzo Martín, Alcalde[330]

1851
José Francisco Sena, Alcalde[331]

1855
Francis A. Cunningham, Mayor[332]

1857
Jesús María Baca y Salazar, Alcalde Mayor[333]

City of Santa Fe Incorporated on June 17, 1891

1891–1892
William T. Thorton, Mayor[334]

1892–1893
Manuel Valdes, Mayor

1893–1894
Ralph E. Twitchell, Mayor

1894–1895
J. H. Sloan, Mayor

1895–1896
Charles F. Easley, Mayor

1896–1897
Pedro Delgado, Mayor

1897–1898
Charles A. Spiess, Mayor

1898–1899
J. R. Hudson, Mayor

1899–1901
J. H. Sloan, Mayor

1901–1902
Amado Chávez, Mayor

1902–1904
I. Sparks, Mayor

1904–1906
A. R. Gibson, Mayor

1906–1908
Thomas B. Catron, Mayor

1908–1910
José Sena, Mayor

1910–1912
Arthur Seligman, Mayor

Eleventh Period of the Cabildo de la Villa de Santa Fe
United States of America
State of New Mexico, 1912–Present

1912–1914
Celso López, Mayor

1914–1918
William G. Sargent, Mayor

1918–1920
Edward R. Davies, Mayor

1920–1922
Thomas Z. Winter, Mayor

1922–1924
Charles C. Closson, Mayor

1924–1926
Nathan Jaffa, Mayor

1926–1928
Edward L. Safford, Mayor

1928–1932
James C. McConvery, Mayor

1932–1934
David Chávez, Jr., Mayor

1934–1936
Charles B. Barker, Mayor

1936–1938
Frank Andrews, Mayor

1938–1942
Alfredo Ortiz, Mayor

1942–1948
Manuel Luján, Sr., Mayor

1948–1952
Frank S. Ortiz, Mayor

1952–1956
Paul Huss, Mayor

1956–1962
Leo Murphy, Mayor

1962–1968
Pat Hollis, Mayor

1968–1972
George A. Gonzáles, Mayor

1972–1976
Joséph Valdes, Mayor

1976–1978
Samuel W. Pick, Mayor

1978–1982
Arthur E. Trujillo, Mayor

1982–1986
Louis R. Montaño, Mayor

1986–1994
Samuel W. Pick, Mayor

1994–1998
Debbie Jaramillo, Mayor

1998–2006
Larry A. Delgado, Mayor

2006–As of 2010
David Coss, Mayor

Contributors

Michael J. Alarid, in 2009, is a PhD Candidate in the Department of History at The Ohio State University. Originally from Rancho Cucamonga, California, Michael holds a BA in History from the University of Oregon and an MA in American Studies from the University of Dallas. His dissertation, *Caudillo Justice: Intercultural conflict and social change in Santa Fe, New Mexico, 1837-53*, utilizes the framework of caudillismo to examine criminality and institutions of social control during the transition of New Mexico from a Mexican state into an American territory. In 2009, Michael was an Office of the State Historian Scholar at the New Mexico State Archives and Records, during which time he conducted research within the primary document collections and presented his findings at the New Mexico State Archives and Records. He has also presented his research at the Fray Angélico Chávez History Library, the American Folklore Society Annual Meeting, the Annual Conference of the Rocky Mountain Council for Latin American Studies, and the Ohio Academy of History Conference.

Robert K. Dean has been managing editor of *The Santa Fe New Mexican* since 1992. A native of Montana, he earned undergraduate degrees in journalism, history, and politics at the University of Montana and a master's degree in history from Norwich University in Vermont. He also worked as a newspaper reporter and editor in Montana and Washington state.

Barbara De Marco, after receiving a degree in Romance Philology from the University of California, Berkeley, began editing documents relating to the 1680 Pueblo Revolt as part of a long-range project to publish Spanish editions of primary texts documenting the exploration and settlement of the present-day American Southwest ("The Cíbola Project," directed by Jerry Craddock at the University of California, Berkeley). A related interest in methods of Franciscan catechesis has engaged her in the iconography of pictorial catechisms produced in Mexico in the early sixteenth century. In 2007 she was awarded a Mellon Fellowship at the John Carter Brown Library to study their unique collection of eighteenth-century pictorial catechisms. At present she also serves as editor of the journal *Romance Philology*.

Malcolm Ebright is a historian, an attorney, and director of the Center for Land Grant Studies. His most recent book (with Rick Hendricks), *The Witches of Abiquiú: The Governor, the Priest, the Genízaro Indians, and the Devil*, won a prize for the best history book in 2006 from the Historical Society of New Mexico. Ebright has often testified as an expert witness in litigation dealing with land grants and water rights and has written numerous books and award-winning articles on New Mexico land and water history, including *The Tierra Amarilla Grant: A History of Chicanery* and *Land Grants and Lawsuits in Northern New Mexico*. He continues to work with Hispanic and Native American communities, helping them protect their land and water rights by developing an accurate history of their community and their land grant.

José Antonio Esquibel is a native of Albuquerque with family roots in northern New Mexico. Over the past twenty-four years he has conducted extensive historical research of archival documents of New Mexico, Mexico, and Spain. He is the author of over one hundred articles and co-author of three award-winning books related to New Mexico history. He is co-author with Charles M. Carrillo of *A Tapestry of Kinship: The Web of Influence among Escultores and Carpinteros in the Parish of Santa Fe, 1790–1860*.

Albert J. Gallegos retired from the State of New Mexico with twenty-seven years of service. He served as Deputy Superintendent of Insurance and Director of Risk Management and now serves as Honorary Consul of Spain in Santa Fe and is also on the Board of Directors of the National Hispanic Cultural Center in Albuquerque. Mr. Gallegos has been involved in the community of Santa Fe for thirty-five years promoting Spanish culture, traditions and history and has been recognized by the State of New Mexico, City of Santa Fe, Spain and Mexico for his volunteer work. He has completed his family genealogy going back twenty-five generations and has researched in the archives of New Mexico, Mexico and Spain and has authored articles regarding his research in genealogy.

Gerald T. E. González, JD, a native New Mexican, holds a BS degree in mathematics from Highlands University. A former Air Force pilot, he is a decorated veteran of the Vietnam conflict. Following his military service, he earned his law degree at Harvard Law School where he was an editor for the *Harvard Civil Rights-Civil Liberties Law Review*. Following law school, he engaged in private law practice in Albuquerque, New Mexico before serving in a succession of government positions with the federal government, the state of New Mexico, and various New Mexico municipalities and counties. He is the author of "Reies Lopez Tijerina and Modern Land Grant Struggles," and "New Mexico's Struggle for Statehood," published in *Nuevo Mexico*, a modern history of New Mexico. He has just completed a translation of the Juan Martínez de Montoya document relating to Santa Fe's pre-1610 founding. His poetry has been published in *New Mexico Magazine* and *La Luz*.

Stanley M. Hordes, PhD, Adjunct Research Professor at the Latin American and Iberian Institute of the University of New Mexico, received his PhD in Colonial Mexican History from Tulane University in 1980. He has served as Curator of Colonial Archives at the Louisiana State Museum, Historian for the National Park Service, and New Mexico State Historian. Hordes operates a historical consulting firm, HMS Associates, Inc., and serves as the Chair of the New Mexico Commission of Public Records. He is the author of *To the End of the Earth: A History of the Crypto-Jews of New Mexico* which was awarded the Gaspar Perez de Villagra prize by the Historical Society of New Mexico.

James E. Ivey is a Research Historian for the Intermountain Regional Office of the National Park Service in Santa Fe. He was a contract historical archeologist in Texas for ten years, worked on several Alamo excavations, and has specialized in the land tenure, cultural, and architectural history of the Spanish colonial southwest.

John L. Kessell is the founding editor of the Vargas Project and Professor Emeritus of History at the University of New Mexico. He is most recently the author of *Pueblos, Spaniards, and the Kingdom of New Mexico*, from which much of his chapter in this book is taken. His other books include *Kiva, Cross, and Crown: the Pecos Indians and New Mexico, 1540–1840* and *The Missions of New Mexico since 1776*.

Frances Levine, PhD, has been Director of the Palace of the Governors, New Mexico History Museum in Santa Fe since 2002. A native of Connecticut, Frances received her BA in anthropology from the University of Colorado, Boulder and a MA and PhD in anthropology from Southern Methodist University, Dallas. She came to the museum from her former position as the Dean of Arts and Sciences at Santa Fe Community College where she taught classes in New Mexico history and the ethnohistory of the Pueblo and Hispanic communities of the Southwest. She is the author of numerous professional publications on the archaeology and history of Santa Fe and New Mexico.

Nancy Owen Lewis received her doctorate in anthropology from the University of Massachusetts and is director of scholar programs at the School for Advanced Research. Her book, *A Peculiar Alchemy: A Centennial History of SAR 1907–2007*, which she co-authored with Kay Hagan, was named Best Book in History by the 2008 New Mexico Book Awards. She is currently conducting research on the impact of tuberculosis on New Mexico culture. This work has been funded by grants from the Office of the State Historian and the Historical Society of New Mexico.

Valerie Martínez is a poet, translator, teacher, librettist, and collaborative artist. Her books include *Absence, Luminescent*; *World to World*; *A Flock of Scarlet Doves*; *Each and Her*; *And They Called It Horizon*; *Lines and Circles: A Celebration of Santa Fe Families*; and *Reinventing the Enemy's Language*. She is Executive Director of Littleglobe, an artist-run non-profit that collaborates with communities on art and community dialogue projects. Valerie was Santa Fe's Poet Laureate for 2008–2010.

Judy Reed is a native Santa Fean and recently retired from the National Park Service as an archeologist after thirty-four years. Her current endeavors are centered on historical research and writing. She is the daughter of Errett Lujan who was a three-and-one-half-year prisoner of war of the Japanese after surrendering on Bataan in 1942. Judy is now writing a non-fiction account of her father's experiences during WW II that is inspired by his war diaries.

Orlando A. Romero was born in Santa Fe in 1945 and is best known for his work as a columnist for two different newspapers in Santa Fe. He is also the author of two books, *Nambe Year One* and *Adobe, Building and Living with Earth*; the recipient of an NEA Fellowship for creative writing; and has been named Eminent Scholar by the Commission on Higher Education. He has lectured extensively here and abroad.

Joseph P. Sánchez, PhD, is superintendent of Petroglyph National Monument and the Spanish Colonial Research Center at the University of New Mexico. He is also founder and editor of the *Colonial Latin American Historical Review*. Dr. Sánchez has held professorships at the University of Arizona and the University of New Mexico. He has researched in archives in Spain, Mexico, France, Italy, and England and has published several studies on the Spanish frontiers in California, Arizona, New Mexico, Texas and Alaska. Internationally recognized, he was inducted into the knightly *Order de Isabel la Católica* by King Juan Carlos of Spain.

Marc Simmons is a professional author and historian who has published more than forty books on New Mexico and the American Southwest. His popular "Trail Dust" column is syndicated in several regional newspapers. In 1993, King Juan Carlos of Spain admitted him to the knightly *Order de Isabel la Católica* for his contributions to Spanish colonial history.

Samuel E. Sisneros received his MA in Borderlands History with emphasis on Public History from the University of Texas at El Paso. Prior to his career as a public school Art/Spanish teacher he traveled extensively to Central and South American and Mexico. He has worked as an archivist at the New Mexico National Hispanic Cultural Center and is currently, as of 2009, a senior archivist at the New Mexico State Records Center and Archives.

Cordelia Thomas Snow, an historic sites archaeologist, is a Pennsylvanian who traveled west to the University of New Mexico for a BA in anthropology/archaeology. After graduation and a brief sojourn with the Park Service at Minute Man National Historical Park in Concord, Massachusetts, she returned to New Mexico to raise a family and work at the Laboratory of Anthropology. In the fall of 1973, museum officials made arrangements to remove the old wood floors in the west end of the Palace of the Governors and asked her to see what was there before new flooring was installed. As a result, on January 4, 1974, she, David McNeece and others literally fell into the remains of the 17th century Palace of the Governors and the experience changed her life forever. More than 30 years later she, a long-time employee of the Archaeological Records Management Section (ARMS) of the Historic Preservation Division, is still trying to determine all she can about early Spanish settlers in Santa Fe and northern New Mexico between 1540 and the mid-20th century.

David H. Snow attended and boarded at St. Michael's High School (1951–54). He obtained a BA in anthropology from the University of New Mexico and a graduate degree in anthropology from Brandeis University in 1969. He was employed as an archaeologist with the Museum of New Mexico's Laboratory of Anthropology until 1983, when he left to pursue contract archaeological and historical work at Cross-Cultural Research Systems. He is recognized by the State's Historical Preservation Division as a professional historian, and continues to research and consult after retirement in 2001.

Robert L. Spude is an historian with the National Park Service based in Santa Fe. He received his PhD in history from the University of Illinois, Urbana-Champaign. Over the past thirty years, he has worked at various posts with the National Park Service, from Augusta, Georgia to Anchorage, Alaska. With colleagues Arthur Gomez and Joseph Sánchez, he is co-author of a history of New Mexico.

Linda Tigges has been the principal for Tigges Planning Consultants, Inc. since 1982, working with residential, commercial, and non-profit development in Santa Fe. She is a certified historian on the New Mexico State Historic Preservation and City of Santa Fe Archaeological Review Committee lists and has written many archival reports and historic documents. When working with the City of Santa Fe Planning Division, she was staff for the Historic Design Review Committee and drafted the city's Archaeological Ordinance, also staffing the Archaeological Review Committee.

William Wroth, PhD, is a cultural historian who specializes in the Hispanic and Native American cultures of the Southwest and Mexico. His publications include *Hispanic Crafts of the Southwest* (1977), *Christian Images in Hispanic New Mexico* (1982), *Images of Penance, Images of Mercy* (1991), and *Ute Indian Arts and Culture from Prehistory to the New Millennium* (2000). In 2006 he contributed 31 essays on 19th-century New Mexico history to the website of the New Mexico Office of the State Historian. He has served as Curator of the Taylor Museum of the Colorado Springs Fine Arts Center and as guest curator for exhibitions at the Museum of International Folk Art, the American Craft Museum and other institutions. He is co-curator, with Robin Farwell Gavin, of the exhibition "Converging Streams: Art of the Hispanic and Native American Southwest," at the Museum of Spanish Colonial Art in Santa Fe and co-editor of the book of the same title, published in 2010.

About the 400th Anniversary of Santa Fe

The year 2010 marked the 400th anniversary of Santa Fe, New Mexico from the establishment of the city as a "villa" in 1610 by the Spanish. This makes Santa Fe the oldest capital city in the United States.

A number of cultures played key roles in Santa Fe's development: Native Americans who settled long before 1610, and Hispanic, European and African Americans of diverse backgrounds. These lives and stories created a cross-cultural tapestry of interdependence that over time has made Santa Fe one of the most diverse and rich cultural communities in the United States.

To commemorate this event, The Santa Fe 400th Anniversary Inc, a 501(c)(3) non-profit corporation, was created to design and produce a wide variety of activities that would honor all cultures, heritage, legacies and lasting contributions, that connect the founding past with the promise of tomorrow. One of these projects was this anthology, *All Trails Lead to Santa Fe*.

Board of Directors:

    Maurice Bonal, Chairman and President of the Board
    Troy Lopez, Vice Chairman
        Owner, Tony Lopez Roofing Sevice and Fiesta Council Member
    Jessica C de Baca, Treasurer
        Operations Manager, Big Jo Hardware, Inc

Mary Chavez, Secretary
: Senior Vice President & Banking Officer of 1st National Bank

Martin Wayne Aguilar
: 2007/2008 Governor of Pueblo of San Ildefonso

Stuart Ashman
: Cabinet Secretary, Department of Cultural Affairs
: New Mexico Department of Public Safety

Adrian Bustamante
: Historian

Charles Carrillo
: Carver and Painter of Sacred Figures

Rudy Fernandez
: Santa Fe Fiesta Council Member and Retired Realtor

José Garcia
: Genealogist and Civic Volunteer

Gerald T. E. González
: Majority Media Rep for the Senate Majority Leader

Gregory Heltman
: Founder and General Director of the Santa Fe Symphony and Chorus

Jennifer Hobson
: Deputy Cabinet Secretary, New Mexico Tourism Department

Jeff Jinnett
: President, Santa Fe Dining

Herman Lovato
: Bureau Chief of Information Technology Division/Application Support for the New Mexico Department of Public Safety; Director of Santa Fe Opera and Fiesta Council Member

Paul Margetson
: General Manager of Hotel Santa Fe

Mark Mitchell
: Governor of Tesuque Pueblo

Albert "Gaby" Montoya
: 2009 President of Fiesta Council

Peter Pacheco
: Vice President and Loan Officer for Century Bank

Andres Romero
: Retired Engineer and Fiesta Council Member

Gilbert Romero
  Past Prsident of the Caballeros de Vargas
Connie Tsosie Gaussoin
  Award-winning Artist of the Picuris Pueblo and Navajo Tribe

Monument to Kit Carson in an illustration from *Illustrated New Mexico, 1885*, by W. G. Ritch. The monument still stands in front of the Federal Courthouse in Santa Fe.

The 400TH Anniversary of Santa Fe Book Committee

When the Santa Fe 400th Commemorative events committees were formed, among them was the History Task Force Committee. Within the History Task Force there were various subcommittees created that included a lecture series, plaza plaques, and a book.

For the book, a "Call For Papers Committee" was organized to encourage scholars, including historians, anthropologists, and writers to submit previously unpublished works to be included in an anthology on the history of Santa Fe to commemorate its official founding in 1610. The committee was comprised of individuals who were either historians, archaeologists, archivists or had previous publications in related fields.

The anthology's title, *All Trails Lead To Santa Fe*, was chosen because it reflected what the committee felt was the diversity of what they wanted and hoped to include. The committee selected 19 of the submissions and an introduction for the core text that the committee felt reflected Santa Fe's diverse and complex prehistory and history, to periods in between and up to WWII. The anthology, it was hoped, would inspire other scholars and writers to pursue further research and future publications regarding Santa Fe in years to come. The intent of the anthology was also to complement existing publications on the history of Santa Fe.

—Orlando Romero
Chair, Call for Papers Committee

Members of the committee:

Adrian H. Bustamante, PhD, Retired Professor, Chairman

Cordelia Thomas Snow, Historic Sites Archaeologist

Sandra Jaramillo, Director of the New Mexico State Records Center and Archives

Joseph P. Sánchez, PhD, Superintendent of Petroglyph National Monument and Spanish Colonial Research Center

Gerald T. E. González, Attorney and Historical Researcher

Orlando Romero, Retired Director of the Fray Angélico Chávez History Library and Author

Publisher Acknowledgements

Sunstone Press gratefully acknowledges the following:

Maurice Bonal, Adrian Bustamante, Orlando Romero and the entire Book Committee for making this book possible.

Laura Holt for contributing her services in the preparation of the index.

Barbara Barlow for her assistance and many suggestions.

Sandra Brintnall for helping to make our days easier and for answering endless questions.

André Dumont for assistance in locating many of the illustrations and maps in this book.

NOTES

Preface

1. Clarence Haring, *The Spanish Empire in America* (Gloucester, Massachusetts: Peter Smith 1973, original printing 1947), pp. 147-148. Haring writes "The urban tradition was much stronger in the history of Spain than in that of England. The Mediterranean institution of the free city state, the *civitas* perpetuated in the Roman Empire as the unit of local administration had been implanted in the Hispanic peninsula during the flourishing days of Roman occupation; and this Roman municipal tradition ... became ... deeply rooted in the mind and habits of the inhabitants of Spain."
2. Marc Simmons, *Yesterday in Santa Fe: Episodes in a Turbulent History* (Santa Fe: Sunstone Press, 1989), p. 10. See also, Hubert Howe Bancroft *History of Arizona and New Mexico* (San Francisco: The History Company, 1889), fn 27, p. 158, which reads "A few years ago, since 1889, a grand celebration was held of the 300th (or 350th or 400th, it matters not which) anniversary of the founding!"
3. Bancroft, *History*, pp vii-viii.
4. Ibid., p. 159.
5. Ibid., p. 158.
6. Francisco de Thoma, *Historia de Nuevo México* (New York: American Book Company, 1896), p. 72.
7. Ralph Emerson Twitchell, *Old Santa Fe: The Story of New Mexico's Ancient Capital* (Santa Fe: Santa Fe New Mexican Publishing Corporation, 1925; New Edition, Santa Fe: Sunstone Press, 2007, with foreword by Richard Melzer, PhD)
8. Ibid., p. 17.
9. Ibid., pp. 13-14.
10. Lansing Bloom, translator, "Instructions for Don Pedro de Peralta, Governor and Captain General of New Mexico, in the Place of Don Joan de Oñate," *El Palacio*, Vol. XXIV, No. 24, June 16, 1928, p. 466.
11. France V. Scholes, "Juan Martínez de Montoya, Settler and Conquistador of New Mexico," *New Mexico Historical Review*, (19:4) 1944 p. 341.
12. Marc Simmons, *Yesterday in Santa Fe: Episodes of a Turbulent History* (Santa Fe: Sunstone Press, 1989), p. 13.

13. Robert McGeagh, *Juan de Oñate's Colony in the Wilderness: An Early History of the American Southwest* (Santa Fe: Sunstone Press, 1990), p. 40.
14. Marc Simmons, *The Last Conquistador: Juan de Oñate and the Settling of the Far Southwest* (Norman: University of Oklahoma Press, 1991), p. 195.
15. Ibid., 182.
16. David J. Weber, *The Spanish Frontier in North America* (New Haven: Yale University Press, 1992), p. 90 and 195.
17. Ibid., p. 90.
18. Ibid., p. 78.
19. Beverly Becker, "Santa Fe: Est. ~~1610~~ 1607," *El Palacio*, Winter 1994–1995, pp 14-16.
20. Ibid., p.14.
21. France V. Scholes, Juan Martínez de Montoya *New Mexico Historical Review* (1944), pp. 337-338,
22. Ibid., 14.
23. John Kessell, *Spain in the Southwest: A Narrative History of Colonial New Mexico, Arizona, Texas, and California* (Norman: University of Oklahoma Press, 2002), p. 97-98.

Chapter 2
A City Different Than We Thought,
Land Grants in Early Santa Fe, 1598–1900

1. Cordelia T. Snow, "A Hypothetical Configuration of the Early Santa Fe Plaza Based on the 1573 Ordenances or the Law of the Indies," in Linda Tigges, ed., *Santa Fe Historic Plaza Study I: With Translations from Spanish Colonial Documents* (Santa Fe, 1990), 56-57.
2. Cordelia Thomas Snow, "Dispelling Some Myths of Santa Fe, New Mexico, or Santa Fe of the Imagination," in *Current Research on the Late Prehistory and Early History of New Mexico* (Albuquerque: New Mexico Archaeological Council, 1992), 215-20.
3. In 1883, civic boosters who were more interested in tourism than accurate history staged a "Tertio Millenial Centennial" to commemorate the founding of Santa Fe in 1550, a completely fictitious date. Fray Angelico Chavez, "Santa Fe's Fake Centennial of 1883," *El Palacio* (1955) 62: 315.
4. Critics have seen Caliban as "an American Indian," or as "Shakespeare's sole representation of the human population of the New World." W. Gordon Zeeveld, *The Temper of Shakespeare's Thought* (New Haven, 1974), p. 250; in William Shakespeare, *The Tempest* (United Kingdom: Thomas Nelson and Sons, 1999), p. 105, third Arden edition, edited by Virgina Mason Vaughan and Alden T. Vaughan.
5. The books, passed on to Shakespeare by his friend the Earl of Southampton, were Silvester Jourdain's *A Discovery of the Barmudas, Otherwise called the Ile of Divels* (1610), and "William Strachey's Account" in J. H. Lefroy's *Memorials of the Bermudas* (London: 1877), 22-54, cited in George F. Wilson, *Saints and Strangers*, (New York: Reynal and Hitchcock, 1945), 465.
6. Miguel de Cervantes Saavedra, *The Adventures of Don Quixote* (Great Britain: Penguin Books, 1950). Governor's Mendizábal (1659–1661) and Peñalosa (1661–1664) were

said to have copies of *Don Quixote* on their bookshelves. France V. Scholes, "Civil Government and Society in New Mexico," *NMHR* 10 (April 1935), 103.

7. The "oldest house," with tree ring dates of 1740–1767 may not be older than that. A structure in the approximate location of the "oldest house" is shown on the 1766 Urrutia map, but there are clearly older structures in Santa Fe. John Gaw Meem, preface, *Old Santa Fe Today* (Albuquerque: UNM Press, 1991), 74.

8. See the Santa Fe City Grant, SG 88, Roll 20, fr. 1326 et seq.; the Villa de Santa Fe Grant, PLC 19, Roll 34, fr. 1573, et seq.; and the City of Santa Fe Grant, PLC 80, Roll 42, fr. 6, et seq.

9. For an example of a "ghost grant," a grant whose title papers were valid, was recommended for confirmation and surveyed by the Surveyor General, but was never submitted to the Court of Private Land Claims, see the Luis de Armenta grant, Bowden, "Private Land Claims," 2: 370-75.

10. George P. Hammond and Agapito Rey, eds., *The Rediscovery of New Mexico* (Albuquerque: University of New Mexico Press, 1966), 36-7, 280.

11. George P. Hammond and Agapito Rey, eds., *Don Juan de Oñate: Colonizer of New Mexico, 1595–1628* (Albuquerque: University of New Mexico Press, 1953), 1: 17. *When Cultures Meet: Remembering San Gabriel del Yunge Oweenge* (Santa Fe: Sunstone Press, 1987).

12. In 1591 Castaño de Sosa crossed a river (probably the Santa Fe River) "which was frozen so hard that the horses were able to cross without breaking the ice." George P. Hammond and Agapito Rey, eds., *The Rediscovery of New Mexico* (Albuquerque: University of New Mexico Press, 1966), 280.

13. France V. Scholes, "Juan Martínez de Montoya, Settler and Conquistador of New Mexico," *NMHR* 19: (1944), 341

14. Hammond and Rey, *Rediscovery of New Mexico*, 36-7, 280 and Bloom, "When was Santa Fe Founded?" *New Mexico Historical Review* IV (1929): 188-194.

15. George P. Hammond and Agapito Rey, eds., *Don Juan de Oñate: Colonizer of New Mexico, 1595–1628* (Albuquerque: University of New Mexico Press, 1953), 2: 1087.

16. Kuapoge has been translated as "bead water place," or "the place of the Olivella shells, from which they make the beads they so highly prize." John Peabody Harrington, *The Ethnography of the Tewa Indians* (Washington, DC: Government Printing Office, 1916), 459-65. These names suggest the possibility that Kuapoge may have been the center of a Olivella shell bead distribution network reaching all the way to Mesoamerica, similar to the Hohokam shell bead distribution network, described in Richard Nelson, *Hohokam Marine Shell Exchange and Artifacts* (Tucson: Arizona State Museum, 1991) and similar as well to the turquoise trade network between Cerrillos and Mesoamerica, Phil C. Weigand and Acelia Garcia de Weigand, "A Macroeconomic Study of the Relationships between the Ancient Cultures of the American Southwest and Mesoamerica," in Virginia Fields and Victor Zamudio-Taylor, *The Road to Aztlan: Art from a Mythic Homeland* (Los Angeles: Los Angeles County Museum of Art, 2001), 184-95.

17. Historian Lansing B. Bloom believed that by the first part of May 1610, the fields of the villa had been planted. Bloom, "When was Santa Fe Founded?" p. 194. Lansing Bartlett Bloom and Ireneo L. Chaves, trans., "Ynstruccion a Peralta por Vi-roy," *NMHR* 4 (April

1929): 178-87; Governor Peralta's Instructions, Hammond and Roy, *Oñate* 2:1087-91; Marc Simmons, "The Naming of Santa Fe," in Simmons, *Yesterday in Santa Fe: Episodes in a Turbulent History* (Santa Fe: Sunstone Press, 1989), 13.

18. "Ynstruccion A Peralta por Vi-Roy," *NMHR* 4 (April 1929): 179-180.

19. Joseph P. Sánchez, "The Peralta-Ordóñez Affair and the Founding of Santa Fe," in David Grant Noble, ed. *Santa Fe: History of an Ancient City* (Santa Fe: School of American Research Press, 1989), 28-31.

20. Marc Simmons, "Tlascalans in the Spanish Borderlands," *NMHR* 39 (April 1964): 108-10. The will of Salvador Montoya refers to a tract bounded by "*tierras de los Mexicanos*," SANM I: 512. Although some scholars doubt that the Mexican Indians in Analco were Tlascalans (Adams and Chavez, 37-38, n. 64) the evidence cited by Simmons makes a strong case for mostly Tlascalans in Analco, especially the Franciscan report referring to "the chapel of San Miguel which before [the revolt] served as the parish church of the Tlascalan Indians," Memorial of Fray Salvador de San Antonio, *et al.*, December 18, 1693 in *Documentos para Servir a la Historia de Nuevo México* (Madrid, 1962), p. 347.

21. The *Recopilación* provided for three classes of municipalities in order of their size: *ciudad*, *villa*, or *pueblo*. "The classification of a municipality as *ciudad*, *villa* or *pueblo* . . . was more than a mere formality since these terms implied definite ranking according to prestige and importance. Also the number of municipal magistrates and councilmen allowed by law depended upon the status of the community." Marc Simmons, "Settlement Patterns and Village Plans in Colonial New Mexico," *Journal of the West* 8 (January 1969): 8-9, n. 9.

22. For the Pueblo Revolt see, Charles Wilson Hackett, ed. *Revolt of the Pueblo Indians of New Mexico and Otermín's Attempted Reconquest, 1680–1682* (Albuquerque: University of New Mexico Press, 1942) 2 vol., passim, and Andrew Knaut, *The Pueblo Revolt of 1680: Conquest and Resistance in Seventeenth-Century New Mexico* (Norman: University of Oklahoma Press, 1995).

23. Edict by Vargas, El Paso, September 20, 1693 in Kessell, Hendricks and Dodge eds., *To The Royal Crown Restored* (Albuquerque: University of New Mexico Press, 1995) p. 375.

24. SANM I: 8 and SANM I: 169. The case of *Arias de Quiros v. the Cabildo of Santa Fe* is discussed in Malcolm Ebright, *Land Grants and Lawsuits in Northern New Mexico* (Albuquerque: University of New Mexico Press, 1994), 91-96.

25. Gaspar Ortiz y Alarid was a land grant speculator who engaged in property transactions around Santa Fe. Petition of Santa Fe County Probate Judge Gaspar Ortiz y Alarid, City of Santa Fe Grant, SG 88, Roll 21, fr. 1328-35.

26. Petition of Santa Fe County Probate Judge Gaspar Ortiz y Alarid, City of Santa Fe Grant, SG 88, Roll 21, fr. 1328-35.

27. Opinion of Surveyor General Proudfit, City of Santa Fe Grant, SG 88, Roll 21, fr. 1336-38.

28. J. J. Bowden, "Private Land Claims in the Southwest," 6 vols. (MA thesis, Southern Methodist University, 1968) 2: 329.

29. By the time the Court of Private Land Claims was established a backlog of 116 grants had been approved and were awaiting congressional action. Congress had not approved a grant since early in 1879. Ebright, *Land Grants and Lawsuits*, 45.

30. Bruce T. Ellis, "Fraud Without Scandal: The Roque Lovato Grant and Gaspar Ortiz y Alarid," *NMHR* 57 (January 1982): 43-59.
31. Petition of the Board of County Commissioners of Santa Fe County. July 14, 1892, Villa de Santa Fe Grant, PLC 19, Roll 34, fr. 1574–1578.
32. Answer and Demurrer by the United States, Villa de Santa Fe Grant, PLC 19, Roll 34, fr. 1574–1578. For more on Tipton and Flipper see, Ebright, *Land Grants and Lawsuits*, 134-35.
33. Bowden, "Private Land Claims," 2: 331.
34. Petition of the City of Santa Fe, City of Santa Fe Grant, PLC 80, Roll 42, fr. 7-12.
35. Demurrer by the United States, City of Santa Fe Grant, PLC 80, Roll 42, fr. 15-16.
36. Bowden, "Private Land Claims," 2: 332.
37. Amended petition of the City of Santa Fe, Villa de Santa Fe Grant, PLC 80, Roll 42, fr. 37-43.
38. Answer of the U.S. to the amended petition, Villa of Santa Fe Grant, PLC 80, Roll 42, fr. 153-160.
39. Answer of seventeen defendants with grants inside the Santa Fe League, Villa of Santa Fe Grant, PLC 80, Roll 42, fr. 148-51.
40. Dissenting opinion of Justice Murray, Villa of Santa Fe Grant, PLC 80, Roll 42, fr. 189-201. Grants rejected because they overlapped the Santa Fe league and were trumped by the CPLC confirmation of the Santa Fe league were the Talaya Hill, Chamiso Arroyo, Juan Cayetano Lovato, Antonio Dominguez, Manuel Tenorio, Juan Antonio Flores, Juan Felipe Rodríguez, Juan Antonio Archuleta, Leonardo Gonzales, Antonio Armijo, Juan José Archuleta, José Romulo de Vera and Caterina Maese grants.
41. Transcription and translation of *Recopilación, Book 4, Chapter 5, Law 6*, Villa of Santa Fe Grant, PLC 80, Roll 42, fr. 54-57.
42. Majority opinion, Villa of Santa Fe Grant, PLC 80, Roll 42, fr. 177-88.
43. *San Francisco v. LeRoy*, 138 U.S. 656 (1891), and *Brownsville v. Cavazos*, 100 U.S. 138 (1897).
44. For a brief discussion of *empresario* grants and a map of the *empresario* grants in Texas, see A. Ray Stephens and William M. Holmes, *Historical Atlas of Texas* (Norman: University of Oklahoma Press, 1989), 22.
45. In practice, *empresario* contracts in Texas in the 1820s and 1830s required the *empresario* to bring in at least 100 families. Andrés Reséndez, *Changing National Identities at the Frontier: Texas and New Mexico, 1800–1850* (Cambridge: Cambridge University Press, 2004), 37-38.
46. The settlers were each to provide "a breeding sow, twenty breeding ewes from Castille, and six hens and a cock." Translation of *Recopilación, Book 4, Chapter 5, and Law 6*, Villa of Santa Fe Grant, PLC 80, Roll 42, fr. 54-7.
47. Dissenting opinion of Justice Murray, Villa of Santa Fe Grant, PLC 80, Roll 42, fr. 189-202.
48. *U.S. v. Santa Fe*, 165 U.S. 675 (1897).
49. Ralph Emerson Twitchell, *Old Santa Fe: The Story of New Mexico's Ancient Capital* (Chicago: The Rio Grande Press: 1963), 417-18.
50. *U.S. v. Santa Fe*, 165 U.S. 675 (1897), 676, 691.
51. *U.S. v. Santa Fe*, 165 U.S. 675 (1897), 683.

52. Justice White famously interpreted the language of the Sherman Antitrust Act prohibiting all business combinations in restraint of trade to outlaw only unreasonable restraints on trade, ushering in the concept of judicial subjectivity in both statutory and constitutional interpretation. Kermit Hall, ed. *The Oxford Companion to the Supreme Court of the United States* (New York: Oxford University Press, 1992), 927-28, 968.
53. *U.S.* v. *Santa Fe*, 165 U.S. 675 (1897), 694-700.
54. *San Francisco* v. *LeRoy*, 138 U.S. 656 (1891), 664-67.
55. Bowden, "Private Land Claims," 2: 340-41.
56. *U.S.* v. *Santa Fe*, 167 U.S. 675 at 676 and 691.
57. "Ynstruccion a Peralta por Vi-roy," *NMHR* 4 (April 1929), 179. This order from Viceroy Velasco was dated March 39, 1609.
58. "Ynstruccion a Peralta por Vi-roy," *NMHR* 4 (April 1929), 187.
59. Twitchell's *Old Santa Fe: The Story of New Mexico's Ancient Capital* (Chicago: The Rio Grande Press, 1963), is an example of his historical scholarship.
60. Declaration of Pedro García, August 25, 1680, translated in Charles Wilson Hackett and Charmion Clair Shelby, *Revolt of the Pueblo Indians of New Mexico and Otermín's Attempted Reconquest* (Albuquerque: University of New Mexico Press, 1942), 23-26. Two of the daughters born to Petrona Nieto were: Petrona Nieto, and Josefa, who kept her mother's surname of Pacheco.
61. Colin G. Calloway, *The Shawnees and the War for America* (New York: Viking; the Penguin Library of American Indian History, 2007), xxxii-xxxiii.
62. John Demos, *The Unredeemed Captive: A Family Story from Early America* (New York: Alfred A. Knopf, 1994), passim. The title comes from the subsequent refusal of Eunice Williams (age 7 at the time of her capture), to be redeemed, preferring instead to live among the Mohawks with her Mohawk husband.
63. "When she died in 1753, Juana Hurtado owned a rancho with three houses and managed extensive herds of cattle and flocks of sheep." Malcolm Ebright and Rick Hendricks, *The Witches of Abiquiú: The Governor, the Priest, the Genízaro Indians and the Devil* (Albuquerque: University of New Mexico Press, 2006), 33-34. James F. Brooks, *Captives & Cousins: Slavery, Kinship, and Community in the Southwest Borderlands* (Chapel Hill: University of North Carolina Press, 2002), 99-103.
64. Chavez, *New Mexico Families*, 83, citing AGN, Mex. Inquisicion, f. 190. David H. Snow, "So Many Mestizos, Mulatos, and Zambohigos: Colonial New Mexico's People Without History," paper presented at the Oct. 11-14, 1995, Annual Meeting of the Western History Association, Denver, Colorado.
65. John L. Kessell and Rick Hendricks eds., *By Force of Arms: The Journals of Don Diego de Vargas* (Albuquerque: University of New Mexico Press, 1992), 444. Petrona had three daughters during her captivity, not three sons and daughters.
66. Declaration of Sargento Mayor don Fernándo de Chávez, Guadalupe del Paso, April 5, 1681 in Hackett and Shelby, *Revolt*, 2: 17.
67. Kessell and Hendricks, *By Force of Arms*, 525-30.
68. Record and list of payments made to settlers. El Paso, September 22 – October 16, 1681. Payments and enlistments made on September 27, 1681. Hackett and Shelby, *Revolt* 2: 119-120.

69. Kessell and Hendricks, *By Force of Arms*, 525-530, 488.
70. Fray Angélico Chávez, *New Mexico Roots, Ltd.*, 1482. Petrona Pacheco the younger first appears on a 1712 tool distribution list.
71. Diego De Vargas, Distribution of livestock and supplies, Santa Fe, May 1, 1697 in John L. Kessell, Rick Hendricks and Meredith Dodge, eds., *Blood on the Boulders: The Journals of Don Diego de Vargas, New Mexico, 1694–1697, Book 2* (Albuquerque: University of New Mexico Press, 1998), 1138-4.
72. On August 1, 1700, Aguilera met Nieto at his home and performed a rudimentary survey starting: ". . . from a small cedar standing behind the house, and some piles of stones, running in a straight line to the main road (Camino Real), and from a small acequia to a pile of small stones separating the lands of Domingo de la Barreda, and from said pile of stones running in a straight line to the ruins of an old house behind said house of Domingo de la Barreda to the river, and running along the same to the first cedar." SANM I: 638.
73. In a 1697 deed from Antonio Gutierrez de Figueroa to Antonio de Aguilera the land described was bounded on one side by the Camino Real and on the west by Cristóbal Nieto, SANM I: 4. See illustration on page 72 for the approximate location of the Nieto grant based on this deed.
74. Chávez, *New Mexico Families*, 243; José Antonio Esquibel "Notes on Cristóbal Nieto (and others)," unpublished manuscript in the possession of the author.
75. Fray Angélico Chávez, *Origins of New Mexico Families* (Santa Fe: Museum of New Mexico Press, 1992), 242-43.
76. Deed from Simón Nieto to Juan García de Noriega, September 25, 1728. SANM I: 642. Fray Angélico Chávez, *New Mexico Families*, 217.
77. Simón Nieto also purchased two *fanegas* of corn-planting land in the area in 1707 from José Manuel Gilthomey who said he received it by royal grant. The land was bounded by Salvador Archuleta on one side and Captain Luis Maese on the other. Deed from José Manuel Gilthomey to Simón Nieto, December 5, 1707. SANM I: 639.
78. Virgina Langham Olmsted, comp., *Spanish and Mexican Censuses of New Mexico, 1750 to 1830* (Albuquerque: The New Mexico Genealogical Society, 1981), 9.
79. "*Hija de la Iglesia.*" *Diligencia Matrimonia*, 1711, no. 5, SRCA, Santa Fe.
80. Partition of land at Pueblo Quemado (Agua Fria) between Francisco Nieto and Jacinto Perea, Santa Fe, July 10, 1765. SANM I: 644. Alfred B. Thomas, *After Coronado: Spanish Exploration Northeast of New Mexico, 1696–1727* (Norman: University of Oklahoma Press, 1935), 227.
81. Deed from Jacinto Perea to Juan Tafoya, 1761, Puesto del Pino, Santa Fe. SANM I: 985.
82. El Pino (Cristóbal Nieto) Grant, PLC 81, Roll 42, fr. 482-83.
83. David H. Snow, "A Note on Encomienda Economics in Seventeenth Century New Mexico," in Weigle et al., ed., *Hispanic Arts and Ethnohistory in the Southwest*, 354.
84. SANM I: 644.
85. Petition by Juan Nieto for confirmation of the El Pino (Cristóbal Nieto) grant, El Pino grant, PLC 81, Roll 42, fr. 455-57.
86. J. J. Bowden, "Private Land Claims in the Southwest," 6 vols., MA thesis, Southern Methodist University, 1969, 2: 269.

87. Claimant's map, El Pino grant, PLC 81, Roll 42, fr. 524-27.
88. As David Benavides has pointed out "fairness is ensured in our adversarial system because [then] each party has the services of a zealous advocate." David Benavides, "Lawyer-Induced Partitioning of New Mexico Land Grants: An Ethical Travesty." Center for Land Grant Studies Research Paper, www.southwestbooks.org.
89. Deraignment of title, El Pino grant, PLC 81, Roll 42, fr. 529.
90. The Sebastián de Vargas grant claim was based solely on a mention of Sebastián de Vargas in the Juan de Leon Brito grant. As was true of at least half of the grants submitted to the CPLC by lawyer James Purdy, there was no grant document, only a mention of the grant or parcel of land in the description of an adjoining parcel. Another basis for assuming that there may have been a grant were statements by witnesses that Donaciano Vigil had told them that he had seen the grant papers in the archives. However there is no mention of a grant to Sebastián de Vargas in the index prepared by Vigil of the documents in the New Mexico archives. Nor is there any mention of such a grant in eighteenth century lists of documents found in the New Mexico archives. Sebastián de Vargas grant, SG 137, Roll 25, fr. 1286–1472; Sebastián de Vargas grant, PLC 6, Roll 33, fr. 745 et seq. The Sebastián de Vargas grant was confirmed by the Land Claims Court on a split decision: Justices Fuller and Stone recommended confirmation of the entire grant, Chief Justice Reed and Justice Murray recommended rejection of the entire grant, and Justice Sluss voted to confirm the east tract but reject the western tract. Bowden, "Spanish and Mexican Land Grants," 2: 314-18. The grant was surveyed to contain 13,434 acres.
91. Answer of seventeen defendants with grants inside the Santa Fe League, Villa of Santa Fe Grant, PLC 80, Roll 42, fr. 148-51. Dissenting opinion of Justice Murray, Villa of Santa Fe Grant, PLC 80, Roll 42, fr. 189-202. *U.S.* v. *Santa Fe*, 165 U.S. 675 (1897).
92. James F. Brooks, *Captives & Cousins*, 56.
93. Genízaros were a class of mixed blood former captives that by 1776 would comprise fourteen percent of the population of Santa Fe. Malcolm Ebright and Rick Hendricks, *The Witches of Abiquiú: The Governor, the Priest, the Genízaro Indians, and the Devil* (Albuquerque: University of New Mexico Press, 2006), 30.
94. France V. Scholes, "Juan Martínez de Montoya, Settler and Conquistador of New Mexico," *NMHR* 19: (1944), 341. Scholes made a clear distinction between "some sort of post or settlement" at Santa Fe and the founding of a villa, which he says occurred in 1610. Scholes clearly did not believe the Martínez de Montoya document was evidence of a 1607 founding of Santa Fe. But the unsigned *El Palacio* article seems to discredit Scholes' opinion by stating "he never saw the documents in London," when Scholes himself states "the documents mentioned above were owned by Maggs Bros. of London *when I saw them*" (emphasis added).
95. "Santa Fe, Est. 1610/1607," *El Palacio* (Winter, 1994–1995): 14-16.
96. James Ivey, "An Uncertain Founding: Santa Fe." *Common-Place* 3 (2003): 7, *www.common-place.org/vol-03/no-04/santa-fe* (accessed 25 November 2008).
97. David Weber, "Santa Fe," in James C. Kelly and Barbara Clark Smith, eds., *Jamestown, Quebec, Santa Fe: Three North American Beginnings* (Washington, DC: Smithsonian Books, 2007). In this article Weber states almost parenthetically "Captain Juan Martinez

de Montoya, who founded Santa Fe [in 1608] was to replace Oñate as governor."
98. See Chapter 4, José Antonio Esquibel, "Thirty-eight Adobe Houses, The Villa of Santa Fe in the Seventeenth Century, 1608–1699."
99. Edict by Vargas. El Paso, September 20, 1693 in Kessell, Hendricks and Dodge eds., *To The Royal Crown Restored*, p. 375.
100. For a detailed discussion of grazing land for the presidial horseherd, see Chapter 11, Linda Tigges, "The Pastures of the Royal Horse Herd of the Santa Fe Presidio, 1692–1740."
101. Testimony of Hernando Martín in the lawsuit *Antonio Sisneros v. Lorenzo* over loss of a mule. Santa Fe, 1697. SANM II: 64a.
102. State Historian Estevan Rael-Gálvez stated: "Some are starting to say they were here as early as 1598, when Oñate came and settled in Ohkay Owingeh—they may have stopped and started building here," Marin Sandy, ed., "Where Credit is Due," in *Santa Fean: The History Issue* (February/March 2009), 28. John L. Kessell, *Spain in the Southwest: A Narrative History of Colonial New Mexico, Arizona, Texas, and California* (Norman: University of Oklahoma Press, 2002), 394, n. 3; Carroll L. Riley, personal communication, December 18, 2008. The will of Salvador Montoya refers to a tract bounded by "*tierras de los Mexicanos*," SANM I: 512. A deed from Andrés Montoya, *el viejo*, to Bernadino de Sena in 1729 for land south of the river, is bounded by *tierras de San Miguel*, SANM I: 840. Eleanor B. Adams and Fray Angelico Chavez, *The Missions of New Mexico, 1776* (Albuquerque: University of New Mexico Press, 1956); Marc Simmons, "Tlascalans in the Spanish Borderlands," *NMHR* 39 (April 1964): 108-10.
103. Tomás Martínez Saldaña and Estevan Arellano, "*La riqueza botanica del Rio Grande: Dales a conocer a los tlaxcaltecas . . . dle Virrey Luis de Velasco*," in *Boletín del Archivo Histórico del Agua Año 13 enero-abril 2008* (Coyacan, México: Comision Nacional del Agua, 2008), 44-5.
104. Ayer, Hodge, and Lummis, *The Memorial of Fray Alonso de Benavides, 1630* (Chicago, 1916), pp. 22-23; Adams and Chávez, *The Missions of New Mexico, 1776* (Albuquerque; The University of New Mexico Press, 1956), pp. 37-38; George Kubler, *The Rebuilding of San Miguel at Santa Fe in 1710* (Colorado Springs: Taylor Museum of the Colorado Springs Fine Arts Center, 1939), p. 6, France Scholes, "Church and State in New Mexico 1610–1650," *NMHR* 11 (1936): 333.
105. Carroll Riley, *Kachina and Cross,* 129-30.
106. Declaration of Pedro de la Cruz, September 14, 1632 in France V. Scholes, "The First Decade of the Inquisition in New Mexico," 240-41; David Snow, "So Many Mestizos," 10.
107. Chavez, *New Mexico Families*, 83.
108. Cordelia T. Snow, "A Hypothetical Configuration of the early Santa Fe Plaza Based on the 1573 Ordenances or the Law of the Indies," in Linda Tigges, ed., *Santa Fe Historic Plaza Study I: With Translations from Spanish Colonial Documents* (Santa Fe, 1990), 56-57.
109. Cordelia Thomas Snow, "Dispelling Some Myths of Santa Fe, New Mexico, or Santa Fe of the Imagination," in *Current Research on the Late Prehistory and Early History of New Mexico* (Albuquerque: New Mexico Archaeological Council, 1992), 215-20.
110. Cordelia T. Snow, "A Hypothetical Configuration of the early Santa Fe Plaza Based on the 1573 Ordenances or the Law of the Indies," in Linda Tigges, ed., *Santa Fe Historic*

Plaza Study I: With Translations from Spanish Colonial Documents (Santa Fe, 1990), 56-57. Jason S. Shapiro, *Before Santa Fe: Archaeology of the City Different* (Santa Fe: Museum of New Mexico Press, 2008), X, 127-29; Stephen S. Post, Stephen C. Lentz, Mathew Barbour, Susan Moga, Nancy J. Akins, and Eric Blinman, "Third Interim Report on the Data Recovery Program at LA 1051, El Pueblo de Santa Fe." Museum of New Mexico, Office of Archaeological Studies, submitted to the New Mexico Historic Preservation Division, NMCRIS Activity No. 90579, MNM #41,776, Santa Fe.

111. Chris Wilson, *The Myth of Santa Fe: Creating a Modern Regional Tradition* (Albuquerque: University of New Mexico Press, 1997), passim.
112. Gilbert R. Cruz, *Let There by Towns: Spanish Municipal Origins in the American Southwest, 1610–1810* (College Station: Texas A&M University Press, 1988), 67, 69.
113. Fray Angelico Chavez and Eleanor Adams, *The Missions of New Mexico, 1776* (Albuquerque, University of New Mexico Press, 1956), 39.
114. J. K. Shiskin, "The Wonderful Year of 1880," in *La Gaceta, El Boletín del Corral de Santa Fe Westerners* 5 (1970): 5-6.

Chapter 3
The Viceroy's Order Founding the Villa of Santa Fe, A Reconsideration, 1605–1610

1. Hubert Howe Bancroft, *History of Arizona and New Mexico* (San Francisco: The History Company, 1889), pp. 158-59.
2. Adolph Bandelier, *Final Report of Investigations Among the Indians of the Southwestern United States, Carried On Mainly in the Years From 1880 to 1885* (Cambridge: University Press, 1890) part I, p. 124, n. 1. The ellipsis in the quotation is as Bandelier presented it. The full quotation is: "La Villa de santa fee centro del Nuevo Mexico, esta en treinta y siete grados en retalinia del sur, teniendo por el Occidente la mar a distancia de 200 leguas, descubriola el año de 1605: el adelantado Don Juan de Oñate llevando en su compania a[l]gunos soldados, y Religiosos de me seraphi[ca] Religion, y por Presidente al Padre Predicador Fr. Francisco de Escobar." Archivo General de las Indias, Estado, 43, n. 1, f.3v.
3. Adolph Bandelier, *The Gilded Man (El Dorado) and Other Pictures of the Spanish Occupancy of America* (New York: D. Appleton and Co., 1893), pp. 286-87.
4. Ralph Emerson Twitchell, *The Leading Facts of New Mexican History*, two volumes (Cedar Rapids: The Torch Press, 1911), Vol. I, pp. 332, 333, n. 336. New Edition, Sunstone Press, Santa Fe, 2007
5. This statement overlooks that San Agustín, the capital of La Florida, was established in 1565.
6. Lansing B. Bloom, "New Mexico Under Mexican Administration, 1821–1846," *Old Santa Fe*, 1(July, 1913)1:9.
7. Ralph Emerison Twitchell, "Editorial," *Old Santa Fe*, 1(July, 1913)1:226-27.
8. Lansing Bloom to Ralph Emerison Twitchell, "Editorial," *Old Santa Fe*, 1(January, 1914)3:336-37, quoting Benjamin Read, *Illustrated History of New Mexico*, (Santa Fe: New Mexican Printing Co., 1912), p. 246.

9. Ralph Emerison Twitchell, "Editorial," *Old Santa Fe*, 1(January, 1914)3:336-37.
10. Ralph Emerison Twitchell, *Old Santa Fe: The Story of New Mexico's Ancient Capitol* (Santa Fe: Santa Fe New Mexican Publishing Corporation, 1925), pp. 18-19. New Edition, Sunstone Press, Santa Fe, 2007.
11. George Hammond, "Don Juan de Oñate and the Founding of New Mexico: A New Investigation Into the Early History of New Mexico in the Light of a Mass of New Materials Recently Obtained from the Archivo General de Indias, Seville, Spain," *New Mexico Historical Review*, 1(January, 1926)1:42.
12. Hammond, "Oñate," *New Mexico Historical Review*, 2(April, 1927)2:143 and n. 691, citing the "Instrucción á Don Pedro de Peralta gobernador y capitan-general de la Nueva Mexico en lugar de Don Juan de Oñate," March 30, 1609, Archivo General de las Indias, 58-3-16.
13. Lansing Bloom, "Instructions for Don Pedro de Peralta Governor and Captain General of New Mexico, in the Place of Don Juan de Oñate," *El Palacio*, 24(June 16, 1928)24:466-473.
14. Hammond, with Agapito Rey, later published his own translation of the Instructions: "Instructions to Don Pedro de Peralta, Who Has Been Appointed Governor and Captain General of the Provinces of New Mexico in Place of Don Juan de Oñate, Who Has Resigned the Said Offices, March 30, 1609," George P. Hammond and Agapito Rey, *Don Juan de Oñate, Colonizer of New Mexico, 1595–1628* (Albuquerque: University of New Mexico Press, 1953), part 2, pp. 1087-91.
15. Lansing Bloom, transcriber, and Ireneo L. Chaves, translator, "Instructions to Peralta by Vice-Roy," *New Mexico Historical Review* 4 (April 1929)2:178-87.
16. Lansing Bloom, "When Was Santa Fe Founded?", *New Mexico Historical Review* 4(April 1929)2:188-94.
17. Fray Alonso de Benavides, *Fray Alonso de Benavides' Revised Memorial of 1634; With Numerous Supplementary Documents Elaborately Annotated*, Frederick Webb Hodge, George P. Hammond, and Agapito Rey, eds. and annotaters (Albuquerque: University of New Mexico Press, 1945), pp. 68, 273-74.
18. Benavides, *Benavides 1634*, p. 68 n. 86, 273-74.
19. France V. Scholes, "Juan Martínez de Montoya, Settler and Conquistador of New Mexico," *New Mexico Historical Review* 19 (October 1944) 4:337-42.
20. Scholes, "Martínez de Montoya," p. 341.
21. One scholar who accepted the evidence presented by Scholes about the Martinez de Montoya founding of Santa Fe before 1608 was Jack Forbes, who cites Scholes's article in *Apache, Navaho and Spaniard* (Norman: University of Oklahoma Press, 1960), pp. 112-13.
22. "D[on] Juan Saens Maurigade, vecino de esta Corte, Sobre que se incluya en la descendencia directa del Capitan D[on] Juan Martínez de Montoya, Descubridor, Conquistador y Poblador que fue en las Americas y Governador del Nuevo Mexico," Juan Martínez de Montoya Collection, 1785–1835, AC 143, Angelico Chavez Library, Palace of the Governors, Santa Fe, New Mexico.
23. Scholes, "Martínez de Montoya," p. 338.
24. Juan Martínez de Montoya to governor Cristobal de Oñate, August 10, 1608, "Juan Martínez de Montoya, Descubridor," pp. 18, 18v.

25. Carroll L. Riley, *The Kachina and the Cross: Indians and Spaniards in the Early Southwest* (Salt Lake City: University of Utah Press, 1999), pp. 92, 103.
26. Bloom and Chaves, "Instructions," p. 178.
27. This change in emphasis for the goals of the colony was made explicit in the orders sent by the Viceroy to both Martínez de Montoya and Peralta; Viceroy Luis de Velasco, "Montoya Appointed Governor: Appointment of Juan Martínez de Montoya as Governor, February 27, 1608," in Hammond and Rey, *Oñate*, p. 1053; Viceroy Luis de Velasco, "Peralta Appointed Governor: Appointment of Don Pedro de Peralta as Governor of New Mexico, March 30, 1609," in Hammond and Rey, *Oñate*, p. 1085.
28. Bloom and Chaves, "Instructions," pp. 178-87. The English translation has been revised somewhat for this article.
29. Translations of the applicable Laws of the Indies are included in David H. Snow, "Review of Agrarian and Linear Land Measurement of Land From 17th Century Documents in Colonial New Mexico," pp. 85-108, and Cordelia T. Snow, "Hypothetical Configurations of the Early Santa Fe Plaza Based on the 1573 Ordenances or the Law of the Indies," pp. 55-73, in *Santa Fe Historic Plaza Study I: With Translations from Spanish Colonial Documents*, Linda Tigges, ed. (Santa Fe: City Planning Department, 1990).
30. Most of the known historical evidence about the early plan of Santa Fe has been assembled in Tigges, *Plaza Study I*.
31. Max Moorehead, *The Presidio, Bastion of the Spanish Borderlands* (Norman: University of Oklahoma Press, 1975), "Villa of Santa Fe in 1766," plate 17.
32. Lota M. Spell, "The Grant and First Survey of the City of San Antonio," *Southwestern Historical Quarterly (SWHQ)* 66(July 1962):75-78.
33. James Ivey, "A Reconsideration of the Survey of the Villa de San Fernando in 1731," *Southwestern Historical Quarterly*, 111(January 2008)1, pp. 250-81.
34. Bloom and Chaves, "Instructions," pp. 180, 181. Translations by James Ivey.
35. Lansing Bloom translated "vecindades" as "properties" in the 1928 *El Palacio* article (Bloom, "Instructions," p. 468) and left it as "vecindades" in the *New Mexico Historical Review* article the next year (Bloom and Chaves, "Ynstuccion," pp. 180, 181). Hammond and Rey translated the term as "districts (*vecindades*)" in Hammond and Rey, *Oñate*, part II, p. 1088. For the meaning of "vecindad" in my interpretation above, see, for example, Real Academia Española, *Diccionario de la lengua Castellana*, vol. S-Z (Madrid: Real Academia Española, 1739), p. 428, col. 1, Vecindad: "[3] Significa tambien la razon de vecino en un pueblo, por la habitacion, ú domicilio en el tiempo determinado por la ley." "Razon," in this case, means more or less "allotment of land."
36. Snow, "1573 Ordinances," p. 59.
37. Thomas C. Barnes, Thomas H. Naylor, and Charles W. Polzer, *Northern New Spain: A Research Guide* (Tucson, AZ: University of Arizona Press, 1981).
38. A *pie* was one-third of a vara, or about 0.915 feet (11 inches).
39. James Ivey, "A Reconsideration of the Survey of the Villa de San Fernando in 1731," *Southwestern Historical Quarterly*, 111(January 2008)1, pp. 250-81.
40. J. Bawden, "Private Land Claims in the Southwest," M.A. thesis, Southern Methodist University, 1969, part 2, vol. 2, "The Santa Fe Grant," pp. 324-342.
41. United States v. Santa Fe, 165 U.S. 675 (1897); Bawden, "The Santa Fe Grant," p. 340.

42. Bawden, "The Santa Fe Grant," p. 341.

Chapter 4
Thirty-eight Adobe Houses,
The Villa of Santa Fe in the Seventeenth Century, 1608–1699

1. Archivo General de la Nación, México (AGN), Inquisición (Inq.), t. 596, leg. 2, no. 24, f. 121.
2. Marc Simmons, *The Last Conquistador: Juan de Oñate and the Settling of the Far Southwest* (Norman: University of Oklahoma Press, 1991), 148-149.
3. Juan Martinez de Montoya Collection, Box 1, f.18ff, Fray Angélico Chávez Library, Santa Fe.
4. Juan Martinez de Montoya Collection, Box 1, f.18ff, Fray Angélico Chávez Library, Santa Fe.
5. Amalio Huarte, ed. *Relaciones de los Reinados de Carlos V y Felipe II* (Madrid: Sociedad de Bilbliófilos Españoles, 1941), 248; and Carlos Navarro y Rodrigo, *El cardenal Cisneros: Estudio biográfico* (Madrid: G. Estrada, 1869), 152.
6. Juan Martinez de Montoya Collection, Box 1, f.18ff, Fray Angélico Chávez Library, Santa Fe.
7. Juan Martinez de Montoya Collection, Box 1, f.18ff, Fray Angélico Chávez Library, Santa Fe.
8. Simmons, *The Last Conquistador*, 157.
9. Frederick Webb Hodge, George P. Hammond, and Agapito Rey, eds., *Fray Alonso de Benavides' Revised Memorial of 1634* (Albuquerque: University of New Mexico Press, 1945), 68.
10. Simmons, *The Last Conquistador*, 164-169.
11. AGN, Inq., t. 583, exp. 3, f. 297r; and AGN, Inq., t. 586, f. 49r.
12. AGN, Inq., t. 592, f. 288r.
13. Archivo General de las Indias, Sevilla (AGI), México, 27, N63, leg. 6, f. 1v.
14. AGI, México, 27, N40, leg. 1, f.1v.
15. AGI, México, 27, N40, leg. 2, 1r.
16. AGI, México, 27, N40, exp. 7, f. 1v: Decree of King, February 27, 1608.
17. AGI, México, 27, N63, leg. 4, f. 2r.
18. AGI, México, 27, N63, leg. 6, ff. 1r-2v; and George P. Hammond and Agapito Rey, eds., *Don Juan de Oñate, Colonizer of New Mexico* (Albuquerque: University of New Mexico Press, 1953), Vol. I, 1087-1088.
19. AGI, México, N63, leg. 4, f. 2r.
20. Hammond and Rey, *Don Juan de Oñate, Colonizer of New Mexico*, 1096, citing AGI, México, 128, Memorial of Fray Francisco de Velasco, April 9, 1609.
21. Hammond and Rey, *Don Juan de Oñate, Colonizer of New Mexico*, 1096.
22. AGN, Inq., t. 356, f. 268r.
23. AGN, Inq., t. 356, f. 269v; and Fray Angélico Chávez, *Origins of New Mexico Families In the Spanish Colonial Period* (Santa Fe: Museum of New Mexico Press, 1992), 36.

24. AGN, Inq., t. 586, f. 49; AGN, Inq. t. 583, exp. 3, f. 297; and Chávez, *Origins*, 41.
25. AGN, Inq., t. 356, f. 270r; and AGN, Inq., t. 356, f. 303r.
26. AGN, Inq., t. 356, f. 268; and AGN, Inq., t. 316, f. 172v.
27. AGN, Inq., t. 356, f. 267; AGN, Inq., t. 356, f. 311; and Chávez, *Origins*, 71.
28. AGN, Inq., t. 356, f. 268v.
29. AGN, Inq., t. 356, f. 269; and AGN, Inq. t. 372, leg. 16, f. 6.
30. AGI, Patronato, 244, R7, leg. 14, f. 14v.
31. AGN, Inq., t. 316, f. 150v.
32. AGN, Inq., t. 316, f. 150v.
33. AGN, Inq., t. 316, f. 150v.
34. AGN, Inq., t. 316, f. 150v.
35. AGI, México, 27, N63, leg. 6, f. 1v; and Charles Wilson Hackett, *Historical Documents relating to New Mexico, Nueva Vizcaya, and Approaches Thereto, to 1773* (Washington, DC: Carnegie Institution of Washington, 1937), III:47.
36. AGN, Inq., t. 316, f. 152v.
37. AGN, Ramo de Concurso de Peñalosa, vol. 3, exp. 455, leg. 1, no. 2, f. 4r (*plaza principal*); AGI, Ramo de Concurso de Peñalosa, t. 1. leg. 1, ff. 33r (*plaza real*); AGI, Patronato, 244, R7, exp. 14, f. 13r (*plaza pública and plaza mayor*); and Hackett, *Historical Documents*, III:51 (*plaza mayor*).
38. AGN, Ramo de Concurso de Peñalosa, vol. 3, exp. 455, leg. 1. no. 1, f. 126.
39. AGN, Inq., t. 585, f. 82r; AGN, Inq., t. 629, exp. 2, f. 118r ; and AGN, Ramo de Concurso de Peñalosa, vol. 3, exp. 455, leg. 1, no. 2, f. 4r.
40. AGN, Inq., t. 596, f. 21r; also AGN, Inq. t. 608, exp. 6, f. 417r.
41. AGN, Inq., t. 608, exp. 6, f. 417r.
42. AGN, Inq., t. 316, f. 151v.
43. AGN, Inq., t. 316, f. 151v.
44. AGI, México, 29, N45a, leg.2, ff.4v-5r.
45. Hodge, Hammond and Rey, eds., *Fray Alonso Benavides' Revised Memorial*, 8.
46. AGN, Inq., t. 304, f. 187r, and AGN, Inq. t. 356, f. 308r; AGN, Inq., t. 372, exp. 16, f. 12v.
47. Hackett, ed., *Historical* Documents, III:108 and 119.
48. Hackett, ed., *Historical Documents*, III:69 and 119.
49. Biblioteca Nacional de Madrid, MS 19258, photos 15-16.
50. AGI, México, 304; and France V. Scholes, "Documents for the History of the New Mexican Missions in the Seventeenth Century, in *New Mexico Historical Review* 4 (1929), 46.
51. AGI, Patronato 244, R7, leg. 17, f. 1v.; Hackett, *Historical Documents*, III:56.
52. AGI, Patronato, Mexico, 29, leg 14, f. 33v; and AGN, Ramo de Concurso de Peñalosa, vol. 3, exp. 455, leg. 1, no. 2, f. 4r.
53. AGI, Patronato, 244, R7, leg. 14, f. 33v.
54. AGI, Patronato, 244, R7, exp. 14, ff. 18v and 28r; AGN, Ramo de Concurso de Peñalosa, vol. 3, exp. 455, leg. 1, no. 2, f. 4r; AGN, Ramo de Concurso de Peñalosa, vol. 2, exp. 495, leg. 1, no. 4, f. 245r; and AGN, Tierras, t. 3268, f. 253v.
55. AGN, Ramo de Concurso de Peñalosa, vol. 2, exp 495, leg. 1, no. 7, f. 167r

56. AGN, Tierras, t. 3268, leg. 1, no. 6, ff.3r-4r.
57. AGN, Tierras, t. 3268, leg. 1, no. 6, ff.2v.
58. AGN, Tierras, t. 3268, leg. 1, no. 6, f.3r.
59. AGN, Ramo de Concurso de Peñalosa, vol. 3, exp. 455, leg 1, no. 1, ff.79v-80r.
60. AGN, Ramo de Concurso de Peñalosa, vol. 3, exp. 455, leg., 1, no. 1, f. 73r.
61. AGN, Ramo de Concurso de Peñalosa, vol. 3, exp. 455, leg., 1, no. 1, f. 74r.
62. AGN, México, Ramo de Concurso de Peñalosa, vol. 1, leg. 1, no. 2, f. 233ff; and AGN, Tierras, t. 326, ff. 231r-231v, and 418v-419r.
63. AGN, Tierras, t. 3268, f. 247r-247v.
64. AGN, Tierras, t. 3268, f. 58r.
65. AGI, Patronato 244, R7, leg. 14, ff. 8r and 12v
66. AGN, Ramo de Concurso de Peñalosa, vol. 3, exp. 455, leg. 1, no. 1, ff. 73-80v, 91, 103v, and 109v.
67. José Antonio Esquibel, "References to the *Casas Reales de Palacio* on the Villa de Santa Fe: The Palace of the Governor, 1659–1663," unpublished manuscript, 2005.
68. AGN, Tierras, t. 3268, ff. 208-208v.
69. AGI, Patronato, 244, R7, leg. 20, ff.8r and 10v; AGI, Patronato, 244, R7, leg. 14, ff. 14r, 17v and 23r.
70. AGI, Patronato, 244, R7, leg. 14, f.17v.
71. AGN, Provincias Internas, t. 37, ff. 112r-114r.
72. AGN, Inq., t. 421, f. 238r.
73. AGN, Inq.., t. 608, exp. 6, f. 417r.
74. AGI, Patronato, 244, R7, leg. 14, f.9v.
75. Elinore M. Barrett, *Conquest and Catastrophe: Changing Rio Grande Pueblo Settlement Patterns in the Sixteenth and Seventeenth Centuries* (Albuquerque: University of New Mexico Press, 2002), 172.
76. AGI, Patronato 244, R7, leg. 15, f.2v.
77. Biblioteca Nacional de México, leg. 1, no. 32.
78. John L. Kessell, Rick Hendricks, and Meredith D. Dodge, eds. To the Royal Crown Restored: The Journals of Don Diego de Vargas, 1692–1694 (Albuquerque: University of New Mexico Press, 1995), 529-533.

Chapter 5
The History of Santa Fe Plaza, 1610–1720

1. John W. Reps, *Town Planning in Frontier America* (Columbia and London: University of Missouri Press, 1980), p. 24-29; Clarance Haring, *The Spanish Empire in America* (New York: Harcourt, Brace and World, 1949), p. 103.
2. Thomas Chávez, "Santa Fe: Established ~~1610~~ 1607," *El Palacio,* Vol. 100, no. 1 (Winter 1994–1995), pp. 14-16.
3. John Francis Bannon, *The Spanish Borderlands Frontier, 1513–1821* (New York: Holt, Rinehart and Winston, 1970), pp. 36-41.
4. Joseph P. Sánchez, "The Peralta-Ordóñez Affair and the Founding of Santa Fe," in

Santa Fe: History of an Ancient City, (Santa Fe: School of Advanced Research, 2008), pp. 15-23, p. 18; Fray Angelico Chávez, "Santa Fe Church and Convent Sites in the Seventeenth and Eighteenth Centuries," *New Mexico Historical Review* (hereafter cited as *NMHR*), Vol. 24, no. 2 (April 1949), pp. 89-90.

5. Bruce T. Ellis, "Santa Fe's Seventeenth Century Plaza, Parish Church, and Convent Reconsidered," in Albert H. Schroeder, Editor, *Collected Papers in Honor of Marjorie Ferguson Lambert* (Albuquerque: Archaeological Society of New Mexico, 1976), pp. 185-192; Boyd C. Pratt and David H. Snow, "The North Central Regional Overview: Strategies for the Comprehensive Survey of the Architectural and Historic Archaeological Resources of North Central New Mexico," unpublished report prepared for the New Mexico State Historic Preservation Division, 1988, Volume I, pp. 161-162; Cordelia Thomas Snow, "The Plazas of Santa Fe, New Mexico, 1610–1776," unpublished manuscript, 1988.

6. Eg. Ralph Emerson Twitchell, *Old Santa Fe* (Chicago: Rio Grande Press, 1965 (originally published in 1925)), p. 51, New Edition, Sunstone Press, Santa Fe 2007; Pratt and Snow, *op. cit.*, pp. 161-162; C.T. Snow, *op. cit.*, pp. 1-6; Stanley M. Hordes, "Archival Study," in Christine Rudecoff, *Archival and Archaeological Research at the Water Street Parking Lot, Laboratory of Anthropology Notes, No. 388* (Santa Fe: Museum of New Mexico, 1987).

7. Hordes, *op. cit.*; New Mexico State Records Center and Archives (hereafter cited as NMSRCA), Spanish Archives of New Mexico (hereafter cited as SANM), Series I, No. 411, Ysabel Jorge, petition for lands and house formerly belonging to her grandfather, Capitan Antonio Baca (May 17, 1696) (this *expediente* contains other conveyances through 1708), f. 1-6v; Chávez, *Origins of New Mexico Families in the Spanish Colonial Period* (Santa Fe: Historical Society of New Mexico, 1954), pp. 9-10; France V. Scholes, *Church and State in New Mexico, 1610–1650* (Albuquerque: University of New Mexico Press, 1937), pp. 138, 175.

8. See John Leddy Phelan, "Authority and Flexibility in the Spanish Imperial Bureaucracy," *Administrative Science Quarterly*, Vol. 5, no. 1 (June 1960), pp. 47-65.

9. Reps, *op. cit.*, pp. 33, 35.

10. Charles Wilson Hackett and Charmion Claire Shelby, *Revolt of the Pueblo Indians and Otermin's Attempted Reconquest,1680–1682* (Albuquerque: University of New Mexico Press, 1942), pp. xxiv-lxvii; 11-19, 112-115.

11. Cordelia Snow, *op. cit.*, pp. 13-18.

12. This position is supported by Twitchell, *op. cit.*, pp. 53, 84, 136, Sánchez, *op. cit.*, p. 16; and Kessell, "By Force of Arms: Vargas and the Spanish Restoration of Santa Fe," in Noble, *op. cit.*, pp. 37-46, p. 38.

13. José Manuel Espinosa, *Crusaders of the Rio Grande: The Story of Don Diego de Vargas and the Reconquest and Refounding of New Mexico* (Chicago: Institute of Jesuit History, 1942), p. 66.

14. Twitchell, *op. cit.*, pp. 136-138; Espinosa, *op. cit.*, p. 66; Kessell, *op. cit.*; NMSRCA, SANM II, No. 94a.

15. John L. Kessell and Rick Hendricks (eds.), *By Force of Arms: The Journals of Don Diego de Vargas, 1691–1693* (Albuquerque: University of New Mexico Press, 1992), pp. 387-399; Espinosa, *op. cit.*, pp. 60-65; Espinosa, *First Expedition of Vargas into New Mexico, 1692*

(Albuquerque: University of New Mexico Press, 1940), pp. 79-94.
16. Kessell and Hendricks, *op. cit.*, pp. 400-402; Espinosa, *Crusaders*, pp. 65-66.
17. Kessell, "By Force of Arms: Vargas and the Spanish Restoration of Santa Fe," p. 41; Espinosa, *Conquerors*, pp. 151-162.
18. NMSRCA, SANM II, No. 65 (1697). This document consists of a *repartimiento* (distribution) of goods to colonists in Santa Fe that had survived the famine of 1695–1696. The list of colonists included 413 *españoles* (presumably native of New Mexico), 75 persons from the Mexico City area, 79 persons from Zacatecas, and 470 listed as coming from Zacatecas and Sombrerete; see also Clevy Strout, "The Resettlement of Santa Fe, 1695: The Newly Found Muster Roll," *NMHR*, Vol. 53, no. 2 (July 1978), pp. 261-270.
19. NMSRCA, SANM II, No. 74 (May 22, 1698).
20. Twitchell, *op. cit.*, pp. 140, 147.
21. NMSRCA, SANM I, No. 294 (1703); No. 295 (1704); and No. 929 (1703); Chávez, *Origins*, p. 134.
22. Chávez, "Santa Fe Church and Convent Sites," pp. 85-93.
23. NMSRCA, SANM I, No. 425 (1701) and No. 821 (1701); Chávez, *Origins*, pp. 169-170.
24. NMSRCA, SANM I, Nos. 77 (1704); 483 (1706); 489 (1711); Chávez, *Origins*, pp. 228, 269-271.
25. NMSRCA, SANM II, No. 79 (October 4, 1701); Chávez, *Origins*, p. 278.
26. NMSRCA, SANM I, No. 1198 (1705).
27. See for example, NMSRCA, SANM II, No. 172 (March 28, 1712), describing the house of Diego de Velasco, and SANM I, No. 168 (1716), which offers details on the house sold on the south side of the plaza by Juan de la Mora Pineda to Juan Ruíz de Cordero.
28. NMSRCA, SANM I, Nos. 1073 (1714); and 1073 (1714).
29. NMSRCA, SANM I, Nos. 8 (1715); 290 (1702); 298 (1708); 312 (1716): 404 (1716); 481 (1704); and 1072 (1714).
30. NMSRCA, SANM I, No. 8 (1715).
31. NMSRCA, SANM I, Nos. 3 (1697); 8 (1715); 303 (1713); and 482 (1706).
32. NMSRCA, SANM I, Nos. 298 (1708); 489 (1711); 491 (1713); and 929 (1703).
33. Kessell, *op. cit*, pp. 41-44.
34. NMSRCA, Twitchell Collection, No. 242 (July 7, 1708).
35. NMSRCA, SANM II, No. 253 (July 15, 1716); NMSRCA, Twitchell Collection, No., 243 (July 15, 1716).
36. NMSRCA, SANM II, No. 307 (1720).
37. NMSRCA, SANM II, Nos. 225 (July 2, 1715); and 296 (May 7, 1719).
38. NMSRCA, SANM II, No. 179 (September 16, 1712).
39. NMSRCA, SANM II, No. 172 (March 28, 1712); see also Elizabeth Howard West, "The Right of Asylum in New Mexico in the Seventeenth and Eighteenth Centuries," *NMHR*, Vol. 41, no. 2 (April 1966), pp. 115-153.
40. NMSRCA, SANM II, No. 296 (May 7, 1719).
41. NMSRCA, SANM II, No. 267 (January 20, 1716).

Chapter 6
A Window to the Past, The San Miguel
and La Conquistador Chapels and Their Builders, 1610–1776

1. Kubler, *The Rebuilding of San Miguel*. See also, A. von Wuthenau, "The Spanish Military Chapels in Santa Fe," page 180, note 12.
2. Throughout the 17th century, San Miguel was consistently referred to as an *ermita* or hermitage. According to church historian Conrad Harkins, O. F. M. (personal communication June 2, 2004), an *ermita* was defined as "a small place, usually isolated, where individual friars from a province withdrew from their places or convents and their normal responsibilities for a longer or shorter interval to devote themselves to a contemplative life of prayer and silence." It appears the word *ermita* probably had other connotations during the 17th century from the modern usage.
3. Scholes, France V. "Church and State," page 38.
4. Scholes, "Church and State," page 38; my emphasis.
5. Ivey, *In the Midst of a Loneliness*, page 41. According to Ivey, before 1640 in New Mexico, the Franciscans constructed the baptismal area under the choir loft. After that date, the baptistry was placed in a separate room.
6. Giffords, *Sanctuaries of Earth, Stone and light* page 44; Ivey, "The Architectural Background of the New Mexico Missions," pages 45-50.
7. Bloom, "A Glimpse of New Mexico," page 370.
8. Bloom, "A Glimpse of New Mexico," page 370.
9. Bloom, "A Glimpse of New Mexico," page 370.
10. Hodge, Hammond and Rey, *Revised Memorial*, 129.
11. Hodge, Hammond and Rey, *Revised Memorial*, 2.
12. Hodge, Hammond and Rey, *Revised Memorial*, 3.
13. Hodge, Hammond and Rey, *Revised Memorial*, 128-129, emphasis added. Giffords, *Sanctuaries of Earth Stone and Light*, page 157 defines transepts as, "…armlike extensions at right angles to the naves in cruciform churches, intersect immediately in front of the sanctuary." The transept is separated from the sanctuary where the altar is housed by the communion rail.
14. Kubler, *San Miguel*, 6. Scholes, Church and State, 333.
15. Mrs. Edward E. Ayer, *The Memorial of Fray Alonso de Benavides 1630*
16. Hodge, Hammond and Rey, *Revised Memorial*, 68.
17. Stubbs and Ellis, *Archaeological Investigations*, pages 1-7.
18. Giffords, *Sanctuaries of Earth, Stone, and Light*, page 75
19. Margo, *N. S. Guadalupe* and Scholes," Mission Documents," page 195
20. Scholes, "Mission Documents," page 198.
21. Scholes, "Church and State," page 333.
22. Kessell et al., *To the Royal Crown Restored* page 112; Hodge, Hammond and Rey, *Revised Memorial* page 114.
23. Kessell et al, *To the Royal Crown Restored*, 477.
24. Kessell et al., *Blood on the Boulders* page 68. There is no indication in the Vargas Journals of where this church was located. Mid-18th deeds and other land transfers would seem to

place the church in the area around present Washington Avenue and Paseo de Peralta.
25. Esquibel and Colligan, *The Spanish Recolonization of New Mexico*.
26. Esquibel and Colligan, *The Spanish Recolonization of New Mexico*, page 7.
27. Fray Angélico Chávez, Families, page 254; Strout, "Resettlement of Santa Fe, 261-263.
28. Chávez, *Origins of New Mexico Families* page 176; Kubler, *San Miguel*, 21-22, 26. According to art historian Robin Farwell Gavin, the bulto of San Miguel presently found in the main niche in the altarscreen at San Miguel was probably the figure that was escorted through New Mexico to raise funds for the restoration.
29. Chávez, *Families*, 286.
30. SANM I: 825, Andres Montoya to Bernadino de Sena; SANM I: 826, Sevastiana de Mondragon to Bernardino de Sena; SANM I:860, Last Will and Testament of Bernardino de Sena.; Esquibel and Carrillo, *A Tapestry of Kinship,* pages 16 and 25.
31. SANM I:836; SANM I:837; SANM I:850; SANM I:860.
32. Chávez, *Families*, 286; SANM I:860. Syndics were laymen who handled funds for the Franciscans and other mendicant orders. The fact that Sena was a syndic at age 25 is an indication of the extraordinary trust placed in him by the Franciscans in Santa Fe.
33. Chávez, *Families*, page 208; Esquibel and Colligan, *The Spanish Recolonization of New Mexico* pages 12 and 24; Kubler *San Miguel*, 17, 23; Kessell et al., *Blood on the Boulders*, page 670, n. 15.
34. Chávez, *Families*, 226.
35. Kubler, *San Miguel*, 20, 23, 27; Chávez, *Families*, 191, 309.
36. Chávez, *Families*, 191.
37. SANM II :253.
38. Chávez, *Families*, 309.
39. Chávez, *Families*, 309.
40. SANM I: 737
41. Chávez, *Families*, 309-310; SANM II:172; aside from building barges to cross the Rio Grande at El Paso del Norte, one wonders if Diego Velasco ever did any repair work at Nuestra Señora de Guadalupe. See also Esquibel and Carrillo, *A Tapestry of Kinship*, page 11.
42. Kessell et al., *By Force of Arms*, page 300 n. 1; Chávez, Santa Fe's Own: A History of Fiesta, page 9; SANM I:183.
43. Kessell et al, *By Force of Arms*, page 477, n. 5.
44. SANM I:169, Petition of Diego Arias and proceedings undertaken concerning a pond in the cienega.
45. Esquibel and Colligan, *The Spanish Recolonization of New Mexico*, page 32. See also, Esquibel and Carrillo, *A Tapestry of Kinship*, page 11.
46. Kessell et al., *To the Royal Crown Restored*, page 58.
47. SANM I:489. The fact that Magdalena de Ogama appears to have been an *Indio de Mexico* and owned land on the west side of the plaza suggests that not all Indians in Santa Fe were forced to live in the Barrio de Analco.
48. SANM I:183; SANM I:489.
49. Chávez, *Families*, pages 264, 388.
50. Chávez, *Families*, page 312.

51. Kubler, *San Miguel*, 17-20; 23-17; Chávez, *Families*, page 188.
52. Esquibel and Colligan, the Spanish Recolonization of New Mexico, pages 217-218; Gerald Gonzales, personal communication, March 14, 2009;
53. Kessell et al, *To the Royal Crown Restored*, pages 56-58
54. Kubler, *San Miguel*, 20, 27.
55. Stubbs and Ellis, 1-4.
56. Stubbs and Ellis, 1-4.
57. Kubler, *San Miguel*, 5
58. Adams and Chávez, *Missions of New Mexico, 1776*, page 27
59. Adams and Chávez, *Missions of New Mexico, 1776*, page 38.
60. Adams and Chávez, *Missions of New Mexico, 1776*, page 38.
61. Chávez, "Santa Fe Church and Convent Sites," page 85-93; Kessell et al. *That Disturbances Cease*, page 403; page 440 n. 1; SANM I: 169. Bruce Ellis, *Bishop Lamy's Cathedral*, page 55, provides references that indicate construction of the new parroquia may have started as early as 1712.
62. SANM I:169.
63. Chávez, *Our Lady of the Conquest*, page 29.
64. Ellis, *Bishop Lamy's Cathedral*, pages 47-57, 157-173.
65. It should be noted that in the original Spanish, Juan de Medina is identified only as *maestro*. Chávez, *Our Lady of the Conquest*, page 93.
66. Chávez, *Our Lady of the Conquest*, page 39.
67. Kessell et al. Blood on the Boulders, page 126.
68. SANM I:169.
69. Chávez, *Families*, page 236.
70. Chávez, *Families*, pages 309-310; SANM II:172.
71. Ellis, *Bishop Lamy's Cathedral*, pages 56-57; 157-158.
72. Adams and Chávez, *Missions of New Mexico, 1776*, page 24.
73. Fray Angélico Chávez, Our *Lady of the Conquest*, page 76. Juan Lorenzo de Medina was also called upon to inspect the tanque constructed in the cienega by Diego Arias in 1715–1716, SANM I:169, Petition of Diego Arias re tanque in the Cienega and Inspection of the Entrances and Exits of Santa Fe.
74. Giffords, *Sanctuaries of Earth, Stone and Light*, page 74-75.
75. Esquibel and Carrillo, *A Tapestry of Kinship*.

Chapter 7
Barrio de Analco, Its Roots in Mexico and Role in Early Colonial Santa Fe, 1610–1780

1. Cyprian J. Lynch, ed., *Benavides' Memorial of 1630* (Washington: Academy of American Franciscan History, 1954), pp. 23-24. Some of the Españoles were of Mestizo origin, or had Mestizo or even Indian spouses, as Benavides acknowledges in his *Revised Memorial of 1634*, p. 68: "Most of them [the Españoles in Santa Fe] are married to Spanish or Indian women or to their descendants."

2. For a comprehensive study of the original configuration of the Santa Fe plaza and its *casas reales*, see Cordelia Thomas Snow, "The Plazas of Santa Fe, New Mexico, 1610–1776" in *El Palacio*, vol. 94, no. 2 (1988), pp. 40-51. For a recent summary history of Santa Fe, see William Wroth, "Santa Fe," New Mexico Office of the State Historian, 2006 (www.newmexicohistory.org/filedetails.php?fileID=392).

3. On pre-Conquest urban pattern and social structure see James Lockhart, *The Nahuas after the Conquest* (Stanford: Stanford University Press, 1992), and Charles Gibson, *The Aztecs under Spanish Rule* (Stanford: Stanford University Press, 1964).

4. See Charles Hannaford and Michael Taylor, "Finding Elysium: When Territorial Santa Fe Brewed its Own Beer, " in *Archeology in Your Backyard* (Santa Fe: City of Santa Fe, n.d., ca. 1998), pp. 117-132; and Linda Tigges, "Soils, Tests, the *Cienega*, and Spanish Colonial Occupation in Downtown Santa Fe" in Linda Tigges, ed., *Santa Fe Historical Plaza Study* (Santa Fe: City Planning Department, 1990), pp. 75-84. A photograph of the Bishop's Garden, ca. 1880, showing a large pond, is in the Princeton University Library collection.

5. Other Spanish towns and cities in colonial Mexico with a neighboring Barrio de Analco are Villa Juárez in Oaxaca, Celaya in Guanajuato, and the city of Puebla.

6. John K. Chance, *Conquest of the Sierra: Spaniards and Indians in Colonial Oaxaca* (Norman: University of Oklahoma Press, 1989), pp. 33-34, citing *Papeles de Analco* in the Archivo Parroquial de Villa Alta. See also Antonio García Cubas, *Diccionario Geográfico, Histórico y Biográfico de los Estados Unidos Méxicanos* (México: Antigua Imprenta de Murguia, 1888–1891), vol. 1, pp. 187-188. On the ambiguous status of *Indios naborías*, see William L. Sherman, *Forced Native Labor in Sixteenth-Century Central America* (Lincoln: University of Nebraska Press, 1979), p. 102.

7. Rodney Anderson, *Guadalajara Censuses Project* (www.fsu.edu/~guadalaj); María Gracia Castillo Ramírez, "Analco: un barrio en la historia" in *Alteridades*, No. 15 (1998).

8. Charles Gibson, *The Aztecs under Spanish Rule*, p. 370.

9. P. J. Bakewell, "Zacatecas: An Economic and Social Outline of a Silver Mining District, 1547–1700" in Ida Altman and James Lockhart, eds. *Provinces of Early Mexico* (Los Angeles: UCLA Latin American Center Publications, 1976 [1984]), pp. 199-229; and Peter Gerhardt, *The North Frontier of New Spain* (Princeton: Princeton University Press, 1982), 157-160.

10. José de Arlegui, *Crónica de la provincia de n.s.p.s. Francisco de Zacatecas* (México: Cumplido, 1851) (first published in 1737), pp. 31-32, 219. Atanasio G. Saravia, *Obras I: Apuntes para la Historia de Nueva Vizcaya* (México: Universidad Nacional Autónoma de México, 1993), p. 261. H. H. Bancroft *History of the North Mexican States and Texas; 1531–1889* (San Francisco: The History Company, 1886), p. 596.

11. The Indians and other individuals not of Español status on the expedition have been inventoried by David H. Snow, *New Mexico's First Colonists: The 1597–1600 Enlistments for New Mexico under Juan de Oñate, Adelante & Gobernador* (Albuquerque: Hispanic Genealogical Research Center of New Mexico, 1998). See also, for Mexican Indians brought to New Mexico on earlier expeditions, Carroll L. Riley, "Mesoamerican Indians in the Early Southwest," in *Ethnohistory* Vol. 21, No. 1 (1974), pp. 25-36.

12. Caso's nephew, Alonso González, interviewed during the Acoma trial in 1599, was

described as "a mestizo and native of the city of Mexico." Archivo General de Indias (AGI), Patronato, legajo 22, ramo 13, ff. 1036r-1085r (94r-143r); ff. 1086r-1131v., translated in Jerry R. Craddock, ed and John H. R. Polt, trans., *The Trial of the Indians of Acoma, 1598–1599* (Berkeley: Research Center for Romance Studies, 2008), p. 21.

13. George P. Hammond and Agapito Rey, eds. and trans., *Don Juan de Oñate, Colonizer of New Mexico, 1595–1628* (Albuquerque: University of New Mexico Press, 1953), pp. 416-419.

14. France V. Scholes, "The Supply Service of the New Mexican Missions in the Seventeenth Century" in *New Mexico Historical Review*, Vol. 5, No. 1 (January, 1930), pp. 93-115.

15. Translation of AGI, *Contaduria*, 726, Appendix IV in Fray Alonso de Benavides, *Revised Memorial of 1634*, Frederick Webb Hodge, et al., eds. and trans. (Albuquerque: University of New Mexico Press, 1945), pp. 123-124.

16. Much of this information is drawn from unpublished research notes by José Antonio Esquibel, "Indios Méxicanos of 17th-century New Mexico" and "Vecinos and Residents of New Mexico 1659–1663, and 1667," with my gratitude for his generosity in sharing them. Vargas's census of the *Indios Méxicanos* is translated in John L. Kessell, et al., *To the Royal Crown Restored* (Albuquerque: University of New Mexico Press, 1995), pp. 56-58. Otermín's muster of October 1680 is translated in Charles Wilson Hackett, *The Revolt of the Pueblo Indians and Otermín's Attempted Reconquest, 1680–1682* (Albuquerque: University of New Mexico Press, 1942), vol. 1, p. 136ff. Juan Chamiso's name (also spelled Chamizo) most likely derives from the colonial *casta* designation "Chamizo" (meaning literally half burned stick) which was usually used to describe the caste (racial type) resulting from the union of a *coyote* and an *india*. See Ilona Katzew, *Casta Painting: Images of Race in Eighteenth-century Mexico* (New Haven: Yale University Press, 2005), *passim*. The adding of racial designation to a person's name was a common practice in colonial Mexico, especially since many Indians and mixed-castes were given only first and middle names and not surnames. For instance, Antonio Coyote and Francisco Coyote are listed (immediately after the governor and immediately preceding the cacique) in the 1750 census of Tesuque Pueblo (see Virginia Olmsted, *Spanish and Mexican Censuses of New Mexico, 1750–1830* (Albuquerque: New Mexico Genealogical Society, 1981).

17. "…otro dia por la mañana se descubrio el exerçito del henemigo en el llano de las milpas de san Miguel y casas de los mexicanos, saqueandolas con tanta desverguensa que se aloxaron en ellas para poner sitio a la Villa con la demas jente que aguardaban." Archivo General de la Nación (AGN), Provincias Internas 37, fol. 6r. My thanks to Barbara De Marco for providing a copy of the microfilm of the original document and her careful transcription of this and the following document. My translation differs slightly from that in Hackett, *Revolt of the Pueblo Indians*.

18. "El dia martes trese del dicho mes como a las nueve de la mañana se nos aparesieron en el varrio de Analco en el sementerio de la hermita de san Miguel y en la otra parte del rio de la Villa todos los yndios de las nasiones de Tanos y Pecos y Queres de san Marcos en arma dando alaridos de guerra." AGI Guadalajara 138, fol. 520r. A certified copy, dated September 15 of Otermín's letter of September 8 written in Socorro to Fray Francisco de Ayeta, regarding the 1680 Pueblo Revolt and the siege of Santa Fe. Transcription by

Barbara De Marco. This copy contains a scribal error: the use of the word "sementerio" (cemetery) instead of "sementera" (cultivated field). It appears that Otermín in writing to Ayeta used the Spanish word "sementera" instead of the Nahuatl "milpa" (perhaps thinking authorities in Spain would not be familiar with the latter term). The scribe copying it then mistakenly wrote "sementerio." The text is translated in Charles Wilson Hackett, *Historical Documents Relating to New Mexico, Nueva Vizcaya, and Approaches Thereto* (Washington: Carnegie Institution, 1923–1937), vol. 3, p. 330.

19. AGI Guadalajara 138, fol. 521r – 522r, translated in Hackett, *Historical Documents*, vol. 3, p. 330.
20. AGN, Provincias Internas 37, fol. 6v. Diego de Vargas in reporting his arrival at Santa Fe in September 1692 also uses the term "milpa" to refer to the fields of the Indians. He notes that the Indians in possession of the villa "were warned [of his coming] by the Indians who were sleeping in the milpas through which I passed" (Kessell et al., *To the Royal Crown Restored*, p. 187).
21. According to Carlos de Sigüenza y Góngora, in the re-conquest Vargas liberated 74 Mestizos and Genízaros who had been living in captivity among the Pueblos ("Consiguieron su libertad setenta y quarto Mestizos, y Genizaros, que de los muchos que quedaron en cautiverio se hallaron vivos") See Sigüenza y Góngora, *Mercurio Volante con la Noticia de la recuperacion de las Provincias del Nuevo Mexico conseguida por D. Diego de Vargas....* (México: Antuerpia, 1693), p. 18; facsimile reprint in Irving Albert Leonard, trans. & ed., *The Mercurio Volante of Don Carlos de Sigüenza y Góngora...* (Los Angeles: Quivira Society, 1932), p. 125. These 74 individuals no doubt included some of the Mexican Indian residents of Barrio de Analco who were captured in August 1680 when the Tanos, Queres, and Pecos warriors took possession of Analco in their siege of Santa Fe.
22. Francisco Xavier, "Certification [and] notice of departure," [Santa Fe, August 21, 1680], translated in Charles Wilson Hackett, *The Revolt of the Pueblo Indians*, vol. 1, p. 19.
23. Hackett, *The Revolt of the Pueblo Indians*, vol. 1, pp. 136ff. Among the many servants mentioned in Spanish households are those of Governor Otermín whose 30-member entourage of family and servants included Españoles, Mulatos, and Indians, and the entourage of the Father Guardian [head friar] whose 30 individuals included "attendants and servants."
24. John L. Kessell, et al., *To the Royal Crown Restored*, pp. 56-58, 91-92.
25. George Kubler, ed., *The Rebuilding of San Miguel at Santa Fe in 1710* (Colorado Springs: Taylor Museum, 1939), p.19, 25 (transcription and translation of "Testimonio del Gasto de la Capilla del glorioso San Miguel echo por el Capitan Don Agustín Flores de Vergara....", Huntington Library, Ritch Collection, no. 48). On Magadalena de Ogama, see also Spanish Archives of New Mexico (SANM) I, nos. 489 and 1071. At least seven households of Mexican Indians returned to Santa Fe in 1693 with Vargas; see José Antonio Esquibel, "The Formative Era for New Mexico's Colonial Population: 1693–1700" in Claire Farrago and Donna Pierce, eds. *Transforming Images* (University Park: Pennsylvania State University Press, 2006), p. 70 and p. 285n24.
26. John L. Kessell, et al., *To the Royal Crown Restored*, p. 477.
27. Kubler, George, ed., *The Rebuilding of San Miguel at Santa Fe in 1710*, p. 15, 20.

28. SANM I no. 1138, "Bentura Bustamante, communication to the governor, protesting the treatment of the Genízaro Indians of Santa Fe. (Copy made in Arispe),1780." My thanks to Cordelia Snow for calling this document to my attention. Bustamante is named as the "Lieutenant of the Genízaro Indians of the Villa of Santa Fe." He traveled to Sonora with four companions and spoke in behalf of 33 fellow petitioners. For a discussion of this document, see James F. Brooks, "'Lest We Go In Search of Relief to Our Lands and Our Nation': Customary Justice and Colonial Law in the New Mexico Borderlands, 1680–1821" in Christopher L. Tomlins and Bruce H. Mann, eds. *The Many Legalities of Early America* (Chapel Hill: University of North Carolina Press, 2001), pp. 150-180. And also his *Captives & Cousins: Slavery, Kinship, and Community in the Southwest Borderlands* (Chapel Hill: University of North Carolina Press, 2002), pp. 138-142.
29. For a summary of scholarly literature on the Tlaxcalan northern migrations and discussion of the rights granted to them, see Patricia Martinez, "'Noble' Tlaxcalans: Race and Ethnicity in Northeastern New Spain, 1770–1810" (Austin: University of Texas, PhD dissertation, 2004), pp. 2-47. See also David B. Adams, "The Tlaxcalan Colonies of Spanish Coahuila and Nuevo León" (Austin: University of Texas, PhD dissertation, 1971). Adams found no evidence of a Tlaxcalan settlement in Santa Fe.
30. David Brugge, "Captives and Slaves on the Camino Real" in June-el Piper, ed., *El Camino Real de Tierra Adentro* (Santa Fe: Bureau of Land Management, 1999), vol. 2 pp. 103-110.
31. Later, in 1794 the eastern community of San Miguel del Bado was founded and its founders included 12 Genízaro families from the Barrio de Analco. The new community most likely took its name from the venerable San Miguel church in Analco.
32. Yet the memory of the Barrio de Analco as an Indian/Genízaro community survived well into the twentieth century. Anita Gonzalez Thomas who was born in Santa Fe in the early 1900s told historian Marc Simmons a children's rhyme which suggests that the social gap between the Españoles of Santa Fe and the Indian/Genízaros of Barrio de Analco was very much alive: "La torre de San Miguel/ Se desmorese de la risa/ De ver a las analqueñas/ Con enaguas y sin camisas" (The tower of San Miguel almost dies laughing to see the Analco girls with skirts and without shirts) (Marc Simmons, personal communication, 2008).

Chapter 8
In Her Own Voice, Doña Teresa Aguilera y Rocha and Intrigue in the Palace of the Governors, 1659–1662

1. France V. Scholes (1937–1941) published a synopsis of the administration of Bernardo López de Mendizábal, and the trial of the Governor and his wife Teresa de Aguilera y Roche, in his series of articles, "Troublous Times in New Mexico, 1659–1670," *New Mexico Historical Review*, vols. 12, 13 and 15, republished as *Troublous Times in New Mexico 1659–1670*, Historical Society of New Mexico, Publications in History, Vol. XI, (Albuquerque: University of New Mexico Press, 1942) and used for subsequent citations.

2. José Antonio Esquibel compiled information on the service that Juan Chamiso, a master mason, provided to Governor López de Mendizábal in this seventeenth century renovation of the Palace. Chamiso was a Mexican Indian from the Valley of Mexico who seems to have been responsible for overseeing these renovations. Chamiso (also spelled Chamico) and his household of 20 family members and servants were among those who fled the colony during the Pueblo Revolt of 1680. Jose Antonio Esquibel, *Juan Chamiso, Albañil Maestro: Research and Summary Notes*. 2005. Used by permission of the author. Hackett, Charles W. (editor) and C. C. Shelby (translator) *The Revolt of the Pueblo Indians of New Mexico and Otermin's Attempted Reconquest 1680*–1682, Vol. I and II (Albuquerque: University of New Mexico Press, 1942), Vol. I, p. 157.
3. Ward Alan Minge (1979), defines *efectos del país* as the domestic products and manufactured goods produced in New Mexico and traded south throughout the Spanish Colonial and Mexican periods. *Efectos del País:* A History of Weaving Along the Río Grande, in *Spanish Textile Tradition of New Mexico and Colorado, Museum of International Folk Art (*Santa Fe: Museum of New Mexico Press, 1979).
4. Paul Kraemer and Cordelia Snow, "When the Palace was a Store; Economics in Seventeenth Century New Mexico," in *Newsletter of the Compadres del Palacio* (Santa Fe: Museum of New Mexico, 1997) Vol. 6, No. 1, pp. 4-7 and Scholes, *op. cit.*, 34-36, 44-45, 111-112.
5. Carroll L. Riley. *The Kachina and the Cross: Indians and Spaniards in the Early Southwest* (Salt Lake City: University of Utah Press, 1999), pp. 162-168.
6. Stanley M. Hordes. *To the End of the Earth: A History of the Crypto-Jews of New Mexico* (New York: Columbia University Press, 2005), pp. 161-65; Ramon A. Gutierrez. *When Jesus Came the Corn Mothers Went Away, Marriage, Sexuality and Power in New Mexico, 1500–1846* (Stanford: Stanford University Press, 1991), pp. 115-127.
7. Carroll L. Riley, *op. cit.*, pp. 184-185; Carrol L. Riley, "Bernardo López de Mendizábal; Could He Have Prevented the Pueblo Revolt?," *El Palacio*, 2007, Vol. 112, No. 3, pp. 38-46.
8. Scholes, *Troublous Times*, p. 20.
9. *Ibid.*, pp. 20-23.
10. *Ibid.*, pp. 24-28.
11. *Ibid.*, pp. 28-30, 52-84.
12. *Ibid.*, pp. 30-31.
13. *Ibid.*, p. 151.
14. Juan Manso was also the younger brother of Fray Tomás Manso, administrator of the New Mexico mission supply service and former Custodian of the New Mexico Franciscans. Fray Juan Ramírez was his successor. Scholes, *op. cit.*, pp. 2-3, 10.
15. Scholes, *op. cit.*, pp. 35-39.
16. Hordes, *op. cit.*, pp. 134 and 165-66, n. 2.
17. Scholes, *op. cit.*, pp. 38-47.
18. *Ibid.*, p. 38.
19. Scholes notes that in short order, more than 1600 masks, prayer sticks and figures were collected and destroyed. *Ibid.*, p. 98.
20. *Ibid.*, pp. 97-101, 108-110.

21. *Ibid.*, pp. 91-92.
22. *Ibid.*, pp. 90-105.
23. *Ibid.*, pp. 129-130.
24. *Ibid.*, p. 116.
25. See notes 29 and 46 and accompanying text.
26. Scholes, *op. cit.*, pp. 111-120.
27. *Ibid.*, pp. 136-137; Charles W. Hackett. *Historical Documents Relating to New Mexico, Nueva Vizcaya, and the Approaches Thereto*, Vol. III (Washington: Carnegie Institute of Washington, 1937), pp. 233, 240.
28. Scholes, *op. cit.*, pp. 159-160.
29. Petition, Polonia Varela vezina destas provincias del Nuebo México, Vol. 425, ff. 633r-645r, Ramo de Inquisición, Archivo General de la Nación; *Ibid.*, tomo 571, exp. 8, f. 214-216 and 230. Fray Angelico Chávez calls the matter involving Polonia Varela a "cause célèbre of the period." See Fray Angelico Chávez, *Origins of New Mexico Families*, revised ed. (Santa Fe: Museum of New Mexico Press, 1992), pp. 359-360.
30. Susan Wallace, wife of Lew Wallace who was Governor of New Mexico from 1878–1881, and who lived in the Palace during his term, describes a letter written in 1692 to Antonio Eusebio de Cubero, Secretary of Governor Don Diego de Vargas, by his lady love from Seville, Spain. Susan E. Wallace, *The Land of the Pueblos* (New York: John Alden, 1888; New Edition, Santa Fe: Sunstone Press, 2006), pp. 114-120.
31. Mary E. Giles. *Women in the Inquisition: Spain and the New World* (Baltimore: John Hopkins University Press, 1999). The volume edited by Giles presents case studies of fourteen women tried before the Inquisition in Spain and the New World for a variety of offenses—secret practice of Judaism, blasphemy, bigamy, and practicing as religious visionaries—a practice specifically forbidden to women. For the virtues, expectations and education of women in seventeenth century Spain and New Spain, see the work of Meredith D. Dodge and Rick Hendricks, *Two Hearts, One Soul. The Correspondence of the Condesa de Galve, 1688–1696* (Albuquerque: University of New Mexico Press, 1993).
32. Clark Colahan, "María de Jesús de Agreda: The Sweetheart of the Holy Office" in Mary E. Giles, *Women in the Inquisition: Spain and the New World*, pp. 155-170). See also John L. Kessell. *Kiva, Cross and Crown* (Washington, DC: National park Service, 1979), pp. 150-152.
33. The description here is compiled from the following sources: Hordes, *op. cit.*, pp. 57-59. Seymour B. Liebman, *Los Judíos en México y América Central (Fé, Llamas e Inquisición)*. (Mexico D.F.: Siglo Veintiuno Editores, S.A., 1971), pp. 113-120, 122-125.
34. Prisión y embargo de bienes de Doña Teresa de Aguilera y Roche, Santa Fe, August 27, 1662, fols. 396r-397r, Ramo de Concurso de Peñalosa, tomo 1, AGN.
35. The inventory—which reflects Doña Teresa's wealth and position in the upper class— consisted of 128 lots of various items. To illustrate the extent of her personal possessions and give a cross section of the kinds of goods that could be found circulating in Santa Fe at the time, an abridged version of the inventory and accompanying formalities follows:

In said Villa, ... said year, month and day, ... I went to the house and residence of Doña Teresa de Aguilera y Roche and having shut the doors as the Illustrious Tribunal of the

Inquisition ordered and required, I embargoed all of the goods which belonged to Doña Teresa de Aguilera, which are as follows:

1 — First a bed made of red ebony wood which has four pillars with headboards in two parts and five crossboards and fifty-eight balusters—thirty five small ones and four large ones—all made of red ebony wood, along with eight iron screws, nine posts and eleven boards, all of which comprise the bed....

This initial lot detailing the components of her bed is followed by 127 numbered lots. The diversity of clothing, textiles and leather goods in those lots is remarkable. A cross-section consists of: petticoats of green *baieta*; a locally made carpet; doublets of cashmere; some castanets; coarse cloth; bracelets of coral and abalone; green petticoats of coarse cotton; towels of local cotton; a doublet of chamois; a fan; flax bonnets; a small belt of gold with thirty-eight equal-sized pieces, one with its stones which look like diamonds, two of the fastening pieces lack two stones, and three large pieces with nine stones each and the joining piece with stones, all ill-treated; two yards of linen and a yard of narrow linen; a canopy of blue linen; blue narrow embroidered linen; Rouen linen; Roeun linen embroidered with tufted silk; linen washcloths embroidered with lace of this land; crimson ribbon; three yards of old point lace; local white point lace; a bundle of silver lace point; a painted elk hide; a yard of strings of sham lace; black point lace; ribbon roses of various colors; linen roses; *manta*; crimson damask; gold point lace; a cross made of manatee hide; pieces of black watered satin; a corset and *turca* of watered satin; a scarlet cloak; a bonnet of blue embroidered silk; flowered silk; net silk stockings of two colors; watered silk; a bed canopy of Chinese silk; a yard of rose-colored taffeta; white taffeta; wool bedsheets; purple skirts of coarse wool cloth of this land; and a wool table cloth from Hopi.

Similarly, the list of utensils and tools in the list was extensive. A sampling: a small box for bottles with four small bottles; a brass basin; a brass hand warmer; a chinese porcelain; three coconut shell vessels with silver feet; a small copper scoop; a small copper coal pan; a jug for chocolate along with two platters, five plates and a cup from la Puebla; two little chests for storing salt; a little chest for storing chocolate; a chocolate cup from Michoacán; a pouch with three shaving razors; a hand mill with a silver base; fourteen cups made by the Apaches and large clay jar; a small gilded mirror; four hand mills for making vanilla paste; an old kitchen hatchet; and a *metate* and its *mano* from New Spain.

Other significant items that were inventoried included a large desk with eleven drawers—for which the items in each drawer were individually listed; a small trunk with sewing equipment; a large trunk with its lock and key; a small writing desk; a small writing desk of tortoise shell; and Doña Teresa's coach with all its equipment and trappings. And also included in the inventory were Doña Teresa's two slaves: "the *mulatilla* named Clara who appeared to be thirty-nine years old ... Also the *mulatillo* named Diego, a laborer who appeared to be seven or eight years of age, along with both were papers showing they were slaves."

Various religious items also showed up in the inventory: "a figure of Christ half a *vara* in size with a canopy of blue linen;" "a sash of purple netting for devotion to Our Lady;"

"a small silver reliquary of Our Lady and San Juan, and other paper reliquaries and two rosaries;" and "a book titled *Angeli Custodis*."

The inventory ended in the usual formal fashion:

> All the preceding goods were inventoried by said Fray Father Commissary with assistance from the previously mentioned *Alguacil Mayor*, Don Juan Manso and the Recetor ... [Francisco] de León and the others who are the Maese de Campo Pedro Luzero de Godoy and the President Secretary. He did so, putting everything in closed boxes, tied and labeled and which say on each one: "*Fisco [Real]*". He did this in said house and loaded two wagons and stored them in the *convento* of Santo Domingo so they would be stored there and similarly, he required said *Alguacil* to take Doña Teresa de Aguilera her goods. And he put her in a room that is next to the church against the wall of the cemetery. And [put] the clothes in a little office until time to send her to Mexico City as your Lordship ordered. And he said the present inventory is being left open in case some pertinent goods have been left out which the aforesaid will rectify. And as for the chocolate [that was inventoried—] it should be used with [the Father Commissary's] permission so that it will be done without misunderstanding.

Prisión y embargo de bienes de Doña Teresa de Aguilera y Roche, Santa Fé, August 27, 1662, fols. 397r-400v, Ramo de Concurso de Peñalosa, tomo 1, AGN.

36. Scholes, *op. cit.*, pp. 142,149.
37. *Ibid.*, pp. 150-157.
38. Hordes, *op. cit.*, p. 155; Scholes, *op. cit.*, p. 153.
39. Scholes, *op. cit.*, pp. 158-165; María Magdalena Coll More, "'Fio Me a de Librar Dios Nuestro Señor de Mis Falsos Acusadores': Doña Teresa de Aguilera y Roche al Tribunal de la Inquisición (1664, Mexico)," Romance Philology, Vol. 53, Special Issue, Part 2 (1999–2000), p. 296.
40. Chávez, *op. cit.*, p. 7.
41. El Señor fiscal del Santo Oficio contra Doña Teresa Aguilera y Roche, testimony of Pedro de Artiaga, Santa Fe, October 24, 1661, ff. 18r-18v, Ramo de Inquisición, tomo 596, exp. 1, AGN.
42. *Ibid*, testimony of Josepha de Sandoval, f. 26v.
43. *Ibid.*, testimony of Antonia Ysabel, f. 23r.
44. Ana Rodrigues is apparently the daughter of Alonso Rodrigues and Ynez de Anaya—sister of Cristóbal de Anaya who was arrested by the Inquisition along with Mendizábal and Doña Teresa. See Chavez, *op. cit.*, p. 94. Alonso Rodrigues, Cristóbal de Anaya, Ynez de Anaya, Ynez' brother Francisco de Anaya and her father—also Francisco de Anaya—all had befriended Mendizábal and Doña Teresa in Mexico City. They had fled to Mexico City following a dispute with Governor Manso, but returned to New Mexico in 1659 with Mendizábal. Scholes, *op. cit.*, pp. 35-36.
45. Pedro de Valdes was a nephew of former Governor Juan Manso. Scholes, *op. cit.*, p. 108.
46. Juan Griego was the father of Isabel Bernal, wife of Juan González Bernal and sister-in-

law of Diego González Bernal. Chavez, *op. cit.*, p. 40. See also notes 25 and 29, *supra*.
47. Siete pliegos de papel escritos que presenta Doña Teresa de Aguilera en la Audiencia, f. 148r, Ramo de Inquisición, tomo 596, exp. I, AGN.
48. Stanley Hordes reads the Spanish term to be a *zapote*, and kind of fruit. He also notes that this behavior appears to be a form of crypto-Jewish behavior or observance. Hordes, *op. cit.*, p. 158. See also David M. Gitlitz, *Secrecy and Deceit: The Religion of the Crypto-Jews* (Philadelphia: Jewish Publication Society of America, 1996, pp. 277, 280, 305 n. 12, 627.
49. Siete pliegos de papel escritos que presenta Doña Teresa de Aguilera en la Audiencia, f. 148r, Ramo de Inquisición, tomo 596, exp. I, AGN.
50. *Ibid.*, f. 148r, Ramo de Inquisición, tomo 596, exp. I, AGN.
51. Jusepa was Josepha de Sandoval, wife of Pedro de Artiaga.
52. Siete pliegos de papel escritos que presenta Doña Teresa de Aguilera en la Audiencia, ff. 148r-148v, Ramo de Inquisición, tomo 596, exp. I, AGN.
53. Scholes, *op. cit.*, pp. 7-8, 40.
54. Chávez, *op. cit.*, pp. 19, 25.
55. Scholes, *op. cit.*, pp. 215-216, 227.
56. *Ibid.*, p. 144.
57. Siete pliegos de papel escritos que presenta Doña Teresa de Aguilera en la Audiencia, f. 153v, Ramo de Inquisición, tomo 596, exp. I, AGN.
58. Scholes, *op. cit.*, p. 8.
59. Scholes, *op. cit.*, pp. 44-45; Siete pliegos de papel escritos que presenta Doña Teresa de Aguilera en la Audiencia, f. 154r, Ramo de Inquisición, tomo 596, exp. I, AGN.
60. Siete pliegos de papel escritos que presenta Doña Teresa de Aguilera en la Audiencia, ff. 150r-150v, Ramo de Inquisición, tomo 596, exp. I, AGN.
61. *Ibid.*, ff. 150v-151r.
62. *Ibid.*, f. 151r.
63. *Ibid.*, f. 152v.
64. *Ibid.*
65. *Ibid.*, f. 152r.
66. *Ibid.*, ff. 152v-153r. Additional details concerning this incident emerged in the Inquisition's charges against Mendizábal. One of the charges presented during Mendizábal's June 16, 1663 hearing before the Inquisitors states: "So unbridled was the concupiscence of the accused that he availed himself of the authority of his office to assist him in his misdeeds to the degree that women who had committed crimes for which he was to examine them were not free from his barbarous lust. Such ... occurred with ... Petrona Gamboa who was also detained in the same house for ... investigating the death of her sister. The accused kept her in his wife's dressing-room and sent to have her called ... to take an oath; but before she reached the room where the secretary was, there was another, used as a harness room; there he knew her carnally, and later went on with the judicial processes for which he had summoned her." Charles W. Hackett, *op. cit.*, p. 210.
67. Siete pliegos de papel escritos que presenta Doña Teresa de Aguilera en la Audiencia, f. 151r, Ramo de Inquisición, tomo 596, exp. I, AGN.

68. *Ibid.*, ff. 148r-148v.
69. Scholes, *op. cit.*, pp. 166-167
70. *Ibid.*, p. 157.
71. *Ibid.*, pp. 166-168.

Chapter 9
On Establishing A Presidio in Santa Fe 1678–1693

1. Vargas' eventual success in re-establishing a Spanish presence in New Mexico is well documented in the several volumes produced by John Kessell and his colleagues at the University of New Mexico. The chapter on "Northern Rebellions" in Naylor and Polzer 1986 (which pre-dates the publication of the Kessell volumes on Vargas; see p. 24, note 32), does not include Santa Fe and the 1680 Pueblo Revolt: "No documents dealing with this well-known historical episode have been included because the subject of this study is not the chronology of Indian rebellions, but the changing role of the presidio as a frontier institution." (p. 24)

   Weber, in his discussion of the Marquis de Rubí's 1766–1768 inspection tour of the frontier defenses, states that the presidio at Santa Fe was "established in 1693" (1992:208-209); however, Kessell, who describes the establishment of a 100-man presidio at Santa Fe as part of the "second phase" of Vargas' recolonization of New Mexico (1987:254), makes clear that the company left El Paso on 4 October 1693 but was still not in possession of Santa Fe at the end of that same year. Espinosa does not discuss the date of the establishment of the presidio, but refers only to the viceregal decree that granted Vargas the right to "enlist one hundred soldiers for the establishment of a presidio at Santa Fe, wherever and in whatever manner might be most convenient." (1988:40)

   On the physical location of the presidio, Nostrand states that the presidio established after Vargas' successful recolonization "was not a formal fortress but instead a company of soldiers whose quarters, guardhouse, and military chapel were somewhat scattered throughout the *villa*. Before the 1680 revolt a walled adobe fortress had existed immediately north of and contiguous with the Palace of the Governors, yet that fort was manned by colonists, not by soldiers, and technically was not a presidio. The old fort was partially restored in 1715, yet even after that date the presidio troops seem to have lived at points around the *villa*—until 1791, when a one-hundred man barracks and other modifications were completed in a major two-year renovation." (1992:38-39 and note 26)

   Bunting describes the problematic nature of reconstructing the earlier architecture, but nonetheless places the garrison within the structure known as the Palace of the Governors: "One other secular structure which has enjoyed almost continuous occupancy since it was begun in 1610, is the Palace of the Governors in Santa Fe. It has, however, been so often and so heavily remodeled that it is difficult to visualize its original appearance. Excavations on the palace carried out in 1973-75 by the staff of the Museum of New Mexico have provided more questions than answers. In the seventeenth century the palace housed the governor and his household, the provincial administrative offices, the jail, and the military garrison.... [I]t occupied the whole area between the present plaza and the Federal Building two blocks to the north." (1976:80) Moorhead, citing Ralph Emerson Twitchell's 1924 article on the Palace of the Governors, writes: "The architectural history of the urban presidio of Santa Fe is at once intriguing and confusing ... the original fort predated the establishment of a formal presidial company there. It was a huge rectangle extending more than four hundred feet along the north side of the town plaza and more than eight hundred feet behind it, enclosed on three sides by an adobe wall with barracks lining its interior and on the fourth side largely by the palace of the governors.... This early fortress served as a refuge for the inhabitants of Santa Fe and the nearby villages during the Pueblo Revolt of 1680, and breastworks were erected on the roofs during the crisis, but the stronghold was abandoned to the Indians after a five-day siege.... In 1703 the plaza was without defenses and the troops' quarters were scattered over the town and its environs.... In 1760, according to Bishop Pedro Tamarón, Santa Fe had no formal fortress or presidio." (1975:172-173)

2. In 1630 Fray Benavides published the first version of his *Memorial*, dedicated to King Philip IV. The relevant passage in the Cedula reads (transcription retains the original spelling): "Fray Alonso de Venabides, en diferentes memoriales que ha dado, me ha echo relazion [que] a asistido en essas provinçias y en el nuebo reyno de Mexico mas tiempo de treinta años a la predicazion y administrazion de los santtos sacramentos a los españoles y yndios y en la pasificazion y comberzion de los ynfieles ... " (AGI Guadalajara 138, fol. 154r-v). A second version of the *Memorial* was published in 1634; see Forrestal 1954:ix-xiv. The 1630 *Memorial* was published by Mrs. Edward Ayer, with notes by Frederick W. Hodge and Charles F. Lummis (Chicago: Donnelley & Son, 1916); the 1634 *Memorial* was published by George P. Hammond and Agapito Rey in the Coronado Cuarto Centennial series. (Albuquerque: University of New Mexico Press, 1945)

3. The most thorough presentation of the background and events of the 1680 Pueblo Revolt, in English, remains Hackett 1942.

4. It seems that it was Vargas himself who informed Ayeta that the Spanish crown was finally reasserting its possession of the northern kingdom. On 12 October 1692, writing "from this villa of Santa Fe, capital of the kingdom of New Mexico, newly restored to and conquered for the royal crown," Vargas informed his son-in-law of his successful reentry into New Mexico. Making reference to the failed attempt to reconquer the province in the year immediately after the Revolt, he mentions Father Ayeta, and his intention to inform him of the most recent events: "In 1681, the Rev. Father fray Francisco de Ayeta (who resides at the Convento Grande in Mexico City), procurator general of the Holy Gospel Province of Our Father St. Francis for the entire kingdom of New Spain, left for Santa Fe in the governor's company.... I could wish for no better chronicler of this important undertaking than this father, who came in that capacity. As I have said, he came with the then governor, but they did not succeed.... Though it was considered a desperate situation, with divine favor and at my own expense, I have now achieved the unexpected.... I have just arrived [at the Villa of Santa Fe] from the pueblos and nations

of the interior as far as the Taos, the most distant. I am writing this father, although briefly, so that he will be informed of everything and because he will rejoice." (Kessell et al. 1989:171-172)

5. Of the documents mentioned in this chapter, all but the 1693 *memorial* were published in volume three of the Bandelier papers, *Historical Documents Relating to New Mexico…*, edited by Charles Hackett (1937). Unlike the first two volumes in that series, which offer both Spanish texts and English translations, the third volume contains only English translations which, as Hackett himself explains in the preface, were based on transcriptions found among the Bandelier papers. Whenever these were incomplete, he made use of "complete transcripts of the same documents that were to be found in other transcript collections that were available to him." (iii)

6. Father Ayeta's 1693 *memorial* has never been published in English. A transcription of the Spanish text was first published (De Marco 2000) in a special issue of the journal *Romance Philology*, dedicated to "Documenting the Colonial Experience, with Special Regard to Spanish in the American Southwest" (De Marco and Craddock 1999–2000). The excerpts from the 1693 *memorial* that appear here in English are my own translation. Excerpts from Spanish documents are based on my own transcriptions.

7. Rubén Cobos includes the term *cuera* in his *Dictionary of New Mexico and Southern Colorado Spanish*: "a kind of thick rawhide jacket worn by Colonial New Mexico cavalry (XVIIIth century)…."

Chapter 10
Vargas at the Gate, The Spanish Restoration of Santa Fe, 1692–1696

1. Vargas's 1692 campaign journals and his correspondence with the viceroy appear in John L. Kessell and Rick Hendricks, eds., *By Force of Arms: The Journals of don Diego de Vargas, New Mexico, 1691–1693* (Albuquerque: University of New Mexico Press, 1992), 341-626 (quotations, 389, 412). See also J. Manuel Espinosa, *Crusaders of the Río Grande: The Story of Don Diego de Vargas and the Reconquest and Refounding of New Mexico* (Chicago: Institute of Jesuit History, 1942).

2. Irving A. Leonard, ed., *The Mercurio Volante of Don Carlos de Sigüenza y Góngora: An Account of the First Expedition of Don Diego de Vargas into New Mexico in 1692* (Los Angeles: The Quivira Society, 1932).

3. Kessell and Hendricks, *By Force*, 431. For a biographical sketch of Ojeda, see John L. Kessell, Rick Hendricks, and Meredith D. Dodge, eds., *To the Royal Crown Restored: The Journals of don Diego de Vargas, New Mexico, 1692–1694* (Albuquerque: University of New Mexico Press, 1995), 552 n. 61.

4. Kessell, Hendricks, and Dodge, *To the Royal Crown*, 483, 485.

5. John L. Kessell, Rick Hendricks, and Meredith D. Dodge, eds., *Blood on the Boulders: The Journals of don Diego de Vargas, New Mexico, 1694–1697* (Albuquerque: University of New Mexico Press, 1998), 1: 68-69.

6. Kessell, Hendricks, and Dodge, *To the Royal Crown*, 495-519 (quotations, 503, 506).

7. Ibid., 469.

8. Ibid., 519-42 (quotation, 528). Kessell and Hendricks, *By Force,* 421-34, 510-12.
9. Kessell, Hendricks, and Dodge, *Blood on the Boulders,* 1: 74.
10. Kessell, Hendricks, and Dodge, *To the Royal Crown,* 555-64 (quotation, 563).
11. Ibid., 538-42 (quotations, 540, 542).
12. Kessell, Hendricks, and Dodge, *Blood on the Boulders,* 1: 33.
13. John L. Kessell, *Kiva, Cross, and Crown: The Pecos Indians and New Mexico, 1540–1840* (Washington, DC: National Park Service, 1979), 262-70. Kessell, Hendricks, and Dodge, *Blood on the Boulders,* 1: 293, 315.
14. See Rick Hendricks, "Pueblo-Spanish Warfare in Seventeenth-Century New Mexico: The Battles of Black Mesa, Kotyiti, and Astialakwa," in Robert W. Preucel, ed., *Archaeologies of the Pueblo Revolt: Identity, Meaning, and Renewal in the Pueblo World* (Albuquerque: University of New Mexico Press, 2002), 180-97; Joe S. Sando, *Nee Hemish: A History of Jemez Pueblo* (Albuquerque: University of New Mexico Press, 1982), 120-21; and Kessell, Hendricks, and Dodge, *Blood on the Boulders.*
15. Kessell, *Kiva, Cross, and Crown,* 271-74. Kessell, Hendricks, and Dodge, *Blood on the Boulders,* 1: 398-402.
16. See John B. Colligan, *The Juan Páez Hurtado Expedition of 1695: Fraud in Recruiting Colonists for New Mexico* (Albuquerque: University of New Mexico Press, 1995), and José Antonio Esquibel and John B. Colligan, *The Spanish Recolonization of New Mexico: An Account of the Families Recruited at Mexico City in 1693* (Albuquerque: Hispanic Genealogical Research Center of New Mexico, 1999).
17. Kessell, Hendricks, and Dodge, *Blood on the Boulders,* 2: 698.
18. See J. Manuel Espinosa, ed., *The Pueblo Indian Revolt of 1696 and the Franciscan Missions in New Mexico: Letters of the Missionaries and Related Documents* (Norman: University of Oklahoma Press, 1988).
19. Kessell, Hendricks, and Dodge, *Blood on the Boulders,* 2: 678.
20. Espinosa, *Pueblo Indian Revolt of 1696,* 174-75.
21. Kessell, Hendricks, and Dodge, *Blood on the Boulders,* 2: 740-41.
22. Ibid., 732.
23. Ibid., 734.
24. Espinosa, *Pueblo Indian Revolt of 1696,* 182.
25. Stefanie Beninato, "Popé, Pose-yemu, and Naranjo: A New Look at Leadership in the Pueblo Revolt of 1680," *New Mexico Historical Review* 65 (October 1990), 422-23. Espinosa, *Pueblo Indian Revolt of 1696,* 278 n. 2.
26. Kessell, Hendricks, and Dodge, *Blood on the Boulders,* 2: 888.
27. John L. Kessell, *Spain in the Southwest: A Narrative History of Colonial New Mexico, Arizona, Texas, and California* (Norman: University of Oklahoma Press, 2002), 201-203.
28. Rick Hendricks, "Pedro Rodríguez Cubero: New Mexico's Reluctant Governor, 1697–1703," *New Mexico Historical Review* 68 (January 1993), 13-39. The struggle between Vargas and Rodríguez Cubero is detailed in John L. Kessell, Rick Hendricks, Meredith D. Dodge, and Larry D. Miller, eds., *That Disturbances Cease: The Journals of don Diego de Vargas, New Mexico, 1697–1700* (Albuquerque: University of New Mexico Press, 2000).
29. Kessell, Hendricks, Dodge, and Miller, eds., *A Settling of Accounts: The Journals of don*

Diego de Vargas, New Mexico, 1700–1704 (Albuquerque: University of New Mexico Press, 2002).
30. Ibid., 227.
31. Donna Pierce, ed., *!Vivan las Fiestas!* (Santa Fe: Museum of New Mexico Press, 1985). See also Ronald L. Grimes, *Symbol and Conquest: Public Ritual and Drama in Santa Fe* (Albuquerque: University of New Mexico Press, 1992). The tricultural dynamics of the annual Santa Fe Fiesta are explored in a video documentary by Jeanette DeBouzek and Diane Reyna, *Gathering Up Again: Fiesta in Santa Fe* (Santa Fe, New Mexico: Quotidian Independent Documentary Research, 1992). Kessell, Hendricks, Dodge, and Miller, eds., *A Settling of Accounts*, 251-66, offer a brief assessment of Vargas's New Mexico years.

Chapter 11
The Pastures of the Royal Horse Herd of the Santa Fe Presidio, 1692–1740

1. Noyes, *Los Comanches*, University of New Mexico Press. 1993, pages xxiii–xxiv.
2. See Elizabeth John, *Storms Brewed and Other Men's Worlds,* University of Nebraska Press. 1975, pages 231-233; T.R. Fehrenbach, *Comanches,* Anchor Books,1975, pages 86-91; Pekka Hämäläinen, *The Comanche Empire,* Yale University Press, New Haven, 2008, pages 18-67; and Frank Raymond Secoy, *Changing Military Patterns of the Great Plains Indians,* University of Nebraska Press, 1953, pages 6-30.
3. The Faraónes were a tribe of Apaches generally located west of the Rio Grande.
4. The sense of being surrounded by hostile tribes continued through the century. Writing in 1786, Viceroy Bernardo de Gálvez stated that the province of New Mexico "is very distant and surrounded in all directions by different enemies" and that "the troops must operate, if not by themselves, with only the aid of the Spanish settlers and the Indians of the pueblos." Bernard de Gálvez. *Instructions for Governing the Interior Provinces of New Spain, 1786,* The Quivira Society, Berkeley, 1951, page 72.
5. George P. Hammond, and Agapito Rey, editors. *The Rediscovery of New Mexico*. Albuquerque, University of New Mexico Press, Albuquerque, 1996, pages 36-37.
6. Alfred Barnaby Thomas, *Teodoro de Croix,* University of Oklahoma, Norman, 1941, page 57.
7. H.P. Walker in writing about the use of the horses in the west in the early 1800s states that "Cowboys and Indians who relied on horses for their livelihood worked strings of at least six or eight mounts. The horse could not keep up its strength over a long period of time on a diet of nothing but buffalo grass, and grain was not readily available." H. P.Walker. *The Wagonmasters*, University of Oklahoma Press, 1966, page 102.
8. Secoy, pages 6-10.
9. Secoy, pages 78-83.
10. John, pages 312-313; Colin G. Calloway. *One Vast Winter Count.* University of Nebraska Press, Lincoln. 2003, pages 284-286.
11. John, pages 323-324.
12. Spanish Archives of New Mexico (SANM) II: Twitchell No. 99. microfilm, New Mexico State Archives.

13. Rick Hendricks and John P. Wilson. *The Navajos in 1705.* Roque *Madrid's Campaign Journal.* University of New Mexico Press, Albuquerque, 1996, page 2.
14. Hendricks, page 3.
15. Hendricks, pages 1-4.
16. Hendricks, page xxi.
17. Alfred Barnaby Thomas, *After Coronado.* University of Oklahoma Press, 1935. pages 84-93.
18. Lansing Bloom. "A Campaign Against the Moqui Pueblos". *New Mexico Historic Review,* VI, April 1931, Vol. 2, pages 158-201.
19. Thomas. *After Coronado,* pages 99-110.
20. Thomas. *After Coronado,* pages 133-136.
21. SANM II: 329; John, pages 267-268.
22. SANM II: page 362.
23. SANM II: page 395-396.
24. SANM II: pages 443.
25. SANM II: pages 425. Translated by Richard Salazar.
26. An alferez was a kind of second lieutenant.
27. Pinart Collection, P-E 46:1, Bancroft Library. University of California, Berkley
28. Pinart Collection P-E 46:2. Complete transcriptions and translations of the two Pinart documents are at the end of the notes.
29. An explanation for the lack of military campaigns in the later 1730s may be found in the climate studies carried out for the Arroyo Hondo Pueblo excavations by the School of American Research. The tree ring data show that starting in the early 1730s, precipitation dropped markedly, with the drought not ending until the 1740s. It may be that the drought deterred both the raids on New Mexico and the campaigns against them. Martin R. Rose, Jeffrey S. Dean, and William J. Robinson. *The Past Climate of Arroyo Hondo New Mexico Reconstructed from Tree Rings,* School of American Research Press, Santa Fe, 1981, page 105.
30. In spite of their detailed regulations, some of the worst fears of the military were met later in 1777 when the Apaches raided Chihuahua stealing the entire horse herd of 400 horses and killing five guards. The Apaches easily escaped because the garrison had no mounts on which to pursue them. Bob Bernard. *The Vice-Regency of Antonio María Bucareli in New Spain, 1771–1779,* University of Texas, Austin, 1962, page 134.
31. John Kessell and Rick Hendricks, editors. *By Force of Arms.* University of New Mexico Press, Albuquerque, 1992, pages 349-354.
32. John Kessell and Rick Hendricks, editors. *A Settling of Accounts.* University of New Mexico Press, Albuquerque, 2003. page 74. In this case, *monte* may mean "brush" rather than "wooded area". Haggard, J. Villasana. *Handbook for Translators of Spanish Historical Documents,* University of Texas, 1941.
33. John Kessell and Rick Hendricks, editors. *Royal Crown Restored.* University of New Mexico Press, Albuquerque, 1993, page 429. A flying squadron was intended to move more quickly that the regular military without the heavy leather jackets and some of the other equipment that the other soldiers had. They were not always assigned to a specific location. Thomas H. Naylor and Charles W. Pozer. *Pedro Rivera and the Military Regulations of the Northern New Spain, 1724–1729.* University of Arizona Press, Tucson, 1988, page 4.

34. Kessell, *Royal Crown Restored,* page 429.
35. Kessell, *Royal Crown Restored,* pages 429-430.
36. Hendricks, page 29.
37. Thomas, *After Coronado,* page 84.
38. Thomas, *After Coronado,* page 87.
39. Thomas, *After Coronado,* pages 90-93.
40. Bloom, page 179.
41. Bloom, pages179-186.
42. Thomas. *After Coronado,* page 28.
43. Thomas, *After Coronado,* pages 133-136.
44. Bandelier, "Expedition of Pedro de Villasur", in *Contributions to the History of the Southwestern Portion of the United States,* page 194, in Hotz, *The Segesser Hides Paintings,* page 186.
45. SANM II: 321b.
46. Donald T. Garate. *Juan Bautista de Anza.* University of Nevada Press, Reno, 2003, pages 211-213.
47. Garate, *Juan Bautista de Anza,* page 85.
48. Diana Hadley, Thomas H. Naylor, and Mardith K. Schuetz-Miller. *The Presidio and Militia on the Northern Frontier of New Spain, A Documentary History. The Central Corridor and the Texas Corridor, 1700–1765.* Vol. 2, Part 2, University of Arizona Press, Tucson, 1997, pages 43,123.
49. Naylor, page 130.
50. Naylor, page 245.
51. Naylor, page 260.
52. Sidney Brinkerhoff and Odie B. Faulk. *Lancers of the King.* Arizona Historical Foundation, Phoenix, 1965, page 23.
53. Fernando de la Concha. "*Advice on Governing New Mexico*", *New Mexico Historical Review.* XXIV, 1949, pages 236-254.
54. Mark Simmons. *Spanish Government in New Mexico.* University of New Mexico Press, Albuquerque, 1968, page 124.
55. Kessell, *Royal Crown Restored,* page 429.
56. Naylor, pages 269-278.
57. Henrietta Martinez Christmas. *Military Records. Colonial New Mexico. Notas y Revistas.* Hispanic Genealogical Research Center, Albuquerque, 2004, pages 56-116.
58. Concha, page 253.
59. SANM II: 2092.
60. Garate, *Juan Bautista de Anza,* 99-100. It is possible that the intention was that the *caballada* be kept together and be driven from pasture to pasture as the grass was used up, as suggested by Simmons when writing about the horse herd in the later eighteenth century. (Simmons, page 124.) But reviewing the locations assigned by Olavidé, it is more likely that at this time, the herd was divided up among the pastures, perhaps along with the presidio cattle and other animals. In the later years, with more settlers located in the *Cieneguilla* area west of the villa, the pastures seem to have shifted to a larger single pasture in the Galisteo Basin. An 1805 government document written for

the northern frontier sets forth presidio privileges for the citizens. It states that settlers could add five or six horses to the presidio caballada, but not whole herds. The herds of the settlers could graze in the Presidio pastures, but had to follow those of the presidio at distance of two to three leagues. SANM I: 1812.

61. Pinart, P-E:46:1.
62. Pinart, P-E:46:2.
63. Kessell. *Royal Crown Restored*, page 111.
64. John Kessell and Rick Hendricks, editors. *Blood on the Boulders*. University of New Mexico Press, Albuquerque, 1998, page 603; SANM II:471.
65. New Mexico Land Grants, Surveyor General Documents (SG) No. 63: roll 19, frame 782-785, microfilm, New Mexico State Archives.
66. SG roll 39, frame 19, 53; Herbert O. Brayer. *Pueblo Indian Land Grants in "Rio Abajo", New Mexico*, page 121.
67. Snow, Cordelia Thomas. "The Evolution of a Frontier: An Historical Interpretation of Archaeological Sites" in Jan V. Biella and Richard C. Chapman. *Archeological Investigations in Cochiti Reservoir, New Mexico*. Vol. 4, pages 217-289. See also Herbert O. Brayer. Pueblo Indian Land Grants of the "Rio Abajo", New Mexico, pages 116-123.
68. SANM I: 319. pages 1-2,\.
69. SANM I: 773
70. Kessell, *By Force of Arms*, page 386.
71. Kessell, *By Force of Arms*, page 481 footnote 36.
72. The area is also shown in this location on a map prepared by Hal Jackson in his guide to the Camino Real in *Following the Royal Road*, University of New Mexico Press, 2006, page 32.
73. Kessell, *Royal Crown Restored*, page 111.
74. Kessell, *That Disturbances Cease*. University of Texas, Austin, 2002, page 47.
75. Kessell, *Blood on the Boulders*. page 826.
76. Kessell, *Royal Crown Restored*, page 111.
77. J.H. Simpson. *Journal of a Military Reconnaissance from Santa Fe, New Mexico, to the Navajo Country Made in 1849*. University of Oklahoma Press, Norman, Oklahoma,1964, page 8.
78. In his report on the livestock distribution of 1697, Vargas says that Peláez was company captain, military leader in charge of escorting cattle and horses to the colony. Kessell, *Blood on the Boulders*, pages 1157–1158.
79. SG 387: R 30, F 391-393; Kessell, *To the Royal Crown Restored*, pages 177-178, footnote 41.
80. Lujan was also a solider from the El Paso Presidio. Kessell, *That Disturbances Cease*, pages 99-100.
81. SG 387: roll 30, frame 394.
82. SG 59: roll 19, frame 194-197.
83. SG 59: roll 19, frame 100.
84. U.S. House of Representatives (HR), Misc. Doc. #181, 1872, 42nd Congress, 2nd Session, page 112, microfilm, New Mexico State Library, Santa Fe.
85. SG 102: roll 23, frames 26-28.

86. SANM I: 1081.
87. Kessell, *Royal Crown Restored,* page 467.
88. SG 121, roll 24, frame 776; New Mexico Land Grants Private Land Claims of the Surveyor General (PLC) Case 98, roll 43, frame 933, microfilm, New Mexico State Archives.
89. PLC 98, roll 43, frame 953.
90. PLC 276, roll 54, frame 268.
91. H.R. Misc. #181, pages 50 and 51.
92. PLC, roll 42, frame 670.
93. Rod Hall, resident of Galisteo, personal communication, February 12, 2009.
94. John Kessell. *Kiva Cross and Crown* University of New Mexico Press, Albuquerque, 1979, page 357.
95. SANM I: 2114.
96. H.R. Misc. 181, page 91.
97. H.R. Misc. 181, page 93.
98. Kessell, *Royal Crown Restored,* page 111.
99. Linda Tigges. "Soils, Tests, the Cienega, and Spanish Colonial Occupation in Downtown Santa Fe", in *Santa Fe Historic Plaza Study I*. City of Santa Fe Planning Department, Santa Fe, 1990, pages 75-83.
100. Ebright, *Land Grants and Lawsuits in Northern New Mexico,* pages 90-95.
101. SANM I: 1251.
102. SANM I: 491.
103. SANM I: 10.
104. SANM I: 169.
105. SANM I: 1251.
106. John O. Baxter. *Las Carneradas*. University of New Mexico Press, Albuquerque, 1987, page 23; SANM II:495,496.
107. The location is also shown on a map in Hal Jackson's *Following the Royal Road,* page 25.
108. SG 115: roll 24, frames 59 and 60.
109. Kessell, *Royal Crown Restored*, page 111.
110. Kessell, *By Force of Arms,* page 169.
111. This discussion is based on information from Ebright's *Land and Lawsuits in Northern New Mexico*, pages 90-96 and SANM I: 8 and 169.
112. Pinart, P-E 46: 2.
113. Pinart, P-E 46: 2.
114. Pinart, P-E, 46:1.
115. Daniel Tyler. *Ejido Lands in New Mexico in Spanish and Mexican Land Grants and the Law*. Edited by Malcolm Ebright. Sunflower University Press, Manhattan, Kansas, 1988, page 24.
116. Tyler, page 26.
117. Gálvez, *Instruccions,* 1786, page 39.
118. Thomas, A.B., "*Governor Mendinueta's Proposals for the Defense of New Mexico, 1772–1778*", *New Mexico Historical Review,* Vol. 5, pages 28 and 29.
119. Thomas, A.B., *Forgotten Frontiers,* page 63.

120. Thomas, A.B., *Teodoro de Croix and the Northern Frontier of New Spain, 1776–178,* page 56.
121. Gálvez, *Instruccions*, 1786, page 39.
122. Frank McNitt. *Navajo Expedition,* University of Oklahoma Press, Norman, 1964, pages 170-174.

TWO DOCUMENTS FROM THE PINART COLLECTION, P-E 46:1 and 2, BANCROFT LIBRARY, UNIVERSITY OF CALIFORNIA, BERKELEY. Translated and Transcribed by Richard Salazar, March 2002

English Translation of Letter from Alferez Juan Joseph Moreno to Henrique de Olavidé y Micheleña, Governor and Captain General, Santa Fe 1737. (P-E: 46-1)

The Lieutenant, Alferez and Sergeant of the Company of this Royal Presidio appear before Your Lordship in the best form which is proper and say that it has been more than three years that we have been experiencing the loss of weight which has occurred to the horse herd of this Royal Presidio because there is absolutely no place for them to graze, and if there is one, it is at such a distance from this garrison, which causes grave damage to them [horses]. What is even worse is that which is experienced by the soldiers, who do double duty, and requires more men [to do it], and who are needed at the Presidio. The defense, garrison and security of this Kingdom require that the horses be fat [in good condition] and at hand for any invasion by the Indians or hostility by enemies which occurs on a daily basis because the Kingdom is surrounded by them. There are grazing places in close proximity to the Presidio where they were grazed before, which are, Caja del Rio, Santa Cruz, La Majada de Dominguez, Las Bocas, Los Cerrillos, San Marcos, and Maragua, and are sufficient to maintain them the entire year without having to take them some thirty or forty leagues, as is the case. The reason that the horses are not grazed at these said places is none other than because it is said that they are owned by someone and their herds, cattle and sheep, are given the first priority to graze upon them instead of the horse herd which belongs to the King, which serves to safeguard not only the Kingdom, but also the same herds, which are kept close at hand, fattened and kept from being taken by the enemies. In attention to this, as well as to that which makes us immediately look for places which are good and available for grazing, and having found them, which are those mentioned above with all the required conveniences, so that we will not be blamed as being irresponsible if anything happens and we cannot comply with our obligation because the horse herd is at such a far distance, we present this to Your Lordship so that as Captain General of this Kingdom he will order, by promulgating a *banda* throughout the jurisdiction, that no resident who is in the area or lives there, will take any herd into those grazing areas mentioned as being for the horse herd. If they insist that they are the owners of any of the places we will recognize them [lands] as being vacant and without legitimate owners who can impede the use. When this happens Your Lordship will impose upon them a specific punishment so that it does not occur. To Your Lordship we ask and petition that he order this be done and determined as we have asked which is in justice and what is necessary, etc.

Juan Joseph Moreno

Spanish Transcription of Letter from Alferez Juan Joseph Moreno to Henrique de Olavidé y Micheleña, Governor and Captain General, Santa Fe 1737. (P-E: 46-1)

El Theniente, Alferez y Sargento de la Compania deste Real Presidio parecemos ante Vuestra Senoria en la major forma que aya lugar y decimos que por cuanto ham as de tres anos que estamos experimentando lo ascaicido y flaca que se halla la cavallada de este dicho Real Presidio motivado de que no tiene absolutamente comedero alguno y si se halla es sumamente distante de esta guarnicion cediendo este alojamiento en grave perjuicio de ella, y lo que es mas el que experimentan los soldados con el doble travajo en su custodia y augmento de hombres, los que hacen falta en el Presidio; y por que la defensa, guarnicion y segura de el Reyno, no es otro que el que esten los cavallos gordos y a mana para qualquiera sublevacion de Yndios o hostilidad de enemigos que diariamente amenaza por lo rodeado que el Reyno esta de ellos; y aver como ay immediatos al Presidio parajes para comedores de dicha cavallada que son los mismos en donde antes ha pastado, conviene a saver la Caja del Rio, Santa Cruz, La Majada de Dominguez, Las Vocas, Los Zerrillos, San Marcos y Maragua sufficient para mantenerse el ano sin que sea preciso retirarse treinta o quarenta leguas como sucede; y la causa de que en los parajes suso dichos no paste dicha cavallada, no es otra que la de decirse tener duenos, y sus ganados assi menor como maior es primero que pasten en ellos, que la cavallada del Rey, que es la que guarda no tan solo el Reyno. vecindad y Presidio, sino aun los mismos ganados. pues los defienden con tenerla a prompta y gorda de que los enemigos sela lleven. En esta atencion y en la de que nos toca immediatamente buscar parajes mas comodos y utiles para su pasto y aviendolos hallado, que son los referidos con las convenencias que se saven, para que en ningun tiempo senos culpe de amisos, ni suseda lo que amenasa de tenerla retirada en cumplimiento de nuestra obligacion, hacemos a Vuestra Senoria esta representacion para que como Capitan General de este dicho Reyno se sirva mandar, promulgar bando en toda la jurisdicion para que ningun vezino estante ni morador, entre ganados alguno en los comedores mensionados dela cavallada, aunque se preteste por qualquiera ser dueno de alguno de dichos parajes, respecto de que los conocemos por despoblados y sin dueno lexitimo que lo pueda empedir y caso que assi suceda les impondra Vuestra Senoria zierta pena para que no llegue a suceder atendiendo Vuestra Senoria pedimos y suplicamos se sirva mandar hacer y determinar como llebamos pedido que es justicia y en los necessario, ut supra.

Juan Joseph Moreno

English Translation of Letter from Henrique de Olavidé y Micheleña, Governor and Captain General to Alferez Juan Joseph Moreno, Santa Fe 1737. (P-E: 46-2)

Enrique de Olavidé y Micheleña, Governor and Captain General of this Kingdom of New Mexico and Its Provinces, Castellan of His Forces and Presidios for His Majesty, etc.

Whereas a written presentation has be made to me by the Lieutenant, Alferez and Sergeant of this Company, in order that the horse herd of this Royal Presidio be placed in the places assigned for that purpose [grazing], which are, the Caja del Rio, Santa Cruz, La Majada de Dominguez, Las Bocas, Los Cerrillos, San Marcos and Maragua, being that they are ancient pasture lands for that use, as well as being closer to this Villa, and these places now have tall grasses for pastures, an abundance of water and are much more secure from the enemies, in addition to being a benefit for this Royal Presidio in that they are closer at hand and less work for the soldiers and require less people for its maintenance, since if they were thirty or forty leagues away it would require more than double the number of the guard [for the horses] who are needed at this said Royal Presidio; and because the defense of it consists of the robust, prompt and immediate [availability] due to the incidents which occur on a daily basis in the wake of a revolt and invasion by the enemies, and there being no fundamental right nor reason where some particular residents wish to have large numbers of herds of cattle and sheep and to pasture them at said places, as they are assigned for the said horse herd, and considering them as they should be considered as *ejidos* of His Majesty (who God may guard) reserved for His Royal Presidio and garrison of this Kingdom (although in it there is no exempt for its maintenance), having, as I have, for the good of the presentation, and not because some of the said residents want to have herds, the Royal Presidio shall have the fundamental right to its used by said horse herd. As such I order all the residents and settlers of this Villa, those of Santa Cruz and other jurisdictions of this Kingdom who have personal or other herds [herds on *partido* basis], whether they be cattle or sheep, they are not to enter nor pasture in the seven mentioned places as they are reserved as pasture lands for the Royal Presidio's horse herd. If someone for some reason or motive wants to do so in contravention to the order, they will incur the penalty of a fifty peso fine, applied by a third party, for the benefit of the Royal Council, expenses for justice and the accuser. They are to be irremissibly removed without exemption within fifteen days, counted from the date of publication of this *bando*. Those who have herds in said places are to remove them from there, and those not complying will receive the same punishment So that this notice is made available to everyone so that they cannot plead ignorance, I order that this be made public and affixed in the places accustomed to, in all of the jurisdictions of this said Kingdom, making everyone aware of it and certifying it at the bottom [of the page] so as to show that it was executed. So that it is valid I signed it at this said Villa of Santa Fe on the 24th day of the month of July, 1737, with my assisting witnesses due to the lack of a Public and Royal Scribe, which there are none in this Kingdom.

Henrique de Olavidé y Micheleña

Spanish Transcription of Letter from Henrique de Olavidé y Micheleña, Governor and Captain General to Alferez Juan Jose Moreno, Santa Fe 1737. (P-E: 46-2)

Don Enrique de Olavidé y Micheleña, Governador y Capitan General de este Reyno de la Nueva Mexico y sus Provincias, Castellano de Sus Fuerzas y Presidios por Su Majestad, ut supra.

En quanto se me ha hecho representacion por escrito presentado por el Theniente, Alferez y

Sargento de esta Compania en orden a que se ponga la cavallada de este Real Presidio en los parajes asignados para ello, que son, La Caja del Rio, Santa Cruz, La Majada de Dominguez, Las Vocas, Los Serrillos, San Marcos, y Maragua, por ser comederos antiguos de ella, y estar mas immediate a esta Villa y tener como tienen dichos parajes sus pastos crecidos, abundancia de agua, y mucho mas segura de enemigos; y lo que es mas el beneficia que de ello se sigue a este dicho Real Presidio en tenerlo a mana y el poco trabajo de los soldados, y menos numero de gente para su custodia, por que de estar retirada treinta o quarenta leguas se dobla el numero de su guardia la que hace falta en este dicho Real Presidio, y por que la defensa de el consiste en lo robusto, prompta y immediate, por los accidentes que diariamente amenasar de sublevacion e invacion de enemigos, y no aver como ay fundamento rason ni derecho per donde algunos vecinos particulares quierian tener crecido numero de ganado assi maior como menor, pastandolo en dichos parajes, siendo como son asignados para dicha cavallada, y conciderandolos, como se deven conciderar por egidos de Su Magestad que Dios guarde) reservados para su Real Presidio guarnicion de este Reyno (aunque en el no ay lugar exempto para su manutencion) teniendo segun tengo abien dicha representacion y que no porque algunos de dichos vecinos quieran tener ganados, los ha de pastar lo fundamental de dicho Real Presidio que es dicha cavallada. Por tanto mando a todos los vecinos y moradores de esta Villa, la de Santa Cruz y demas jurisdiciones de este Reyno que tubiesen ganado assi maior como menor suio propio, o ageno no lo entren ni pasten en los mensionados siete parajes por quedar como quedan reservados para comederos de la cavallada de este Real Presidio. Y si alguno por algun pretexto o motivo lo quisiere hacer assi en contravencion de lo mandado, incurra en la pen a de cinquenta pesos de multa aplicados por terceras partes para la Real Camara, gastos de Justicia y denunciador, que se le sacaran irremisiblemente con la prevencion de que dentro de quinze dias contados desde la publicasion de este, ayan de sacar y saquen los que tubiesen algun ganado en dichos parajes, y no executandolo asi incurriran en la misma pena. Y para que llegue a noticia de todos a fin de que ninguno pueda alegar ignorancia, mando assi mismo que en todas las jurisdiciones de este dicho Reyno sea publicado y fixado en las partes y lugares acostumbrados, sacando testimonio de el y poniendo a el pie de este certificazion de averlo assi executado. Y para que conste lo firme en esta dicha Villa de Santa Fee en veinte y quatro dias del mes de Julio de setecientos treinta y siete con los testigos de mi assistencia a falta de Escribano Real y Publico que no lo ay en este dicho Reyno y ba en el presente papel par no correr el sellado en estas partes.

Henrique de Olavidé y Michelena

Chapter 12
It Happened in Old Santa Fe, The Death of Governor Albino Pérez, 1835–1837

1. *The Santa Fe New Mexican*, June 15, 1901, p. 1.
2. Ibid.
3. Ibid.
4. Ibid.

5. Ibid.
6. Benjamin M. Read, *Historia Ilustrada de Nuevo Mexico* (Santa Fe, 1911) pp. 518-519, contains a brief biography of Demetrio Pérez. New Edition, Sunstone Press, Santa Fe, 2010.
7. Lansing Bloom, "New Mexico Under Mexican Administration: *Old Santa Fe*, Vol. II (July 1914-April 1915), p, 4,
8. *Ibid.*, p. 3.
9. *Ibid.*, p. 4.
10. "El Ciudadano Albino Pérez, Coronel de Caballería del Ejército permanente Jefe Político y Militar del Territorio del Nuevo México a sus conciudadanos... Santa Fe, 26 de Junio de 1835;" Governors Papers, 1835, Mexican Archives of New Mexico; hereinafter cited as MANM, University of New Mexico microfilm.
11. Charles F. Coan, *A History of New Mexico*, Vol. I (Chicago, 1925) pp. 320-321.
12. *Ibid.*
13. Order from Albino Pérez, October 16, 1835; Ritch Papers, reel 2, frame no. 153, University of New Mexico microfilm.
14. Read, *Illustrated History*, pp. 373-374.
15. Josiah Gregg, *Commerce of the Prairies*, Vol. I (New York, 1844), p. 130.
16. Bloom. *Op. cit.*, p. 13.
17. Ralph Emerson Twitchell, *The Leading Facts of New Mexican History* (Cedar Rapids, 1912), Vol. II, p. 57. New Edition, Sunstone Press, Santa Fe, 2007.
18. Twitchell, *op. cit.*, p. 58.
19. *Ibid.*, p. 59.
20. *Ibid.*, pp. 56-57.
21. Bloom. o*p. cit.*, p.13.
22. *Ibid.*, p. 15.
23. *Ibid.*, p. 16.
24. Twitchell, *op. cit.*, p. 58.
25. Ibid.
26. Gregg, op. cit. P. 130.
27. *Ibid.*
28. Benjamin Read Papers, MANM, Reel 24, frame 807.
29. Gregg. *op. cit.*, p. 130.
30. Ibid.
31. Depositions and certificates testifying to the loyalty of Donaciano Vigil in the fight with the insurrectionists in August, 1837, Ritch Papers, reel 24, frame 169.
32. Gregg, *op. cit.*, p. 131.
33. Ibid.
34. See Gregg, p. 131 for details regarding Abreu's death.
35. Ibid. p. 132
36. Marc Simmons, *Hispanic Albuquerque, 1706–1846.* (University of New Mexico Press, 2003), p. 139.
37. Ibid., p. 139.
38. Translated by Joseph P. Sánchez and Robert Bacalski in Joseph P. Sánchez, "Año

Desgraciado, 1837: The Overthrow of New Mexico's Jefe Político Albino Perez, *Atisbos: Journal of Chicano Research*, Fall 1978, p. 182.
39. Ralph Emerson Twitchell, *The History of the Military Occupation of the Territory of New Mexico, From 1846 to 1851, By the Government of the United States* (Danville, Ill.: 1909). New Edition, Sunstone Press. Santa Fe, 2007.

Chapter 13
"She Was Our Mother," New Mexico's Change of National Sovereignty and Juan Bautista Vigil y Alarid, The Last Mexican Governor of New Mexico.

1. Kearney was placed in command of the United States Army of the west during the United States-Mexico war. He took Santa Fe with a force of fifteen thousand soldiers strong and immediately after went on to occupy California.
2. Ralph Emerson Twitchell, *The Military Occupation of the Territory of New Mexico from 1846 to 1851 by the Government of the United States* (Denver, 1909) 74-77; New Edition, Sunstone Press, Santa Fe, 2007. Included in this publication is a reproduction of Vigil y Alarid's original Spanish proclamation with his signature along with an English translation. Twitchell's footnote cites the Vigil Papers-New Mexico Historical Society, Santa Fe, New Mexico as the source of the original document. The Historical Society of New Mexico Collection at the New Mexico State Records Center and Archives contains a typed English transcription but no original. Sister Mary Loyola, in *The American Occupation of New Mexico,* cites the Vigil Papers and also the Ritch Collection at the Huntington Library, (R.I, 242.) The finding aid for the Ritch Collection has no listing for this citation or document. The Bloom-McFie Collection at the New Mexico State Records Center and Archives contains a typed transcription of the Spanish text but it varies slightly from the text purported to be the original in Twitchell's book. Robert Tórrez and other historians, who have also extensively searched for the original, believe that this document has been lost.
3. Twitchell, *The Military Occupation…*, 75.
4. See Genaro M. Padilla, *My History, Not Yours: The Formation of Mexican American Autobiography* (University of Wisconsin Press, 1993). Padilla offers a profound analysis of Vigil y Alarid's response to Kearny's proclamation. He proposes that his speech was not only a call for accommodation to U.S. dominance but also a strategy for survival, which he said was full of "rhetorical switches", encoded with reminders of Mexican cultural continuity. Padilla states that Vigil y Alarid's proclamation "operated as an early example of multivoiced encodation, a rhetorical appeasement that made the occupation sufferable." Padilla continued: "With resentment embedded in accommodation, he quietly articulated the Nuevomexicano's fidelity to the homeland that would not be summarily dissolved by conquest, governmental reorganization, or dispossession."
5. *Patria Chica* is a regional attachment to a home, community or native landscape.
6. The Nuevomexicanos may have sent Abert to far away places to get rid of him, similar to the sixteenth-century Pueblo Indians directing the Spanish in their quest for the Gran Quivira. They would tell them of gold in far away places to get them out of their communities.

7. Abert, James William, *U.S. Army Corps of Topographical Engineers: Lieut. J.W. Aberts New Mexico Report, 1846-'47* (Albuquerque: Horn and Wallace, 1962) 48-52,77,97,108-109,116-118.
8. Abert,107.
9. For the most comprehensive overview of the history of New Mexico under the administration of Mexico see David J. Weber, *The Mexican Frontier, 1821–1845: The American Southwest under Mexico* (Albuquerque: University of New Mexico Press, 1982).
10. Angela Moyano Pahissa, *México y Estados Unidos: Orígenes de una relación 1819–1861 (México, 1987)* and Martín González de la Vara, "El translado de familias al norte de Chihuahua y la conformación de una región fronteriza, 1848–1854"*Frontera Norte* (Tijuana, Mexico, El Colegio de la Frontera Norte, Vol. 11, 1994).
11. Ralph Emerson Twitchell, *Leading Facts of New Mexican History, Vol. II* (Iowa: The Torch Press, 1912) 197-198; New Edition, Sunstone Press, Santa Fe, 2007. See also William A. Keleher, *Turmoil in New Mexico, 1846–1868* (Santa Fe: Rydal Press, 1952; New Edition, Sunstone Press, Santa Fe, 2008), and Sister Mary Loyola, "The American Occupation of New Mexico, 1821–1852." NMHR 14 (April 1939): 143-99.
12. Much discontent with the American occupation led to an insurrection by several Hispanos and Pueblo Indians discussed further on in this essay.
13. George I. Sánchez, *Forgotten People: A Study of New Mexicans* (Albuquerque: Calvin Horn, Publisher Inc., 1967).
14. For a thorough look into cultural and racial identity in New Mexico see: John Nieto Phillips, *The Language of Blood, The Making of the Spanish American Identity in New Mexico. 1880s to 1930s* (Albuquerque: University of New Mexico Press, 2004).
15. David J. Weber, *Myth and the History of Hispanic Southwest* (Albuquerque: University of New Mexico Press, 1988).
16. Fray Angélico Chávez, *But Time and Chance, The Story of Padre Martínez of Taos, 1793–1867* (Santa Fe: Sunstone Press, 1981).
17. See Janet Lecompte, *Rebellion in Rio Arriba, 1837* (Albuquerque: University of New Mexico Press, 1985).
18. Manuel Alvarez, Annotation & Ed, Thomas E. Chávez, *Conflict and Acculturation: Manuel Alvarez's 1842 Memorial* (Santa Fe: Museum of New Mexico Press, 1989).
19. Robert J. Tórrez has written several articles dealing with New Mexico under the Mexican administration such as "The Celebration of 16th of September and Other Expressions of Mexican Patriotism in New Mexico, 1821–1846" (Manuscript, New Mexico State Archives, 1998), "What 16 de Setiempre Means to Nuevo Mexico." (Albuquerque Tribune, September 15, 2001) p.C1., "Celebrations of Mexican Independence and Fracas at the Palace in 1844." (Compadres, Newsletter of the Friends of the Palace of the Governors, November 1997).
20. Tórrez, "The Celebration of 16th de Setiembre…" 20.
21. For an extensive chronology of Vigil y Alarid's life as a bureaucrat and politician see: Wayne A. Harper, *Juan Bautista Vigil y Alarid, A New Mexico Bureaucrat* (M.A. Thesis, Brigham Young University, 1985). This is a very good study of Vigil y Alarid's career. The thesis concludes with a call for further research on selected topics, which this essay hopes to address in part.

22. Raymond Salas and Margaret Leonard Windham, *New Mexico Marriages, Churches of Immaculate Conception of Tomé and Our Lady of Belén* (New Mexico Genealogical Society, 1994) 34. His exact birth date is hard to determine due to the fact that his baptismal record has not been located.

   It is appropriate here to discuss Vigil y Alarid's family life which was left out of this narrative so as not to distract from his political life. Rafaela was a widow to Ramón Chávez with whom she bore a son named Cristóbal Chávez, (September 13, 1801 at Tomé). He was brought into the Vigil y Alarid family and raised by them in Santa Fe. It appears that Juan Bautista Vigil y Alarid and Rafaela Sánchez didn't give birth to any children. The baptismal registries for the churches of Tomé, Belen and Santa Fe do not list any children born to them although they show up as godparents to various children. Two in particular indicate that they adopted or took in Indian children. Left as "expuestos" (dropped off) at their home, were María Guadalupe (March 17, 1817), a three year old Ute Indian, and María Trinidad (April 18, 1825), six year old Navajo. Both entries noted that their parents were unknown. It is not until the 1821 Census of Santa Fe that we get a better picture of Vigil y Alarid's household. Listed is Don Juan Vigil, married, 33, Doña Rafaela Sánchez, spouse, 34, Juan Cristoval, son, 19, and the following most likely extended family or domestic servants: Guadalupe, 12, Rafaela, 2 and Antonio 4. Their family situation could have been the cause of their tumultuous marriage. On April 9, 1835 Rafaela filed for divorce under the grounds that her husband imposed a bad life on her. The judge did not grant the separation and recommended reconciliation (MANM, reel 22, Fr.114). They lived together on and off until her death in 1851 where she died at the home of her son, Cristoval, in Sausal, New Mexico (See: Belen burials August 31, 1880 which notes that her remains were transferred to Belen. Her death date is also mentioned). The only other census that Vigil y Alarid's family appears is in the 1860 census of Santa Fe. Here he is listed as Juan. B. Vigil y Alarid, 67. Listed in his household are Juana María Vigil, 15, and Juan de Mata, 11. They could have been relatives or domestic servants. Not listed in this household is Inéz Vigil y García who in a 1863 Santa Fe district court hearing, states that she is the daughter of Ignacia García (who died when she was a child) and claims to have been raised by Juan Bautista Vigil y Alarid and refers to him as her natural father. She could be his daughter and Ignacia his concubine or she could have also been the illegitimate daughter of his nephew Juan Nepomuceno Vigil who was mentioned as holding her against her will. Regardless of their true relationship to Vigil y Alarid, his shaky and aged signature is on Inez's testimony. Perhaps he signed it to help free her from Nepomuceno (Inéz Vigil y García vs. Juan Nepomuceno Vigil, Santa Fe, May 12, 1863, Santa Fe County Territorial District Court Records, State Records Center and Archives, Santa Fe, New Mexico).

23. Twitchell, *Leading Facts..*, 9-12.
24. [B.S.M.?] New Mexico to Br. Juan Rafael Rascón, El Paso del Norte, May? 1824, Mexican Archives of New Mexico hear after MANM (Microfilm, New Mexico State Archives, r.4, f. 0159-0160.
25. Although there is no mention of the relationship between Juan Bautista Vigil y Alarid and José Rafael Alarid it is very likely the later was Vigil y Alarid's uncle. Church records reveal that Vigil y Alarid's maternal grandparents were José Ignacio Alarí and María

Loreto Benavides. A January 22, 1776 Santa Fe Cathedral baptismal record for a José Rafael Alarid gives his parent's names as José Ignacio Alarí and María Loreto Benavides.

26. David J. Weber, *The Mexican Frontier, 1821–1845: The American Southwest under Mexico* (Albuquerque: University of New Mexico Press, 1982) 22-25.

27. Sección extraordinaria de 10 de Agosto 1824, MANM (Microfilm, New Mexico State Archives, r.4, f. 0215-0216).

28. Charlotte Marie Nelson Parraga "*Santa Fe de Nuevo Mexico: a study of a frontier city based on an annotated translation of selected documents (1825-1832) from the Mexican Archives of New Mexico*" (MA thesis, Ball State University, 1976), 107-133, 182-190, 204-208.

29. Transcriptions of Bent's letters are included in "Notes and Documents, The Charles Bent Papers." *New Mexico Historical Review*, Vol. 29, July 1954, 315-317.

30. The Juan B. Vigil here is undoubtedly the Juan Bautista Vigil y Alarid of this study. I have not been able to find any other Juan B. Vigil who was of the educated class nor political clout living in this area at this time besides Vigil y Alarid.

31. David Sandoval, "*Trade and the 'Manito' Society in New Mexico, 1821–1848*" (PhD, Dissertation, University of Utah, 1978) p. 193.

32. Twitchell, *Leading Facts…*, 73-80 and Weber, *The Mexican Frontier…*, 266-267.

33. Maríano Otero, "Comunicación que sobre las negociaciones diplomáticos habidos en la casa de Alfaro," in *Algunos documentos Sobre El Tratado de Guadalupe*, Archivo Histórico Diplomático Mexicano, no. 31 (México, D.F.: Editorial Porrua, 1970), 69. This is my translation from the original text written in Spanish. The text is quoted in a letter written to the President of México on September 16, 1847 from Mariano Otero, Governor of Jalisco, who later became Secretary of Foreign Affairs. The original quote is as follows: "*Si, como dice el Excelentísimo Señor Ministro de Relaciones, la República no puede abandonar a Nuevo México, porque no le es dado vender como un rebaño esos beneméritos mexicanos que abandonados a su suerte, sin protección y olvidando sus quejas, se han levantado contra los invasores y derramado su sangre por seguir perteneciendo a la familia mexicana.*"

34. Twitchell, *Leading Facts…*, 233-236.

35. Samuel E. Sisneros, "*Los Emigrantes Nuevomexicanos: The 1849 Repatriation to Guadalupe and San Ignacio, Chihuahua, México*" (MA thesis, University of Texas at El Paso, 2001).

36. Documents dealing with Vigil y Alarid's life in northern Chihuahua are found in the Ciudad Juárez Municipal Archives hereafter referred to as CJMA.

37. Gobierno de Estado de Chihuahua to Ministro de Relaciones Exteriores, October 3, 1853. (Archivo de la Secretaría de Relaciones Exteriores de México) leg. 2-12-2902, Doc.16, No.47.

38. Interestingly, María Trinidad emigrated also to Guadalupe, Chihuahua where she must have just arrived before her death on September 21, 1850. The Guadalupe church burial record notes that she was the adult daughter of Don Juan Vigil but didn't mention a mother. It appears that no other family members besides she and Vigil y Alarid emigrated to México.

39. Certification of election results signed by Ramón Ortiz, José Sánchez and Juan Bautista Vigil y Alarid. Ayuntamiento de Ciudad Juárez Archives (Microfilm, UTEP Library, MF 495, r.16, 0116).

40. Various correspondences from Miguel Castro to the Chief Magistrate. Dated from June 13 to July 13, 1852. Ciudad Juárez Municipal Archives (Microfilm, UTEP Library, MF 513, p.2, r.37).
41. Samuel E. Sisneros, "El Paseño, Padre Ramón Ortiz: 1814–1896." *Password*, Vol. 44, No.3, Fall, 1999, 107-121.
42. Exoneración de Don. Ramón Ortiz …y nombramiento de Guadalupe Miranda para sustiturlo. March 1853, ASREM leg. 2-12-2902.
43. Idem., Doc.16, No.47.
44. Ciudad Juárez Cathedral Archives, May 22, 1855 (Microfilm, UTEP Library, 489, r.13).
45. It is not given where Vigil y Alarid was when he wrote this letter. My research has shown that Vigil y Alarid was living the town of Guadalupe from 1850–1852 to 1858–1859.
46. Given that Vigil y Alarid made many enemies with local authorities it is possible that Vigil fabricated this whole incident " continuing with his old habits", but no evidence exists to disprove his accusations nor does the note from Manuel Alvarado, the Bishop's secretary (attached to the end of Vigil's letter), protest the letter as an outright fabrication. Alvarado simply directed the priest (no name mentioned) to prudently fix this situation and if the accusations were true he was to write to the authorities in Chihuahua. The priest assigned to the parish in Guadalupe at this time was Don José Antonio Otero who, in 1853, was stationed in Guadalupe by Bishop Zubiría, where he served until his death in 1864. Father Otero was a native New Mexican and was the parish priest in Socorro, New Mexico, just before he left to repatriate to Guadalupe with many of his parishioners. Otero was one of the first parish priests in New Mexico not to accept the authority of the new "American" bishop to New Mexico, Juan Bautista Lamy, who was strategically placed by the United States government because it feared the political power of the native Mexican clergy (Otero's communication on Lamy's entrance, 14 July 1851, Archives of the Archdiocese of Santa Fe, New Mexico, Patentes, Book LXXI -Microfilm UTEP Library, r. #525). Assuming that the subject of Vigil y Alarid's accusation was Father Otero, then most likely Father Otero brought this woman with him from his parish in Socorro, New Mexico.
47. CJMA, *MF513,pt.2,r.39, sec 2,0104-0116.* The citizens of Guadalupe an San Ignacio adhered to the Plan de Tacubaya which led up to the Guerra de Reforma. The Plan de Tacubaya was an attempt by the conservatives or church party to overthrow the Liberal constitutional government. In Chihuahua, in the early months of 1858, there were out bursts of rebellion; some headed by priests. The main commanders of the revolt in Chihuahua were Tomás and José María Zuloaga, brothers of the ex-president Luis Zuloaga.
48. They crossed over the border to the town of Boscheville, and as rebels, as they were called, continued to return to their colonies to harass the few citizens who remained. It is not known exactly where Boscheville was, but most likely it was near present day Fabens, Texas, down river from San Elizario. In June of 1859, 267 citizens from Guadalupe grouped together in Boscheville to sign a petition to the State of Chihuahua asking for independence from the Cantón Bravos and the ability to name their own local authorities. For more on this see: Sisneros, "Los Emigrantes Nuevomexicanos." 90-92.
49. Eighth U.S. Territorial Census, 1860, Santa Fe County, New Mexico (Microfilm, SRCA, r.#1).

50. Rafael Chacón, ed. Jacqueline Dorgan Meketa, *Legacy of Honor, The Life of Rafael Chacón, A Nineteenth-Century New Mexican* (Albuquerque: UNM Press, 1986) 72-73. Rafael Chacón (1833–1925) included in his memoirs two poems by Doctor Juan Bautista Vigil y Alarid as he called him. Also Dorgan-Maketa included a foot note that as a young postmaster, Vigil y Alarid painted a large allegorical backdrop to be used for a dramatic presentation on the Santa Fe plaza for the celebration of Mexico's Independence from Spain.
51. Juan Bautista Vigil Land Grant, SANM-I, SG Report #26 (Microfilm, SRCA, r. 16, f. 201). A note at the end of these documents reveals that the original documents were returned to the Surveyor General in 1871. Although they are not included with the land grant records housed at the State Archives and their whereabouts are unknown. Even though it was not adjudicated and passed in Congress it was one of the seven largest Spanish land grants in New Mexico.
52. Harper, 71.
53. Alvin R. Sunseri, *Seeds of Discord, New Mexico in the Aftermath of the American Conquest, 1846–1861* (Chicago: Nelson Hall, 1979) 115.
54. For recent scholarship on New Mexico land ownership, law and race see: Laura E. Gomez, *Manifest Destinies, The Making of the Mexican American Race*. (New York University Press, 2007).
55. David G. Gutiérrez "Migration, Emergent Ethnicity, and the 'third Space': The Shifting Politics of Nationalism in Greater Mexico." The Journal of American History, Vol 82, September 2, 1999.480-517. The "third space," as Gutiérrez calls it, caused its inhabitants to sharply define their loyalties. As a result of the United States-Mexico war, Gutiérrez asserts, the "third space" was created. It became an "intermediate social space" where those Mexican citizens that remained in territory acquired by the United States, called their "ancestral home." This third space on one hand "marginalized" and "racialized" the native people who were soon becoming a minority or "foreigners in their native land" as David Weber put it. The repatriation of 1849 along with resistance to United States political and cultural dominance, which continues to this day in New Mexico, attests to Gutiérrez's claims. The forms of nationalism discussed in this paper share a common thread. Nuevomexicanos and their leaders were patriotic to the Republic of Mexico, although they often would adjust this patriotism to fit their immediate practical needs. They shifted from an official form of nationalism- la Madre Patria, which involved celebration and warfare, to a popular form, which was concerned with ideas (Hidalgo's independence) of commitment to family and local community mentioned previously as Patria Chica.
56. Andrés Reséndez, "National Identity on the Shifting Border: Texas and New Mexico in the Age of Transformation, 1821–1848." The Journal of American History, Vol. 82, September 2, 1999, 668-688. Reséndez counters the traditional thought that a national state identity "wins out" over local loyalties and a national identity overrides the ethnic or family allegiances. He suggests that the issue of national identity should be analyzed from bottom to top. The ordinary peoples' needs, interests, opinions, and hopes, Reséndez states, were not necessarily national but they determined the outcome of the state imposed nationalism.

57. Sunseri, 115. Letter found in the State Dept. Territorial Papers, New Mexico, 1851–1872 (Microfilm, UTEP Library, MF 11622.T17, r.1).
58. Archives of the Archdiocese of Santa Fe, Santa Fe burial records (Microfilm, New Mexico State Archives, r. 88, f. 0102).

Chapter 14
They Came From the East, Importing Homicide, Violence and Misconceptions of Soft Justice into Early Santa Fe, New Mexico, 1847–1853

1. Author's Note: I have defined Anglo settlers as both those who have recently arrived from the United States and the small population of Americans who had settled in New Mexico before the U.S. Mexican War. For the purposes of this chapter, I am including both soldiers and the small population of European settlers in this category of analysis.
2. New Mexico State Records Center and Archives, "Records of the United States Territorial and New Mexico District Courts for Santa Fe County 1847–1951." Box 1-3. Anglo Crime was 96/773(pop) =.124 and Hispanic Crime was 309/4285 =.072.
3. New Mexico State Records Center and Archives, "Records of the United States Territorial and New Mexico District Courts for Santa Fe County 1847–1951." Box 1-3. The homicide rate for the Nuevo Mexicano community was 23.3 per 100,000 per year, which is a relatively normal rate. The Anglo settler homicide rate was 221.9 per 100,000 per year, making them ten times more likely to commit homicide.
4. New Mexico State Records Center and Archives, "Records of the United States Territorial and New Mexico District Courts for Santa Fe County 1847–1951." Box 1-3. The overall homicide rate in Santa Fe from 1847–1853, including both Anglo settlers and Nuevo Mexicanos, was 53.7 per 100,000 per year, more than double the rate of 23.3 per 100,000 per year within the older New Mexican community.
5. Author's Note: For the purpose of this article, I define Nuevo Mexicanos as those New Mexicans of mixed Spanish, Mexican, and Native American ancestry who were born in New Mexico.
6. Jill Mocho, *Murder and Justice in Frontier New Mexico 1821–1846*, (Albuquerque, New Mexico: University of New Mexico Press, 1997), Mocho found records for only eleven homicides throughout the twenty-five year Mexican Period. Though Mocho concedes there are likely missing records, the dearth of New Mexico homicides during the Mexican Period reveals a society far less prone to violence before American settlement. Hereafter referred to as Mocho.
7. District Court Records, Box 1-3, (1847–1853), the actual number of adjudicated cases is certainly much higher, but documentation of the proceedings remains lost. Gilbreath, who has thoroughly researched the topic, claims that there was only one capital punishment in Santa Fe during this period, but already evidence of a second individual, Andrew Jackson Simms, has been documented here. Having conducted my research, I contend that the missing files, if discovered, would reveal 40% guilty verdicts, that punishments outside of hanging were assigned those determined guilty, and that 60% were either dismissed or found not guilty.

8. Many case files from this era are incomplete, especially for cases that were never prosecuted. Rather than making an assumption that incomplete cases were never prosecuted, this study leaves the possibility open that verdicts were simply lost. Statistically, this is why rates are implemented, rather then using aggregate numbers as foundational data.
9. Laws, pp 63.
10. Laws, pp 65.
11. The Exchange Hotel, once known as the Inn at the End of the Trail or La Fonda, was purchased in 1847 by Anglo settlers. The building was not altered until it was purchased again in the 20th century by a corporation that demolished it and built the new Hotel La Fonda, which remains at the original site on the plaza.
12. Monte, a game sometimes called "find the lady," uses three cards: the jack of spades, jack of clubs, and usually the queen of hearts. The dealer uses slight of hand to shuffle the cards and individual bets on the card believed to be the queen.
13. In Faro, cards are laid out in this manner (see below), individuals place bets on which cards they believe will be drawn, and the dealer draws twice. The first card drawn is the loser, and the money bet on it goes to the dealer. The second pays at equal odds. Like most gambling, the odds are always with the house.
14. *Santa Fe Weekly Gazette*, 19 November 1853, pp 2, the article contained here was written by an eyewitness, who was present throughout the affair, hereafter designated *SFWG*.
15. West Gilbreath, *Death on the Gallows: The Story of Legal Hangings in New Mexico, 1847–1923*, (Silver City, New Mexico: High Lonesome Books, 2002) pp 215, hereafter designated Gilbreath.
16. Fray Angelico Chavez & Thomas E. Chavez, *Wake for a Fat Vicar: Father Juan Felipe Ortiz, Archbishop Lamy, and the New Mexican Catholic Church in the Middle of the Nineteenth Century,* (Albuquerque, New Mexico: LPD Press, 2004), pp 56-58. The Texans attacked Santa Fe in 1841, but were easily defeated and marched back to Mexico City. Most of the Texans died on the March, and animosity between the two parties never subsided. Anglo Settlers and Nuevo Mexicanos alike despised the Texans, and were always mindful of another potential Texas invasion. Hereafter designated Chavez & Chavez.
17. *SFWG*, 19 November 1853, pp 2, Stephenson offered his gun as collateral.
18. *SFWG*, 19 November 1853, pp 2.
19. *SFWG*, 19 November 1853, pp 2.
20. *SFWG*, 19 November 1853, pp 2.
21. Author's Note: All available sources, the conversations related, the language of the trial, and the decision to condemn without the authority of the Alcaldes make it overwhelmingly likely that the lynch mob was comprised primarily of Anglo settlers with a smattering of observers from the old New Mexican community.
22. SFWG, 19 November 1853, pp 2.
23. Gilbreath, pp 215, Gilbreath has uncovered evidence of 155 lynching's in the New Mexico Territory between 1851–1893. Another Texan, whose name remains unknown, had been lynched 14 June 1851 in Santa Fe.
24. Robert J. Torrez, *Myth of the Hanging Tree: Stories of Crime and Punishment in Territorial*

New Mexico, (Albuqurque: University of New Mexico Press, 2008), pp 42-43, hereafter designated Torrez.
25. Michael Foucault, *Discipline & Punish: The Birth of the Prison*, (New York, New York: Vintage Books, 1995), pp 7-9, hereafter designated Foucault.
26. Clinton Brook and Frank Reeve, *Forts and Forays: James A. Bennettz, a Dragoon in New Mexico, 1850–1856*, (Albuquerque, New Mexico: The University of New Mexico Press, 1948.), pp 27, hereafter designated Brook and Reeve.
27. Brook and Reeve, pp 27.
28. Gilbreath, pp 215-219.
29. SFWG, 19 November 1853, pp 2.
30. New Mexico State Records Center and Archives, "Records of the United States Territorial and New Mexico District Courts for Santa Fe County 1847–1951," Box 1-3, hereafter designated District Court Records.
31. New Mexico State Records Center and Archives, "Governors' Office Affiliates, Governors' letterbook," Serial #13892, 1853–1862, pp 167-68, hereafter designated Governors' Book.
32. Gilbreath, pp 148, Gilbreath was unaware of the conviction and execution and Andrew Jackson Simms.
33. District Court Records, "New Mexico v. Henry Wheeler," (1849)
34. 1850 United States Census, Santa Fe County, Santa Fe City, pp 85.
35. Santa Fe New Mexican, 28 November 1849, pp 2, two days later Captain Papin was buried with full military honors.
36. 1850 United States Census, Santa Fe County, Santa Fe City, pp 85, regulators of the justice system prided themselves on expeditious punishments and two months was longer than citizens normally waited for punishment. The Census lists Wheeler as in Jail for the crime of murder.
37. Torrez, pp25-25.
38. SFWG, 19 November 1853, pp 2, 8 January 1853, pp 2, 17 December, 1853 pp 2.
39. District Court Records, Box 1-3, all jury lists in the 12 Anglo homicide cases are comprised exclusively of Anglo jurors.
40. District Court Records, "New Mexico v. Pablo Rael," (1848).
41. 1850 United States Census, Santa Fe County, pp 26, Rael is listed as non-working and the far column declares him "insane," having "killed his wife and sister."
42. Mocho, pp19.
43. Torrez, pp 53, Torrez insinuates that New Mexican juries were unwilling to pass the sentence against individuals with a Spanish surname and uses Andrew Jackson Simms as an example of the New Mexican community willing to deal capital punishment.
44. District Court Records, "Territory v. A.J. Simms," (1849).
45. District Court Records, "New Mexico v. Manuel Sandoval," (1849).
46. 1850 United States Census, Santa Fe County, Santa Fe City, pp 85, Sandoval is listed in jail, having been convicted of the crime of manslaughter.
47. District Court Records, "New Mexico v. James C. Brady," (1848).
48. District Court Records, "New Mexico v. James C. Brady," Indictment by John Tulles, pp1. (1848).

49. District Court Records, "New Mexico v. James C. Brady," Indictment by Hugh N. Smith, pp1. (1848).
50. District Court Records, "New Mexico v. James C. Brady," Notes of Attorney Allen Clark, pp1-2. (1848).
51. District Court Records, "New Mexico v. James C. Brady," Jury List, pp1. (1848), of the 12 jury members listed, only 2, John Abell and Charles Giddings, remain in the Territory by 1850.
52. District Court Records, "New Mexico v. James C. Brady," Witness Summons," (1848).
53. District Court Records, "New Mexico v. O.P. Anderson," Indictment by *Alcalde* J. Smith, (1852).
54. District Court Records, "New Mexico v. O.P. Anderson," Indictment by *unknown Author*, (1852).
55. District Court Records, Court Docket Book, 1850–1853, pp 20, 28-29.
56. District Court Records, Court Docket Book, 1850–1853, pp 16.
57. District Court Records, Court Docket Book, 1850–1853, pp 80.
58. District Court Records, Court Docket Book, 1850–1853, pp 113.
59. Stephen G. Hyslop, *Bound for Santa Fe: The Road to New Mexico and the American Conquest, 1806–1848,* (Norman, Oklahoma: University of Oklahoma Press, 2002), pp 268, Hyslop documents numerous accounts of traditional fandangos by early travelers from the United States, hereafter designated Hyslop.
60. Brook and Reeve, pp 15, 20, Bennett's account of these two fandangos are diametrically opposed, the first of a traditional fandango in San Miguel del Bado and the second a commodified fandango in Santa Fe.
61. District Court Records, "New Mexico v. Christian Mild," Inquest by Sheriff E.L. Vaughn, (1853).
62. Emily E. Keita, "The New Mexico Fandango," (Wagontracks: Vol. 19, Issue no. 3 May, 2005), Traditionally, drinking was kept to a minimum, but Anglo settlers, soldiers, and European settlers were more given to excess at these soirées. Hereafter designated Keita.
63. Tomas Jaehn, *Germans in the Southwest: 1850–1920,* (Albuquerque: University of New Mexico Press, 2005), pp 31, The German population in the American Southwest was very small and Jaehn's book the definitive book on their activities in New Mexico. Though the case happens before Jaehn's study begins and is therefore omitted from his work, the Inquest of Sheriff E.L. Vaughn clearly identifies Christian Mild as an early German immigrant.
64. Keita, pp 3, traditional fandangos were held by wealthy Nuevo Mexicanos at the cost of the host, who used the occasion to better relations between his person and the other classes of citizens. Everyone was invited who wished to attend without cost, and all were welcome to the event.
65. District Court Records, "New Mexico v. Christian Mild," Inquest by Sheriff E.L. Vaughn, pp 1-2, (1853).
66. District Court Records, "New Mexico v. Christian Mild," Inquest by Sheriff E.L. Vaughn, pp 1-9, (1853).
67. District Court Records, "New Mexico v. Christian Mild," Indictment by Hugh N. Smith, pp 1-2, (1853).

68. C. Castro, J. Castro, J. Campillo, L. Auda and G. Rodriguez "Mexico y Sus Alrededores," (Alicante: Miguel de Cervantes Virtual Library, 2006), Casimiro Castro y J. Campillo, "Trajes Mexicanos: A Fandango," (1855), pp XXIX, the artist portrays a traditional fandango as would occur in the Mexican countryside. Only eight years removed from Mexican rule, this depiction mirrors fandangos in Santa Fe, which were filled with peoples of all classes and ethnic origins. As in the picture, Santa Fe fandangos featured ornately decorated rooms with crucifixes, pictures of saints, and damsels waltzing with men of all backgrounds. The depiction here is of a more humble fandango, very common in the countryside, but ornate fandangos with champagne and fine foods were held at wealthier homes and within the Palace of the Governors. The fandango remained an important part of Santa Fe culture after American settlers arrived, though they became increasingly violent when whiskey drinking Americans participated. Nuevo Mexicanos had used the fandango to transcend cultural and class barriers; wealthy Nuevo Mexicanas could be seen waltzing with poor farmers, Native Americans with Nuevo Mexicanas, and wealthy elites with poor *vecinas*. As more settlers arrived, American participation increased and the function of the fandango as a social bonding institution was permanently altered into an event directed toward entertainment. Keita, 1-13.
69. District Court Records, "New Mexico v. Christian Mild," Inquest by Sheriff E.L. Vaughn, pp 1-2, (1853).
70. District Court Records, "New Mexico v. Christian Mild," Inquest by Sheriff E.L. Vaughn, pp 2, (1853).
71. District Court Records, "New Mexico v. Christian Mild," Inquest by Sheriff E.L. Vaughn, pp 2, (1853).
72. District Court Records, "New Mexico v. Christian Mild," Inquest by Sheriff E.L. Vaughn, pp 2, (1853).
73. District Court Records, "New Mexico v. Christian Mild," Inquest by Sheriff E.L. Vaughn, pp 2-3, (1853).
74. District Court Records, "New Mexico v. Christian Mild," Inquest by Sheriff E.L. Vaughn, pp 3, 9, (1853).
75. District Court Records, "New Mexico v. Christian Mild," Inquest by Sheriff E.L. Vaughn, pp 10, (1853).
76. District Court Records, "New Mexico v. Christian Mild," Inquest by Sheriff E.L. Vaughn, pp 3, (1853).
77. District Court Records, "New Mexico v. Christian Mild," Inquest by Sheriff E.L. Vaughn, pp 4, (1853).
78. District Court Records, "New Mexico v. Christian Mild," Inquest by Sheriff E.L. Vaughn, pp 1-10, (1853).
79. District Court Records, "New Mexico v. Christian Mild," Inquest by Sheriff E.L. Vaughn, pp 5, (1853).
80. Congressional Globe, House of Representatives, 32nd Congress, 1st Session, "Contested Election in New Mexico - Mr. Weightman," 15 March, 1853, pp 330, hereafter designated Globe.
81. District Court Records, Boxes 1-3, (1847–1853), It is important to note that the Nuevo

Mexicanos invited to participate in the jury process were landed, and most of them were elites. Still, Nuevo Mexicano elites were better able to both interact culturally and linguistically.

82. District Court Records, Boxes 1-3, Commencing in late 1848, Nuevo Mexicanos are listed in the jury lists and witnesses in the majority of cases, including those that do not involve Nuevo Mexicano litigants.
83. District Court Records, "New Mexico v. A. J. Simms," (1849), Simms traveled from Santa Fe to Taos, and there committed the murder. The case was tried in Santa Fe County as it was the residence of Simms.
84. District Court Records, "New Mexico v. A .J. Simms, Indictment dated July, pp 1, (1849).
85. District Court Records, "New Mexico v. A. J. Simms, Indictment dated July, pp 2, (1849).
86. District Court Records, "New Mexico v. A. J. Simms, instructions to the Santa Fe County Sheriff, (1849).
87. *Santa Fe New Mexican*, 28 November 1849, pp 2, the prison sentence was carried out, as Simms is described as being in jail awaiting his execution.

Chapter 15
King Maker in the Back Room, Editor Max Frost and Hardball Politics in the Late-Territorial Period, 1876–1909

1. National Archives and Records Administration, Washington, DC, U. S. Army, Register of Enlistments, 1798–1914, January 1867.
2. Ibid., May 1870.
3. *Santa Fe New Mexican*, September 28, 1876.
4. "Passing of Frost: New Mexico's Blind Boss a Picturesque Figure," *Stevens Point Journal*, March 18, 1909.
5. Richard Melzer, Foreword to 2007 Edition of *The Military Occupation of New Mexico: Facsimile of Original 1909 Edition* by Ralph Emerson Twitchell (Santa Fe, New Mexico: Sunstone Press, 2007).
6. Lilian Whiting, *The Land of Enchantment: From Pike's Peak to the Pacific* (New York: Little, Brown, and Company, 1910), 226.
7. Laura E. Gomez, *Manifest Destinies: The Making of the Mexican American Race* (New York: New York University, 2007), 4.
8. Porter A. Stratton, *The Territorial Press of New Mexico 1834–1912* (Albuquerque, New Mexico: University of New Mexico Press, 1969), 202-203.
9. Howard R. Lamar, *The Far Southwest, 1846–1912: A Territorial History* (New Haven, Connecticut: Yale University Press, 1966), 14.
10. Ibid., 129.
11. Marion Dargan, "New Mexico's Fight for Statehood 1895–1912," *New Mexico Historical Review* 18 (April 1943): 148.
12. Ibid., 14 (April 1939): 141.

13. Register of Enlistments, 1867.
14. National Archives and Records Administration, Washington, DC, U. S. Department of Commerce, Bureau of the Census, Decennial Census of the United States, 1900.
15. *Santa Fe New Mexican*, October 14, 1909.
16. Register of Enlistments, 1867.
17. Ibid., 1875.
18. Rebecca Robbins Raines, *Getting the Message Through: A Branch History of the U. S. Army Signal Corps* (Washington, DC: Center of Military History, 1996), 43.
19. Register of Enlistments, 1875.
20. Jeremy Agnew, *Life of a Soldier on the Western Frontier* (Missoula, Montana: Mountain Press Publishing, 2008), 141.
21. *Santa Fe New Mexican*, October 14, 1909.
22. Max Frost, *New Mexico: Its Resources, Climate, Geography* (Santa Fe, New Mexico: New Mexican Printing Co., 1894), 4.
23. "Passing of Frost," *Stevens Point Journal*, March 18, 1909.
24. U. S. War Department, *Annual Report of the Chief Signal-Officer, to the Secretary of War: For the Year* (Washington: Government Printing Office, 1878), 117.
25. *Santa Fe New Mexican*, September 28, 1876.
26. Ibid., January 20, 1877.
27. Ibid.
28. Robert J. Torrez, Introduction to *New Mexico in 1876–1877: A Newspaperman's View, the Travels and Reports of William D. Dawson,* edited by Robert J. Torrez, (Los Ranchos de Albuquerque, New Mexico: Rio Grande Books, 2007), 11.
29. U. S. Department of the Interior, National Park Service, Fairview Cemetery, Santa Fe, New Mexico, National Register of Historic Places Registration Form, Prepared by Corinne P. Sze, Fairview Cemetery Preservation Association, August 2004.
30. LaMoine Langston, "The History of Montezuma Lodge No. 1, Santa Fe," *A History of Masonry in New Mexico 1877–1977* (Roswell, New Mexico: Hall-Poorbaugh Press, 1977).
31. *Santa Fe New Mexican*, October 14, 1909.
32. Department of the Interior, Fairview Cemetery, 2004.
33. *Santa Fe New Mexican*, October 14, 1909.
34. "Passing of Frost," *Stevens Point Journal*, March 18, 1909.
35. Henry Norris Copp, *Public Land Laws Passed by Congress from April 1, 1882, to January 1, 1890* (Washington, DC: Office of the Librarian of Congress, 1890), 15.
36. George W. Julian, "Land Stealing in New Mexico," *North America Review* 145 (July 1887): 19.
37. Ibid., 20-22.
38. Lamar, *The Far Southwest*, 123-124.
39. Julian, "Land Stealing,"17-32.
40. Ibid., 20.
41. Ibid. 28.
42. "New-Mexico's Land Ring: Gigantic Swindles Accomplished in the Territory," *New York Times*, May 18, 1884.

43. Miguel Antonio Otero, *My Life on the Frontier, Vol. 2: Facsimile of Original 1939 Edition* (Santa Fe, New Mexico: Sunstone Press, 2007), 83-96.
44. Ibid., 83.
45. Julian, "Land Stealing," 28.
46. Stephen W. Dorsey, " 'Land Stealing in New Mexico.' A Rejoinder," *North American Review* 147 (October 1887): 408-409.
47. Frost, *New Mexico*, 3.
48. Ralph Emerson Twitchell, *The Leading Facts of New Mexican History, Vol. I: Facsimile of Original 1911 Edition* (Santa Fe, New Mexico: Sunstone Press, 2007), 498-499; Stratton, *The Territorial Press*, 228.
49. *Santa Fe New Mexican*, October 14, 1909.
50. Copp, *Public Land Laws*, 330.
51. Missouri State Archives, Jefferson, Missouri., Missouri Marriage Records, 1805–2002.
52. Decennial Census, 1900.
53. Decennial Census, 1880 and 1900; John William Leonard, *Who's Who in Finance and Banking* (New York: Who's Who in Finance Inc., 1922), 514.
54. Lamar, *The Far Southwest*, 144.
55. *Santa Fe New Mexican*, January, 25, 1890.
56. *Rio Grande Republican*, June 11, 1909.
57. *Santa Fe New Mexican*, December 31, 1893.
58. Stratton, *The Territorial Press*, 27.
59. Frost, *New Mexico*.
60. George B. Anderson, *History of New Mexico: Its Resources and People* (Los Angeles: Pacific States Publishing, 1907), 469-470.
61. *Santa Fe New Mexican*, August 8, 1903.
62. Ibid., January 25, 1897.
63. L. Bradford Prince, *New Mexico's Struggle for Statehood: Sixty Years of Effort to Obtain Self Government* (Santa Fe, New Mexico: The New Mexican Printing, 1910), 3-4. New Edition, Sunstone Press, Santa Fe, 2010.
64. Stratton, *The Territorial Press*, 204.
65. Prince, *New Mexico's Struggle*, 102-103.
66. *Santa Fe New Mexican*, April 26, 1898.
67. Ibid., August 3, 1903.
68. Ibid., September 16, 1906.
69. Ibid., May 10, 1902.
70. *Rio Grande Republican*, December 19, 1908.
71. Whiting, *The Land of Enchantment*, 225.
72. Dargan, "New Mexico's Fight," 14, 141.
73. U. S. Department of Commerce, U. S. Census Bureau, New Mexico's Resident Population, 1850–2000, www.census.gov.
74. *Santa Fe New Mexican*, June 28, 1902.
75. Prince, *New Mexico's Struggle*, 107.
76. *Santa Fe New Mexican*, June 16, 1906.
77. Prince, *New Mexico's Struggle*, 111.

78. Holm O. Bursum to Max Frost, August 23, 1906, Manuscripts Collection, Center for Southwestern Research, University Libraries, University of New Mexico, Albuquerque. (CSWR in subsequent references)
79. Max Frost to Holm O. Bursum, September 7, 1906 (CSWR).
80. Holm O. Bursum to Max Frost, October 15, 1906 (CSWR).
81. *Santa Fe New Mexican*, January 21, 1909.
82. "Passing of Frost," *Stevens Point Journal*, March 18, 1909.
83. *Santa Fe New Mexican*, October 18, 1909.
84. "Shouting, Broke His Jaw: Queer Accident to Col. Max Frost, Blind Editor of Santa Fe," *New York Times*, December 1, 1906.

Chapter 16
Progressive Santa Fe, 1880–1912

1. Ralph Emerson Twitchell, *The Leading Facts of New Mexican History, Vol. II* (Santa Fe: Sunstone Press, reprint 2007 reprint of 1912 edition), p. 499.
2. *New Mexican* quote from July 17, 1891, October 14, 23, 1909; "The Blind Editor of Santa Fe" *Kansas City Star*, January 13, 1907; Porter A. Stratton, *The Territorial Press of New Mexico, 1834–1912* (Albuquerque: University of New Mexico Press, 1969), pp. 226; Herbert H. Lang, "The New Mexico Bureau of Immigration 1880–1912," *New Mexico Historical Review* (July 1976), pp. 193-214; F. Stanley, *Ciudad Santa Fe, 1846–1912* (Pampa, Texas: Pampa Press, 1965), pp. 162-67.
3. *Kansas City Star* quote from February 29, 1884, October 10, 1884; general histories cover this era, see Henry J. Tobias and Charles E. Woodhouse, *Santa Fe, a Modern History, 1880–1990* (Albuquerque: University of New Mexico Press, 2001), pp. 16-26; Chris Wilson, *The Myth of Santa Fe, Creating a Modern Regional Tradition* (Albuquerque: University of New Mexico Press, 1997), pp. 56-7, 63-71; F. Stanley, *Ciudad Santa Fe*, pp. 221-30; Ralph Emerson Twitchell, *Old Santa Fe, the Story of New Mexico's Ancient capital* (Santa Fe: Sunstone Press, reprint 2008 of 1925 edition), 410, *passim*.; and Oliver La Farge, *Santa Fe, the Autobiography of a Southwestern Town* (Norman: University of Oklahoma Press, 1959), which is a compilation of clippings from the *New Mexican*; Agnes Wright Spring, *Good Little Bad Man, the Life of Colorado Charley Utter* (Boulder, Colorado: Pruett Publishing Company, 1968), pp. 119-21; *McKenny's Business Directory…1882–1883* (Oakland and San Francisco: Pacific Press, 1883), p. 341.
4. *Kansas City Star*, February 8, 1886, June 26, 1893; *St. Louis Republican* July 8, 1888; *Harpers Weekly* April 21, 1886, July 19, 1890; Chicago *Inter Ocean*, December 21, 1891, May 9, 1892.
5. Keith L. Bryant, *History of the Atchison, Topeka & Santa Fe Railway* (Lincoln: University of Nebraska Press, 1974), pp. 134-8; Gordon Chappell, *To Santa Fe by Narrow Gauge, the D&RG's 'Chili Line'* (Golden Colorado Railroad Museum, 1969), pp. 24-25; *New Mexican* November 11, 1890, May 21, December 16, 1891.
6. *New Mexican* February 18, 1890, February 5, 13, March 4, 10, 13, 16, quote in 24, April quote in 2, 4, 22, 24, quote in August 24, 1891.

7. *New Mexican* March 22, May quote in 17, 28, June 1, quote in 2, 3, 1891; June 3, 1891 issue gives vote of 707 for and 102 against with an 80% voter turn out.
8. *New Mexican* July 1, 2, 1891; the *New Mexican* published early city council minutes, see July 13; Twitchell, *Leading Facts*, v. 2, p.435.
9. *New Mexican* quote in April 2, 4, 6, 19, August 9, 1892; March 31, 1893; Baca is omitted from most lists of mayors, but served after the death of mayor Hudson, Twitchell, *Santa Fe*, p. 416.
10. *New Mexican* April 2, 4, 1892, February 19, 1896; Consuelo Bergere Mendenhall reminiscence in John Pen La Farge, *Turn Left at the Sleeping Dog, Scripting the Santa Fe Legend, 1920–1955* (Albuquerque: University of New Mexico Press, 2001), p 31.
11. *New Mexican* May 5, 1893, September 22, 1894, March 17, June 16, 1897; Twitchell *Leading Facts*, v. 2, pp. 529-30; Minutes, July 9, 1892–December 27, 1898, Records, Woman's Board of Trade and Library Association, Museum of New Mexico, Chavez Library.
12. *New Mexican* October 25, 1899, June 15, 1900, September 7, 1915; Ruth Laughlin, *Cabelleros, The Romance of Santa Fe and the Southwest* (Santa Fe: Sunstone Press, 2007 reprint of 1945 edition), p. 111-2.
13. Richard Melzer, "Foreword," in Twitchell, *Leading Facts*, v. 2, no page number; Myra Ellen Jenkins, "A Dedication to the Memory of Ralph Emerson Twitchell, 1859–1925, *Arizona & the West* (Summer 1966), pp. 103-6; Twitchell's name as a youth included "Waldo," which he dropped later in New Mexico, see census enumeration sheets on Ancestry.com for Ann Arbor, Michigan, 1860, sheet 42, and Kansa City, Missouri, 1880, sheet 113, which lists him with the middle initials "W. E."; the Twitchell papers lack records of his mayoral years, "Ralph Emerson Twitchell Papers, 1896–1986," Museum of New Mexico, Fray Angelico Chavez History Library.
14. *New Mexican* September 19, 1891, March 22, 1893; Twitchell, *Leading Facts*, v. 2, p. 16; *Kansas City Star* December 6, 1893; Ralph Emerson Twitchell, *History of the Military Occupancy of the Territory of New Mexico, 1846–1851* (Santa Fe: Sunstone Press, 2008, reprint of 1909 edition), pp. 12-13; *Albuquerque Journal* March 21, 1910.
15. Quote from *New Mexican* October 7, 1893, various "local" items in *New Mexican* April 1893-April 1894; Twitchell details the city land grant issue in his *Santa Fe*, p. 421.
16. *New Mexican* February 13, April 24, September, October 4, 1893.
17. *New Mexican* March 30, 1894; *San Francisco Weekly Examiner* March 11, 1897; *Kansas City Star* June 26, 1893; on the murder of Francisco Chavez see *El Boletin Popular* May 31, 1894 and Tobias Duran, "Francisco Chavez, Thomas B. Catron, and Organized Political Violence in Santa Fe in the 1890s," *New Mexico Historical Review* (July 1984), pp. 291-310.
18. *New Mexican*, March 18, 1889, January 13, 1893, December 8, 1909; *Albuquerque Journal* April 8, 1910, April 2, 1914; Mendenhall reminiscence in La Farge, *Turn Left at the Sleeping Dog*, p 33.
19. Stratton, *The Territorial Press*, p. 203.
20. *Colorado Springs Gazette* March 2, 1906; *Albuquerque Journal* April 14, 1907; *Kansas City Star* January 5, 1908.
21. *New Mexican* May 1, 1891; *Salt Lake Telegram* March 8, 1909; *Colorado Springs Gazette*

Telegraph February 14, 1913; *Kansas City Star* June 8, 1915.
22. *San Francisco Bulletin* September 3, 1881.
23. *An Illustrated History of New Mexico* (Chicago: Lewis Publishing Company, 1895), pp. 321-2.
24. *New Mexican* December 19, 1896, August 1, 1898, March 18, 1899.
25. *New Mexican* August 13, November 16, 1898, January 5, March 8, 31, April 13,1899, October 29, 1901; *Albuquerque Journal* February 21, 1908; 1900 and 1910 census enumeration sheets for Santa Fe digitized on Acestry.com; Oswald G. Baca, "Infectious Diseases and Smallpox Politics in New Mexico's Rio Abajo, 1847–1920," *New Mexico Historical Review* (January 2000), pp. 107-128; Sandra Schackle, *Social Housekeepers, Women Shaping Public Policy in New Mexico, 1920–1940* (Albuquerque: University of New Mexico Press, 1992), pp.11-19.
26. Twitchell, *Leading Facts*, v. 2, p. 395; Tobias and Woodhouse, *Santa Fe*, pp. 24-28.
27. David Myrick, *New Mexico's Railroads* (Golden: Colorado Railroad Museum, 1970), *passim*.
28. Vernon J. Glover, "Short Line Through a Lonely Land: The New Mexico Central," in Charles Albi, Kenton Forrest, and Richard Cooley, eds., *Journeys Through Western Rail History*, Colorado Rail Annual No. 22 (Golden: Colorado Railroad Museum, 1997), pp. 62-107; *New Mexican* May 20, 1897, June 15, 1900.
29. *New Mexican* September 9, 1899; Glover, "New Mexico Central," p. 93.
30. *New Mexico Business Directory…1905* (Denver: Gazetteer Publishing Company, 1905), pp. 456-7.
31. *New Mexican* September 9, 1899.
32. Twitchell, *Santa Fe*, 457-8; *New Mexican* October 13, 1893, April 23, 1898, January 12, 1899, March 15, 20, June 5, 1900, January 23, 1911; *New Mexico Business Directory, 1905–1906*, p. 462; Emily Abbink, *New Mexico's Palace of the Governors, History of an American Treasure* (Santa Fe: Museum of New Mexico Press, 2007), p. 94.
33. *New Mexican* September 5, October 4, 1899, June 15, 1900; Prince prepared the entries about his ancestors in L. H. Bailey, *The Standard Cyclopedia of Horticulture* (New York: MacMillan, 1917), pp. 1590–1591; Twitchell, *Leading Facts*, v. 2, p. 502; Twitchell, *Santa Fe*, p. 475.
34. *Albuquerque Journal* March 6, 1919; *Kansas City Star* January 13, 1907.
35. *Albuquerque Journal*, September 30, 1908, June 12, 1910; *New Mexican* January 3,March 12, 20, June 22, 1910; *New Mexico Business Directory 1905–1906*, p. 469; *New Mexico Business Directory, 1909*, p. 604; Tara M. Plewa, "Acequia Agriculture, Water, Irrigation, & Their Defining Roles in Santa Fe History," in David Grant Noble, ed, *Santa Fe, History of an Ancient City* (Santa Fe: School for Advanced Research Press, 2008), pp. 95-107; Maria E. Montoya in "L. Bradford Prince: the Education of a Gilded Age Politician," *New Mexico Historical Review* (April 1991), pp. 179-201; L. Bradford Prince Papers, New Mexico State records Center and Archives do not include information on his irrigation or horticulture interests.
36. *Illustrated History of New Mexico*, pp. 501-3; *New Mexican Review* July 12, 1906; Ameliia Sena Sanchez in La Farge, *Turn Left at the Sleeping Dog*, p. 105; Victor Westphall, *Thomas Benton Catron and His Era* (Tucson: University of Arizona press, 1973), p. 298.

37. Paul Horgan, *Lamy of Santa Fe, His Life and Times* (New York: Farrar, Straus and Giroux, 1975), p. 372; Dianna Everett, "The Public School Debate in New Mexico, 1850–1891" *Arizona & the West* (Summer 1984), pp. 107-134, quote p. 124; *St. Louis Republican* July 8, 1888 on Sena as teacher; *New Mexican* December 19, 1896, May 6, 1903; Jon Wallace, "Protestants, Catholics, and the State, The Origins of Public Education in Territorial New Mexico, 1846–1912," *New Mexico Historical Review* (Winter 2008), pp. pp. 57-92.
38. Rosemary Nusbaum, *Terra Dulce, Reminiscences from the Jesse Nusbaum Papers* (Santa Fe: Sunstone Press, 1980), 43-44; *New Mexican* July 13, 1990, *Albuquerque Journal* June 27, 1911.
39. Wilson, *The Myth of Santa Fe*, passim.; *New Mexican* October 14, 23, 1909.
40. *New Mexican* February 22, 1915.
41. Doris Meyer, "The Unpublished Manuscripts of Benjamin Read," *New Mexico Historical Review* (January 2001), pp. 47-64.
42. Reminiscences of Amalia Sena Sanchez, Consuelo Bergere Mendenhall, and Anita Gonzales Thomas in La Farge, *Turn Left at the Sleeping Dog*, passim.; Paul Horgan, *The Centuries of Santa Fe* (New York: E. P. Dutton, 1956), pp. 335-350; Reminiscences of Ruth Laughlin, daughter of progressive lawyer Napolean Bonaparte Laughlin, in her *Cabelleros*, pp. 83, 87-95, 101-102.
43. "Locals" column and "Gleanings by a Peripatetic Pen" column, *New Mexican*, January 3—December 30, 1910; *New Mexican* May 5, 11, 1910.
44. Donald Duke, *Santa Fe…The Railroad Gateway to the American West* (San Marino, California: Golden West Books, 1997), pp. 301-2; Keith L. Bryant, Jr., "The Atchison, Topeka and Santa Fe Railway and the Development of the Taos and Santa Fe Art Colonies," *Western Historical Quarterly* (October 1978), pp. 437-453; Victoria E. Dye, *All Aboard for Santa Fe, Railway Promotion of the Southwest, 1890s to 1930s* (Albuquerque: University of New Mexico Press, 2005), pp. 14-20.
45. Laughlin, *Cabelleros*, quote 128.

Chapter 17
The Cure at the End of the Trail,
Seeking Health While Transforming a City, 1880–1940

1. Josiah Gregg, *Commerce of the Prairies* (Norman: University of Oklahoma Press, 1954). First published in 1844.
2. Bureau of Immigration, *New Mexico: The Tourists Shrine* (Santa Fe: New Mexican Printing Co., 1882). New Mexico Territorial Bureau of Immigration Records, 1959-114, New Mexico State Records Center and Archives (NMSRCA), Santa Fe, New Mexico.
3. Sheila M. Rothman, *Living in the Shadow of Death: Tuberculosis and the Social Experience of Illness in American Society* (New York: Basic Books, 1994), 19, 45.
4. W.D. Bizzell, *Climate of the United States with Reference to Pneumonia and Consumption* (Transaction of the St. Med. Association, 1875), 40.
5. Stephen Sayles, "Stages for Statehood, 1912," in *New Mexico in Maps, Second Edition*, ed. Jerry L. Williams (Albuquerque: University of New Mexico Press, 1986), 132.

6. Nancy Owen Lewis and Kay Hagan, *A Peculiar Alchemy: A Centennial History of SAR* (Santa Fe: School for Advanced Research Press, 2007), 3.
7. Charles Montgomery, *The Spanish Redemption* (Berkeley: University of California Press, 2002), 93, 108.
8. Chris Wilson, *The Myth of Santa Fe: Creating a Modern Regional Tradition* (Albuquerque: University of New Mexico Press, 1997), 78.
9. Bureau of Immigration, *New Mexico the Tourists Shrine.*
10. Montgomery, *The Spanish Redemption,* 93.
11. Edward Willcocks Meany, *Santa Fe, as a Health Resort* (Santa Fe: New Mexican Printing Company, 1890).
12. *Santa Fe: The Climatic Mecca* (Santa Fe: New Mexican Printing Co., ca 1892), E. H. Plummer Papers, 1965-001, NMSRCA, Santa Fe, New Mexico.
13. "Food for the Angry Flames," *The Santa Fe New Mexican,* June 15, 1896.
14. Clark Kimball and Marcus J. Smith, *The Hospital at the End of the Santa Trail: A Photographic History of St. Vincent Hospital* (Santa Fe: Rydal Press, 1977), 14.
15. Marcus J. Smith, *St. Vincent Hospital 1851–1979: A Struggle for Survival at the End of the Santa Fe Trail* (Unpublished manuscript, 1979), 282, Fray Angélico Chávez History Library, Santa Fe, New Mexico.
16. George Curry, *Report of the Governor of New Mexico to the Secretary of the Interior for the Fiscal Year Ended June 30, 1908.* Governor George Curry Papers, 1959-092, NMSRCA, Santa Fe, New Mexico.
17. Smith, *St. Vincent Hospital 1851–1979,* 285.
18. "Fort Marcy Proclamation," *Santa Fe New Mexican,* January 13, 1904.
19. Max. Frost and Paul A. F. Walter, *Santa Fe County: The Heart of New Mexico, Rich in History and Resources*" (Santa Fe: Bureau of Immigration of New Mexico, 1906), 33.
20. Ibid, 33.
21. Ibid, 31.
22. "Dying 'Lungers' Come to New Mexico and Regain their Health." *Santa Fe New Mexican,* November 16, 1959.
23. *Santa Fe New Mexican,* June 1, 1906 and August 1, 1906.
24. *Sunmount, Santa Fe, New Mexico: The Land of the Large and Charitable Air* (no date), University of Arizona Library Special Collections, Tucson, Arizona.
25. "100 Per Cent Have Been Cured," *Santa Fe New Mexican,* September 18, 1911.
26. *Rules and Hints for Patients*: *Sunmount Sanatorium, Santa Fe, New Mexico* (no date), University of Arizona Library Special Collections, Tucson, Arizona.
27. L. G. Rice, "Cardinal Principles for Health Seekers," *Killgloom Gazette* 1, No. 4 (May 1914): 1, Albuquerque and New Mexico Pamphlet Collection, MSS 112 BC, Center for Southwest Research (CSWR), Albuquerque, New Mexico.
28. LeRoy Peters, "Certain Types of Advanced Tuberculosis an Economic Asset." *Medical Journal and Record* (January 7, 1925), Mrs. Howard E. Roosa Papers, 1926–1947, Center for Southwest Research, Albuquerque, New Mexico.
29. "Report of the Governor of New Mexico to the Secretary of the Interior, 1901," 371-372, Governor Miguel A. Otero Papers, 1959-090, NMSRCA, Santa Fe, New Mexico.
30. *Rules and Hints for Patients.*

31. LeRoy Peters, "Some Observations on Diet in Tuberculosis," *Killgloom Gazette* 1, No. 7 (1914): 1, CSWR.
32. Rice, "Cardinal Principles for Health Seekers."
33. *Sunmount Tent City, Santa Fe New Mexico* (ca 1907). University of Arizona Library Special Collections, Tucson, Arizona.
34. LeRoy Peters, "Changing Concepts of Tuberculosis During Twenty-Five Years," *Southwestern Medicine* 24 (1940): 47-48.
35. "Dying 'Lungers," *Santa Fe New Mexican*, November 16, 1959.
36. Mark Caldwell, *The Last Crusade: The War on Consumption, 1862–1954* (New York: Atheneuim, 1988), p. 116.
37. "Consumptives Unwelcome in Texas" *Journal of the American Medical Association* 52 (April 3, 1909), 1118.
38. Jake W. Spidle, Jr., *Doctors of Medicine in New Mexico* (Albuquerque: University of New Mexico Press, 1986), 159.
39. C. M. Mayes, "The Indigent Consumptive Proposition," *Journal of the New Mexico Medical Society.* 5, No. 2, (1909), 18-21.
40. James R. Thorpe: *The Town of Santa Fe, New Mexico [A.D. 1604]: The Bishop's Lodge, Santa Fe* (Boulder: The Taylor Company, 1921).
41. Established by the Archaeological Institute of American in 1907, the School of American Archaeology was renamed the School of American Research in 1917. In 2006 it became the School for Advanced Research on the Human Experience.
42. Wilson, *The Myth of Santa Fe,* 123.
43. Beatrice Chauvenet, *John Gaw Meem: Pioneer in Historic Preservation* (Santa Fe: Museum of New Mexico Press, 1985), 6.
44. Jerry Williams and Steve Fox, "The Healthseeker Era, 1880–1940" in *New Mexico in Maps, Second Edition,* ed. Jerry L. Williams, 131.
45. Witter Bynner, "Alice and I," *New Mexico Quarterly Review* 19 (1949), 36-37.
46. Wayne Mauzy, "Sunmount Vital Force in City Life," *Santa Fe New Mexican*, August 24, 1949.
47. Richard Melzer, *Buried Treasures: Famous and Unusual Gravesites in New Mexico History* (Santa Fe: Sunstone Press, 2007), 375.
48. "Dying Lungers," *Santa Fe New Mexican*, November 16, 1959.
49. Spidle, *Doctors of Medicine in New Mexico*, 87.
50. J. W. Kerr, "Public Health Administration in New Mexico." Influenza Outbreak, 1918, Governor Washington E. Lindsey Papers, 1959-096, NMSCRA, Santa Fe, New Mexico.
51. LeRoy Peters, "Changing Concepts of Tuberculosis During Twenty-Five Years," *Southwestern Medicine* 24 (1940), 47-48.

Chapter 18
Santa Fe in World War II, 1940–1947

Abbreviations Used in Notes

NMAG: New Mexico Adjutant General collection at the New Mexico State Records Center and Archives, Santa Fe, New Mexico.
FACHLPA: Fray Angélico Chávez History Library and Photo Archives, Palace of the Governors, Museum of New Mexico, Santa Fe, New Mexico.
GJEMP: Governor John E. Miles Papers at the New Mexico State Records Center and Archives, Santa Fe, New Mexico.
NMSRCA: New Mexico State Records Center and Archives, Santa Fe, New Mexico.

1. Colonel Stephen M. Mellnik, GSC, "The Life and Death of the 200th Artillery (AA)," *Coast Artillery Journal*, LXXXX, no 2, (March-April 1947) 7, NMSRCA.
2. Eva Jane Matson, *It Tolled for New Mexico*, (Las Cruces, New Mexico: Yucca Tree Press, 1994), data extracted from "Biographical Lists for the 200th and 515th Coast Artillery Regiments," pp 246-427.
3. Saburō Ienaga, *The Pacific War 1931–1945* (New York: Pantheon Books, 1978) 5.
4. E. Bartlett Kerr, *Surrender and Survival* (New York: William Morrow, 1985) 25.
5. Richard John Daly, *Me: A Biography for My Children* (in possession of author, 2002) 107.
6. Theodore H. White, *In Search of History* (New York: Harper and Row, 1978) 70.
7. NMAG, acc 1973-019, sub-series 18.3, NMSRCA.
8. Ibid.
9. John Pershing Jolly, "200th Coast Artillery (AA) and its 'Child' the 515th Coast Artillery (AA) Period 1939–1945," *History National Guard of New Mexico 1606–1963*, (New Mexico State Adjutant General's Office: 1964) 67, NMSRCA-library.
10. Francis VanBuskirk, personal communication-interview (2007).
11. Dorothy Cave, *Beyond Courage: Our Regiment Against Japan, 1941–1945* (Santa Fe, New Mexico: Sunstone Press, 2006) 20.
12. John Pershing Jolly, "200th Coast Artillery (AA) and its 'Child' the 515th Coast Artillery (AA) Period 1939–1945," *History National Guard of New Mexico 1606–1963*, (New Mexico State Adjutant General's Office: 1964) 65, NMSRCA-library.
13. Francis VanBuskirk, personal communication-interview, 2007.
14. Richard John Daly, *Me: A Biography for My Children* (in possession of author, 2002) 78.
15. Ibid.
16. GJEMP, acc 1959-105, box 2, folder 156, NMSRCA.
17. Saburō Ienaga, *The Pacific War 1931–1945* (New York: Pantheon Books, 1978) 154.
18. Richard John Daly, *Me: A Biography for My Children* (in possession of author, 2002) 80-81.
19. John Pershing Jolly, "200th Coast Artillery (AA) and its 'Child' the 515th Coast Artillery (AA) Period 1939–1945," *History National Guard of New Mexico 1606–1963*, (New Mexico State Adjutant General's Office: 1964) 67, NMSRCA-library.
20. Dorothy Cave, *Beyond Courage: Our Regiment Against Japan, 1941–1945*, (Santa Fe, New

Mexico: Sunstone Press, 2006) 37; Richard John Daly, *Me: A Biography for My Children* (in possession of author, 2002) 83.
21. Harry E. Steen, *Experiences in World War 2 in the Far East: The Philippines and Niigata, Japan,* (September 1992) 5, Oral History, Air Defense Artillery School, Historian's Files, Fort Bliss, Texas.
22. John Pershing Jolly, "200th Coast Artillery (AA) and its 'Child' the 515th Coast Artillery (AA) Period 1939–1945," *History National Guard of New Mexico 1606–1963,* (New Mexico State Adjutant General's Office: 1964) 69, NMSRCA-library.
23. *Albuquerque Journal* (18 November 1941) 1.
24. John Pershing Jolly, "200th Coast Artillery (AA) and its 'Child' the 515th Coast Artillery (AA) Period 1939–1945," *History National Guard of New Mexico 1606–1963,* (New Mexico State Adjutant General's Office: 1964) 2-3, NMSRCA-library.
25. Francis VanBuskirk, personal communication-interview, 2007.
26. John Pershing Jolly, "200th Coast Artillery (AA) and its 'Child' the 515th Coast Artillery (AA) Period 1939–1945," *History National Guard of New Mexico 1606–1963,* (New Mexico State Adjutant General's Office: 1964) 67, NMSRCA-library.
27. Richard John Daly, *Me: A Biography for My Children* (possession of author, 2002) 86; Harry E. Steen, *Experiences in World War 2 in the Far East: The Philippines and Niigata, Japan* (September 1992) 9, Oral History, Air Defense Artillery School, Historian's Files, Fort Bliss, Texas.
28. Richard John Daly, *Me: A Biography for My Children* (in possession of author, 2002) 86.
29. Richard M. Gordon, *Horyo: Memoirs of an American POW* (St. Paul, Minnesota: Paragon House, 1999) 63.
30. Richard John Daly, *Me: A Biography for My Children* (in possession of author, 2002) 80, 87.
31. Ibid, 101; Francis Van Buskirk (personal communication, 2007).
32. Harry E. Steen, *Experiences in World War 2 in the Far East: The Philippines and Niigata, Japan* (September 1992) 11, Oral History, Air Defense Artillery School, Historian's Files, Fort Bliss, Texas.
33. Shuji Fujii to Governor John Miles (8 December 1941), GJEMP, acc 1959-105, box 18, folder 533.
34. "A Proclamation by the Governor" (8 December 1941), GJEMP, acc 1959-105, box 5, folder 156.
35. Civil Protection Committee to Governor John Miles, (December 1941), GJEMP, acc 1959-105, box 9, folder 305.
36. John Pershing Jolly, "200th Coast Artillery (AA) and its 'Child' the 515th Coast Artillery (AA) Period 1939–1945," *History National Guard of New Mexico 1606–1963,* (New Mexico State Adjutant General's Office: 1964) 692-3, NMSRCA-library.
37. United Brothers of Carpenters and Joiners to Gov. Miles (17 December 1941); Star Lumber Co. to Gov Miles (undated); Santa Fe Central Labor Union to Gov Miles (30 December 1941); Santa Fe Lions Club to Gov Miles (18 Dec 1941); Kruger and Bigelow, Jr. to Gov. Miles (11 December 1941); Dept of Public Welfare to Gov Miles (11 December 1941), GJEMP, acc 1959-105, box 10, folder 340.
38. Allen R. Bosworth, *America's Concentration Camps* (New York: W.W. Norton, 1967) 56.
39. War Relocation Authority, Administrative Manual, 1942, chapter 10, GJEMP.

40. Edward Brett and Donna Brett, "Santa Fe's Shameful 'Jap Trap'" (15 February 1984) 11, *Santa Fe Reporter*.
41. Jerre Mangione, *An Ethnic at Large: A Memoir of America in the Thirties and Forties*, (New York: G P Putnam's Sons, 1978) 320.
42. Department of Commerce, Bureau of Census, Table 1, GJEMP, acc 1959-105, box 10, folder 343, NMSRCA.
43. Michael Gilewitch, *Moyeh* (no date) 3-31, Archives, Air Defense Artillery Museum, Fort Bliss, Texas.
44. Manny Lawton, *Some Survived: An Epic Account of Japanese Captivity During World War II*, (Chapel Hill, North Carolina, 1984) 5.
45. Colonel Wibb Cooper, *Medical Department Activities in the Philippines from 1941 to 6 May 1942*, (West Point, New York: 1946), 35, Nininger Collection, as referenced in Elizabeth M. Norman, *We Band of Angels* (New York: Random House, 1999) 51.
46. Harry E. Steen, *Experiences in World War 2 in the Far East: The Philippines and Niigata, Japan* (September 1992) 18, Oral History, Air Defense Artillery School, Historian's Files, Fort Bliss, Texas.
47. Manny Lawton, *Some Survived: An Epic Account of Japanese Captivity During World War II*, (Chapel Hill, North Carolina, 1984) 5.
48. John W. Whitman, *Bataan: Our Last Ditch* (New York: Hippocrene Books, 1990) 468.
49. Harry E. Steen, *Experiences in World War 2 in the Far East: The Philippines and Niigata, Japan* (September 1992) 18, Oral History, Air Defense Artillery School, Historian's Files, Fort Bliss, Texas.
50. General Orders Number 14 (9 March 1942), Washington, DC
51. Governor John Miles to All Department Heads (9 January 1942) GJEMP, acc 1959-105, box 3, folder 110.
52. Henry Stimson to Governor Miles (December 1941), GJEMP, acc 1959-105, box 18, folder 533.
53. GJEMP, (1942) acc 1959-105, box 3, folder 110.
54. National Reclamation Association Bulletin (20 May 1942)1, 3, GJEMP, acc 1959-105, box 10, folder 342.
55. Ibid. 4.
56. James Matsu to Governor John Miles (3 February 1942) GJEMP, acc 1959-105, box 10, folder 342.
57. New Mexico State Prison Board to Immigration and Naturalization Service (2 Mar 1942) NMAG, acc 1973-019, sub-series 18.3.
58. Captain Antonio Martin *Report on Visit*, (15-16 Feb 1945), National Archives, RG 59, Special War Problems Division: Santa Fe folder, box 20, copy at FACHLPA; W.F. Kelly, Department of Justice, *Re: the Santa Fe Internment Camp* (17 October 1945), acc 304, box 4, folder 2, FACHLPA.
59. Loyd Jensen to W.F. Kelly (20 January 1944), National Archives, RG 85, INS Internment Camp in New Mexico, copy at FACHLPA.
60. Eva Ammen and Mathilde Ammen to Governor Miles (13 March 1942), GJEMP, acc 1959-105, box 18, folder 534.
61. GJEMP, acc 1959-105, box 18, folder 534; GJEMP, acc 1959-105, box 10, folder 34.

62. Press Release (7 April 1942), GJEMP, acc 1959-105, box 5, folder 167.
63. John W. Whitman, *Bataan: Our Last Ditch* (New York: Hippocrene Books, 1990) 567.
64. *The Santa Fe New Mexican* (9 April 1942).
65. Eva Jane Matson, *It Tolled for New Mexico* (Las Cruces, New Mexico: Yucca Tree Press, 1994) 22.
66. Richard John Daly, *Me: A Biography for My Children* (in possession of author, 2002) 93. Ibid. 107; Michael Gilewitch, *Moyeh* (no date) 3,39, Archives, Air Defense Artillery Museum, Fort Bliss, Texas; John Pershing Jolly, "200th Coast Artillery (AA) and its 'Child' the 515th Coast Artillery (AA) Period 1939–1945," *History National Guard of New Mexico 1606–1963,* (New Mexico State Adjutant General's Office: 1964) 75, NMSRCA-library; John W. Whitman, *Bataan: Our Last Ditch* (New York: Hippocrene Books, 1990) 567.
67. Richard John Daly, *Me: A Biography for My Children* (in possession of author, 2002) 93. Ibid. 107.
68. E. Bartlett Kerr, *Surrender and Survival* (New York: William Morrow, 1985) 51-52.
69. Michael Gilewitch, *Moyeh* (no date) 4.4-4.6, Archives, Air Defense Artillery Museum, Fort Bliss, Texas.
70. *The Santa Fe New Mexican* (9 April 1942) 1.
71. Proclamation (9 April 1942), GJEMP, acc 1959-105, box 5, folder 157.
72. Colonel Memory H. Cain to Mrs. Myers (no date), Sgt. William Myers collection, acc 1971-025, box 5903, NMSRCA.
73. Gavan Daws, *Prisoners of the Japanese* (New York: William Morrow & Co., 1994) 159.
74. Michael Gilewitch, *Moyeh* (no date) 4.32, Archives, Air Defense Artillery Museum, Fort Bliss, Texas.
75. Governor John E. Miles papers, 1 May 1942, acc 1959-105, box 5, folder 157, NMSRCA.
76. Governor Miles Press Release (28 May 1942) Governor Miles papers, acc 1959-105, box 5, folder 167, NMSRCA.
77. "Maybe Not Art But New Mexico Loves It", *Albuquerque Tribune* (18 June 1942).
78. Secretary of State Washington, DC to Governor Miles (20 May 1942), Governor Miles papers, acc 1959-105, box 10, folder 342, NMSRCA.
79. Governor Miles to Oregon Governor Charles A. Sprague (3 November 1942) Governor Miles papers, acc 1959-105, box 10, folder 342, NMSRCA.
80. Lloyd to Governor Miles (April 1942) Governor Miles papers, acc 1959-105, box 10, folder 342, NMSRCA.
81. Captain Antonio Martin, *Report on Visit,* (20 & 22 April 1943), National Archives, RG 59, Special War Problems Division: Santa Fe folder, box 20.
82. Allen R. Bosworth, *America's Concentration Camps* (New York: W.W. Norton & Co Inc, 1967) 232.
83. Ivan Williams to W.F. Kelly (30 March 1945), National Archives, RG 85, INS, file 1300/P.
84. Captain Antonio Martin, *Report on Visit,* (15-16 Feb 1945), National Archives, RG 59, Special War Problems Division, box 20, Santa Fe folder.
85. Ivan Williams to W.F. Kelly (30 March 1945), National Archives, RG 85, INS, file 1300/P.

86. Edward Brett and Donna Brett, "Santa Fe's Shameful 'Jap Trap'" (15 Feb 1984) *Santa Fe Reporter*, 11.
87. unknown to Jerre Mangione, *Re: Santa Fe Camp Data* (14 October 1943) 1-2, acc 304, box 2, folder 7, FACHLPA.
88. Captain Antonio Martin, *Report on Visit* (20 & 22 April 1943), National Archives, RG 59, Special War Problems Division, box 20, Santa Fe folder.
89. Francisco de Amat, *Report* (26 May 1942), Koichiro Okada collection, acc 304, box 4, folder 2, FACHLPA.
90. Captain Antonio Martin, *Report on Visit*, (10-11 July 1944), National Archives, RG 59, Special War Problems Division: Sant Fe folder, box 20.
91. Edward Brett and Donna Brett, "Santa Fe's Shameful 'Jap Trap'" (15 Feb 1984) *Santa Fe Reporter*, 11.
92. unknown to Jerre Mangione, *Re: Santa Fe Camp Data* (14 October 1943) 1, acc 304, box 2, folder 7, FACHLPA; Koichiro Okada, *Appendix 1: Significant Dates and Events of the Nikkei Ethnohistory* (undated) 7, acc 304, box 2, folder 8, FACHLPA.
93. Ivan Williams to W.F. Kelly, *History of the Santa Fe Camp* (9 August 1945), National Archives, RG 85, INS Internment Camp in New Mexico.
94. Captain Antonio Martin, *Report on Visit*, (20 & 22 April 1943), National Archives, RG 59, Special War Problems Division: Santa Fe folder, box 20.
95. Allen R. Bosworth, *America's Concentration Camps* (New York: W.W. Norton, 1967) 231-232.
96. *Albuquerque Journal* (5 Jan 1944); Captain Antonio Martin, *Report on Visit*, (20 & 22 April 1943), National Archives, RG 59, Special War Problems Division: Santa Fe folder, box 20.
97. Brother Tim Coldwell, *A History of Bruns General Hospital and Its Subsequent Acquisition by St. Michael's College: 1942–1947* (1977), research paper, vertical file, FACHLPA.
98. "Bruns in Way of Becoming Finest Hospital of Type in US," (19 April 1945) *The Santa Fe New Mexican*, 1 & 3.
99. Gussie Fauntleroy, "Bruns Hospital had Big Impact in Little Time," *The Santa Fe New Mexican* (29 August 1999).
100. Brother Tim Coldwell, *A History of Bruns General Hospital and Its Subsequent Acquisition by St. Michael's College: 1942–1947* (May 1977), research paper, vertical file, FACHLPA.
101. Gussie Fauntleroy, "Bruns Hospital had Big Impact in Little Time," *The Santa Fe New Mexican* (29 August 1999).
102. *Bruns Annual Report* (1943); *Bruns Annual Report* (1944); *Bruns Annual Report* (1945), Military Reference and Research Branch, Medical History Division, Fort Detrick, Maryland, copies at FACHLPA.
103. *The Santa Fe New Mexican* (2 November 1943).
104. *Bruns Echo, Souvenir edition* (1946) NMAG, box 13626.
105. plan view drawing of Bruns General Hospital complex, oversized file, NMSRCA; Debra Voisin-Halsey, "Military Hospital Recalled," *Journal North* (19 June 1982).
106. Michael Gilewitch, *Moyeh* (no date) 4-78, Archives, Air Defense Artillery Museum, Fort Bliss, Texas.
107. Richard Gordon, *Horyo* (St. Paul, Minnesota: Paragon House, 1999) 138.

108. Thomas Allen and Norman Polmar, *Code Name Downfall*, (New York: Simon and Schuster, 1995) 160.
109. Errett L. Lujan, POW diary (22 May 1943) in possession of author.
110. Thomas Allen and Norman Polmar, *Code Name Downfall*, (New York: Simon and Schuster, 1995); "Super-Fortress Blasts Jap Homeland," *The Santa Fe New Mexican* (15 June 1944).
111. *Bruns Annual Report* (1944) Military Reference and Research Branch, Medical History Division, Fort Detrick, Maryland, copies at FACHLPA; "Bruns in Way of Becoming Finest Hospital of Type in US," *The Santa Fe New Mexican* (19 April 1945) 1, 3.
112. *Bruns Annual Report* (1944) Military Reference and Research Branch, Medical History Division, Fort Detrick, Maryland, copy at FACHLPA; "Santa Fe Inn Taken Over January 20 for Annex" *The Santa Fe New Mexican* (12 January 1944).
113. "Recreation, Reconditioning Programs Popular at Bruns," *The Santa Fe New Mexican* (9 October 1944).
114. Brother Tim Coldwell, *A History of Bruns General Hospital and Its Subsequent Acquisition by St. Michael's College: 1942–1947* (1977), research paper, vertical file, FACHLPA.
115. "100 Vacant Jobs at Bruns; Officers Say Need Acute" (9 June 1945), *The Santa Fe New Mexican*.
116. *Bruns Annual Report* (1945) 1, Military Reference and Research Branch, Medical History Division, Fort Detrick, Maryland copy at FACHLPA.
117. Thomas Allen and Norman Polmar, *Code Name Downfall* (New York: Simon and Schuster, 1995) 208-209.
118. *Bruns Annual Report* (1945) 1, 6, Military Reference and Research Branch, Medical History Division, Fort Detrick, Maryland, copy at FACHLPA.
119. John Pershing Jolly, "200th Coast Artillery (AA) and its 'Child' the 515th Coast Artillery (AA) Period 1939–1945," *History National Guard of New Mexico 1606–1963*, (New Mexico State Adjutant General's Office: 1964) 77-78, NMSRCA-library.
120. Koichiro Okada, *Appendix 1: Significant Dates and Events of the Nikkei Ethnohistory,"* (undated) acc 304, box 2, folder 8, FACHLPA.
121. John Pershing Jolly, "200th Coast Artillery (AA) and its 'Child' the 515th Coast Artillery (AA) Period 1939–1945," *History National Guard of New Mexico 1606–1963*, (New Mexico State Adjutant General's Office: 1964) 13, NMSRCA-library.
122. Brigadier General Charles G. Sage, *General Orders No. 6* (6 December 1946) State of New Mexico, Office of the Adjutant General, Santa Fe.
123. "In Bruns Plea," *The Santa Fe New Mexican* (19 November 1946).
124. Santa Fe City Resolution (18 November 1946).
125. Brother Tim Coldwell, *A History of Bruns General Hospital and Its Subsequent Acquisition by St. Michael's College: 1942–1947* (1977), research paper, vertical file, FACHLPA.
126. Koichiro Okada, *Appendix 1: Significant Dates and Events of the Nikkei Ethnohistory* (undated) 9, acc 304, box 2, folder 8, FACHLPA.
127. "Ambassador," *The Quan*, Volume 65, Number 1 (July 2009), Wellsburg, West Virginia.

Chapter 19
Alcaldes and Mayors of Santa Fe, 1613–2008

1. Viceroy Luis de Velasco, Instructions, March 30, 1609, Mexico City, Archivo General de las Indias (AGI), México, 27, N. 63, exp 5., f. 1r.
2. List of Ministers of Justice and War, October 2, 1661, Archivo General de la Nación, México (AGN), Ramo de Concurso de Peñalosa, vol. 3, leg. 1, no. 2, f. 6ff.
3. In 1639, the *cabildo* of the Villa de Santa Fe was regarded "as head of these provinces." Charles Wilson Hackett, *Historical Documents relating to New Mexico, Nueva Vizcaya, and Approaches Thereto, to 1773* (Washington, D.C: Carnegie Institution of Washington, 1937), Vol. III, 56.
4. Governor Alonso Pacheco de Heredia, *Auto*, July 26, 1640, Santa Fe, AGI, Patronato 244, R. 7, exp. 14, f.33v.
5. List of Property Owners in Santa Fe, 1836, Spanish Archives of New Mexico, Series I (SANM I), 1314.
6. Fray Juan de Salas, *Relación*, 1640, Santo Domingo Pueblo, AGI, Patronato, 244, R7, exp. 14, f. 18v; Governor Alonso Pacheco de Heredia, *Auto*, January 6, 1640, Santa Fe, AGI, Patronato, 244, R7, exp. 14, f. 28r; Edict of the *Residencia* of Governor Bernardo López de Mendizábal, September 30, 1661, Santa Fe, AGN, Ramo de Concurso de Peñalosa, vol. 3, exp. 455, leg. 1, no. 2, f. 4r; Proceedings in Case against Don Diego de Peñalosa y Briceño, 1662, AGN, Ramo de Concurso de Peñalosa, vol. 2, exp. 495, leg. 1, no. 4, f. 245r; and Proceedings in Case against Don Bernardo López de Mendizábal, May 16, 1662, Santa Fe, AGN, Tierras, t. 3268, leg. 2, no. 34, f. 253v.
7. Orders of Compliance by the *Cabildo*, 1713–1715, Santa Fe, SANM I, 1110.
8. The phrase in Spanish reads: "*Fiesta Jurada por la villa por patrona de los rayos.*" Orders of Compliance by the *Cabildo*, 1713–1715, Santa Fe, SANM I, 1110.
9. The Feast of the Naval Battle appears to be a reference to the Battle of Lepanto, October 7, 1571.
10. Inventory of the *Cabildo* Archives and Fiscal Accounting, 1715, Santa Fe, SANM I, 1110; Inventory of the *Cabildo* Archives, 1715, Santa Fe, SANM I, 1136; Inventory of the Proceedings of *Alcalde* Don José Bustamante y Tagle, 1749, Santa Fe, SANM I, 1084; and Proceedings of *Cabildo* Meetings, 1845, Santa Fe, SANM I, 1174.
11. Santa Fe was elevated in status from a villa to a ciudad (city) in July–August 1819. Archives of the Archdiocese of Santa Fe (AASF), Roll 31, Santa Fe Marriages, 1758–1857.
12. Incorporation Proclamation, Office of Probate Court, Santa Fe County, June 17, 1891. The official seal of the City of Santa Fe bears the date of July 13, 1891, for the formal organization of the incorporation.
13. Félix Martínez, Election of Local Officials, January 1, 1716, Santa Fe, Spanish Archives of New Mexico, Series II (SANM II), 240.
14. Draft Letter Regarding Difficulties with Electing *Alcaldes Ordinarios* in New Mexico, July 13, 1797, Santa Fe, SANM II, 1451.
15. Miguel Sena, Proceedings over the Destruction of a Reservoir, 1835–1836, Santa Fe, SANM I, 1313.

16. María Dolores Sandoval, Proceedings against *Alcalde* Juan García, Los Tanques, SANM I, 148.
17. María Dolores Sandoval, Proceedings against *Alcalde* Juan García, Los Tanques, SANM I, 148.
18. Ramón Abreu, Communication to Felipe Sena, 1837, Santa Fe, SANM I, 1216.
19. Governor Manuel Armijo, Letterbook of Communications, 1840–1842, SANM I, 1317.
20. Governor Manuel Armijo, Letterbook of Communications, 1840–1842, SANM I, 1317.
21. Fray Francisco Pérez Guerta, *Relación*, 1611–1617, New Mexico, AGN, Inquisición, t. 316, f. 155 (Juan de Escarramad).
22. Fray Francisco Pérez Guerta, *Relación*, 1611–1617, New Mexico, AGN, Inquisición, t. 316, ff. 162r , 163r, and 163v (Juan Ruiz de Cáceres).
23. Fray Francisco Pérez Guerta, *Relación*, 1611–1617, New Mexico, AGN, Inquisición, t. 316, f. 165r; and Fray Angélico Chávez, *Origins of New Mexico Families in the Spanish Colonial Period* (Santa Fe: Museum of New Mexico Press, 1992), hereafter ONMF, 14 (Juan de Vitoria Carvajal).
24. Fray Francisco Pérez Guerta, *Relación*, 1611–1617, New Mexico, AGN, Inquisición, t. 316, f. 172v (Asencio de Archuleta).
25. *Captain* Francisco Pérez Granillo, *Declaración*, 1626, Santa Fe, AGN, Inquisición, t. 356, f. 264v (Francisco Pérez Granillo).
26. Captain Bartolomé Romero, *Declaración*, September 26, 1628, Pueblo of Santa Clara, AGN, Inquisición, t. 304, f. 187r (Bartolomé Romero).
27. Captain Diego de Santa Cruz, *Declaración*, January 19, 1631, San Francisco de Sandía, AGN, Inquisición, t. 372 exp. 16, ff. 1 and 4–4v (Diego de Santa Cruz).
28. Captain Francisco Gómez de Torres, Settlement of Estate, October 1636, Santa Fe, Biblioteca Nacional de México, leg. 1, no. 7, p. 503 (Francisco Gómez).
29. Charles Wilson Hackett, Historical Documents, 3:49, 53, 61 (Roque Medón de Casaus).
30. Charles Wilson Hackett, Historical Documents, 3:49, 53, 61 (Francisco de Madrid)
31. Tim MacCurdy, "From Spain to Pajarito and The De La Hubbel-Gutierrez Story (The Caesar of Santa Fe)", in *La Bandera*, 3:2, 6 (Antonio Baca).
32. Certification of the *Cabildo*, July 26, 1643, Santa Fe, AGI, Patronato, 244, R.7, exp. 14, f. 33v (Matías Romero).
33. Certification of the *Cabildo*, July 26, 1643, Santa Fe, AGI, Patronato, 244, R.7, exp.14, f. 33v (Francisco de Madrid).
34. Scholes, *Church and State of New Mexico,* 176 (Francisco Durán y Chaves).
35. Captain Juan Luján, *Declaración*, October 29, 1661, Santa Fe, AGN, Ramo de Concurso de Peñalosa, exp. 605, vol. 1, leg 1, no. 1, f.211r. (Francisco de Madrid).
36. Proceedings in Case against Don Diego de Peñalosa y Briceño, 1662, Santa Fe, AGN, Ramo de Concurso de Peñalosa, exp. 605, vol. 1, leg. 1, no. 2, f.197r; and Proceedings in Case against Doña Teresa de Aguilera y Roche, 1663, Santa Fe and Mexico City, AGN, Inquisición, t. 596. f. 72r (Francisco Gómez Robledo).
37. Proceedings in Case against *Captain* Diego Romero, 1660, Santa Fe, AGN, Inquisición, t. 586, f. 3r (Diego Romero).
38. Captain Bartolomé Romero, *Petición*, October 20, 1661, Santa Fe, AGN, Tierras, t. 3268, leg. 2, no. 32, f. 50r-50vr; Sebastián de Herrera Corrales, *Declaración*, September

28, 1661, AGN, Inquisición t. 596, f. 16v; and Chávez, ONMF, 95 & 97 (Bartolomé Romero II).

39. Captain Pedro de Leyva, *Declaración*, October 29, 1661, Santa Fe, AGN, Inquisición, t. 596, f. 26r; and *Captain* Juan Domínguez de Mendoza, Testimony, October 29, 1661, Santa Fe, AGN, Ramo de Concurso de Peñalosa, vol. 3, leg. 1, no. 1, f. 218r (Pedro de Leyva).

40. Proceedings in Case against Don Diego de Peñalosa y Briceño, July 7, 1662, Santa Fe, AGN, Ramo de Concurso de Peñalosa, vol. 3, leg 1, no. 1, f. 39v; and Chávez, ONMF, 3 (Francisco de Anaya Almazán).

41. *Sargento Mayor* Diego López del Castillo, *Declaración*, August 16, 1662, Santa Fe, AGN, Ramo de Concurso de Peñalosa, vol. 3, leg 1, no. 1 f. 39v and f. 101v (Diego López del Castillo).

42. *Maese de Campo* Juan Domínguez de Mendoza, Title of Lieutenant Captain General and Visitador General, October 6, 1663, Santa Fe, Biblioteca Nacional de Madrid MS 19258, f. 33 (Juan Domínguez de Mendoza).

43. *Maese de Campo* Tomé Domínguez de Mendoza in the name of *Captain* Don Diego de Peñalosa Briceño, Embargo of Goods, 1663, Santa Fe, AGN, Ramo de Concurso de Peñalosa, exp 455, vol 3, leg. 1 no.10, 160ff (Tomé Domínguez de Mendoza).

44. Captain Juan Domínguez de Mendoza, *Declaración*, October 31, 1664, Santa Fe, AGN, Tierras, t. 3268, f.409r-409v (Juan Domínguez de Mendoza).

45. Edict Concerning a Council of War, February 18-16, 1668, Santa Fe, Biblioteca Nacional de Mexico, leg. 1, doc. 29 (Bartolomé Romero III).

46. Edict Concerning a Council of War, February 18-16, 1668, Santa Fe, Biblioteca Nacional de Mexico, leg. 1, doc. 29 (Pedro Lucero de Godoy).

47. *Maese de Campo* Juan Domínguez de Mendoza, Certification of Services, January 26, 1672, Santa Fe, Biblioteca Nacional de Madrid, MS 19258, ff. 48-49 (Juan Domínguez de Mendoza).

48. Spanish Archives of New Mexico, Series II (SANM II), 4; see also, Ralph Emerson Twitchell, *Spanish Archives of New Mexico* (The Torch Press, 1914; New Edition, Sunstone Press, 2008), Vol. II, 48 and 49; and Chávez, ONMF, 113 (Francisco Xavier).

49. SANM II, 4 and 8b; and Twitchell, *Spanish Archives of New Mexico*, Vol. II, 49 and 71; Chávez, ONMF, 60; John L. Kessell and Rick Hendricks, eds., *By Force of Arms: The Journals of Don Diego de Vargas, 1691–1693* (Albuquerque: University of New Mexico Press) 204; and Charles W. Hackett, *Revolt of the Pueblo Indians of New Mexico and Otermín's Attempted Reconquest, 1680–1682* (Albuquerque: University of New Mexico Press, 1942), I:137 (Juan Lucero de Godoy).

50. SANM II, 4; and Twitchell, *Spanish Archive of New Mexico*, Vol. II, 48 (Gregorio de Valdes).

51. SANM II, 8b (Lorenzo de Madrid).

52. Hackett, *Revolt of the Pueblo Indians*, I: 45 and 107.

53. SANM II, 13 (Francisco Xavier).

54. Spanish Archives of New Mexico, Series I (SANM I), 728 (Juan Lucero de Godoy).

55. AGN, Provincias Internas, t. 35, ff. 71-75 (Francisco Ramírez de Salazar).

56. Certification of Documents Showing the Services of Maestre de Campo Don Juan

Domínguez de Mendoza, October 3, 1684, El Paso, Biblioteca Nacional de Madrid, M.S. 19258, photos 2-5 (Lorenzo de Madrid).
57. Certification of Documents Showing the Services of Maestre de Campo Don Juan Domínguez de Mendoza, October 3, 1684, El Paso, Biblioteca Nacional de Madrid, M.S. 19258, photos 2-5 (Juan Severino de Zuballe).
58. John L. Kessell and Rick Hendricks, eds., *By Force of Arms: The Journals of Don Diego de Vargas, 1691–1693* (Albuquerque: University of New Mexico Press, 1992), 208 n.30 (Francisco Gómez Robledo).
59. SANM II, 45 and 50 (Juan Lucero de Godoy).
60. John L. Kessell, Rick Hendricks, and Meredith D. Dodge, eds., *To The Royal Crown Restored: The Journals of Don Diego de Vargas, New Mexico, 1692–1694* (Albuquerque: University of New Mexico Press, 1995), 169 n.10, (José Telles Jirón).
61. SANM II, 52; and Kessell, Hendricks and Dodge, *To the Royal Crown Restored*, 37 and 49 (Francisco de Anaya Almazán).
62. Kessell, Hendricks and Dodge, *To the Royal Crown Restored*, 37 (Antonio Montoya).
63. Kessell and Hendricks, *To the Royal Crown Restored*, 203 n.8 (Alfonso Rael de Aguilar).
64. Kessell and Hendricks, *To the Royal Crown Restored*, 422 and 440 (Lorenzo de Madrid).
65. SANM II, 51; Kessell and Hendricks, *To the Royal Crown Restored*, 564; and John L. 66. Kessell, Rick Hendricks, and Meredith D. Dodge, *Blood on the Boulders: The Journals of Don Diego de Vargas, New Mexico, 1694–97*, (Albuquerque, University of New Mexico Press, 1998), I:186 (Lorenzo de Madrid).
66. Kessell and Hendricks, *To the Royal Crown Restored*, 77 n.18 (Francisco Romero de Pedraza).
67. SANM I, 479; and State of New Mexico Records Center and Archives (SNMRCA), Linda Tigges Special Collection, Documents 114, 115 & 116, and T479 I; SNMRCA, Linda Tigges Special Collection, Santa Fe Historic Plaza Study III book 19271, 19272 and 19273 (Francisco Romero de Pedraza).
68. John L. Kessell, Rick Hendricks, Meridith D. Dodge, and Larry D. Miller, *That Disturbance Cease: The Journals of Don Diego de Vargas, New Mexico, 1697–1700* (Albuquerque: University of New Mexico, 2000), 37 (Lorenzo de Madrid).
69. SANM I, 411; and Kessell, Hendricks and Dodge, *Blood on the Boulders*, II: 787 (Lorenzo Madrid).
70. SANM I, 411 (Antonio de Aguilera y Isasi).
71. SANM I, 411; and Kessell, Hendricks and Dodge, *Blood on the Boulders*, II: 847, 852, 853, and 855.
72. Kessell, Hendricks and Dodge, *Blood on the Boulders*, II: 1158 (Diego Montoya)
73. SANM I, 3, 729, 730, and 929; and Kessell, Hendricks and Dodge, *Blood on the Boulders*, II: 1139 and 1157 (Diego Arias de Quirós).
74. SANM I, 4, 76 (Diego Arias de Quirós).
75. Antonio Lucero de Godoy was the first signatory for petitions issued by the *Cabildo de Santa Fe* in December 1698 and February 1699, and it is presumed that the first signatory was one of the *alcaldes ordinarios*. See Kessell, Hendricks, Dodge and Miller, *That Disturbances Cease*, 172 and 179.
76. Antonio de Aguilera Isasi was the second signatory for petitions issued by the *Cabildo de*

Santa Fe in December 1698 and February 1699, and it is presumed that the first two signatories was one of the *alcaldes ordinarios*. See Kessell, Hendricks, Dodge and Miller, *That Disturbances Cease*, 172 and 179.

77. Kessell, Hendricks, Dodge and Miller, *That Disturbances Cease*, 179 (Antonio Lucero de Godoy).
78. SANM I, 758, 819, 820, 886, and 929; Kessell, Hendricks, Dodge and Miller, *That Disturbances Cease,* 179; and SNMRCA, Linda Tigges Special Collection, Twitchell (T) 758a Series I (I), and T411 I. (Antonio de Aguilera y Isasi).
79. SANM I, 924 and 925 (Agustín Sáez).
80. SANM I, 5, 270, 289, 291, 638, and 678 (Antonio de Aguilera y Isasi).
81. Francisco Romero de Pedraza was the second signatory for three petitions issued by the *Cabildo de Santa Fe* in July 1700, and it is presumed that the first two signatories were the *alcaldes ordinarios*. Kessell, Hendricks, Dodge and Miller, *That Disturbances Cease,* 380 and 383.
82. Fray Angélico Chávez, "New Mexico Roots, Ltd.," (Santa Fe: n.p., 1982), 285, DM 1701, no. 1, Santa Fe (Francisco Romero).
83. SANM I, 77, 230, 296, 424, 483, 480, 732, 821, 927, and 1136; and SANM II, 83 and SNMRCA, Linda Tigges Special Collection, T424 I, T425 I, T483 I, T821 I, T732 I, T77 I, and T79 I (José Rodríguez).
84. SANM I, 291 (Antonio de Aguilera y Isasi).
85. SANM I, 678; SANM II, 86; and Kessell, Hendricks and Dodge, *Blood on the Boulders*, II: 958 n.59 (Antonio de Montoya I).
86. SANM I, 290, 292, 483 and 928; and SANM II, 83 (José Rodríguez).
87. SANM I, 155 and 929 (Antonio Montoya)
88. SANM I, 293; Kessell and Hendricks, *By Force of Arms*, 319 n.5 (Lorenzo de Madrid).
89. SANM I, 481 (Lorenzo de Madrid); and SNMRCA Linda Tigges, Special Collection, T481 I, and T1704 Series II (II).
90. SANM II, 100 (Diego Arias de Quirós).
91. SANM I, 155 and 481(Antonio de Montoya).
92. SANM I, 483 and 932; SANM II, 120; and SNMRCA, Linda Tigges Special Collection, T932 I (Juan de Ulibarrí).
93. SANM I, 158 and 735; and SANM II, 119 (Diego Arias de Quirós).
94. SANM II, 124 (Alonso Rael de Aguilar).
95. SANM I, 411 (Diego Arias de Quirós).
96. SANM I, 130, 134, 175, and 1028; and SANM II, 130 (Alonso Rael de Aguilar).
97. SANM I, 639; and SANM II, 130 (Antonio de Montoya).
98. SANM I, 157, 298, 299, 411, and 679 (Juan García de la Riva).
99. SANM I, 159; and SNMRCA, Linda Tigges Special Collection, T1972 I (Juan de Ulibarrí).
100. SANM I, 428, 640, 825 and 826 (Diego Arias de Quirós).
101. SANM I, 160, 489; and SNMRCA, Linda Tigges Special Collection, T489 I (Diego Arias de Quirós).
102. SANM I, 489 (Juan de Ulibarrí).
103. SANM I, 300 (Alfonso Rael de Aguilar).

104. SANM I, 429, 492, 737, 738; and SNMRCA, Linda Tigges Special Collection, T429 I (Diego Arias de Qurós).
105. SANM I, 301, 302, 432, 937; SANM II, 172; and SNMRCA, Linda Tigges Special Collection, T 491 I, T429 I, and 301 I (Alonso Rael de Aguilar).
106. SANM I, 491; and SNMRCA, Linda Tigges Special Collection, T491 I (Juan Páez Hurtado).
107. SANM I, 258, 303, 305, 411, 431, 491, 1110, 1136 and; and SNMRCA, Linda Tigges Special Collection, T491 I and T303 I (Juan Páez Hurtado).
108. SANM II, Reel 23 ff. 65–110 (Antonio Montoya).
109. SANM I, 2, 163, 164, 165, 258, 303, 403, 934, and 1110; and SNMRCA, Linda Tigges Special Collection, T1 I, T304, T258 I (Juan García de la Riva).
110. SANM I, 181, 495, 498, 1072 and 1073; and SNMRCA, Linda Tigges Special Collection, T498 I (Francisco Bueno de Bohórquez y Corcuera).
111. SANM I, 304; and SNMRCA, Linda Tigges Special Collection, T432 I (Juan García de la Riva).
112. SANM I, 1072 (Juan de Ulibarrí).
113. SANM I, 181, 233, 1074; and SNMRCA, Linda Tigges Special Collection, T233 I (Diego Arias de Quirós).
114. SANM I, 497, 832 and 1110; and SANM II, 225 (Juan Páez Hurtado).
115. SANM I, 434, 499, 831, 1030, 1110, and 1136 (Juan García de la Riva).
116. SANM, 219, 235 and 680 (Alonso Rael de Aguilar).
117. SANM I, 307, 308, 680 and 935 (Diego Arias de Quirós).
118. SANM I, 11, 79, 168, 234, 404, 502, 731, 833, and 1030; SANM II, 240 and 273 (Juan García de la Riva).
119. SANM I, 10, 80, 312; SANM II, 240 and SNMRCA, Linda Tigges Special Collection, T80 I, T312 I, and T10 I (Francisco Lorenzo de Casados).
120. SANM II, 240 (Salvador Montoya).
121. SANM I, 233, 936 (Diego Arias de Quirós).
122. SANM II, Reel 23, ff. 65-110 (Francisco Bueno de Bohórquez y Corcuera).
123. SANM I, 504 (Juan García de la Riva).
124. SANM I, 235 (Salvador Montoya).
125. SANM I, 170, 171, 438, 505, 716, 939, 835, 938 and 939; SANM II, 286; and SNMRCA, Linda Tigges Special Collection, T939 I and T716 I (Francisco Bueno de Bohórquez y Corucera).
126. SANM I, 742, 940 and 1075; SANM II, 304 (Francisco Bueno de Bohórquez y Corcuera).
127. SANM I, 506 and 717; SANM II 312; and SNMRCA, Linda Tigges Special Collection, T717 I and T13 I (Francisco Bueno de Bohórquez y Corcuera).
128. SANM II, 308 (Miguel Tenorio de Alba).
129. SANM I, 13, 81, 508, 743, 744; and SNMRCA, Linda Tigges Special Collection, T743 I and T744 I (Francisco Bueno de Bohórquez y Corcuera).
130. SANM II, Reel 23, ff, 65-110 (Juan de Pineda).
131. SANM I, 746 (Diego Arias de Quirós).
132. SANM I, 439, 508, 682, 1031, 1032, 1033, and 1034; SANM II, 317; and SNMRCA, Linda Tigges Special Collection, T682 I, T439 I, and T1033 I (Francisco Bueno de Bohórquez y Corcuera).

133. SANM I, 15 and 946 (Diego Arias de Quirós).
134. SANM I, 81, 509, 836, and 1206; AGN, Provincias Internas, t. 183, ff. 404-435 ; and SNMRCA, Linda Tigges Special Collection, T81 I (Francisco Bueno de Bohórquez y Corcuera).
135. SANM I, 1034; (Francisco Bueno de Bohórquez y Corcuera).
136. SANM I, 837; SANM II, 334; and Kessell, Hendricks and Dodge, *Blood on the Boulders*, 671 n.23 (Miguel José de la Vega y Coca).
137. SANM II, 340 (Francisco José de Casados).
138. SANM I, 405, 511, 837, 838, and 945; and SANM II, 336 (Miguel José de la Vega y Coca).
139. SANM II, 340 (Antonio Montoya).
140. SANM II, 340; Francisco Afán de Rivera, Certified Copy of Last Will and Testament, August 6, 1725, Santa Fe, Archivo Histórico de Parral, Roll 1725C, frs. 1893–99; and SNMRCA, Linda Tigges Special Collection, Ortiz Family Papers (OP) 1726S (Miguel Joséph de la Vega y Coca).
141. SANM I, 16, 17, 440, 512, 746, 947 and 1035; SANM II, 343a; and SNMRCA, Linda Tigges Special Collection, T15 I and T16 I (Diego Arias de Quirós).
142. SANM I, 442, 642, 747, 839, 840, and 947; and SANM II, 350 (Diego Arias de Quirós).
143. SANM I, 444 (Antonio Montoya).
144. SNMRCA, Linda Tigges Special Collection, T514 I and T331 I (Antonio Montoya).
145. SANM I, 175, 176, 443, 514, 748, 840, and 948; SANM II, 355a, and SNMRCA, Linda Tigges Special Collection, T748 I and T948 I (Diego Arias de Quirós).
146. SANM I, 1036, and 1037; SANM II, 351; and SNMRCA, Linda Tigges Special Collection, T1036 (Diego Arias de Quirós).
147. SANM I, 749; and SANM II, 358 (Diego Arias de Quirós).
148. SANM I, 758, 951, and 1220; SANM II, 373; and SNMRCA, Linda Tigges Special Collection, T758 I, T236 I (Antonio de Ulibarrí).
149. SANM I, 236, 357, 952, 953, 1105, 1219, 1220, 1224, 1227, 1228, and 1229; SANM II, 386; and SNMRCA, Linda Tigges Special Collection T1228 I, T1229 I, and T1105 I (Antoino de Ulibarrí).
150. SANM I, 953 (Francisco Guerrero).
151. SANM I, 521 and 522 (Antonio Montoya II).
152. SANM I, 19, 1230; SANM II, 400; and SANMRCA, Linda Tigges Special Collection, T953 I (Antonio de Ulibarrí).
153. SANM I, 1022 (Antonio de Ulibarrí).
154. Archives of the Archdiocese of Santa Fe (AASF), Roll 40, Santa Fe Burials, 1726–1834, January 22, 1736 (Antonio Montoya II).
155. SANM I, 1223 (Antonio de Ulibarrí).
156. SANM I, 1256; SANM II: 416; and SNMRCA, Linda Tigges Special Collection, T1256 I (Antonio de Ulibarrí).
157. Malcolm Ebright, *Land Grants and Lawsuits in Northern New Mexico* (Albuquerque: University of New Mexico Press, 1994), 97 (Juan García).
158. SANM I, 21, 22, 179, 327, 522, 756, 757, and 844; SANM II, 423; Kessell, Hendricks and Dodge, *Blood on the Boulders*, 1160 n.5 and 958 n.59; and SNMRCA, Linda Tigges

Special Collection, T179 IS, T444 I, and T521 I (Antonio Montoya).
159. SANM I: 756 (Juan Rodríguez).
160. SANM I, 19, 23, 88, 90, 91, 328, 329, 330, 331, 757, 844, 957, 958, 959, 960, 1042 and 1352; SANM II, 89; and SNMRCA, Linda Tigges Special Collection, T89 I, T90 I, T23 I, T91 I, T329 I, T330 I, T959 I, T960 I, and T23 I (Antonio Montoya).
161. SANM I, 526 and 1352 (Juan Páez Hurtado).
162. SANM I, 272, 525 (Antonio Montoya).
163. SNMRCA, Linda Tigges Special Collection, Delgado-Jenkins Papers (D-J) Miscellaneous (MISC) 1 (Juan Páez Hurtado).
164. SANM I, 24, 85, 87, 180, 239, 332, 333, 445, 627, 961, 962, 1043, 1078 and 1079 (Antonio de Ulibarrí).
165. SANM I, 647 (Francisco Guerrero).
166. SANM I, 26, 237, 964A, 964B, and 1043; and SNMRCA, Linda Tigges Special Collection, T964 I (Antonio de Ulibarrí).
167. SANM I, 93, 335, 336, 337, 762, 763, and 764 (Antonio de Ulibarrí).
168. SANM I, 31, 336, 337, 338, 339, 765, 966, and 1346 (Antonio de Ulibarrí).
169. SANM I, 181 and 337 (Antonio Ulibarrí).
170. SANM I, 1084 (José de Bustamante de Tagle)
171. SANM I, 648 (Antonio de Ulibarrí).
172. SANM I, 336, 345, 346, 969 and 1084; SANM II, 512 (José Bustamante y Tagle).
173. SANM II, 52 (Bernardo Bustamante y Tagle).
174. SANM I, 190, 242, 348, 349, 969 and 1084 (José de Bustamante y Tagle).
175. SANM I, 1079 (Antonio de Ulibarrí).
176. SANM I, 30, 446, 539, 970 and 974 (Manuel Gallegos).
177. SANM I, 243, 344, 351, 352 and 1084; and SNMRCA, Linda Tigges Special Collection, T351 I, T190 I, and T349 I (José de Bustamante y Tagle).
178. SANM I, 274 and 350; SANM II, 521; and SNMRCA, Linda Tigges Special Collection, T350 I (Manuel Gallegos).
179. SANM I, 98, 192, 770, 977, 978, and 1052; SNMRCA: Linda Tigges Special Collection, T977 I, T78 I, T192 I, T407 I, T549 I, and OP, 1754S MISC (Nicolás Ortiz).
180. SANM I, 447 (Manuel Gallegos).
181. SANM I, 31, 355, 407, 548, 549, 977, 978, and 1052; SNMRCA, Linda Tigges Special Collection, T977 I, T78 I, T192 I, T407 I, T549 I and OP 1754S MISC (Nicolás Ortiz).
182. SANM I, 1078 (Antonio de Ulibarrí).
183. SANM I, 194, 356, 408, 550, 551, 689, 772, 855, and 979 (Francisco Guerrero).
184. SANM I, 856, 857, 858, and 859 (Francisco Guerrero).
185. SANM I, 553, 980; and SANM II, 540 (Francisco Guerrero).
186. SANM I, 34, 554, 651, 859, 860, 861, and 982 (Francisco Guerrero).
187. SANM I, 35, 102, 357, 555, 854, 983, and 984 (Francisco Guerrero).
188. SANM I, 37, 336, 358, 570, 652, and 862; and SNMRCA, Linda Tigges Special Collection, 1758 SRCA, D-J pages 5 and 6, D-J MISC 1, D-J MISC 2W, and T772 I, T356 I, T408 I, T857 I, T980 I, T553 I, T34 I, T554 I, T861 I, T983 I, T854 I, D-J

1760S, T358 I, and O174 Santa Fe County Deeds (SFCD) (Francisco Guerrero).
189. Museum of New Mexico, History Library, Delgado Collection, transcribed by Edmundo R. Delgado (Felipe Tafoya).
190. SANM I, 358, 556 (Francisco Guerrero).
191. SANM I, 985 (Manuel Gallegos).
192. SANM I, 38, 104, 273, 274, 448, 775, 776, 986, 1055, and 1056; and SNMRCA, Linda Tigges Special Collection, T273 I, T104 I, T274 I, T1055 I, T1056 I, T106 I, T988 I (Manuel Gallegos).
193. SANM I, 106, 775, 863 and 988 (Manuel Gallegos).
194. SANM I, 987 (Carlos Fernández).
195. SANM I, 109, 244, 245, 449, 451, 593, 777 and 989 (Francisco Guerrero).
196. SANM I, 360, 452, 453, 644, 782, 860, 867, 868, 1023, and 1352; and SNMRCA, Linda Tigges Special Collection, T583 II, T575 I, T570 I, T867 I, T1190 II, T276 I, T578 I, T364 I (Francisco Guerrero).
197. SANM I, 280 (Tomás Antonio Sena).
198. SANM I, 247,571, 575, 784, 867, 868, 991, 992, 1023, and 1190 (Francisco Guerrero).
199. SANM I, 787 (Felipe Tafoya).
200. SANM I, 41, 42, 50, 112, 199, 276, 365, 574, 577, 578, 580, 583, 653, 693, 785 (Francisco Guerrero).
201. SANM I, 419 (Manuel García Pareja).
202. SANM I, 654 (Vicente Sena).
203. SANM I, 248, 569 and 871 (Francisco Guerrero).
204. SANM I, 248, 370, 455, 585, 586, 587, 787 and 1237; and SNMRCA, Linda Tigges Special Collection, T248 I, T181 I, T455 I, T586 I, T657 I, T278 I, 276 I, Pinart Collection 53:5M and 364 I, and Delgado Papers (DP) 1 (Felipe Tafoya).
205. SANM I, 44, 278, 367, 456, 457, 657, 788, and 995 (Felipe Tafoya).
206. SANM I, 249 (Manuel García Pareja).
207. SANM I, 115, 379, 790 (Felipe Tafoya).
208. SANM I, 459, 591, 794; and SNMRCA, Linda Tigges Special Collection, SNMRCA: Misc. 1771S, DP 2, DP 3, Twit: 65S, T267 I, T47 I, T119 I, T658 I (Manuel García Pareja).
209. SANM I, 696 (Felipe Tafoya).
210. SANM I, 45, 409, 459, 795, 796, 797, 879, 996, 1024, 1059 (Manuel García Pareja).
211. SANM I, 409 (Manuel Gallegos).
212. SANM I, 118, 267 (Manuel García Pareja).
213. SANM I, 47, 119, 594 (Manuel García Pereja).
214. SANM I, 866 (Francisco Guerrero).
215. SANM I, 798 and 799 (Manuel García Pareja).
216. SANM I, 249 (Manuel García Pareja).
217. SANM I, 658; and SNMRCA, Linda Tigges Special Collection, DP 11 (Francisco Guerrero).
218. SANM I, 1003 (Antonio José Ortiz).
219. SANM I, 364, 785 (Francisco Guerrero).

220. SNMRCA, Linda Tigges Special Collection, T370 I (Felipe Tafoya).
221. SANM I, 1259 (Antonio José Ortiz).
222. SANM I, 800; and SNMRCA, Linda Tigges Special Collection, SNMRCA:Misc. 1778S (José Miguel de la Pena).
223. SANM I, 427861; and SNMRCA, Linda Tigges Special Collection, DP 13S (Felipe Tafoya).
224. SNMRCA, Linda Tigges Special Collection, SRCA:Misc. 1778 (Antonio José Ortiz).
225. SANM I, 1144 (Antonio José Ortiz).
226. SNMRCA, Linda Tigges Special Collection, DP 20, DP 18B, Donaciiano Vigil Papers (DV)1784 II, T662 I, D 389 SFCD, T 280 I, V 120 SFCDS, T999 I, DP 11B, H 669 SFCD, DP 6, T374 I, A 90 SFCD, DP 4B, DP 5, DP 16B; SNMRCA:Misc.1794S, SNMRCA Hinojos Papers (HP) 1795A, HP 1795B, SNMRCA, Vigil papers Box 7 Folder 311; and for the year of 1793 see Museum of New Mexico, History Library, Delgado Collection, transcribed by Edmundo R. Delgado; Ebright, *Land Grants and Lawsuits of Northern New Mexico*, 175; and John L. Kessell, *Kiva, Cross and Crown: The Pecos Indians and New Mexico, 1540–1840* (Washington, DC: National Park Services, U. S. Department of the Interior, 1979), 353 (Antonio José Ortiz).
227. SANM I, 120, 280, 462, and 662 (Antonio José Ortiz).
228. SANM I, 562 (Manuel García Pareja).
229. SANM I, 881, 1261, and 1342; and SANM II, Misc. Documents, 1784 (Antonio José Ortiz).
230. SANM I, 1261 (José Miguel de la Peña).
231. SANM I, 597, 999 (Antonio José Ortiz).
232. SANM I, 1354 (José Campos Redondo).
233. See note 226 (Antonio José Ortiz).
234. SANM I, 572 (Manuel García Pareja).
235. SANM I, 121 (1789), 374 and 598 (1791) and 598 (1789); see also note 226 (Antonio José Ortiz)
236. SANM I, 465 (1794); see also note 226 (Antonio José Ortiz).
237. SNMRCA: Linda Tigges Special Collection, SNMRCA:Misc.1799 B, T124 I (José Miguel de la Peña).
238. SANM I, 124, 128, 604 and 1277; and SNMRCA, Linda Tigges Special Collection, SNMRCA:Misc. 1800AS, SNMRCA:Misc. 1800 (José Miguel de la Peña).
239. SANM I, 604 (Francisco Montoya).
240. SNMRCA, Linda Tigges Special Collection, E 394 SFCD (José Miguel de la Peña).
241. SANM II, 1602 (Juan Rafael Ortiz).
242. SNMRCA, Linda Tigges Special Collection, SNMRCA:Misc. 1803S (José Antonio Beita).
243. SANM I, 54, 125, 887; and SNMRCA, Linda Tigges Special Collection, DV 1803S (Pedro Bautista Pino).
244. SNMRCA, Linda Tigges Special Collection, OP 1804S (Manuel Delgado).
245. SNMRCA, Linda Tigges Special Collection, T665 I (José Francisco Ortiz).
246. SANM I, 604 (Francisco Montoya).
247. SNMRCA, Linda Tigges Special Collection, 471 SFCDS (Bartolomé Fernández).

248. SANM I, 663 (Manuel Delgado).
249. SANM I, 604 (Francisco Montoya).
250. SNMRCA, Linda Tigges Special Collection, V135 SFCDS (Juan Rafael Ortiz).
251. SANM I, 1003 (José Campos Redondo).
252. SNMRCA, Linda Tigges Special Collection, O 229 SFCD and SNMRCA, Ortiz Bustamante papers (Diego Montoya).
253. SNMRCA, Linda Tigges Special Collection, B 204 SFCD and Misc. Business Transactions 1791–1824 page 13 (José Miguel Tafoya).
254. SANM I, 888 (José Miguel Tafoya).
255. SNMRCA: Linda Tigges Special Collection, HP 1812 (José Miguel Trujillo).
256. SANM I, 1277 (Juan Cristóbal Vigil).
257. SANM I, 666; and SNMRCA, Linda Tigges Special Collection, T 171S, A-1 189 SFCD, T 666 I (Matías Ortiz).
258. SANM I, 666 and 703 (Matías Ortiz).
259. SANM I, 889; and SNMRCA, Linda Tigges Special Collection, A-1 189 SFCD, T666 I, T 293 , HP 1815A (Juan Estévan Pino).
260. SANM I, 602 (Matías Ortiz).
261. SANM I, 263 (José Francisco Baca).
262. SANM I, 707; SANM II, 2854; and SNMRCA, Linda Tigges Special Collection, T665 I (José Francisco Ortiz).
263. SANM I, 383 (José Francisco Ortiz).
264. SNMRCA, Linda Tigges Special Collection, AASF 1821M (Juan Rafael Ortiz).
265. SANM I, 58, 133, 616, 892, 893, and 894 (Pedro de Armendarís).
266. SANM I, 617 (José Francisco Baca).
267. SANM I, 670 (Santiago Abreu).
268. SANM I, 266 and 670; and SNMRCA, Linda Tigges Special Collection, CCRPTS. PRG #2 OPT. 9 Twit II: 1224, T670 I (José Ignacio Ortiz).
269. SANM I, 254 (José Francisco Baca).
270. SANM I, 470 (José María Martínez).
271. SANM I, 267, 469 and 724; and SNMRCA, Linda Tigges Special Collection, B 230 SFCD (Juan Vigil).
272. SANM I, 305, 810; and SNMRCA, Linda Tigges Special Collection, T810 I (Vicente Baca).
273. Article in the New Mexico Office of the State Historian by William H. Worth (Juan Bautista Vigil y Alarid).
274. According to research by Heather Devine, Antione Robidoux was an *alcalde* of Santa Fe in 1830. A primary source has not yet been consulted to confirm this assertion. See Heather Devine, *People Who Own Themselves: Aboriginal Ethnogenesis in a Canadian Family, 1660–1990* (Calgary: University of Calgary Press, 2004), 71. Also, Hugh M. Lewis indicates Antione Robidoux was involved in Santa Fe politics between 1830–1832 and was the first non-New Mexican to serve as an *alcalde* in Santa Fe, but he does indicate a year for which Robidoux was *alcalde*. See Hugh M. Lewis, *Robidoux Chronicles: Ethnohistory of the French American Fur Trade* (Victoria, B.C.: Trafford Publishing, 2006), 77 (Antoine Robidoux).

275. SANM I, 394 and 471 (José Ignacio Ortiz).
276. SANM I, 627; and SNMRCA, Linda Tigges Special Collection, D-J 1830 (Domingo Fernández).
277. SANM I, 145, 395, 627, and 903 (Pablo Montoya).
278. SANM I, 627 (Domingo Fernández).
279. SANM I, 627; and SNMRCA, Linda Tigges Special Collection, HP 1831 SRCA (Francisco Archibeque).
280. SANM I, 395 (Vicente Martínez).
281. SANM I, 144, 146, 147, 905, 906 and 907; and SNMRCA, Linda Tigges Special Collection, CCRPTS. PRG #2 OPT 9, Code C, T909 & T905 I (Juan García).
282. SANM I, 627 (Francisco Rascón).
283. SANM I, 144 (Pablo Montoya).
284. SANM I, 148, 674 and 1014 (Francisco Baca y Ortiz).
285. SANM I, 148 (Juan García).
286. SANM I, 712; SNMRCA, Linda Tigges Special Collection, J 48 SFCD (Manuel Antonio Sena).
287. SANM I, 222, 813; and SNMRCA, Linda Tigges Special Collection, B 601 SFCD (Santiago Abreu).
288. SANM I, 902 (Juan Gallegos).
289. SANM I, 67 and 1313; and SNMRCA, Linda Tigges Special Collection, HP 1835B (Manuel Dorotero Pino).
290. SNMRCA, Linda Tigges Special Collection, CCRTTS. PRG #2 OPT. 9–Twit: 77 (José Maria Ribera).
291. SANM I, 1313 (Francisco Ortiz y Delgado).
292. SANM I, 909; and SNMRCA, Linda Tigges Special Collection, T909 I (Francisco Trujillo).
293. SANM I, 675 and 713 (Agustín Durán).
294. SANM I, 1378 (Gregorio Sánchez).
295. SANM I, 713 (Don Juan Rafael Ortiz).
296. SNMRCA, Linda Tigges Special Collection, Donaciano Vigil Papers # 68 page 8 (Luis Robidoux).
297. SNMRCA, Linda Tigges Special Collection, T1216 I (Ramón Abreu).
298. SANM I, 713; and State of New Mexico Records Center and Archives, Donaciano Vigil Collection box 2 folder 53 and 54 (Francisco Ortiz y Delgado).
299. SANM I, 1216 (Felipe Sena).
300. SANM I, 472 (Juan García).
301. SANM I, 713 (Francisco Baca y Ortiz).
302. SANM I, 1316; and SNMRCA, Linda Tigges Special Collection, T1316C I, T1316A I, T1316B I (Manuel Doroteo Pino).
303. SANM I, 913 (Antonio Sena).
304. SANM I, 913; and SNMRCA, Linda Tigges Special Collection, T913A I (Felipe Sena).
305. Luis Robidoux is said to have been an *alcalde* of Santa Fe in 1739, but a primary source has not been consulted to confirm this assertion. See Lewis, *Robidoux Chronicles*, 105; Dan Thrapp, *Encyclopedia of Frontier Biography* (Lincoln: University of Nebraska Press,

1991), 3:105; and Devine, *People Who Own Themselves*, 71.
306. SANM I, 912 (Gaspar Ortiz).
307. Manuel Álvarez is said to have served as an *alcalde* in 1840, but a primary source has not been consulted to confirm this assertion. See Lewis, *Robidoux Chronicles*, 106 (Manuel Alvarez).
308. SANM I, 1016; and SNMRCA, Linda Tigges Special Collection, A 94 SFCDS (Domingo Fernández).
309. SANM I, 1317; and SNMRCA, Linda Tigges Special Collection, J 50 SFCD (Francisco Ortiz y Delgado).
310. SANM I, 1317 (Justo Pino).
311. SANM I, 1317 (Albino Chacón).
312. SANM I, 1317 (Simón Apodaca).
313. SANM I, 1317 (Antonio Montoya).
314. SANM I, 1317 (Pedro José Perea).
315. SANM I, 398; SNMRCA, Linda Tigges Special Collection, Twit: 112M (Antonio Sena).
316. SNMRCA, Linda Tigges Special Collection, HP 1843 SNMRCA (Francisco Ortiz y Delgado).
317. SANM I, 1233; and SNMRCA, Linda Tigges Special Collection, J 50 SFCD (Santiago Armijo).
318. SANM I, 1169 (Francisco Sena).
319. SANM I, 814 (José Francisco Baca y Terrus).
320. SANM I, 70, 71, 73, 74, 152, 633, 714, 715, 726, and 1169; and SNMRCA, Linda Tigges Special Collection, T152 I, T170 SFCD, T474 I, T726 I, Loretto Papers: 1B, C 170 SFCD (Tomás Ortiz).
321. SANM I, 1169 (Francisco Ortiz y Delgado).
322. SANM I, 475 (Santiago Flores).
323. SANM I, 919 (José Francisco Baca y Terrus).
324. SANM I, 154, 919; and SNMRCA, Linda Tigges Special Collection, S 139 SFCD, HP 1845BS (Francisco Ortiz y Delgado).
325. SANM I, 636 (José Miguel Romero).
326. SANM I, 154, 636 (Trinidad Barcelo).
327. SNMRCA, Linda Tigges Special Collection, A 87 SFCD (Henry Maidew).
328. SNMRCA, Linda Tigges Special Collection, A 81 SFCD (Rufus Bench).
329. SNMRCA: Linda Tigges Special Collection, A 96 SFCD, B 298 SFCD (José Francisco Sena).
330. Court Case 177 US 104, 120, Santa Fe, December 31, 1845 in the footnotes (Lorenzo Martín).
331. SNMRCA, Linda Tigges Special Collection, B 298 SFCD (José Francisco Sena).
332. SNMRCA, Linda Tigges Special Collection, B 113 SFCD (Francis A. Cunningham).
333. SNMRCA, Linda Tigges Special Collection, B 314 SFCDS (Jesús María Baca y Salazar).
334. The names of the mayors of the City of Santa Fe for the years 1891 to the present day are accounted for in City records, mainly from City Council minutes, and were provided by the City of Santa Fe for use in this compilation.

INDEX

A

Abert, J.W., 15, 36, 281–282
Abó, 209–210
Abreu, Ramón, 273, 425
Abreu, Santiago, 42, 272, 274; as *alcalde*, 423, 424
acequia madre, 90, 141, 154, 167
acequias, 136
Acoma Pueblo, 53; and revolt of 1696, 232
African American community in Santa Fe, 343–344
Agua Fria village, 42–43
Aguilar, Nicolás de, 184
Aguilera, Antonio de, 80
Aguilera y Isasi, Antonio de, 412, 413
Aguilera y Rocha, Teresa, 30; accusation of Jewish practice, 180, 194, 207; and the Inquisition, 179–208
Alamo -- Chavez and Nieto land grant, 95
Alarid, Canuto, 347
Alarid, Jesus María, 274
Alarid, Jóse Rafael, 285–286
Alarid, María Francisca, 285
Alarid, Michael J., 31–32, 301–316, 431
Albuquerque, 67, 140
alcaldes ordinarios, 33, 124, 403–428
Alencaster, Real, 244
Alvarez, Manuel, 284, 287
Anaya, Cristóbal de, 184
Anaya, Joseph de, 154–155
Anaya Almazán family and the *cabildo de Santa Fe*, 124
Anaya Almazán, Francisco de, 124, 225, 229, 235–236; as *alcalde ordinario*, 410, 412; land grant, 82–83, 95, 259–260; and Pecos Pueblo, 230
Anderson, Oliver P., 311
Andrews, Frank, 428
Andrews, William H. "Bull", 350
Ángeles, Beatríz de los, 52–53
Apache Indians, 36, 40, 47, 112, 140; alliances with Spanish, 243; raids on pueblos, 182, 209–210, 235; warfare with Spanish, 47, 108, 238–240, 242
Apodaca, Juana, 141
Apodaca, Simón, 425
Aragón, Francisco [López] de, 124
Archibeque, Francisco, 424
archival records, 65, 68, 130; stored in the *casas reales*, 111
Archivo General de Indias, Guadalajara, 214
Archivo General de Indias, Seville, Spain, 77, 97, 99, 117, 121
Archuleta, Asencio de, 409
Archuleta, Juan Antonio, 95
Archuleta, Juan José, 95
Archuleta, Salvador de, 157
Archuleta and Gonzales Land Grant, 95
Argüello Carvajal, Francisco de, 123
Arias de Quirós, Diego, 90, 138, 157; as *alcalde ordinario* and *alcalde mayor*, 406, 412–416; and *Ciénega de Santa Fe*, 68–69, 154, 259, 261; land grant, 95
Armendáriz, Pedro de, 423
Armenta, Luis, 95
Armijo, Antonio, 95
Armijo, Manuel, 31, 268, 272–275, 279, 284, 285; plot to assassinate, 287–288
Armijo, Perfecto, 358
Armijo, Santiago, 425
Armijo, Vizente, 155
Arroyo de las Máscaras, 61
Artiaga, Pedro de, 194, 201–203
asamblea territorial, 20
Atanasio Domínguez, Francisco, 42–43, 91, 155–156, 158, 200

525

Atchison, Topeka and Santa Fe Railroad, 341, 342, 349–350, 358, 362
Atkinson, Henry, 259–260
Ayeta, Francisco de, 30, 209–216

B

Baca, Antonio, 133, 135, 139, 410
Baca, Bartolomé, 287
Baca, Gerónima, 139
Baca, José Francisco, 423
Baca, Vicente, 423
Baca y Ortiz, Francisco, 424, 425
Baca y Ortiz, José Francisco, 408–409
Baca y Salazar, Jesús María, 426
Baca y Terrus, José Francisco, 425, 426
Baker, Grafton, 311
Balón, Francisco "Pancho", 52, 122, 171
Bancroft, Hubert Howe, 22–23, 97
Bandelier, Adolph, 61, 77, 97, 107; and Oldest House, 58, *60*
Barba Martín, Alonso, 118
Barcelo, Trinidad, 426
Barker, Charles B., 428
Barreda, Domingo de la, 90
barrio, 166–167
Barrio de Analco, 29, 54, 57, 65, 88–90, 126–127, 132, 163–178, *165*, *166*, *175*, *177*; governance, 175–176; and San Miguel Chapel, 147–156; settlement for Mexican Indians, 67–68, 101–102; and Tlaxcalan Indians, 49, 51
Barrio de Analco, Guadalajara, 168
Barrio de San Francisco, 29, 147–148
Bartlett, Cora, 344
Bartlett, Ed, 343, 344
Bas Gonzales, Antonia, 138
Bautista de Anza, Juan, 244, *245*, 263
Bautista de Zaragoza, Juan, 186
Bautista Pino, Pedro, 422
Becker, Beverly, 25–26
Beita, José Antonio, 422
Benavides, Alonso de, 52–53, 100, 114, 122, 132, 149–151, 164; and *La Conquistadora*, 127; and María Coronel y Arana, 186; and Mexican Indians, 170–171
Bench, Rufus, 426
Bent, Charles, 287–288

Bernal, Catalina, 199–200
Bernal, Pascuala, 118
Bernalillo, 140
Bloom, Lansing B., 23, 76–77, 98, 99, 107
Bohórquez, Isabel de, 118
Bohórquez y Corcuera, Francisco Bueno de, 406, 414, 415
Bolsas, Antonio, 61, 226, 227
Bolt, William H., 312
Bolton, Herbert E., 77
Bowden, J.J., 67, 83–84
Brady, James C., 310
Brito, Agustín, 171
Brito, Cristobal, 52–53
Brito, Diego, 155, 171, 174
Brito, Juan de Leon, 95
Broeske, Fritz, 149, 156
Brooks, James, 87
Brown, Robert O., 380–381, 381, 382
Brown, William Henry, 165, 166
Bruns, Earl Harvey, 397
Bruns Army Hospital, 33, 383–384, 397–401
Bruns Army Hospital annex, 399
Bursum, Holm O., 332–333
Bustamante de Tagle, José de, 417, 418
Bustamente expedition (Governor), 240, 243
Bynner, Witter, 379–380

C

cabildo de Santa Fe, 20–22, 68–69, 124, 128, 403–428
Caja de Rio land grant, 248, 250, 257, 260
Camino Real de Tierra Adentro, 21, 30, 135, 140
Campo Redondo, José, 422
Cañada Ancha, 95
Cañada de los Alamos land grant, 95
Cárdenas, Juan de, 206
Carlos II, (king), 210–213
Casados, Francisco José de, 415
Casados, Francisco Lorenzo de, 408, 414
casas reales, 45, 134
Caso Barahona, Juan del, 169–170
Cassidy, Gerald, 379
Castaño de Sosa, Gaspar, 52, 67

Castro, Miguel, 289–290
Catholic Church, 115–116, 126–127; conversion efforts, 112, 131
Catron, Thomas B., 73, 74, 345, 427; and funding for capitol building and penitentiary, 341; and Santa Fe Ring, 327; and school system, 355–356; and smallpox, 348
Chacón, Albino, 425
Chacón, Fernando, 408
Chacon Medina Salazar y Villaseñor, José, 141, 153, 155–156
Chamiso, Juan, 126–127, 171, 180
Chamiso Arroyo - Marquez and Padilla land grant, 95
Chapman, Kenneth, 377
Chávez, Amado, 355–356, 427
Chávez, Angélico, 157, 283–284
Chávez, David, Jr., 428
Chavez, Francisco, 347
Chávez, Francisco Javier, 285
Chavez, Ireneo L., 99
Chávez, Mariano, 274
Chávez, Thomas E., 14, 25–26, 101, 284
Chicago, Rock Island & Pacific Railroad, 350–351
Chicago & Santa Fe Smelter, 341
Chililí, 209–210
Chiriños Martínez de Cervantes, Juan Manuel, 153
Chistoe, Felipe, 232, 235
Chisum, John, 321–322
chocolate, 125, 180, 199, 229
Ciénega de Santa Fe, 68–69, 72–73, 136, 141; and horse pasture, 257–258, 260–261
Cieneguilla, 257, 259–261
Ciudad Juárez, Mexico, 147
clay, 40
Cleveland, Grover, 327, 329
Closson, Charles C., 427
Cochiti Pueblo, 42, 53; and reconquest, 228, 230; and revolt of 1696, 231–232
Codallos y Rabel, Joaquin, 253, 259
College of Christian Brothers, 401
Comanche Indians, 238–240
Concha, Fernando de, 244
Coronel y Arana, María, 186

Coss, David, 428
Craycraft, Aaron B., 353
crime in Territorial Period Santa Fe, 301–316
Crisostome, Juana, 174
Cristóbal Nieto Grant, 65, 77–86, 95
Croix, Teodoro, 263
Cruz, Agustín de la, 155
Cruzat y Gongóra campaign, 240
crypto-Jews, 180, 194, 207
Cuervo y Valdes, Francisco, 49, 140, 258–259; warfare with Indians, 239–240
Cunningham, Francis A., 426
Curry, George, 366
Cutting, Bronson, 380

D

Daly, Richard, 389
Dargan, Marion, 320–321
Davies, Edward R., 427
Davis, Theodore R., 304
Davis, W.W.H., 37, 44, 57–58
Dawson, William, 321–322
De Marco, Barbara, 30, 209–217, 432
Dean, Robert K., 32, 317–334, 431
Delgado, Larry A., 428
Delgado, Manuel, 255–256, 422
Delgado, Pedro, 427
Dendahl, Henry, 357
Denver & Rio Grande Railroad, 342, 349–350
Diego el Mexicano, 155, 174
Díez, José, 223, 231–232
Dios Peña, Juan de, 257
Domingo de Mendoza, Gaspar, 250
Domínguez, Antonio, 95
Domínguez, Joseph, 143
Domínguez, Juana, 139
Domínguez, Manuel, 143
Domínguez de Mendoza, Antonio (Tomé), 139, 200–201, 410
Domínguez de Mendoza, Juan, 200–201, 410, 411
Dorman, Harry H., 378
Doroteo Pino, Manuel, 424, 425
Dorsey, Stephen W., 327
Durán, Agustín, 424

Duran, José, 95
Dúran, Nicolás and Maria, 125
Durán de Chaves, Pedro, 118
Durán de Chavez, Isabel, 200
Durán y Chávez, Fernando, I, 410
Durango, Mexico, 169

E
Easley, Charles F., 427
Ebright, Malcolm, 28, 432
education in New Mexico, 271, 273, 355
El Alamo, 257, 260–261
El Pino Grant, 78, 82–85, *84*, 88
El Zepe, 230
Elkins, Stephen B., 344; and Santa Fe Ring, 327
Ellis, Bruce T., 133, 155
Encinas, Ramon, 58
encomiendas, 82, 101, 119, 122, 134, 164, 183
Escarramad, Juan de, 409
Escarramán, Julián de, 186
Escobar, Francisco de, 115
Esquibel, José Antonio, 14, 27, 28–29, 33, 88, 109–128, 403–428, 432
Esquibel, Juan José, 273
Eulate, Juan de, 149, 178
Exchange Hotel, *303–304*

F
fandangos, 311–313
Faraón Apaches, 235, 238–240, 242
Farfán, Francisco, 152–153
Federal Court House, 75
Fernández, Bartolomé, 422
Fernández, Carlos, 418
Fernández, Domingo, 257, 424, 425
Fernandez de Córdoba y Cardona, Diego, 122
Fiesta de Santa Fe, 144, 154, 236
Flipper, Henry, 72
Flores, Juan Antonio, 95
Flores, Santiago, 425
Flores de Vergara, Agustín, 153, 155, 175–176
Flores Mogollón, Juan Ignacio, 69, 72–73, 141, 259, 261, 406

Fort Marcy, 75, 344, 365–366
Franciscan friars, 112, 115, 122, 126–127, 179–180; deaths in Indian raids, 210; and revolt of 1696, 233
Francisco de Anaya Almazan Grant, 82–83
Freitas, Nicolás de, 184, 188, 206
Frost, Max, 32, 317–334, *323–324*, *340*, 356–357; charged with registering fradulent land claim, 327–328; and city politics, 345–346; and gambling and prohibition, 347–348; and health seekers, 367, 368; and irrigation movement, 354–355; and land grant claims, 325–328; and marriage, 328; and Masonic and Odd Fellows Lodges, 319, 322, 333; and railroads in Santa Fe, 350; and Santa Fe New Mexican, 318–321, 329–333, 334, 339–342; and Santa Fe Ring, 318–319, 326–328; and Signal Corps, 320–321; and statehood, 319, 320, 328, 330–333; and territorial militia and National Guard, 322
Fuentes, Cristobal, 255
Fuller, Thomas C., 73
Fulweiler, Victoria, 365

G
Galisteo Basin, 39
Galisteo Pueblo, 39, 42, 257–258; Indian laborers, 180
Gallegos, Albert J., 33, 403–428, 432–433
Gallegos, Diego, 250–251
Gallegos, Juan, 424
Gallegos, Manuel, 417–418
Galvan, Juana, 87
Gálvez (Viceroy), 263
Gamboa, Petrona de, 205, 206
Garate, Donald, 243
Garcia, Evans, 400
Garcia, Francisco, 58
García, Joseph, 311
García, Juan, 82, 408, 416, 424, 425
Garcia, Lazaro, 82
Garcia, Marcelino, 354
García de la Riva, Juan, 48; as *alcalde ordinario*, 406, 414
García de San Francisco, (Fray), 184, 206
García Holgado, Alvaro, 124

García Pareja, Manuel, 419, 420
Genízaros, 176, 178
Gibson, Adelbert R., 352–353, 355, 367, 427
Giffords, Gloria, 148
Gildersleeve, Charles H., 327
Girón de Tejeda, Tomas, 154
Gómez, Francisco, 118, 125, 410
Gomez, Manuel, 54–55
Gómez Robledo, Francisco, 124–125, 184, 410, 411
Gongora, Cristóbal, 155
Gonzales, José, 274–275
Gonzales, Salvador, 95
Gonzales Lobon, Juan, 43–44
González, Andrés, 153, 158–159
González, Antonia, 188
González, George A., 428
González, Gerald T.E., 30, 179–208, 433
González, Sebastian, 186
González Bernal, Diego, 185, 186
González Bernal, Juan, 186
González Lobón, Diego, 185
Gould, George, 350
Gran Quivira, 113
Gregg, Josiah, 270–271, 273–274, 361
Griego, Juan, 114, 118, 197–199
Griego, Juana, 138
Griego, María, 95, 138
Guadalajara, Jalisco, 168
Guadalajara family and the *cabildo de Santa Fe*, 124
Guerrero, Francisco, 406, 416–420
Gutiérrez, Isabel, 80
Gutiérrez, Jusepe, 169–170
Gutiérrez de Umaña, Antonio, 170

H

Hacienda del Alamo, 95
Hackett, Charles W., 77
Hagerman, Herbert J., 331
Hallenbeck, Cleve, 152, 159, 245
Hammond, George P., 77, 98–99, 100
Hano Village, *41*, 41
Harrington, J.P., 38–39, 61
Henderson, Alice Corbin, 379
Henderson, William Penhallow, 379

Hermita de Nuestra Señora, 136
Herrera, Miguel de, 142–143, 154, 158
Hewett, Edgar L., 77, 377–378
Hidalgo, Miguel, 284, 285, 292
Hodge, Frederick W., 77, 100
Hoffman, Edward, 310
Hollis, Pat, 428
Hopewell, Willard S., 350, 355
Hopi Pueblo, 40–41; and revolt of 1696, 232, 234; warfare with Spanish, 239–240, 242
Hordes, Stanley M., 29, 129–145, 433
horse herds and the colonists, 238, 259, 261–262
horse herds and the presidio, 238–264
horses and Native Americans, 237–239, 243
Hudson, J.R., 427
Hurtado, Juan Páez, 152, 154, 235
Hurtado, Juana, 78
Huss, Paul, 428

I

Indian slaves, 182
Inés, Doña, 52, 62, 118
Inquisition, 90, 179–208; process, 186–188
Inquisition headquarters in Mexico City, *190*, *191*, *192*, *193*
instructions for founding Villa de Santa Fe, 13, 22, 77, 115–116, *117*, *121*, 131–132, 144
irrigation movement, 354–355
Isleta Pueblo, 53
Ivey, James E., 28, 97–107, 148, 433

J

Jackson, William Henry, 175
Jaffa, Nathan, 427
Japanese Internment Camp, 33, 392–393, 395–397, 400–401
Jaramillo, Debbie, 428
Javier, Francisco, 220
Jemez Pueblo, 53, 54; and reconquest, 228–230; and revolt of 1696, 233
Jesus de Agreda, María, 186
Jicarilla Apaches, 36, 243
Jiménez, Lázaro, 115
John, Elizabeth, 239

Johnson, Henry, 343
Jorge, Isabel, 95
Jorge de Bela, Ysabel, 133, 139
Jornado del Muerto land grant, 292–293
Julian, George W., 325–327
Jumanas, 209–210
Jurado, Joseph, 188

K

Kachina, 44–47, *46*
Kearny, Stephen Watts, 31, 275, 277, 279; proclamation, 295–296
Kearny Code, 302, 308
Keres Indians, 37–38
Kerr, J.W., 380–381
Kessell, John L., 26–27, 30, 157, 219–236, 433
Kidder, Alfred V., 77
kivas, 55–56, *224*
Klah, Hasteen, 40
Kuapoge, 40, 67
Kubler, George, 148, 151, 155

L

La Cienega, 37–38
La Cieneguilla de Cochiti, 230
La Conquistadora, 127, 158, 225
La Conquistadora Chapel, 29, 147, 157–160, *159*
La Gotera land grant, 257
La Majada de Dominguez land grant, 248, 254–255, 257, 260
la parroquia, 132, 138, 144
Laguna Pueblo, 53, 54
Lamar, Howard, 320
Lamar, Mirabeau Bonaparte, 288
Lamy, Jean Baptiste, 355, 363
Lamy, Juan B., 363
land grants, 133, 138, 139–140, 325–328
Las Bocas, 248–249, 253–254, 257, 260
Laughlin, Ruth, 359
Laws of the Indies. *see* Reales Ordenanzas
Lee, Louis, 288
Lenoia, Maria Antonia, 310
Leon, Juan de, 155
Leon Brito, Juan de, 52, 95
Levine, Frances, 30, 179–208, 434

Lewis, Janet, 379
Lewis, Nancy Owen, 32, 361–382, 434
Leyba, José de, 95
Leyva, Pedro de, 410
Limpia Concepción de Nuestra Señora, 120, 127
Lincoln Avenue, 141, 144
Lindsey, Washington E., 380
López, Celso, 427
Lopez, Martín, 51
López, Pedro, 155
López de Mendizábal, Bernardo, 30, 44–46, 124, 125, 126; and the Inquisition, 179–208
López de Santa Anna, Antonio, 268–269, 275
López del Castillo, Diego, 410
López Gallardo, Pedro, 153, 158–159
López Holguin, Juan, 118
López Sambrano, Diego, 220
Lorenzo de Medina, Juan, 159
Loretto Chapel, *165*
Los Cerrillos land grant, 248, 255–256, 257, 260
Los Jumanos, 113
Lovato, Juan Cayetano, 95
Lovato, Roque, 95; land grant, 70
Lucas, José, 125
Lucero, José Antonio, 95
Lucero de Godoy, Antonio, 124, 412–413
Lucero de Godoy family and the *cabildo de Santa Fe*, 124
Lucero de Godoy, Juan, 43, 95, 124, 411
Lucero de Godoy, Pedro, 124, 185, 411
Lujan, Ana, 95
Lujan, Francisco, 255
Luján, Manuel, Sr., 394, 400, 428
Luján, Miguel, 224, 226

M

Madrid, Francisco de, 118, 124, 410
Madrid, Francisco de, II, 410
Madrid, Lorenzo de, 48, 411, 412, 413
Madrid, Roque de, 43, 78, 90, 228; land grant, 95; and revolt of 1696, 232; warfare with Indians, 240, 242

Madrid family and the *cabildo de Santa Fe*, 124
Maes and Gallegos land grant, 95
Maese, Catarina, 95
Maese, Francisca, 80
Maese, Luis, 95
Maggs Bros. Ltd., 24, 26, 101
Maidew, Henry, 426
Malacate, Antonio, 222–223, 228, 230
Mang, Fred E., Jr., 224
Manifest Destiny, 281, 317, 319, 333
Manrique, José, 256
Manso, Juan, 55, 183–184, 188, 197
Manso Indians, 54
Manuel, Salvador, 155
Manzano, N.M., 282
Maragua land grant, 248–249, 256–257, 260
Marcos, Diego, 230
Marín del Valle, Francisco Antonio, 406
Marqués de Peñuela, Governor, 141
Márquez, Antonia, 139
Márquez, Francisco, 124
Martín, Domingo, 95
Martin, Hernando, 48
Martín, Lorenzo, 426
Martín Serrano, Hernán, 114, 118, 125
Martínez, Antonio, 283–284
Martínez, Félix, 48, 53, 55, 140–142, 240, 242–243
Martínez, José María, 423
Martinez, Pedro, 58
Martínez, Valerie, 35, 434
Martínez, Vicente, 424
Martínez de Montoya, Juan, 13–15, 37, 100–103; and Apache Indians, 47; appointed as governor, 14, 115; certificate of services, 14, 24–28, 88–91, 113–114
Masonic Lodge, 318, 319, 322, 333
Matsu, James, 392
Mauzy, Wayne, 380
Mayes, C.M., 376
Maynez, Alberto, 54, 258
mayors of Santa Fe, 33
McAfee, Larry B., 397
McConvery, James C., 428
McCutcheon, John T., 177

McGeagh, Robert, 24, 25
McKibben, Dorothy, 380
McNitt, Frank, 263–264
Meany, Edward Willcocks, 364–365
Medina, Diego de, 139
Medina, Juan Lorenzo de, 157
Medón de Casaus, Roque, 410
Meem, John Gaw, 378–379
Melgarejo, Diego de, 202–204
Mendinueta (Governor), 263
Mendoza campaign, 240
Mera, Frank, 355, 368–371, 375, 379, 382
Mera, H.P., 355, 368–369
Merritt, 315–316
Mestas, Juan de, 125
Mexican Indians, 29, 49–52, 65, 67–68, 76, 90, 122–123; in Barrio de Analco, 54–55, 101–102, 126, 132, 163–164, 167–168; and Pueblo Revolt, 171–173
Mexican Republic rule of New Mexico, 268–277; and loyalty of New Mexicans, 280–281
Mexicas, 176–177
Meyers, Datus, 379
Miera de Pacheco map, 250–251
Mild, Christian, 312, 315
Miles, John E., 386, 389–391, 393, 395
military garrison in Santa Fe, 112–114
Mitchell, F.H., 367
Mocho, Jill, 302
Montaño, Louis R., 428
Montoya, Andrés, 82, 157
Montoya, Antonio, 425
Montoya, Antonio de, I, 406, 412–414
Montoya, Antonio, II, 415–417
Montoya, Diego, 412, 422
Montoya, Francisco, 421, 422
Montoya, Pablo, 424
Montoya, Salvador, 48, 55, 58, 154; as *alcalde ordinario*, 408, 414, 415
Montoya, Tony, 400
Moraga, Antonia de, 55, 259
Morán, Matías, 171
Moreno, Juan José, 240–241, 248–250, 253, 257, 259–261
Morley, Sylvanus, 378
Mower, Horace, 311

Murphy, Leo, 428
Murray, W.W., 73–74
Museum of New Mexico, 356, 377
Musgrave, Arthur, 379

N

Nambe Pueblo, 53
Naranjo, Lucas, 233–234
National Guard Armory, 385
National Irrigation Congress, 354
Native Americans and Santa Fe, 28, 37–62
Navajo Indians, 40, 47, 112, 140; and reconquest, 228–229; warfare with Spanish, 108, 238–240
New Mexican, 318–321, 329–333, 334; and Progressive issues, 341–343; and Santa Fe building style, 363
New Mexico Bureau of Immigration, 329, 340, 354, 380; and tuberculosis, 361, 363, 376
New Mexico Central Railway, 350–353, *352*, 355
New Mexico Historical Society, 353
New Mexico Horticulture Society, 354
New Mexico National Guard, 33, 383–400
New Mexico National Guard 200th Coast Artillery Antiaircraft Regiment, 383, 386–395, 398–401
New Mexico State Legislature, 20
New Mexico State Records Center, 130
New Mexico statehood, 328, 330–333
New Mexico Territorial Legislature, 20
Newlands Reclamation Act, 354–355
Nieto, Cristóbal, 77–80, *81*; land grant, 65, 77–86, 95
Nieto, Dawn, *81*, 86–87
Nieto, Francisco, 79, 80–83, *81*, 84–85
Nieto, Juan, 83–85, *87*
Nieto, Lucía, 79, 80, *81*, 83, 85
Nieto, María [Magdalena], 79, 80, 85
Nieto, Petrona, 79, *81*
Nieto, Simón, 79, 80–81, *82*, 85
Nieto genealogy, *81*
Noble, David Grant, 27
Noriega, Miguel de, 202–204
Nuestra Señora de Guadalupe Church, 147, 150–151

Nusbaum, Jesse L., 370, 381

O

Odd Fellows Lodge, 322
Ogama, Magdalena de, 55, 154, 174
Ogapoge, 40, 67
Ohkay Owingeh Pueblo, 78–79, 90, 112, 131
Ojeda, Bartolomé de, 128, 222–223, 228–229, 235; and revolt of 1696, 232
Olavidé y Micheleña, Enrique de, 248–250, 253, 261–263; warfare with Indians, 240–241
Oldest House, 57–60, *59*, *60*
Olguín, Isabel, 139
Olguín, Salvador, 80, 85
Oñate, Cristóbal de, 14, 101–102, 115
Oñate, Juan de, 13–15, 22–27, 67, 131; accusations against, 115; established *cabildo*, 20; and founding of Santa Fe, 97, 98–101, 112, 114; and Mexican Indians, 169–170; and Tlaxcalan Indians, 50
Ordinances of 1573. *see* Reales Ordenanzas
Ordóñez, Isidro de, 115, 119, 122, 148
Ortiz, Alfredo, 428
Ortiz, Antonio, 358
Ortiz, Antonio José, 406, 420, 421
Ortiz, Francisco, 256
Ortiz, Frank S., 428
Ortiz, Gaspar, 425
Ortiz, José Francisco, 422, 423
Ortiz, José Ignacio, 423, 424
Ortiz, Juan Rafael, 422, 423, 424
Ortiz, Matías, 422, 423
Ortiz, Nicolás, 418
Ortiz, Ramón, 289–290
Ortiz, Tomás, 425
Ortiz Niño Ladrón de Guevara, Nicolás, 140, 250
Ortiz y Alarid, Gaspar, 70, 106
Ortiz y Delgado, Francisco, 409, 424–426
Ortiz y Pino, Mela, 399
Otermín, Antonio de, 134–135, 211, 213; and Pueblo Revolt, 171–172; reconquest attempt, 173
Otero, Miguel Antonio, 326–327, 328, 371
Otero, Miguel, Jr., 380

P

Pacheco, Esquipula, 58
Pacheco, Felipe, 95
Pacheco, Francisco, 229
Pacheco, Geronimo, 79, 90
Pacheco, Josefa, 79, 80–83, *81*, 85, 87–88
Pacheco, Joseph, 95
Pacheco, María, 205
Pacheco, Sebastiana, 79, *81*
Pacheco Nieto, Petrona, 77–83, *81*, 90
Padilla, Maria Rita, 58, 82
Padilla land grant, 95
Páez Hurtado, Juan, 142, 154, 231, 259; as *alcalde ordinario*, 406, 414, 417; warfare with Indians, 240, 242
Pain, Maud, 328
Palace Avenue, 141
Palace of the Governors, *57*, 67, 104, 111, 120, 126, 144; condition, 121, 141, 142; construction and remodeling, 180; and Museum of New Mexico, 356, 378; and New Mexico Historical Society, 353, 357; and Pueblo Revolt, 56, 136, 223
Papin, Alexander, 308
Parkhurst, T. Harmon, 352
Parsons, Sheldon, 379
Patania, Frank, 380
Payo de Rivera (archbishop and viceroy), 211–212
Pecos National Historical Park, *224*
Pecos Pueblo, 258; and reconquest, 137, 226, 228, 230; work on San Miguel Chapel, 155
Peinado, Alonso de, 132
Peláez, Jacinto, 254
Peña, José Miguel de la, 420–422
Peñalosa Briceño y Berdugo, Diego Dionisio de, 179, 181, 183–185, 197
Peñuela, Marquis de la, 141, 153, 155–156
Peralta, Pedro de, 22–27, 67, 77, 90; excommunicated by Fray Ordóñez, 148; and founding of Santa Fe, 13–15, 97, 99–103, 107, 131–132, 133–134; as governor, 102, 115–116, 118, 119, 122; and Mexican Indians, 170
Perea, Jacinto, 79, 80, 82–83, 87–88
Perea, Pedro José, 425

Pérez, Albino, 31, 42, 267–277
Pérez, Demetrio, 60–61, 267
Pérez, Gaspar, 124
Pérez de Bustillo, Catalina, 118
Pérez de Bustillo, Yumar, 133
Pérez Granillo, Francisco, 200–201, 409
Peters, LeRoy, 372, 375, 382
Pick, Samuel W., 428
Picuris Pueblo, 53; and revolt of 1696, 233, 234
Pindi ruin, 43
Pineda, Juan de, 415
Pino, Juan Estevan, 272, 422
Pino, Justo, 425
Pino, Manuel Doroteo, 424, 425
Pino, Pedro Bautista, 422
Piro Indians, 54
Plan de Iguala of 1821, 284
plaza of Santa Fe, 29, 120, 129–145, *145*, *357*; reconstruction after Pueblo Revolt, 137–139
poetry, 35
Pojoaque Pueblo, 53
Popé, 61, 134
Pope, William H., 74
Posada, Alonso de, 184, 188
Posadas, Alonso de, 97–98
presidio of Santa Fe, 209–216, 237–264
Prince, L. Bradford, 77, 353–354, 357; and irrigation movement, 354–355
Proudfit, James K., 70, 106
Pueblo Blanco, 39
Pueblo Colorado, 39
Pueblo dances, 44–47
Pueblo Indians, 37–38; and death of Albino Pérez, 268, 273–274; and *encomiendas*, 119, 122, 180–181; and reconquest, 219–234; relations with Spanish, 164, 243; religious practices, 180, 184; social and economic relations with Spanish, 111–112, 119–120, 123, 127–128
Pueblo Revolt of 1680, 134–137, 171–173, 213
Pueblo Revolt of 1696, 231–234
Pueblo Shé, 39
Purdy, James, 70, 73, 75, 77, 82–85

Q

Quaking leaf water, 38
Quarái, 209–210
Quasin, Francisco, 125
Quintana, Luis de, 220
Quirós, Cristóbal de, 118

R

Rael, Juan del, 170
Rael, Pablo, 309
Rael de Aguilar Alfonso; land grant, 95
Rael de Aguilar, Alonso, 255, 412, 413, 414
railroads, 341, 342, 349–353
Ramírez, Alonso, 124, 405
Ramírez, Juan, 181–182, 184, 185, 206
Ramírez, Nicolás, 155
Ramírez de Salazar, Francisco, 411
Rascón, Francisco, 424
Read, Benjamin M., 23, 357
Reales Ordenanzas, 103, 130–131, 132–134, 144, 148
Rebellion of 1837, 273, 274, 284
Rebellion of 1847, 284–285
reconquest of Santa Fe, 136–137
Recopilación de Leyes de los Reyes de las Indias, 70, 72, 73–75
Redondo, José Campo, 422
Reed, Joseph R., 73
Reed, Judy, 33, 383–401, 434
Rencher, Abraham, 307–308
Rey, Agapito, 100
Reynolds, Matthew, 72
Ribera, Ana de, 153
Ribera, José Maria, 424
Rice, L.G., 371–373
Riley, Carroll, 101
Río Chiquito, 133
Rios, Juan de los, 153
Ritch, W.G., 145, 298–299, 304
Rivenburg, Grant, 354
Rivenburg, Ida, 344
Rivera, Pedro de, 243
Robidoux, Luis, 424
Robledo, Ana, 118, 125, 188
Roche, Juan, 125
Rodelo, Juan, 155
Rodrigues, Ana, 197
Rodríguez, Esteban, 139
Rodríguez, Felipe, 155
Rodríguez, José, 413
Rodríguez, Juan, 417
Rodríguez, Juan Felipe, 95
Rodríguez, Melchor, 139
Rodríguez, Sebastián, 139
Rodríguez Bellido, Juan, 118
Rodríguez Cubero, Francisco, 139
Rodríguez Cubero, Pedro, 80, 83, 138–139, 234–235; and land for Franciscan convento, 157; and Vargas, 141
Rodríguez de San Antonio, Salvador, 223–224
Rojas Liscano, Pedro de, 155
Romero, Ana María, 143, 144
Romero, Bartolomé, 126
Romero, Bartolomé II, 410
Romero, Bartolomé III, 411
Romero, Diego, 184, 410
Romero, Francisco, 413
Romero, Jesus, 312
Romero, José Miguel, 426
Romero, Mateo, 124
Romero, Matías, 410
Romero, Orlando A., 17–18, 434–435
Romero clan and the *cabildo de Santa Fe*, 124
Romero de Pedraza, Francisco, 412, 413
Romo de Vera, José, 95
Roosevelt, Theodore, 344, 366
Roque Lovato grant, 70, 95
Rosa, Luis de la, 288
Rosas, Luis de, 45, 133, 169, 186
Roybal, Ignacio, 95
Ruiz de Cáceres, Juan, 409

S

Sáez, Agustín, 139, 413
Safford, Edward I., 428
Sage, Charles G., 386
Saint Francis Cathedral, 144
Salas, Antonio de, 188, 198
Salas family and the *cabildo de Santa Fe*, 124
Salinas, 209–210
San Antonio, Texas, 103–106
San Buenaventura de los Jumanos, 113

San Cristobal land grant, 257
San Cristóbal Pueblo, 39; Indian laborers, 180
San Felipe Pueblo, 53; and reconquest, 228–229
San Fernando de Bexar, 103–106
San Francisco de Santa Fé, Real Campo de Españoles, 22
San Francisco Street, 135, 140, 144
San Gabriel, 13–14, 52, 102, 114–115, 116, 131; decline in importance, 112, 113–114
San Ildefonso Pueblo, 53; and revolt of 1696, 233
San Juan Bautista de Mexicaltzingo, Jalisco, 168
San Juan de los Caballeros, 22
San Juan Pueblo, 53, 78–79, 90, 112, 131
San Lázaro Pueblo, 39; Indian laborers, 180
San Marcos land grant, 248, 256, 257, 260, 263
San Marcos Pueblo, 37–38
San Miguel Chapel, 29, *50*, 126, 132, 147–156, *149, 152, 156, 166*; restoration efforts, 55, 174–175; and Tlaxcalan Indians, 49–51, 53
Sánchez, George I., 283
Sánchez, Gregorio, 424
Sánchez, Joseph P., 19–33, 267–277, 435
Sánchez, María Encarnación Rafaela, 285
Sánchez, Ysidro, 142, 144
Sandoval, Josepha de, 194, 198, 199, 202–204, 206
Sandoval, Manuel, 310
Santa Ana Pueblo, 53; and reconquest, 228–229; and revolt of 1696, 232
Santa Anna, Antonio López de, 268–269, 275
Santa Clara Pueblo, 53; and revolt of 1696, 233
Santa Cruz de la Cañada, 67, 137, 140, 152, 234; and rebellion of 1837, 273; and revolt of 1696, 231, 232, 233
Santa Cruz, Diego de, 410
Santa Cruz land grant, 248, 250–253, 257, 260
Santa Fe: alcaldes and mayors, 33, 115–116; building style, 122, 351–353, 356, 358–359, 362–363, 378, 385; as capital, 20–21, 350; crime in Territorial Period, 301–316; drawings, *15, 18*, 34, 36, *298–299*; famines and epidemics, 137–138; founding, 13–15, 88–91, 101–107, 130–132; grants, 65–95, *76, 95*, 103–107; and health seekers, 345–347, 352, 361–382; incorporation, 341–343; maps, *6–7, 69, 71*, 92–93, 249, *297–299*, 359, 385; military garrison, 112–114; name, 72–73; plaza, 120; police force, 346–347; population, 122–123, 137, 164, 362; presidio at, 209–216, 237–264; public health, 348–349; after Pueblo Revolt, 223; reconquest, 30, 68, 136–139, 213, 219–236, 241, 256; roads, 356; school system, 355–356; selection of site, 119; settlement pattern and land use, 68, 89; status as "villa", 116, 124–125; water system and sewers, 348–349
Santa Fe Cabildo, 20–22, 68–69, 124, 128, 403–428
Santa Fe Central Railway, 350–353, *352*, 355
Santa Fe County Board of County Commissioners, 72
Santa Fe Grant, 66–77, *71*
Santa Fe Irrigation and Improvement Company, 354–355
Santa Fe Lake, *39*
Santa Fe League, 65, 75–76, *76*
Santa Fe New Mexican, 318–321, 329–333, 334; and Progressive issues, 341–343; and Santa Fe building style, 363
Santa Fe Ring, 318–319, 326–328
Santa Fe Trail, 21–22, 269, 356
Santa María, patron saint of Santa Fe, 120, 127
Santander, Diego de, 206
Santo Domingo Pueblo, 42, 53; and rebellion of 1837, 274; and reconquest, 230
Sargent, William G., 427
Sarracino, Francisco, 272, 274
Scallion, Gillion, 305–307
Schmidt, Gustavus, 74
Scholes, France V., 23–24, 77, 88, 100–101; and Ermita de San Miguel, 151; and Maggs Bros. documents, 25–26
School of American Archaeology, 377
Scottish Rite Temple, 318, 322, 356

Sebastián de Vargas Grant, 84, *84*
Secoy, Frank, 239
Segesser hide paintings, 244, *246–247*
Seligman, Arthur, 355, 357, 378, 427
Seligman, Bernard, 343
Sena, Antonio, 425
Sena, Bernardino de, 153, 157
Sena, Felipe, 425
Sena, Francisco, 425
Sena, José, 348, 355–356, 427
Sena, José Francisco, 426
Sena, Manuel Antonio, 424
Sena, Miguel, 272
Sena, Tomás Antonio, 419
Sena, Vicente, 419
Senecú, 209–210
Serna, Antonio de la, 125
Severino de Zuballe, Juan, 411
Shelby Street, 141, 144
shell, 40
Sherman, William T., 363, 364
Shuster, Will, 32, 379
Sierra Mosca grant, 70
Simito, Lorenzo, 54–55
Simmons, Marc, 13–15, 24–25, 244, 435
Simms, Andrew Jackson, 307–308, 309–310, 315–316
Simpson, James H., 254
Sisneros, Antonio, 48
Sisneros, Samuel E., 31, 279–297, 435
Sisters of Charity, 363
Slaughter, William, 343–344
Sloan, John H., 348–349, 427
small pox, 348–349
Smith, Hugh N., 305–306
Snow, Cordelia Thomas, 29, 133, 135, 147–160, 435
Snow, David H., 27–28, 37–63, 133, 436
Sombrero, Domingo and Francisca, 122–123
Sosa de Canela, Juan, 259
Sotelo Osorio, Felipe de, 150
Southern Athapaskans, 40
Spanish Archives of New Mexico, 130
Sparks, Ishmael, 352, 355, 427
Speis, Charles, 348
Spencer, T. Rush, 70

Spiess, Charles A., 427
Spude, Robert L., 32, 339–359, 436
St. Vincent Hospital, 363, 366
St. Vincent Sanatorium, 32, 363–365, *364*, 377, 380–382, *381*
Stinson, Katherine, 380
Stoner, J.J., *6–7*, 298–299
Stratton, Porter, 319–320
Strock, Glen, 86
Stubbs, Stanley, 155
Sumner, Edwin, 263–264
Sunmount Sanatorium, 352, 367–376, *369–374*, 379–380, 382; as Bruns Hospital Annex, 399–400
Surveyor General of New Mexico, 66
sweat-lodges, 55

T

Tadeo, Francisca, 171
Tafoya, Felipe, 418, 419, 420; land grant, 95
Tafoya, José Miguel, 422
Talaya Hill land grant, 95
Tano Indians, 38–39, 42, 61; and reconquest, 219–220, 223, 226–228; and revolt of 1696, 231, 233
Taos Pueblo, 42, 53, 229; and revolt of 1696, 233
Taos Rebellion of 1847, 284–285
Tapia, Tomás, 95
Tarascan Indians, 51–52, 168
Taylor, Patrick, 147
Telles Jirón, José, 412
Tenorio, Manuel, 95
Tenorio de Alba, Miguel, 415
Territorial Period, 310–316, 317–334, 339–359, 361–378; legal system and crime, 301–316; militia, 322
Tesuque, Domingo of, 128
Tesuque Pueblo, 42, 44, 53, 61, *62*; occupation of Santa Fe during Pueblo Revolt, 61
Tewa Indians, 38–41; and reconquest, 219–220, 223, 226–228, 230; and revolt of 1696, 231, 233, 234
Texas, 281
Texas-Santa Fe Expedition, 287–288
Thoma, Francisco de, 22–23

Thomas, A.B., 243
Thornton, William T., 329, 342–343, 347, 427
Tigges, Linda, 30–31, 237–266, 409–428, 436
Tipton, Will, 70, 72
Tiwa Indians, 54
Tlaxcalan Indians, 29, 49–55, 67–68, 101–102, 126, 163–164; in Barrio de Analco, 167–168, 176–177
Torquemada, Juan de, 44
torreones, 55–56, *56*, 67; on the Palace of the Governors, 142
Tórrez, Robert, 284–285
Torrez, Robert J., 308
Town of Galisteo Land Grant, 258
trade, 125, 180, 222, 229; with Indians, 237, 239; regulation of, 269–270
Treaty of Guadalupe Hidalgo, 285, 288–289
Trejo, Felipe, 389
Treviño, Juan, 61
Trujillo, Andres, 95
Trujillo, Arthur E., 428
Trujillo, Diego, 138
Trujillo, Francisco, 424
Trujillo, José Miguel, 422
tuberculosis, 32, 352, 361–382, 397, 399–400; among Indians in New Mexico, 380–381
Tupatú, Luis, 128, 220–222
Twitchell, Ralph Emerson, 23, 77, 97–98, 107, 282–283, *346*, 356; about Max Frost, 339–340; as mayor, 427; and Oldest House, 57–58, *59*; and railroads in Santa Fe, 349–350; and Santa Fe politics, 345–347
Tyler, Daniel, 262

U

Ulibarrí, Antonio de, 406, 416, 417, 418
Ulibarrí, Juan de, 413, 414
Umviro, Diego, 222
Urban Montaño, Antonio, 256, 263
Urrútia, Joseph de, 49, 52; 1766 map of Santa Fe, *92–93*, 103, 133, 140
U.S. Congress, 75
U.S. Court of Private Land Claims, 65–66, 70, 72–75, 77, 83–85, 107
U.S. Supreme Court, 74–76, 107
Utaca, Juan, 124
Ute Indians, 60–61; and revolt of 1696, 232; warfare with Spanish, 238–240
Utter, Buckskin Charlie, 341

V

Valdés, Gregorio de, 411
Valdes, Joséph, 428
Valdes, Manuel, 342–343, 427
Valdes, Pedro de, 197–198
Valdez, Domingo, 95
Valle, José del, 153
Valverde expedition (Governor), 240, 243
VanBuskirk, Frances, 389
Varela, Alonso, 118
Varela, Luisa, 139
Varela, Polonia, 186
Vargas, Diego de, 30, 54, 61, 128, *221*, 253–254; arrested, 141; census of refugees from New Mexico, 173–174; establishing settlement pattern, 68, 89; and grants of land, 133, 138, 139–140, 259–261; named governor of New Mexico, 136–139; and Our Lady of the Conquest, 151; reconquest of Santa Fe, 135–137, 144, 219–236, 241–242; and Tlaxcalan Indians, 50–51; warfare with Indians, 239
Vargas, Francisco de, 232
Vargas, Sebastián de, *84*, 95
Vaughn, E.L., 312–313
Vega Márquez, María de la, 118
Vega y Coca, Miguel José de la, 406, 415, 416
Veitia, Diego de, 141
Velasco, Cristóbal de, 152–153
Velasco, Diego de, 142–143, 153–154, 155, 157–159
Velasco, Francisco de, 116
Velasco, Luís de, II, 14, 67, 99; instructions for founding Villa de Santa Fe, 13, 22, 77, 114–116, *117*, 120
Velez Cachupin, Tomás, 255–256, 258, 262–263
Vernal, Catalina, 55
Vierra, Carlos, 377, 378

Vigil, Domingo, 285
Vigil, Donaciano, 258
Vigil, Juan, 423
Vigil, Juan Cristóbal, 422
Vigil y Alarid, Juan Bautista, 31, 272, 277, 279–297; Acceptance of Allegiance speech, 296–297; as *alcalde*, 424; in Guadalupe, Chihuahua, MX., 289–292; and land grant claims, 292–294
Villa Alta, Oaxaca, 167–168
Villalpando, Catalina de, 143
Villanueva, Catalina de, 118
Villasur expedition, 240, 243
Vitoria Carvajal, Juan de, 409

W

Waldo, Henry, 349–350
Wallace, Lew, 91, *94*; sketch of Palace of the Governors, 57
Walter, Paul A.F., 77, 99, 362, 367, 368
Washington Avenue, 141, 144
Webber, E.T., 342
Weber, David J., 25, 283
Weightman, Richard W., 313–314
Wheeler, Henry, 308
White, Edward D., 74–76
Whitty, Eulalia, 365
Wilson, Chris, 363
Winter, Thomas Z., 427
Winters, Yvor, 379
Wirth, Nancy Meem, 379
Woman's Board of Trade and Library Association, 344
Workman, William, 287
World War II, 33, 383–401; and Japanese internment, 383, 390, 392–393, 395–397, 400
Wroth, William, 29, 163–178, 436

X

Xavier, Francisco, 173, 411

Y

Ye, Juan de, 128, 222–223, 226, 228–229
Ye, Lorenzo de, 229, 230, 231–232
Yope, Cristóbal de, 128

Z

Zacatecas, Mexico, 168–169
Zamora, Catalina de, 188
Zapata Telles Jirón, María, 139
Zárate Salmerón, Gerónimo, 53
Zeinos, Diego, 230
Zia Pueblo, 53; and reconquest, 228–229
Zuni Pueblo, 54; and revolt of 1696, 232

www.ingramcontent.com/pod-product-compliance
Lightning Source LLC
Chambersburg PA
CBHW080720300426
44114CB00019B/2434